S0-AGW-112

Business Law

Principles for Today's Commercial Environment

Third Edition

Twomey | Jennings

CENGAGE
Learning™

Australia • Brazil • Japan • Korea • Mexico • Singapore • Spain • United Kingdom • United States

Business Law: Principles for Today's Commercial Environment, Third Edition

Business Law: Principles for Today's Commercial Environment, 3rd Edition
David P. Twomey | Marianne M. Jennings

© 2011 Cengage Learning. All rights reserved.

Executive Editors:
Maureen Staudt
Michael Stranz

Senior Project Development Manager:
Linda deStefano

Marketing Specialist:
Courtney Sheldon

Senior Production/Manufacturing Manager:
Donna M. Brown

PreMedia Manager:
Joel Brennecke

Sr. Rights Acquisition Account Manager:
Todd Osborne

Cover Image:
Getty Images*

*Unless otherwise noted, all cover images used by Custom Solutions, a part of Cengage Learning, have been supplied courtesy of Getty Images with the exception of the Earthview cover image, which has been supplied by the National Aeronautics and Space Administration (NASA).

ALL RIGHTS RESERVED. No part of this work covered by the copyright herein may be reproduced, transmitted, stored or used in any form or by any means graphic, electronic, or mechanical, including but not limited to photocopying, recording, scanning, digitizing, taping, Web distribution, information networks, or information storage and retrieval systems, except as permitted under Section 107 or 108 of the 1976 United States Copyright Act, without the prior written permission of the publisher.

For product information and technology assistance, contact us at
Cengage Learning Customer & Sales Support, 1-800-354-9706

For permission to use material from this text or product,
submit all requests online at **cengage.com/permissions**
Further permissions questions can be emailed to
permissionrequest@cengage.com

This book contains select works from existing Cengage Learning resources and was produced by Cengage Learning Custom Solutions for collegiate use. As such, those adopting and/or contributing to this work are responsible for editorial content accuracy, continuity and completeness.

Compilation © 2010 Cengage Learning
ISBN-13: **978-1-111-52173-8**

ISBN-10: **1-111-52173-5**

Cengage Learning
5191 Natorp Boulevard
Mason, Ohio 45040
USA

Cengage Learning is a leading provider of customized learning solutions with office locations around the globe, including Singapore, the United Kingdom, Australia, Mexico, Brazil, and Japan. Locate your local office at:
international.cengage.com/region.
Cengage Learning products are represented in Canada by Nelson Education, Ltd.
For your lifelong learning solutions, visit **www.cengage.com/custom.**
Visit our corporate website at **www.cengage.com.**

Printed in the United States of America

BRIEF CONTENTS

Part 1

THE LEGAL AND SOCIAL ENVIRONMENT OF BUSINESS

Chapter 1

THE NATURE AND SOURCES OF LAW

Why have law? If you have ever been stuck in a traffic jam or jostled in a crowd leaving a stadium, you have observed the need for order to keep those involved moving in an efficient and safe manner. The interruptions and damages from Internet viruses demonstrate the need for rules and order in this era of new technology. When our interactions are not orderly, whether at our concerts or through our e-mail, all of us and our rights are affected. The order or pattern of rules that society uses to govern the conduct of individuals and their relationships is called **law**. Law keeps society running smoothly and efficiently.

A. Nature of Law and Legal Rights

Law consists of the body of principles that govern conduct and that can be enforced in courts or by administrative agencies. The law could also be described as a collection or bundle of rights.

1. Legal Rights

A **right** is a legal capacity to require another person to perform or refrain from performing an act. Our rights flow from the U.S. Constitution, state constitutions, federal and state statutes, and ordinances at the local levels, including cities, counties, and boroughs. Within these sources of rights are also duties. A **duty** is an obligation of law imposed on a person to perform or refrain from performing a certain act.

Duties and rights coexist. No right exists in one person without a corresponding duty resting on some other person or persons. For example, if the terms of a lease provide that the premises will remain in a condition of good repair so that the tenant can live there comfortably, the landlord has a corresponding duty to provide a dwelling that has hot and cold running water.

2. Individual Rights

The U.S. Constitution gives individuals certain rights. Those rights include the right to freedom of speech, the right to due process or the right to have a hearing before any freedom is taken away, and the right to vote. There are also duties that accompany individual rights, such as the duty to speak in a way that does not cause harm to others. For example, individuals are free to express their opinions about the government or its officials, but they would not be permitted to yell "Fire!" in a crowded theater and cause unnecessary harm to others. The rights given in the U.S. Constitution are rights that cannot be taken away or violated by any statutes, ordinances, or court decisions. These rights provide a framework for the structure of government and other laws.

3. The Right of Privacy

One very important individual legal right is the right of privacy, which has two components. The first is the right to be secure against unreasonable searches and seizures by the government. The Fourth Amendment of the U.S. Constitution guarantees this portion of the **right of privacy**. A police officer, for example, may not search your home unless the officer has a reasonable suspicion (which is generally established through a warrant) that your home contains evidence of a crime, such as illegal drugs. If your home or business is searched unlawfully, any items obtained during that unlawful search could be excluded as evidence in a criminal trial because of the Fourth Amendment's exclusionary rule. **For Example,** in the murder trial of O.J. Simpson, Judge Lance Ito excluded some of the evidence the police had obtained from inside Mr. Simpson's Ford Bronco, which was parked on the street outside his home. Judge Ito ruled that the officers should have first obtained a warrant for the locked vehicle, which was not going to be taken anywhere because Mr. Simpson was out of town at that time.

A second aspect of the right of privacy protects individuals against intrusions by others. Your private life is not subject to public scrutiny when you are a private citizen. This right is provided in many state

Wilson v Layne, 526 US 603 (1999)

When Warrants are involved, No Brief Photographs

In the early morning hours of April 16, 1992, a special team of Deputy U.S. Marshals and police officers executed warrants that had been issued against Dominic Wilson, who was wanted for robbery, theft, and assault and who had a "use caution" warning posted on law enforcement files and records. The team was accompanied by a reporter and a photographer from the *Washington Post*, who had been invited by the marshals to accompany them as part of a Marshals Service ride-along policy.

The officers, with media representatives in tow, entered the dwelling noted in the warrant at 6:45 A.M. The home they entered and that was on the arrest warrant actually belonged to Dominic's parents, Charles and Geraldine Wilson. Charles and Geraldine were still in bed. When they heard the officers enter the home, Charles Wilson, dressed only in a pair of briefs, ran into the living room to investigate. He angrily cursed the officers. Geraldine Wilson then entered the living room to investigate, wearing only a nightgown. She observed her husband being restrained by the armed officers. Dominic Wilson was not in the house, and the officers left. However, the *Washington Post* photographer had already taken numerous pictures of the confrontation between the police and Charles Wilson. The *Washington Post* never published its photographs of the incident.

The Wilsons filed suit against the officers for invasion of their privacy and violation of their Fourth Amendment rights. The district court found that the officers could be held liable. The Court of Appeals reversed and found that the officers had immunity. The U.S. Supreme Court granted *certiorari* because of several conflicting circuit decisions on the issue of cameras and reporters being present during arrests and warrant executions.

JUDICIAL OPINION

REHNQUIST, Chief Justice . . . In 1604, an English court made the now-famous observation that "the house of every one is to him as his castle and fortress, as well for his defence against injury and violence, as for his repose." In his Commentaries on the Laws of England, William Blackstone noted that "the law of England has so particular and tender a regard to the immunity of a man's house, that it stiles it his castle, and will never suffer it to be violated with impunity: agreeing herein with the sentiments of ancient Rome . . . . For this reason no doors can in general be broken open to execute any civil process; though, in criminal causes, the public safety supersedes the private."

The Fourth Amendment embodies this centuries-old principle of respect for the privacy of the home: "The right of the people to be secure in their persons, houses, papers, and effects, against unreasonable searches and seizures, shall not be violated, and no Warrants shall issue, but upon probable cause, supported by Oath or affirmation, and particularly describing the place to be searched, and the persons or things to be seized."

Our decisions have applied these basic principles of the Fourth Amendment to situations, like the one in this case, in which police enter a home under the authority of an arrest warrant in order to take into custody the suspect named in the warrant. We decided that "an arrest warrant founded on probable cause implicitly carries with it the limited authority to enter a dwelling in which the suspect lives when there is reason to believe the suspect is within."

Here, of course, the officers had such a warrant, and they were undoubtedly entitled to enter the Wilson home in order to execute the arrest warrant for Dominic Wilson. But it does not necessarily follow that they were entitled to bring a newspaper reporter and a photographer with them. In *Horton v California*, 496 US 128, 140, 110 S.Ct. 2301, 110 L.Ed.2d 112 (1990), we held "[i]f the scope of the search exceeds that permitted by the terms of a validly issued warrant or the character of the relevant exception from the warrant require-ment, the subsequent seizure is unconstitu-tional without more." While this does not mean that every police action while inside a home must be explicitly authorized by the text of the warrant, the Fourth Amendment does require that police actions in execution of a warrant be related to the objectives of the authorized intrusion . . . Certainly the presence of reporters inside the home was not related to the objectives of the authorized intrusion. Respon-dents concede that the reporters did not engage in the execution of the warrant, and did not assist the police in their task. The reporters therefore were not present for any reason related to the justification for police entry into the home—the apprehension of Dominic Wilson.

This is not a case in which the presence of the third parties directly aided in the execution of the warrant. Where the police enter a home under the authority of a warrant to search for stolen property, the presence of third parties for the purpose of identifying the stolen property has long been approved by this Court and our common-law tradition.

Respondents argue that the presence of the *Washington Post* reporters in the Wilsons' home nonetheless served a number of legitimate law enforcement purposes. They first assert that officers should be able to exercise reasonable discretion about when it would "further their law enforcement

Continued

mission to permit members of the news media to accompany them in executing a warrant." But this claim ignores the importance of the right of residential privacy at the core of the Fourth Amendment. It may well be that media ride-alongs further the law enforcement objectives of the police in a general sense, but that is not the same as furthering the purposes of the search. Were such generalized "law enforcement objectives" themselves sufficient to trump the Fourth Amendment, the protections guaranteed by that Amendment's text would be significantly watered down.

Respondents next argue that the presence of third parties could serve the law enforcement purpose of publicizing the government's efforts to combat crime, and facilitate accurate reporting on law enforcement activities. There is certainly language in our opinions interpreting the First Amendment which points to the importance of "the press" in informing the general public about the administration of criminal justice. No one could gainsay the truth of these observations, or the importance of the First Amendment in protecting press freedom from abridgment by the government. But the Fourth Amendment also protects a very important right, and in the present case it is in terms of that right that the media ride-alongs must be judged.

Surely the possibility of good public relations for the police is simply not enough, standing alone, to justify the ride-along intrusion into a private home. And even the need for accurate reporting on police issues in general bears no direct relation to the constitutional justification for the police intrusion into a home in order to execute a felony arrest warrant.

Finally, respondents argue that the presence of third parties could serve in some situations to minimize police abuses and protect suspects, and also to protect the safety of the officers. While it might be reasonable for police officers to themselves videotape home entries as part of a "quality control" effort to ensure that the rights of homeowners are being respected, or even to preserve evidence. The Washington Post reporters in the Wilsons' home were working on a story for their own purposes. They were not present for the purpose of protecting the officers, much less the Wilsons. A private photographer was acting for private purposes, as evidenced in part by the fact that the newspaper and not the police retained the photographs. Thus, although the presence of third parties during the execution of a warrant may in some circumstances be constitutionally permissible, the presence of these third parties was not.

The reasons advanced by respondents, taken in their entirety, fall short of justifying the presence of media inside a home. We hold that it is a violation of the Fourth Amendment for police to bring members of the media or other third parties into a home during the execution of a warrant when the presence of the third parties in the home was not in aid of the execution of the warrant.

QUESTIONS

1. How long has the right to privacy in one's home been a judicial issue?

2. What arguments do law enforcement officials make to justify including third parties in arrests and service of warrants?

3. Does the Court find that the arguments justify the presence of the reporters?

4. What if the Humane Society brought along reporters when it was investigating a private home for possible animal abuse? Would this action be a breach of privacy?

constitutions and exists through interpretation at the federal level in the landmark case of *Roe v Wade*,[1] in which the U.S. Supreme Court established a right of privacy that gives women the right to choose whether to have an abortion.

These two components of the right to privacy have many interpretations. These interpretations are often found in statutes that afford privacy rights with respect to certain types of conduct. **For Example,** a federal statute provides a right of privacy to bank customers that prevents their banks from giving out information about their accounts except to law enforcement agencies conducting investigations. Some laws protect the rights of students. **For Example,** the Family Educational Rights and Privacy Act of 1974 (FERPA, also known as the *Buckley Amendment*) prevents colleges and universities from disclosing students' grades to third parties without the students' permission. From your credit information to your Social Security number, you have great privacy protections.

[1] 410 US 113 (1973).

ethics&the law

Googling Job Applicants

A recent survey shows a new component in the background searches performed by potential employers of job applicants:

- 61 percent of professional service firms, including accounting, consulting, engineering, and law firms, do Google searches on their job candidates.

- Fifty percent of professional services hired by employers to do background checks use Google.

One employer commented that a Google search is so simple that it would be irresponsible not to conduct such a

search. Experts tell college students to remember that what may seem to be something noncontroversial in your youth can later come back to haunt you when you begin your professional career. Their advice is to watch what you put in MySpace, Facebook, and all other Internet sites. Discuss privacy rights and whether there is any legal issue when information is posted voluntarily on the Internet. Is there an ethical issue with these types of searches?

Source: Sandhya Bathija , "Have a Profile on MySpace? Better Keep It Clean," *National Law Journal,* June 4, 2007, 10.

4. Privacy and Technology

Technology creates new situations that may require the application of new rules of law. Technology has changed the way we interact with each other, and new rules of law have developed to protect our rights. Today, business is conducted by computers, wire transfers of funds, e-mail, electronic data interchange (EDI) order placements, and the Internet. We still expect that our communication is private. However, technology also affords others the ability to eavesdrop on conversations and intercept electronic messages. The law has stepped in to reestablish that the right of privacy still exists even in these technologically nonprivate circumstances. Some laws now make it a crime and a breach of privacy to engage in such interceptions of communications.[2] (See Chapter 11)

e-commerce&cyberlaw

Employers, E-mail, and Privacy

Scott Kennedy, a computer system administrator for Qualcomm Corporation in San Diego, California, discovered that somebody had obtained unauthorized access (or "hacked into," in popular parlance) the company's computer network. Kennedy contacted the Federal Bureau of Investigation (FBI). Working together, Kennedy and the FBI were able to trace the intrusion to a computer on the

University of Wisconsin at Madison network. They contacted Jeffrey Savoy, the University of Wisconsin computer network investigator, who found evidence that someone using a computer on the university network was in fact hacking into the Qualcomm system and that the user had gained unauthorized access to the university's system as well. Savoy traced the source of intrusion to a

---

[2] *State v Christensen,* 79 P3d 12 (CA Wash 2003).

e-commerce&cyberlaw

continued

computer located in university housing, the room of Jerome Heckenkamp, a computer science graduate student at the university. Savoy knew that Heckenkamp had been terminated from his job at the university computer help desk two years earlier for similar unauthorized activity.

While Heckenkamp was online and logged into the university's system, Savoy, along with detectives, went to Heckenkamp's room. The door was ajar, and nobody was in the room. Savoy entered the room and disconnected the network cord that attached the computer to the network. In order to be sure that the computer he had disconnected from the network was the computer

that had gained unauthorized access to the university server, Savoy wanted to run some commands on the computer. Detectives located Heckenkamp, explained the situation, and asked for Heckenkamp's password, which Heckenkamp voluntarily provided. Savoy then ran tests on the computer and copied the hard drive without a warrant. When Heckenkamp was charged with several federal computer crimes, he challenged the university's access to his account and Savoy's steps that night, including the copy of the hard drive, as a breach of his privacy. Was Heckenkamp correct? Was his privacy breached?

[U.S. v Heckenkamp, 482 F3d 1132 (CA 9 2007).]

B. Sources of Law

Several layers of law are enacted at different levels of government to provide the framework for business and personal rights and duties. At the base of this framework of laws is constitutional law. Constitutional law is the branch of law that is based on the constitution for a particular level of government. A **constitution** is a body of principles that establishes the structure of a government and the relationship of that government to the people who are governed. A constitution is generally a combination of the written document and the practices and customs that develop with the passage of time and the emergence of new problems. In each state, two constitutions are in force: the state constitution and the federal Constitution.

Statutory law includes legislative acts. Both Congress and the state legislatures enact statutory law. Examples of congressional legislative enactments include the Securities Act of 1933 (Chapter 46), the Sherman Antitrust Act (Chapter 5), the bankruptcy laws (Chapter 35), and consumer credit protection provisions (Chapter 33). At the state level, statutes govern the creation of corporations, probate of wills, and the transfer of title to property. In addition to the

state legislatures and the U.S. Congress, all cities, counties, and other governmental subdivisions have some power to adopt ordinances within their sphere of operation. Examples of the types of laws found at this level of government include traffic laws, zoning laws, and pet and bicycle licensing laws.

Administrative regulations are rules promulgated by state and federal administrative agencies, such as the Securities and Exchange Commission and the National Labor Relations Board. These regulations generally have the force of statutes.

Even individuals and businesses create their own laws, or **private law**. Private law consists of the rules and regulations parties agree to as part of their contractual relationships. **For Example,** landlords develop rules for tenants on everything from parking to laundry room use. Employers develop rules for employees on everything from proper computer use to posting pictures and information on bulletin boards located within the company walls. Homeowner associations have rules on everything from your landscaping to the color of your house paint.

Law also includes principles that are expressed for the first time in court decisions. This form of law is called **case law**. When a court decides a new question or problem, its decision becomes a **precedent**, which stands as the law in future cases that involve that particular problem.

Using precedent and following decisions in similar cases is the doctrine of **stare decisis**. However, the rule of *stare decisis* is not cast in stone. Judges have some flexibility. When a court finds an earlier decision to be incorrect, it overrules that decision. For Example, in 1954, the U.S. Supreme Court departed from the general rule of *stare decisis* in *Brown v Board of Education*.[3] In that case, the Court decided that its 1896 decision *Plessy v Ferguson*,[4] that held separate facilities for blacks were equal to facilities for whites, was incorrect.

Court decisions do not always deal with new problems or make new rules. In many cases, courts apply rules as they have been for many years, even centuries. These time-honored rules of the community are called the **common law**. Statutes sometimes repeal or redeclare the common law rules. Many statutes depend on the common law for definitions of the terms in the statutes.

Law also includes treaties made by the United States and proclamations and executive orders of the president of the United States or of other public officials.

C. UNIFORM STATE LAWS

To facilitate the national nature of business and transactions, the National Conference of Commissioners on Uniform State Laws (NCCUSL), composed of representatives from every state, has drafted statutes on various subjects for adoption by the states. The best example of such laws is the Uniform Commercial Code (UCC).[5] (See Chapters 23–31, Chapter 34.) The UCC regulates the sale and leasing of goods; commercial paper, such as checks; funds transfers; secured transactions in personal property;

banking; and letters of credit. Having the same principles of law on contracts for the sale of goods and other commercial transactions in most of the 50 states makes doing business easier and less expensive. Other examples of uniform laws across the states include the Model Business Corporations Act (Chapter 44), the Uniform Partnership Act (Chapter 42), and the Uniform Residential Landlord Tenant Act (Chapter 51). The Uniform Computer Information Transactions Act (UCITA) as well as the Uniform Electronic Transactions Act (UETA) are new technology statutes that have been adopted or are under consideration for passage by the states. These two uniform laws and versions of them take contract law from the traditional paper era to the paperless computer age.

D. CLASSIFICATIONS OF LAW

Law is classified in many ways. **Substantive law** creates, defines, and regulates rights and liabilities. **Procedural law** specifies the steps that must be followed in enforcing those rights and liabilities. For example, the laws that grant employees protection against discrimination are substantive laws. The regulations of the Equal Employment Opportunity Commission (EEOC) for bringing suits against or investigations of employers for discrimination charges are procedural laws. The laws that prohibit computer theft are substantive laws. The prosecution of someone for computer theft follows procedural law. Law may also be classified in terms of its origin from Roman (or civil) law, from English common law based on customs and usages of the community,[6] or from the law merchant. Law may be classified according to subject matter, such as the law of contracts, the law of real estate, or the law of wills.

---

[3] 349 US 294 (1954).

[4] 163 US 537 (1895).

[5] The UCC has been adopted in every state, except that Louisiana has not adopted Article 2, Sales. Guam, the Virgin Islands, and the District of Columbia have also adopted the UCC. The NCCUSL has adopted amendments to Article 8, Investment Securities (1977 and 1994), and Article 9, Secured Transactions (1999, and as amended 2001). There have been new articles of the UCC: Article 2A, Leases, and Article 4A, Funds Transfers. The United Nations Convention on Contracts for the International Sale of Goods (CISG) has been adopted as the means for achieving uniformity in sale-of-goods contracts on an international level. Provisions of CISG were strongly influenced by Article 2 of the UCC.

[6] For example, in *Washington State Grange v Washington Republican Party*, 552 US 442 (2008), Justice Antonin Scalia wrote, "Washington's law is like a law that encourages Oscar the Grouch (Sesame Street's famed bad-taste resident of a garbage can) to state a "preference" for Campbell's at every point of sale, while barring the soup company from disavowing his endorsement, or indeed using its name at all, in those same crucial locations." In *BMW of North America, Inc. v Gore*, 517 US 559 (1996), Justice Scalia, in his dissenting opinion, wrote, "One expects the court to conclude, 'To thine own self be true.'"

sports&entertainment law

On March 17, 2005, former and current major league baseball (MLB) players, Commissioner Bud Selig, and the parents of young baseball players who had taken their own lives after taking steroids testified before the U.S. House of Representatives Government Reform Committee. The House held the hearings to determine whether government regulation of baseball is necessary.

Committee Chair Tom Davis made an opening statement with the following excerpts:

Fourteen years ago, anabolic steroids were added to the Controlled Substance Act as a Schedule III drug, making it illegal to possess or sell them without a valid prescription. Today, however, evidence strongly suggests that steroid use among teenagers—especially aspiring athletes—is a large and growing problem.

Today we take the committee's first steps toward understanding how we got here, and how we begin turning those numbers around. Down the road, we need to look at whether and how Congress should exercise its legislative powers to further restrict the use and distribution of these substances.

Our specific purpose today is to consider MLB's recently negotiated drug policy; how the testing policy will be implemented; how it will effectively address the use of prohibited drugs by players; and, most importantly, the larger societal and public health ramifications of steroid use.

Mark McGwire, now a retired MLB player and a record holder, stated during the hearings:

Asking me, or any other player, to answer questions about who took steroids in front of television cameras, will not solve this problem. If a player answers 'no,' he simply will not be believed. If he answers 'yes,' he risks public scorn and endless government investigations. My lawyers have advised me that I cannot answer these questions without jeopardizing my friends, my family, or myself. I intend to follow their advice.*

Give a list of all the laws, rights, and duties you can find in this information.

* http://reform.house.gov/GovReform/Hearings/EventSingle.aspx? EventID=1637. Click on Mark McGwire

Law is at times classified in terms of principles of law and principles of equity. The early English courts were very limited as to the kinds of cases they could handle. Persons who could not obtain relief in those courts would petition the king to grant them special relief according to principles of **equity** and justice. In the course of time, these special cases developed certain rules that are called *principles of equity*. In general, the rules of equity apply when the remedies provided at law cannot provide adequate relief in the form of monetary damages. At one time, the United States had separate law courts and equity courts. Except in a few states, these courts have been combined so that one court applies principles of both law and equity. A party may ask for both legal and equitable remedies in a single court.[7] **For Example,** suppose a homeowner contracts to sell his home to a buyer. If the homeowner then refuses to go through

---

[7] For example, Jennifer Lopez and Marc Anthony filed suit against the manufacturer of a British company that produces baby carriages for using their images on its Web site and in ads without permission; they asked for $5 million in damages as well as an injunction to stop use of their photos and likenesses in the company's ads. *Lopez v Silver Cross*, 2009 WL 481386 (CD Cal).

with the contract, the buyer has the legal remedy of recovering damages. The rules of equity go further, when appropriate, and could require the owner to actually transfer the ownership of the house to the buyer. Such remedies require a court order for specific conduct, known as *specific performance.* Equitable remedies may also be available in certain contract breaches (see Chapter 2, 12 and 20).

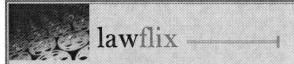

And Justice for All (1979) (R)

An excellent film that gives an overview of the judicial system in Maryland. Rights, precedent, and the role of lawyers are all topics for satire and analysis in the movie.

Check out LawFlix at **www.cengage.com/ blaw/dvl** to access movie clips that illustrate business law concepts.

MAKE THE CONNECTION

SUMMARY

Law provides rights and imposes duties. One such right is the right of privacy, which affords protection against unreasonable searches of our property and intrusion into or disclosure of our private affairs.

Law consists of the pattern of rules established by society to govern conduct and relationships. These rules can be expressed as constitutional provisions, statutes, administrative regulations, and case decisions. Law can be classified as substantive or procedural, and it can be described in terms of its historical origins, by the subject to which it relates, or in terms of law or equity.

The sources of law include constitutions, federal and state statutes, administrative regulations, ordinances, and uniform laws generally codified by the states in their statutes. The courts are also a source of law through their adherence to case precedent under the doctrine of *stare decisis* and through their development of time-honored principles called the common law.

LEARNING OUTCOMES

After studying this chapter, you should be able to clearly explain:

A. NATURE OF LAW AND LEGAL RIGHTS

L.O.1 Discuss the nature of law and legal rights
See *Wilson v Layne,* p. 5.
See E-Commerce and Cyberlaw, p. 7.

B. SOURCES OF LAW

L.O.2 List the sources of law
See the **For Example,** discussion of landlords developing rules for tenants on everything from parking to laundry room use on p. 8.
See the Sports & Entertainment Law discussion of steroids in baseball on p. 10.

C. UNIFORM STATE LAWS

L.O.3 Explain uniform state laws
See the list and explanation of uniform laws on p. 9.

D. CLASSIFICATIONS OF LAW

LO.4 Describe the classifications of law
See the discussion of law, equity, and substantive law on pp. 9 and 10.

See footnote 7 with the discussion of the Jennifer Lopez/Marc Anthony suit on p. 10.

KEY TERMS

administrative regulations	equity	right of privacy
case law	law	right
common law	precedent	*stare decisis*
constitution	private law	statutory law
duty	procedural law	substantive law

QUESTIONS AND CASE PROBLEMS

1. Glenda Brunette, a 60-year old widow, operates a pedigreed cat breeding business on her 11-acre ranch and avocado farm in Ojai, California. You can enter Brunette's ranch only by passing through a locked gate that has a "No Trespass" sign. Concerned citizens reported to the Humane Society that Brunette was "selling cats that looked sick, with eyes matted shut and covered in flies and feces." The Humane Society, a quasi-public body in California, can investigate reports of animal cruelty, impound animals, place liens on property, and bring criminal charges against citizens. The Humane Society obtained a warrant to search Brunette's property and invited Tim Dewar of the *Ojai Valley News* to come along and photograph the search of the ranch. Dewar came in his own car and arrived after the Humane Society had severed the lock on the gate. When he arrived, Dewar went in and began photographing the search, the animals, and Brunette. Brunette filed suit against Dewar and the *Ojai Valley News* for invasion of her privacy. Can she recover damages? Be sure to refer to the *Wilson v Layne* case (on p. 5) as you consider your answer. *Brunette v Humane Society of Ventura County,* 294 F3d 1205 (CA 9).

2. The Family Educational Rights and Privacy Act (FERPA) protects students' rights to keep their academic records private. What duties are imposed and upon whom because of this protection of rights? Discuss the relationship between rights and duties.

3. List the sources of law.

4. What is the difference between common law and statutory law?

5. Classify the following laws as substantive or procedural:

   a. A law that requires public schools to hold a hearing before a student is expelled

   b. A law that establishes a maximum interest rate for credit transactions of 24 percent

   c. A law that provides employee leave for the birth or adoption of a child for up to 12 weeks

   d. A law that requires the county assessor to send four notices of taxes due and owing before a lien can be filed (attached) to the property

6. What do uniform laws accomplish? Why do states adopt them? Give an example of a uniform law.

7. Cindy Nathan is a student at West University. While she was at her 9:00 A.M. anthropology class, campus security entered her dorm room and searched all areas, including her closet and drawers. When Cindy returned to her room and

discovered what had happened, she complained to the dorm's senior resident. The senior resident said that this was the university's property and that Cindy had no right of privacy. Do you agree with the senior resident's statement? Is there a right of privacy in a dorm room?

8. Professor Lucas Phelps sent the following e-mail to Professor Marlin Jones: "I recently read the opinion piece you wrote for the *Sacramento Bee* on affirmative action. Your opinion is incorrect, your reasoning and analysis are poor, and I am embarrassed that you are a member of the faculty here at Cal State Yolinda." Professor Jones forwarded the note from Professor Phelps to the provost of the university and asked that Professor Phelps be disciplined for using the university e-mail system for harassment purposes. Professor Phelps objected when the provost contacted him: "He had no right to forward that e-mail to you. That was private correspondence. And you have no right of access to my e-mail. I have privacy rights." Do you agree with Professor Phelps? Was there a breach of privacy?

9. Under what circumstances would a court disregard precedent?

10. What is the difference between a statute and an administrative regulation?

11. What is the difference between a remedy in equity and other forms of judicial remedies?

12. Give examples of areas covered by federal laws. Give examples of areas covered by city ordinances. What are the limitations on these two sources of laws? What could the laws at these two levels not do?

13. What is the principle of *stare decisis?*

14. List some purposes of law that you were able to spot in reading this chapter.

15. During the 2001 baseball season, San Francisco Giants player Barry Bonds hit 73 home runs, a new record that broke the one set by Mark McGwire in 2000 (72 home runs). FN Be sure to read the text box on p.9 for more background on McGwire's hitting prowess. When Mr. Bonds hit his record-breaking home run, the ball went into the so-called cheap seats. Alex Popov was sitting in those seats and had brought along his baseball glove for purposes of catching any hits that might come into the stands. Everyone sitting in the area agreed that Mr. Popov's glove touched Bonds's home-run ball. Videotape also shows Mr. Popov's glove on the ball. However, the ball dropped and, following a melee among the cheap-seat fans, Patrick Hayashi ended up with Bonds's home-run ball. Mr. Popov filed suit for the ball, claiming it as his property. Such baseballs can be very valuable. The baseball from Mr. McGwire's record-breaking home run in 2000 sold for $3 million. List those areas of law that will apply as the case is tried and the owner of the baseball is determined.

Chapter 2

THE COURT SYSTEM AND DISPUTE RESOLUTION

Despite carefully negotiated and well-written contracts and high safety standards in the workplace or in product design and production, businesses can still encounter disputes that may result in a lawsuit. **For Example,** you could hire the brightest and most expensive lawyer in town to prepare a contract with another party and believe the final agreement is "bulletproof." However, even a bullet-proof contract does not guarantee performance by the other party, and a lawsuit for damages may be necessary.

Business disputes can be resolved in court or through alternative means. This chapter covers the structure of the court system and the litigation process as well as alternative means used outside the court system to resolve disputes.

A. THE COURT SYSTEM

A **court** is a tribunal established by government to hear and decide matters brought before it, provide remedies when a wrong has been committed, and prevent possible wrongs from happening. A court could award money damages to a business party for a breach of contract, but it could also issue an injunction to halt patent infringement. **For Example,** in 2006, a court's threat to issue an injunction to shut down operation of the BlackBerry wireless e-mail device system resulted in a settlement of the patent infringement case between Research in Motion, Ltd. (RIM), the BlackBerry service provider, and NTP, Inc., the company that had won its patent infringement case against RIM for the technology used in the BlackBerry device.[1]

1. The Types of Courts

Every type of court is given the authority to decide certain types or classes of cases. The power to hear cases is called **jurisdiction**. One form of jurisdiction, **subject matter jurisdiction**, covers the type of proceedings that the court holds. A court with **original jurisdiction** is the trial court or the court with the authority to conduct the first proceedings in the case. **For Example,** a court of original jurisdiction would be one where the witnesses actually testify, the documents are admitted into evidence, and the jury, in the case of a jury trial, is present to hear all the evidence and to make a decision.

Other types of subject matter jurisdiction are applicable to courts. A court with **general jurisdiction** has broad authority over different types of cases. The authority of a court with general jurisdiction can extend to both general civil and criminal cases. When a general jurisdiction trial court hears criminal cases, it conducts the trials of those charged with crimes. When a general trial court exercises its civil jurisdiction, it uses its authority to hear civil disputes, such as breach of contract cases and disputes about leases between landlords and tenants.

A court with **limited** or **special jurisdiction** has the authority to hear only particular kinds of cases. **For Example,** many states have courts that can hear only disputes in which the damages are $10,000 or less. Many types of courts have special jurisdiction, including juvenile courts, probate courts, and domestic relations courts. States vary in the names they give these courts, but all are courts of special or limited jurisdiction because they have very narrow authority for their subject matter jurisdiction. In the federal system, courts with limited or special jurisdiction include bankruptcy courts and the U.S. Tax Court.

A court with **appellate jurisdiction** reviews the work of a lower court. **For Example,** a trial court may issue a judgment that a defendant in a breach of contract suit should pay $500,000 in damages. That defendant could appeal the decision to an appellate court and seek review of the decision itself or even the amount of the damages.[2] An **appeal** is a review of the trial and decision of the lower court. An appellate court does not hear witnesses or take testimony. An appellate court, usually a panel of three judges, simply reviews the transcript and evidence from the lower court and determines whether there has been

---

[1] RIM eventually settled the suit with NTP by agreeing to pay $612.5 million.
[2] A case that is sent back for a redetermination of damages is remanded for what is known as *remittur*.

Yates v State, 171 SW 3D 215 (TEX APP 2005)

Law and Order on TV and in the Court

Andrea Pia Yates (Appellant) and Russell Yates were married on April 17, 1993. Their first child, Noah, was born in February 1994; their second child, John, was born in December 1995; and their third child, Paul, was born in September 1997. During this time, the Yates family moved from place to place living in a recreational vehicle. In 1998, they moved from the recreational vehicle to a converted bus and continued to live in a trailer park. At one point, appellant told her husband she felt depressed and overwhelmed, and he suggested that she talk to her mother and a friend.

In February 1999, a fourth child, Luke, was born. On June 18, 1999, Andrea suffered severe depression and tried to commit suicide by taking an overdose of an antidepressant that had been prescribed for her father. She was admitted to the psychiatric unit of Methodist Hospital. After her release six days later, she began seeing a psychiatrist as an outpatient. On July 20, 1999, her husband found Andrea in the bathroom, holding a knife to her neck. She was admitted to Spring Shadows Glen Hospital where a physician classified her among the five sickest patients she had ever seen. When she was discharged, her treating physician warned Mr. Yates that having another baby could result in a severe psychotic episode. Following her release in August 1999, the Yates family moved from the converted bus to a house and Yates began home-schooling Noah. In November 2000, Andrea had

her fifth child, Mary. Several months later her father died and Andrea experienced another depression and resulting hospitalization. Upon her discharge, her treating physician recommended that someone stay with her at all times and that she not be left alone with her children.

During April 2001, Mr. Yates' mother came to the house each day to help. Andrea's mother-in-law described Andrea as almost catatonic, unresponsive, trembling, and scratching her head until she created bald spots. She did not eat. On May 3, Andrea filled a bathtub with water, but could not give a good reason for doing so. When asked, she said, "I might need it." She was readmitted to the hospital for ten days from May 4 until May 14.

On June 20, 2001, at 9:48 A.M., appellant called 9-1-1 and told the operator that she needed a police officer to come to her home. She also called Yates at his work and told him that he needed to come home, but would not say why. As Yates was leaving, he called her and asked if anyone was hurt, and she said that the kids were hurt. He asked, "Which ones?" She responded, "All of them."

Within minutes of the 9-1-1 call, several police officers arrived at the Yates' home. They discovered four dead children, soaking wet and covered with a sheet, lying on appellant's bed. The fifth child, Noah, was still in the bathtub, floating face down.

Mrs. Yates was charged with capital murder and entered a plea of "not guilty by reason of insanity."

At trial, ten psychiatrists and two psychologists testified regarding Andrea's mental illness. The tenth psychiatrist, Dr. Park Dietz, who interviewed Yates and was the State's sole mental-health expert in the case, testified that Yates, although psychotic on June 20, knew that what she did was wrong. Dr. Dietz reasoned that because Yates indicated that her thoughts were coming from Satan, she must have known they were wrong; that if she believed she was saving the children, she would have shared her plan with others rather than hide it as she did; that if she really believed that Satan was going to harm the children, she would have called the police or a pastor or would have sent the children away; and that she covered the bodies out of guilt or shame.

On cross-examination, Yates's counsel asked Dr. Dietz about his consulting work with the television show *Law & Order*, which Yates was known to watch. The testimony was as follows:

Q. Now, you are, are you not, a consultant on the television program known as *Law & Order?*

A. Two of them.

Q. Okay. Did either one of those deal with postpartum depression or women's mental health?

A. As a matter of fact, there was a show of a woman with postpartum depression who drowned her children in the bathtub and was found insane and it was aired shortly before the crime occurred.

The second mention of *Law & Order* came during Dr. Lucy Puryear's testimony. Dr. Puryear, a defense expert witness, was cross-examined by the State regarding her evaluation of appellant. The State specifically asked about her failure to inquire into whether or not Yates had seen *Law & Order*. Dr. Puryear testified as follows:

Q. You know she watched *Law & Order* a lot; right?

A. I didn't know. No.

Q. Did you know that in the weeks before June 20th, there was a *Law & Order* episode where a woman killed her children by drowning them in a bathtub, was defended on the basis of whether she was sane or insane under the law, and the diagnosis was postpartum depression and in the program the

Continued

person was found insane, not guilty by reason of insanity? Did you know that?

A. No.

Q. If you had known that and had known that Andrea Yates was subject to these delusions, not that she was the subject of a delusion of reference, but that she regularly watched *Law & Order* and may have seen that episode, would you have changed the way you went about interviewing her, would you have interviewed whether she got the idea somehow she could do this and not suffer hell or prison?

A. I certainly wouldn't have asked her that question. No.

Q. Would you have—you didn't have to ask her that question, but you could have explored that?

A. If I had known she watched that show, I would have ask [ed] her about it, yes.

In his final argument at the guilt-innocence phase of the trial, appellant's attorney referred to Dr. Dietz's testimony by stating, "Or maybe even we heard some evidence that she saw some show on TV and knew she could drown her children and get away with it."

The prosecutor, in his final argument, made the following reference to Dietz's testimony about the *Law & Order* episode:

> She gets very depressed and goes into Devereux. And at times she says these thoughts came to her during that month. These thoughts came to her, and she watches Law & Order regularly, she sees this program. There is a way out. She tells that to Dr. Dietz. A way out.

The jury returned a guilty verdict. Mrs. Yates's counsel discovered that Dr. Dietz had given false testimony. The producer of *Law & Order* spoke to counsel by telephone and said he could not recall such an episode. An attorney representing the producer, after talking to Dr. Dietz and researching the shows, verified to counsel that there was no show with a plot as outlined by Dr. Dietz. Dr. Dietz acknowledged that he had made an error in his testimony. Mrs. Yates appealed the guilty verdict on the grounds that the testimony about the show constituted reversible error.

JUDICIAL OPINION

NUCHIA, Justice… The State recognizes that the State's knowing use of perjured testimony that is likely to materially affect the judgment violates the Due Process Clause of the Fourteenth Amendment of the United States Constitution. The State argues that it did not know that the testimony was false, did not use the false information, and the information was not material. We agree that this case does not involve the State's knowing use of perjured testimony. At the hearing on appellant's motion for mistrial, appellant did not complain that there had been prosecutorial misconduct. Rather, appellant stated, [M]ake no mistake, the issue is not whether or not the State was aware and we have no reason to believe the State was aware that such a program did not exist. The issue is that the defense of insanity was rebutted by the testimony of Dr. Dietz relative to an act of premeditation, that is a planned and/or a deceptive act on Mrs. Yates' part, that is something that would give her an idea, a way out of these particular allegations. And that was relayed to this jury and we believe that the jury relied upon the presentation of Dr. Dietz as well as the cross-examination by [the State's attorney] of Dr. Puryear relative to this particular issue.

It is uncontested that the testimony of Dr. Dietz regarding his consultation on a *Law & Order* television show having a plot remarkably similar to the acts committed by appellant was untrue and that there was no *Law & Order* television show with such a plot. However, the State asserts that it is "very questionable whether it can be said that the trial prosecutors used Dr. Dietz' testimony on cross-examination, especially in light of the fact that it played absolutely no role in the development of Dr. Dietz' conclusion that the appellant knew that her conduct was wrong. . . ."

The record reflects that the State used Dr. Dietz's testimony twice. First, the State used the testimony to cross-examine Dr. Puryear, who had seen appellant for several months while appellant was in the county jail, asking Dr. Puryear whether she knew that appellant watched *Law & Order* and whether she knew that there was an episode with a plot line mirroring appellant's acts. In so doing, the State repeated those facts that were common to appellant's acts and the referenced episode, thus emphasizing those facts already stated by Dr. Dietz. Second, the State connected the dots in its final argument by juxtaposing appellant's depression, her dark thoughts, watching *Law & Order* and seeing "a way out." Thus, the State used Dr. Dietz's false testimony to suggest to the jury that appellant patterned her actions after that *Law & Order* episode. We emphasize that the State's use of Dr. Dietz's false testimony was not prosecutorial misconduct. Rather, it served to give weight to that testimony.

The State argues that Dr. Dietz's testimony regarding the *Law & Order* episode was not material. The State asserts that "there is no reasonable likelihood" that the testimony "could

Continued

have affected the judgment of the jury," but does not make any argument to support such a conclusory statement. We conclude that the testimony, combined with the State's cross-examination of Dr. Puryear and closing argument, was material. The materiality of the testimony is further evidenced by the fact that appellant's attorney felt compelled to address it in his own closing argument.

The State also asserts that Dr. Dietz did not suggest that appellant used the plot of the show to plan killing her children. Although it is true that Dr. Dietz did not make such a suggestion, the State did in its closing argument.

Five mental health experts testified that appellant did not know right from wrong or that she thought what she did was right. Dr. Dietz was the only mental health expert who testified that appellant knew right from wrong. Therefore, his testimony was critical to establish the State's case. Although the record does not show that Dr. Dietz intentionally lied in his testimony, his false testimony undoubtedly gave greater weight to his opinion.

We conclude that there is a reasonable likelihood that Dr. Dietz's false testimony could have affected the judgment of the jury. We further conclude that Dr. Dietz's false testimony affected the substantial rights of appellant. We reverse the trial court's judgment and remand the cause for further proceedings.[3]

QUESTIONS

1. What was Mrs. Yates' family and mental health history?

2. What was the significance of the *Law & Order* show testimony?

3. Why does the appellate court find that the false testimony about the *Law & Order* segment was reversible error?

reversible error. A reversible error is a mistake in applying the law or a mistake in admitting evidence that affected the outcome of the case. An appellate court can **affirm** or **reverse** a lower court decision or **remand** that decision for another trial or additional hearings.

2. The Federal Court System

The federal court system consists of three levels of courts. Figure 2.1 illustrates federal court structure.

(A) FEDERAL DISTRICT COURTS. The **federal district courts** are the general trial courts of the federal system. They are courts of original jurisdiction that hear both civil and criminal matters. Criminal cases in federal district courts are those in which the defendant is charged with a violation of federal law (the U.S. Code). In addition to the criminal cases, the types of civil cases that can be brought in federal district courts include (1) civil suits in which the United States is a party, (2) cases between citizens of different states that involve damages of $75,000 or more, and (3) cases

that arise under the U.S. Constitution or federal laws and treaties.

Federal district courts are organized within each of the states. There are 94 federal districts (each state has at least one federal district and there are 89 federal districts in the United States with the remaining courts found in Puerto Rico, Guam, etc.). Judges and courtrooms are assigned according to the caseload in that geographic area of the state.[4] Some states, such as New York and California, have several federal districts because of the population base and the resulting caseload. Figure 2.2 shows the geographic structure of the federal court system, including the appellate circuits.

The federal system has additional trial courts with limited jurisdiction, differing from the general jurisdiction of the federal district courts. These courts include, for example, the federal bankruptcy courts, Indian tribal courts, Tax Court, Court of Federal Claims, Court of Veterans Appeals, and the Court of International Trade.

(B) U.S. COURTS OF APPEALS. The final decision in a federal district court can be appealed to a court with

---

[3] Mrs. Yates was found to be criminally insane in her 2006 retrial and is now institutionalized.
[4] For complete information about the courts and the number of judgeships, go to 28 USC §§ 81-144 and 28 USC §133.

FIGURE 2-1 | **The Federal Court System**

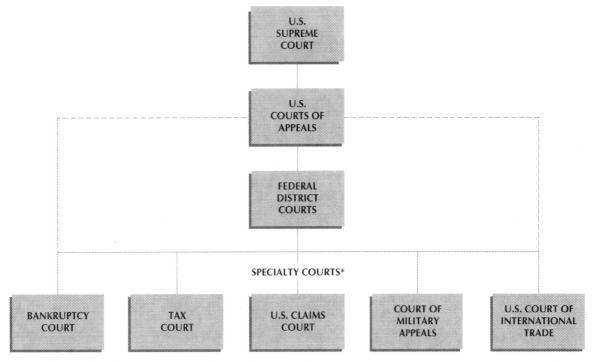

*Appeals often go directly to U.S. Courts of Appeals.

appellate jurisdiction. In the federal court system, the federal districts are grouped together geographically into 12 judicial circuits, including one for the District of Columbia. Additionally, a thirteenth federal circuit, called the *Federal Circuit,* hears certain types of appeals from all of the circuits, including specialty cases such as patent appeals. Each circuit has an appellate court called the U.S. Court of Appeals, and the judges for these courts review the decisions of the federal district courts. Generally, a panel of three judges reviews the cases. However, some decisions, called **en banc** decisions, are made by the circuit's full panel of judges. **For Example,** in 2003, the Ninth Circuit heard an appeal on a father's right to challenge the requirement

that his daughter recite the Pledge of Allegiance in the public school she attended. The contentious case had so many issues that the Ninth Circuit issued three opinions and the third opinion was issued after the case was heard *en banc.*[5]

(c) U.S. SUPREME COURT. The final court in the federal system is the U.S. Supreme Court. The U.S. Supreme Court has appellate jurisdiction over cases that are appealed from the federal courts of appeals as well as from state supreme courts when a constitutional issue is involved in the case or a state court has reversed a federal court ruling. The U.S. Supreme Court does not hear all cases from the federal courts of appeals

[5] *Newdow v U.S. Congress,* 292 F3d 597, 602 (CA 9 2002) (*Newdow I*); *Newdow v U.S. Congress,* 313 F3d 500, 502 (CA 9 2002) (*Newdow II*); and *Newdow v U.S. Congress,* 328 F3d 466, 468 (CA 9 2003) (*Newdow III*). The U.S. Supreme Court eventually heard the case. *Elkgrove Unified School District v Newdow,* 542 US 1 (2004). Another *en banc* hearing occurred at the Ninth Circuit over the issues in the California gubernatorial recall election. The three-judge panel held that the voting methods in California violated the rights of voters and therefore placed a stay on the election. However, the Ninth Circuit then heard the case *en banc* and reversed the decision of the original three-judge panel. The recall election then proceeded.

FIGURE 2-2 | **The Thirteen Federal Judicial Circuits**

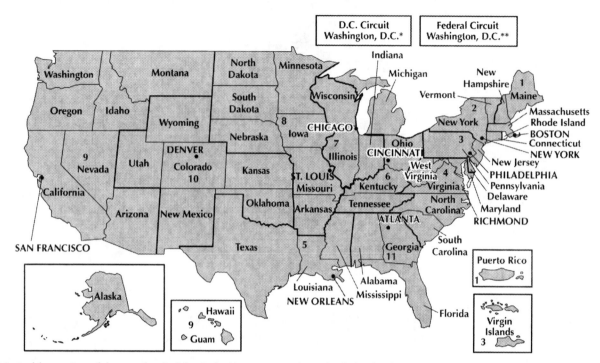

*A sizable portion of the caseload of the D.C. Circuit comes from the federal administrative agencies and offices located in Washington, D.C., such as the Securities and Exchange Commission, the National Labor Relations Board, the Federal Trade Commission, the Secretary of the Treasury, and the Labor Department, as well as appeals from the U.S. District Court of the District of Columbia.

**Rather than being defined by geography like the regional courts of appeals, the Federal Circuit is defined by subject matter, having jurisdiction over such matters as patent infringement cases, appeals from the Court of Federal Claims and the Court of International Trade, and appeals from administrative rulings regarding subject matter such as unfair import practices and tariff schedule disputes.

but has a process called granting a **writ of *certiorari***, which is a preliminary review of those cases appealed to decide whether a case will be heard or allowed to stand as ruled on by the lower courts.[6]

The U.S. Supreme Court is the only court expressly created in the U.S. Constitution. All other courts in the federal system were created by Congress pursuant to its Constitutional power. The Constitution also makes the U.S. Supreme Court a court of original jurisdiction. The U.S. Supreme Court serves as the trial court for cases involving ambassadors, public ministers, or consuls and for cases in which two states are involved in a lawsuit. **For Example,** the U.S. Supreme Court has served for a number of years as the trial court for a Colorado River water rights case in which California, Nevada, and Arizona are parties.

3. State Court Systems

(A) GENERAL TRIAL COURTS. Most states have trial courts of general jurisdiction that may be called superior courts, circuit courts, or county courts. These courts

---

[6] For example, the Supreme Court refused to grant *certiorari* in a Fifth Circuit case on law school admissions at the University of Texas. However, it granted *certiorari* in a later case involving law school admissions at the University of Michigan. *Gratz v Bollinger*, 539 US 244 (2003).

of general and original jurisdiction usually hear both criminal and civil cases. Cases that do not meet the jurisdictional requirements for the federal district courts would be tried in these courts. Figure 2.3 illustrates a sample state court system.

(B) SPECIALTY COURTS. Most states also have courts with limited jurisdiction, sometimes referred to as *specialty courts.* **For Example,** most states have juvenile courts, or courts with limited jurisdiction over criminal matters that involve defendants who are under the age of 18. Other specialty courts or lesser courts in state systems are probate and family law courts.

(C) CITY, MUNICIPAL, AND JUSTICE COURTS. Cities and counties may also have lesser courts with limited jurisdiction, which may be referred to as *municipal courts* or *justice courts.* These courts generally handle civil matters in which the claim made in the suit is an amount below a certain level, such as $5,000 or $10,000. These courts may also handle misdemeanor types of offenses, such as traffic violations or violations of noise ordinances, and the trials for them.

(D) SMALL CLAIMS COURTS. Most states also have **small claims courts** at the county or city level. These are courts of limited jurisdiction where parties with small amounts in dispute may come to have a third party, such as a justice of the peace or city judge, review their disputes and determine how they should be resolved. A true small claims court is one in which the parties are not permitted to be represented by counsel. Rather, the parties present their cases to the judge in an informal manner without the strict procedural rules that apply in courts of general jurisdiction. Small claims courts provide a faster and inexpensive means for resolving a dispute that does not involve a large amount of claimed damages.

(E) STATE APPELLATE COURTS. Most states also have intermediate-level courts similar to the federal courts of appeals. They are courts with appellate jurisdiction that review the decisions of lower courts in that state. Decisions of the general trial courts in a state would be appealed to these courts.

(F) STATE SUPREME COURTS. The highest court in most states is generally known as the *state supreme court,* but a few states, such as New York, may call their highest court the *court of appeals;* Maine and Massachusetts, for example, call their highest court the *supreme judicial court.* State supreme courts primarily have appellate jurisdiction, but some states' courts do have original jurisdiction, such as in Arizona, where counties in litigation have their trial at the supreme court level. Most state supreme courts also have a screening process for cases. They are required to hear some cases, such as criminal cases in which the defendant has received the death penalty. A decision of a state supreme court is final except in those circumstances in which a federal law or treaty or the U.S. Constitution is involved. Cases with these federal subject matter issues can then be appealed to the U.S. Supreme Court.

FIGURE 2-3 | *Sample State Court System*

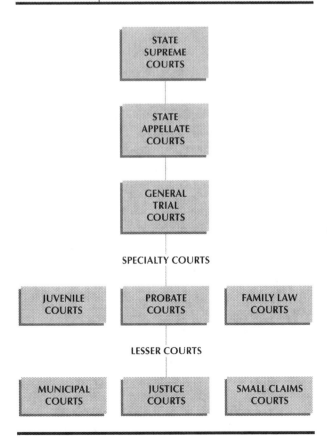

B. Court Procedure

Once a party decides to use the court system for resolution of a dispute, that party enters a world with specific rules, procedures, and terms that must be used to have a case proceed.

4. Participants in the Court System

The **plaintiff** is the party that initiates the proceedings in a court of original jurisdiction. In a criminal case in which charges are brought, the party initiating the proceedings would be called the **prosecutor**. The party against whom the civil or criminal proceedings are brought is the **defendant**. A **judge** is the primary officer of the court and is either an elected or an appointed official who presides over the matters brought before the court. Attorneys or lawyers are representatives for the plaintiff and the defendant for purposes of presenting their cases. Lawyers and clients have a privilege of confidentiality know as the **attorney-client privilege**. Lawyers cannot disclose what their clients tell them unless the client is committing, or plans to commit, a crime.

A **jury** is a body of citizens sworn by a court to reach a verdict on the basis of the case presented to them. Jurors are chosen for service based on lists compiled from voter registration and driver's license records.

5. Which Law Applies—Conflicts of Law

When a lawsuit is brought, there is not just the question of where a case will be tried but also of what law will be applied in determining the rights of the parties. The principle that determines when a court applies the law of its own state—the law of the forum—or some foreign law is called *conflict of laws*. Because there are 50 state court systems and a federal court system, as well as a high degree of interstate activity, conflicts of law questions arise frequently.

Some general rules apply. For example, the law of the state in which the court is located governs the case on procedural issues and rules of evidence. In contract litigation, the court applies the law of the state in which the contract was made for determining issues of formation. Performance disputes and damages for nonperformance are generally governed by the law of the state where the contract is to be performed. International contracts follow similar rules. **For Example,** a California court will apply Swiss law to a contract made in Switzerland that is to be performed in that country.

However, it is becoming more common for the parties to specify their choice of law in their contract. In the absence of a law-selecting provision in the contract, there is a growing acceptance of the rule that a contract should be governed by the law of the state that has the most significant contacts with the transaction.

For Example, assume the buyer's place of business and the seller's plant are located in Nebraska, and the buyer is purchasing goods from the seller to resell to Nebraska customers. Many courts will hold that this is a contract governed by the law of Nebraska. In determining which state has the most significant contacts, the court considers the place of contracting, negotiating, and performing; the location of the subject matter of the contract; and the domicile (residence), states of incorporation, and principal place of business of the parties.

6. Initial Steps in a Lawsuit

The following steps in a lawsuit generally apply in cases brought in courts of original jurisdiction. Not every step applies in every case, but understanding litigation steps and terms is important for businesspeople.

(A) Commencement of a Lawsuit. A lawsuit begins with the filing of a **complaint**. The complaint generally contains a description of the wrongful conduct and a request for damages, such as a monetary amount. **For Example,** a plaintiff in a contract suit would describe the contract, when it was entered into, and when the defendant stopped performance on the contract. A copy of the contract would be attached to the complaint.

(B) Service of Process. Once the plaintiff has filed the complaint with the proper court, the plaintiff has the responsibility of notifying the defendant that the lawsuit has been filed. The defendant must be served with **process**. Process, often called a *writ, notice,* or *summons,* is delivered to the defendant and includes a copy of the complaint and notification that the defendant must appear and respond to the allegations in the complaint.

(C) THE DEFENDANT'S RESPONSE AND THE PLEADINGS. After the defendant is served with process in the case, the defendant is required to respond to or **answer** the complaint within the time provided under the court's rules. In answering the plaintiff's complaint, the defendant has several options. For example, the defendant could make a **motion to dismiss**, which is a request to the court to dismiss the lawsuit on the grounds that, even if everything the plaintiff said in the complaint were true, there is still no right of recovery. A motion to dismiss is also called a **demurrer**.

A defendant could also respond and deny the allegations. **For Example,** in a contract lawsuit, the defendant-seller could say he did not breach the contract but stopped shipment of the goods because the plaintiff-buyer did not pay for the goods in advance as the contract required. A defendant could also **counterclaim** in the answer, which is asking the court for damages as a result of the underlying dispute. **For Example,** the defendant-seller in the contract lawsuit might ask for damages for the plaintiff-buyer's failure to pay as the contract required.

All documents filed in this initial phase of the case are referred to as the **pleadings**. The pleadings are a statement of the case and the basis for recovery if all the facts alleged can be proved.

(D) DISCOVERY. The Federal Rules of Civil Procedure and similar rules in all states permit one party to obtain from the adverse party information about all witnesses, documents, and any other items relevant to the case. **Discovery** requires each side to name its potential witnesses and to provide each side the chance to question those witnesses in advance of the trial. Each party also has the opportunity to examine, inspect, and photograph books, records, buildings, and machines. Even examining the physical or mental condition of a party is part of discovery when it has relevance in the case. The scope of discovery is extremely broad because the rules permit any questions that are likely to lead to admissible evidence.

Deposition.

A **deposition** is the testimony of a witness taken under oath outside the courtroom; it is transcribed by a court reporter. Each party is permitted to question the witness. If a party or a witness gives testimony at the trial that is inconsistent with her deposition testimony, the prior inconsistent testimony can be used to **impeach** the witness's credibility at trial

Depositions can be taken either for discovery purposes or to preserve the testimony of a witness who will not be available during the trial. Some states now permit depositions to be videotaped. A videotape is a more effective way of presenting deposition testimony than reading that testimony at trial from a reporter's transcript because jurors can see the witness and the witness's demeanor and hear the words as they were spoken, complete with inflection.[7]

Other Forms of Discovery.

Other forms of discovery include written **interrogatories** (questions) and written **requests for production of documents**. These discovery requests can be very time consuming to the answering party and often lead to pretrial legal disputes between the parties and their attorneys as a result of the legal expenses involved.

(E) MOTION FOR SUMMARY JUDGMENT. If a case has no material facts in dispute, either party can file a **motion for summary judgment**. Using affidavits or deposition testimony obtained in discovery, the court can find that there are no factual issues and decide the case as a matter of law. **For Example,** suppose that the parties can agree that they entered into a life insurance contract but dispute whether the policy applies when there is a suicide. The facts are not in dispute; the law on payment of insurance proceeds in the event of a suicide is the issue. Such a case is one that is appropriate for summary judgment.

---

[7] At the civil trial of O.J. Simpson for the wrongful death of Nicole Brown Simpson and Ronald Goldman, Daniel Petrocelli used a videotape of Mr. Simpson's deposition very effectively in impeaching Mr. Simpson's testimony at trial. Daniel Petrocelli, *Triumph of Justice: The Final Judgment on the Simpson Saga* (New York: Crown, 1998).

(F) DESIGNATION OF EXPERT WITNESSES. In some cases, such as those involving product safety, the parties may want to designate an expert witness. An **expert witness** is a witness who has some special expertise, such as an economist who gives expert opinion on the value of future lost income or a scientist who testifies about the safety of a prescription drug. There are rules for naming expert witnesses as well as for admitting into evidence any studies or documents of the expert.[8] The purpose of these rules is to avoid the problem of what has been called *junk science,* or the admission of experts' testimony and research that has not been properly conducted or reviewed by peers.

7. The Trial

(A) SELECTING A JURY. Jurors drawn for service are questioned by the judge and lawyers to determine whether they are biased or have any preformed judgments about the parties in the case. Jury selection is called ***voir dire* examination.** For Example, in the trial of Martha Stewart, the multimedia home and garden diva, it took a great deal of time for the lawyers to question the potential jurors about their prior knowledge concerning the case, which had received nationwide attention and much media coverage. Lawyers have the opportunity to remove jurors who know parties in the case or who indicate they have already formed opinions about guilt or innocence. The attorneys question the potential jurors to determine if a juror should be *challenged for cause* (e.g., when the prospective juror states he is employed by the plaintiff's company). Challenges for cause are unlimited, but each side can also exercise six to eight peremptory challenges.[9] A peremptory challenge is an arbitrary challenge that may be used to strike (remove) a juror except for racial reasons.

(B) OPENING STATEMENTS. After the jury is called, the opposing attorneys make their **opening statements** to the jury. An opening statement, as one lawyer has explained, makes a puzzle frame for the case so jurors can follow the witnesses and place the pieces of the case—the various forms of evidence—within the frame.

(C) THE PRESENTATION OF EVIDENCE. Following the opening statements, the plaintiff then begins to present his case with witnesses and other evidence. A judge rules on the **admissibility** of evidence. Evidence can consist of documents, testimony, and even physical evidence.

In the case of testimony, the attorney for the plaintiff conducts **direct examination** of his witnesses during his case, and the defense attorney conducts **cross-examination** of the plaintiff's witnesses. The plaintiff's attorney can then ask questions again of his witnesses in what is called **redirect examination**. Finally, the defense attorney may question the plaintiff's witnesses again in **recross-examination**. This procedure is followed with all of the plaintiff's witnesses, and then the defendant presents her case after the plaintiff's case concludes. During the defendant's case, the lawyer for the defendant conducts direct examination of the defendant's witnesses, and the plaintiff's lawyer can then cross-examine the defendant's witnesses.

(D) MOTION FOR A DIRECTED VERDICT. A motion for a **directed verdict** asks the court to grant a verdict because even if all the evidence that has been presented by each side were true, there is either no basis for recovery or no defense to recovery. For example, in some states, the defendant can make a motion for a directed verdict after the plaintiff's case is concluded. The defendant's motion argues that even if the plaintiff's case were 100 percent true, there is no basis in law for recovery. It is also possible for either side to move for a directed verdict after both sides have presented their cases. The defendant is arguing the same position as stated earlier, that there is no basis for recovery even assuming all facts to be true. The plaintiff is arguing that even if everything the defendant presented were 100 percent true, there was nothing in the defense case that challenged the plaintiff's right to recovery.

(E) SUMMATION. After the witnesses for both parties have been examined and all the evidence has been presented, each attorney makes another address to the jury. These statements are called **summations** or

---

[8] *Daubert v Merrell Dow Pharmaceuticals, Inc.,* 509 US 579 (1993).
[9] The number of peremptory challenges varies from state to state and may also vary within a particular state depending on the type of case. For example, in Arizona, peremptory challenges are unlimited in capital cases.

ethics & the law

Qualcomm filed suit against Broadcom for alleged patent infringement. Broadcom made a discovery request from Qualcomm for copies of e-mail and other correspondence among and between Qualcomm employees and others in their industry. Qualcomm lawyers turned over a handful of e-mails but did not turn over 200,000 pages of e-mails, memoranda, and other company documents,

all of which had important information that undercut Qualcomm's patent infringement claim. In fact, Qualcomm's legal counsel, while preparing a key Qualcomm witness for her testimony, stripped over 50 pages of e-mails from her email archives. Evaluate the ethics of Qualcomm's lawyer [**Qualcomm, Inc. v Broadcom, Inc., 539 F Supp 2d 1214 SD Cal 2007**]

thinking things through
Why Do We Require Sworn Testimony?

There is a difference between what people say in conversation (and even what company executives say in speeches and reports) and what they are willing to say under oath. Speaking under oath often means that different information and recollections emerge. The oath is symbolic and carries the penalty of criminal prosecution for perjury if the testimony given is false.

The *Wall Street Journal* has reported that the testimony of executives in the Microsoft antitrust trial and their statements regarding their business relationships outside the courtroom are quite different. For example, the following quotations indicate some discrepancies. Eric Benhamou, the chief executive officer (CEO) of Palm, Inc., said:

> We believe that the handheld opportunity remains wide open.... Unlike the PC industry, there is no monopoly of silicon, there is no monopoly of software.

However, at the Microsoft trial, another officer of Palm, Michael Mace, offered the following testimony:

> We believe that there is a very substantial risk that Microsoft could manipulate its products and its standards in order to exclude Palm from the marketplace in the future.

Likewise, Microsoft has taken different positions inside and outside the courtroom. For example, an attorney for Microsoft stated that Microsoft had "zero deployments of its interactive TV middleware products connected to cable systems in the United States." However, Microsoft's marketing materials provide as follows:

> Microsoft's multiple deployments around the world now including Charter-show Microsoft TV is ready to deploy now and set the standard for what TV can be.*

Explain why the executives had differing statements. For more information on the Microsoft antitrust cases, go to **www.usdoj.gov** or **www.microsoft.com**.

* Rebecca Buckman and Nicholas Kulish, "Microsoft Trial Prompts an Outbreak of Doublespeak," *Wall Street Journal*, April *5, 2002, B1, B3.

closing arguments; they summarize the case and suggest that a particular verdict be returned by the jury.

(F) MOTION FOR MISTRIAL. During the course of a trial, when necessary to avoid great injustice, the trial court may declare that there has been a **mistrial**. The declaration of a mistrial terminates the trial and requires that it start over with a new jury. A mistrial can be declared for jury or attorney misconduct. **For Example,** if a juror were caught fraternizing with one of the lawyers in the case, objectivity would be compromised and the court would most likely declare a mistrial.

(G) JURY INSTRUCTIONS AND VERDICT. After the summation by the attorneys, the court gives the jurors **instructions** on the appropriate law to apply to the facts presented. The jury then deliberates and renders its verdict. After the jury verdict, the court enters a judgment. If the jury is deadlocked and unable to reach a verdict, the case is reset for a new trial at some future date.

(H) MOTION FOR NEW TRIAL; MOTION FOR JUDGMENT N.O.V. A court may grant a judgment *non obstante veredicto* or a **judgment n.o.v.** (notwithstanding the verdict) if the verdict is clearly wrong as a matter of law. The court can set aside the verdict and enter a judgment in favor of the other party. Perhaps one of the most famous judgments n.o.v. occurred in Boston in 1997 when a judge reversed the murder conviction of nanny Louise Woodward, who was charged with the murder of one of her young charges.

8. Posttrial Procedures

(A) RECOVERY OF COSTS/ATTORNEY FEES. Generally, the prevailing party is awarded costs. Costs include filing fees, service-of-process fees, witness fees, deposition transcript costs, and jury fees. Costs do not include compensation spent by a party for preparing the case or being present at trial, including the time lost from work because of the case and the fee paid to the attorney, although lost wages from an injury are generally part of damages.

Attorney fees may be recovered by a party who prevails if a statute permits the recovery of attorney fees or if the complaint involves a claim for breach of contract and the contract contains a clause providing for recovery of attorney fees.

(B) EXECUTION OF JUDGMENT. After a judgment has been entered or all appeals or appeal rights have ended, the losing party must pay that judgment. The winning party can also take steps to execute, or carry out, the judgment. The **execution** is accomplished by the seizure and sale of the losing party's assets by the sheriff according to a writ of execution or a writ of possession.

Garnishment is a common method of satisfying a judgment. When the judgment debtor is an employee, the appropriate judicial authority in the state garnishes (by written notice to the employer) a portion of the employee's wages on a regular basis until the judgment is paid.

C. ALTERNATIVE DISPUTE RESOLUTION (ADR)

Parties can use means other than litigation to resolve disagreements or disputes. Litigation takes significant time and money, so many businesses use alternative methods for resolving disputes. Those methods, which include arbitration, mediation, and several other formats, are enjoying increasing popularity. Figure 2.4 provides an overall view of dispute resolution procedures.

9. Arbitration

In **arbitration**, arbitrators (disinterested persons selected by the parties to the dispute) hear evidence and determine a resolution. Arbitration enables the parties to present the facts before trained experts familiar with the industry practices that may affect the nature and outcome of the dispute. Arbitration first reached extensive use in the field of commercial contracts and is encouraged as a means of avoiding expensive litigation and easing the workload of courts.[10]

---

[10] *Warfield v Beth* Israel Deaconess Medical Center, Inc. 910 NE2d 317, 454 Mass 390, (2009). Arbitration has existed in the United States since 1920 when New York passed an arbitration statute. For a look at the history of arbitration, see Charles L. Knapp, "Taking Contracts Private: The Quiet Revolution in Contract Law," 71 *Fordham L. Rev.* 761 (2002).

FIGURE 2-4 | **Dispute Resolution Procedures**

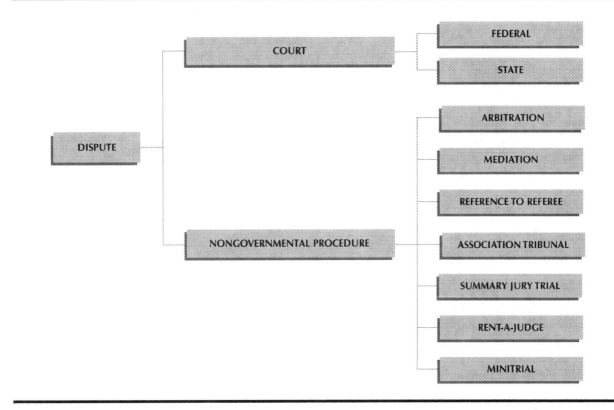

A number of states have adopted the Uniform Arbitration Act.[11] Under this act and similar statutes, the parties to a contract may agree in advance that all disputes arising under it will be submitted to arbitration. In some instances, the contract will name the arbitrators for the duration of the contract. The uniform act requires a written agreement to arbitrate.[12]

The Federal Arbitration Act[13] provides that an arbitration clause in a contract relating to an interstate transaction is valid, irrevocable, and enforceable. When a contract subject to the Federal Arbitration Act provides for the arbitration of disputes, the parties are bound to arbitrate in accordance with the federal statute even if the agreement to arbitrate would not be binding under state law.

(A) MANDATORY ARBITRATION. In contrast with statutes that merely regulate arbitration when it is selected voluntarily by the parties, some statutes require that certain kinds of disputes be submitted to arbitration. In some states, by rule or statute, the arbitration of small claims is required.

(B) SCOPE OF ARBITRATION. When arbitration is required by statute, the terms of the statute will define the scope of the arbitration. When the parties have voluntarily agreed to arbitrate, their agreement will control the scope of the dispute. Because arbitration is now favored, any doubt as to its scope will be decided in favor of arbitration by the arbitrator.[14]

---

[11] On August 3, 2000, the National Conference of Commissioners on Uniform State Laws unanimously passed major revisions to the Uniform Arbitration Act (UAA). These revisions were the first major changes in 45 years to the UAA, which is the basis of arbitration law in 49 states, although not all states have adopted it in its entirety. Thirty-five states and the District of Columbia have adopted the 1955 version. Only 13 states have adopted the UAA 2000 revisions. Donald L. Carpo & John B. LaRocco, "A Comparison of Litigation, Arbitration, and Mediation," 63 *Dispute Resolution* J. 48 (2008).

[12] Fawzy v Fawzy, 973 A2d 347 (NJ 2009).

[13] 9 USC § 114 *et seq.*

[14] *First Options v Kaplan*, 514 US 938 (1995). See also *Hialeah Automotive, LLC v Basulto*— So2d —, 2009 WL 187584 (Fla App).

(C) FINALITY OF ARBITRATION. Most parties provide, within their arbitration agreements, that the decision of the arbitrator will be final. Such a clause is binding on the parties, even when the decision seems to be wrong, and can be set aside only if there is clear proof of fraud, arbitrary conduct, or a significant procedural error.[15]

If the arbitration is mandatory under statute or rule, the losing party generally may appeal such arbitration to a court.[16] The appeal proceeds just as though there had never been any prior arbitration. This new court proceeding is called a **trial *de novo*** and is necessary to preserve the constitutional right to a jury trial. As a practical matter, however, relatively few appeals are taken from arbitration decisions.

10. Mediation

In **mediation**, a neutral person acts as a messenger between opposing sides of a dispute, carrying to each side the latest settlement offer made by the other. The mediator has no authority to make a decision, although in some cases the mediator may make suggestions that might ultimately be accepted by the disputing parties.

The use of mediation has the advantage of keeping discussions going when the disputing parties have developed such fixed attitudes or personal animosity that direct discussion between them has become impossible.

11. MedArb

In this new form of alternative dispute resolution (ADR), the arbitrator is also empowered to act as a mediator. Beyond just hearing a case, the arbitrator acts as a messenger for the parties on unresolved issues.

12. Reference to a Third Person

Many types of transactions provide for **reference to a third person**, in which a third person or a committee makes an out-of-court determination of the rights of persons. **For Example,** employees and an employer

may have agreed as a term of the employment contract that claims of employees under retirement plans will be decided by a designated board or committee. In a sales contract, the seller and buyer can select a third person to determine the price to be paid for goods. Construction contracts often include a provision for disputes to be referred to the architect in charge of the construction with the architect's decision being final.

These referrals often eliminate the disputes or pursuit of remedies. **For Example,** fire insurance policies commonly provide that if the parties cannot agree on the amount of the loss, each will appoint an appraiser, the two appraisers will appoint a third appraiser, and the three will determine the amount of the loss the insurer is required to pay.

13. Association Tribunals

Many disputes never reach the courts because both parties to a dispute belong to a group or an association, and the **association tribunal** created by the group or association disposes of the matter. Trade associations commonly require their members to employ out-of-court methods of dispute settlement. **For Example,** the National Association of Home Builders requires its member builders to employ arbitration. The National Automobile Dealers Association provides for panels to determine warranty claims of customers. The decision of such panels is final as to the builder or dealer, but the consumer can still bring a regular lawsuit after losing before the panel. Members of an association must use the association tribunal, which means they cannot bypass the association tribunal and go directly to a law court.[17]

14. Summary Jury Trial

A **summary jury trial** is a dry-run or mock trial in which the lawyers present their claims before a jury of six persons. The object is to get the reaction of a sample jury. No evidence is presented before this jury, and it bases its opinion solely on what the lawyers state. The determination of the jury has no binding effect, but it has value in that it gives the lawyers some idea of what a

---

[15] *Apache Bohai Corp. LDC v Texaco China BV*, 480 F.3d 397 (CA 5 2007).
[16] *U.S. v Park Place Associates*, 563 F3d 907 (CA 9 2009).
[17] The securities industry follows this process as well.

e-commerce&cyberlaw

Referred to as the "Google Mistrial," a federal judge in Florida declared a mistrial after a juror told that judge that he had been doing research on the Internet on the drug trial in which he was serving When the judge declared the mistrial, eight other jurors confessed that they had been doing the same thing.

Judges have long warned jurors about using outside sources, including the Internet, but BlackBerries and iPhones have proven to be mighty tempting for jurors. Some jurors are using Facebook to announce when verdicts are coming. One juror even looked up evidence that had been excluded by the judge in the case. When asked why he violated the judge's order, the juror said simply, "Well, I was curious."

A judge in Arkansas is reviewing a request for a reversal of a $12.6 million jury verdict against a company from one of the company's lawyers based on the court's discovery that one of the jurors was using Twitter to send out postings about how the trial was proceeding. An excerpt from the posting follows:

> "Oh, and nobody buy Stoam. It's bad mojo and they'll probably cease to Exist now that their wallet is $12m lighter ... So, Jonathan, what did you do today? Oh nothing really, I just gave away TWELVE MILLION DOLLARS of somebody else's money."*

What is the problem with jurors using these electronic tools during their cases?

* John Schwartz, "As Jurors Turn to Google and Twitter, Mistrials Are Popping Up," *New York Times*, March 18, 2009, A1.

---

jury might think if there were an actual trial. This type of ADR has special value when the heart of a case is whether something is reasonable under all circumstances. When the lawyers and their clients see how the sample jury reacts, they may moderate their positions and reach a settlement.

15. Rent-A-Judge

Under the **rent-a-judge plan**, the parties hire a judge to hear the case. In many states, the parties voluntarily choose the judge as a "referee," and the judge acts under a statute authorizing the appointment of referees. Under such a statute, the referee hears all evidence just as though there were a regular trial, and the rented judge's determination is binding on the parties unless reversed on appeal if such an appeal (like a court trial) is permitted under the parties' agreement. In some jurisdictions, the parties can agree that the decision of the judge selected as referee will be final.

16. Minitrial

When only part of a case is disputed, the parties may stay within the framework of a lawsuit but agree that only the disputed issues will be taken to trial and submitted to a jury. When there is no real dispute over the liability of the defendant but the parties disagree as to the damages, the issue of damages alone may be submitted to the jury. This shortened trial is often called a **minitrial**. A minitrial may use a retired judge to listen to the evidence on just the disputed issues and decide the case. The agreement of the parties for the minitrial may specify whether this decision will be binding on the parties. As a practical matter, the evaluation of a case by a neutral person often brings the opposing parties together to reach a settlement.

17. Judicial Triage

The court systems, experiencing heavy caseloads, now practice **judicial triage**. Judges examine cases from a timeliness perspective. For example, in asbestos cases, judges are now evaluating plaintiffs on the basis of "how sick they are" and expediting trials for those plaintiffs who are the most ill from the alleged effects of asbestos that are the subject of their suits. The trials of those who do not have medical documentation of current illness are postponed and placed on the inactive docket until the court can get to them or until the plaintiffs become sick. Using triage, one judge has been able to bring to trial 40 percent of all asbestos cases brought since 1992.[18]

18. Contract Provisions

The parties' contract may pave the way for the settlement of future disputes by containing clauses requiring the parties to use one of the procedures already described. In addition, contracts may provide that no action may be taken until after the expiration of a specified cooling-off period. Contracts may also specify that the parties should continue in the performance of their contract even though a dispute between them still exists.

19. Disposition of Complaints and Ombudsmen

In contrast with the traditional and alternative procedures for resolving disputes are the procedures aimed at removing the grounds for a complaint before it develops into a dispute that requires resolution. **For Example,** the complaint department in a

department store is often be able to iron out a difficulty before the customer and the store are locked in an adversarial position that could end in a lawsuit. Some states have a public official, called an **ombudsman**, who receive complaints and then make recommendations for improvements.

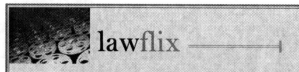

lawflix

Class Action (1991) (R)

Here is a good movie to illustrate discovery and the ethics of withholding paperwork.

Twelve Angry Men (1957) G

A movie that shows the jury process, rights of parties in court, jury instructions, and group think, all wrapped up in terrific dialogue.

Check out LawFlix at **www.cengage.com/blaw/dvl** to access movie clips that illustrate business law concepts.

MAKE THE CONNECTION

SUMMARY

Courts have been created to hear and resolve legal disputes. A court's specific power is defined by its jurisdiction. Courts of original jurisdiction are trial courts, and courts that review the decisions of trial courts are appellate courts. Trial courts may have general jurisdiction to hear a wide range of civil and criminal matters, or they may be courts of limited jurisdiction—such as a probate court or the Tax Court—with the subject matter of their cases restricted to certain areas.

The courts in the United States are organized into two different systems: the state and federal court systems. There are three levels of courts, for the most part, in each system, with trial courts, appellate courts, and a supreme court in each. The federal courts are federal district courts, federal courts of appeals, and the U.S. Supreme Court. In the states, there may be specialized courts, such as municipal, justice, and small claims courts, for trial courts. Within the courts of original jurisdiction, there are rules for procedures in all

---

[18] Susan Warren, "Swamped Courts Practice Plaintiff Triage," *Wall Street Journal,* January 27, 2003, B1, B3.

matters brought before them. A civil case begins with the filing of a complaint by a plaintiff, which is then answered by a defendant. The parties may be represented by their attorneys. Discovery is the pretrial process used by the parties to find out the evidence in the case. The parties can use depositions, interrogatories, and document requests to uncover relevant information.

The case is managed by a judge and may be tried to a jury selected through the process of *voir dire*, with the parties permitted to challenge jurors on the basis of cause or through the use of their peremptory challenges. The trial begins following discovery and involves opening statements and the presentation of evidence, including the direct examination and cross-

examination of witnesses. Once a judgment is entered, the party who has won can collect the judgment through garnishment and a writ of execution.

Alternatives to litigation for dispute resolution are available, including arbitration, mediation, MedArb, reference to a third party, association tribunals, summary jury trials, rent-a-judge plans, minitrials, judicial triage, and the use of ombudsmen. Court dockets are relieved and cases consolidated using judicial triage, a process in which courts hear the cases involving the most serious medical issues and health conditions first. Triage is a blending of the judicial and alternative dispute resolution mechanisms.

LEARNING OUTCOMES

After studying this chapter, you should be able to clearly explain:

A. THE COURT SYSTEM

LO.1 Explain the federal and state court systems
  See Figure 2-1 on p. 19 and accompanying text.
  See Figure 2-3 on p. 21 and accompanying text.

B. COURT PROCEDURE

LO.2 Describe court procedures
  See the discussion of steps in litigation that begins on p. 22.
  See the **For Example** discussion of the Martha Stewart *voir dire* example on p. 24.

C. ALTERNATIVE DISPUTE RESOLUTION (ADR)

LO.3 List the forms of alternative dispute resolution and distinguish among them
  See the discussion of arbitration that begins on p. 26.
  See the discussion of other forms of ADR, mediation, minitrials, rent-a-judge, MedArb, judicial triage, and referral to a third party that begins on p. 28.
  See the discussion of employee and employer referrals of disputes to a designated board or committee on p. 28.

KEY TERMS

admissibility
affirm
answer
appeal
appellate jurisdiction
arbitration
association tribunal
attorney-client privilege
complaint
counterclaim
court
cross-examination

defendant
demurrer
deposition
direct examination
directed verdict
discovery
en banc
execution
expert witness
federal district courts
garnishment
general jurisdiction

impeach
instructions
interrogatories
judge
judgment n.o.v.
judicial triage
jurisdiction
jury
limited jurisdiction
mediation
minitrial
mistrial

motion for summary judgment	prosecutor	reversible error
motion to dismiss	recross-examination	small claims courts
ombudsman	redirect examination	special jurisdiction
opening statements	reference to a third person	subject matter jurisdiction
original jurisdiction	remand	summary jury trial
plaintiff	rent-a-judge plan	summations
pleadings	requests for production of documents	trial *de novo*
process	reverse	*voir dire* examination
		writ of *certiorari*

QUESTIONS AND CASE PROBLEMS

1. List the steps in a lawsuit. Begin with the filing of the complaint, and explain the points at which there can be a final determination of the parties' rights in the case.

2. Distinguish between mandatory and voluntary arbitration. What is the difference between mediation and arbitration?

3. Ralph Dewey has been charged with a violation of the Electronic Espionage Act, a federal statute that prohibits the transfer, by computer or disk or other electronic means, of a company's proprietary data and information. Ralph is curious. What type of court has jurisdiction? Can you determine which court?

4. Jerry Lewinsky was called for jury duty. When *voir dire* began, Jerry realized that the case involved his supervisor at work. Can Jerry remain as a juror on the case? Why or why not?

5. Carolyn, Elwood, and Isabella are involved in a real estate development. The development is a failure, and Carolyn, Elwood, and Isabella want to have their rights determined. They could bring a lawsuit, but they are afraid the case is so complicated that a judge and jury not familiar with the problems of real estate development would not reach a proper result. What can they do?

6. Larketta Randolph purchased a mobile home from Better Cents Home Builders, Inc., and financed her purchase through Green Tree Financial Corporation. Ms. Randolph signed a standard form contract that required her to buy Vendor's Single Interest insurance, which protects the seller against the costs of repossession in the event of default. The agreement also provided that all disputes arising from the contract would be resolved by binding arbitration. Larketta found that there was an additional $15 in finance charges that were not disclosed in the contract. She and other Green Tree customers filed a class-action suit to recover the fees. Green Tree moved to dismiss the suit because Larketta had not submitted the issue to arbitration. Larketta protests, "But I want the right to go to court!" Does she have that right? What are the rights of parties under a contract with an arbitration clause? [*Green Tree Financial Corp. v Randolph*, 531 US 79]

7. John Watson invested $5,000,000 in SmartRead, Inc., a company that was developing an electronic reading device. Within a few months, the $5,000,000 was spent but SmartRead never developed the reading device. John filed suit against directors of SmartRead for their failure to supervise SmartRead's CEO in his operation of the company. The directors used an expert on corporate governance to testify that the directors had done all that they could to oversee the company. The expert did not disclose that he had served as a director of a company and had been found to be negligent in his role there and had been required to pay $370,000 to shareholders. The directors won the case. Is there anything Watson can do?

8. Indicate whether the following courts are courts of original, general, limited, or appellate jurisdiction:

   a. Small claims court

   b. Federal bankruptcy court

c. Federal district court

d. U.S. Supreme Court

e. Municipal court

f. Probate court

g. Federal court of appeals

9. The Nursing Home Pension Fund filed suit against Oracle Corporation alleging that Larry Ellison, the company's CEO, misled investors in 2001 about the true financial condition of the company. During the time of the alleged misrepresentation, Mr. Ellison was working with a biographer on his life story and there are videotapes of Mr. Ellison's interviews with his biographer as well as e-mails between the two that discuss Oracle. Could the Nursing Home Pension Fund have access to the tapes and e-mails? Explain how. [*Nursing Home Pension Fund, Local 144 v Oracle Corp.*, 380 F3d 1226 (CA 9)]

10. Mostek Corp., a Texas corporation, made a contract to sell computer-related products to North American Foreign Trading Corp., a New York corporation. North American used its own purchase order form, on which appeared the statement that any dispute arising out of an order would be submitted to arbitration, as provided in the terms set forth on the back of the order. Acting on the purchase order, Mostek delivered almost all of the goods but failed to deliver the final installment. North American then demanded that the matter be arbitrated. Mostek refused to do so. Was arbitration required? [*Application of Mostek Corp.,* 120 App Div 2d 383, 502 NYS2d 181]

11. Ceasar Wright was a longshoreman in Charleston, South Carolina, and a member of the International Longshoremen's Association (AFL-CIO). Wright used the union hiring hall. The collective bargaining agreement (CBA) of Wright's union provides for arbitration of all grievances. Another clause of the CBA states: "It is the intention and purpose of all parties hereto that no provision or part of this Agreement shall be violative of any Federal or State Law."

On February 18, 1992, while Wright was working for Stevens Shipping and Terminal Company (Stevens), he injured his right heel and back. He sought permanent compensation from Stevens and settled his claims for $250,000 and another $10,000 in attorney fees. Wright was also awarded Social Security disability benefits.

In January 1995, Wright, whose doctor had approved his return to work, returned to the hiring hall and asked to be referred for work. Wright did work between January 2 and January 11, 1995, but when the companies realized Wright had been certified as permanently disabled, they deemed him not qualified for longshoreman work under the CBA and refused to allow him to work for them.

Wright did not file a grievance under the union agreement but instead hired a lawyer and proceeded with a claim under the Americans with Disabilities Act. The district court dismissed the case because Wright had failed to pursue the grievance procedure provided by the CBA. Must Wright pursue the dispute procedure first, or can he go right to court on the basis of his federal rights under the Americans with Disabilities Act? [*Wright v Universal Maritime Service Corp.*, 525 US 70]

12. Winona Ryder was arrested for shoplifting from Saks Fifth Avenue in California. One of the members of the jury panel for her trial was Peter Guber, a Hollywood executive in charge of the production of three films in which Ms. Ryder starred, including *Bram Stoker's Dracula, The Age of Innocence,* and *Little Women.* If you were the prosecuting attorney in the case, how could you discover such information about this potential juror, and what are your options for excluding him from selection? [Rick Lyman, "For the Ryder Trial, a Hollywood Script," *New York Times,* November 3, 2002, SL-1]

13. What is the difference between the role of a trial court and the role of an appellate court? What functions do they perform, and how do they perform them?

14. Martha Simms is the plaintiff in a contract suit she has brought against Floral Supply, Inc., for its failure to deliver the green sponge Martha needed in building the floral designs she sells to exclusive home decorators. Martha had to obtain the sponge from another supplier and was late on seven deliveries. One of Martha's customers has been called by Martha's lawyer as a witness and is now on the witness stand, testifying about Martha's late performance and the penalty she charged. The lawyer for Floral Supply knows that Martha's customer frequently waives penalties for good suppliers. How can Floral Supply's lawyer get that information before the jury?

Chapter 3

BUSINESS ETHICS, SOCIAL FORCES, AND THE LAW

Each day businesspeople work together on contracts and projects. Their completion of the work is partially the result of the laws that protect contract rights. Much of what businesspeople do, however, is simply a matter of their word. Executives arrive at a 9:00 A.M. meeting because they promised they would be there. An employee meets a deadline for an ad display board because she said she would. Business transactions are completed through a combination of the values of the parties and the laws that reflect those values and the importance of one's word in business.

This chapter takes you behind the rules of law to examine the objectives in establishing rules for business conduct. Both social forces and business needs contribute to the standards that govern businesses and their operations.

A. WHAT IS BUSINESS ETHICS?

Ethics is a branch of philosophy dealing with values that relate to the nature of human conduct and values associated with that conduct. Balancing the goal of profits with the values of individuals and society is the focus of **business ethics**. Some economists make the point that insider trading is an efficient way to run that market. To an economist, inside information allows those with the best information to make the most money. This view ignores some issues: What about those who trade stock who do not have access to that information? Is the philosophy fair to them? What will happen to the stock market if investors perceive there is not a level playing field? In the U.S. Supreme Court decision *United States v O'Hagan*[1] on insider trading, Justice Ruth Ginsburg noted, "Investors likely wouldn't invest in a market where trading based on misappropriated nonpublic information is unchecked." The field of business ethics deals with the balance between society's values and the need for businesses to remain profitable.

1. The Law as the Standard for Business Ethics

Philosophers debate the origin of moral and ethical standards as well as which of those standards should be applied. One view of ethics is simply following what codified or **positive law** requires. The test of whether an act is legal is a common moral standard used frequently in business. Codified law, or law created by governmental authority, is used as the standard for ethical behavior. Absent illegality, all behavior is ethical under this simple standard. The phrase "AS IS," on a contract (see Chapter 25 for further discussion), means by law that there are no warranties for the goods being sold. **For Example,** if a buyer purchases a used car and the phrase "AS IS" is in the contract, the seller has no legal obligation, in most states, if the transmission falls apart the day after the buyer's purchase. Following a positive law standard, the seller who refuses to repair the transmission has acted ethically. However, ethical standards are different. We know there was no legal obligation to fix the transmission, but was it fair that the car fell apart the day after it was purchased?

2. The Notion of Universal Standards for Business Ethics

Another view of ethics holds that standards exist universally and cannot be changed or modified by law. In many cases, universal standards stem from religious beliefs. In some countries today, the standards for business are still determined by religious tenets. **Natural law** imposes higher standards of behavior than those required by positive law and they must be followed even if those higher standards run contrary to codified law. **For Example,** in the early nineteenth century when slavery was legally permissible in the United States, a positive law standard supported slavery. However, slavery violates the natural law principle of individual freedom and would be unethical. **Civil disobedience** is the remedy natural law proponents use to change positive law.

Former Supreme Court Justice Sandra Day O'Connor, who was second in her class at Stanford Law School (the late Chief Justice William Rehnquist

[1] 521 US 657 (1997).

was first), was offered a job as a receptionist for a law firm while her male classmates were hired as attorneys. At that time, no law prohibited discrimination against women, so law firms' hiring practices, using only a positive law standard, were ethical. However, if the natural law standard of equality is applied, the refusal to hire Sandra O'Connor as a lawyer, a position for which she was qualified, was a violation of the natural law principle of equality and unethical.

3. The Standard of Situational Business Ethics or Moral Relativism

Situational ethics or **moral relativism** is a flexible standard of ethics that considers circumstances and motivation before attaching the label of right or wrong to conduct. The classic example of moral relativism: Would it be unethical to steal a loaf of bread to feed a starving child? A question a Florida court faced was whether to go forward with the prosecution for arson of a man who set fire to an abandoned property in his neighborhood that was used as a crack-cocaine house. In both cases, the law has been broken. The first crime is theft, and the second crime is arson. Neither person, either the bread thief or the arsonist, denied committing the crime. The issue in both cases is not whether the crime was committed but whether the motivation and circumstances excuse the actions and eliminate the punishment. An employee embezzles money from her employer because she is a single parent trying to make ends meet. Was her conduct unethical? The conduct is illegal, but moral relativism would consider the employee's personal circumstances in determining whether it is ethical.

Businesses use moral relativism standards frequently in their international operations. Bribery is illegal in the United States, but, as many businesses argue, it is an accepted method of doing business in other countries.[2]

---

thinking things through

Corrupt Climates: Good or Bad for Business?

As you examine the following list of countries, those in the column labeled "Least Corrupt" (countries in which government officials are least likely to accept bribes) and those in the column marked

"Most Corrupt" (countries in which government officials are most likely to accept bribes), can you comment on the business climates in them?

Least Corrupt (Least Likely to Accept Bribes)		Most Corrupt (Most Likely to Accept Bribes)	
Denmark	Luxembourg	Somalia	Zimbabwe
New Zealand	Austria	Myanmar	Uzbekistan
Sweden	Hong Kong	Iraq	Turkmenistan
Singapore	Germany	Haiti	Kyrgyzstan
Finland	Norway	Afghanistan	Cambodia
Switzerland	Ireland	Sudan	Venezuela
Iceland	United Kingdom	Guinea	Sierra Leone
Netherlands	Belgium	Chad	Guinea-Bissou
Australia	Japan	Equatorial Guinea	Gambia
Canada	USA	Congo, Democratic Republic	Congo Republic

*From 2008 Transparency International annual survey, **http://www.transparency.org**.

---

[2] The United States, Mexico, Korea, and most of the countries in the European Union have joined together and signed a resolution denouncing bribery, specifically noting that its practice is neither legally nor culturally accepted in their nations.

The standard of moral relativism is used to allow behavior in international business transactions that would be a violation of the law in the United States. **For Example,** Google and other Internet service providers have agreed to do business in China despite the restrictions the Chinese government places on the use of the Internet and the content of search engines. Such restrictions in the United States would be an unconstitutional violation of our First Amendment. In China, however, government control of information is legal. Google and others testified before Congress that some entry, however restricted, was better for the Chinese people than no access at all. Their decision weighed the conflicting values and concluded that they would use the standard of honoring the law of China despite the censorship.

4. The Business Stakeholder Standard of Behavior

Businesses have different constituencies, referred to as **stakeholders**, often with conflicting goals for the business. Shareholders, for example, may share economists' view that earnings, and hence dividends, should be maximized. Members of the community where a business is located are also stakeholders in the business and have an interest in preserving jobs. The employees of the business itself are stakeholders and certainly wish to retain their jobs. Balancing the interests of these stakeholders is a standard used in resolving ethical dilemmas in business.

As Figure 3-1 indicates, stakeholder analysis requires a view of an issue from different perspectives in the light of day. **Stakeholder analysis** requires measurement of the impact of a decision on various groups but also requires that public disclosure of that decision be defensible. The questions provide insight in a variety of situations and ethical dilemmas. For example, if a lender gives a loan to a debtor without checking income, the lapse seems harmless. But, suppose someone purchases that loan believing the debtor met the standards and the lender verified income. The debtor defaults on the loan. The purchaser has to write down or write off the loan. If enough loans that were not documented go into default, you create the kind of ripples in the real estate and stock markets that occurred in late 2008. Stakeholder analysis helps you to see that the decisions we make in business are not made in isolation or limited in their impact.

In other ethical dilemmas, a business faces the question of taking voluntary action or simply complying with the law. Some experts maintain that the shareholders' interest is paramount in resolving these conflicts among stakeholders. Others maintain that a business must assume some responsibility for social issues and their resolution. Economist Milton Friedman expresses his views on resolving the conflicts among stakeholders as follows:

A corporate executive's responsibility is to make as much money for the shareholders as possible, as long as he operates within the rules of the game. When an

---

FIGURE 3-1 | ***Guidelines for Analyzing a Contemplated Action***

1. DEFINE THE PROBLEM FROM THE DECISION MAKER'S POINT OF VIEW.
2. IDENTIFY WHO COULD BE INJURED BY THE CONTEMPLATED ACTION.
3. DEFINE THE PROBLEM FROM THE OPPOSING POINT OF VIEW.
4. WOULD YOU (AS THE DECISION MAKER) BE WILLING TO TELL YOUR FAMILY, YOUR SUPERVISOR, YOUR CEO, AND THE BOARD OF DIRECTORS ABOUT THE PLANNED ACTION?
5. WOULD YOU BE WILLING TO GO BEFORE A COMMUNITY MEETING, A CONGRESSIONAL HEARING, OR A PUBLIC FORUM TO DESCRIBE THE ACTION?
6. WITH FULL CONSIDERATION OF THE FACTS AND ALTERNATIVES, REACH A DECISION ABOUT WHETHER THE CONTEMPLATED ACTION SHOULD BE TAKEN.

executive decides to take action for reasons of social responsibility, he is taking money from someone else—from the stockholders, in the form of lower dividends; from the employees, in the form of lower wages; or from the consumer, in the form of higher prices. The responsibility of the corporate executive is to fulfill the terms of his contract. If he can't do that in good conscience, then he should quit his job and find another way to do good. He has the right to promote what he regards as desirable moral objectives only with his own money.[3]

Many businesses feel an obligation to solve social problems because those problems affect their stakeholders. For example, programs such as flextime, job sharing, and telecommuting as work are not legal requirements but voluntary options businesses offer their employees to accommodate family needs. These options are a response to larger societal issues surrounding children and their care but may also serve as a way to retain a quality workforce that is more productive without the worry of poor child care arrangements.

Some businesses are also involved in their communities through employees' volunteer work and companies' charitable donations. For example, Bill Gates, the CEO of Microsoft who is ranked as the richest man in the United States, in 2003 pledged $3 billion for fighting AIDS and providing childhood vaccine programs around the world. In 2008,

corporations gave a total of $15.6 billion to charity. Overall charitable giving in the United States in 2008 reached over $300 billion for the first time. Many companies also provide support for employees to participate in volunteer programs in their communities.

B. Why is Business Ethics Important?

Ethics and values represent an important part of business success. Business ethics is important for more than the simple justification that "it's the right thing to do." This section covers the significance of ethics in business success.

5. The Importance of Trust

Capitalism succeeds because of trust. Investors provide capital for a business because they believe the business will provide a return on their investment. Customers are willing to purchase products and services from businesses because they believe the businesses will honor their commitments to deliver quality and then stand behind their product or service. Businesses are willing to purchase equipment and hire employees on the assumption that investors will continue to honor their commitment to furnish

ethics & the law

Rapper Lil Wayne used lyrics from the Rolling Stones 1965 song, "Playing With Fire," in his "Playing With Fire" song that was part of his *The Carter III* CD. Abkco Music filed an infringement suit against Lil Wayne for using the lyrics after it had denied him permission. Abkco was going to grant permission to Lil until it read all of the songs lyrics, described as "explicit, sexist, and offensive." The suit was

settled when Lil Wayne agreed to remove the song from the CD and from iTunes. The Rolling Stones did not seek damages, only that the song be removed. Why did Abkco and the Rolling Stones take this position? Who are the stakeholders? Are there any constitutional issues here?

Source: Ethan Smith, "Rapper to Pull Song in Copyright Fight," *Wall Street Journal,* January 30, 2009, B8.

---

[3] "Interview: Milton Friedman," *Playboy,* February 1973. 1973 *Playboy.*

the necessary funds and will not withdraw their promises or funds. Business investment, growth, and sales are a circle of trust. Although courts provide remedies for breaches of agreements, no economy could grow if it were based solely on positive law and court-mandated performance. It is the reliance on promises, not the reliance on litigation, that produces good business relationships.

6. Business Ethics and Financial Performance

Studies centering on a business's commitment to values and its financial performance suggest that those with the strongest value systems survive and do so successfully. According to the book *Building and Growing a Business Through Good Times and Bad* by Louis Grossman and Marianne Jennings,[4] an in-depth look at companies with 100 years of consistent dividends produced a common thread: the companies' commitment to values. All firms studied had focused on high standards for product quality, employee welfare, and customer service.

Poor value choices do have an effect on financial performance. A study of the impact of just breaches of federal law by companies showed that for five years after their regulatory or legal misstep, these companies were still struggling to recover the financial performances they had achieved prior to their legal difficulties.[5]

Over the past five years, there have been devastating stories of companies' fates after ethical lapses. After Enron announced that it would restate its income because it had been spinning off its debt obligations into off-the-book-entities, its price per share dropped from $83 on January 14, 2001, to $0.67 on January 14, 2002.[6] By the time former Enron CEO Jeffrey Skilling and its former chairman, the late Kenneth Lay, were convicted of multiple federal felonies, Enron stock was trading at $0.15 per share, a figure that was up four cents from the pre-verdict value of $0.11. Columbia

Health Care's share price dropped 58 percent and it experienced a 93 percent drop in earnings after it was charged with overbilling for Medicare reimbursements. Its share price dropped from $40 to $18. The nation's largest hospital chain had to spin off 100 hospitals and has paid record fines to settle the charges.[7] When the subprime lender New Century Financial announced that it was finally writing down all the subprime loans it had made that had gone into default but that it had been concealing, it was forced to declare bankruptcy because it was insolvent. On January 1, 2007, New Century had $1.75 billion in market capitalization, but by the middle of March, that figure was $55 million and its stock was delisted by the New York Stock Exchange.

Insurance broker Marsh & McLennan paid $850 million to former clients to settle price-fixing charges brought by then-New York Attorney General Eliot Spitzer. The 134-year-old company saw a drop in both its earnings (64 percent) and its share price (40 percent).[8] The financial crunch resulted in 3,000 employees losing their jobs. AIG, the insurance giant, paid $1.64 billion, the largest penalty ever by a U.S. company, to settle charges that it smoothed its earnings over time. The fine came after the company was forced to reduce its reported earnings by $1.3 billion.[9] The company also issued an apology as part of the settlement: "Providing incorrect information to the investing public and regulators was wrong and is against the values of our current leadership and employees."[10] Its $73 share price dropped to $50 before the financial reporting allegations were settled. But AIG continued to underestimate its needed reserves and losses for the subprime mortgage market it had insured. By the fall of 2008, AIG had to be rescued by the federal government with a funds bailout. The company continues to struggle as its dependence on federal funding draws attention to all of its activities.

---

[4] Greenwood Press (2002).

[5] Melinda S. Baucus and David A. Baucus, "Paying the Piper: An Empirical Examination of Longer-Term Financial Consequences of Illegal Corporate Behavior," 40 *Academic Management J.* 129 (1997).

[6] From stock price chart, **www.enron.com**.

[7] Lucette Lagnado, "Columbia/HCA Warns of Profit Decline," *Wall Street Journal*, September 10, 1987, A3.

[8] Ian McDonald, "After Spitzer Probe, Marsh CEO Tries Corporate Triage," *Wall Street Journal*, August 29, 2005 A1, A5.

[9] Ian McDonald and Liam Pleven, "AIG Reaches Accord with Regulators, Stock Rises But May Still Be a Bargain," *Wall Street Journal*, February 10, 2006, C1, C4.

[10] Gretchen Morgenson, "AIG Apologizes and Agrees to $1.64 Billion Settlement," *New York Times*, February 10, 2006, C1, C5.

ethics & the law

In March 2009, after it received government assistance, AIG announced the payment of $100 million in bonuses to various executives and managers in the company. There was a great hue and cry from regulators, legislators, and the public. However, AIG maintained it was contractually obligated to pay the bonuses. For a time, AIG had to cover its name on its New York office building because of public protests. The executives who received the bonuses received death threats. Evaluate the ethical issues related to the bonus payments. Evaluate the ethical issues in the public response to those bonuses. Be sure to discuss AIGs argument on the legal requirements for the bonuses.

7. The Importance of A Good Reputation

Richard Teerlink, the CEO of Harley-Davidson, once said, "A reputation, good or bad, is tough to shake.[11] A breach of ethics is costly to a firm not only in the financial sense of drops in earnings and possible fines. A breach of ethics also often carries with it a lasting memory that affects the business and its sales for years to come. **For Example,** the Peanut Corporation of America had to declare bankruptcy in 2009 after government officials discovered that its plant was the source of salmonella poisonings among those customers who had eaten peanut products that used Peanut Corporation's product as their base. Records showed that Peanut Corporation continued to produce the product even after salmonella warnings and questions arose. The company's name and image became so damaged that it could not continue to make sales. When an ethical breach occurs, businesses lose that component of trust important to customers' decisions to buy and invest.

8. Business Ethics and Business Regulation: Public Policy, Law, and Ethics

When business behavior results in complaints from employees, investors, or customers, laws or regulations are often used to change the behavior. **For Example,** the bankruptcy of Lehman Brothers, the near-collapse of Bear Stearns, and the losses at Merrill Lynch and AIG in 2008-2009 all resulted from the subprime mortgage financial derivative investment market, a market that had previously been a relatively regulation-free environment. The companies had billions of dollars of exposure because of their sales and purchases of financial instruments that were tied to the subprime mortgage market that ultimately resulted in high rates of foreclosure and nearly worthless loans. Congress, the Securities and Exchange Commission (SEC), and the Federal Reserve all stepped in to regulate virtually all aspects of mortgage transactions, including the lenders and others who were involved in packaging the loans into financial products.

Confusion among consumers about car leasing and its true costs and the fees applicable at the end of the lease terms caused the Federal Reserve to expand its regulation of credit to car leases. Figure 3-2 depicts the relationships among ethics, the social forces of customers and investors, and the laws that are passed to remedy the problems raised as part of the social forces movement.

From the nutrition facts that appear on food packages to the type of pump at the gas station, government regulation of business activity is evident. Legislation and regulation are responses to activities of businesses that are perfectly legal but raise questions of fairness that cause customer and investor protests.

Businesses that act voluntarily on the basis of value choices often avoid the costs and the sometimes

---

[11] David K. Wright, *The Harley-Davidson Motor Co.: An Official Ninety-Year History* (Milwaukee: Motorbook International, 1993).

FIGURE 3-2 | **The Endless Cycle of Societal Interaction**

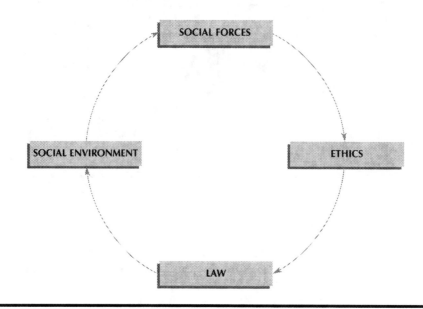

ethics & the law

Ethics, Trust, and Markets

The cover of *Fortune* magazine from May 14, 2001, featured a picture of Wall Street financial analyst Mary Meeker and the words, "Can we ever trust again?"* The inside story focused on the relationship of underwriters, analysts, and brokerage houses with the high-tech companies whose stocks they were touting and selling. They had continued to pump the virtues of stock shares they knew had overinflated prices. When the dot-com market bubble burst, the losses to shareholders were catastrophic. The analysts, underwriters, and brokers had not violated the law. Those in the financial markets had too much at stake to be honest with investors.

In 2002, when companies beyond the dot-coms, such as Enron, WorldCom, and Tyco, experienced write-downs for some fairly creative accounting practices gone awry, the market once again looked at analysts, wondering how they had failed to catch the accounting issues. The cover of *Fortune* read, "In Search of the Last Honest Analyst."**

During 2007, *Fortune* ran a cover with the pictures of the CEOs of the major Wall Street investment firms (such as Merrill Lynch, Bear Stearns, and Lehman Brothers) who had managed to lose trillions of investors pension and 401(k) plans to risky investments in subprime mortgages that were marketed as low-risk investments. The covers headline asked, "What Were They Smoking?"***

What do the covers of this business magazine convey about the importance of trust and its role in markets?

* "Can We Ever Trust Again?" *Fortune*, May 14, 2000 (cover).

** "In Search of the Last Honest Analyst," *Fortune*, June 10, 2002 (cover).
*** Cover, *Fortune*, November 26, 2007.

arbitrariness of legislation and regulation. Voluntary change by businesses is less costly and is considered less intrusive.

Businesses that respond to social forces and the movements of the cycle of societal interaction often gain a competitive advantage. Businesses that act irresponsibly and disregard society's views and desire for change speed the transition from value choice to enforceable law. Businesses should watch the cycle of social forces and follow trends there to understand the values attached to certain activities and responses. These values motivate change either in the form of voluntary business activity or legislation. All values that precipitate change have one of several basic underlying goals. These underlying goals are discussed in the following sections.

(A) PROTECTION OF THE STATE. A number of laws exist today because of the underlying goal or value of protection of the state. Laws that condemn treason are examples of laws passed to preserve the government of the state. Another less dramatic set of laws offering protection to the state are the tax codes, which provide authority for collecting taxes for the operation of government facilities and enforcement agencies. The U.S Patriot Act and airport security regulations are also examples of government programs and regulations created with the protection and security of the state as the goal.

(B) PROTECTION OF THE PERSON. A second social force is protection of the person. From the earliest times, laws have been developed to protect the individual from being injured or killed. Criminal laws are devoted to protection of individuals and their properties. In addition, civil suits permit private remedies for wrongful acts toward people and their property. Over time, the protection of personal rights has expanded to include the rights of privacy and the protection of individuals from defamation. Contract rights are protected from interference by others. Laws continue to evolve to protect the reputations, privacy, and mental and physical well-being of individuals.

(C) PROTECTION OF PUBLIC HEALTH, SAFETY, AND MORALS. Food-labeling regulations are an example of laws grounded in the value of protecting the safety and health of individuals. Food and restaurant

inspections, mandatory inoculation, speed limits on roadways, mandatory smoke detectors and sprinkler systems in hotels, and prohibitions on the sale of alcohol to minors are all examples of laws based on the value of safety for the public. Zoning laws that prohibit the operation of adult bookstores and movie theaters near schools and churches are examples of laws based on moral values.

(D) PROTECTION OF PROPERTY: ITS USE AND TITLE. Someone who steals another's automobile is a thief and is punished by law with fines and/or imprisonment. A zoning law that prohibits the operation of a steel mill in a residential area also provides protection for property. A civil suit brought to recover royalties lost because of another's infringement of one's copyrighted materials is based on federal laws that afford protection for property rights in nontangible or intellectual property (see Chapter 10). Laws afford protection of title for all forms of property. The deed recorded in the land record is the legal mechanism for protecting the owner's title. The copyright on a software program or a song protects the creator's rights in that intellectual property. The title documents issued by a department of motor vehicles afford protection of title for the owner of a vehicle.

Those who have title to property are generally free to use the property in any manner they see fit. However, even ownership has restrictions imposed by law. A landowner cannot engage in activities on his property that damage another's land or interfere with another's use of land. A business may operate a factory on its real property, but if the factory creates a great deal of pollution, adjoining landowners may successfully establish it as a nuisance (see Chapter 49) that interferes with their use and enjoyment of their land. The law affords remedies for such a nuisance that might include an injunction, or court order, limiting the hours of the factory's operation or requiring scrubbers on the emissions towers.. Environmental laws also emerged as regulation of land use in response to concerns about legal, but harmful, emissions by companies.

(E) PROTECTION OF PERSONAL RIGHTS. The desire for individual freedom to practice religion and to enjoy freedom from political domination gave rise to the colonization of the United States and, eventually, the

American Revolution. The desire for freedom from economic domination resulted in the free enterprise philosophy that exists in the United States today. Individual freedoms and personal rights continue as a focus of value discussions followed by legislation if those individual rights are violated.

(F) Enforcement of Individual Intent. When we voluntarily enter into a contract, we have a responsibility to fulfill the promises made in that agreement. Principles of honesty and the honoring of commitments are the ethical values at the heart of the parties' conduct in carrying out contracts. If, however, the parties do not keep their promises, the law does enforce transactions through sets of rules governing requirements for them. For Example, the law will carry out the intentions of the parties to a business transaction.

Laws exist to honor the intent of parties because not all commitments are fulfilled voluntarily. The law may impose requirements that a transaction or agreement be in writing to ensure that the intent of the parties is adequately documented and fulfilled (see Chapter 17). The law may also place restrictions on honoring intentions. A contract to commit a murder may be evidenced by intent and fully documented in writing. However, the intent of the parties will not be honored because of the social values manifested in the protection of individuals and individuals' rights and safety.

(G) Protection From Exploitation, Fraud, and Oppression. Many laws have evolved because businesses took advantage of another group. The law has given some groups or individuals protection because of excesses by businesses in dealing with them. Minors, or persons under legal age (see Chapter 14), are given special protections under contract laws that permit them to disaffirm their contracts so they are not disadvantaged by excessive commitments without the benefit of the wisdom of age and with the oppressive presence of an adult party.

The federal laws on disclosure in the sales of securities and shareholder relations (see Chapters 45 and 46) were developed following the 1929 stock market crash when many investors lost all they had because of the lack of candor and information by the businesses in which they were investing.

(H) Furtherance of Trade. Some laws are the result of social forces seeking to simplify business and trade. Installment sales and credit transactions, and their accompanying laws and regulations, have made additional capital available for businesses and provided consumers with alternatives to cash purchases. The laws on checks, drafts, and notes have created instruments used to facilitate trade.

(I) Protection of Creditors and Rehabilitation of Debtors. Society seeks to protect the rights of creditors and to protect them from dishonest or fraudulent acts of debtors. Statutes that make it a fraud for a debtor to conceal property from a creditor also protect creditors. Mortgages, security interests, and surety relationships (see Chapters 32, 34, and 49) are mechanisms created by law to provide creditors the legal mechanisms for collecting their obligations.

When collection techniques became excessive and exploitative, new laws on debtors' rights were enacted. Debtors' prisons were abolished. Congress mandated disclosure requirements for credit contracts. The Fair Debt Collections Practices Act (see Chapter 33) limited collection techniques. The remedy of bankruptcy was afforded debtors under federal law to provide them an opportunity to begin a new economic life when their existing debts reached an excessive level and could no longer be paid in a timely fashion (see Chapter 35).

(J) Stability and Flexibility. Stability is particularly important in business transactions. When you buy a house, for example, you want to know not only what the exact meaning of the transaction is under today's law but also that the transaction will have the same meaning in the future.

Because of the desire for stability, courts will ordinarily follow former decisions unless there is a strong reason to depart from them. Similarly, when no former case bears on the point involved, a court will try to reach a decision that is a logical extension of some former decision or that follows a former decision by analogy rather than strike out on a new path to reach a decision unrelated to the past.

The typical modern statute, particularly in the area of business regulation, often contains an escape clause by which a person can "escape" from the operation of the statute under certain circumstances.

For Example, a rent control law may impose a rent ceiling, that is, a maximum rent a landlord can charge a tenant. The same law may also authorize a higher charge when special circumstances make it just and fair to allow such an exception. For example, the landlord may have made expensive repairs to the property or taxes on the property may have increased substantially.

C. How to Recognize and Resolve Ethical Dilemmas

Business managers often find themselves in circumstances in which they are unclear about right and wrong and are confused about how to resolve the dilemmas they face. A recent survey showed that 98 percent of all Fortune 500 companies have codes of ethics designed to help their employees recognize and resolve ethical dilemmas. Nearly 90 percent of those firms provide their employees some form of training in ethics.[12] Almost 80 percent of companies now have an ethics officer. These codes of ethics provide employees information about categories of behavior that constitute ethical breaches. Regardless of the industry, the type of business, or the size of the company, certain universal categories can help managers recognize ethical dilemmas. Figure 3-3 provides a list of those categories.

9. Categories of Ethical Behavior

(A) Integrity and Truthfulness. Mark Twain once wrote, "Always tell the truth. That way you don't have to remember anything." As discussed earlier, trust is a key component of business relationships and of the free enterprise system. Trust begins with the belief that honesty is at the heart of relationships. Many contract remedies in law are based on the failure of the parties to be truthful with each other. If you purchase a home that has been certified as termite free but you discover termites in the home shortly after you move in, someone has not been truthful. If you also discover that two termite inspections were

FIGURE 3-3 | ***Categories of Ethical Behavior***

1. INTEGRITY AND TRUTHFULNESS
2. PROMISE KEEPING
3. LOYALTY—AVOIDING CONFLICTS OF INTEREST
4. FAIRNESS
5. DOING NO HARM
6. MAINTAINING CONFIDENTIALITY

conducted and that the first one, which revealed there were termites, was concealed from you, your trust in both the sellers and their exterminators is diminished.

An assurance that a seller has the expertise to handle your project is important in building that relationship. If you discover later that the seller lacks the expertise, you are harmed by the delay and possible poor work that has been done. Investors become skeptical when offerings do not carry with them a very basic level of honesty in their disclosures. Honesty is necessary for the wheels of commerce to turn.

Integrity is the adherence to one's values and principles despite the costs and consequences. **For Example,** an executive contracted with a variety of companies to sell his hard-to-find computer components. When he was approached by one of his largest customers to break a contract with a small customer, the executive refused. The customer assured the executive it would be his last order with the company if he did not get more components. Despite facing the threat of losing a multimillion-dollar customer, the executive fulfilled his promises to the small purchasers. The executive kept his word on all of his contracts and demonstrated integrity.

(B) Promise Keeping. If we examine the types of things we do in a day, we would find that most of them are based on promises. We promise to deliver goods either with or without a contract. We promise to pay the dentist for our dental work. We promise to provide someone with a ride. Keeping those promises, regardless of whether there is a legal obligation to do

[12] Survey of the Society for Human Resource Management and Ethics Resource Center (2005).

ethics & the law

Lying to Get into a Top School

The University of California at Berkeley has implemented a new step in its admission process. The Haas School of Business has begun running background checks on students who have applied to determine whether the information in their applications is correct. The Wharton School implemented a similar procedure and charges applicants a $35 fee for these background checks.

Of the 100 students admitted to Berkeley in the fall of 2003, 5 students were found to have offered false information on their admissions applications. The most common type of false information was the job titles they held, and the second most common type was their number of years of work experience. Haas admissions officers indicated that had the students not lied, they otherwise met the GMAT score and GPA standards for admission to Haas.

What risk do the students take in lying on their applications? What are the long-term consequences?

Source: "Cheaters Dont Make the Grade at Berkeley Business School," **www.azcentral.com**, March 14, 2003, AP wire reports.

so, is a key component of being an ethical person and practicing ethical business. Keeping promises is also evidence of integrity.

The issue of employee downsizing is debated with the underlying question of whether the downsized employees had a promise from their company of continued employment. As we consider stakeholder analysis the ethical issue surrounding the question is whether there are promises to others who are at risk. Weren't shareholders promised a return on their investment? Weren't suppliers promised payment? In many circumstances, the question is not *whether* a

sports & entertainment law

Image, Morals, and Cereal

Olympic champion Michael Phelps was photographed apparently smoking a bong pipe at a party at the University of South Carolina. When the picture made its way onto the Internet, the companies that carry Mr. Phelps' image for their products were listed on the Internet. Those companies include the following:

- Kellogg's
- Subway
- Speedo
- Visa
- Omega
- PureSport
- 505 Games*
- Mazda (China only)

After the picture appeared, Kelloggs canceled its contract with Mr. Phelps. What legal right would a company have to cancel its agreement with Mr. Phelps? What is a "morals clause" and how is it used?

* Indicates that endorsement was signed after the Olympics.

promise will be kept but rather *which* promise will be kept. The strategic issue is whether businesses should make commitments and promises in circumstances that create a very thin margin of profit and perhaps even thinner margin for error. Over the long term, the importance of a company's keeping its promises to all stakeholders translates into its reputation.

(c) LOYALTY—AVOIDING CONFLICTS OF INTEREST. An employee who works for a company owes allegiance to that company. Conduct that compromises that loyalty is a **conflict of interest**. For Example, suppose that your sister operates her own catering business. Your company is seeking a caterer for its monthly management meetings. You are responsible for these meetings and could hire your sister to furnish the lunches for the meetings. Your sister would have a substantial contract, and your problems with meal logistics would be solved. Nearly all companies have a provision in their codes of ethics covering this situation. An employee cannot hire a relative, friend, or even her own company without special permission because it is a conflict of interest. Your loyalty to your sister conflicts with the loyalty to your employer, which requires you to make the best decision at the best price.

A conflict of interest arises when a purchasing agent accepts gifts from suppliers, vendors, or manufacturers' representatives. The purchasing agent has introduced into the buy-sell relationship an element of *quid pro quo,* or the supplier's expectation that the gift will bring about a return from the agent in the form of a contract. Some companies have zero tolerance for conflicts and establish a complete prohibition on employees accepting any gifts from suppliers and manufacturers. For Example, Wal-Mart buyers are not permitted to accept even a cup of coffee from potential merchandise suppliers, and Amgen's buyers can go out to dinner with a supplier only if Amgen pays.

(d) FAIRNESS. In business transactions in which the buyer was not told about the crack in the engine block or the dry well on the property, a typical response is "That's not fair. I wouldn't have bought it if I'd known." A question often posed to the buyer in response is "Wouldn't you have done the same thing?" We feel differently about such situations, depending on whether we are the victims of unfairness or whether we hold the superior knowledge in the transaction. The ethical standard of fairness requires both sides to ask these questions: "How would I want to be treated? Would this information make a difference to me?" Imposing our own standards and expectations on our own behavior in business transactions produces fairness in business.

(e) DOING NO HARM. Imagine selling a product that your company's internal research shows presents significant health dangers to its users. Selling the product without disclosure of the information is unfair. There is the additional ethical breach of physical harm to your customers and users. Ford designed and sold its Pinto with a fundamental flaw in the placement of the car's gas tank. Rear-end collisions in which a Pinto was involved resulted, even at very low speeds, in fires that engulfed the car so quickly that occupants could not always escape from it. An internal memo from engineers at Ford revealed that employees had considered doing an analysis of the risk of the tanks versus the cost of redesign but never did. The late Peter Drucker's advice on ethics for businesses is *primum non nocere*, or "above all, do no harm." Such a rule might have helped Ford.

(f) MAINTAINING CONFIDENTIALITY. Often the success of a business depends on the information or technology that it holds. If the competitive edge that comes from the business's peculiar niche or knowledge is lost through disclosure, so are its profits. Employees not only owe a duty of loyalty to their employers, but they also owe an obligation of confidentiality. Employees should not use, either personally or through a competitor, information they have obtained through their employer's work or research. Providing customer lists or leads is a breach of employees' obligation of confidentiality.

In addition, managers have responsibilities regarding their employees' privacy. Performance evaluations of individual employees are private and should never be disclosed or revealed, even in one-on-one conversations outside the lines of authority and the workplace.

10. Resolving Ethical Dilemmas

Recognizing an ethical dilemma is perhaps the easiest part of business ethics. Resolution of that dilemma is

e-commerce&cyberlaw

Piggybacking on Wireless Networks

A new issue that has evolved because of technology could require legal steps to stop it. People are "piggybacking" or tapping onto their neighbors wireless Internet connection. The original subscriber pays a monthly fee for the service, but without security, people located in the area are able to tap into the wireless network, which bogs down the speed of the service. Once limited to geeks and hackers, the practice is now common among the ordinary folk who just want free Internet service.

One college student said, "I dont think its stealing. I always find people out there who arent protecting their connection, so I just feel free to go ahead and use it."* According to a recent survey, only about 30 percent of the 4,500 wireless networks onto which the surveyors logged were encrypted.

An apartment dweller said she leaves her connection wide open because "I'm sticking it to the man. I open up my network, leave it wide open for anyone to jump on." One of the users of anothers wireless network said, "I feel sort of bad about it, but I do it anyway. It just seems harmless." She said that if she gets caught, "I'm a grandmother. They're not going to yell at an old lady. I'll just play the dumb card."

Some neighbors offer to pay those with wireless service in exchange for their occasional use rather than paying a wireless company for full-blown service. However, the original subscribers do not really want to run their own Internet service.

Do you think we need new legislation to cover this activity? What do you think of the users statements? Is their conduct legal? Is it ethical?

* Michael Marriott, "Hey Neighbor, Stop Piggybacking on My Wireless," *New York Times*, March 5, 2006, A1, A23.

more difficult. The earlier section on stakeholders offers one model for resolution of ethical dilemmas (see Figure 3-1). Other models have been developed to provide managers analytical methods for resolving dilemmas in a timely fashion.

(A) BLANCHARD AND PEALE THREE-PART TEST. Dr. Kenneth Blanchard, author of books on the *One-Minute Manager,* and the late Dr. Norman Vincent Peale developed a model for evaluating ethical breaches that is widely used among Fortune 500 companies.[13] To evaluate situations, ask the following three questions: Is it legal? Is it balanced? How does it make me feel?

In answering the questions on legality, a manager should look to positive law both within and outside the company. If the proposed conduct would violate antitrust laws, the manager's analysis can stop there. If the proposed conduct would violate company policy, the manager's analysis can stop. In the field of business ethics, there is little room for civil

disobedience. Compliance with the law is a critical component of a successful ethics policy in any company.

The second question on balance forces the manager to examine the ethical value of fairness. Perhaps the decision to downsize must be made, but couldn't the company offer the employees a severance package and outplacement assistance to ease the transition?

The final question of the Blanchard and Peale model is conscience based. Although some managers may employ any tactics to maximize profits, this final question forces a manager to examine the physical impact of a decision: Does it cause sleeplessness or appetite changes? Personalizing business choices often helps managers to see the potential harm that comes from poor ethical choices.

(B) THE FRONT-PAGE-OF-THE-NEWSPAPER TEST. This simple but effective model for ethical evaluation helps a manager visualize the public disclosure of proposed

[13] Kenneth Blanchard and Norman Vincent Peale, *The Power of Ethical Management* (New York: William Morrow, 1986).

conduct. When he temporarily took over as the leader of Salomon Brothers after its bond-trading controversy, Warren Buffett described the newspaper test as follows:

Contemplating any business act, an employee should ask himself whether he would be willing to see it immediately described by an informed and critical reporter on the front page of his local paper, there to be read by his spouse, children, and friends. At Salomon, we simply want no part of any activities that pass legal tests but that we, as citizens, would find offensive.[14]

(C) LAURA NASH MODEL. In her work, business ethicist Laura Nash has developed a series of questions to help businesspeople reach the right decision in ethical dilemmas. These are her questions: Have you defined the problem accurately? How would you define the problem if you stood on the other side of the fence? How did this situation occur in the first place? What is your intention in making this decision? How does the intention compare with the probable results? Whom could your decision or action injure? Can you discuss your decision with the affected parties? Are you confident that your position will be as valid over a long period of time as it seems now? Could you discuss your decision with your supervisor, coworkers, officers, board, friends, and family?

The Nash model requires an examination of the dilemma from all perspectives. Defining the problem and how the problem arose provides the business assistance in avoiding the dilemma again. **For Example,** suppose that a supervisor is asked to provide a reference for a friend who works for her. The supervisor is

---

ethics & the law

Burger King, Coke, and Numbers

Coca-Cola has admitted that it paid a consultant $10,000 to drive up the demand for its Frozen Coke beverage being test-marketed in Burger Kings in the Richmond, Virginia, area. The consultant used the money to make donations to Boys and Girls Clubs. The clubs then provided meal coupons to the children in exchange for them doing their homework. The impressive demand that resulted from the Richmond area test market led Burger King to invest $65 million to put the machines in restaurants around the country. However, the demand was not what it had been falsely alleged to be, and the result is that, following a six-week investigation by a law firm hired by the Coca-Cola board, Coca-Cola admitted that the marketing studies were inflated.

The board investigation followed an allegation in a lawsuit filed by a former employee, Matthew Whitley. Whitley was terminated following his questioning of an expense claim by the consultant and his resulting investigation that produced an internal memo describing the consultants work on driving up the demand.

Coca-Cola also issued an earnings restatement of $9 million based on an investigation of those allegations. The *Wall Street Journal* was following the Whitley lawsuit when the underlying issues emerged, and it reported the marketing scheme.* Coca-Cola settled with Burger King by paying $21 million.

Was this conduct ethical? Was it fraud? What does Mr. Whitleys termination say about the company? Does he have protection? Why do you think the marketing managers decided to involve the consultant and report the false demand? What effect does this incident have on Burger Kings relationship with Coke? How do you think the story played on the front page of the *Wall Street Journal?***

---

* Chad Terhune, "Coke Employees Acted Improperly in Marketing Test," *Wall Street Journal*, June 18, 2003, A3, A6;Sherri Day, "Coke Confirms Product Test Was Rigged," *New York Times*, June 18, 2003, C1, C10.
** Marianne Jennings, one of the authors of this text, has done consulting work for Coca-Cola since this incident. Why is this disclosure important?

---

[14] Janet Lowe, *Warren Buffett Speaks: Wit and Wisdom from the World's Greatest Investor* (New York: Wiley, 1997).

hesitant because the friend has not been a very good employee. The ethical dilemma the manager believes she faces is whether to lie or tell the truth about the employee. The real ethical dilemma is why the supervisor never provided evaluation or feedback indicating the friend's poor performance. Avoiding the problem in the future is possible through candid evaluations. Resolving the problem requires that the supervisor talk to her friend now about the issue of performance and the problem with serving as a reference.

One final aspect of the Nash model that businesspeople find helpful is a question that asks for a perspective on an issue from family and friends. The problem of groupthink in business situations is very real. As businesspeople sit together in a room and discuss an ethical dilemma, they can persuade each other to think the same way. The power of consensus can overwhelm each person's concerns and values. There is a certain fear in bringing up a different point of view in a business meeting. Proper perspective is often lost as the discussion centers around numbers. Therefore, bringing in the views of an outsider is often helpful. For example, when McNeil, the manufacturer of Tylenol, faced the cyanide poisonings from contaminated capsules sold in the Chicago area, it had to make a decision about the existing Tylenol inventory. It was clear to both insiders and outsiders that the poison had not been put in the capsules at McNeil but after delivery to the stores. Despite the huge numbers involved in the recall and the destruction of inventory, the McNeil managers made the decision easily because they viewed the risk to their own families, that is, from the outside. From this standpoint, the issue became a question of human life, not of numbers.[15]

(D) WALL STREET JOURNAL MODEL. The *Wall Street Journal* presented a simple, three-prong test for resolving ethical dilemmas known as the three-C model: (1) Will this conduct be in compliance with the law? (2) What contribution does this decision make to the shareholders? To the community? To the employees? (3) What are the consequences of this decision? This model requires an examination of the impact of a choice, which then produces a different perspective on a course of conduct. **For Example,** Sears paid $475

lawflix

Breaking Away (1979) (PG)

In this story about "cutters" (a nickname for natives of Bloomington, Indiana), a recent high school graduate trains to be a first-class bike rider. He idolizes the Italian world racing team and enters an Indiana race to have the opportunity to compete with them. He does well in the race and manages to catch up and keep pace with the Italian team. As he rides alongside his idols, one of the members of the Italian team places a tire pump in his spoke. His bike crashes, he loses the race and is injured. He becomes disillusioned. Is this experience like business? Do unethical tactics get you ahead? Do nice guys finish last? Are there sanctions for unethical conduct?

Jaws (1975) (PG 13)

The movie that shot Steven Spielberg to directorial legend brings us the classic business dilemma of what to do when you have a high-risk/low-probability event that you know about but about which the public has no knowledge. Do you stop? But what about the economic losses?

Hoosiers (1986) (PG)

Often called the "greatest sports movie ever made," this story of a coach with a history and a small-town team presents several life-defining ethical moments. In one, with advancement to the finals on the table, Coach Norman Dale grapples with whether he should allow one of his injured players to continue when he has no depth on his bench. What do you do when your values are in conflict?

The Family Man (2000) (PG 13)

Nicolas Cage plays a Wall Street billionaire who is suddenly given a suburban life in New Jersey with all of its family life and financial constraints. He is forced to examine who he really is and what is important.

You can view a clip of these movies and others that illustrate business law concepts at the LawFlix site, located at **www.cengage.com/blaw/dvl**.

---

[15] "Brief History of Johnson & Johnson" (company pamphlet, 1992).

million in fines and penalties for its unauthorized collection of debts from debtors who were in bankruptcy or had debts discharged in bankruptcy. Such collection beyond what the law allows did not comply with the law.[16] The contribution to the company was more collections and hence more cash, but the consequences were the large fine and the damage to

Sears's reputation for putting its interests above the law and above the interests of other creditors who conducted themselves within the limits of the bankruptcy law. Sears may have resented the fact that debtors had not paid, but the company was not justified in taking the law into its own hands or profiting at the expense of other creditors.

MAKE THE CONNECTION

SUMMARY

Business ethics is the application of values and standards to business conduct and decisions. These values originate in various sources from positive (codified) law to natural law to stakeholder values. Business ethics is important because trust is a critical component of good business relationships and free enterprise. A business with values will enjoy the additional competitive advantage of a good reputation and, over the long term, better earnings. When businesses make decisions that violate basic ethical standards, they set into motion social forces and cause the area of abuse to be regulated, resulting in additional costs and restrictions for business.

Voluntary value choices by businesses position them for a competitive advantage.

The categories of ethical values in business are truthfulness and integrity, promise keeping, loyalty and avoiding conflicts of interest, fairness, doing no harm, and maintaining confidentiality.

Resolution of ethical dilemmas is possible through the use of various models that require a businessperson to examine the impact of a decision before it is made. These models include stakeholder analysis, the Blanchard and Peale test, the front-page-of-the-newspaper test, the Laura Nash model, and the *Wall Street Journal* model.

LEARNING OUTCOMES

After studying this chapter, you should be able to clearly explain:

A. WHAT IS BUSINESS ETHICS?

LO.1 Define business ethics
See the discussion of the definition, balancing the goal of profits with the values of individuals and society, on p. 36.

B. WHY IS BUSINESS ETHICS IMPORTANT?

LO.2 Discuss why ethics are important in business
See "The Importance of Trust" on p. 39.

See "Business Ethics and Financial Performance" on p. 40.
See "The Importance of a Good Reputation" on p. 41.

C. HOW TO RECOGNIZE AND RESOLVE ETHICAL DILEMMAS

LO.3 Describe how to recognize and resolve ethical dilemmas

[16] Leslie Kaufman, "Sears Settles Suit on Raising of Its Credit Card Rates," *New York Times*, March 11, 1999, C2.

See "Integrity and Truthfulness" on p. 45
See "Promise Keeping" on p. 45
See "Loyalty—Avoiding Conflicts of Interest" on p. 47.
See "Fairness" on p. 47.
See "Doing No Harm" on p. 47.
See "Maintaining Confidentiality" on p. 47.

See "Resolving Ethical Dilemmas" on p. 47.
See "Blanchard and Peale Three-Part Test" on p. 48.
See "The Front-Page-of-the-Newspaper Test" on p. 48.
See "Laura Nash Model" on p. 49.
See "*Wall Street Journal* Model" on p. 50.

KEY TERMS

business ethics
civil disobedience
conflict of interest
ethics

integrity
moral relativism
natural law
positive law

primum non nocere
situational ethics
stakeholder analysis
stakeholders

QUESTIONS AND CASE PROBLEMS

1. Marty Mankamyer, the president of the United States Olympic Committee (USOC), resigned in early February 2003 following reports in *The Denver Post* that indicated she had demanded a commission from a fellow real estate broker in the Colorado Springs area, the home of the USOC, who had sold property to Lloyd Ward, the CEO of the USOC. Mr. Ward had purchased a 1.3-acre lot in Colorado Springs for $475,000 and had paid the listing broker, Brigette Ruskin, a commission. Ms. Mankamyer allegedly demanded a portion of the commission from Ms. Ruskin, and Ms. Ruskin sent her a check. Ms. Mankamyer had shown Mr. Ward and his wife properties in the area when they were being considered for the job and when he was considering taking the job. However, Mrs. Ward indicated that Ms. Mankamyer did not identify herself as a real estate agent and that she assumed that Ms. Mankamyer was showing the properties as a "goodwill gesture."[17] What conflicts of interest do you see here?

2. Ann Elkin, who works for Brill Co., has been sent out to conduct two customer evaluations, which have gone much more quickly than Ann

anticipated. Her supervisor does not expect Ann back until after lunch. It is now 10:30 A.M., and Ann would like to run some personal errands and then go to lunch before returning to work at 1:00 P.M. Should Ann take the time? Would you? Why or why not? Be sure to consider the categories of ethical values and apply one or two models before reaching your conclusion.

3. Fred Sanguine is a New York City produce broker. Ned Santini is a 19-year-old college student who works for Sanguine from 4:00 A.M. until 7:00 A.M. each weekday before he attends classes at Pace University. Fred has instructed Ned on the proper packing of produce as follows: "Look, put the bad and small cherries at the bottom. Do the same with the strawberries and blueberries. Put the best fruit on top and hide the bad stuff at the bottom. This way I get top dollar on all that I sell." Ned is uncomfortable about the instructions, but, as he explains to his roommate, "It's not me doing it. I'm just following orders. Besides, I need the job." Should Ned just follow instructions? Is the manner in which the fruit is packed unethical? Would you do it? Why or why not? Is anyone really harmed by the practice?

---

[17] Richard Sandomir, "U.S. Olympic Chief Resigns in a Furor Over Ethics Issues," *New York Times*, February 5, 2003, A1, C17; Bill Briggs, *Realtor Waving Red Flag*, **www.denverpost.com**, February 4, 2003.

4. Alan Gellen is the facilities manager for the city of Milwaukee and makes all final decisions on purchasing items such as chairs, lights, and other supplies and materials. Alan also makes the final decisions for the award of contracts to food vendors at event sites. Grand Beef Franks has submitted a bid to be one of the city's vendors. Alan went to school with Grand Beef's owner, Steve Grand, who phones Alan and explains that Grand Beef owns a condominium in Maui that Alan could use. Steve's offer to Alan is: "All it would cost you for a vacation is your airfare. The condo is fully stocked with food. Just let me know." Should Alan take the offer? Would you? Be sure to determine which category of ethical values this situation involves and to apply several models as you resolve the question of whether Alan should accept the invitation.

5. Television network CNBC and other television networks have been working to develop policies for their business correspondents and guests on their business shows because of a practice known as *pump-and-dump,* the practice of a Wall Street professional or network business correspondent appearing on television to tout a particular stock as being a good buy. Often, unbeknown to the viewing audience, the guest or correspondent promoting the stock has a large holding in it and, after the television show runs and the stock price creeps up, sells his or her interest at a higher price than would have been possible before the show on which the person raved about the stock. What category of ethical issue exists here? If you were a network executive, what would you do to remedy the problem? Could the government regulate such practices? What kind of regulation could it impose?

6. Adam Smith wrote the following in *The Theory of Moral Sentiments:*

   In the practice of the other virtues, our conduct should rather be directed by a certain idea of propriety, by a certain taste for a particular tenor of conduct, than by any regard to a precise maxim or rule; and we should consider the end and foundation of the rule, more than the rule itself.[18]

Do you think Adam Smith adhered to positive law as his ethical standard? Was he a moral relativist? Does his quote match stakeholder analysis? What would his ethical posture be on violating the law?

7. A new phenomenon for admissions to MBA programs is hiring consultants to help applicants hone their applications. About 20 percent of those who apply to the top MBA programs have hired consultants at a cost of $150 to $200 per hour to help them say and do the right things to be admitted. The total cost for most who use a consultant is $5,000. The consultants help with personal essays and applications. One admissions officer points out that one function of the consultant is to draw out and emphasize skills that the applicant may not see as important. For example, playing the piano is looked upon favorably because it shows discipline and focus. However, admissions committees are becoming adept at spotting the applications via consultant because, as the faculty describe it, these essays and applications have a certain "sameness" to them. The Fuqua School at North Carolina suggests that students simply call the admissions office and get comparable advice for free. Is it ethical to use an admissions consultant? When would you cross a line in using the consultant on the essay?

8. Oprah Winfrey named James Frey's autobiographical book, *A Million Little Pieces,* to her television book club. The impact of the book's inclusion in the Oprah Book Club was the sale of 10 million copies, making it the fastest-selling book in the club's history. The book allegedly addressed Mr. Frey's addictions and recovery. However, on January 8, 2006, the Web site The Smoking Gun found significant and multiple discrepancies between Frey's accounts of his life experiences in the book and what really happened. For example, Frey wrote that he spent 87 days in prison. In reality, he spent 3 hours. When the discrepancies initially emerged, Ms. Winfrey defended Mr. Frey, saying the book was the

---

[18] Adam Smith, *The Theory of Moral Sentiments* (Arlington House, 1969; originally published in 1769).

"essential truth" about his life. She also called the controversy "much ado about nothing."

The public reaction was different, and Ms. Winfrey had Mr. Frey on her show, or, as some critics labeled it, "had him into the woodshed." Ms. Winfrey told Mr. Frey, "I feel really duped. You betrayed millions of readers. Why would you lie?"

In the week following his Oprah appearance, Mr. Frey sold 50,000 copies of *A Million Little Pieces*, but the publisher for his next book canceled his contract. However, Mr. Frey rebounded and found another publisher for a book released in 2008. Was there truthfulness in his book? Mr. Frey said the book was a "creative novel memoir" that had not been intended to be autobiographical. Does this clarification help? Were Mr. Frey's actions ethical? Evaluate Ms. Winfrey's initial response.

9. The state of Arizona mandates emissions testing for cars before drivers can obtain updated registrations. The state hires a contractor to conduct the emissions tests in the various emissions-testing facilities around the state. In October 1999, the Arizona attorney general announced the arrest of 13 workers at one of the emissions-testing facilities for allegedly taking payoffs of between $50 to $200 from car owners to pass their cars on the emissions tests when those cars fell below emissions standards and would not have been registered. Nearly half of the staff at the emissions facility were arrested.

Why is it a crime for someone working in a government-sponsored facility to accept a payment for a desired outcome? Do the payoffs to the workers really harm anyone?

10. The president and athletic director at the University of California at Los Angeles (UCLA) fired the school's basketball coach because an expense form he had submitted for reimbursement had the names of two students he said had joined him for a recruiting dinner. The students had not been to the dinner. The coach was stunned because he had been at UCLA for eight years and had established a winning program. He said, "And to throw it all away on a meal?" Do you agree with the coach's assessment? Was it too harsh to fire him for one inaccurate expense form? Did the coach commit an ethical breach?

11. A new trend is emerging in health insurance: premium increases based on claims. It is common practice in the auto insurance industry, for example, for insurers to revisit your premium each year and adjust it based on factors such as your driving record or number of accidents. However, health insurers have generally evaluated their insured's health only once, at the outset, when issuing a policy. The reevaluation of health and premiums was a practice that ended in the 1950s because the insurers feared regulators would impose limitations on premiums. At least one health insurer, however, has begun to evaluate the health of its insureds annually and to adjust policy premiums accordingly. Even without examination of insureds, some insurers have increased the insureds' premiums based simply on the nature of their claims for the year and the possibility that more claims will arise. Those who are healthy are in favor of this annual review. Perceiving themselves as the equivalent of good drivers, they want to pay less when they stay healthy. The health discount is, in their minds, the equivalent of the safe driver discount. However, those who are less healthy argue that people buy insurance so it will be there when they need it, and the coverage should apply without regard to claims. Consider the ethical issues in this type of pricing for health insurance.

12. David A. Vise, a Pulitzer Prize winner and a reporter for the *Washington Post,* wrote the book *The Bureau and the Mole.* When the book hit the market, Mr. Vise purchased 20,000 copies via Barnes & Noble.com, taking advantage of both free shipping offered by the publisher and a discounted initial price. Mr. Vise's book had already hit the *New York Times'* bestseller list in the week before the purchases. He used the books he purchased to conduct online sales of autographed copies of the books, and then returned 17,500 books and asked for his money back. However, that return of 17,500 books represented more books than a publisher generally

runs for a book. Mr. Vise said that he did not intend to manipulate the market or profit from the transactions. He said his only intent was to "increase awareness of *The Bureau and the Mole.*" Mr. Vise's editor offered to pay Barnes & Noble for any expenses it incurred. Was it ethical to do what Mr. Vise did? Was he within his rights to return the books? What are his remedies? Does Barnes & Noble have any rights?

13. Suzy Wetlaufer, editor of the *Harvard Business Review,* interviewed former General Electric CEO Jack Welch for a piece in the business magazine. In December 2001, she asked that the piece be withdrawn because her objectivity might have been compromised. Those at the magazine did another interview and published that interview in the February issue of the magazine. Editorial director of the magazine, Walter Kiechel, who supervised Ms. Wetlaufer, acknowledged as true a report in the *Wall Street Journal* about an alleged affair between Ms. Wetlaufer and Mr. Welch and that Mr. Welch's wife had called to protest the article's objectivity. Mr. Welch refused to confirm or deny an affair with Ms. Wetlaufer, who was divorced. Some staff members asked that Ms. Wetlaufer resign from her $277,000-per-year job, but she refused. Their objections were that she compromised her journalistic integrity. Mr. Kiechel, on the other hand, noted that she did "the right thing in raising her concerns."[19] About six weeks later, Ms. Wetlaufer did resign from her position as editor, announcing that she would be spending time with her four children. Do you think there was a conflict of interest because of the affair between Welch and Wetlaufer?[20] Note: Mr. Welch and Ms. Wetlaufer have married and have written a book together. They now write a semiweekly column for *BusinessWeek* magazine.

14. Piper High School in Piper, Kansas, a town located about 20 miles west of Kansas City, experienced national attention because of questions about students and their term papers for a botany class.

Christine Pelton, a high school science teacher, had warned students in her sophomore class not to use papers posted on the Internet for their projects. When their projects were turned in, Ms. Pelton noticed that the writing in some of the papers was well above the students' usual quality and ability. She found that 28 of her 118 students had taken substantial portions of their papers from the Internet. She gave these students a zero grade on their term paper projects with the result that many of the students were going to fail the course for that semester. The students' parents protested, and the school board ordered Ms. Pelton to raise the grades. She resigned in protest. She received a substantial number of job offers from around the country following her resignation. Nearly half of the high school faculty as well as its principal announced their plans to resign at the end of the year. Several of the parents pointed to the fact that there was no explanation in the Piper High School handbook on plagiarism. They also said that the students were unclear about what could be used, when they had to reword, and when quotations marks were necessary. The annual Rutgers University survey on academic cheating has revealed that 15 percent of college papers turned in for grades are completely copied from the Internet. Do you think such copying is unethical? Why do we worry about such conduct? Isn't this conduct just a function of the Internet? Isn't it accepted behavior?

15. Pharmaceutical companies, faced with the uphill battle of getting doctors to take a look at their new products, have created complex systems and programs for enticing doctors to come, sit, and absorb information about the new products. Following is a list of the various type of benefits and gifts that drug companies have given doctors over the past few years to entice them to consider prescribing their new offerings:

- An event called "Why Cook?" in which doctors were given the chance to review drug studies and product information at a restaurant as

---

[19] Del Jones, "Editor Linked with Welch Finds Job at Risk," *USA Today,* March 5, 2002, 3B.
[20] Ms. Wetlaufer and Mr. Welch are now married and have collaborated on books and a *BusinessWeek* column.

their meals were being prepared—they could leave as soon as their meals were ready, and they were treated to appetizers and drinks as they waited

- Events at Christmas tree lots where doctors can come and review materials and pick up a free Christmas tree

- Flowers sent to doctors' offices on Valentine's Day with materials attached

- Manicures as they study materials on new drugs

- Pedicures as they study materials on new drugs

- Free car washes during which they study materials

- Free books with materials enclosed

- Free CDs with materials attached

- Bottles of wine with materials attached

- Events at Barnes & Noble where doctors can browse and pick out a book for themselves for free as long as they also take some materials on a new drug

Some doctors say that they can enjoy dinner on a drug company as often as five times per week. The American Medical Association (AMA) frowns on the "dine-and-dash" format because its rules provide that dinners are acceptable only as long as the doctors sit and learn something from a featured speaker. The AMA also limits gifts to those of a "minimal value" that should be related to their patients, such as note pads and pens with the new drug's name imprinted on them. The chairman of the AMA Committee on Ethics says the following about gifts, "There are doctors who say, 'I always do what's best for my patients, and these gifts and dinners and trips do not influence me.' They are wrong."[21] In which category of ethical issues do these gifts fall? Do you think doctors act ethically in accepting gifts, meals, and favors? The Food and Drug Administration recently issued rules about such favors and perks. Why?

[21] Chris Adams, "Doctors on the Run Can 'Dine 'n' Dash' in Style in New Orleans," *Wall Street Journal*, May 14, 2001, A1, A6.

Chapter 4

THE CONSTITUTION AS THE FOUNDATION OF THE LEGAL ENVIRONMENT

This chapter introduces you to the powers of government and to the protections that you have for your rights. The Constitution of the United States establishes the structure and powers of government but also the limitations on those powers. This Constitution forms the foundation of our legal environment.

A. The U.S. Constitution and the Federal System

By establishing a central government to coexist with the governments of the individual states, the U.S. Constitution created a federal system. In a **federal system**, a central government has power to address national concerns, while the individual states retain the power to handle local concerns.

1. What a Constitution Is

A **constitution** is the written document that establishes the structure of the government and its relationship to the people. The U.S. Constitution was adopted in 1789 by the 13 colonies that had won their independence from King George.[1]

2. The Branches of Government

The U.S. Constitution establishes a **tripartite** (three-part) government: a **legislative branch** (Congress) to make the laws, an **executive branch** (the president) to execute or enforce the laws, and a **judicial branch** (courts) to interpret the laws. The national legislature or Congress is a **bicameral** (two-house) body consisting of the Senate and the House of Representatives. Members of the Senate are popularly elected for a term of six years. Members of the House of Representatives are popularly elected for a term of two years. The president is elected by an electoral college whose membership is popularly elected. The president serves for a term of four years and is eligible for reelection for a second term. Judges of the United States are appointed by the president with the approval of the Senate and serve for life, subject to removal only by impeachment because of misconduct. (See Chapter 2 for a discussion of the federal court system.)

B. The U.S. Constitution and the States

The Constitution created certain powers within the national government that would have been exercised by the individual states, which are given their powers by the people of the state. Figure 4.1 illustrates the delegation of powers. Likewise, the states, as the power-granting authorities, reserved certain powers for themselves.

3. Delegated and Shared Powers

(A) DELEGATED POWERS. The powers given by the states to the national government are described as *delegated powers*. Some of these **delegated powers** are given exclusively to the national government. For example, the national government alone may declare war or establish a currency.

(B) SHARED POWERS. The powers delegated to the national government that may still be exercised by the states are **shared powers**. For Example, the grant of power to the national government to impose taxes did not destroy the state power to tax. In other cases, a state may provide regulation along with, but subject to the supremacy of, federal law. For Example, regulation of the use of navigable waterways within a state is an example of joint state and federal regulation.

4. Other Powers

(A) STATE POLICE POWER. The states possess the power to adopt laws to protect the general welfare, health, safety, and morals of the people. This authority is called the **police power**. For Example, states may require that businesses be licensed with state agencies to protect persons dealing with the business. State exercise of the police power may not unreasonably interfere with federal powers.

[1] To examine the U.S. Constitution, go to **www.constitution.org** and click on "Founding Documents," or refer to Appendix 2.

FIGURE 4-1 | *Governments of the United States*

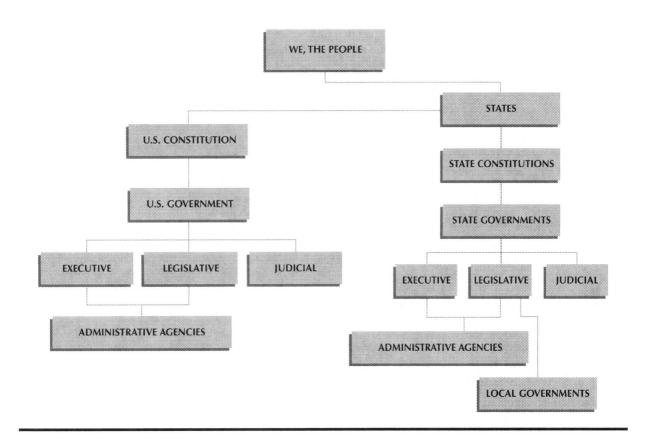

(B) PROHIBITED POWERS. The Constitution also prohibits both states and the federal government from doing certain things. **For Example,** neither states nor the national government may adopt *ex post facto* **laws**, which make criminal an act that has already been committed but was not criminal when it was committed. Laws that increase the penalty for an act already committed above the penalty in force when the act was committed are also *ex post facto* laws.

5. Federal Supremacy

Federal law bars or preempts conflicting state regulation when a federal law regulates that particular subject. Federal law also preempts state action when congressional intent to regulate exclusively can be inferred from the details of congressional regulation.

Preemption means that the federal regulatory scheme is controlling.

(A) EXPRESS FEDERAL REGULATION. The Constitution and statutes passed by Congress are the supreme law of the land. They cancel out any conflicting state law.[2] When a direct conflict exists between federal and state statutes, federal law prevails.

In some cases, however, no obvious conflict occurs because the federal statute covers only part of the subject matter. In such cases, the question becomes whether a state law can regulate the areas not regulated by Congress or whether the partial regulation made by Congress preempts, or takes over, the field so as to preclude state legislation.

(B) SILENCE OF CONGRESS. In some situations, the silence of Congress in failing to cover a particular

[2] U.S. Const., Art VI, cl 2. *Cuomo v Clearinghouse Ass'n, LLC,* 129 S Ct 2710 (2009).

Wyeth v Levine, 129 S Ct 1187 (2009)*

The Folk Singer Who Staged a Protest against Preemption

Diana Levine, a folk singer from Vermont, suffered from migraine headaches. She was being administered Wyeth Laboratory's Phenergan through a drip IV. Either because the IV needle entered Levine's artery or the drug escaped from the vein into her surrounding tissue, Ms. Levine developed gangrene. Doctors amputated her right hand and eventually her forearm. Levine could no longer work as a professional musician. Levine filed suit against both the clinic that administered the drug and Wyeth. She was awarded $7.4 million and Wyeth appealed on the grounds that the FDA approval of the drug preempted state tort suits by patients.

JUDICIAL OPINION

STEVENS, Justice …Generally speaking, a manufacturer may only change a drug label after the FDA approves a supplemental application. There is, however, an FDA regulation that permits a manufacturer to make certain changes to its label before receiving the agency's approval. Among other things, this "changes being effected" (CBE) regulation provides that if a manufacturer is changing a label to "add or strengthen a contraindication, warning, precaution, or adverse reaction" or to "add or strengthen an instruction about dosage and administration that is intended to increase the safe use of the drug product," it may make the labeling change upon filing its supplemental application with the FDA; it need not wait for FDA approval. Wyeth argues that the CBE regulation is not implicated in this case because a 2008 amendment provides that a manufacturer may only change its label "to reflect newly acquired information." Resting on this language (which Wyeth argues simply reaffirmed the interpretation of the regulation in effect when this case was tried), Wyeth contends that it could have changed Phenergan's label only in response to new information that the FDA had not considered. And it maintains that Levine has not pointed to any such information concerning the risks of IV-push administration.

We need not decide whether the 2008 CBE regulation is consistent with the FDCA and the previous version of the regulation, as Wyeth and the United States urge, because Wyeth could have revised Phenergan's label even in accordance with the amended regulation. As the FDA explained in its notice of the final rule, "'newly acquired information'" is not limited to new data, but also encompasses "new analyses of previously submitted data."

Wyeth argues that if it had unilaterally added such a warning, it would have violated federal law governing unauthorized distribution and misbranding. But strengthening the warning about IV-push administration would not have made Phenergan a new drug…. And the very idea that the FDA would bring an enforcement action against a manufacturer for strengthening a warning pursuant to the CBE regulation is difficult to accept.

Absent clear evidence that the FDA would not have approved a change to Phenergan's label, we will not conclude that it was impossible for Wyeth to comply with both federal and state requirements.

We conclude that it is not impossible for Wyeth to comply with its state and federal law obligations and that Levine's common-law claims do not stand as an obstacle to the accomplishment of Congress' purposes in the FDCA. Accordingly, the judgment of the Vermont Supreme Court is affirmed.

DISSENTING OPINION

Justice ALITO, with whom THE CHIEF JUSTICE and Justice SCALIA join, dissenting. This case illustrates that tragic facts make bad law. The Court holds that a state tort jury, rather than the Food and Drug Administration (FDA), is ultimately responsible for regulating warning labels for prescription drugs. That result cannot be reconciled with *Geier v American Honda Motor Co.*, 529 US 861, 120 S Ct 1913, 146 L Ed 2d 914 (2000), or general principles of conflict preemption. I respectfully dissent. The Court frames the question presented as a "narro[w]" one—namely, whether Wyeth has a duty to provide "an adequate warning about using the IV-push method" to administer Phenergan. But that ignores the antecedent question of who—the FDA or a jury in Vermont —has the authority and responsibility for determining the "adequacy" of Phenergan's warnings. Moreover, it is unclear how a "stronger" warning could have helped respondent, after all, the physician's assistant who treated her disregarded at least six separate warnings that are already on Phenergan's labeling, so respondent would be hard pressed to prove that a seventh would have made a difference.

As noted above, when the FDA approved Phenergan's label, it was textbook medical knowledge that the "antecubital fossa" creates a high risk of inadvertent intra-arterial injection, given the close proximity of veins and arteries. According to the physician's assistant who injured respondent, however, "[i]t never crossed my mind" that an antecubital injection of Phenergan could hit an artery. Oblivious to the risks emphasized in Phenergan's warnings, the physician's assistant pushed a

---

* For an earlier decision that concluded differently on preemption, see *Riegel v Medtronic*, 552 U.S. 312 (2008).

Continued

double dose of the drug into an antecubital artery over the course of "[p]robably about three to four minutes," notwithstanding respondent's complaints of a "'burn[ing]'" sensation that she subsequently described as "'one of the most extreme pains that I've ever felt,'" And when asked why she ignored Phenergan's label and failed to stop pushing the drug after respondent complained of burning pains, the physician's assistant explained that it would have been "just crazy" to "worr[y] about an [intra-arterial] injection" under the circumstances.

The FDA, however, did not think that the risks associated with IV push—especially in the antecubital space—were "just crazy." That is why Phenergan's label so clearly warns against them.

To be sure, state tort suits can peacefully coexist with the FDA's labeling regime, and they have done so for decades. But this case is far from peaceful coexistence.

The FDA told Wyeth that Phenergan's label renders its use "safe." But the State of Vermont, through its tort law, said: "Not so."

The state-law rule at issue here is squarely preempted. Therefore, I would reverse the judgment of the Supreme Court of Vermont.

QUESTIONS

1. What argument does Wyeth make to establish preemption protection against the suit?

2. What does the majority of the court say about the right of Wyeth to change its label and how does that right affect the preemption argument?

3. What is the concern of the dissenting judges about allowing the suit?

subject area indicates that Congress does not want any law on the matter. However, when national uniformity is essential, the silence of Congress generally means that the subject has been preempted for practical reasons by Congress and that no state law on the subject may be adopted.

(c) EFFECT OF FEDERAL DEREGULATION. The fact that the federal government removes the regulations from a regulated industry does not automatically give the states the power to regulate that industry. If under the silence-of-Congress doctrine the states cannot regulate, they are still barred from regulating after deregulation. **For Example,** deregulation of banks in the 1980s did not mean that the states could step in and regulate those banks.[3]

C. INTERPRETING AND AMENDING THE CONSTITUTION

The Constitution as it is interpreted today has changed greatly from the Constitution as originally written. The change has been brought about by interpretation, amendment, and practice.

6. Conflicting Theories

Shortly after the Constitution was adopted, conflict arose over whether it was to be interpreted strictly, so as to give the federal government the least power possible, or broadly, so as to give the federal government the greatest power that the words would permit. These two views may be called the *bedrock view* and the *living-document view*, respectively.

In the **bedrock view**, or strict constructionist or originalist view, the purpose of a constitution is to state certain fundamental principles for all time. In the **living-document view**, a constitution is merely a statement of goals and objectives and is intended to grow and change with time.

Whether the Constitution is to be liberally interpreted under the living-document view or narrowly interpreted under the bedrock view has a direct effect on the Constitution. For the last century, the Supreme Court has followed the living-document view. This view has resulted in strengthening the power of the federal government, permitting the rise

---

[3] *New York v Trans World Airlines*, 556 NYS2d 803 (1990). See also footnote 2 and the *Cuomo* case from 2009.

of administrative agencies, and expanding the protection of human rights.

One view is not selected to the exclusion of the other. As contradictory as these two views sound, the Constitution remains durable. We do not want a set of New Year's resolutions that will soon be forgotten. At the same time, we know that the world changes, and therefore, we do not want a constitution that will hold us tied in a straitjacket of the past.

In terms of social forces that make the law, we are torn between our desire for stability and our desire for flexibility. We want a constitution that is stable. At the same time, we want one that is flexible.

7. Amending the Constitution

The U.S. Constitution has been amended in three ways: (1) expressly, (2) by interpretation, and (3) by practice. Figure 4.2 illustrates these three methods of amendment.

(A) CONSTITUTIONAL METHOD OF AMENDING. Article V of the Constitution gives the procedure to be followed for amending the Constitution. Relatively few changes have been made to the Constitution by this formal process, although thousands of proposals have been made. Since the time of its adoption, there have been only 27 amendments to the Constitution.

(B) AMENDMENT BY JUDICIAL INTERPRETATION. The U.S. Supreme Court has made the greatest changes to the written Constitution by interpreting it. Generally, interpretation is used to apply the Constitution to a new situation that could not have been foreseen when the written Constitution was adopted.

(C) AMENDMENT BY PRACTICE. In practice, the letter of the Constitution is not always followed. Departure from the written Constitution began as early as 1793 when George Washington refused to make treaties as required by the Constitution, by and with the consent of the Senate. Washington began the practice of the president's negotiating a treaty with a foreign country and then submitting it to the Senate for approval. This practice has been followed since that time. Similarly, the electoral college was originally intended to exercise independent judgment in selecting the president, but it now automatically elects the official candidate of the party that elected the majority of the members of the electoral college.

8. The Living Constitution

The living Constitution has the following characteristics.

(A) STRONG GOVERNMENT. One of the characteristics of the new Constitution is strong government. Business enterprises are highly regulated and the economy is controlled through monetary policy.

(B) STRONG PRESIDENT. Instead of being merely an officer who carries out the laws, the president has become the political leader of a party, exerting strong influence on the lawmaking process.

(C) ECLIPSE OF THE STATES. Under constitutional interpretations, all levels of government have powers that they never possessed before, but the center of gravity has shifted from the states to the nation. When the Constitution was adopted in 1789, the federal

FIGURE 4-2 | ***Amending the U.S. Constitution***

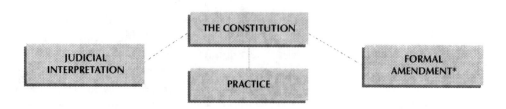

*Article V of the U.S. Constitution specifies the procedure for adopting amendments.

government was to have only the very limited powers specified in Article I, Section 8, of the Constitution. Whatever regulation of business was permissible was to be imposed by the states. Today, the great bulk of the regulation of business is adopted by the federal government through Congress or its administrative agencies. As the U.S. economy moved from the local community stage to the nationwide and then international stages, individual states could no longer provide effective regulation of business. Regulation migrated to the central government.

(D) ADMINISTRATIVE AGENCIES. These units of government were virtually unheard of in 1789, and the Constitution made no mention of them. The vast powers of the new Constitution are exercised to a very large degree by administrative agencies. They are in effect a fourth branch of the government, not provided for in the written Constitution. More importantly, the administrative agencies are the ones that come in contact with the majority of businesspersons and citizens.

Agencies have had a significant amount of power delegated to them. The members and heads of the agencies, boards, or commissions are not elected by the voters (see Chapter 6). They are appointed by the president and, at certain levels of appointment in the agency, must be approved by Congress.

D. FEDERAL POWERS

The federal government possesses powers necessary to administer matters of national concern.

9. The Power to Regulate Commerce

The desire to protect commerce from restrictions and barriers set up by the individual states was a prime factor leading to the adoption of the Constitution of 1789. To protect commerce, Congress was given Article I, Section 8, Clause 3—now known as the **commerce clause**—the power "to regulate commerce with foreign nations, and among the several states, and with the Indian tribes."[4]

Until 1937, the Supreme Court held that this provision gave Congress the power to control or regulate only that commerce crossing a state line, such as an interstate railway train or an interstate telegraph message.

(A) THE COMMERCE POWER BECOMES A GENERAL WELFARE POWER. In 1937, the Supreme Court began expanding the concept of interstate commerce. By 1946, the power to regulate interstate commerce had become very broad. By that year, the power had expanded to the point that it gave authority to Congress to adopt regulatory laws that were "as broad as the economic needs of the nation."[5] By virtue of this broad interpretation, Congress can regulate manufacturing, agriculture, mining, stock exchanges, insurance, loan sharking, monopolies, and conspiracies in restraint of trade. The far reach of the interstate commerce power is seen in the Freedom of Access to Clinic Entrances Act,[6] which prohibits obstruction of entrances to clinics.[7]

The case that was the beginning point in the transition of the commerce clause was *NLRB v Jones & Laughlin Steel,* 301 US 1 (1937). The "affectation" doctrine expanded the authority of the federal government under the commerce clause. At that time, the Court concluded, "If it is interstate commerce that feels the pinch, it does not matter how local the squeeze."

(B) THE COMMERCE CLAUSE TODAY. Today, judicial review of the commerce clause typically finds some connection between the legislation and congressional authority. However, in the past five years, the U.S. Supreme Court has found some areas Congress may not regulate and has placed some limitations on the commerce clause. These constraints on the commerce clause focus on the nature of the underlying activity being regulated. So long as the federal regulation relates to economic/ commercial activity, it is constitutional. If, however, the underlying activity is not economic and has only an economic impact, the Supreme Court has imposed restrictions on congressional authority under the commerce clause.

---

[4] For more details on the actual language in the U.S. Constitution, go to **www.constitution.org** and click on "Founding Documents," or refer to Appendix 2.
[5] *American Power & Light Co. v Securities and Exchange Commission,* 329 US 90 (1946).
[6] 18 USC § 248.
[7] The act is constitutional. *United States v Wilson,* 73 F3d 675 (7th Cir 1995), *cert denied,* 519 US 806 (1996).

(C) THE COMMERCE POWER AS A LIMITATION ON STATES. The federal power to regulate commerce not only gives Congress the power to act but also prevents states from acting in any way that interferes with federal regulation or burdens interstate commerce. **For Example,** if the federal government establishes safety device regulations for interstate carriers, a state cannot require different devices.

States may not use their tax power for the purpose of discriminating against interstate commerce, because such commerce is within the protection of the national government. **For Example,** a state cannot impose a higher tax on goods imported from another state than it imposes on the same kind of goods produced in its own territory.

State regulations designed to advance local interests may conflict with the commerce clause. Such regulations are invalid. A state cannot refuse to allow an interstate waste collector to conduct business within the state on the grounds that the state already has enough waste collectors.

Granholm v Heald, 544 US 460 (2005)

Whining About Wine

Like many other states, Michigan and New York regulate the sale and importation of alcoholic beverages, including wine, through a three-tier distribution system. Separate licenses are required for producers, wholesalers, and retailers. Both the regulations and statutory frameworks in New York and Michigan prohibit out-of-state wine producers from selling their wines directly to consumers there. In-state wineries can sell directly to consumers. The impact of the prohibition on the out-of-state wine producers is that they are required to pay wholesaler fees and cannot compete with in-state wine producers on direct-to-consumer sales. The direct-to-consumer sales avenue has been a means for small wineries to compete. Also, technological improvements, in particular the ability of wineries to sell wine over the Internet, have helped make direct shipments an attractive sales channel.

Several wine producers filed suit in their federal districts challenging these laws that prohibit direct shipment. The district court granted summary judgment for the state of Michigan. The Sixth Circuit Court of Appeals reversed on the grounds that the out-of-state restrictions violated the commerce clause. The state of Michigan appealed. In the New York case, the district court found the out-of-state restrictions violative of the Commerce Clause and Second Circuit Court of Appeals reversed and upheld the New York statute as constitutional. The out-of-state wine producers appealed, and the Supreme Court agreed to hear the cases to resolve the conflict in the circuits.

JUDICIAL OPINION

KENNEDY, Justice …We consolidated these cases and granted certiorari on the following question: "'Does a State's regulatory scheme that permits in-state wineries directly to ship alcohol to consumers but restricts the ability of out-of-state wineries to do so violate the … Commerce Clause…?'"

Time and again this Court has held that, in all but the narrowest circumstances, state laws violate the Commerce Clause if they mandate "differential treatment of in-state and out-of-state economic interests that benefits the former and burdens the latter." This rule is essential to the foundations of the Union. The mere fact of nonresidence should not foreclose a producer in one State from access to markets in other States. States may not enact laws that burden out-of-state producers or shippers simply to give a competitive advantage to in-state businesses. This mandate "reflect[s] a central concern of the Framers that was an immediate reason for calling the Constitutional Convention: the conviction that in order to succeed, the new Union would have to avoid the tendencies toward economic Balkanization that had plagued relations among the Colonies and later among the States under the Articles of Confederation."

The rule prohibiting state discrimination against interstate commerce follows also from the principle that States should not be compelled to negotiate with each other regarding favored or disfavored status for their own citizens. States do not need, and may not attempt, to negotiate with other States regarding their mutual economic interests. Rivalries among the States are thus kept to a minimum, and a proliferation of trade zones is prevented.

Laws of the type at issue in the instant cases contradict these principles. They deprive citizens of their right to have access to the markets of other States on equal terms. State laws that protect local wineries have led to the enactment of statutes under which some States condition the right of out-of-state wineries to make direct wine sales to in-state consumers on a reciprocal right in the shipping State. The current patchwork of laws—with some States banning direct shipments altogether, others doing so only for out-of-state

Continued

wines, and still others requiring reciprocity—is essentially the product of an ongoing, low-level trade war. Allowing States to discriminate against out-of-state wine "invite [s] a multiplication of preferential trade areas destructive of the very purpose of the commerce clause."

The discriminatory character of the Michigan system is obvious. Michigan allows in-state wineries to ship directly to consumers, subject only to a licensing requirement. Out-of-state wineries, whether licensed or not, face a complete ban on direct shipment. The differential treatment requires all out-of-state wine, but not all in-state wine, to pass through an in-state wholesaler and retailer before reaching consumers. These two extra layers of overhead increase the cost of out-of-state wines to Michigan consumers. The cost differential, and in some cases the inability to secure a wholesaler for small shipments, can effectively bar small wineries from the Michigan market.

The New York regulatory scheme differs from Michigan's in that it does not ban direct shipments altogether. Out-of-state wineries are instead required to establish a distribution operation in New York in order to gain the privilege of direct shipment.

The New York scheme grants in-state wineries access to the State's consumers on preferential terms. The suggestion of a limited exception for direct shipment from out-of-state wineries does nothing to eliminate the discriminatory nature of New York's regulations. In-state producers, with the applicable licenses, can ship directly to consumers from their wineries. Out-of-state wineries must open a branch office and warehouse in New York, additional steps that drive up the cost of their wine. For most wineries, the expense of establishing a bricks-and-mortar distribution operation in 1

State, let alone all 50, is prohibitive. It comes as no surprise that not a single out-of-state winery has availed itself of New York's direct-shipping privilege. We have "viewed with particular suspicion state statutes requiring business operations to be performed in the home State that could more efficiently be performed elsewhere." *Pike v. Bruce Church, Inc.* 397 U.S. 137, 145, 90 S.Ct. 844, 25 L.Ed.2d 174 (1970). New York's in-state presence requirement runs contrary to our admonition that States cannot require an out-of-state firm "to become a resident in order to compete on equal terms."

We have no difficulty concluding that New York, like Michigan, discriminates against interstate commerce through its direct-shipping laws.

Affirmed as to judgment of the Sixth Circuit Court of Appeals; reversed and remanded as to judgment of the Second Circuit Court of Appeals.

NOTE: There was a strong dissent in the case that indicated that because of the 21st Amendment the federal government (and the court) could not be involved in state liquor regulation and that the Commerce Clause could not be applied to these state laws on liquor sales.

QUESTIONS

1. What do the Michigan and New York statutes require?

2. Why did the U.S. Supreme Court grant *certiorari* in the cases? Why do you think the court heard and decided the two cases together?

3. What is the economic impact of the statutes on wineries, both in- and out-of-state? On wholesalers? On consumers?

10. The Financial Powers

The financial powers of the federal government include the powers to tax and to borrow, spend, and coin money.

(A) THE TAXING POWER. The federal Constitution provides that "Congress shall have power to lay and collect taxes, duties, imposts and excises, to pay the debts and provide for the common defence and general welfare of the United States."[8] Subject to the express and implied limitations arising from the Constitution, the states may impose such taxes as they desire and as their own individual constitutions and statutes permit. In addition to express constitutional limitations, both national and local taxes are subject to the unwritten limitation that they be imposed for a public purpose. Taxes must also be apportioned. A business cannot be taxed for all of its revenues in all 50 states. There must be apportionment of taxes, and there must be sufficient connection with the state.

[8] U.S. Const., Art 1, § 8, cl 1. To read more of the U.S. Constitution, refer to Appendix 2, or go to **www.constitution.org** and click on "Founding Documents."

Quill v North Dakota, 504 US 298 (1992)

A Quill In Your State Means Taxes In The Coffer

FACTS: Quill is a Delaware corporation with offices and warehouses in Illinois, California, and Georgia.None of its employees works or lives in North Dakota, and it owns no property in North Dakota.

Quill sells office equipment and supplies; it solicits business through catalogs and flyers, advertisements in national periodicals, and telephone calls. Its annual national sales exceed $200 million, of which almost $1 million are made to about three thousand customers in North Dakota. The sixth largest vendor of office supplies in the state, it delivers all of its merchandise to its North Dakota customers by mail or common carriers from out-of-state locations.

As a corollary to its sales tax, North Dakota imposes a use tax upon property purchased for storage, use, or consumption within the state. North Dakota requires every "retailer maintaining a place of business in" the state to collect the tax from the consumer and remit it to the state. In 1987, North Dakota amended its statutory definition of the term "retailer" to include "every person who engages in regular or systematic solicitation of a consumer market in th[e] state." State regulations in turn define "regular or systematic solicitation" to mean three or more advertisements within a 12-month period. Thus, since 1987, mail-order companies that engage in such solicitation have been subject to the tax even if they maintain no property or personnel in North Dakota.

Quill has taken the position that North Dakota does not have the power to compel it to collect a use tax from its North Dakota customers. Consequently, the state, through its tax commissioner, filed this action to require Quill to pay taxes (as well as interest and penalties) on all such sales made after July 1, 1987. The trial court ruled in Quill's favor.

The North Dakota Supreme Court reversed, and Quill appealed.

JUDICIAL OPINION

STEVENS, J. ... This case, like *National Bellas Hess, Inc. v Department of Revenue of Ill.*, 386 U.S. 753, 87 S.Ct. 1389, 18 L.Ed.2d 505 (1967), involves a State's attempt to require an out-of-state mail-order house that has neither outlets nor sales representatives in the State to collect and pay a use tax on goods purchased for use within the State. In *Bellas Hess* we held that a similar Illinois statute violated the Due Process Clause of the Fourteenth Amendment and created an unconstitutional burden on interstate commerce. In particular, we ruled that a "seller whose only connection with customers in the State is by common carrier or the United States mail" lacked the requisite minimum contacts with the State.

In this case the Supreme Court of North Dakota declined to follow *Bellas Hess* because "the tremendous social, economic, commercial, and legal innovations" of the past quarter-century have rendered its holding "obsole[te]."

As in a number of other cases involving the application of state taxing statutes to out-of-state sellers, our holding in *Bellas Hess* relied on both the Due Process Clause and the Commerce Clause.

The Due Process Clause "requires some definite link, some minimum connection, between a state and the person, property or transaction it seeks to tax," and that the "income attributed to the State for tax purposes must be rationally related to 'values connected with the taxing State.'" Prior to *Bellas Hess*, we had held that that requirement was satisfied in a variety of circumstances involving use taxes. For example, the presence of sales personnel in the State, or the maintenance of local retail stores in the State, justified the exercise of that power because the seller's local activities were "plainly accorded the protection and services of the taxing State." We expressly declined to obliterate the "sharp distinction ... between mail order sellers with retail outlets, solicitors, or property within a State, and those who do no more than communicate with customers in the State by mail or common carrier as a part of a general interstate business."

Our due process jurisprudence has evolved substantially in the 25 years since *Bellas Hess*, particularly in the area of judicial jurisdiction. Building on the seminal case of *International Shoe Co. v. Washington*, 326 U.S. 310, 66 S.Ct. 154, 90 L.Ed. 95 (1945), we have framed the relevant inquiry as whether a defendant had minimum contacts with the jurisdiction "such that the maintenance of the suit does not offend 'traditional notions of fair play and substantial justice.'"

Applying these principles, we have held that if a foreign corporation purposefully avails itself of the benefits of an economic market in the forum State, it may subject itself to the State's ***in personam*** jurisdiction even if it has no physical presence in the State.

Comparable reasoning justifies the imposition of the collection duty on a mail-order house that is engaged in continuous and widespread solicitation of business within a State. In "modern commercial life" it matters little that such solicitation is accomplished by a deluge of catalogs rather than a phalanx of drummers: the requirements of due process are met irrespective of a corporation's lack of physical presence in

Continued

the taxing State. Thus, to the extent that our decisions have indicated that the Due Process Clause requires physical presence in a State for the imposition of duty to collect a use tax, we overrule those holdings as superseded by developments in the law of due process.

In this case, there is no question that Quill has purposefully directed its activities at North Dakota residents, that the magnitude of those contacts are more than sufficient for due process purposes, and that the use tax is related to the benefits Quill receives from access to State. We therefore agree with the North Dakota Supreme Court's conclusion that the Due Process Clause does not bar enforcement of that State's use tax against Quill.

[Affirmed]

QUESTIONS

1. Did Quill Corporation own any property in North Dakota? Were any Quill offices or personnel located in North Dakota?

2. How did Quill come to have customers in North Dakota?

3. Will Quill be subject to North Dakota's use tax?

4. Is there a jurisdictional difference between pamphlets being present in a state and the presence of salespeople in that state?

e-commerce&cyberlaw

Internet and Interstate

Collection of sales tax from Internet stores has been a stickler of an issue for businesses, state revenue officials, and the U.S. Supreme Court. All three were grappling with how to collect, what to collect, and whether anybody had any authority to collect. Internet sales represent a large, untapped source of revenue. A study from the Center for Business and Economic Research at the University of Tennessee estimates the lost tax revenue from untaxed Internet sales as $21 billion in 2008.

The merchants involved fell into several different legal groups in terms of their theories on whether tax was owed and whether they should just pay it, with or without the states having the authority to tax:

1. Those stores with physical presences in states (Wal-Mart and J.C. Penney) that just collected sales tax as if they were collecting it in a store in that state where the Internet purchaser was located

2. Those stores without a physical presence (Amazon) that did collect taxes, particularly in those states known for taking a hard-line approach

3. Those stores without a physical presence that do not collect taxes and maintain that it is unconstitutional to do so

4. Those stores with or without a physical presence that have collected taxes but held them until everyone could figure out the legal status of the companies.

What are the constitutional issues in this taxation question?

Note: Amazon.com filed suit in 2008 challenging New York's statute that authorized the collection of sales taxes from online company sales to New York residents.

Source: Robery Guy Matthews, "Some States Push to Collect Sales Tax from Internet Stores," *Wall Street Journal*, Sept. 30, 2005, B1–B4.

(B) THE SPENDING POWER. The federal government may use tax money and borrowed money "to pay the debts and provide for the common defence and general welfare of the United States."[9]

(C) THE BANKING POWER. The Constitution is liberally interpreted to allow the federal government to create banks and to regulate banks created under state laws. For example, the Federal Reserve System is responsible for this regulatory oversight of banks.

E. CONSTITUTIONAL LIMITATIONS ON GOVERNMENT

The constitutional limitations discussed in the following sections afford protections of rights for both persons and businesses.

11. Due Process

The power of government is limited by both the Fifth and Fourteenth Amendments to the Constitution. Those amendments respectively prohibit the national government and state governments from depriving any person "of life, liberty, or property without due process of law."[10]

(A) WHEN DUE PROCESS RIGHTS ARISE. As a result of liberal interpretation of the Constitution, the **due process clause** now provides a guarantee of protection against the loss of property or rights without the chance to be heard. These amendments also guarantee that all citizens are given the same protections. **For Example,** the Supreme Court has extended the due process clause to protect the record or standing of a student.[11] A student cannot lose credit in a course or be suspended or expelled without some form of a hearing.

Because there are so many areas in which due process rights exist and require a chance to be heard, speeding up due process has resulted in the creation of **quasi-**

judicial proceedings. In these types of proceedings, the parties need not go through the complex, lengthy, and formal procedures of a trial (described in Chapter 2). Rather, these proceedings have a hearing officer or administrative law judge (see Chapter 6) who conducts an informal hearing in which the rules of evidence and procedure are relaxed.

For Example, a student taking a grade grievance beyond a faculty member's decision will generally have his case heard by a panel of faculty and students as established by college or university rules. An employer appealing its unemployment tax rate will have the appeal heard by an administrative law judge.

(B) WHAT CONSTITUTES DUE PROCESS? Due process does not require a trial on every issue of rights. Shortcut procedures, such as grade grievance panels, have resulted as a compromise for providing the right to be heard along with a legitimate desire to be expeditious in resolving these issues.

12. Equal Protection of the Law

The Constitution prohibits the states and the national government from denying any person the equal protection of the law.[12] This guarantee prohibits a government from treating one person differently from another when there is no reasonable ground for classifying them differently.

(A) REASONABLE CLASSIFICATION. Whether a classification is reasonable depends on whether the nature of the classification bears a reasonable relation to the wrong to be remedied or to the object to be attained by the law. The judicial trend is to permit the classification to stand as long as there is a rational basis for the distinction made.[13] Whether a rational basis exists is determined by answering whether the lawmaking body has been arbitrary or capricious.

The equal protection clause is the basis of many of the U.S. Supreme Court's most complicated decisions. **For Example,** during the 2000 presidential election, the U.S. Supreme Court faced an issue of equal protection with regard to the challenge then–vice president and

---

[9] U.S. Const., Art 1, § 8, cl 1. See **www.constitution.org**, or Appendix 2.

[10] For more information on the language of the Fifth and Fourteenth Amendments, see the U.S. Constitution in Appendix 2, or go to **www.constitution.org**.

[11] That is, a student cannot be expelled without a chance to have his or her side of the story reviewed.

[12] U.S. Constitution, Fourteenth Amendment as to the states; modern interpretation of due process clause of the Fifth Amendment as to national government. Congress adopted the Civil Rights Act to implement the concept of equal protection.

[13] *Ileto v Glock, Inc.*, 565 F3d 1126 (CA 9 2009)

presidential candidate Al Gore made to the undervotes in Florida's ballots. However, then-presidential candidate George W. Bush argued that counting the undervotes in some counties and not in others and applying different standards for counting or not counting the infamous dimpled chads, hanging chads, and other undervotes was unconstitutional because it deprived other Florida voters of equal protection because each vote is intended to count equally. Recounts in only some counties while using varying standards resulted in some counties being given greater weight in Florida's presidential election. The U.S. Supreme Court agreed in a 7–2 decision that the recounts were unconstitutional on equal protection grounds.[14] However, the justices split 5–4 on the correct remedy for the unconstitutional recounts.

(B) IMPROPER CLASSIFICATION. Laws that make distinctions in the regulation of business, the right to work, and the right to use or enjoy property on the basis of race, national origin, or religion are invalid. Also invalid are laws that impose restrictions on some, but not all, persons without any justification for the distinction.[15] **For Example,** a state statute taxing out-of-state insurance companies at a higher rate than in-state insurance companies violates the equal protection clause.[16]

13. Privileges and Immunities

The federal Constitution declares that "the citizens of each state shall be entitled to all privileges and immunities of citizens in the several states."[17] The so-called **privileges and immunities clause** means that a person going into another state is entitled to make contracts, own property, and engage in business to the same extent as the citizens of that state. **For Example,** a state cannot bar someone who comes from another state from engaging in local business or from obtaining a hunting or fishing license merely because the person is not a resident of that state.

14. Protection of the Person

The Constitution has no general provision declaring that the government shall not impair rights of persons. The Constitution does not mention the phrase "unalienable right" that was part of the Declaration of Independence.[18] However, the Bill of Rights, the first 10 amendments to the Constitution, does provide protections for freedom of speech, jury trials, and freedom of religion and association.[19] The Bill of Rights provides for the due process protections discussed earlier as well as those that prohibit unlawful searches and seizures. The Second Amendment provides for the right to keep and bear arms, an issue that has resulted in some conflicting decisions that the U.S. Supreme Court has begun to address.[20]

During the last six decades, the Supreme Court has been interpreting the rights in these amendments and has been finding constitutional protection for a wide array of rights of the person that are not expressly protected by the Constitution. **For Example,** judicial interpretations have concluded that the Constitution provides for the right of privacy, the right to marry the person one chooses,[21] protection from unreasonable zoning, protection of parental control, protection from discrimination because of poverty, and protection from gender discrimination.[22]

---

[14] *Bush v Gore*, 531 US 98 (2000).
[15] *Associated Industries of Missouri v Lohman*, 511 US 641 (1994).
[16] *Metropolitan Life Ins. Co. v Ward*, 470 US 869 (1985).
[17] U.S. Const., Art IV, § 2, cl 1. See **www.constitution.org** and click on "Founding Documents" to access more language of the Constitution, or see Appendix 2.
[18] The term *unalienable right* is employed in reference to natural right, fundamental right, or basic right. Apart from the question of scope of coverage, the adjective *unalienable* emphasizes the fact that the people still possess the right rather than having surrendered or subordinated it to the will of society. The word *alien* is the term of the old common law for transferring title or ownership. Today, we would say *transfer* and, instead of saying unalienable rights, would say *nontransferable* rights. Unalienable rights of the people were therefore rights that the people not only possessed but also could not give up even if they wanted to. Thus, these rights are still owned by everyone. It is important to note that the Declaration of Independence actually uses the word "unalienable" when describing the rights eventually placed in the Constitution as Amendments I–X, the Bill of Rights, not "inalienable."
[19] *North Coast Women's Care Medical Group, Inc. v San Diego County Superior Court*, 189 P 3d 959 (Ca 2008).
[20] *District of Columbia v Heller*, 128 S Ct 2783(2008).
[21] *Akron v Akron Center for Reproductive Health, Inc.*, 462 US 416 (1983); but see *Colorado v Hill, cert granted*, 527 US 1068 (2000). For more on commercial speech, see *Greater New Orleans Broadcasting Association, Inc., v U.S.* 527 US 173 (1999) and *U.S. v Philip Morris USA Inc.*, 566 F3d 1095 (CA DC 2009).
[22] In some cases, the courts have given the due process and equal protection clauses a liberal interpretation in order to find a protection of the person, thereby making up for the fact that there is no express constitutional guarantee of protection of the person. *Davis v Passman* 442 US 228 (1979) (due process); *Orr v Orr*, 440 US 268 (1979) (equal protection).

thinking things through

Sweating It Out on Free Speech

In 1996, Nike was inundated with allegations about its labor practices in shoe factories around the world. Nike responded to the negative reports and allegations with a series of releases, advertisements, and op-ed pieces in newspapers around the country. *New York Times* columnist Bob Herbert wrote two columns that were sharply critical of Nike's conditions in plants throughout Asia. The columns compared then-CEO Philip Knight's compensation with the $2.20 per day wages of Nike workers in Indonesia.

After the columns appeared, CEO Knight wrote a letter to the editor in response to them. In that letter, he wrote, "Nike has paid, on average, double the minimum wage as defined in countries where its products are produced under contract. History shows that the best way out of poverty for such countries is through exports of light manufactured goods that provide the base for more skilled production."*

Marc Kasky filed suit against Nike in California, alleging that the op-ed pieces and letters in response to negative op-ed pieces about Nike violated the False Advertising Act of California. The act permits state agencies to take action to fine corporate violators of the act as well as to obtain remedies such as injunctions to halt the ads.

Nike challenged the suit on the grounds that such an interpretation and application of the advertising regulation violated its rights of free speech. The lower court agreed with Kasky and held that the advertising statute applied to Nike's defense of its labor practices, even on the op-ed pages of newspapers. The California Supreme Court, 45 P.3d 243 (Cal. 2002), ruled that Nike could be subject to regulatory sanctions for false advertising. Nike appealed to the U.S. Supreme Court. Should Nike's editorial be protected by the First Amendment? Discuss where this type of speech fits.

The opinion handed down in this case is only one sentence: "The writ of certiorari is dismissed as improvidently granted." 539 US 654 (2003). Is this letter protected speech?

* Roger Parloff, "Can We Talk?" *Fortune*, September 2, 2002, 102–110.

15. The Bill of Rights and Businesses as Persons

The Bill of Rights provides protections for individuals and also for corporations. **For Example,** the Fourth Amendment (see Chapter 8) provides protections against unreasonable searches. Individuals enjoy that protection in their homes, and corporations enjoy that protection with their files, offices, and business records. Businesses also enjoy freedom of speech protections under the First Amendment. The First Amendment provides that "Congress shall make no law … abridging the freedom of speech …"[23]

The U.S. Supreme Court has clarified the free speech rights of business through classification of the

lawflix

The Candidate (1972) (PG)

The movie depicts an idealist running for office who finds himself caught in the political process of fundraising, image-building, and winning. A number of scenes with speeches, fundraising, and principles in conflict provide excellent discussion issues with respect to government structure, the First Amendment, and campaign contributions.

Check out LawFlix at **www.cengage.com/blaw/dvl** to access movie clips that illustrate business law concepts.

[23] To read the full language of the First Amendment, go to Appendix 2, or to **www.constitution.org** and click on "Founding Documents."

types of business speech. One form of business or commercial speech is advertising. This form of speech in which businesses tout their products is subject to regulation and restriction on form, content, and placement, and such regulation has been deemed constitutional. (See Chapters 25 and 33 for more information on the regulation of advertising.)

However, there are other forms of commercial speech. Businesses do have the right to participate in political processes such as creating political action committees and supporting or opposing ballot initiatives. Businesses often take positions and launch campaigns on ballot initiatives that will affect the taxes they will be required to pay.

MAKE THE CONNECTION

SUMMARY

The U.S. Constitution created the structure of our national government and gave it certain powers. It also placed limitations on those powers. It created a federal system with a tripartite division of government and a bicameral national legislature.

The national government possesses some governmental powers exclusively, while both the states and the federal government share other powers. In areas of conflict, federal law is supreme.

The U.S. Constitution is not a detailed document. It takes its meaning from the way it is interpreted. In recent years, liberal interpretation has expanded the powers of the federal government. Among the powers of the federal government that directly affect business

are the power to regulate commerce; the power to tax and to borrow, spend, and coin money; and the power to own and operate businesses.

Among the limitations on government that are most important to business are the requirements of due process and the requirement of equal protection of the law. In addition, government is limited by the rights given to individuals such as freedom of speech, freedom of religion, and equal protection. The equal protection concept of the U.S. Constitution prohibits both the federal government and the state governments from treating one person differently from another unless there is a legitimate reason for doing so and unless the basis of classification is reasonable.

LEARNING OUTCOMES

After studying this chapter, you should be able to clearly explain:

A. THE U.S. CONSTITUTION AND THE FEDERAL SYSTEM

LO.1 Describe the U.S. Constitution and the Federal System

See the discussion of the **tripartite** (three-part) government on p. 58.

B. THE U.S. CONSTITUTION AND THE STATES

LO.2 Explain the relationship between the U.S. Constitution and the States

See the discussion of the federal system on p. 58.
See Figure 4.1 for an illustration of the delegation of powers.

C. INTERPRETING AND AMENDING THE CONSTITUTION

LO.3 Discuss interpreting and amending the Constitution

See the discussion of the bedrock and constructionist views on p. 61.

D. FEDERAL POWERS

LO.4 List and describe the significant federal powers

See the discussion of the commerce power on p. 63.

See the discussion of the taxing power on p. 65.

See the discussion of the banking power on p. 68.

E. CONSTITUTIONAL LIMITATIONS ON GOVERNMENT

LO.5 Discuss constitutional limitations on governmental power

See the discussion of the Bill of Rights on p. 70.

See the discussion of the Fourth Amendment on p. 70.

See the discussion of due process on p. 68.

See the **For Example** discussion of a student taking a grade grievance beyond a faculty member's decision on p. 68.

KEY TERMS

bedrock view
bicameral
commerce clause
constitution
delegated powers
due process clause
ex post facto laws

executive branch
federal system
judicial branch
legislative branch
living-document view
police power
preemption

privileges and immunities
    clause
quasi-judicial proceedings
shared powers
tripartite

QUESTIONS AND CASE PROBLEMS

1. Federal law requires most interstate truckers to obtain a permit that reflects compliance with certain federal requirements. The 1965 version of the law authorized states to require proof that a truck operator had such a permit. By 1991, 39 states had demanded such proof, requiring a $10 per truck registration fee and giving each trucker a stamp to affix to a multistate "bingo card" carried in the vehicle. Finding this scheme inefficient and burdensome, Congress created the current Single State Registration System (SSRS), which allows a trucking company to fill out one set of forms in one state, thereby registering in every participating state through which its trucks travel.

   A subsection of Michigan's Motor Carrier Act imposes on truck companies operating in interstate commerce an annual fee of $100 for each self-propelled motor vehicle operated by or on

   behalf of the motor carrier. The American Truckers Association (ATA) and others challenged the $100 fee as preempted by the extensive federal regulation of interstate trucking and trucking companies. The ATA and others appealed to the U.S. Supreme Court. What should the U.S. Supreme Court do? Be sure to discuss what portion of the Constitution applies to this issue. [*American Trucking Associations, Inc. v Michigan Public Service Com'n,* 545 US 429]

2. J.C. Penney, a retail merchandiser, has its principal place of business in Plano, Texas. It operates retail stores in all 50 states, including 10 stores in Massachusetts, and a direct mail catalog business. The catalogs illustrated merchandise available for purchase by mail order. The planning, artwork, design, and layout for these

catalogs were completed and paid for outside of Massachusetts, primarily in Texas, and Penney contracted with independent printing companies located outside Massachusetts to produce the catalogs. The three major catalogs were generally printed in Indiana, while the specialty catalogs were printed in South Carolina and Wisconsin. Penney supplied the printers with paper, shipping wrappers, and address labels for the catalogs; the printers supplied the ink, binding materials, and labor. None of these materials was purchased in Massachusetts. Printed catalogs, with address labels and postage affixed, were transported by a common carrier from the printer to a U.S. Postal Service office located outside Massachusetts, where they were sent to Massachusetts addressees via third- or fourth-class mail. Any undeliverable catalogs were returned to Penney's distribution center in Connecticut.

Purchases of catalog merchandise were made by telephoning or returning an order form to Penney at a location outside Massachusetts, and the merchandise was shipped to customers from a Connecticut distribution center. The Massachusetts Department of Revenue audited Penney in 1995 and assessed a use tax, penalty, and interest on the catalogs that had been shipped into Massachusetts. The position of the department was that there was a tax due of $314,674.62 on the catalogs that were used by Penney's Massachusetts customers. Penney said such a tax was unconstitutional in that it had no control or contact with the catalogs in the state. Can the state impose the tax? Why or why not? [*Commissioner of Revenue v J.C. Penney Co., Inc.*, 730 NE2d 266 (Mass)]

3. Alfonso Lopez, Jr., a 12th-grade student at Edison High School in San Antonio, Texas, went to school carrying a concealed .38-caliber handgun and five bullets. School officials, acting on an anonymous tip, confronted Lopez. Lopez admitted that he had the gun. He was arrested and charged with violation of federal law, the Gun-Free School Zones Act of 1990. Lopez moved to dismiss his indictment on the grounds that the provision of the Gun-Free School Zones Act with which he was charged was unconstitutional in

that it was beyond the power of Congress to legislate controls over public schools. The district court found the statute to be a constitutional exercise of congressional authority.

Lopez was found guilty and sentenced to two years in prison. He appealed and challenged his conviction on the basis of the commerce clause. The Court of Appeals agreed with Lopez, found the Gun-Free School Zones Act an unconstitutional exercise of congressional authority, and reversed the conviction. The U.S. Attorney appealed. Who should win at the U.S. Supreme Court and why? [*United States v Lopez*, 514 US 549]

4. The University of Wisconsin requires all of its students to pay, as part of their tuition, a student activity fee. Those fees are used to support campus clubs and activities. Some students who objected to the philosophies and activities of some of the student clubs filed suit to have the fees halted. What constitutional basis do you think they could use for the suit? [*Board of Regents of Wisconsin System v Southworth*, 529 US 217]

5. The Crafts' home was supplied with gas by the city gas company. Because of some misunderstanding, the gas company believed that the Crafts were delinquent in paying their gas bill. The gas company had an informal complaint procedure for discussing such matters, but the Crafts had never been informed that such a procedure was available. The gas company notified the Crafts that they were delinquent and that the company was shutting off the gas. The Crafts brought an action to enjoin the gas company from doing so on the theory that a termination without any hearing was a denial of due process. The lower courts held that the interest of the Crafts in receiving gas was not a property interest protected by the due process clause and that the procedures the gas company followed satisfied the requirements of due process. The Crafts appealed. Were they correct in contending that they had been denied due process of law? Why or why not? [*Memphis Light, Gas and Water Division v Craft*, 436 US 1]

6. Alexis Geier was injured in an accident while driving a 1987 Honda Accord that did not have passive safety restraints. When her Honda Accord was manufactured, the U.S. Department of Transportation required passive safety restraints on some, but not all, vehicles. Geier and her parents filed suit against Honda for its negligence in not equipping the Honda Accord with a driver's-side airbag. Geier alleged that because Honda knew of the safety standard but did not voluntarily comply with it (it was not required to do so under the federal regulations), it was negligent under state negligence standards for liability and should be held liable. The district court granted Honda summary judgment based on Honda's argument that safety requirements for cars were set exclusively by the federal government. The Court of Appeals affirmed, and Geier appealed. What would be the effect of a decision that requires a car company to comply with state-by-state standards of negligence? Would a state court finding of negligence be a constitutional exercise of state power? Should the U.S. Supreme Court affirm or reverse the summary judgment for Honda? [*Geier v American Honda Motor Co.,* 529 US 1913]

7. Montana imposed a severance tax on every ton of coal mined within the state. The tax varied depending on the value of the coal and the cost of production. It could be as high as 30 percent of the price at which the coal was sold. Montana mine operators and some out-of-state customers claimed that this tax was unconstitutional as an improper burden on interstate commerce. Decide. [*Commonwealth Edison Co. v Montana,* 453 US 609]

8. Ollie's Barbecue is a family-owned restaurant in Birmingham, Alabama, specializing in barbecued meats and homemade pies, with a seating capacity of 220 customers. It is located on a state highway 11 blocks from an interstate highway and a somewhat greater distance from railroad and bus stations. The restaurant caters to a family and white-collar trade, with a take-out service for "Negroes." (Note: This term is used by the Court in its opinion in the case.) In the 12 months preceding the passage of the Civil Rights Act, the restaurant purchased locally approximately $150,000 worth of food, $69,683 or 46 percent of which was meat that it bought from a local supplier who had procured it from outside the state. Ollie's has refused to serve Negroes in its dining accommodations since opening in 1927, and since July 2, 1964, it has been operating in violation of the Civil Rights Act. A lower court concluded that if it were required to serve Negroes, it would lose a substantial amount of business. The lower court found that the Civil Rights Act did not apply because Ollie's was not involved in "interstate commerce." Will the commerce clause permit application of the Civil Rights Act to Ollie's? [*Katzenbach v McClung,* 379 US 294]   yes

9. Ellis was employed by the city of Lakewood. By the terms of his contract, he could be discharged only for cause. After working for six years, he was told that he was going to be discharged because of his inability to generate safety and self-insurance programs, because of his failure to win the confidence of employees, and because of his poor attendance. He was not informed of the facts in support of these conclusions and was given the option to resign. He claimed that he was entitled to a hearing. Is he entitled to one? Why or why not? [*Ellis v City of Lakewood,* 789 P 2d 449 (Colo. App.)]   Due Process

10. The Federal Food Stamp Act provided for the distribution of food stamps to needy households. In 1971, section 3(e) of the statute was amended to define households as limited to groups whose members were all related to each other. This was done because of congressional dislike for the lifestyles of unrelated hippies who were living together in hippie communes. Moreno and others applied for food stamps but were refused them because the relationship requirement was not satisfied. An action was brought to have the relationship requirement declared unconstitutional. Is it constitutional? Discuss why or why not. [*USDA v Moreno,* 413 US 528]   unconstitutional

11. New Hampshire adopted a tax law that in effect taxed the income of nonresidents working in

New Hampshire only. Austin, a nonresident who worked in New Hampshire, claimed that the tax law was invalid. Was he correct? Explain. [*Austin v New Hampshire*, 420 US 656]

12. Following a boom in cruise ship construction, the ships are now looking for ports at which they can dock in order to begin voyages, most of which begin in the United States. With so many new ships, the companies are trying to establish connections with cities that are not ordinarily considered cruise ship docks. The companies pursue these alternatives because the traditional docking cities of New York, Seattle, Miami, Los Angeles, and Houston have become crowded with cruise ship traffic. The following issues have arisen:

- Without proper scheduling and departures, cruise ships often end up waiting in the harbor for three to eight hours; as a result, ports such as Tampa, a nontraditional cruise ship port, are experiencing traffic jams of ships waiting to dock.

- The presence of the large boats and the resulting number of tourists cause overwhelming flooding of the often-quaint alternative ports such as Charleston, South Carolina. Charleston residents worry that tourists from the cruise ships flooding their city will result in irreversible destruction of the town's preserved landmarks and quaint looks.

- Rising water levels in ports such as New Orleans mean that the tall ships cannot clear power lines and have to be redirected to ports nearby that are not prepared, as when New Orleans had to redirect a 2,974-passenger cruise ship to Gulfport, Mississippi.

- The port facilities are not adequate to handle all of the boats, the passengers, and even the ships' fueling needs.

Most cruise ship lines are incorporated outside of the United States, and they do not pay federal income taxes and are certainly not subject to state income taxes even though the most passengers come from the United States.[24] Can the ships be taxed to cover the harbor expenses? Can they be required by states and cities to pay docking fees, or are they internationally exempt companies?

13. A federal statute prohibited granting federal funds to libraries that did not control access to pornographic Internet sites on library computers so that children did not gain access and were not exposed to such sites as they used the public facilities. The American Library Association challenged the prohibition as a violation of First Amendment rights.

Are free speech rights violated with the funding regulation? [*U.S. v American Library Association*, 539 US 194; lower court decision at 201 F Supp 2d 401]

---

[24] Nicole Harris, "Big Cruise Ships Cause Traffic Jams in Ports," *Wall Street Journal*, August 20, 2003, B1–B6.

Chapter 5

GOVERNMENT REGULATION OF COMPETITION AND PRICES

The government can regulate not just businesses but also business competition and prices. Antitrust legislation and a regulatory scheme help to ensure that businesses compete fairly.

A. POWER TO REGULATE BUSINESS

The federal government may regulate any area of business to advance the nation's economic needs.[1] Under the police power, states may regulate all aspects of business so long as they do not impose an unreasonable burden on interstate commerce or any activity of the federal government. (See Chapter 4 for a discussion of the protections and limits of the commerce clause.) Local governments may also exercise this police power to the extent a state permits them to do so.

1. Regulation, Free Enterprise, and Deregulation

Milton Friedman, the Nobel economist, has written that government regulation of business interferes with the free enterprise system. Under a true free enterprise system, market forces would provide the necessary protections for airline safety, food purity, and safe drugs through the forces of demand and supply. Sometimes, however, the demand response, or market reaction, to problems or services is not rapid enough to prevent harm, and government regulation steps in to stop abuses. For example, the Federal Trade Commission (FTC) stepped in to curb the tactics and practices of telemarketers when the number of consumer complaints increased dramatically without any industry self-regulation.

There has been some deregulation in certain industries. The collapse of companies such as Lehman Brothers and New Century Financial as well as the financial woes of companies such as Merrill Lynch and Bear Stearns (situations that stemmed from the meltdown of the subprime mortgage markets) have revealed that more oversight is necessary for Wall Street investment firms, financial analysts, and mortgage lenders. Consequently, Congress is in the process of regulating bond rating agencies, the mortgage process, appraisals, and investment banking operations.

2. Regulation of Production, Distribution, and Financing

To protect the public from harm, government may prohibit false advertising and labeling, and establish health and purity standards for cosmetics, foods, and drugs. Licenses may be required to be able to deal in certain goods, and these licenses may be revoked for improper conduct or violations of statutes and regulations.[2] The government may also regulate markets themselves: the quantity of a product that may be produced or grown and the price at which the finished product may be sold. For example, agricultural products markets and commodities have significant government constraints. Government may also engage in competition with private enterprises or own and operate an industry. **For Example,** the U.S. Postal Service competes directly with UPS and FedEx for the delivery of packages as well as for overnight delivery services.

The financing of business is directly affected by the national government, which creates a national currency and maintains the Federal Reserve banking system. State and other national laws may also affect financing by regulating financing contracts and documents, such as bills of lading and commercial paper.

3. Regulation of Unfair Competition

Each of the states and the federal government have statutes and regulations that prohibit unfair methods of competition. Unfair competition is controlled by both statutes and administrative agencies and regulations.

Congress has enacted the Federal Trade Commission Act,[3] which makes all "unfair methods of competition … and unfair or deceptive acts or practices"[4] unlawful and created the Federal Trade

---

[1] *SKF, USA, Inc. v Customs and Border Protection*, 556 F3d 1337 (CA 9 2009).
[2] *Culver v Maryland Ins. Com'r*, 931 A2d 537 (Md App 2007).
[3] 15 USC § 41 *et seq.*
[4] To review the Federal Trade Commission Act, go to **www.ftc.gov**.

Commission (FTC) to administer the act. The FTC has taken enforcement steps against refusals to sell, boycotts, market restrictions, disparagement of competitors' products, and unlawful methods of billing and collection. The FTC regulates false and misleading advertising and controls even the statements on packaged foods to ensure that the nutritional content of the food described on the label is accurate **For Example,** Beech-Nut Baby Food Company paid significant fines in the late 1980s for representing its baby apple juice to actually contain apple juice. The product was made from a very good-tasting chemical concoction, but it had no apple juice. Such misrepresentation on the label was a violation of Section 5 of the Federal Trade Commission Act that prohibits unfair methods of competition. Business missteps, from false advertising to boycotts, constitute unfair methods of competition prohibited under the FTC Act.[5]

B. REGULATION OF MARKETS AND COMPETITION

CPA 4. Regulation of Prices

Governments, both national and state, may regulate prices. Price regulation may be delegated to an administrative officer or agency. Prices in various forms are regulated, including not only what a buyer pays for goods purchased from a store (through controls on price fixing—see discussion that follows) but also through limits on interest rates and rent controls.

(A) PROHIBITION ON PRICE FIXING. Agreements among competitors, as well as "every contract, combination … or conspiracy" to fix prices, violate Section 1 of the Sherman Act.[6] Known as *horizontal price-fixing,* any agreements to charge an agreed-upon price or to

set maximum or minimum prices between or among competitors are *per se*—in, through, or by themselves—a violation of the Sherman Act. An agreement among real estate brokers to never charge below a 6 percent commission is price-fixing.[7] **For Example,** in 2001, Christie's and Sotheby's auction houses settled an antitrust lawsuit for charging the same commissions for many years.[8]

(B) PROHIBITED PRICE DISCRIMINATION. The **Clayton Act** and **Robinson-Patman Act** prohibit price discrimination.[9] **Price discrimination** occurs when a seller charges different prices to different buyers for "commodities of like grade and quality," with the result being reduced competition or a tendency to create a monopoly.[10]

Price discrimination prohibits charging different prices to buyers as related to marginal costs. That is, volume discounts are permissible because the marginal costs are different on the larger volume of goods. However, the Robinson-Patman Act makes it illegal to charge different prices to buyers when the marginal costs of the seller for those goods are the same. Any added incentives or bonuses are also considered part of the price.

For Example, offering one buyer free advertising while not offering it to another as an incentive to buy would be a violation of the Robinson-Patman Act. The Clayton Act makes both the giving and the receiving of any illegal price discrimination a crime.

CPA State statutes frequently prohibit favoring one competitor by giving a secret discount when the effect is to harm the competition.[11] A state may prohibit either selling below cost to harm competitors or selling to one customer at a secret price that is lower than the price charged other customers when there is no economic justification for the lower price.[12] Some state statutes specifically permit sellers to set prices so that they can match competitive prices, but not to undercut a competitor's prices.[13]

---

[5] In many states, such a seller would also be guilty of committing a deceptive trade practice or violating a consumer protection statute.
[6] To view the full language of Section 1 of the Sherman Act, see 15 USC § 1.
[7] *McClain v Real Estate Board of New Orleans, Inc.*, 441 US 942 (1980).
[8] Carol Vogel and Ralph Blumenthall, "Ex-Chairman of Sotheby's Gets a Year and a Day for Price-Fixing," *New York Times*, April 12, 2002, A26.
[9] 15 USC §§ 1, 2, 3, 7, 8.
[10] 15 USC § 13a. To read the full Clayton Act, go to **www.usdoj.gov** or **www.justice.gov** and plug in "Clayton Act" in a site search.
[11] *Eddins v Redstone*, 35 Cal Rptr 3d 863 (2006).
[12] In *Weyerhaeuser v Ross-Simons*, 549 U.S. 312 (2007), the U.S. Supreme Court ruled that predatory bidding is also a price discrimination issue. In a monopsony, a buyer tries to control a market by overbidding all its competitors and thereby cornering the market for supplies it needs to produce goods. However, if the bidder is actually just in need of the goods and bids higher for them, there is no anticompetitive conduct.
[13] *Home Oil Company, Inc. v Sam's East, Inc.*, 252 F Supp 1302 (MD Ala 2003).

Utah Pie Co. v Continental Baking Co., 386 US 685 (1967)

Getting a Piece of the Pie Market

Utah Pie Company (petitioner) is a Utah corporation that for 30 years has been baking pies in its plant in Salt Lake City and selling them in Utah and surrounding states. It entered the frozen pie business in 1957 and was immediately successful with its new line of frozen dessert pies—apple, cherry, boysenberry, peach, pumpkin, and mince.

Continental Baking Company, Pet Milk, and Carnation (respondents), based in California, sell pies in Utah primarily on a delivered-price basis.

The major competitive weapon in the Utah pie market was price. Between 1958 and 1961, there was a deteriorating price structure for pies in the Utah market. Utah Pie was selling pies for $4.15 per dozen at the beginning of the period; at the time it filed suit for price discrimination, it was selling the same pies for $2.75 per dozen. Continental's price went from $5.00 per dozen in 1958 to $2.85 at the time suit was filed. Pet's prices went from $4.92 per dozen to $3.46, and Carnation's from $4.82 per dozen to $3.30.

Utah Pie filed suit, charging price discrimination by respondents based on allegations outlined in the opinion that follows. The district court found for Utah Pie. The court of appeals reversed, and Utah Pie appealed.

JUDICIAL OPINION

WHITE, J.... We deal first with petitioner's case against the Pet Milk Company.... Pet's initial emphasis was on quality, but in the face of competition from regional and local companies and in an expanding market where price proved to be a crucial factor, Pet was forced to take steps to reduce the price of its pies to the ultimate consumer. These developments had consequences in the Salt Lake City market which are the substance of petitioner's case against Pet.

First, Pet successfully concluded an arrangement with Safeway, which is one of the three largest customers for frozen pies in the Salt Lake market, whereby it would sell frozen pies to Safeway under the latter's own "Bel-air" label at a price significantly lower than it was selling its comparable "Pet-Ritz" brand in the same Salt Lake market and elsewhere....

Second, it introduced a 20-ounce economy pie under the "Swiss Miss" label and began selling the new pie in the Salt Lake market in August 1960 at prices ranging from $3.25 to $3.30 for the remainder of the period. This pie was at times sold at a lower price in the Salt Lake City market than it was sold in other markets.

Third, Pet became more competitive with respect to the prices for its "Pet-Ritz" proprietary label.... According to the Court of Appeals, in seven of the 44 months Pet's prices in Salt Lake were lower than prices charged in the California markets. This was true although selling in Salt Lake involved a 30- to 35-cent freight cost.

The burden of proving cost justification was on Pet and, in our view, reasonable men could have found that Pet's lower priced "Bel-air" sales to Safeway were not cost justified in their entirety.

The Court of Appeals almost entirely ignored other evidence which provides material support of the jury's conclusion that Pet's behavior satisfied the statutory test regarding competitive injury. This evidence bore on the issue of Pet's predatory intent to injure Utah Pie. As an initial matter, the jury could have concluded that Pet's discriminatory pricing was aimed at Utah Pie; Pet's own management, as early as 1959, identified Utah Pie as an "unfavorable factor," one which "d[u]g holes in our operation" and posed a constant "check" on Pet's performance in the Salt Lake City market. Moreover, Pet candidly admitted that during the period when it was establishing its relationship with Safeway, it sent into Utah Pie's plant an industrial spy to seek information that would be of use to Pet in convincing Safeway that Utah Pie was not worthy of its customers.... Finally, Pet does not deny that the evidence showed it suffered substantial losses on its frozen pie sales during the greater part of time involved in this suit, and there was evidence from which the jury could have concluded that the losses Pet sustained in Salt Lake City were greater than those incurred elsewhere. It would not have been an irrational step if the jury concluded that there was a relationship between the price and the losses.

It seems clear to us that the jury heard adequate evidence from which it could have concluded that Pet had engaged in predatory tactics in waging competitive warfare in the Salt Lake City market. Coupled with the incidence of price discrimination attributable to Pet, the evidence as a whole established, rather than negated, the reasonable possibility that Pet's behavior produced a lessening of competition proscribed by the Act.

Petitioner's case against Continental is not complicated. Continental was a substantial factor in the market in 1957. But its sales of frozen 22-ounce dessert pies, sold under the "Morton" brand, amounted to only 1.3 percent of the market in 1958, 2.9 percent in 1959, and 1.8 percent in 1960. Its problems were primarily that of cost and in turn that of price, the controlling factor in the market. In late 1960 it worked out a co-packing arrangement in California by which fruit would be processed directly from the trees into the finished pies without large intermediate packing, storing, and shipping expenses. Having improved its position, it attempted to increase its share of the Salt Lake City market by utilizing a

Continued

local broker and offering short-term price concessions in varying amounts. Its efforts for seven months were not spectacularly successful. Then in June 1961, it took the steps which are the heart of petitioner's complaint against it. Effective for the last two weeks of June it offered its 22-ounce frozen apple pies in the Utah area at $2.85 per dozen. It was then selling the same pies at substantially higher prices in other markets. The Salt Lake City price was less than its direct cost plus an allocation for overhead…. Utah's response was immediate. It reduced its price on all of its apple pies to $2.75 per dozen…. Continental's total sales of frozen pies increased from 3,350 dozen in 1960 to 18,800 dozen in 1961. Its market share increased from 1.8 percent in 1960 to 8.3 percent in 1961. The Court of Appeals concluded that Continental's conduct had had only minimal effect, that it had not injured or weakened Utah Pies as a competitor, that it had not substantially lessened competition and that there was no reasonable possibility that it would do so in the future.

Even if the impact on Utah Pie as a competitor was negligible, there remain the consequences to others in the market who had to compete not only with Continental's 22-ounce pie at $2.85 but with Utah's even lower price of $2.75 per dozen for both its proprietary and controlled labels…. The evidence was that there were nine other sellers in 1960 who sold 23,473 dozen pies, 12.7 percent of the total market. In 1961 there were eight other sellers who sold less than the year before—18,565 dozen or 8.2 percent of the total—although the total market had expanded from 184,569 dozen to 226,908 dozen. We think there was sufficient evidence from which the jury could find a violation of § 2(a) by Continental.

Section 2(a) does not forbid price competition which will probably injure or lessen competition by eliminating competitors, discouraging entry into the market or enhancing the market shares of the dominant sellers. But Congress has established some ground rules for the game. Sellers may not sell like goods to different purchasers at different prices if the result may be to injure competition to either the sellers' or the buyers' market unless such discriminations are justified as permitted by the Act. In this case there was some evidence of predatory intent with respect to each of these respondents. There was also other evidence upon which the jury could rationally find the requisite injury to competition. The frozen pie market in Salt Lake City was highly competitive. At times Utah Pie was a leader in moving the general level of prices down, and at other times each of the respondents also bore responsibility for the downward pressure on the price structure. We believe that the Act reaches price discrimination that erodes competition as much as it does price discrimination that is intended to have immediate destructive impact. In this case, the evidence shows a drastically declining price structure which the jury could rationally attribute to continued or sporadic price discrimination.

[Reversed]

QUESTIONS

1. Describe the competitors in the Utah Pie frozen pie market.

2. Is it significant that the national competitors were selling their pies at different prices in Utah?

3. Does it matter that the size of the pie market (i.e., number of pies sold) increased during the period examined?

The issue of state antitrust regulation and wide variations in state laws and decisions prompted the creation of the Antitrust Modernization Commission, a group likely to recommend changes in laws and judicial review standards at both the state and federal levels.[14]

(c) PERMITTED PRICE DISCRIMINATION. Price discrimination is expressly permitted when it can be justified on the basis of (1) a difference in grade, quality, or quantity; (2) the cost of transportation involved in performing the contract; (3) a good-faith effort to meet competition; (4) differences in methods or quantities, i.e., marginal cost differences; (5) deterioration of goods; or (6) a close-out sale of a particular line of goods. The Robinson-Patman Act[15] reaffirms the right of a seller to select customers and refuse to deal with anyone. The refusal, however, must be in good faith, not for the purpose of restraining trade.

---

[14] 21st Century Department of Justice Appropriations Authorization Act, Pub. L. No. 107-273, 116 Stat. 1758 (2002), available at **http://amc.gov/pdf/statute/amc_act.pdf**.
[15] 15 USC §§ 13, 21.

Leegin Creative Leather Products, Inc. v PSKS, Inc., 551 US 877 (2007)

Bagging a Customer for Having Sales

Leegin Creative Leather Products, Inc. (Leegin) (petitioner), designs, manufactures, and distributes leather goods and accessories under the brand name "Brighton." The Brighton brand has now expanded into a full line of women's fashion accessories and is sold across the United States in over 5,000 retail stores. PSKS, Inc., (PSKS) (respondent) runs Kay's Kloset, a Brighton retailer in Lewisville, Texas, that carries about 75 different product lines, but was known as the place in that area to go for Brighton. Kay's ran Brighton ads and had Brighton days in its store.

Leegin's president, Jerry Kohl, who also has an interest in about 70 stores that sell Brighton products, believes that small retailers treat customers better, provide customers more services, and make their shopping experience more satisfactory than do larger, often impersonal retailers. In 1997, Kohl released a new strategic refocus for Brighton and instituted the "Brighton Retail Pricing and Promotion Policy," which banished retailers that discounted Brighton goods below suggested prices. In December 2002, Leegin discovered that Kay's Kloset had been marking down Brighton's entire line by 20 percent. Leegin stopped selling to the store.

PSKS sued Leegin for violation of the antitrust laws. Leegin asked to introduce expert testimony describing the procompetitive effects of its pricing policy. The jury awarded PSKS $1.2 million in damages and the judge trebled the damages and reimbursed PSKS for its attorney's fees and costs—for a judgment against Leegin of $3,975,000.80. The Court of Appeals affirmed. Leegin appealed. The U.S. Supreme Court granted *certiorari*.

JUDICIAL OPINION

KENNEDY, Justice

The question presented by the instant case is whether the Court should overrule the *per se* rule and allow resale price maintenance agreements to be judged by the rule of reason, the usual standard applied to determine if there is a violation of § 1. The Court has abandoned the rule of *per se* illegality for other vertical restraints a manufacturer imposes on its distributors. Respected economic analysts, furthermore, conclude that vertical price restraints can have precompetitive effects.

The rule of reason is the accepted standard for testing whether a practice restrains trade in violation of § 1. The rule of reason does not govern all restraints. Some types "are deemed unlawful *per se*." The *per se* rule, treating categories of restraints as necessarily illegal, eliminates the need to study the reasonableness of an individual restraint in light of the real market forces at work, and, it must be acknowledged, the *per se* rule can give clear guidance for certain conduct. Restraints that are *per se* unlawful include horizontal agreements among competitors to fix prices, or to divide markets.

… [T]he *per se* rule is appropriate only after courts have had considerable experience with the type of restraint at issue, and only if courts can predict with confidence that it would be invalidated in all or almost all instances under the rule of reason. Though each side of the debate can find sources to support its position, it suffices to say here that economics literature is replete with procompetitive justifications for a manufacturer's use of resale price maintenance.

The justifications for vertical price restraints are similar to those for other vertical restraints. Minimum resale price maintenance can stimulate interbrand competition—the competition among manufacturers selling different brands of the same type of product—by reducing intrabrand competition—the competition among retailers selling the same brand. The promotion of interbrand competition is important because "the primary purpose of the antitrust laws is to protect [this type of] competition." A single manufacturer's use of vertical price restraints tends to eliminate intrabrand price competition; this in turn encourages retailers to invest in tangible or intangible services or promotional efforts that aid the manufacturer's position as against rival manufacturers. Resale price maintenance also has the potential to give consumers more options so that they can choose among low-price, low-service brands; high-price, high-service brands; and brands that fall in between.

Resale price maintenance can also increase interbrand competition by encouraging retailer services that would not be provided even absent free riding. It may be difficult and inefficient for a manufacturer to make and enforce a contract with a retailer specifying the different services the retailer must perform. Offering the retailer a guaranteed margin and threatening termination if it does not live up to expectations may be the most efficient way to expand the manufacturer's market share by inducing the retailer's performance and allowing it to use its own initiative and experience in providing valuable services. While vertical agreements setting minimum resale prices can have procompetitive justifications, they may have anticompetitive effects in other circumstances. Vertical price restraints also "might be used to organize cartels at the retailer level." A group of retailers might collude to fix prices to consumers and then compel a manufacturer to aid the unlawful arrangement with resale price maintenance. In that instance the manufacturer does not establish the practice to stimulate services or to promote its brand but to give inefficient retailers higher profits.

Continued

Resale price maintenance, furthermore, can be abused by a powerful manufacturer or retailer. A manufacturer might consider it has little choice but to accommodate the retailer's demands for vertical price restraints if the manufacturer believes it needs access to the retailer's distribution network.

Vertical agreements establishing minimum resale prices can have either procompetitive or anticompetitive effects, depending upon the circumstances in which they are formed. Resale price maintenance, it is true, does have economic dangers. If the rule of reason were to apply to vertical price restraints, courts would have to be diligent in eliminating their anticompetitive uses from the market.

[Reversed].

QUESTIONS

1. What reasons did Leegin give for wanting the minimum price established for its retailers?

2. What points does the Court make about not having minimum prices in terms of reducing competition?

3. What risks are there in allowing minimum price requirements?

5. Prevention of Monopolies and Combinations

Monopolies and combinations that restrain trade are prohibited under the federal antitrust laws.

CPA   (A) THE SHERMAN ACT. The **Sherman Antitrust Act** includes two very short sections that control anticompetitive behavior. They provide:

> *[§ 1] Every contract, combination in the form of trust or otherwise, or conspiracy, in restraint of trade or commerce among the several states, or with foreign nations, is declared to be illegal.*
>
> *[§ 2] Every person who shall monopolize or attempt to monopolize, or combine or conspire with any other person or persons to monopolize any part of the trade or commerce among the several states, or with foreign nations, shall be deemed guilty of a felony.*[16]

The Sherman Act applies not only to buying and selling activities but also to manufacturing and production activities. Section 1 of the Sherman Act applies to agreements, conduct, or conspiracies to restrain trade, which can consist of price-fixing, tying, and monopolization. Section 2 prohibits monopolizing or attempting to monopolize by companies or individuals.

(B) MONOPOLIZATION. To determine whether a firm has engaged in monopolization or attempts to monopolize, the courts determine whether the firm has **market power**, which is the ability to control price and exclude competitors. Market power is defined by looking at both the geographic and product markets. **For Example,** a cereal manufacturer may have 65 percent of the nationwide market for its Crispy Clowns cereal (the product market), but it may have only 10 percent of the Albany, New York, market because of a local competitor, Crunchy Characters. Crispy Clowns may have market power nationally, but in Albany, it would not reach monopoly levels.

Having a large percentage of a market is not necessarily a monopoly. The Sherman Act requires that the monopoly position be gained because of a superior product or consumer preference, not because the company has engaged in purposeful conduct to exclude competitors by other means, such as preventing a competitor from purchasing a factory. Perhaps one of the best known monopolization cases involved Microsoft. In the case, the Justice Department alleged that because Microsoft had 90 percent of the market for operating systems it had and used monopoly power to control and

---

[16] 15 USC § 1. Free competition has been advanced by the Omnibus Trade and Competitiveness Act of 1988, 19 USC § 2901 *et seq.*

ethics & the law

Marsh & McLennan

Marsh & McLennan (MMC) is best known as the worlds largest insurance broker with 43,000 employees in its global operations.* MMC had a different way of achieving growth.

MMC should have been obtaining competing bids on employee insurance plans for the companies it represented. However, MMC developed a pay-to-play format for obtaining bids that allowed the insurers and MMC to profit. To be sure (1) that the policies were renewed and (2) that the renewal bonus was a given, MMC had all of its insurers agree to roll over on renewals. For example, if Insurer A was up for renewal, Insurers B and C would submit fake and higher bids that MMC would then take to the corporate client and, of course, recommend renewal at the lower rate. In some cases, MMC did not even have official bids from the competing insurers. MMC sent bids forward that had not even been signed by the insurers who were playing along to receive the same treatment when their renewals came along. Once MCC implemented the pay-to-play system, its insurance revenue became 67.1 percent of its revenue.** Commissions from these arrangements represented one-half of MMCs 2003 income of $1.5 billion.***

One of the companies to complain about MMCs practices was Munich RE. One of its e-mails to an MMC executive (whose name was blacked out) wrote, I am not some Goody Two Shoes who believes that truth is absolute, but I do feel I have a pretty strict ethical code about being truthful and honest. This idea of throwing the quote by quoting artificially high numbers in some predetermined arrangement for us to lose is repugnant to me, not so much because I hate to lose, but because it is basically dishonest. And I basically agree with the comments of others that it comes awfully close to collusion and price-fixing.

Without admitting or denying guilt, MMC settled antitrust charges by agreeing to drop the commission system and pay $850 million to its clients as a means of compensating for what might have been overcharges. MMC also agreed to hire a new CEO. The value of MMCs shares dropped almost 50 percent within 10 days following the mid-October filing of suit by then New York Attorney General Spitzer against the company.[†]

MMCs new CEO fired several senior executives despite the fact that there was no evidence that they had broken the law. When asked why he would fire them, Michael G. Cherkasky, a former district attorney in New York, said, Freedom from criminal culpability is not our standard for executive leadership.[‡]

* Monica Langley and Ianthe Jeanne Dugan, How a Top Marsh Employee Turned the Tables on Insurers, *Wall Street Journal*, October 23, 2004, A1, A9. Some put the number of employees at 60,000. See also Gretchen Morgenson, Who Loses the Most at Marsh? Its Workers, *New York Times*, October 24, 2004, 3–1 (Sunday Business 1) and 9.
** Monica Langley and Ianthe Jeanne Dugan, How a Top Marsh Employee Turned the Tables on Insurers, *Wall Street Journal*, October 23, 2004, A1, A9.
*** Id.

[†] The Chatter, *New York Times*, November 14, 2004, BU2.
[‡] Ian McDonald, After Spitzer Probe, Marsh CEO Tries Corporate Triage, *Wall Street Journal*, August 29, 2005, A1.

market and did so by refusing to sell its operating system to companies that installed Netscape in lieu of or in addition to the Microsoft Explorer browser.[17]

CPA   (c) PRICE-FIXING. The Sherman Act prohibits, as discussed previously, competitors agreeing to set prices. Price-fixing can involve competitors: agreeing to not sell below a certain price, agreeing on

[17] *United States v Microsoft*, 253 F3d 34 (CA DC 2001).

State Oil v Khan, 522 US 3 (1997)

Fill It Up: The Price Is Right and Fixed

Barkat U. Khan and his corporation (respondents) entered into an agreement with State Oil (petitioner) to lease and operate a gas station and convenience store owned by State Oil. The agreement provided that Khan would obtain the gasoline supply for the station from State Oil at a price equal to a suggested retail price set by State Oil, less a margin of 3.25 cents per gallon. Khan could charge any price he wanted, but if he charged more than State Oil's suggested retail price, the excess went to State Oil. Khan could sell the gasoline for less than State Oil's suggested retail price, but the difference would come out of his allowed margin.

After a year, Khan fell behind on his lease payments and State Oil gave notice of and began proceedings for eviction. The court had Khan removed and appointed a receiver for operation of the station. The receiver operated the gas station without the price constraints and received an overall profit margin above the 3.25 cents imposed on Khan.

Khan filed suit, alleging that the State Oil agreement was a violation of Section 1 of the Sherman Act because State Oil was controlling price. The district court held that there was no *per se* violation and that Khan had failed to demonstrate antitrust injury. The Court of Appeals reversed and State Oil appealed.

JUDICIAL OPINION

O'CONNOR, J.... Under § 1 of the Sherman Act, 26 Stat. 209, as amended, 15 U.S.C. § 1, "[e]very contract, combination..., or conspiracy, in restraint of trade" is illegal. In *Albrecht v. Herald Co.*, 390 U.S. 145, 88 S. Ct. 869, 19 L.Ed.2d 998 (1968), this Court held that vertical maximum price fixing is a per se violation of that statute. In this case, we are asked to reconsider that decision in light of subsequent decisions of this Court. We conclude that *Albrecht* should be overruled.

Although the Sherman Act, by its terms, prohibits every agreement "in restraint of trade," this Court has long recognized that Congress intended to outlaw only unreasonable restraints.

As a consequence, most antitrust claims are analyzed "under a rule of reason," according to which the finder of fact must decide whether the questioned practice imposes an unreasonable restraint on competition, taking into account a variety of factors, including specific information about the relevant business, its condition before and after the restraint was imposed, and the restraint's history, nature, and effect.

Some types of restraints, however, have such predictable and pernicious anticompetitive effect, and such limited potential for procompetitive benefit, that they are deemed unlawful per se.

Thus, we have expressed reluctance to adopt per se rules with regard to "restraints imposed in the context of business relationships where the economic impact of certain practices is not immediately obvious."

[I]n *United States v Arnold, Schwinn & Co.*, 388 U.S. 365, 87 S.Ct. 1856, 18 L. Ed. 2d 1249 (1967), the Court reconsidered the status of exclusive dealer territories and held that, upon the transfer of title to goods to a distributor, a supplier's imposition of territorial restrictions on the distributor was "so obviously destructive of competition" as to constitute a per se violation of the Sherman Act. In *Schwinn*, the Court acknowledged that some vertical restrictions, such as the conferral of territorial rights or franchises, could have procompetitive benefits by allowing smaller enterprises to compete, and that such restrictions might avert vertical integration in the distribution process. The Court drew the line, however, at permitting manufacturers to control product marketing once dominion over the goods had passed to dealers.

Albrecht, decided the following Term, involved a newspaper publisher who had granted exclusive territories to independent carriers subject to their adherence to a maximum price on resale of the newspapers to the public. Influenced by its decisions in *Socony-Vacuum*, *Kiefer-Stewart*, and *Schwinn*, the Court concluded that it was per se unlawful for the publisher to fix the maximum resale price of its newspapers.

The Court acknowledged that "[m]aximum and minimum price fixing may have different consequences in many situations," but nonetheless condemned maximum price fixing for "substituting the perhaps erroneous judgment of a seller for the forces of the competitive market."

Nine years later, in *Continental T.V., Inc. v GTE Sylvania Inc.*, 433 U.S. 36, 97 S.Ct. 2549, 53 L.Ed.2d 568 (1977), the Court overruled *Schwinn*, thereby rejecting application of a per se rule in the context of vertical non-price restrictions. The Court acknowledged the principle of *stare decisis*, but explained that the need for clarification in the law justified reconsideration of *Schwinn*:

"Since its announcement, Schwinn has been the subject of continuing controversy and confusion, both in the scholarly journals and in the federal courts. The great weight of scholarly opinion has been critical of the decision, and a number of the federal courts confronted with analogous vertical restrictions have sought to limit its reach."

Thus, our reconsideration of *Albrecht's* continuing validity is informed by several of our decisions, as well as a considerable body of scholarship discussing the effects of vertical restraints. Our analysis is also guided by our general view that the primary purpose of the antitrust laws is to protect interbrand competition. "Low prices," we have

Continued

explained, benefit consumers regardless of how those prices are set, and so long as they are above predatory levels, they do not threaten competition." Our interpretation of the Sherman Act also incorporates the notion that condemnation of practices resulting in lower prices to consumers is "especially costly" because "cutting prices in order to increase business often is the very essence of competition."

So informed, we find it difficult to maintain that vertically-imposed maximum prices could harm consumers or competition to the extent necessary to justify their per se invalidation. As Chief Judge Posner wrote for the Court of Appeals in this case:

"*As for maximum resale price fixing, unless the supplier is a monopsonist he cannot squeeze his dealers' margins below a competitive level; the attempt to do so would just drive the dealers into the arms of a competing supplier. A supplier might, however, fix a maximum resale price in order to prevent his dealers from exploiting a monopoly position.... [S]uppose that State Oil, perhaps to encourage... dealer services... has spaced its dealers sufficiently far apart to limit competition among them (or even given each of them an exclusive territory); and suppose further that Union 76 is a sufficiently distinctive and popular brand to give the dealers in it at least a modicum of monopoly power. Then State Oil might want to place a ceiling on the dealers' resale prices in order to prevent them from exploiting that monopoly power fully. It would do this not out of disinterested malice, but in its commercial self-interest. The higher the price at which gasoline is resold, the smaller the volume sold, and so the lower the profit to the supplier if the higher profit per gallon at the higher price is being snared by the dealer.*"

Further, although vertical maximum price fixing might limit the viability of inefficient dealers, that consequence is not necessarily harmful to competition and consumers.

After reconsidering *Albrecht*'s rationale and the substantial criticism the decision has received, however, we conclude that there is insufficient economic justification for per se invalidation of vertical maximum price fixing. That is so not only because it is difficult to accept the assumptions underlying *Albrecht*, but also because *Albrecht* has little or no relevance to ongoing enforcement of the Sherman Act.

We approach the reconsideration of decisions of this Court with the utmost caution. *Stare decisis* reflects "a policy judgment that 'in most matters it is more important that the applicable rule of law be settled than that it be settled right.'"

But "[s]*tare decisis* is not an inexorable command." In the area of antitrust law, there is a competing interest, well-represented in this Court's decisions, in recognizing and adapting to changed circumstances and the lessons of accumulated experience. Thus, the general presumption that legislative changes should be left to Congress has less force with respect to the Sherman Act in light of the accepted view that Congress "expected the courts to give shape to the statute's broad mandate by drawing on common-law tradition."

In overruling *Albrecht*, we of course do not hold that all vertical maximum price fixing is per se lawful. Instead, vertical maximum price fixing, like the majority of commercial arrangements subject to the antitrust laws, should be evaluated under the rule of reason. In our view, rule-of-reason analysis will effectively identify those situations in which vertical maximum price fixing amounts to anticompetitive conduct.

There remains the question whether respondents are entitled to recover damages based on State Oil's conduct. Although the Court of Appeals noted that "the district judge was right to conclude that if the rule of reason is applicable, Khan loses," its consideration of this case was necessarily premised on *Albrecht*'s per se rule. Under the circumstances, the matter should be reviewed by the Court of Appeals in the first instance. We therefore vacate the judgment of the Court of Appeals and remand the case for further proceedings consistent with this opinion.

[Remanded.]

QUESTIONS

1. What were the price requirements for Khan's lease?

2. What happened when someone else took over Khan's station?

3. What does the court discuss about long-standing precedent and *stare decisis*?

commission rates, agreeing on credit terms, or exchanging cost information. Price is treated as a sensitive element of competition, and discussion among competitors has also been deemed to be an attempt to monopolize.

(D) TYING. It is a violation of the Sherman Act to force "tying" sales on buyers. **Tying** occurs when the seller makes a buyer who wants to purchase one product buy an additional product that he or she does not want.

sports & entertainment law

Celebrity Issues and Antitrust

Public Interest Corporation (PIC) owned and operated television station WTMV-TV in Lakeland, Florida. MCA Television Ltd. (MCA) owns and licenses syndicated television programs. In 1990, the two companies entered into a licensing contract for several first-run television shows. With respect to all but one of these shows, MCA exchanged the licenses on a barter basis for advertising time on WTMV. However, MCA conditioned this exchange on PICs agreeing to license the remaining show, *Harry and the Hendersons,* for cash as well as for barter. *Harry and the Hendersons* was what some in the industry would call a dog, a show that was not very good that attempted to capitalize on a hit movie. PIC agreed to this arrangement, although it did not want *Harry and the Hendersons.* The shows that PIC did want were *List of a Lifetime, List of a Lifetime II, Magnum P.I.,* and 17 other miscellaneous features.

The relationship between the parties was strained over nonpayment, poor ratings performance of *Harry,* and other issues. When litigation resulted, PIC alleged that it had been subjected to an illegal tying arrangement. PIC requested damages for MCAs violation of the Sherman Act. What violation do you think occurred?

Source: Adapted from MCA Television Ltd. v Public Interest Corp., 171 F3d 1265 (CA 11 1998).

The essential characteristic of a tying arrangement that violates Section 1 of the Sherman Act is the use of control over the tying product within the relevant market to compel the buyer to purchase the tied article that either is not wanted or could be purchased elsewhere on better terms. **For Example,** in the Microsoft antitrust case, Microsoft is accused of requiring the purchase and use of its browser as a condition for purchasing its software. The Sherman Act also prohibits professional persons, such as doctors, from using a peer review proceeding to pressure another professional who competes with them in private practice and refuses to become a member of a clinic formed by them.

(E) BUSINESS COMBINATIONS. The Sherman Antitrust Act does not prohibit bigness. However, Section 7 of the Clayton Act provides that "no corporation … shall acquire the whole or any part of the assets of another corporation … where in any line of commerce in any section of the country, the effect of such acquisition may be substantially to lessen competition, or to tend to create a monopoly." If the Clayton Act is violated through ownership or control of competing enterprises, a court may order the violating defendant to dispose of such interests by issuing a decree called a **divestiture order.**[18]

(1) Premerger Notification

When large-size enterprises plan to merge, they must give written notice to the FTC and to the head of the Antitrust Division of the Department of Justice. This advance notice gives the department the opportunity to block the merger and thus avoid the loss that would occur if the enterprises merged and were then required to separate.[19] **For Example,** Time Warner was required to notify the Justice Department and seek approval for its merger with AOL, which the Justice Department eventually gave. However, when World-Com proposed its merger with Sprint, the Justice

---

[18] *California v American Stores Co.,* 492 US 1301 (1989).
[19] Antitrust Improvement Act of 1976, PL 94-435, § 201, PL 94-435, 90 Stat 1383, 15 USC § 1311 *et seq.*

e-commerce&cyberlaw

Email's Revelations

In the U.S. Justice Departments case against Microsoft, a lawyer commented, The Government does not need to put Mr. Gates on the stand because we have his e-mail and memoranda. There were 30 million pages of e-mail used as evidence in the Microsoft trial.

E-mail provides what is known as a *contemporaneous record of events* and has the added bonus that, for whatever psychological reason, those communicating with e-mail tend to be more frank and informal than they would be in a memo. E-mail can also contradict a witnesss testimony and serve to undermine credibility. For example, when asked whether he recalled discussions with a subordinate about whether Microsoft should offer to invest in Netscape, Mr. Gates responded in his deposition, I didnt see that as something that made sense. But Mr. Gatess e-mail included an urging to his subordinates to consider a Netscape alliance: We could even pay them money as part of the deal, buying a piece of them or something.

E-mail is discoverable, admissible as evidence, and definitely not private. Employees should follow the admonition of one executive whose e-mail was used to fuel a million-dollar settlement by his company with a former employee: If you wouldnt want anyone to read it, dont send it in e-mail.

The impact of e-mail in the Microsoft antitrust case on companies and their e-mail policies was widespread. For example, Amazon.com launched a companywide program called Sweep and Keep, under which employees were instructed to purge e-mail messages no longer needed for conducting business. Amazon.com offered employees who immediately purged their e-mail free lattes in the company cafeteria. The company had a two-part program. The first portion included instructions on document retention and deletion. The second part of the program was on document creation and included the following warning for employees: Quite simply put, there are some communications that should not be expressed in written form. Sorry, no lattes this time.

Source: Adapted from Marianne M. Jennings, *Business: Its Legal, Ethical and Global Environment*, 8th ed. (Cincinnati, OH:: West Legal Studies in Business, 2009), ch. 16.

Department refused approval because it believed this would reduce competition in telecommunications too much.[20]

(2) Takeover Laws

Antitrust laws usually focus on whether the combination or agreement is fair to society or to a particular class, such as consumers. Some legislation aims to protect the various parties directly involved in combining different enterprises. Concern arises that one enterprise may in effect be raiding another enterprise. Congress and four-fifths of the states have adopted **takeover laws**, which seek to guard against unfairness in such situations. State laws apply only to corporations chartered in their state.

C. POWER TO PROTECT BUSINESS

In addition to controlling business combinations, the federal government protects others. By statute or decision, associations of exporters, marine insurance associations, farmers' cooperatives, and labor unions are exempt from the Sherman Act with respect to agreements between their members. Certain pooling and revenue-dividing agreements between carriers are exempt from the antitrust law when approved by the appropriate federal agency. The Newspaper Preservation Act of 1970 grants an antitrust exemption to operating agreements entered into by

---

[20] Rebecca Blumenstein and Jared Sandberg, "WorldCom CEO Quits Amid Probe of Firm's Finances," *Wall Street Journal*, April 30, 2002, A1, A9.

newspapers to prevent financial collapse. The Soft Drink Interbrand Competition Act[21] grants the soft drink industry an exemption when it is shown that, in fact, substantial competition exists in spite of the agreements.

The general approach of the U.S. Supreme Court has been that these types of agreements should not be automatically, or *per se*, condemned as a restraint of interstate commerce merely because they create the power or potential to monopolize interstate commerce. It is only when the restraint imposed is unreasonable that the practice is unlawful. The Court applies the rule of reason in certain cases because the practice may not always harm competition.

6. Remedies for Anticompetitive Behavior

(A) CRIMINAL PENALTIES. A violation of either section of the Sherman Act is punishable by fine or imprisonment or both at the discretion of the court. The maximum fine for a corporation is $100 million. A natural person can be fined a maximum of $1,000,000 or imprisoned for a maximum term of ten years or both.

(B) CIVIL REMEDIES. In addition to these criminal penalties, the law provides for an injunction to stop the unlawful practices and permits suing the wrongdoers for damages.

(1) Individual Damage Suit
Any person or enterprise harmed may bring a separate action for **treble damages** (three times the damages actually sustained).

(2) Class-Action Damage Suit by State Attorney General
When the effect of an antitrust violation is to raise prices, the attorney general of a state may bring a class-action suit to recover damages on behalf of those who have paid the higher prices. This action is called a *parens patriae* action on the theory that the state is suing as the parent of its people.

lawflix

Antitrust (2001) (R)
This movie is based on Bill Gates and Microsoft. Check out **www.cengage.com/blaw/dvl** to access movie clips that illustrate business law concepts.

MAKE THE CONNECTION

SUMMARY

Regulation by government has occurred primarily to protect one group from the improper conduct of another group. The police power is the basis for government regulation. Regulation is passed when the free enterprise system fails to control abuses, as with the recent passage of investment banking regulations. Unfair methods of competition are prohibited.

Prices have been regulated both by prohibiting setting the exact price or a maximum price and discrimination in pricing. Price discrimination between buyers is prohibited when the effect of such discrimination could tend to create a monopoly or lessen competition. Price discrimination occurs when the prices charged different buyers are different despite the same marginal costs. However, resale price maintenance is not illegal *per se* if the control is for purposes of providing customer service.

[21] Act of July 9, 1980, PL 96-308, 94 Stat 939, 15 USC § 3501 *et seq.*

The Sherman Antitrust Act prohibits conspiracies in restraint of trade and the monopolization of trade. The Clayton Act prohibits mergers or the acquisition of the assets of another corporation when this conduct would tend to lessen competition or create a monopoly. The Justice Department requires premerger notification for proposed mergers. Violation of the federal antitrust statutes subjects the wrongdoer to criminal prosecution and possible civil liability that can include treble damages.

LEARNING OUTCOMES

After studying this chapter, you should be able to clearly explain:

A. POWER TO REGULATE BUSINESS

LO.1 State the extent to which government can regulate business

> See the **For Example** discussion of the subprime mortgage market on p. 77
> See the Ethics & the Law discussion of Marsh & McLennan on p. 83

B. REGULATION OF MARKETS AND COMPETITION

LO.2 Explain what laws regulate the markets and protect competition

> See the *Utah Pie* case on predatory pricing, p. 79

> See the *Kahn* oil case on price controls, p. 84
> See the *Leegin* case on resale price maintenance, p. 81
> See the Sports & Entertainment Law feature on tying, p. 86

C. POWER TO PROTECT BUSINESS

LO.3 Discuss the powers and remedies available to protect business competition

> See Section 6 for a list of the penalties and remedies on p. 88

KEY TERMS

Clayton Act	price discrimination	takeover laws
divestiture order	Robinson-Patman Act	treble damages
market power	Sherman Antitrust Act	tying

QUESTIONS AND CASE PROBLEMS

1. American Crystal Sugar Co. was one of several refiners of beet sugar in northern California, and it distributed its product in interstate commerce. American Crystal and the other refiners had a monopoly on the seed supply and were the only practical market for the beets. In 1939, all of the refiners began using identical form contracts that computed the price paid to the sugar beet growers using a "factor" common to all the refiners. As a result, all refiners paid the same price for beets of the same quality. Though there was no hard evidence of an illegal agreement, the growers brought suit under the Sherman Act against the refiners, alleging that they conspired to fix a single uniform price among themselves to hold down the cost of the beets. The growers sued for the treble damages available under the Sherman Act. Can they recover? [*Mandeville Island Farms v American Crystal Sugar Co.*, 334 US 219]

2. A Wisconsin statute prohibits "the secret payment or allowance of rebates, refunds, commissions, or unearned discounts" to some customers without allowing them to all customers on the

same conditions when such practices injure or tend to injure competition or a competitor. Kolbe generally gave dealers a 50 percent discount, but it gave Stock Lumber Co. a discount of 54 percent. Other dealers were not informed of this or of the conditions that had to be satisfied to obtain the same discount. Kolbe gave Jauquet, another lumber dealer, only a 50 percent discount and, when asked, expressly stated that it did not give any other dealer a higher discount. When Jauquet learned of the higher discount given to Stock, it brought suit against Kolbe for violation of the Wisconsin statute. Did Kolbe violate the statute? [*Jauquet Lumber Co., Inc. v Kolbe & Kolbe Millwork, Inc.*, 476 NW2d 305 (Wis App)]

3. The major record companies settled an antitrust suit brought by 40 state attorneys general against them for alleged price-fixing in the sale of CDs. The record companies agreed to pay $67.4 million to consumers who purchased CDs during the period from 1995 to 2000. The consent decree stipulated that the record companies had required retailers that accepted subsidies from record companies for advertising CDs not to advertise CDs for sale at a price agreed upon in advance. The record companies said that the policy helped keep independent retailers in business because they could not afford to price at Wal-Mart levels. Wal-Mart always advertised CDs for sale at a price below the floor agreed to by the subsidized independent retailers and the record companies. The record companies did not admit any wrongdoing and, in addition to agreeing to the $67.4 million, also agreed to provide 5.5 million CDs to libraries, schools, and nonprofit organizations (worth $75.7 million).[22] What antitrust violation were the attorneys general alleging? Is a minimum price a violation of antitrust laws?

4. The Three Tenors (Luciano Pavarotti, Placido Domingo, and Jose Carreras) made a record of their live performances together once every four years. The first two CDs and videos in the series,

made by Time Warner, sold millions, with both becoming two of the highest-volume opera recordings in history. However, by the third performance and CD and video, the public demand was not as great, and Time Warner believed the first two releases would cannibalize the sales for the third. As a result, all parties involved in the sales of these CDs and tapes had to agree not to discount the first two performance tapes so that the third would have an opportunity to sell. The Federal Trade Commission (FTC) stumbled across the information on the pricing program when its staff members located a memo on the marketing plan and advertising constraints as it was reviewing documents for the proposed Time Warner/EMI Music merger proposal, a merger that fell through after European officials balked at the idea. The FTC pursued the case, and Time Warner settled the charges by agreeing not to restrain competition or set prices in the future. Is establishing a minimum price a violation of the Sherman Act? Is restricting advertising a violation of the Sherman Act?

5. Hines Cosmetic Co. sold beauty preparations nationally to beauty shops at a standard or fixed-price schedule. Some of the shops were also supplied with a free demonstrator and free advertising materials. The shops that were not supplied with them claimed that giving the free services and materials constituted unlawful price discrimination. Hines replied that there was no price discrimination because it charged everyone the same. What it was giving free was merely a promotional campaign that was not intended to discriminate against those who were not given anything free. Was Hines guilty of unlawful price discrimination? Explain.

6. Moore ran a bakery in Santa Rosa, New Mexico. His business was wholly intrastate. Meads Fine Bread Co., his competitor, engaged in an interstate business. Meads cut the price of bread in half in Santa Rosa but made no price cut in any other place in New Mexico or in any other state.

---

[22] Claudia Deutsch, "Suit Settled over Pricing of Recordings at Big Chains," *New York Times*, October 1, 2002, C1, C10; David Lieberman, "States Settle CD Price-fixing Case," *USA Today*, October 1, 2002, 3B.

This price-cutting drove Moore out of business. Moore then sued Meads for damages for violating the Clayton and Robinson-Patman Acts. Meads claimed that the price-cutting was purely intrastate and, therefore, did not constitute a violation of federal statutes. Was Meads correct? Why or why not? [*Moore v Meads Fine Bread Co.*, 348 US 115]

7. A&P Grocery Stores decided to sell its own brand of canned milk (referred to as *private label* milk). A&P asked its longtime supplier, Borden, to submit an offer to produce the private label milk. Bowman Dairy also submitted a bid, which was lower than Borden's. A&P's Chicago buyer then contacted Borden and said, "I have a bid in my pocket. You people are so far out of line it is not even funny. You are not even in the ballpark." The Borden representative asked for more details but was told only that a $50,000 improvement in Borden's bid "would not be a drop in the bucket." A&P was one of Borden's largest customers in the Chicago area. Furthermore, Borden had just invested more than $5 million in a new dairy facility in Illinois. The loss of the A&P account would result in underutilization of the plant. Borden lowered its bid by more than $400,000. The Federal Trade Commission charged Borden with price discrimination, but Borden maintained it was simply meeting the competition. Did Borden violate the Robinson-Patman Act? Does it matter that the milk was a private label milk, not its normal trade name Borden milk? [*Great Atlantic & Pacific Tea Co., Inc. v FTC*, 440 US 69]

8. Department 56 is a company that manufactures and sells collectible Christmas village houses and other replica items to allow collectors to create the whimsical "Snow Village" town or "Dickens Christmas." Department 56 has only authorized dealers. Sam's Club, a division of Wal-Mart Stores, Inc., began selling Department 56 pieces from the Heritage Village Collection. Susan Engel, president and CEO of Department 56, refused to sell Department 56 products to Wal-Mart. Does her refusal violate any antitrust laws?

9. Dr. Edwin G. Hyde, a board-certified anesthesiologist, applied for permission to practice at East Jefferson Hospital in Louisiana. An approval was recommended for his hiring, but the hospital's board denied him employment on grounds that the hospital had a contract with Roux & Associates for Roux to provide all anesthesiological services required by the hospital's patients. Dr. Hyde filed suit for violation of antitrust laws. Had the hospital done anything illegal? [*Jefferson Parish Hosp. Dist. No. 2 v Hyde*, 466 US 2]

10. BRG of Georgia, Inc. (BRG), and Harcourt Brace Jovanovich Legal and Professional Publications (HJB) are the nation's two largest providers of bar review materials and lectures. HJB began offering a Georgia bar review course on a limited basis in 1976 and was in direct, and often intense, competition with BRG from 1977 to 1979 when the companies were the two main providers of bar review courses in Georgia. In early 1980, they entered into an agreement that gave BRG an exclusive license to market HJB's materials in Georgia and to use its trade name "Bar/Bri." The parties agreed that HJB would not compete with BRG in Georgia and that BRG would not compete with HJB outside of Georgia. Under the agreement, HJB received $100 per student enrolled by BRG and 40 percent of all revenues over $350. Immediately after the 1980 agreement, the price of BRG's course was increased from $150 to more than $400. Is their conduct illegal under federal antitrust laws? [*Palmer v BRG of Georgia, Inc.*, 498 US 46]

11. Favorite Foods Corp. sold its food to stores and distributors. It established a quantity discount scale that was publicly published and made available to all buyers. The top of the scale gave the highest discount to buyers purchasing more than 100 freight cars of food in a calendar year. Only two buyers, both national food chains, purchased in such quantities, and therefore, they alone received the greatest discount. Favorite Foods was prosecuted for price discrimination in violation of the Clayton Act. Was it guilty?

12. Run America, Inc., manufactures running shoes. Its shoe is consistently rated poorly by *Run Run Run* magazine in its annual shoe review. The number one shoe in *Run Run Run*'s review is the Cheetah, a shoe that Run America has learned is manufactured by the parent company of the magazine. Is this conduct a violation of the antitrust laws? Do you think it is ethical to run the shoe review without disclosing ownership?

13. The Quickie brand wheelchair is the most popular customized wheelchair on the market. Its market share is 90 percent. Other manufacturers produce special-use wheelchairs that fold, that are made of mesh and lighter frames, and that are easily transportable. These manufacturers do not compete with Quickie on customized chairs. One manufacturer of the alternative wheelchairs has stated, "Look, it's an expensive market to be in, that Quickie market. We prefer the alternative chairs without the headaches of customizations." Another has said, "It is such a drain on cash flow in that market because insurers take so long to pay. We produce chairs that buyers purchase with their own money, not through insurers. Our sales are just like any other product." Quickie entered the market nearly 40 years ago and is known for its quality and attention to detail. Buying a Quickie custom chair, however, takes time, and the revenue stream from sales is slow but steady because of the time required to produce custom wheelchairs. Has Quickie violated the federal antitrust laws with its 90 percent market share? Discuss.

14. Gardner-Denver is the largest manufacturer of ratchet wrenches and their replacement parts in the United States. Gardner-Denver had two different lists of prices for its wrenches and parts. Its blue list had parts that, if purchased in quantities of five or more, were available for substantially less than its white list prices. Did Gardner-Denver engage in price discrimination with its two price lists? [*D. E. Rogers Assoc., Inc. v Gardner-Denver Co.*, 718 F2d 1431 (6th Cir)]

15. The Aspen ski area consisted of four mountain areas. Aspen Highlands, which owned three of those areas, and Aspen Skiing, which owned the fourth, had cooperated for years in issuing a joint, multiple-day, all-area ski ticket. After repeatedly and unsuccessfully demanding an increased share of the proceeds, Aspen Highlands canceled the joint ticket. Aspen Skiing, concerned that skiers would bypass its mountain without some joint offering, tried a variety of increasingly desperate measures to recreate the joint ticket, even to the point of in effect offering to buy Aspen Highland's tickets at retail price. Aspen Highlands refused even that. Aspen Skiing brought suit under the Sherman Act, alleging that the refusal to cooperate was a move by Aspen Highlands to eliminate all competition in the area by freezing it out of business. Is there an antitrust claim here in the refusal to cooperate? What statute and violation do you think Aspen Skiing alleged? What dangers do you see in finding the failure to cooperate to be an antitrust violation? [*Aspen Skiing Co. v Aspen Highlands Skiing Corp.*, 472 US 585]

Chapter 6

ADMINISTRATIVE AGENCIES

L
ate in the nineteenth century, a new type of governmental structure began to develop to meet the highly specialized needs of government regulation of business: the administrative agency. The administrative agency is now typically the instrument through which government makes and carries out its regulations.

A. NATURE OF THE ADMINISTRATIVE AGENCY

An **administrative agency** is a government body charged with administering and implementing legislation. An agency may be a department, independent establishment, commission, administration, authority, board, or bureau. Agencies exist on the federal and state levels. One example of a federal agency is the Federal Trade Commission (FTC), whose structure is shown in Figure 6.1.

1. Purpose of Administrative Agencies

Federal administrative agencies are created to carry out general policies specified by Congress. Federal agencies include the Securities Exchange Commission (SEC), the Consumer Product Safety Commission (CPSC),

and the Food and Drug Administration (FDA). The law governing these agencies is known as **administrative law**.

State administrative agencies also exist and may have jurisdiction over areas of law affecting business, such as workers' compensation claims, real estate licensing, and unemployment compensation.

2. Uniqueness of Administrative Agencies

The federal government and state governments alike are divided into three branches: executive, legislative, and judicial. Many offices in these branches are filled by persons who are elected. In contrast, members of administrative agencies are ordinarily appointed (in the case of federal agencies, by the president of the United States with the consent of the Senate).

In the tripartite structure, the judicial branch reviews actions of the executive and legislative branches to ensure that they have not exceeded their constitutional powers. However, the major governmental agencies combine legislative, executive, and judicial powers (see Figure 6.2). These agencies make the rules, conduct inspections to see that the rules have been or are being obeyed, and sit in judgment to determine whether there have been violations of their rules. Because agencies have broad powers, they are

FIGURE 6-1 | **Structure of the Federal Trade Commission**

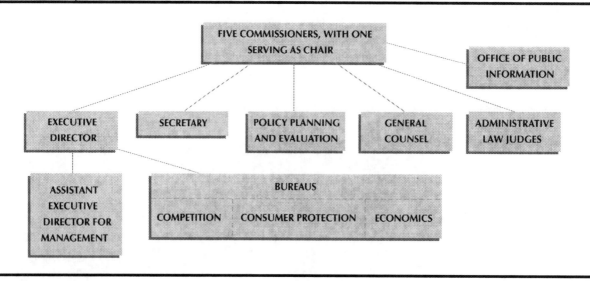

FIGURE 6-2   │   *The Administrative Chain of Command*

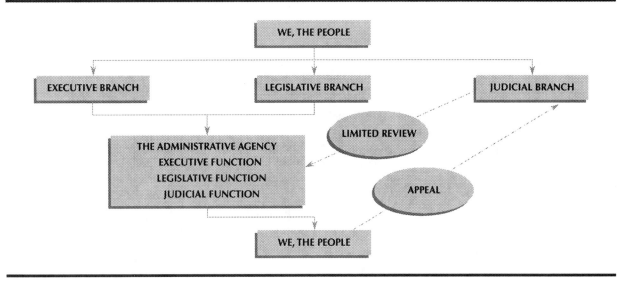

subject to strict procedural rules as well as disclosure requirements (discussed in the following section).

3. Open Operation of Administrative Agencies

The public has ready access to the activity of administrative agencies. That access comes in three ways: (1) open records, (2) open meetings, and (3) public announcement of agency guidelines. The actions and activities of most federal agencies that are not otherwise regulated are controlled by the **Administrative Procedure Act** (APA).[1] Many states have adopted statutes with provisions similar to those of the APA.

(A) OPEN RECORDS. The **Freedom of Information Act**[2] (FOIA) provides that information contained in records of federal administrative agencies is available to citizens on proper request. The primary purpose of this statute is to ensure that government activities be opened to the sharp eye of public scrutiny.[3] To ensure that members of the

public understand how to obtain records, the FOIA provides that [e]ach agency shall publish in the *Federal Register* for the guidance of the public the methods whereby the public may obtain information, make submittals or requests, or obtain decisions.[4] There are exceptions to this right of public scrutiny. They prevent individuals and companies from obtaining information that is not necessary to their legitimate interests and might harm the person or company whose information is being sought.[5] State statutes typically exempt from disclosure any information that would constitute an invasion of the privacy of others. However, freedom of information acts are broadly construed, and unless an exemption is clearly given, the information in question is subject to public inspection. Moreover, the person claiming that there is an exemption that prohibits disclosure has the burden of proving that the exemption applies to the particular request made. Exemptions include commercial or financial information not ordinarily made public by the person or company that supplies

---

[1] Administrative Procedures Act 5 USC 550 *et seq.*
[2] 5 USC 552 *et seq.* The Electronic Freedom of Information Act Amendments of 1996 extend the public availability of information to electronically stored data.
[3] *Brady-Lunny v Massey,* 185 F Supp 2d 928 (CD III 2002).
[4] 5 USC 552(a)(1)(a).
[5] Additional protection is provided by the Privacy Act of 1974, 5 USC § 552a(b); *Doe v U.S. Dept. of Treasury,* 2009 WL 1949119 (DDC).

the information to the agency as part of the agency's enforcement role.[6]

The FOIA's primary purpose is to subject agency action to public scrutiny. Its provisions are liberally interpreted, and agencies must make good-faith efforts to comply with its terms.

(B) OPEN MEETINGS. Under the Sunshine Act of 1976,[7] called the **open meeting law**, the federal government requires most meetings of major administrative agencies to be open to the public. The Sunshine Act[8] applies to those meetings involving deliberations of the agency or those that result in the joint conduct or disposition of official agency business. The object of this statute is to enable the public to know what actions agencies are taking and to prevent administrative misconduct by having open meetings and public scrutiny. Many states also have enacted Sunshine laws.

(C) PUBLIC ANNOUNCEMENT OF AGENCY GUIDELINES. To inform the public of the way administrative agencies operate, the APA, with certain exceptions, requires that each federal agency publish the rules, principles, and procedures that it follows.[9]

B. LEGISLATIVE POWER OF THE AGENCY

An administrative agency has the power to make laws and does so by promulgating regulations with public input.

4. Agency's Regulations as Law

An agency may adopt regulations within the scope of its authority. The power of an agency to carry out a congressional program necessarily requires the formulation of policy and the making of rules to fill any gap left by Congress.[10] If the regulation is not

authorized by the law creating the agency, anyone affected by it can challenge the regulation on the basis that the agency has exceeded its authority. [See Section 11(c), Beyond the Jurisdiction of the Agency.]

An administrative agency cannot act beyond the scope of the authority in the statute that created it or assigned a responsibility to it.[11] However, the authority of an agency is not limited to the technology in existence at the time the agency was created or assigned jurisdiction for enforcement of laws. The sphere in which an agency may act expands with new scientific developments.[12]

When an agency's proposed regulation deals with a policy question that is not specifically addressed by statute, the agency that was created or given the discretion to administer the statute may establish new policies covering such issues. This power is granted regardless of whether the lawmaker intentionally left such matters to the agency's discretion or merely did not foresee the problem. In either case, the matter is one to be determined within the agency's discretion, and courts defer to agencies' policy decisions.[13] For example, the FCC has authority to deal with cell phones and cell phone providers even though when the agency was created, there were only the traditional types of land-line telephones.

Today, regulations adopted by an agency may interpret or clarify the law. In effect, many regulations have the feel of legislation. Courts have come to recognize the authority of an agency even though the lawmaker creating the agency did nothing more than state the goal or objective to be attained by the agency. The modern approach is to regard the administrative agency as holding all powers necessary to effectively perform the duties entrusted to it. When the agency establishes a rational basis for its rule, courts accept the rule and do not substitute their own judgment.[14]

---

[6] *Sun-Sentinel Company v U.S. Dept. of Homeland Security,* 431 F Supp 2d 1258 (SD Fla 2006).
[7] The Government in the Sunshine Act can be found at 5 USC § 552b.
[8] 5 USC 552b(a)(2).
[9] APA codified at 5 USC 552. See Section 5(c) of this chapter for a description of the *Federal Register,* the publication in which these agency rules, principles, and procedures are printed.
[10] *Virginia v Browner,* 80 F3d 869 (4th Cir 1996).
[11] *Zuni Public School Dist. No. 89 v Department of Educ.,* 550 US 81 (2007).
[12] *United States v Midwest Video Corp.,* 406 US 649 (1972) (sustaining a commission regulation that provided that no CATV system having 3,500 or more subscribers shall carry the signal of any television broadcast station unless the system also operates to a significant extent as a local outlet by cablecasting and has available facilities for local production and presentation of programs other than automated services).
[13] *Chevron, U.S.A., Inc. v National Resources Defense Council, Inc.,* 467 US 837 (1984).
[14] *Covad Communications Co. v FCC,* 430 F3d 528 (DC Cir 2006).

Legislatures have met the judicial standard for approval with various types of agencies created for different purposes such as licensing to protect the public, prohibiting unfair methods of competition, or administering the registration of autos and other vehicles. The purposes in these types of statutes include the typical public safety and welfare areas such as ensuring competence and integrity of professionals through the licensing process or ensuring that there are free markets that allow open competition.[15]

5. Agency Adoption of Regulations

(A) CONGRESSIONAL ENABLING ACT. Before an agency can begin rulemaking proceedings, it must be given jurisdiction by congressional enactment in the form of a statute. For example, Congress has enacted broad statutes governing discrimination in employment practices and has given authority to the Equal Employment Opportunity Commission (EEOC) to establish definitions, rules, and guidelines for compliance with those laws. Sometimes an existing agency is assigned the responsibility for new legislation implementation and enforcement. **For Example,** the Department of Labor has been assigned the responsibility to handle the whistle-blower protection provisions of Sarbanes-Oxley that provide protection against retaliation and/or termination to those who report financial chicanery at their companies. The Department of Labor has been in existence for almost a century, but it was assigned a new responsibility and given new jurisdiction by Congress.

(B) AGENCY RESEARCH OF THE PROBLEM. After jurisdiction is established, the agency has the responsibility to research the issues and various avenues of regulation for implementing the statutory framework. As the agency does so, it determines the cost and benefit of the problems, issues, and solutions. The study may be done by the agency itself, or it may be completed by

---

ethics & the law

Flush with Regulation: How Many Gallons and Where

The Energy Policy Act of 1992 requires that toilets installed after the act took effect (1994) use only 1.6 gallons of water rather than the nearly century-old standard of 3.5 gallons. As of 2000, about one-fourth of the nation's toilets were the 1.6-gallon types. The EPA mandated that permits be conditioned on the use of the 1.6-gallon toilets and that inspection approvals be denied if anything but a 1.6-gallon toilet had been installed.

As homeowners have remodeled and replaced older toilets, they have learned that the 3.5-gallon toilets are no longer sold in the United States. However, just across the U.S./Canadian border near Detroit, Canadian hardware stores are doing a land-office business selling 3.5-gallon tanks to U.S. citizens.

Those who are remodeling, and even some who are building new homes, provide for 1.6-gallon toilets in their plans and generally install $100 1.6-gallon toilets from Home Depot in order to pass inspection. They then purchase a standard fixture Canadian toilet for anywhere from $500 to $1,000 because of the high demand, and install it. Plumbing stores all over Canada report that sales are brisk. In a survey conducted in May 2000, the Canadian plumbing store owners said that they sell, on average, one toilet per day to U.S. citizens either via direct sale or shipment.

Do the citizens break any laws by what they do? Is what they do ethical? How could the regulation be challenged? What foundation in administrative law might be used?

---

[15] All of these are examples of the general legislative authority given to agencies. Agencies are given generic commands of law and then create the law's specifics.

someone hired by the agency. **For Example,** before red lights were required equipment in the rear windows of all cars, the Department of Transportation developed a study using taxicabs with the red lights in the rear windows and found that the accident rate for rear-end collisions with taxicabs was reduced dramatically. The study provided justification for the need for regulation as well as the type of regulation itself.

(c) PROPOSED REGULATIONS. Following a study, the agency proposes regulations, which must be published. To provide publicity for all regulations, the **Federal Register Act**[16] provides that proposed administrative regulation be published in the *Federal Register*. This is a government publication published five days a week that lists all administrative regulations, all presidential proclamations and executive orders, and other documents and classes of documents that the president or Congress directs to be published.

The Federal Register Act provides that printing an administrative regulation in the *Federal Register* is public notice of the contents of the regulation to persons subject to it or affected by it, but in addition, the Regulatory Flexibility Act,[17] passed during the Reagan administration, requires that all proposed rules be published in the trade journals of those trades that will be affected by the proposed rules. **For Example,** any changes in federal regulations on real property closings and escrows have to be published in real estate broker trade magazines. In addition to the public notice of the proposed rule, the agency must also include a regulatory flexibility analysis that shall describe the impact of the proposed rule on small entities.[18] The goal of this portion of the APA was to

Motor Vehicles Manufacturers Ass'n v State Farm Mutual Ins. Co., 463 US 29 (1983)

Seats Belts and Air Bags and Rules, Oh My!

FACTS: The U.S. Department of Transportation (DOT), charged with enforcing the National Traffic and Motor Vehicle Safety Act of 1966 and reducing auto accidents, passed Standard 208 in 1967, which required that all cars be equipped with seat belts. When another study showed the DOT that people did not use the belts, the department began a study of passive restraint systems which showed that these devices—automatic seat belts and air bags—could prevent approximately 12,000 deaths a year and over 100,000 serious injuries.

In 1972, after many hearings and comments, the DOT passed a regulation requiring some type of passive restraint system on all vehicles manufactured after 1975. Because of changes in directors of the DOT and the unfavorable economic climate in the auto industry, the requirements for passive restraints were postponed. In 1981, the department proposed a rescission of the passive restraint rule. After receiving written comments and holding public hearings, the agency concluded there was no longer a basis for reliably predicting that passive restraints increased safety levels or decreased accidents. Furthermore, the agency found it would cost $1 billion to implement the rule, and it was unwilling to impose such substantial costs on auto manufacturers.

State Farm filed suit on the rescission of the rule on the basis that it was arbitrary and capricious. The Court of Appeals held that the rescission was, in fact, arbitrary and capricious. The auto manufacturers appealed.

JUDICIAL OPINION

WHITE, J.... The ultimate question before us is whether NHTSA's (National Highway Traffic Safety Administration) rescission of the passive restraint requirement of Standard 208 was arbitrary and capricious. We conclude, as did the Court of Appeals, that it was.

The first and most obvious reason for finding the rescission arbitrary and capricious is that NHTSA apparently gave no consideration whatsoever to modifying the standard to require that airbag technology be utilized. Standard 208 sought to achieve automatic crash protection by requiring automobile manufacturers to install either of two passive restraint devices: airbags or automatic seatbelts. There was no suggestion in the long

---

[16] 44 USC § 1505 *et seq.*
[17] 5 USC § 601 *et seq.*
[18] 5 USC § 603(a).

Continued

rulemaking process that led to Standard 208 that if only one of these options were feasible, no passive restraint standard should be promulgated. Indeed, the agency's original proposed standard contemplated the installation of inflatable restraints in all cars. Automatic belts were added as a means of complying with the standard because they were believed to be as effective as airbags in achieving the goal of occupant crash protection.

The agency has now determined that the detachable automatic belts will not attain anticipated safety benefits because so many individuals will detach the mechanism. Even if this conclusion were acceptable in its entirety, standing alone it would not justify any more than an amendment of Standard 208 to disallow compliance by means of the only technology which will not provide effective passenger protection. It does not cast doubt on the need for a passive restraint standard or upon the efficacy of airbag technology. In its most recent rulemaking, the agency again acknowledged the lifesaving potential of the airbag. Given the effectiveness ascribed to airbag technology by the agency, the mandate of the Safety Act to achieve traffic safety would suggest that the logical response to the faults of detachable seatbelts would be to require the installation of airbags. At the very least this alternative way of achieving objectives of the Act should have been addressed and adequate reasons given for its abandonment. But the agency not only did not require compliance through airbags, it did not even consider the possibility in its 1981 rulemaking. Not one sentence of its rulemaking statement discusses the airbags-only option. We have frequently reiterated that an agency must cogently explain why it had exercised its discretion in a given manner.

For nearly a decade, the automobile industry waged the regulatory equivalent of war against the airbag and lost—the inflatable restraint was proven sufficiently effective. Now the automobile industry has decided to employ a seatbelt system which will not meet the safety objectives of Standard 208. This hardly constitutes cause to revoke the standard itself. Indeed the Motor Vehicle Safety Act was necessary because the industry was not sufficiently responsive to safety concerns. The Act intended that safety standards not depend on current technology and would be "technology-forcing" in the sense of inducing the development of superior safety design.

It is not infrequent that the available data does not settle a regulatory issue and the agency must then exercise its judgment in moving from the facts and probabilities on the record to a policy conclusion. Recognizing that policy making in a complex society must account for uncertainty, however, does not imply that it is sufficient for an agency to merely recite the terms "substantial uncertainty" as a justification for its actions. The agency must explain the evidence which is available, and must offer a "rational connection between the facts found and the choice made."

In this case, the agency's explanation for rescission of the passive restraint requirement is not sufficient to enable us to conclude that the rescission was the product of reasoned decision making. We start with the accepted ground that if used, seatbelts unquestionably would save many thousands of lives and would prevent tens of thousands of crippling injuries. Unlike recent regulations we have reviewed, the safety benefits of wearing seatbelts are not in doubt and it is not challenged that were those benefits to accrue, the monetary costs of implementing the standard would be easily justified.

Since 20 to 50 percent of motorists currently wear seatbelts on some occasions, there would seem to be grounds to believe that seatbelt use by occasional users will be substantially increased by the detachable passive belts. Whether this is the case is a matter for the agency to decide, but it must bring its expertise to bear on the question.

An agency's view of what is in the public interest may change, either with or without a change in circumstances. But an agency changing its course must supply a reasoned analysis. We do not accept all of the reasoning of the Court of Appeals but we do conclude that the agency has failed to supply the requisite "reasoned analysis" in this case. Accordingly, we remand the matter to the NHTSA for further consideration consistent with this opinion.

[Affirmed]

QUESTIONS

1. Why does the DOT want to withdraw the regulation?

2. What does the DOT need to withdraw the regulation?

3. Will the regulation go into effect?

be certain that small businesses were aware of proposed regulatory rules and their cost impact.

(D) PUBLIC COMMENT PERIOD. Following the publication of the proposed rules, the public has the opportunity to provide input on the proposed rules. Called the *public comment period,* this time must last at least 30 days (with certain emergency exceptions) and can consist simply of letters written by those affected that

San Diego Air Sports Center, Inc. v FAA, 887 F2d 966 (9th Cir 1989)

Get Off of My Cloud, er, Parachute

FACTS: San Diego Air Sports (SDAS) Center operates a sports parachuting business in Otay Mesa, California. SDAS offers training to beginning parachutists and facilitates recreational jumping for experienced parachutists. It indicates that the majority of SDAS jumps occur at altitudes in excess of 5,800 feet. The jump zone used by SDAS overlaps the San Diego Traffic Control Area (TCA). Although the aircraft carrying the parachutists normally operate outside the TCA, the parachutists themselves are dropped through it. Thus, the air traffic controllers must approve each jump.

In July 1987, an air traffic controller in San Diego filed an Unsatisfactory Condition Report with the Federal Aviation Administration (FAA), complaining of the strain that parachuting was putting on the controllers and raising safety concerns. The report led to a staff study of parachute jumping within the San Diego TCA. This was followed by a letter in March 1988 from the FAA to SDAS informing SDAS that "[e]ffective immediately parachute jumping within or into the San Diego TCA in the Otay Reservoir Jump Zone will not be authorized." The FAA stated that the letter was final and appealable.

SDAS challenged the letter in federal court on grounds that it constituted rulemaking without compliance with required Administrative Procedure Act (APA) procedures.

JUDICIAL OPINION

BEEZER, C. J... . The Federal Aviation Act requires that rules affecting the use of navigable airspace be issued in accordance with the Administrative Procedure Act (APA). The "principal purpose" of section 553 of the APA is "to provide that the legislative functions of administrative agencies shall so far as possible be exercised only upon public participation." Section 553 of the APA requires agencies to adhere to three steps when promulgating rules: Notice of the proposed rule, opportunity to comment, and an explanation of the rule ultimately adopted. These three requirements have been referred to as "the statutory *minima*" imposed by Congress.

Not every decision made by administrative agencies requires citizen participation. The APA lists four instances when the statutory *minima* do not apply: When the agency is promulgating (1) interpretive rules, (2) general statements of policy, or (3) rules of agency organization, procedure, or practice, or (4) when the requirement of notice and participation are impractical or contrary to public interest.

Congress was concerned that the exceptions to section 553, though necessary, might be used too broadly. The Senate noted that the courts have a "duty ... to prevent avoidance of the requirements of the [Act] by any manner or form of

indirection." We have stated that "[t]he exceptions to section 553 will be 'narrowly construed and only reluctantly countenanced.'"

The FAA letter does not come within either of the first two exceptions. The letter creates an immediate, substantive rule, i.e., that no parachuting will be allowed in the San Diego TCA.

The FAA argues that parachuting created an emergency to which it responded in the letter at issue. It is further argued that a response to an immediate emergency is covered by the fourth exception. This argument is not persuasive. The only accident known to the FAA occurred two years before it issued its letter. Furthermore, the FAA itself claims to have extensively studied the situation before issuing the letter. The FAA does not explain why public participation as required by the APA could not be included in its study.

Finally, the FAA argues that the letter is not a rule at all; rather, the FAA characterizes the letter as an order to which

the requirements set forth in section 553 of the APA does [sic] not apply. We find this argument somewhat mystifying, as there are equally stringent participation requirements for orders. Furthermore, the FAA is wrong; the letter is a rule.

A time-honored principle of administrative law is that the label an agency puts on its actions "is not necessarily conclusive." Equally true, however, is the fact that agencies can issue rules through adjudication (the process by which orders are normally issued) and orders through rulemaking.

In this case no record was kept of the "process" that resulted in the FAA letter; we can only scrutinize the letter itself. The letter clearly promulgates a rule. It states that *all* parachuting by any party will be prohibited in the San Diego TCA from the time it is issued. This comports with this court's statement that "[s]ubstantive rules are those which effect a change in existing law or policy."

The Federal Aviation Act requires that rules affecting the use of navigable airspace be issued in accordance with the APA, In issuing this substantive rule, the FAA failed to do so. A substantive rule is invalid if the issuing agency fails to comply with the APA. Therefore, the petition for review is granted.

QUESTIONS

1. Was the letter a form of regulation?

2. Did the agency skirt procedure?

3. Was SDAS deprived of due process by the letter?

are filed with the agency or of hearings conducted by the agency in Washington, D.C., or at specified locations around the country. An emergency exemption for the 30-day comment period was made when airport security measures and processes were changed following the September 11, 2001, attacks on the World Trade Center and the Pentagon that used domestic, commercial airliners.

(E) OPTIONS AFTER PUBLIC COMMENT. After receiving the public input on the proposed rule, an agency can decide to pass, or promulgate, the rule. The agency can also decide to withdraw the rule. **For Example,** the EEOC had proposed rules on handling religious discrimination in the workplace. The proposed rules, which would have required employers to police those wearing a cross or other religious symbol, met with so much public and employer protest that they were withdrawn. Finally, the agency can decide to modify the rule based on comments and then promulgate or, if the modifications are extensive or material, modify and put the proposed rule back out for public comment again. A diagram of the rule-making process can be found in Figure 6.3.

C. EXECUTIVE POWER OF THE AGENCY

The modern administrative agency has the power to execute the law and to bring proceedings against violators.

6. Enforcement or Execution of the Law

An agency has the power to investigate, to require persons to appear as witnesses, to require witnesses to produce relevant papers and records, and to bring proceedings against those who violate the law. In this connection, the phrase *the law* embraces regulations adopted by an agency as well as statutes and court decisions.

An agency may investigate to determine whether any violation of the law or of its rules generally has occurred. An agency may also investigate to determine whether additional rules need to be adopted, to ascertain the facts with respect to a particular suspected or alleged violation, and to see whether the defendant in a proceeding before it is complying with its final order. An agency may issue subpoenas to obtain information reasonably required by its investigation.[19]

7. Constitutional Limitations on Administrative Investigation

Although administrative agencies have broad enforcement authority, they remain subject to the constitutional protections afforded individuals and businesses.

(A) INSPECTION OF PREMISES. In general, a person has the same protection against unreasonable searches and seizures by an administrative officer as by a police officer. In contrast, when the danger of concealment is great, a warrantless search can be

---

e-commerce&cyberlaw
Complying with Regulations Online

Federal agencies have been adapting to online business. For example, the IRS offers electronic filing of income tax returns. The SEC permits electronic submission of various forms and reports due from companies. Corporations are using the Web to telecast their discussions with

analysts to comply with SEC rules on uniform disclosure of all company information to all investors in the same time frame. All federal agencies are accepting e-mail comments on proposed rules as valid public comments during the public comment periods for proposed rules.

---

[19] *EEOC v Sidley, Austen, Brown and Wood,* 35 F3d 696 (CA 7 2002).

FIGURE 6-3 | ***Steps in Agency Rulemaking***

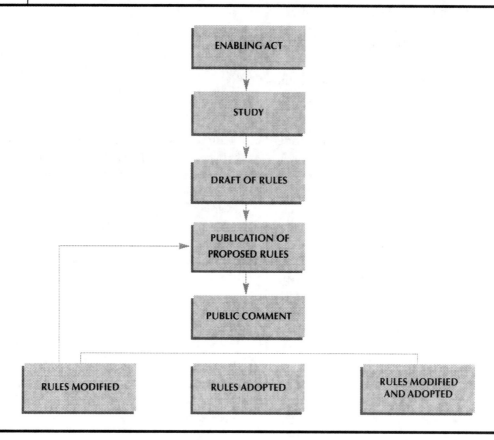

made of the premises of a highly regulated business, such as one selling liquor or firearms. Likewise, when violation of the law is dangerous to health and safety, the law may authorize inspection of the workplace without advance notice or a search warrant when such a requirement could defeat the purpose of the inspection.

(B) AERIAL INSPECTION. A search warrant is never required when the subject matter can be seen from a public place. **For Example,** when a police officer walking on a public sidewalk can look through an open window and see illegal weapons, a search warrant is not required to enter the premises and seize the weapons. Using airplanes and helicopters, law enforcement officers can see from the air; an agency, too, can gather information in this manner.[20]

(C) PRODUCTION OF PAPERS. For the most part, the constitutional guarantee against unreasonable searches and seizures does not afford much protection for papers and records being investigated by an agency. **For Example,** a subpoena to testify or to produce records cannot be opposed on the ground that it is a search and seizure. The constitutional protection is limited to cases of actual physical search and seizure rather than obtaining information by compulsion. Employers must turn over to the Occupational Health and Safety Administration (OSHA) their records on workplace injuries and lost workdays.

The protection afforded by the guarantee against self-incrimination is likewise narrow. It cannot be invoked when a corporate employee or officer in control of corporate records is compelled to produce those records even though he or she would be

[20] *Dow Chemical Co. v United States,* 476 US 1819 (1986).

incriminated by them.[21] The privilege against self-incrimination cannot be invoked if records required to be kept by law are involved.

(D) COMPLIANCE VERIFICATION. To ensure that a particular person or business is obeying the law, including an agency's regulations and orders, the administrative agency may require proof of compliance. At times, the question of compliance may be directly determined by an agency investigation, involving an examination either of a building or plant or of witnesses and documents. An agency may require the regulated person or enterprise to file reports in a specified form.[22]

D. JUDICIAL POWER OF THE AGENCY

Once the investigation of an agency reveals a potential violation of the law, an agency assumes its third role of judicial arbiter to conduct hearings on violations.

8. The Agency as a Specialized Court

An agency, although not a court by law, may be given power to sit as a court and to determine whether any violations of the law or of agency regulations have occurred. The National Labor Relations Board (NLRB) determines whether a prohibited labor practice has been committed. The Federal Trade Commission (FTC) acts as a court to determine whether someone has engaged in unfair competition.

(A) BEGINNING ENFORCEMENT—PRELIMINARY STEPS. Either a private individual or company or an agency may file a written complaint alleging some violation of law or regulation that is within the agency's jurisdiction. This complaint is then served on the company or individual named in the complaint, who then has the opportunity to file an answer to the allegations. There may be other phases of pleading between the parties and the agency, but eventually, the matter comes before the agency to be heard. After a hearing, the agency makes a decision and enters an order either dismissing the complaint or directing remedies or resolutions.

(B) THE ADMINISTRATIVE HEARING. To satisfy the requirements of due process, an agency handling a complaint must generally give notice and hold a hearing at which all persons affected may be present. A significant difference between an agency hearing and a court hearing is that there is no right of trial by jury before an agency. **For Example,** a workers' compensation board may decide a claim without any jury. Similarly, a case in which an employer protests the unemployment tax rate assigned to her company by a state agency has no right to a jury trial. The lack of a jury does not deny due process (see Chapter 4). An administrative law judge (ALJ) hears the complaint and has the authority to swear witnesses, take testimony, make evidentiary rulings, and make a decision to recommend to the agency heads for action.

An agency hearing is ordinarily not subject to the rules of evidence. Another difference between an administrative hearing and a judicial determination is that an agency may be authorized to make an initial determination without holding a hearing. If its conclusion is challenged, the agency then holds a hearing. A court, on the other hand, must have a trial before it makes a judgment. This difference has important practical consequences because the party objecting to the agency's initial determination has the burden of proof and the cost of going forward. The result is that fewer persons go to the trouble of seeking such a hearing, which reduces the number of hearings and the amount of litigation in which an agency becomes involved. The government saves money and time with this abbreviated process.

When an administrative action involves only the individuals directly affected rather than a class of persons or the community in general, the agency must have some form of hearing before it makes a decision. The Supreme Court has held that because a civil service employee may be removed only for cause, it is

---

[21] *Braswell v United States,* 487 US 99 (1988), see also *Armstrong v Guccione,* 470 F3d 89 (CA 2 2006).
[22] *United States v Morton Salt Co.,* 338 US 632 (1950).

a denial of due process for a statute to authorize an agency to remove the employee without a hearing.[23] Just giving the employee the right to appeal such action is not sufficient. Because the employee has a significant interest in continued employment, there must be some form of hearing prior to removing the employee to determine that there were not errors in the administrative action.

(C) STREAMLINED PROCEDURE: CONSENT DECREES. **Informal settlements** or **consent decrees** are practical devices to cut across the procedures already outlined. In many instances, an alleged wrongdoer informally notified that a complaint has been made is willing to change. An agency's informing an alleged wrongdoer of the charge before filing any formal complaint is sound public relations, as well as expeditious policy. A matter that has already gone into the formal hearing stage may also be terminated by agreement, and a stipulation or consent decree may be filed setting forth the terms of the agreement. The Administrative Dispute Resolution Act of 1990 encourages the streamlining of the regulatory process and authorizes federal agencies to use alternative means of dispute resolution.[24]

(D) FORM OF ADMINISTRATIVE DECISION. When an administrative agency makes a decision, it usually files an opinion that sets forth the findings of facts and reasons on which the decision is based. In some instances, a statute expressly requires this type of opinion, but an agency should always file one so that the parties and the court (in the event of an appeal) will understand the agency's action and reasoning.[25]

9. Punishment and Enforcement Powers of Agencies

(A) PENALTY. Within the last few decades, agencies have increasingly been given the power to impose a penalty and to issue orders that are binding on a regulated party unless an appeal is taken to a court, which reverses the administrative decision. As an illustration of the power to impose penalties, the Occupational Safety and Health Act of 1970 provides for the assessment of civil penalties against employers who fail to end dangerous working conditions when ordered to do so by the administrative agency created by that statute.[26]

(B) CEASE-AND-DESIST ORDER. Environmental protection statutes adopted by states commonly give a state agency the power to assess a penalty for violating environmental protection regulations. As an illustration of the issuance of binding orders, the FTC can issue a **cease-and-desist order** to stop a practice that it decides is improper. This order to stop is binding unless reversed on an appeal. **For Example,** the FTC can order a company to stop making claims in ads that have been determined by that agency to be deceptive.

10. Exhaustion of Administrative Remedies

All parties interacting with an agency must follow the procedure specified by the law. No appeal to a court is possible until the agency has acted on the party's matter before it. As a matter of policy, parties are required to exhaust administrative remedies before they may go into court or take an appeal.

As long as an agency is acting within the scope of its authority or jurisdiction, a party cannot appeal before the agency has made a final decision. The fact that the complaining party does not want the agency to decide the matter or is afraid that the agency will reach a wrong decision is not grounds for bypassing the agency by going to court before the agency has acted.

Exceptions to the **exhaustion-of-administrative remedies** requirement are (1) available remedies that provide no genuine opportunity for adequate relief; (2) irreparable injury that could occur if immediate judicial relief is not provided; (3) an appeal to the administrative agency that would be useless; or (4) a substantial constitutional question that the plaintiff has raised.

[23] *Cleveland Board of Education v Loudermill*, 470 US 532 (1985); *Darr v Town of Telluride, Colo.*, 495 F3d 1243 (CA 10 2007).
[24] 5 USC § 571 *et. seq.*
[25] *Jordan v Civil Service Bd., Charlotte*, 570 SE2d 912 (CA NC 2002).
[26] 29 USC § 651 *et seq.*

11. Appeal from Administrative Action and Finality of Administrative Determination

The statute creating the modern administrative agency generally provides that an appeal may be taken from the administrative decision to a particular court. The statute may provide the basis for an appeal. However, judicial precedent holds that courts may review administrative agency decisions on the bases covered in the following sections.

(A) Procedural Issues. If the procedure that an agency is to follow is specified by law, a decision of the agency that was made without following that procedure will be set aside and the matter sent back to the agency to proceed according to the required law.[27] An agency's actions, whether enforcement or rule promulgation, can be set aside if the agency has not followed the procedures required for rule-making or, in the case of enforcement, the due process rights of the charged business or individual.

(B) Substantive Law or Fact Issues. When the question that an agency decides is a question of law, the court on appeal will reverse the agency if the court disagrees with the legal interpretation.[28] This concept is being eroded to some extent by technical aspects of regulation. Courts now accept an agency's interpretation of a statute that involves a technical matter. Courts now tend to accept the agency's interpretation so long as it was reasonable even though it was not the only interpretation that could have been made.

In contrast with an agency's decision on matters of law, a controversy may turn on a question of fact or a mixed question of law and fact. In such cases, a court accepts an agency's conclusion if it is supported by substantial evidence. This means that the court must examine the entire record of the proceedings before the administrative agency to determine if there was substantial evidence to support the administrative findings. So long as reasonable minds could have reached the same conclusion as the agency after considering all of the evidence as a whole, the court must sustain the agency's findings of fact.[29]

A court will not reverse an agency's decision merely because the court would have made a different decision based on the same facts.[30] Because most disputes before an agency are based on questions of fact, the net result is that the agency's decision will be final in most cases.

Courts must give administrative agencies the freedom to do the work delegated to them and should not intervene unless the agency action is clearly unreasonable or arbitrary (see below). The agency action is presumed proper, and a person seeking reversal of the agency action has the burden to prove a basis for reversal.[31]

(C) Beyond the Jurisdiction of the Agency. When the question is whether an administrative action is in harmony with the policy of the statute creating the agency, an appellate court will sustain the administrative action if substantial evidence supports it.

(D) Arbitrary and Capricious. When an agency changes its prior decisions and customary actions, it must give its reasons. In the absence of such an explanation, a reviewing court cannot tell whether the agency changed its interpretation of the law for a valid reason or has made a mistake. The absence of an explanation condemns the agency action as arbitrary and requires reversal.[32]

The greatest limitation on court review of administrative action is the rule that a decision involving discretion will not be reversed in the absence of an error of law or a clear abuse of, or the arbitrary or capricious exercise of, discretion. The courts reason that because agency members were appointed on the basis of expert ability, it would be absurd for the court, which is unqualified technically to make a decision in the matter, to step in and determine whether the agency made the proper choice. Courts will not do so unless the agency has clearly acted

---

[27] *Tingler v State Board of Cosmetology*, 814 SW2d 683 (Mo App 1991).
[28] *Wallace v Iowa State Bd. of Educ.*, 770 NW2d 344 (Iowa 2009).
[29] *Dorchester Associates LLC v District of Columbia Bd. of Zoning Adjustment*, 976 A2d 200 (DC 2009).
[30] *In re Smith*, 121 P3d 150 (Wyo. 2005). An appellate court cannot review the evidence to determine the credibility of witnesses who testified before the administrative agency. *Hammann v City of Omaha*, 17 NW2d 323 (Neb. 1987).
[31] See note 29.
[32] *Lorillard Tobacco Co. v Roth*, 786 NE2d 7 (CA NY 2003).

Mainstream Marketing Services, Inc. v F.T.C., 358 F3d 1228 (10th Cir 2004) cert denied 543 US 812 (2004)

I'll Call You—Maybe During Dinner: The FCC and the National Do-Not-Call List Regulation

FACTS: The Telephone Consumer Protection Act of 1991 (TCPA) granted the FCC the authority to promulgate rules creating a procedure to protect telephone subscribers from receiving unwanted telemarketing calls. In 1994, Congress enacted the Telemarketing Act, which granted the FTC the authority to promulgate rules prohibiting "deceptive or abusive telemarketing practices." Congress specifically found that consumers were being increasingly victimized by telemarketing fraud and other abuses, and it required the FTC in promulgating its rules to (1) define "deceptive telemarketing acts or practices," (2) prohibit abusive patterns of unsolicited telephone calls, (3) restrict the hours of the day when telemarketing calls may be placed, and (4) require telemarketers to promptly disclose to call recipients the nature of their call.

In December 2002, the FTC issued amended rules that prohibit "deceptive or abusive telemarketing acts or practices."

Under the TCPA, the FCC announced its intention to adopt rules similar to the FTC's, enforcing the do-not-call list.

Mainstream Marketing and TMG, independent telemarketing companies based in Colorado, brought suit challenging the FTC's authority to create a national do-not-call list that allows consumers to opt out, alleging that the do-not-call list violates the First Amendment and the APA. The District Court for Colorado held that the FTC's do-not-call rules were unconstitutional on First Amendment grounds, and the District Court for the Western District of Oklahoma held that FTC lacked statutory authority to enact its do-not-call rules. The two appeals by the FCC and FTC were consolidated in the Tenth Circuit.

JUDICIAL OPINION

EBEL, C. J... . The national do-not-call registry is the product of a regulatory effort dating back to 1991 aimed at protecting the privacy rights of consumers and curbing the risk of telemarketing abuse. In the Telephone Consumer Protection Act of 1991 ("TCPA")—under which the FCC enacted its do-not-call rules—Congress found that for many consumers telemarketing sales calls constitute an intrusive invasion of privacy. Moreover, the TCPA's legislative history cited statistical data indicating that "most unwanted telephone solicitations are commercial in nature" and that "unwanted commercial calls are a far bigger problem than unsolicited calls from political or charitable organizations." TCPA

therefore authorized the FCC to establish a national database of consumers who object to receiving "telephone solicitations," which the act defined as commercial sales calls.

Furthermore, in the Telemarketing and Consumer Fraud and Abuse Prevention Act of 1994 ("Telemarketing Act")—under which the FTC enacted its do-not-call rules—Congress found that consumers lose an estimated $40 billion each year due to telemarketing fraud. Therefore, Congress authorized the FTC to prohibit sales calls that a reasonable consumer would consider coercive or abusive of his or her right to privacy.

The national do-not-call registry's telemarketing restrictions apply only to commercial speech. Like most commercial speech regulations, the do-not-call rules draw a line between commercial and non-commercial speech on the basis of content. In reviewing commercial speech regulations, we apply the *Central Hudson* test. *Central Hudson Gas & Elec. Corp. v. Pub. Serv. Comm'n of N.Y.*, 447 U.S. 557, 566, 100 S. Ct. 2343, 65 L.Ed.2d 341 (1980).

Central Hudson established a three-part test governing First Amendment challenges to regulations restricting non-misleading commercial speech that relates to lawful activity. First, the government must assert a substantial interest to be achieved by the regulation. Second, the regulation must directly advance that governmental interest, meaning that it must do more than provide "only ineffective or remote support for the government's purpose." Third, although the regulation need not be the least restrictive measure available, it must be narrowly tailored not to restrict more speech than necessary.

A. Governmental Interests
The government asserts that the do-not-call regulations are justified by its interests in 1) protecting the privacy of individuals in their homes, and 2) protecting consumers against the risk of fraudulent and abusive solicitation. Both of these justifications are undisputedly substantial governmental interests.

B. Reasonable Fit
A reasonable fit exists between the do-not-call rules and the government's privacy and consumer protection interests if the regulation directly advances those interests and is "narrowly tailored". In this context, the narrowly tailored standard does not require that the government's response to protect substantial interests be the least restrictive measure available. All that is required is a proportional response.

Continued

The individuals on the do-not-call list have declared that they do not wish to receive unsolicited commercial telemarketing calls, whereas those who do want to continue receiving such calls will not register.

Additionally, the FTC has found that commercial callers are more likely than non-commercial callers to engage in deceptive and abusive practices. Specifically, the FTC concluded that in charitable and political calls, a significant purpose of the call is to sell a cause, not merely to receive a donation, and that non-commercial callers thus have stronger incentives not to alienate the people they call or to engage in abusive and deceptive practices.

In sum, the do-not-call list directly advances the government's interests—reducing intrusions upon consumer privacy and the risk of fraud or abuse—by restricting a substantial number (and also a substantial percentage) of the calls that cause these problems.

2. Narrow Tailoring

Although the least restrictive means test is not the test to be used in the commercial speech context, commercial speech regulations do at least have to be "narrowly tailored" and provide a "reasonable fit" between the problem and the solution. Whether or not there are "numerous and obvious less-burdensome alternatives" is a relevant consideration in our narrow tailoring analysis.

We hold that the national do-not-call registry is narrowly tailored because it does not over-regulate protected speech; rather, it restricts only calls that are targeted at unwilling recipients. The do-not-call registry prohibits only telemarketing calls aimed at consumers who have affirmatively indicated that they do not want to receive such calls and for whom such calls would constitute an invasion of privacy.

The idea that an opt-in regulation is less restrictive than a direct prohibition of speech applies not only to traditional door-to-door solicitation, but also to regulations seeking to protect the privacy of the home from unwanted intrusions via telephone, television, or the Internet.

For the reasons discussed above, the government has asserted substantial interests to be served by the do-not-call registry (privacy and consumer protection), the do-not-call registry will directly advance those interests by banning a substantial amount of unwanted telemarketing calls, and the regulation is narrowly tailored because its opt-in feature ensures that it does not restrict any speech directed at a willing listener. In other words, the do-not-call registry bears a reasonable fit with the purposes the government sought to advance. Therefore, it is consistent with the limits the First Amendment imposes on laws restricting commercial speech.

The judgments below in [both] cases are REVERSED.

QUESTIONS

1. List the arguments that the telemarketers make to challenge the national do-not-call list.

2. What does the court do with each of the arguments and why?

3. What lessons on business practices do you see with the passage of the rules on the national do-not-call list?

wrongly, arbitrarily, or capriciously. As a practical matter, an agency's action is rarely found to be arbitrary or capricious. As long as an agency has followed proper procedure, the fact that the court disagrees with the agency's conclusion does not make that conclusion arbitrary or capricious. In areas in which economic or technical matters are involved, it is generally sufficient that the agency had a reasonable basis for its decision. A court will not attempt to second-guess the agency about complex criteria with which an administrative agency is intimately familiar. The judicial attitude is that for protection from laws and regulations that are unwise, improvident, or out of harmony with a particular school of thought, the people must resort to the ballot box, not to the court.

Because of limited funding and staff, an agency must exercise discretion in deciding which cases it should handle. Ordinarily, a court will not reverse an agency's decision to do nothing about a particular complaint.[33] That is, the courts will not override an agency's decision to do nothing. Exceptions include acting arbitrarily in those enforcement actions as when an agency refuses to act in circumstances in which action is warranted and necessary.

---

[33] *Heckler v Chaney*, 470 US 821 (1985).

F.C.C. v Fox Television Stations, Inc. 129 S Ct 1800 (2009)

Foul Mouths Can Get You a Foul

FACTS: During the 2002 Billboard Music Awards, which were broadcast over the Fox Television Stations, singer Cher exclaimed, "I've also had critics for the last 40 years saying that I was on my way out every year. Right. So f* * * 'em." During a segment of the similarly broadcast 2003 Billboard Music Awards, when Nicole Richie and Paris Hilton, principals in a Fox television series called "The Simple Life" were presenting an award, Ms. Hilton began their interchange by reminding Ms. Richie to "watch the bad language," but Ms. Richie proceeded to ask the audience, "Why do they even call it 'The Simple Life?' Have you ever tried to get cow s* * * out of a Prada purse? It's not so f* * *ing simple."

Following each of these broadcasts, the Federal Communications Commission (FCC) received numerous complaints from parents whose children were exposed to the language. The FCC found that Fox Television had violated the FCC's indecency standards that prohibited use of the "F word" and discussion of excrement. The FCC issued a notice of fine. Fox and other broadcasters appealed the order. The court of appeals reversed the order, finding that the FCC's reasoning on its standards for indecency was not consistent or grounded in logic. The FCC appealed.

SCALIA, Justice

In 2004, the Commission [held] that a nonliteral (expletive) use of the F- and S-Words could be actionably indecent, even when the word is used only once. The first order to this effect dealt with an NBC broadcast of the Golden Globe Awards, in which the performer Bono commented, "'This is really, really, f* * *ing brilliant.'". Although the Commission had received numerous complaints directed at the broadcast, its enforcement bureau had concluded that the material was not indecent because "Bono did not describe, in context, sexual or excretory organs or activities and… the utterance was fleeting and isolated." The full Commission reviewed and reversed the staff ruling.

The Commission first declared that Bono's use of the F-Word fell within its indecency definition, even though the word was used as an intensifier rather than a literal descriptor. "[G]iven the core meaning of the 'F-Word,' " it said, "any use of that word… inherently has a sexual connotation." The Commission determined, moreover, that the broadcast was "patently offensive" because the F-Word "is one of the most vulgar, graphic and explicit descriptions of sexual activity in the English language," because "[i]ts use invariably invokes a coarse sexual image," and because Bono's use of the word was entirely "shocking and gratuitous."

The order noted that technological advances have made it far easier to delete ("bleep out") a "single and gratuitous use of a vulgar expletive," without adulterating the content of a broadcast.

The order acknowledged that "prior Commission and staff action have indicated that isolated or fleeting broadcasts of the 'F-Word'… are not indecent or would not be acted upon." It

explicitly ruled that "any such interpretation is no longer good law." Because, however, "existing precedent would have permitted this broadcast," the Commission determined that "NBC and its affiliates necessarily did not have the requisite notice to justify a penalty." (the Golden Globes Order is the name given to the decision in the Bono case)

[In the present case] …The order stated … , that the pre-Golden Globes regime of immunity for isolated indecent expletives rested only upon staff rulings and Commission dicta, and that the Commission itself had never held "that the isolated use of an expletive… was not indecent or could not be indecent," Under the new policy, a lack of repetition "weigh[s] against a finding of indecency," but is not a safe harbor.

We find no basis in the Administrative Procedure Act or in our opinions for a requirement that all agency change be subjected to more searching review. The Act mentions no such heightened standard. And our opinion in *State Farm* neither held nor implied that every agency action representing a policy change must be justified by reasons more substantial than those required to adopt a policy in the first instance. That case, which involved the rescission of a prior regulation, said only that such action requires "a reasoned analysis for the change beyond that which may be required when an agency does not act in the first instance."

To be sure, the requirement that an agency provide reasoned explanation for its action would ordinarily demand that it display awareness that it is changing position. An agency may not, for example, depart from a prior policy *sub silentio* or simply disregard rules that are still on the books. And, of course, the agency must show that there are good reasons for the new policy. But it need not demonstrate to a court's satisfaction that the reasons for the new policy are better than the reasons for the old one; it suffices that the new policy is permissible under the statute, that there are good reasons for it, and that the agency believes it to be better, which the conscious change of course adequately indicates.

Judged under the above described standards, the Commission's new enforcement policy and its order finding the broadcasts actionably indecent were neither arbitrary nor capricious. First, the Commission forthrightly acknowledged that its recent actions have broken new ground, taking account of inconsistent "prior Commission and staff action" and explicitly disavowing them as "no longer good law."

Moreover, the agency's reasons for expanding the scope of its enforcement activity were entirely rational. It was certainly reasonable to determine that it made no sense to distinguish between literal and nonliteral uses of offensive words, requiring repetitive use to render only the latter indecent. As the Commission said with regard to expletive use of the F-Word,

Continued

"the word's power to insult and offend derives from its sexual meaning." And the Commission's decision to look at the patent offensiveness of even isolated uses of sexual and excretory words fits with the context-based approach we [have] sanctioned.

There are some propositions for which scant empirical evidence can be marshaled, and the harmful effect of broadcast profanity on children is one of them. One cannot demand a multiyear controlled study, in which some children are intentionally exposed to indecent broadcasts (and insulated from all other indecency), and others are shielded from all indecency. It is one thing to set aside agency action under the Administrative Procedure Act because of failure to adduce empirical data that can readily be obtained. It is something else to insist upon obtaining the unobtainable. Here it suffices to know that children mimic the behavior they observe-or at least the behavior that is presented to them as normal and appropriate. Programming replete with one-word indecent expletives will tend to produce children who use (at least) one-word indecent expletives. Congress has made the determination that indecent material is harmful to children, and has left enforcement of the ban to the Commission. If enforcement had to be supported by empirical data, the ban would effectively be a nullity.

More fundamentally, however, the agency's decision to consider the patent offensiveness of isolated expletives on a case-by-case basis is not arbitrary or capricious. "Even a prime-time recitation of Geoffrey Chaucer's Miller's Tale," we have explained, "would not be likely to command the attention of many children who are both old enough to understand and young enough to be adversely affected." The same rationale could support the Commission's finding that a broadcast of the film Saving Private Ryan was not indecent-a finding to which the broadcasters point as supposed evidence of the Commission's inconsistency. The frightening suspense and the graphic violence in the movie could well dissuade the most vulnerable from watching and would put parents on notice of potentially objectionable material. The agency's decision to retain some discretion does not render arbitrary or capricious its regulation of the deliberate and shocking uses of offensive language at the award shows under review-shows that were expected to (and did) draw the attention of millions of children.

The Second Circuit believed that children today "likely hear this language far more often from other sources than they did in the 1970's when the Commission first began sanctioning indecent speech," and that this cuts against more stringent regulation of broadcasts. Assuming the premise is true (for this point the Second Circuit did not demand empirical evidence) the conclusion does not necessarily follow. The Commission could reasonably conclude that the pervasiveness of foul language, and the coarsening of public entertainment in other media such as cable, justify more stringent regulation of broadcast programs so as to give conscientious parents a relatively safe haven for their children. In the end, the Second Circuit and the broadcasters quibble with the Commission's policy choices and not with the explanation it has given. We decline to "substitute [our] judgment for that of the agency," and we find the Commission's orders neither arbitrary nor capricious.

The judgment of the United States Court of Appeals for the Second Circuit is reversed, and the case is remanded for further proceedings consistent with this opinion.

QUESTIONS

1. Does agency discretion mean that a rule is arbitrary and capricious?

2. What weight does the court give to the argument that children hear this kind of language all the time?

12. Liability of the Agency

The decision of an agency may cause substantial loss to a business by increasing its operating costs or by making a decision that later is shown to be harmful to the economy. An agency is not liable for such loss when it has acted in good faith in the exercise of discretionary powers. An administrator who wrongly denies a person the benefit of a government program is not personally liable to that person.

lawflix

Clear and Present Danger (1994) PG-13

The struggles of Jack Ryan involve more than Colombian drug lords; he must battle the political appointees and their overstepping of their agency's authority. The relationship between agencies and congress is also depicted in the film.

Check out LawFlix at **www.cengage.com/blaw/dvl** to access movie clips that illustrate business law concepts.

MAKE THE CONNECTION

SUMMARY

The administrative agency is unique because it combines the three functions that are kept separate under our traditional governmental system: legislative, executive, and judicial. By virtue of legislative power, an agency adopts regulations that have the force of law, although agency members are not elected by those subject to the regulations. By virtue of the executive power, an agency carries out and enforces the regulations, makes investigations, and requires the production of documents. By virtue of the judicial power, an agency acts as a court to determine whether a violation of any regulation has occurred. To some extent, an agency is restricted by constitutional limitations in inspecting premises and requiring the production of papers. These limitations, however, have a very narrow application in agency actions. When an agency acts as a judge, a jury trial is not required, nor must ordinary courtroom procedures be followed. Typically, an agency gives notice to the person claimed to be acting improperly, and a hearing is then held before the agency. When the agency has determined that there has been a violation, it may order that the violation

stop. Under some statutes, the agency may go further and impose a penalty on the violator.

An appeal to a court may be taken from any decision of an agency by a person harmed by the decision. Only a person with a legally recognized interest can appeal from the agency ruling. No appeal can be made until every step available before the agency has been taken; that is, the administrative remedy must first be exhausted. An agency's actions can be reversed by a court if the agency exceeded its authority, the decision is not based in law or fact, the decision is arbitrary and capricious, or, finally, the agency violated procedural steps.

Protection from secret government is provided by Sunshine laws that afford the right to know what most administrative agency records contain; by the requirement that most agency meetings be open to the public; by the invitation to the public to take part in rulemaking; and by publicity given, through publication in the *Federal Register* and trade publications, to the guidelines followed by the agency and the regulations it has adopted.

LEARNING OUTCOMES

After studying this chapter, you should be able to clearly explain:

A. NATURE OF THE ADMINISTRATIVE AGENCY

LO.1 Describe the nature and purpose of administrative agencies
See Section A(2) for a discussion of the unique nature of agencies, p. 94.

B. LEGISLATIVE POWER OF THE AGENCY

LO.2 Discuss the legislative or rulemaking power of administrative agencies
See the *State Farm* case on p. 98.
See the *San Diego Air Sports* case on p. 100.

See the National Do-Not-Call case on p. 106.

C. EXECUTIVE POWER OF THE AGENCY

LO.3 Explain the executive or enforcement function of administrative agencies
See the *CBS* case on p. 113.

D. JUDICIAL POWER OF THE AGENCY

LO.4 Discuss the judicial power of administrative agencies including the rule on exhaustion of administrative remedies
See the *Mainstream Marketing* case on p. 106.

KEY TERMS

administrative agency
administrative law
Administrative Procedure
   Act
cease-and-desist order

consent decrees
exhaustion-of-
   administrative remedies
Federal Register Act
Federal Register

Freedom of Information
   Act
informal settlements
open meeting law

QUESTIONS AND CASE PROBLEMS

1. Following the events of September 11, 2001, in which four airplanes crashed as a result of the presence of terrorists on those flights, the FAA concluded that it needed to implement new procedures for airports and flights. The new procedures for security and flights took effect when the airports reopened five days later. Why did the FAA not need to go through the promulgation and public comment processes and time periods to have the new rules take effect?

2. Reserve Mining Co. obtained a permit from the Minnesota Pollution Control Agency to dump wastewater into the nearby Beaver River. The permit specified that no more than 1 million fibers per liter could be discharged in the company's wastewater. The agency did not make or file any explanation as to how or why that maximum was selected. Normally, the wastewater that the company generated was kept in a tailings dam with a discharge in the river necessary only in an emergency. Because of a sudden economic downturn, the company foresaw the need to dispose of wastewater in the river and discovered that the discharge it would have to make would likely be between 10 to 15 times the amount of fiber allowed by the permit. Reserve Mining appealed the maximum limitation imposed by the agency. How could Reserve Mining challenge the 1-million-fibers standard? [*Reserve Mining Co. v Minnesota Pollution Control Agency*, 364 NW2d 411 (Minn App)]

3. The Tacoma-Pierce County Health Department conducted an investigation into the quality of care provided by ambulance service providers in its jurisdiction. On the basis of that investigation,

the department issued a set of temporary rules and regulations that established minimum requirements for equipment, drugs, and service availability for ambulance service providers in Pierce County. The *Tacoma News* wanted to publish an article on the matter and sought discovery of everything that had led to the adoption of the regulations, including all details of the investigation made by the health department. The health department objected to disclosing the names of the persons who had volunteered information on which the department had based its action and the names of the ambulance companies. Were the names subject to a Freedom of Information Act (FOIA) request? [*Tacoma News, Inc. v Tacoma-Pierce County Health Dept.*, 778 P2d 1066 (Wash App)]

4. Congress adopted a law to provide insurance to protect wheat farmers. The agency in charge of the program adopted regulations to govern applications for this insurance. These regulations were published in the *Federal Register*. Merrill applied for insurance, but his application did not comply with the regulations. He claimed that he was not bound by the regulations because he never knew they had been adopted. Is he bound by the regulations? [*Federal Crop Ins. Corp. v Merrill*, 332 US 380]

5. Santa Monica adopted a rent control ordinance authorizing the Rent Control Board to set the amount of rents that could be charged. At a hearing before it, the board determined that McHugh was charging his tenants a rent higher than the maximum allowed. McHugh claimed that the action of the board was improper because

there was no jury trial. Is McHugh correct? Why or why not? [*McHugh v Santa Monica Rent Control Board*, 49 Cal 3d 348, 777 P2d 91]

6. New York City's charter authorized the New York City Board of Health to adopt a health code that it declared to have the force and effect of law. The board adopted a code that provided for the fluoridation of the public water supply. A suit was brought to enjoin the carrying out of this program on the grounds that it was unconstitutional and that money could not be spent to carry out such a program in the absence of a statute authorizing the expenditure. It was also claimed that the fluoridation program was unconstitutional because there were other means of reducing tooth decay; fluoridation was discriminatory by benefiting only children; it unlawfully imposed medication on children without their consent; and fluoridation was or may be dangerous to health. Was the code's provision valid? [*Paduano v City of New York*, 257 NYS2d 531]

7. What is the *Federal Register?* What role does it play in rulemaking? What is the difference between the *Federal Register* and the Code of Federal Regulations?

8. The Consumer Product Safety Commission is reconsidering a rule it first proposed in 1997 that would require child-resistant caps on household products, including cosmetics. When the rule was first proposed in 1997, it was resisted by the cosmetics industry and abandoned. However, in May 2001, a 16-month-old baby died after drinking baby oil from a bottle with a pull-tab cap.

  The proposed rule would cover products such as baby oil and suntan lotion and any products containing hydrocarbons such as cleansers and spot removers. The danger, according to the commission, is simply the inhalation by children, not necessarily the actual ingestion of the products. Five children have died from inhaling such fumes since 1993, and 6,400 children under the age of five were brought into emergency rooms and/ or hospitalized for treatment after breathing in hydrocarbons.

There is no medical treatment for the inhalation of hydrocarbons.

  Several companies in the suntan oil/lotion industry have supported the new regulations. The head of a consumer group has said, We know these products cause death and injury. That is all we need to know.[34]

  What process must the CPSC follow to promulgate the rules? What do you think of the consumer group head's statement? Will that statement alone justify the rulemaking?

9. The *Federal Register* contained the following provision from the Environmental Protection Agency on January 14, 2002:

  We, the U.S. Fish and Wildlife Service (Service), announce the re-opening of the comment period on the proposed listing of Lomatium cookii *(Cook's lomatium) and* Limnanthes floccosa ssp. grandiflora *(large-flowered wooly meadowfoam) as endangered species under the Endangered Species Act of 1973, as amended (Act). We are re-opening the comment period to provide the public an opportunity to review additional information on the status, abundance, and distribution of these plants, and to request additional information and comments from the public regarding the proposed rule. Comments previously submitted need not be resubmitted as they will be incorporated into the public record as part of this extended comment period; all comments will be fully considered in the final rule.*

  DATES: We will accept public comments until March 15, 2002.

  What was the EPA doing and why? What could those who had concerns do at that point?

10. Macon County Landfill Corp. applied for permission to expand the boundaries of its landfill. Tate and others opposed the application. After a number of hearings, the appropriate agency granted the requested permission to expand. Tate appealed and claimed that the agency had made a wrong decision on the basis of the evidence presented. Will the court determine whether the correct decision was made? [*Tate v Illinois*

---

[34] Julian E. Barnes, Safety Caps Are Considered for Cosmetics, *New York Times*, October 10, 2001, C1, C8.

Pollution Control Board, 188 Ill App 3d 994, 544 NE2d 1176]

11. The planning commissioner and a real estate developer planned to meet to discuss rezoning certain land that would permit the real estate developer to construct certain buildings not allowed under the then-existing zoning law. A homeowners association claimed it had the right to be present at the meeting. This claim was objected to on the theory that the state's Open Meetings Act applied only to meetings of specified government units and did not extend to a meeting between one of them and an outsider. Was this objection valid?

12. The Michigan Freedom of Information Act declares that it is the state's policy to give all persons full information about the actions of the government and that the people shall be informed so that they may participate in the democratic process. The union of clerical workers at Michigan State University requested the trustees of the university to give them the names and addresses of persons making monetary donations to the university. Michigan State objected because the disclosure of addresses was a violation of the right of privacy. Decide. [*Clerical-Technical Union of Michigan State University v Board of Trustees of Michigan State University*, 475 NW2d 373 (Mich)]

13. The Department of Health and Human Services has proposed new guidelines for the interpretation of federal statutes on gifts, incentives, and other benefits bestowed on physicians by pharmaceutical companies. The areas on which the interpretation focused follow:

    - Paying doctors to act as consultants or market researchers for prescription drugs

    - Paying pharmacies fees to switch patients to new drugs

    - Providing grants, scholarships, and anything more than nominal gifts to physicians for time,

information sessions, and so on, on new drugs[35]

The Office of Inspector General is handling the new rules interpretation and has established a public comment period of 60 days. Explain the purpose of the public comment period. What ethical issues do the regulations attempt to address?

14. On February 1, 2004, CBS presented a live broadcast of the National Football League's Super Bowl XXXVIII, which included a halftime show produced by MTV Networks. Nearly 90 million viewers watched the Halftime Show, which began at 8:30 p.m. Eastern Standard Time and lasted about 15 minutes. The Halftime Show featured a performance with Janet Jackson and Justin Timberlake as a surprise guest for the final minutes of the show.

    Timberlake and Jackson performed his popular song "Rock Your Body" as the show's finale. Their performance, which involved sexually suggestive choreography, portrayed Timberlake seeking to dance with Jackson, and Jackson alternating between accepting and rejecting his advances. The performance ended with Timberlake singing, "…gonna have you naked by the end of this song…", and simultaneously tearing away part of Jackson's bustier. CBS had implemented a five-second audio delay to guard against the possibility of indecent language being transmitted on air, but it did not employ similar precautionary technology for video images. As a result, Jackson's bare right breast was exposed on camera for nine-sixteenths of one second.

    On September 22, 2004, the Commission issued a Notice of Apparent Liability, finding that CBS had apparently violated federal law and FCC rules restricting the broadcast of indecent material. After its review, the Commission determined that CBS was liable for a forfeiture penalty of $550,000 because its actions were willful..

    CBS filed with the FCC for a reconsideration, which was denied. CBS then appealed the case to

---

[35] See 67 *Federal Register* 62057, October 3, 2002. Go to **www.oig.hhs.gov**. See also Robert Pear, U.S. Warning to Drug Makers Over Payments, *New York Times*, October 1, 2002, A1, A23; Julie Appleby, Feds Warn Drugmakers: Gifts to Doctors May Be Illegal, *USA Today*, October 2, 2002, 1A.

the federal Court of Appeals on the grounds that the finding of willfulness as well as the penalty were arbitrary and capricious and violated First Amendment rights. Based on the *Fox Televisions Stations* case, what do you think the decision should be and why. [CBS Corporation, Inc. v FCC, *535 F3d 167 (CA 3 2006)*]

15. The Endangered Species Act (ESA) charges the National Marine Fisheries Service (a federal agency) with the duty to ensure that any proposed action by the Council does not jeopardize any threatened or endangered species. The Steller sea lion is on the list of endangered species. The agency developed a North Pacific marine fishery plan that permitted significant harvest of fish by commercial fisheries in the area. Greenpeace, an environmental group, challenged the agency on the grounds that the plan was not based on a sufficient number of biological studies on the impact of the allowed fishing on the Steller sea lion. Greenpeace's biologic opinion concluded that the fishery plan would reduce the level of food for the sea lions by about 40 percent to 60 percent, if the juvenile fish were not counted in that figure. Greenpeace's expert maintained that counting juvenile fish was misleading because they were not capable of reproducing and the government agency's figure was, as a result, much lower at 22 percent. What would Greenpeace need to show to be successful in challenging the agency's fishery plan? [*Greenpeace, American Oceans Campaign v National Marine Fisheries Service*, 237 F Supp 2d 1181 (WD Wash)]

Chapter 7

THE LEGAL ENVIRONMENT OF INTERNATIONAL TRADE

The success or failure of the U.S. firms doing business in foreign countries may well depend on accurate information about the laws and customs of the host countries. In their domestic operations, U.S. business firms compete against imports from other nations. Such imported goods include Canadian lumber, Mexican machinery, Japanese automobiles, German steel, French wine, Chinese textiles, and Chilean copper. To compete effectively, U.S. firms should learn about the business practices of foreign firms. They should be alert to unfair trade practices that will put U.S. firms at a disadvantage. Such practices may include the violation of U.S. antitrust and antidumping laws or violation of international trade agreements. Individuals from all over the world participate in the U.S. securities markets. Special problems exist in the regulation and enforcement of U.S. securities laws involving financial institutions of countries with secrecy laws.

A. General Principles

Nations enter into treaties and conferences to further international trade. The business world has developed certain forms of organizations for conducting that trade.

1. The Legal Background

Because of the complexity and ever-changing character of the legal environment of international trade, this section will focus on certain underlying elements.

(A) WHAT LAW APPLIES. When there is a sale of goods within the United States, one law typically applies to the transaction. Some variation may be introduced when the transaction is between parties in different states, but for the most part, the law governing the transaction is the U.S. law of contracts and the Uniform Commercial Code (UCC). In contrast, when an international contract is made, it is necessary to determine whether it is the law of the seller's country or the law of the importer's country that will govern. The parties to an international contract often resolve that question themselves as part of their contract, setting forth which country's law will govern should a dispute arise. Such a provision is called a **choice-of-law clause.** **For Example,** U.S. investors Irmgard and Mitchell Lipcon provided capital to underwriters at Lloyd's of London and signed choice-of-law clauses in their investment agreements binding them to proceed in England under English law should disputes arise. When the Lipcons realized that their investments were exposed to massive liabilities for asbestos and pollution insurance claims, they sued in U.S. district court in Florida for alleged U.S. securities acts violations. However, their complaints were dismissed based on the choice-of-law clauses in their contracts. The U.S. court of appeals stated that the Lipcons must "honor their bargains" and attempt to vindicate their claims in English courts under English law. [1]

The major trading countries of the world have entered into a number of treaties. When their citizens deal with each other and their respective rights are not controlled in their contract, their rights and liabilities are determined by looking at the treaty. These treaties are discussed in Section 7 of this chapter, including the United Nations Convention on Contracts for the International Sale of Goods (CISG), which deals with certain aspects of the formation and performance of international commercial contracts for the sale of goods.

(B) THE ARBITRATION ALTERNATIVE. Traditional litigation may be considered too time consuming, expensive, and divisive to the relationships of the parties to an international venture. The parties, therefore, may agree to arbitrate any contractual disputes that may arise according to dispute resolution procedures set forth in the contract.

Pitfalls exist for U.S. companies arbitrating disputes in foreign lands. **For Example,** were a U.S. company to agree to arbitrate a contractual dispute with a Chinese organization in China, it would find that the arbitrator must be Chinese. Also, under Chinese law, only Chinese lawyers can present an

---

[1] *Lipcon v Underwriters at Lloyd's, London,* 148 F2d 1285, 1299 (11th Cir 1998).

arbitration case, even if one party is a U.S. company. Because of situations like this, it is common for parties to international ventures to agree to arbitrate their disputes in neutral countries.

An arbitration agreement gives the parties more control over the decision-making process. The parties can require that the arbitrator have the technical, language, and legal qualifications to best understand their dispute. While procedures exist for the prearbitration exchange of documents, full "discovery" is ordinarily not allowed. The decision of the arbitrator is final and binding on the parties with very limited judicial review possible.

(c) CONFLICTING IDEOLOGIES. Law, for all people and at all times, is the result of the desire of the lawmaker to achieve certain goals. These are the social forces that make the law. In the eyes of the lawmaker, the attainment of these goals is proper and therefore ethical. This does not mean that we all can agree on what the international law should be because different people have different ideas as to what is right. This affects our views as to ownership, trade, and dealings with foreign merchants. **For Example,** a very large part of the world does not share the U.S. dislike of cartels. Other countries do not have our antitrust laws; therefore, their merchants can form a trust to create greater bargaining power in dealing with U.S. and other foreign merchants.

(d) FINANCING INTERNATIONAL TRADE. There is no international currency. This creates problems as to what currency to use and how to make payment in international transactions. Centuries ago, buyers used precious metals, jewels, or furs in payment. Today, the parties to an international transaction agree in their sales contract on the currency to be used to pay for the goods. They commonly require that the buyer furnish the seller a **letter of credit**, which is a commercial device used to guarantee payment to a seller in an international transaction. By this, an issuer, typically a bank, agrees to pay the drafts drawn against the buyer for the purchase price. In trading with merchants in some countries, the foreign country itself will promise that the seller will be paid.

2. International Trade Organizations, Conferences, and Treaties

A large number of organizations exist that affect the multinational markets for goods, services, and investments. A survey of major international organizations, conferences, and treaties follows.

(a) GATT AND WTO. The *General Agreement on Tariffs and Trade* 1994 (GATT 1994) is a multilateral treaty subscribed to by 126 member governments, including the United States.[2] It consists of the original 1947 GATT, numerous multilateral agreements negotiated since 1947, the Uruguay Round Agreements, and the agreement establishing the *World Trade Organization* (WTO). On January 1, 1995, the WTO took over responsibility for policing the objectives of the former GATT organization. Since 1947 and the end of the World War II era, the goal of the GATT has been to liberalize world trade and make it secure for furthering economic growth and human development. The current round of WTO negotiations began in Doha, Qatar, in 2001. As the talks continued in Cancun in 2003, the developed countries and developing countries divided on key issues such as agricultural subsidies. The Doha Round continues in an effort to meet the WTO's objectives of liberalizing world trade.

The GATT is based on the fundamental principles of (1) trade without discrimination and (2) protection through tariffs. The principle of trade without discrimination is embodied in its **most-favored-nation clause**. In treaties between countries, a most-favored-nation clause is one whereby any privilege subsequently granted to a third country in relation to a given treaty subject is extended to the other party to the treaty. In the application and administration of import and export duties and charges under the GATT most-favored-nation clause, all member countries grant each other equal treatment. Thus, no country gives special trading advantages to another. All member countries are equal and share the benefits of any moves toward lower trade barriers. Exceptions to this basic rule are allowed in certain special

---

[2] Russia has applied to join the GATT and is in the final phase of accession to the World Trade Organization. However, to attain this goal, it is widely accepted that Russia will have to provide meaningful market access to member countries in goods and services and have a solid legal and administrative framework that will guarantee the implementation of contractual commitments.

circumstances involving regional trading arrangements, such as the European Union (EU) and the North American Free Trade Agreement (NAFTA). Special preferences are also granted to developing countries. The second basic principle is protection for domestic industry, which should be extended essentially through a tariff, not through other commercial measures. The aim of this rule is to make the extent of protection clear and to make competition possible.

The WTO provides a **Dispute Settlement Body (DSB)** to enable member countries to resolve trade disputes rather than engage in unilateral trade sanctions or a trade war. The DSB appoints panels to hear disputes concerning allegations of GATT agreement violations, and it adopts (or rejects) the panels' decisions. If a GATT agreement violation is found and not removed by the offending country, trade sanctions authorized by a panel may be imposed on that country in an amount equal to the economic injury caused by the violation.

(B) CISG. The *United Nations Convention on Contracts for the International Sale of Goods* (CISG or convention) sets forth uniform rules to govern international sales contracts. National law, however, is sometimes required to fill gaps in areas not covered by the CISG. The CISG became effective on January 1, 1988, between the United States and the 60 other nations that had approved it.[3] The provisions of the CISG have been strongly influenced by Article 2 of the UCC.

However, as set forth in Chapter 23 on sales, several distinct differences exist between the convention and the UCC. Excluded from the coverage of the convention under Article 2 are the sale of goods for personal, family, or household uses and the sale of watercraft, aircraft, natural gas, or electricity; letters of credit; and auctions and securities.[4] The CISG is often viewed by foreign entities as a neutral body of law, the utilization of which can be a positive factor in successfully concluding negotiations of a contract. The parties to an international commercial contract may opt out of the convention. However, absent an express "opt-out provision," the CISG is controlling and preempts all state actions.

(C) UNCTAD. The *United Nations Conference on Trade and Development* (UNCTAD) represents the interests of the less developed countries. Its prime objective is the achievement of an international redistribution of income through trade. Through UNCTAD pressure, the developed countries agreed to a system of preferences, with quota limits, for manufactured imports from the developing countries.

(D) EU. The *European Economic Community* (EEC) was established in 1958 by the Treaty of Rome to remove trade and economic barriers between member countries and to unify their economic policies. It changed its name and became the *European Union* (EU) after the Treaty of Maastricht was ratified on November 1, 1993. The Treaty of Rome containing the governing principles of this regional trading group was signed by the original six nations of Belgium, France, West Germany, Italy, Luxembourg, and the Netherlands. Membership expanded by the entry of Denmark, Ireland, and Great Britain in 1973; Greece in 1981; Spain and Portugal in 1986; and Austria, Sweden, and Finland in 1995. Ten countries joined the EU in 2004: Cyprus, the Czech Republic, Estonia, Hungary, Latvia, Lithuania, Malta, Poland, Slovakia, and Slovenia. Bulgaria, Romania, Croatia, and Turkey expect to join in the coming years.

Four main institutions make up the formal structure of the EU. The first, the European Council, consists of the heads of state of the member countries. The council sets broad policy guidelines for the EU. The second, the European Commission, implements decisions of the council and initiates actions against individuals, companies, or member states that violate EU law. The third, the European Parliament, has an advisory legislative role with limited veto powers. The fourth, the European Court of Justice (ECJ) and the lower Court of First Instance make up the judicial arm of the EU. The courts of member states may refer cases involving questions on the EU treaty to these courts.

The Single European Act eliminated internal barriers to the free movement of goods, persons, services,

[3] 52 Fed Reg 6262.
[4] CISG art. 2(a)–(f).

and capital between EU countries. The Treaty on European Union, signed in Maastricht, Netherlands (the Maastricht Treaty), amended the Treaty of Rome with a focus on monetary and political union. It set goals for the EU of (1) single monetary and fiscal policies, (2) common foreign and /xample of the interrelationship of the msecurity policies, and (3) cooperation in justice and home affairs.

(E) **NAFTA.** The *North American Free Trade Agreement* (NAFTA) is an agreement between Mexico, Canada, and the United States, effective January 1, 1994, that included Mexico in the arrangements previously initiated under the United States–Canada Free Trade Agreement of 1989. NAFTA eliminates all tariffs among the three countries over a 15-year period. Side agreements exist to prevent the exploitation of Mexico's lower environmental and labor standards.

Products are qualified for NAFTA tariff preferences only if they originate in one or more of the three member countries.

Documentation is required in a NAFTA *Certificate of Origin,* except for certain "low-value" items for which the statement of North American origin is recorded on an invoice. NAFTA ensures nondiscriminatory and open markets for a wide range of services and lowers barriers to U.S. investments in both Canada and Mexico. Although NAFTA does not create a common labor market, as does the European Union, the agreement provides temporary access for businesspersons across borders. The *DaimlerChrysler* decision is an example of the interrelationship of the manufacturing and assembly process between the U.S. and Mexico and the tariff preferences when the finished goods are shipped back to the U.S. for sale.

DaimlerChrysler Corp. v U.S., 361 F3d 1378 (Fed Cir 2004)

A Reason to Assemble Cars in Mexico

FACTS: DaimlerChrysler assembles trucks in Mexico utilizing sheet metal components manufactured in the United States. The sheet metal is subject to painting in Mexico, consisting of primer coats followed by a color-treated coat and a clear coat, referred to as the top coats. After the assembly is completed, the trucks are shipped to and sold in the United States. The U.S. Customs Service believes the top coats are subject to duty payments. DaimlerChrysler asserts that the entire painting process is duty free. Subheading 9802.00.80 of the Harmonized Tariffs Schedule of the U.S. (HTSUS) provides duty-free treatment for:

> Articles . . . assembled abroad in whole or in part of fabricated components, the product of the United States, which (a) were exported in condition ready for assembly without further fabrication, (b) have not lost their physical identity in such articles by change in form, shape or otherwise, and (c) have not been advanced in value or improved in condition abroad except by being assembled and except by operations incidental to the assembly process such as cleaning, lubricating and painting. [emphasis added by the court]

From a judgment by the Court of International Trade in favor of the United States, DaimlerChrysler appealed.

Judicial Opinion

PROST, C. J. . . .[T]he United States Supreme Court addressed the application and interpretation of HTSUS 9802.00.80 in *Haggar I*. . . . In answering that question in the affirmative, the Court specifically considered HTSUS 9802.00.80 and noted that it established two different categories of operations incidental to assembly—one specific and unambiguous and the other general and ambiguous. "The statute under which respondent claims an exemption gives direction not only by stating a general policy (to grant the partial exemption where only assembly and incidental operations were abroad) but also by determining some specifics of the policy (finding that painting, for example, is incidental to assembly)." *Haggar I*, 526 U.S. at 393. . .

On appeal, DaimlerChrysler primarily argues that the Supreme Court's analysis in *Haggar I* provides that painting, without limitation, is an operation incidental to assembly. By using the term "painting" generally to describe a category of incidental operations, DaimlerChrysler argues, Congress unambiguously intended to include all painting, regardless of purpose. Because Customs' regulation regarding painting therefore conflicts with the clear statutory language, DaimlerChrysler continues, the Court of International Trade erred as

Continued

a matter of law in applying this regulation so as to deny DaimlerChrysler a partial duty exemption . . .

The government counters that the statute cannot be read to cover all painting, only painting incidental to assembly. It argues that DaimlerChrysler reads too much into the Supreme Court's statements regarding painting in *Haggar I*, which are simply dicta. . . .

We agree with DaimlerChrysler that the Supreme Court in *Haggar I* determined generally that painting is incidental to the assembly process. In order to qualify for the duty exemption, subheading 9802.00.80 requires that articles not be "advanced in value or improved in condition abroad except by being assembled and except by operations incidental to the assembly process such as cleaning, lubricating and *painting.*" HTSUS 9802.00.80 (emphasis added). For purposes of interpreting subheading 9802.00.80, the Court in *Haggar I* found that it established both an unambiguous category and an ambiguous category of operations incidental to assembly. As noted, subheading 9802.00.80 "determin[es] some specifics of the policy (finding that *painting*, for example, *is*

incidental to assembly)." *Haggar I*, 526 U.S. at 393, 119 S.Ct. 1392 (emphases added). Moreover, the Court concluded that subheading 9802.00.80 is "ambiguous in that the agency must use its discretion to determine how best to implement the policy *in those cases not covered by the statute's specific terms.*" *Id.* (emphasis added). . . .

. . . Because subheading 9802.00.80 unambiguously covers painting operations broadly, DaimlerChrysler's entire painting process, including the application of the tops coats, qualifies for the partial duty exemption. . . .

[Reversed]

QUESTIONS

1. What is the question at issue in this case?

2. How did the Court of Appeals decide the case?

3. Discuss the advantages and disadvantages regarding the U.S. economy and employment issues regarding USTSUS 9802.00.80.

(F) REGIONAL TRADING GROUPS OF DEVELOPING COUNTRIES. In recent years, numerous trading arrangements between groups of developing countries have been established.

(G) IMF—WORLD BANK. The *International Monetary Fund* (IMF) was created after World War II by a group of nations meeting in Bretton Woods, New Hampshire. The Articles of Agreement of the IMF state that its purpose is "to facilitate the expansion and balanced growth of international trade" and to "shorten the duration and lessen the disequilibrium in the international balance of payments of members." The IMF helps to achieve such purposes by administering a complex lending system. A country can borrow money from other IMF members or from the IMF by means of **special drawing rights (SDRs)** sufficient to permit that country to maintain the stability of its currency's relationship to other world currencies. The Bretton Woods conference also set up the *International Bank for Reconstruction and Development* (World Bank) to facilitate the lending of money by capital surplus countries—such as the United States—to countries needing economic help and wanting foreign investments after World War II.

(H) OPEC. The *Organization of Petroleum Exporting Countries* (OPEC) is a producer cartel or combination. One of its main goals was to raise the taxes and royalties earned from crude oil production. Another major goal was to take control over production and exploration from the major oil companies. Its early success in attaining these goals led other nations that export raw materials to form similar cartels. **For Example,** copper and bauxite- producing nations have formed **cartels.**

3. Forms of Business Organizations

The decision to participate in international business transactions and the extent of that participation depend on the financial position of the individual firm, production and marketing factors, and tax and legal considerations. There are a number of forms of business organizations for doing business abroad.

(A) EXPORT SALES. A direct sale to customers in a foreign country is an **export sale**. A U.S. firm engaged in export selling is not present in the foreign country in such an arrangement. The export is subject to a tariff by the foreign country, but the exporting firm is not subject to local taxation by the importing country.

(B) AGENCY REQUIREMENTS. A U.S. manufacturer may decide to make a limited entry into international business by appointing an agent to represent it in a foreign market. An **agent** is a person or firm with authority to make contracts on behalf of another—the **principal**. The agent will receive commission income for sales made on behalf of the U.S. principal. The appointment of a foreign agent commonly constitutes "doing business" in that country and subjects the U.S. firm to local taxation.

(C) FOREIGN DISTRIBUTORSHIPS. A **distributor** takes title to goods and bears the financial and commercial risks for the subsequent sale. To avoid making a major financial investment, a U.S. firm may decide to appoint a foreign distributor. A U.S. firm may also appoint a foreign distributor to avoid managing a foreign operation with its complicated local business, legal, and labor conditions. Care is required in designing an exclusive distributorship for an EU country lest it would violate EU antitrust laws.

(D) LICENSING. U.S. firms may select licensing as a means of doing business in other countries. **Licensing** involves the transfer of technology rights in a product so that it may be produced by a different business organization in a foreign country in exchange for royalties and other payments as agreed. The technology being licensed may fall within the internationally recognized categories of patents, trademarks, and "know-how" (trade secrets and unpatented manufacturing processes outside the public domain). These intellectual property rights, which are legally protectable, may be licensed separately or incorporated into a single, comprehensive licensing contract. **Franchising**, which involves granting permission to use a trademark, trade name, or copyright under specified conditions, is a form of licensing that is now very common in international business.

(E) WHOLLY OWNED SUBSIDIARIES. A firm seeking to maintain control over its own operations, including the protection of its own technological expertise, may choose to do business abroad through a wholly owned subsidiary. In Europe the most common choice of

foreign business organization, similar to the U.S. corporate form of business organization, is called the *société anonyme* (S.A.). In German-speaking countries, this form is called *Aktiengesellschaft* (A.G.). Small and medium-sized companies in Europe now utilize a newly created form of business organization called the limited liability company (*Gesellschaft mit beschränkter Haftung,* or "GmbH" in Germany; *Società a responsabilità limitata,* or "S.r.l." in Spain). It is less complicated to form but is restrictive for accessing public capital markets.

A corporation doing business in more than one country poses many taxation problems for the governments in those countries where the firm does business. The United States has established tax treaties with many countries granting corporations relief from double taxation. Credit is normally given by the United States to U.S. corporations for taxes paid to foreign governments.

There is a potential for tax evasion by U.S. corporations from their selling goods to their overseas subsidiaries. Corporations could sell goods at less than the fair market value to avoid a U.S. tax on the full profit for such sales. By allowing the foreign subsidiaries located in countries with lower tax rates to make higher profits, a company as a whole would minimize its taxes. Section 482 of the Internal Revenue Code (IRC), however, allows the Internal Revenue Service (IRS) to reallocate the income between the parent and its foreign subsidiary. The parent corporation is insulated from such a reallocation if it can show, based on independent transactions with unrelated parties, that its charges were at arm's length.[5]

(F) JOINT VENTURES. A U.S. manufacturer and a foreign entity may form a **joint venture**, whereby the two firms agree to perform different functions for a common result. The responsibilities and liabilities of such operations are governed by contract. **For Example,** Hughes Aircraft Co. formed a joint venture with two Japanese firms, C. Itoh & Co. and Mitsui, and successfully bid on a telecommunications space satellite system for the Japanese government.

China has two forms of joint ventures: a *contract joint venture,* which allows the parties to operate as separate entities governed by a contract, and an *equity*

---

[5] *Bausch & Lomb Inc. v Commissioner,* 933 F2d 1084 (2d Cir 1991).

joint venture whereby each party owns a portion of the business. Such an arrangement is governed by the Chinese Foreign Equity Joint Venture Law. This law requires a Chinese limited liability company to be formed and requires the foreign participant to contribute at least 25 percent of the firm's capital.

B. Governmental Regulation

Nations regulate trade to protect the economic interests of their citizens or to protect themselves in international relations and transactions.

4. Export Regulations

For reasons of national security, foreign policy, or short supply of domestic products, the United States controls the export of goods and technology. The Export Administration Act[6] imposes export controls on goods and technical data from the U.S. Since April 2002, the Bureau of Industry and Security (BIS) of the Department of Commerce has issued Export Administration Regulations to enforce export controls.

Export Administration Regulations effective in 1996 simplify the process and enhance export trade by U.S. citizens.[7] The new regulations eliminate the former system of general and validated licenses under which every export required a license. Under the 1996 *Simplification Regulations,* no license is required unless the regulations affirmatively require a license. However, when no license is required, the exporter must fill out a Shipper's Export Declaration and attach it to the bill of lading for shipment with the goods being exported.

(A) Determining If a License Is Needed. To determine whether a product requires a BIS export license, the exporter should review the Commerce Control List (CCL) to see whether the product to be exported is listed. Listed products have Export Control Classification Numbers (ECCNs) that conform to those used by the EU. If a product is on the list, the ECCN code will provide the reason for control, such as national

security, missile technology, nuclear nonproliferation, chemical and/or biological weapons, antiterrorism, crime control, short supply, or UN sanctions.[8] The exporter should then consult the Commerce Country Chart to *determine whether* a license is needed to send the product to its proposed destination. **For Example,** domestic crude petroleum products and western red cedar are on the Commerce Control List because of the "short supply" of these products. As a result, they are controlled to all destinations, and no reference to the Commerce Country Chart is necessary.

(B) Sanctions. Export licenses are required for the export of certain high-technology and military products. a company intending to ship "maraging 350 steel" to a user in Pakistan would find by checking the CCL and the ECCN code for the product that such steel is used in making high-technology products and has nuclear applications. Thus, an export license would be required. Because Pakistan is a nonsignatory nation of the Nuclear Non-Proliferation Treaty, the Department of Commerce would be expected to deny a license application for the use of this steel in a nuclear plant. However, a license to export this steel for the manufacture of high-speed turbines or compressors might be approved. The prospective purchaser must complete a "Statement of Ultimate Consignee and Purchaser" form with the application for an export license. The prospective purchaser must identify the "end use" for the steel and indicate where the purchaser is located and the location in Pakistan where a U.S. embassy official can make an on-site inspection of the product's use. Falsification of the information in the license application process is a criminal offense. Thus, if the exporter of maraging 350 steel asserted that it was to be used in manufacturing high-speed turbines when in fact the exporter knew it was being purchased for use in a nuclear facility, the exporter would be guilty of a criminal offense.[9]

Civil charges may also be brought against U.S. manufacturers who fail to obtain an export license for foreign sales of civilian items that contain any components that have military applications under the

---

[6] The Export Administration Act of 1979 expired in August 1994 and was extended by Executive Orders signed by Presidents Clinton and G. W. Bush. The EAA is now extended annually by presidential notice.

[7] Simplification of Export Regulations, 61 Fed Reg 12,714 (1996).

[8] *Id.*

[9] See *United States v Perez*, 871 F2d 310 (3d Cir 1989), on the criminal application of the Export Administration Regulations to an individual who stated a false end use for maraging 350 steel on his export application to ship this steel to Pakistan.

Arms Control Export Act. For example. between 2000 and 2003, Boeing Co. shipped overseas 94 commercial jets that carried a gyrochip used as a backup system in determining a plane's orientation in the air. This 2-ounce chip that costs less than $2,000 also has military applications and can be used to stabilize and steer guided missiles. Boeing is asserted to have made false statements on shipping documents to get around the export restrictions. Boeing argued that the State Department is without legal authority to regulate its civilian rather than military items. However, Boeing agreed to pay a $15 million fine for the violations.[10]

(c) Expert Assistance. The Department of Commerce's Exporter Assistance Staff provides assistance to exporters needing help in determining whether an export license is needed.[11] Licensed foreign-**freight forwarders** are in the business of handling the exporting of goods to foreign destinations. They are experts on U.S. Department of Commerce export license requirements. Licensed foreign-freight forwarders can attend to all of the essential arrangements required to transport a shipment of goods from the exporter's warehouse to the overseas buyer's specified port and inland destination. They are well versed in all aspects of ocean, air, and inland transportation as well as banking, marine insurance, and other services relating to exporting.

5. Protection of Intellectual Property Rights

U.S. laws protect **intellectual property rights**, which consist of trademarks, copyrights, and patents.

(a) Counterfeit Goods. The importation of counterfeit compact discs, tapes, computer software, and movies into the United States violates U.S. copyright laws. Importing goods, such as athletic shoes, jeans, or watches, bearing counterfeits of U.S. companies' registered trademarks violates the Lanham Act. Importing machines or devices that infringe on U.S. patents violates U.S. patent laws. A full range of remedies is available to U.S. firms under U.S. laws. Possible remedies include injunctive relief, seizure and destruction of counterfeit goods that are found in the United States, damages, and attorney fees. U.S. firms injured by counterfeit trademarks may recover triple damages from the counterfeiters.[12]

Intellectual property rights are also protected by international treaties, such as the Berne Convention, which protects copyrights; the Patent Cooperation Treaty; and the Madrid System of International Registration of Marks (the Madrid Protocol), a treaty providing for the international registration of marks applicable to more than 60 signatory countries, including the United States as of November 2003.[13]

(b) Gray Market Goods. A U.S. trademark holder may license a foreign business to use its trademark overseas. If a third party imports these foreign-made goods into the United States to compete against the U.S. manufacturer's goods, the foreign-made goods are called **gray market goods**. The Tariff Act of 1930 prevents importation of foreign-made goods bearing a U.S. registered trademark owned by a U.S. firm unless the U.S. trademark owner gives written consent.[14] The Lanham Act may also be used to exclude gray market goods.[15]

A gray market situation also arises when foreign products made by affiliates of U.S. companies have trademarks identical to U.S. trademarks but the foreign products are physically different from the U.S. products.

In the *Lever Brothers* case, the U.S. trademark holder sought to exclude the importation of the foreign-made goods by third parties.

---

[10] Associated Press, "Boeing to Pay $15 Million Fine for Export of Military Technology," *The Boston Globe*, April 10, 2006, E3.

[11] Exporter Assistance Staff, U.S. Department of Commerce, Washington, DC 20230.

[12] 15 USC § 1117(b); *Nintendo of America v NTDEC*, 822 F Supp 1462 (D Ariz 1993).

[13] The Agreement on Trade-Related Aspects of Intellectual Property (TRIPS) is a WTO agreement that requires WTO members to adhere to certain treaties and guidelines in respecting copyright, trademark, and patent rights. Enforcement of such rights, however, varies, depending on national law.

[14] 19 USC § 1526(1). The Copyright Act of 1976 may also apply to gray market goods. One provision of this act gives the copyright holder exclusive right to distribute copies of the copyrighted work. Still another section states that once a copyright owner sells an authorized copy of the work, subsequent owners may do what they like with it. The gray market issue occurs when U.S. manufacturers sell their products overseas at deep discounts, and other firms reimport the products back to the United States for resale. The Supreme Court held that a copyrighted label on the products would not protect a U.S. manufacturer's claim of unauthorized importation because the copyright owner's rights cease upon the original sale to the overseas buyer. *Quality King v L'Anza Research*, 523 US 135 (1998).

[15] *Bourdeau Bros. v International Trade Commission*, 444 F3d 1314 (Fed Cir 2006).

Lever Brothers Co. v U.S., 796 F Supp 1 (DC 1992)

Barring Imported Soap!

FACTS: Lever Brothers (Lever U.S.) manufactures a soap under the trademark Shield and a dishwashing liquid under the trademark Sunlight for sale in the United States. A British affiliate, Lever U.K., also makes products using the marks Shield and Sunlight. Because of different tastes of U.S. and U.K. consumers, the products have physical differences. Third parties imported these U.K. products into the United States. The Lanham Act prohibits "copying or simulating a trademark." The U.S. Customs Service refused to bar these foreign products because a markholder cannot "copy or simulate" its own trademark. That is, Lever U.K. could not copy the marks of its affiliated company, Lever U.S. Lever U.S. sought an injunction against the U.S. Customs Service, requiring it to bar these foreign products.

Judicial Opinion

GREENE, D. J. . . . Plaintiff, Lever U.S., is a wholly owned subsidiary of Unilever U.S., Inc., which in turn is wholly owned by Unilever N.V. A British company, Lever U.K., manufactures Shield and Sunlight, and holds the trademark for those words in the United Kingdom. Lever U.K. is a subsidiary of Unilever PLC. The two corporate parents, Unilever N.V. and Unilever PLC, are not under common ownership but are affiliated with one another and are under common control. . . .

The Shield logos on the American and the British versions of the soap are virtually identical. The American product, however, is designed to produce more lather and contains an anti-bacteria agent absent from the British version. The two soaps are also perfumed and colored differently.

The two versions of Sunlight dishwashing detergent have similar lettering but the packaging is different. The detergents themselves are also quite different. The British product is designed for water with a mineral content higher than is generally found in the United States. It therefore does not perform as well as the American Sunlight in the "soft-water" typical of this country. Thus the trademarks of the American and British versions of the two products are identical but the products are physically different.

Third parties have imported the British versions of the products into the United States without the consent of Lever U.S. or Lever U.K. The outward similarities and substantive differences of the American and British products created confusion and dissatisfaction on the part of American consumers who purchased the British products in the belief that they were purchasing the American version or not realizing that there were two different products under the same name.

This case focuses on interpretation of section 42 of the Lanham Act which states that:

> no article of imported merchandise which shall copy or simulate the name of . . . any domestic manufacturer, . . . or which shall copy or simulate a trademark registered in accordance with the provisions of this chapter or shall bear a name or mark calculated to induce the public to believe that the article is manufactured in the United States, . . . shall be admitted to entry at any customhouse of the United States. . . .
>
> *15 U.S.C. § 1124 (1982) (emphasis added).*

Lever U.S. argues that where a foreign company produces goods that bear the same trademark as a U.S. mark holder but that are materially, physically different, the foreign product copies or simulates the domestic trademark within the meaning of section 42 even where the foreign manufacturer is affiliated with the domestic markholder. Defendants argue that a markholder cannot infringe, i.e., "copy or simulate," its own trademark, and that therefore the affiliation of Lever U.S. with Lever U.K. makes all the difference, placing this case outside the scope of section 42.

The Customs Service has permitted the British versions of the two products to enter the United States under its affiliate exception. Under the Customs Service regulation, foreign goods that bear a trademark identical to one owned and recorded by a United States corporation will not be seized by Customs, notwithstanding section 42 of the statute, if "the foreign and domestic trademark or trade name owners are parent and subsidiary companies or are otherwise subject to common ownership or control." 19 C.F.R. 133 (c) (2) (1988).

The Court of Appeals has come to the tentative conclusion that the Lanham Act bars "foreign goods bearing a trademark identical to a valid U.S. trademark but which are physically different, regardless of the trademarks' genuine character abroad or affiliation between the producing firms." *Lever Bros. Co. v. United States* . . . 877 F.2d at 111. However, as indicated, the appellate court remanded the case for consideration of the legislative history and the administrative practice.

Legislative History

The Court of Appeals regarded its reading of the language of section 42 as being "the natural, virtually inevitable" interpretation. . . . It is well established that where the statute

Continued

is clear on its face and the legislative intent is expressed in "reasonably plain terms" by the text, the statutory language controls. . . .

Representative Fritz G. Lanham, the sponsor of the Act, explained that one purpose of the statute was "to protect the public so that it may be confident that, in purchasing a product bearing a particular trademark, which it favorably knows, it will get the product which it asks for and wants to get." H. R. Rep. No. 219 at 2, 79th Cong., 1st Sess. (February 26, 1945) U.S. Code Cong. Serv. 1946, p.1274. In this case, the outward similarities and physical differences between the British and American versions of Shield and Sunlight have already created consumer confusion and dissatisfaction, and they would be likely to do so again in the future. As the House Report on the Lanham Act stated, "Trademarks encourage the maintenance of quality by securing to the producer the benefit of the good reputation which excellence creates." H. R. No. 219 at 3, 1946 U.S. Code Cong. Serv. at 1274, 1275. Thus, the legislative goals of trademark law generally and of the Lanham Act specifically are served by the barring of goods such as those of the British company. . . .

Neither the legislative history of the statute nor the administrative practice of the Customs Service clearly contradicts the plain meaning of section 42. The Court therefore concludes that section 42 of the Lanham Act prohibits the importation of foreign goods that bear a trademark identical to a valid United States trademark but which are physically different, regardless of the validity of the foreign trademark or the existence of an affiliation between the U.S. and foreign markholders.

Plaintiff's motion for summary judgment will be granted and defendants' motion will be denied. . . .

[Judgment for Lever U.S.]

QUESTIONS

1. Why did Lever U.S. want to exclude the two British products?

2. What was the contention of the U.S. Customs Service?

3. Are the legislative goals of the Lanham Act, as expressed by Representative Lanham, served by barring the British soap products?

6. Antitrust

Antitrust laws exist in the United States to protect the U.S. consumer by ensuring the benefits of competitive products from foreign competitors as well as domestic competitors. Competitors' agreements designed to raise the price of imports or to exclude imports from our domestic markets in exchange for not competing in other countries are restraints of trade in violation of our antitrust laws.[16]

The antitrust laws also exist to protect U.S. export and investment opportunities against privately imposed restrictions, whereby a group of competitors seeks to exclude another competitor from a particular foreign market. Antitrust laws exist in other countries where U.S. firms compete. These laws are usually directed not at breaking up cartels to further competition but at regulating them in the national interest.

(A) JURISDICTION. In U.S. courts, the U.S. antitrust laws have a broad extraterritorial reach. Our antitrust laws must be reconciled with the rights of other interested countries as embodied in international law.

The Effects Doctrine

Judge Learned Hand's decision in *United States v Alcoa* established the **effects doctrine**.[17] Under this doctrine, U.S. courts assume jurisdiction and apply the antitrust laws to conduct outside of the United States where the activity of the business firms outside the United States has a direct and substantial effect on U.S. commerce. This basic rule has been modified to

[16] *United States v Nippon Paper Industries Co. Ltd.*, 64 F Supp 2d 173 (1999).
[17] 148 F2d 416 (2d Cir 1945).

require that the effect on U.S. commerce also be foreseeable.

The Jurisdictional Rule of Reason

The jurisdictional rule of reason applies when conduct taking place outside the United States affects U.S. commerce but a foreign state also has a significant interest in regulating the conduct in question. The **jurisdictional rule of reason** balances the vital interests, including laws and policies, of the United States with those of the foreign country involved. This rule of reason is based on **comity**, a principle of international law, that means that the laws of all nations deserve the respect legitimately demanded by equal participants in international affairs.

(B) DEFENSES. Three defenses are commonly raised to the extraterritorial application of U.S. antitrust laws. These defenses are also commonly raised to attack jurisdiction in other legal actions involving international law.

Act-of-State Doctrine

By the **act-of-state doctrine**, every sovereign state is bound to respect the independence of every other sovereign state, and the courts of one country will not sit in judgment of another government's acts done within its own territory.[18] The act-of-state doctrine is based on the judiciary's concern over its possible interference with the conduct of foreign relations. Such matters are considered to be political, not judicial, questions.

The Sovereign Compliance Doctrine

The **sovereign compliance doctrine** allows a defendant to raise as an affirmative defense to an antitrust action the fact that the defendant's actions were compelled by a foreign state. To establish this defense, compulsion by the foreign government is required. The Japanese government uses informal and formal

contacts within an industry to establish a consensus on a desired course of action. Such governmental action is not a defense for a U.S. firm, however, because the activity in question is not compulsory.

The Sovereign Immunity Doctrine

The **sovereign immunity doctrine** states that a foreign sovereign generally cannot be sued unless an exception to the Foreign Sovereign Immunities Act of 1976 applies.[19] The most important exception covers the commercial conduct of a foreign state.[20] **For Example,** receivers for various insurance companies brought suit against the Vatican City State, contending that the Vatican's conduct fell within the commercial activity exception to the FSIA. Martin Frankel had engaged in a massive insurance fraud scheme, using front organizations to acquire and loot several insurance agencies. Masquerading as "David Rose," a philanthropist, he met Monsignor Emilio Cologiovani and convinced him to create a Vatican-affiliated entity, the St. Francis of Assisi Foundation (SFAF), which was used as part of Frankel's scam. The Court of Appeals held, however, that Cologiovani, acting with only apparent authority of the state, could not trigger the commercial activity doctrine.[21]

(C) LEGISLATION. In response to business uncertainty as to when the antitrust laws apply to international transactions, Congress passed the Foreign Trade Antitrust Improvements Act of 1982. This act, in essence, codified the effects doctrine. The act requires a direct, substantial, and reasonably foreseeable effect on U.S. domestic commerce or exports by U.S. residents before business conduct abroad may come within the purview of U.S. antitrust laws.[22]

(D) FOREIGN ANTITRUST LAWS. Attitudes in different countries vary toward cartels and business combinations. Because of this, antitrust laws vary in content and application. **For Example,** Japan has stressed consumer protection against such practices as

---

[18] *Underhill v Hernandez,* 108 US 250, 252 (1897).
[19] See *Verlinden B.V. v Central Bank of Nigeria,* 461 US 574 (1983).
[20] See *Dole Food Co. v Patrickson,* 538 US 468 (2003), for a limited discussion of when a foreign state can assert a defense of sovereign immunity under the Foreign Sovereign Immunities Act of 1976 (FSIA). The FSIA allows certain foreign-state commercial entities not entitled to sovereign immunity to have the merits of a case heard in federal court. The U.S. Supreme Court held in the *Dole Food* case that a foreign state must itself own a majority of the shares of a corporation if the corporation is to be deemed an instrumentality of the state under the FSIA, and the instrumentality status is determined at the time of the filing of the complaint.
[21] *Dale v Cologiovani,* 443 F3d 425 (5th Cir 2006).
[22] PL 97-290, 96 Stat 1233, 15 USC § 6(a).

price-fixing and false advertising. However, with regard to mergers, stock ownership, and agreements among companies to control production, Japanese law is much less restrictive than U.S. law.

Europe is a major market for U.S. products, services, and investments. U.S. firms doing business in Europe are subject to the competition laws of the EU.[23] The Treaty of Rome uses the term *competition* rather than *antitrust*. Articles 85 and 86 of the Treaty of Rome set forth the basic regulation on business behavior in the EU.[24] Article 85(1) expressly prohibits agreements and concerted practices that

1. even indirectly fix prices of purchases or sales or fix any other trading conditions;

2. limit or control production, markets, technical development, or investment;

3. share markets or sources of supply;

4. apply unequal terms to parties furnishing equivalent considerations, thereby placing one at a competitive disadvantage; or

5. make a contract's formation depend on the acceptance of certain additional obligations that, according to commercial usage, have no connection with the subject of such contracts.

Article 85(3) allows for an individual exemption if the agreement meets certain conditions, such as improving the production or distribution of goods, promoting technical or economic progress, and reserving to consumers a fair share of the resulting economic benefits.

Article 86 provides that it is unlawful for one or more enterprises having a dominant market position within at least a substantial part of the EU to take improper advantage of such a position if trade between the member states may be affected. **For Example,** the European Commission fined computer chip maker Intel $1.45 billion for abusing its dominance in the computer chip market by offering rebates which were conditioned on buying less of a rival's products, or not buying them at all. Intel disagrees with the decision and will appeal the matter to the Court of First Instance.[25]

7. Securities and Tax Fraud Regulation in an International Environment

Illegal conduct in the U.S. securities markets, whether this conduct is initiated in the United States or abroad, threatens the vital economic interests of the United States. Investigation and litigation concerning possible violations of the U.S. securities laws often have an extraterritorial effect. Conflicts with the laws of foreign countries may occur.

(A) JURISDICTION. U.S. district courts have jurisdiction over violations of the antifraud provisions of the Securities Exchange Act of 1934 when losses occur from sales to Americans living in the United States.[26] U.S. district courts also have jurisdiction when losses occur to Americans living abroad if the acts occurred in the United States. The antifraud provisions do not apply, however, to losses from sales of securities to foreigners outside the United States unless acts within the United States caused the losses.

(B) IMPACT OF FOREIGN SECRECY LAWS IN SEC ENFORCEMENT. **Secrecy laws** are confidentiality laws applied to home-country banks. These laws prohibit the disclosure of business records or the identity of bank customers. **Blocking laws** prohibit the disclosure, copying, inspection, or removal of documents located in the enacting country in compliance with orders from foreign authorities. These laws impede, and sometimes foreclose, the SEC's ability to police its securities markets properly.

The *Banca Della Suizzera* case demonstrates how the SEC, in certain circumstances, can obtain discovery from foreign financial institutions in spite of secrecy laws.

[23] The European Commission is the executive branch of the EU government and performs most of the EU's regulatory work. The Competition Commission oversees antitrust and mergers for the European Commission. New merger regulations took effect on May 1, 2004. The regulations require the Competition Commission to review proposed mergers and prohibit those mergers when the effects may "significantly impede effective competition" (called the *SIEC test*). The U.S. test prohibits mergers when the effect "may substantially lessen competition. . . ." 15 USC § 18 (2005). The wording of the EU and U.S. tests is relatively similar.
[24] See *Osakeyhtio v EEC Commission*, 1988 Common Mkt Rep (CCH) ¶ 14,491 for discussion of the extraterritorial reach of the European Commission.
[25] James Kanter, "Europe Fines Intel $1.45 Billion in Antitrust Case," *New York Times*, **www.nytimes.com/2009/05/14/bussiness/global/14/compete.html**.
[26] *Kauthar Sdn Bhd v Sternberg*, 149 F3d 659 (7th Cir 1998).

SEC v Banca Della Suzzera Italiana, 92 FRD 111 (SDNY 1981)

The Long Reach of the SEC

FACTS: Banca Della Suizzera Italiana (BSI), a Swiss bank with an office in the United States, purchased certain call options and common stock of St. Joe Minerals Corporation (St. Joe), a New York corporation, immediately prior to the announcement on March 11, 1981, of a cash tender offer by Joseph Seagram & Sons Inc. for all St. Joe common stock at $45 per share. On March 11, 1981, when BSI acted, the stock moved sharply higher in price. BSI instructed its broker to close out the purchases of the options and sell most of the shares of stock, resulting in an overnight profit of $2 million. The SEC noticed the undue activity in the options market and initiated suit against BSI. The SEC, through the Departments of State and Justice, and the Swiss government sought without success to learn the identity of BSI's customers involved in the transactions. The SEC believed that the customers had used inside information in violation of the Securities Exchange Act of 1934. The SEC brought a motion to compel disclosure. BSI objected on the ground that it might be subject to criminal liability under Swiss penal and banking laws if it disclosed the requested information.

Judicial Opinion

POLLACK, D. J. . . .BSI claims that it may be subject to criminal liability under Swiss penal and banking law if it discloses the requested information. However, this Court finds the factors in § 40 of the Restatement of Foreign Relations[1] to tip decisively in favor of the SEC. Moreover, it holds BSI to be "in the position of one who deliberately courted legal impediments. . . and who thus cannot now be heard to assert its good faith after this expectation was realized." BSI acted in bad faith. It made deliberate use of Swiss nondisclosure law to evade in a commercial transaction for profit to it, the strictures of American securities law against insider trading. . . .

The first of the § 40 factors is the vital national interest of each of the States. The strength of the United States' interest in enforcing its securities laws to ensure the integrity of its

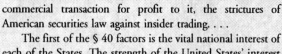

financial markets cannot seriously be doubted. That interest is being continually thwarted by the use of foreign bank accounts. Congress, in enacting legislation on bank record-keeping, expressed its concern over the problem over a decade ago. . . .

The Swiss government, on the other hand, though made expressly aware of the litigation, has expressed no opposition. In response to BSI's lawyers' inquiries, the incumbent Swiss Federal Attorney General . . . said only that a foreign court could not change the rule that disclosure required the consent of the one who imparted the secret and that BSI might thus be subject to prosecution. The Swiss government did not "confiscate" the Bank records to prevent violations of its law. . . .NEITHER THE UNITED STATES NOR THE SWISS GOVERNMENT has suggested that discovery be halted. . . .

The Court of Appeals in *United States v. National City Bank*, 396 F.2d 897 (2d Cir 1968), found the fact that the governments concerned had not intervened of great importance. It observed that "when foreign governments, including Germany, have considered their vital national interests threatened, they have not hesitated to make known their objections. . .to the issuing court." It is true that BSI may be subject to fines and its officers to imprisonment under Swiss law. However, this Court notes that there is some flexibility in the application of that law. Not only may the particular bank involved obtain waivers from its customers to avoid prosecution, but Article 34 of the Swiss Penal Code contains a "State of Necessity" exception that relieves a person of criminal liability for acts committed to protect one's own good, including one's fortune, from an immediate danger if one is not responsible for the danger and one cannot be expected to give up one's good.

Of course, given BSI's active part in the insider trading transactions alleged here, the Swiss government might well conclude—as this Court has—that BSI is responsible for the conflict it is in and that therefore the "State of Necessity"

---

[1] § 40 reads as follows:

§ 40. Limitations on Exercise of Enforcement Jurisdiction. Where two states have jurisdiction to prescribe and enforce rules of law and the rules they may prescribe require inconsistent conduct upon the part of a person, each state is required by international law to consider, in good faith, moderating the exercise of its enforcement jurisdiction, in the light of such factors as

a. vital national interests of each of the states,
b. the extent and the nature of the hardship that inconsistent enforcement actions would impose upon the person,
c. the extent to which the required conduct is to take place in the territory of the other state,
d. the nationality of the person, and
e. the extent to which enforcement by action of either state can reasonably be expected to achieve compliance with the rule prescribed by that state.

Continued

exception should not apply. However, that is certainly no cause for this Court to withhold its sanctions since the dilemma would be a result of BSI's bad faith. A party's good or bad faith is an important factor to consider, and this court finds that BSI, which deposited the proceeds of these transactions in an American bank account in its name and which certainly profited in some measure from the challenged activity, undertook such transactions fully expecting to use foreign law to shield it from the reach of our laws. Such "deliberate courting" of foreign legal impediments will not be countenanced. . . .

It would be a travesty of justice to permit a foreign company to invade American markets, violate American laws if they were indeed violated, withdraw profits and resist accountability for itself and its principals for the illegality by claiming their anonymity under foreign law.. . .

. . . BSI is directed to complete its answers to all of the demands in the SEC's First Interrogatories, pertaining to St. Joe.

[So ordered]

[Authors' Note: Faced with the judge's opinion and the possibility of substantial fines, BSI obtained a waiver of the secrecy laws from its customer and produced the requested information.]

QUESTIONS

1. What are the dominant factors considered by a court when deciding whether to issue a subpoena or discovery order to a foreign bank in a secrecy jurisdiction?

2. Did the court find that the Swiss interest in bank secrecy outweighed the U.S. interest?

3. Did BSI act in good faith?

4. Did the court give significant weight to BSI's potential liability under Swiss law?

The SEC is not limited to litigation when a securities law enforcement investigation runs into secrecy or blocking laws. For example, the SEC may rely on the 1977 Treaty of Mutual Assistance in Criminal Matters between the United States and Switzerland.[27] Although this treaty has served to deter the use of Swiss secrecy laws to conceal fraud in the United States, its benefits for securities enforcement have been limited. It applies only where there is a dual criminality—that is, the conduct involved constitutes a criminal offense under the laws of both the United States and Switzerland.

(c) OFFSHORE TAX EVASION. Switzerland and other countries with histories of banking secrecy have yielded somewhat to United States and EU pressures to help cut down on tax evaders. The U.S. and Switzerland have agreed in an amended tax treaty to increase the amount of tax information they share. Swiss banks have been reluctant to provide client information, asserting that it would violate Swiss privacy laws. For Example, Swiss Bank UBS AG admitted that its bankers and managers referred

U.S. clients to lawyers and accountants who set up secret offshore entities to conceal assets from the IRS, and it agreed to pay $780 million to settle the federal investigation in the U.S. and the Swiss government's investigations. Subsequently the Swiss Financial Markets Supervising Authority ordered UBS to reveal account details to the U.S. authorities for some 250 customers, asserting that "banking secrecy remains intact," while it "doesn't protect tax fraudsters."[28]

8. Barriers to Trade

The most common barrier to the free movement of goods across borders is a tariff. A wide range of nontariff barriers also restricts the free movement of goods, services, and investments. Government export controls used as elements of foreign policy have proven to be a major barrier to trade with certain countries.

(A) TARIFF BARRIERS. A **tariff** is an import or export duty or tax placed on goods as they move into or out

---

[27] 27 UST 2021.
[28] See "The Swiss Bank UBS Is Set to Open Its Secret Files," *New York Times,* **www.nytimes.com/2009/02/19/business/worldbusiness/19ubs.htm**. However, on January 8, 2010 the International Herald Tribune reported that a Swiss court determined that the Authority had exceeded its authority in its order to UBS, and had broken Swiss privacy law.

of a country. It is the most common method used by countries to restrict foreign imports. The tariff raises the total cost, and thus the price, of an imported product in the domestic market. Thus, the price of a domestically produced product not subject to the tariff is more advantageous.

The U.S. Customs and Border Protection Service (Customs) imposes tariffs on imported goods at the port of entry. The merchandise is classified under a tariff schedule, which lists each type of merchandise and the corresponding duty rate (or percentage). Customs also determines the "computed value" of the imported goods under very precise statutory formulas.[29] The total amount of the duty is calculated by applying the duty percentage to the computed value figure.[30] Customs also has authority to investigate fraudulent schemes to avoid or underpay customs duties.[31]

In the *Sabritas* case, an importer challenged Customs' classification of imported taco shells and potato chips.

Sabritas v United States, 998 F Supp 1123 (CIT 1998)

Customs Crunch!

FACTS: Frito-Lay, Inc., owns a Mexican affiliate, Sabritas, S.A. de C.V., and it imports taco shells and *Munchos* potato chips from Mexico to the United States. Customs classified these products as "other bakers' wares" under Section 1905.90.90 of the Tariff Schedule subject to a 10 percent duty rate. Frito-Lay contends before the Court of International Trade that the import of taco shells is properly classified as "bread," which carries duty-free status. It also contends that *Munchos* are properly classified as potato chips and entitled to duty-free treatment.

Judicial Opinion

TSOUCALAS, S. J. . . . The issue of whether an imported article has been classified under an appropriate tariff provision entails a two-step process: (1) ascertaining the proper meaning of specific terms in the tariff provision; and (2) determining whether the article comes within the description of such terms as properly construed. *Sports Graphics, Inc. v. United States*, 24 F.3d 1390, 1391 (Fed.Cir.1994. . . .

[To] determine the common meaning of a tariff term, the Court may utilize standard dictionaries and scientific authorities, as well as its own understanding of the term. The Court may also consider the testimony of credible witnesses as an aid in its understanding, although such testimony is not dispositive.

Taco Shells

Frito-Lay contends its taco shells are not properly classified as other bakers' wares because they are more specifically provided for as bread or, alternatively, as "biscuits and similar baked products" under. . .1905.90.10. Customs disagrees with plaintiff, alleging, mostly through testimonial evidence, that the frying of taco shells necessarily removes them from classification as either bread or biscuits and similar baked products. . . .

An *eo nomine* provision, such as 1905.90.10, includes all forms of the named article, in this case bread. As bread is not specifically defined in the [tariff provision] or in the relevant legislative history, it is necessary for the Court to determine, as a matter of law, the common and commercial meaning of the term bread to decide whether Frito-Lay's taco shells can be classified as such.

Customs maintains that Frito-Lay bases its contention on an intermediate article, the tortilla, and argues that frying baked tortillas substantially transforms them into a different article of commerce such that they are removed from the realm of bread. Indeed, Customs' expert, food scientist Dr. Nicholas Pintauro, defined bread in the following narrow manner:

Bread is a product that is formulated with a cereal grain that's in a flour form, with other ingredients such as shortening, salt, baking powder or a leavening agent and it is prepared as a dough and that dough

---

[29] See Tariff Act of 1930, as amended, 19 USC § 1401a(e).

[30] It is common for importers to utilize customs brokers who research the tariff schedules to see whether a product fits unambiguously under one of the Customs Service's classifications. A broker will also research the classifications given to similar products. It may find that a fax switch may be classified as "other telephonic switching apparatus" at a tariff rate of 8.5 percent or "other telegraphic switching apparatus" with a tariff of 4.7 percent. Obviously, the importer desires to pay the lower rate, and the broker with the assistance of counsel will make a recommendation to the Customs Service for the lower rate, and Customs will make a ruling. The decisions of the Customs Service are published in the *Customs Bulletin*, the official weekly publication of the Customs Service. See *Command Communications v Fritz Cos.*, 36 P3d 182 (Colo App 2001).

[31] *U.S. v Inn Foods, Inc.*, 560 F3d 1338 (Fed Cir 2009).

Continued

has to be treated, which we call kneading so that you could develop the protein that's in the cereal portion of that dough so that the protein is in the form that would encapsulate the gas that's generated by the leavening agent so that you get a rise out of the dough and then at the proper time, in the form of a loaf, that dough is baked.

Tr. 164-65. Dr. Pintauro's definition necessarily precludes any unleavened or fried products from falling within the common and commercial meaning of bread. Nothing could be further from the truth. . . .

First, **Sharon T. Herbst,** *Barron's Cooking Guide: Food Lover's Companion* 49 (1990) (emphasis added), recognizes that a bread may be fried, as it defines bread as a "staple . . . made from flour, water (or other liquid) and usually a LEAVENER [that] can be baked . . . fried or steamed." The Court also deems it exceptionally significant that two recognized bread treatises devote entire chapters to fried breads. *See* **Judith Jones,** *The Book of Bread* (1982) & **Dolores Casela,** *A World of Breads* (1966).

To contend that the common and commercial meaning of bread is limited to baked leavened (or even unleavened) products ignores the reality that flat, fried, usually ethnic breads exist in the United States market and are generally accepted as forms of bread. As Dr. Pintauro noted on cross-examination, "ethnic bread is bread. Period." Tr. 236; *see also* Tr. 132 (testimony that tortillas, of which hard taco shells are a type, are consumed throughout the United States, but primarily in the south and southwest); *Atwood-Stone Co. v. United States* 5 Ct. Cust.App. 472, 474 (CCPA 1914) ("The term 'bread'. . .is broad enough to cover all articles of food made from the flour or meal of grain, whether it will 'raise' or not"). The taco shells at issue, in particular, are not only found in obscure Mexican restaurants, but also on grocery store shelves and in the world's largest Mexican food chain, Taco Bell, which operates outlets across the United States. Tr. 45–46; 132–33.

Contrary to Customs' argument, therefore, the Court finds that the hard, flat, corn-based taco shells at issue are not "bread of de minimis commercial significance" or an "ancient or obscure product" but, rather, articles that are commonly and commercially known as bread in the United States. . . .

Munchos

Frito-Lay contends its *Munchos* should be classified under. . . A2005.20.20 because they are fabricated, as opposed to natural, potato chips, and so, are a type of potato chips. . . .

In opposition, Customs contends *Munchos* are not prepared or preserved potatoes, and so, cannot be classified

under. . .A2005, Customs further points to several physical characteristics that differentiate *Munchos* from natural potato chips, including bulk density, color, texture and flavor. Finally, Customs claims that the process of producing *Munchos*, as well as the ingredient composition and merchandising of *Munchos*, differ greatly from those of potato chips. . . .

Potato chips are consistently defined in food and non-food related sources as snack articles produced from thin slices of whole potatoes that are fried. For instance, *Webster's Third New International Dictionary* at 1774, defines a potato chip as "a thin slice of raw white potato fried crisp in deep fat.". . .

Munchos are composed of several ingredients, including dehydrated potato flakes, corn meal and potato starch, while potato chips are produced entirely from sliced raw whole potatoes. . . .

The physical characteristics of *Munchos* in their final form also set them apart from conventional, natural potato chips. . . .

Upon consideration of the proffered testimonial and documentary evidence and based on the Court's *in camera* inspection of the subject potato crisps, the Court agrees with [Customs] that Munchos are not a form of potato chips and are, therefore, removed from the scope of the . . . provision for potato chips.

Conclusion

Consequently, the Court concludes that Customs properly classified plaintiff's import *Munchos* potato crisps under 1905.90.90. The court also concludes that plaintiff's import taco shells are properly classified as bread under 1905.90.10 and orders Customs to reliquidate these items accordingly.

QUESTIONS

1. Summarize the matter before the court.

2. What decisional process does the court follow in determining whether an imported article is properly classified under the appropriate tariff provision by the Customs Service?

3. Compare Frito-Lay's *Munchos* to its Lay's Potato Chips and Pringles potato chips. Review the ingredients of each product and the merchandising of each product. Should all of these products be subject to the same tax treatment by the Customs Service?

(B) NONTARIFF BARRIERS. Nontariff barriers consist of a wide range of restrictions that inhibit the free movement of goods between countries. An import quota, such as a limitation on the number of automobiles that can be imported into one country from another, is such a barrier. More subtle nontariff barriers exist in all countries. **For Example,** Japan's complex customs procedures resulted in the restriction of the sale of U.S.-made aluminum baseball bats in Japan. The customs procedures required the individual uncrating and "destruction testing" of bats at the ports of entry. Government subsidies are also nontariff barriers to trade.

One U.S. law—the Turtle Law—prohibits the importation of shrimp from countries that allow the harvesting of shrimp with commercial fishing technology that could adversely affect endangered sea turtles. **For Example,** two U.S. importers sought an exemption, representing that their Brazilian supply of shrimp was caught in the wild by vessels using turtle excluder devices (TEDs). Because Brazil had failed to comply with the U.S. Turtle Law by requiring TEDs on its commercial shrimp fleet, even though it had seven years to do so, the exemption was not granted.[32]

(C) EXPORT CONTROLS AS INSTRUMENTS OF FOREIGN POLICY. U.S. export controls have been used as instruments of foreign policy in recent years. **For Example,** the United States has sought to deny goods and technology of strategic or military importance to unfriendly nations. The United States has also denied goods such as grain, technology, and machine parts, to certain countries to protest or to punish activities considered violative of human rights or world peace.

9. Relief Mechanisms for Economic Injury Caused by Foreign Trade

Certain U.S. industries may suffer severe economic injury because of foreign competition. U.S. law provides protection against unfair competition from foreigners' goods and provides economic relief for U.S. industries, communities, firms, and workers adversely affected by import competition. U.S. law also provides certain indirect relief for U.S. exporters and producers who encounter unfair foreign import restrictions.

(A) ANTIDUMPING LAWS AND EXPORT SUBSIDIES. Selling goods in another country at less than their fair value is called **dumping**. The dumping of foreign goods in the United States is prohibited under the Tariff Act of 1930, as amended including the antidumping laws contained in the Uraguay Round Agreement Act of 1994.[33] Proceedings in antidumping cases are conducted by two federal agencies, which separately examine two distinct components. The International Trade Administration (ITA) of the Department of Commerce (commonly referred to in cases as simply "Commerce") investigates whether specified foreign goods are being sold in the United States at less than fair value (LTFV). The International Trade Commission (ITC) conducts proceedings to determine if there is an injury to a domestic industry as a result of such sales. Findings of both LTFV sales and injury must be present before remedial action is taken. Remedial action might include the addition of duties to reflect the difference between the fair value of the goods and the price being charged in the U.S. Commerce and ITC decisions may be appealed to the Court of International Trade. Decisions of this court are reviewable by the U.S. Court of Appeals for the Federal Circuit and then the U.S. Supreme Court.

A settlement may be reached through a suspension agreement, whereby prices are revised to eliminate any LTFV sales and other corrective measures are taken.

American producers have to take the initiative and shoulder the expense of assisting government's enforcement of antidumping laws, and when antidumping laws are violated, producers are entitled to a reward as injured parties.[34]

The 1979 act also applies to subsidy practices by foreign countries. If subsidized goods are sold in the United States at less than their fair value, the goods may be subject to a countervailing duty.

---

[32] *Earth Island Institute v Christopher*, 948 F Supp 1062 (Ct Int'l Trade 1996). See *Turtle Island Restoration Network v Evans*, 284 F3d 1282 (Fed Cir 2002), on the continuing litigation on this topic and the clash between statutory enforcement and political and diplomatic considerations.
[33] 19 USC § 1675b (2000). See *Allegheny Ludlum Corp. v United States*, 287 F3d 1365 (Fed Cir 2002).
[34] The Continued Dumping and Subsidy Offset Act of 2000 (the Byrd Amendment), 19 USC 1679c(a) (2000).

Canada and Mexico may appeal countervailing duty assessments by the United States to an arbitration panel established under NAFTA. The NAFTA panel, however, can determine only whether the U.S. determinations were made in accordance with U.S. law. An appeal can also be made by member states to the WTO Dispute Settlement Body, which can determine whether the United States breached its obligations under the WTO.

(B) RELIEF FROM IMPORT INJURIES. Title II of the Trade Act of 1974[35] provides relief for U.S. industries, communities, firms, and workers when any one or more of them are substantially adversely affected by import competition. The Department of Commerce, the secretary of labor, and the president have roles in determining eligibility. The relief provided may be temporary import relief through the imposition of a duty or quota on the foreign goods. Workers, if eligible, may obtain readjustment allowances, job training, job search allowances, or unemployment compensation.

For Example, trade adjustment assistance, including unemployment compensation and training and relocation allowances, was provided for former employees of Johnson Controls Battery Group plants in Garland, Texas; Bennington, Vermont; and Owosso, Michigan; because surveys of the customers of those plants by the Department of Labor indicated that increased imports of aftermarket batteries, the products produced at these closed plants, caused the shutdowns. Former workers of the closed Louisville battery plant were not provided assistance because this plant produced new car batteries, and the work was shifted to another Johnson Controls plant in the United States.[36]

(C) RETALIATION AND RELIEF AGAINST FOREIGN UNFAIR TRADE RESTRICTIONS. U.S. exporters of agricultural or manufactured goods or of services may encounter unreasonable, unjustifiable, or discriminatory foreign import restrictions. At the same time, producers from the foreign country involved may be benefiting from trade agreement concessions that allow producers from that country access to U.S. markets. Prior trade acts and the Omnibus Trade and Competitiveness Act of 1988 contain broad authority to retaliate against "unreasonable," "unjustifiable," or "discriminatory" acts by a foreign country.[37] The authority to retaliate is commonly referred to as "Section 301 authority." The fear or actuality of the economic sting of Section 301 retaliation often leads offending foreign countries to open their markets to imports. Thus, indirect relief is provided to domestic producers and exporters adversely affected by foreign unfair trade practices.

Enforcement of the act is entrusted to the U.S. trade representative (USTR), who is appointed by the president. Under the 1988 act, mandatory retaliatory action is required if the USTR determines that (1) rights of the United States under a trade agreement are being denied or (2) actions or policies of a foreign country are unjustifiable and a burden or restrict U.S. commerce. The overall thrust of the trade provisions of the 1988 act is to open markets and liberalize trade.

10. Expropriation

A major concern of U.S. businesses that do business abroad is the risk of expropriation of assets by a host government. Firms involved in the extraction of natural resources, banking, communications, or defense-related industries are particularly susceptible to nationalization. Multinational corporations commonly have a staff of full-time political scientists and former Foreign Service officers studying the countries relevant to their operations to monitor and calculate risks of expropriation. Takeovers of U.S.-owned businesses by foreign countries may be motivated by a short-term domestic political advantage or the desire to demonstrate political clout in world politics. Takeovers may also be motivated by long-term considerations associated with planned development of the country's economy.

Treaty commitments, or provisions in other international agreements between the United States and the host country, may serve to narrow expropriation uncertainties. Treaties commonly contain provisions whereby property will not be expropriated except for

---

[35] PL 93-618, 88 Stat 1978, 19 USC §§ 2251, 2298.
[36] 20 F Supp 2d 1288 (Ct Int'l Trade 1998). See also *Former Employees of Merrill Corp. v U.S.*, 387 F Supp 2d 1336 (Ct Int'l Trade 2005).
[37] PL 100-418, 102 Stat 1346, 15 USC § 4727.

public benefit and with the prompt payment of just compensation.

One practical way to mitigate the risk of investment loss as a result of foreign expropriation is to purchase insurance through private companies, such as Lloyd's of London. Commercial insurance is also available against such risks as host governments' arbitrary recall of letters of credit and commercial losses resulting from embargoes.

The Overseas Private Investment Corporation (OPIC) is a U.S. agency under the policy control of the secretary of state. OPIC supports private investments in less developed, friendly countries. OPIC also offers asset protection insurance against risk of loss to plant and equipment as well as loss of deposits in overseas bank accounts to companies that qualify on the basis of the involvement of a "substantial U.S. interest."

11. The Foreign Corrupt Practices Act

There are restrictions on U.S. firms doing business abroad that disallow payments to foreign government officials for getting business from their governments. The Foreign Corrupt Practices Act of 1977 requires strict accounting standards and internal control procedures to prevent the hiding of improper payments to foreign officials. The act prohibits any offers, payments, or gifts to foreign officials—or third parties

who might have influence with foreign officials—to influence a decision on behalf of the firm making the payment. It provides for sanctions of up to $1 million against the company and fines and imprisonment for the employees involved. Moreover, the individuals involved may be responsible for damages as a result of civil actions brought by competitors under federal and state antiracketeering acts.[38]

The act does not apply to payments made to low-level officials for expediting the performance of routine government services.

lawflix

The In-Laws (1979) (PG)

Review the segment in the film in which money is paid by a dictator for the sale of U.S. currency plates. The dictator's plan is to create worldwide inflation. List the various laws and conventions Peter Falk and Alan Arkin violate through their sale of the plates.

Check out LawFlix at **www.cengage.com/ blaw/dvl** to access movie clips that illustrate business law concepts.

ethics & the law

Combating Bribery of Foreign Public Officials in International Business Transactions

Prior to 1999, German law prohibited bribery of domestic public officials (and did not prohibit bribery of foreign officials). Siemens AG, headquartered in Germany and Europe's largest engineering conglomerate, conducts business throughout the world. Employees were allowed to withdraw up to €1 million for bribes from three "cash desks" set up at Siemens's offices to facilitate the obtaining of government contracts throughout the

world. And, until 1999, Siemens claimed tax deductions for these bribes, many of which were listed as "useful expenditures."

The Organization for Economic Cooperation and Development (OECD) works on global issues, endeavoring to help member countries sustain economic growth and employment. OECD adopted its Anti-Bribery Convention on November 21, 1997; its regulations came into effect in

[38] PL 95-213, 94 Stat 1494, 15 USC § 78a nt.

Continued

1999. In 1999, member countries, including Germany, adopted laws combating bribery of foreign public officials in international business transactions. However, between 2001 and 2004 some $67 million was withdrawn from the Siemens "cash desks." The bribery had continued! Mark Pieth, chairman of the working group on bribery at the OECD, said: "People felt confident that they were doing nothing wrong."* With some 470,000 employee jobs at Siemens depending on the ability to obtain engineering and high-tech contracts throughout the world, were Siemens contracting agents justified in continuing to make "useful expenditures" to save jobs and their company from ruin? How could these expenditures be a bad thing?

On December 11, 2008, Siemens AG pleaded guilty to criminal violations of the United States Foreign Corrupt Practices Act and received a total criminal fine of $450 million. It also reached a settlement with the U.S. Securities and Exchange Commission for violation of the FCPA's antibribery, books and records, and internal control provisions and agreed to pay $350 million in disgorgement of profits. Moreover, it agreed

to fines and disgorgement of profits of $569 million to settle an investigation by the Munich Public Prosecutor's Office. Seimens's bribery was a bad thing because bribery and corruption were criminal acts. Moreover, it allowed the corporation to have an inherently unfair competitive advantage over other contract bidders. The convention helps ensure that public works projects are awarded on the basis of sound economic judgment rather than on the basis of who offers the biggest bribe. The notoriety of the Siemens prosecutions should send a strong and clear message to all trading partners that parties to the convention must not engage in bribery to obtain business deals.** Siemens's current board member Peter Solmssen believes it is a myth that firms have to pay bribes to do business in developing countries, and believes that Siemens can increase sales without paying bribes.***

* "The Siemens Scandal: Bavarian Baksheesh," *The Economist*, **www .economist.com/business/displaystory.cfm?story_id=12814642**.

** The current members of the Anti-Bribery Convention are Argentina, Australia, Austria, Belgium, Brazil, Bulgaria, Canada, Chile, Czech Republic, Denmark, Estonia, Finland, France, Germany, Greece, Hungary, Iceland, Ireland, Israel, Italy, Japan, Korea, Luxemburg, Mexico, Netherlands, New Zealand, Norway, Poland, Portugal, Slovak Republic, Slovenia, South Africa, Spain, Sweden, Switzerland, Turkey, United Kingdom, and the United States.

*** "Siemens Settlement: Relief, But Is It Over?" *Business Week*, **www .businessweek.com/print/globalbiz/content/dec2008/gb20081215_ 941906.htm**.

MAKE THE CONNECTION

SUMMARY

The World Trade Organization, a multilateral treaty subscribed to by the United States and most of the industrialized countries of the world, is based on the principle of trade without discrimination. The United Nations Convention on Contracts for the International Sale of Goods provides uniform rules for international sales contracts between parties in contracting nations. The European Union is a regional trading group that includes most of western Europe. The North American Free Trade Agreement involves

Mexico, Canada, and the United States and eliminates all tariffs between the three countries over a 15-year period.

U.S. firms may choose to do business abroad by making export sales or contracting with a foreign distributor to take title to their goods and sell them abroad. U.S. firms may also license their technology or trademarks for foreign use. An agency arrangement or the organization of a foreign subsidiary may be required to participate effectively in foreign markets.

This results in subjecting the U.S. firm to taxation in the host country. However, tax treaties commonly eliminate double taxation.

The Export Administration Act is the principal statute imposing export controls on goods and technical data.

In choosing the form for doing business abroad, U.S. firms must be careful not to violate the antitrust laws of host countries. Anticompetitive foreign transactions may have an adverse impact on competition in U.S. domestic markets. U.S. antitrust laws have a broad extraterritorial reach. U.S. courts apply a "jurisdictional rule of reason," weighing the interests of the United States against the interests of the foreign country involved in making a decision on whether to hear a case. Illegal conduct may occur in U.S. securities markets. U.S. enforcement efforts sometimes run into foreign countries' secrecy and blocking laws that hinder effective enforcement.

Antidumping laws offer relief for domestic firms threatened by unfair foreign competition. In addition, economic programs exist to assist industries, communities, and workers injured by import competition.

The Foreign Corrupt Practices Act restricts U.S. firms doing business abroad from paying public officials "commissions" for getting business contracts from the foreign governments.

LEARNING OUTCOMES

After studying this chapter, you should be able to clearly explain:

A. GENERAL PRINCIPLES

LO.1 Explain which country's law will govern an international contract should a dispute arise

> See the choice of law example where the U.S. court required the Lipcons to "honor their bargains" and vindicate their claims in an English court on p. 116.

LO.2 Identify seven major international organizations, conferences, and treaties that affect the multinational markets for goods, services, and investments

> See the discussion of the GATT-WTO, CISG, UNCTAD, EU, NAFTA, IMF-World Bank, and OPEC beginning on p. 117.

LO.3 List the forms of business organizations for doing business abroad

> See the discussion of export sales, appointing of an agent, foreign distributorships, licensing, subsidiaries, and joint ventures beginning on p. 120.

B. GOVERNMENTAL REGULATION

LO.4 Explain the tariff barriers and nontariff barriers to the free movements of goods across borders

> See the *Sabritas* case on the applicability of tariff barriers on p. 130.
> See the U.S. embargo on all Brazilian shrimp example because of Brazil's failure to require turtle excluder devices on its shrimp boats p. 132.

LO.5 Explain U.S. law regarding payment to foreign government officials as a means of obtaining business contracts with other governments, and compare U.S. law to laws and treaties applicable to most First World nations

> See the Ethics & the Law discussion of the tax deductions for "useful expenditures" (bribes) claimed by Siemens AG, p. 134.

KEY TERMS

act-of-state doctrine
agent
blocking laws
choice-of-law clause

comity
Dispute Settlement Body (DSB)
distributor

dumping
effects doctrine
export sale
franchising

freight forwarders

gray market goods

intellectual property rights

joint venture

jurisdictional rule of
  reason

letter of credit

licensing

most-favored-nation
  clause

principal

secrecy laws

sovereign compliance
  doctrine

sovereign immunity
  doctrine

special drawing rights
  (SDRs)

tariff

QUESTIONS AND CASE PROBLEMS

1. How does the selling of subsidized foreign goods in the United States adversely affect free trade?

2. Able Time Inc. imported a shipment of watches into the United States. The watches bore the mark "TOMMY," which is a registered trademark owned by Tommy Hilfiger. U.S. Customs seized the watches pursuant to the Tariff Act, which authorizes seizure of any "merchandise bearing a counterfeit mark." Tommy Hilfiger did not make or sell watches at the time of the seizure. Able argues that because Tommy Hilfiger did not make watches at the time of the seizure, the watches it imported were not counterfeit, and the civil penalty imposed by Customs was unlawful. The government argues that the mark was counterfeit and the Tariff Act does not require the owner of the registered mark to make the same type of goods as those bearing the offending mark. Decide. [*U.S. v Able Time, Inc.*, 545 F3d 824 (9th Cir 2008)].

3. PepsiCo has registered its PEPSI trademarks in the U.S. Patent and Trademark Office. PEPSI products are bottled and distributed in the United States by PepsiCo and by authorized bottlers pursuant to Exclusive Bottling Appointment agreements, which authorize local bottlers to bottle and distribute PEPSI products in their respective territories. Similarly, PepsiCo has appointed local bottlers to bottle and distribute PEPSI products in Mexico within particular territories. Pacific Produce, Ltd., has been engaged in the sale and distribution within the United States and Nevada of PEPSI products that were manufactured and bottled in Mexico

and intended for sale in Mexico ("Mexican product"). The Mexican product sold by Pacific Products in the United States has certain material differences from domestic PEPSI products sold by PepsiCo: (1) it contains inferior paper labels that improperly report nutritional information; (2) it does not comply with the labeling standards followed by PepsiCo in the United States; (3) it is sold in channels of trade different from PepsiCo's authorized distribution channels without "drink by" notice dates on the Mexican product and monitoring on the Mexican product for proper shipment and storage conditions; and (4) it conflicts with the bottle return policies of PepsiCo. The Mexican product with its "Marca Reg" and Spanish language bottle caps is well received by consumers in Pacific Produce distribution channels. Classify the goods being sold by Pacific Produce. State the applicable law governing a dispute between PepsiCo and Pacific Produce. How would you decide this case? [*PepsiCo, Inc. v Pacific Produce, Ltd.*, 2001 US Dist LEXIS 12085]

4. Ronald Sadler, a California resident, owned a helicopter distribution company in West Germany, Delta Avia. This company distributed U.S.-made Hughes civilian helicopters in western Europe. Sadler's German firm purchased 85 helicopters from Hughes Aircraft Co. After export licenses were obtained in reliance on the purchaser's written assurance that the goods would not be disposed of contrary to the export license, the helicopters were exported to Germany for resale in western Europe. Thereafter, Delta Avia exported them to North Korea, which was a

country subject to a trade embargo by the United States. The helicopters were converted to military use. Sadler was charged with violating the Export Administration Regulations. In Sadler's defense, it was contended that the U.S. regulations have no effect on what occurs in the resale of civilian helicopters in another sovereign country. Decide.

5. Mirage Investments Corp. (MIC) planned a tender offer for the shares of Gulf States International Corp. (GSIC). Archer, an officer of MIC, placed purchase orders for GSIC stock through the New York office of the Bahamian Bank (BB) prior to the announcement of the tender offer, making a $300,000 profit when the tender offer was made public. The Bahamas is a secrecy jurisdiction. The bank informed the SEC that under its law, it could not disclose the name of the person for whom it purchased the stock. What, if anything, may the SEC do to discover whether the federal securities laws have been violated?

6. United Overseas, Ltd. (UOL), is a U.K. firm that purchases and sells manufacturers' closeouts in Europe and the Middle East. UOL's representative, Jay Knox, used stationery listing a UOL office in New York to solicit business from Revlon, Inc., in New York. On April 1, 1992, UOL faxed a purchase order from its headquarters in England to Revlon's New York offices for the purchase of $4 million worth of shampoo. The purchase order on its face listed six conditions, none of which referred to a forum selection clause. When Revlon was not paid for the shampoo it shipped, it sued UOL in New York for breach of contract. UOL moved to dismiss the complaint because of a forum selection clause, which it stated was on the reverse side of the purchase order and provided that "the parties hereby agree to submit to the jurisdiction of the English Courts disputes arising out of the contract." The evidence did not show that the reverse side of the purchase order had been faxed with the April 1992 order. Should the court dismiss the complaint based on the "forum selection clause"? Read Chapter 32 on letters of credit and advise Revlon how to avoid similar litigation in the future. [*Revlon, Inc. v United Overseas, Ltd.,* 1994 WL 9657 (SDNY)]

7. Reebok manufactures and sells fashionable athletic shoes in the United States and abroad. It owns the federally registered Reebok trademark and has registered this trademark in Mexico as well. Nathan Betech is a Mexican citizen residing in San Diego, California, with business offices there. Reebok believed that Betech was in the business of selling counterfeit Reebok shoes in Mexican border towns, such as Tijuana, Mexico. It sought an injunction in a federal district court in California ordering Betech to cease his counterfeiting activity and to refrain from destroying certain documents. It also asked the court to freeze Betech's assets pending the outcome of a Lanham Act lawsuit. Betech contended that a U.S. district court has no jurisdiction or authority to enter the injunction for the activities allegedly occurring in Mexico. Decide. [*Reebok Int'l, Ltd. v Marnatech Enterprises, Inc.,* 970 F2d 552 (9th Cir)]

8. Assume that before the formation of the European Union, the lowest-cost source of supply for a certain product consumed in France was the United States. Explain the basis by which, after the EU was formed, higher-cost German producers could have replaced the U.S. producers as the source of supply.

9. A complaint was filed with the U.S. Commerce Department's ITA by U.S. telephone manufacturers AT&T, Comidial Corp., and Eagle Telephones, Inc., alleging that 12 Asian manufacturers of small business telephones, including the Japanese firms Hitachi, NEC, and Toshiba and the Taiwanese firm Sun Moon Star Corp., were dumping their small business phones in the U.S. market at prices that were from 6 percent to 283 percent less than those in their home markets. The U.S. manufacturers showed that the domestic industry's market share had dropped from 54 percent in 1985 to 33 percent in 1989. They asserted that it was doubtful if the domestic industry could survive the dumping. Later, in a hearing before the ITC, the Japanese and

Taiwanese respondents contended that their domestic industry was basically sound and that the U.S. firms simply had to become more efficient to meet worldwide competition. They contended that the United States was using the procedures before the ITA and ITC as a nontariff barrier to imports. How should the ITC decide the case? [*American Telephone and Telegraph Co. v Hitachi*, 6 ITC 1511]

10. Campbell Soup Co. imports tomato paste from a wholly owned Mexican subsidiary, Sinalopasta, S. A. de C.V. It deducted $416,324 from the computed value of goods shipped to the United States, which was the cost of transportation of the finished tomato paste from Sinalopasta's loading dock in Mexico to the U.S. border. The deduction thus lowered the computed value of the goods and the amount of duty to be paid the U. S. government by Campbell Soup Co. United States Customs questioned this treatment of freight costs. Tariff Act § 140a(e)(1)(B) requires that profits and general expenses be included in calculating the computed value of goods, which in part quantify the value of the merchandise in the country of production. Is Campbell's position correct? [*Campbell Soup Co., Inc. v United States*, 107 F3d 1556 (Fed Cir)]

11. Roland Staemphfli was employed as the chief financial officer of Honeywell Bull, S.A. (HB), a Swiss computer company operating exclusively in Switzerland. Staemphfli purportedly arranged financing for HB in Switzerland through the issuance of promissory notes. He had the assistance of Fidenas, a Bahamian company dealing in commercial paper. Unknown to Fidenas, the HB notes were fraudulent. The notes were prepared and forged by Staemphfli, who lost all of the proceeds in a speculative investment and was convicted of criminal fraud. HB denied responsibility for the fraudulently issued notes when they came due. Fidenas's business deteriorated because of its involvement with the HB notes. It sued HB and others in the United States for violations of U.S. securities laws. HB defended, arguing that the U.S. court did not have jurisdiction over the transactions in

question. Decide. [*Fidenas v Honeywell Bull, S.A.*, 606 F2d 5 (2d Cir)]

12. Marc Rich & Co., A.G., a Swiss commodities trading corporation, refused to comply with a grand jury subpoena requesting certain business records maintained in Switzerland and relating to crude oil transactions and possible violations of U.S. income tax laws. Marc Rich contended that a U.S. court has no authority to require a foreign corporation to deliver to a U.S. court documents located abroad. The court disagreed and imposed fines, froze assets, and threatened to close a Marc Rich wholly owned subsidiary that did business in the state of New York. The fines amounted to $50,000 for each day the company failed to comply with the court's order. Marc Rich appealed. Decide. [*Marc Rich v United States*, 707 F2d 633 (2d Cir)]

13. U.S. Steel Corp. formed Orinoco Mining Co., a wholly owned corporation, to mine large deposits of iron ore that U.S. Steel had discovered in Venezuela. Orinoco, which was incorporated in Delaware, was subject to Venezuela's maximum tax of 50 percent on net income. Orinoco was also subject to U.S. income tax, but the U.S. foreign tax credit offset this amount. U.S. Steel purchased the ore from Orinoco in Venezuela. U.S. Steel formed Navios, Inc., a wholly owned subsidiary, to transport the ore. Navios, a Liberian corporation, was subject to a 2.5 percent Venezuelan excise tax and was exempt from U.S. income tax. Although U.S. Steel was Navios's primary customer, it charged other customers the same price it charged U.S. Steel. U.S. Steel's investment in Navios was $50,000. In seven years, Navios accumulated nearly $80 million in cash but had not paid any dividends to U.S. Steel. The IRS used IRC § 482 to allocate $52 million of Navios's income to U.S. Steel. U.S. Steel challenged this action, contending Navios's charges to U.S. Steel were at arm's length and the same it charged other customers. Decide. [*United States Steel Corp. v Commissioner*, 617 F2d 942 (2d Cir)]

14. National Computers, Inc., a U.S. firm, entered into a joint venture with a Chinese computer

manufacturing organization, TEC. A dispute arose over payments due the U.S. firm under the joint venture agreement with TEC. The agreement called for disputes to be arbitrated in China, with the arbitrator being chosen from a panel of arbitrators maintained by the Beijing arbitration institution, Cietac. What advantages and disadvantages exist for the U.S. firm under this arbitration arrangement? Advise the U.S. firm on negotiating future arbitration agreements with Chinese businesses.

15. Sensor, a Netherlands business organization wholly owned by Geosource, Inc., of Houston, Texas, made a contract with C.E.P. to deliver 2,400 strings of geophones to Rotterdam by September 20, 1982. The ultimate destination was identified as the USSR. Thereafter, in June 1982, the president of the United States prohibited shipment to the USSR of equipment manufactured in foreign countries under license from U.S. firms. The president had a foreign policy objective of retaliating for the imposition of martial law in Poland, and he was acting under regulations issued under the Export Administration Act of 1979. Sensor, in July and August of 1982, notified C.E.P. that as a subsidiary of a U.S. corporation, it had to respect the president's embargo. C.E.P. filed suit in a district court of the Netherlands asking that Sensor be ordered to deliver the geophones. Decide. [*Compagnie Européenne des Pétroles v Sensor Nederland,* 22 ILM 66]

Chapter 8

CRIMES

Society sets certain standards of conduct and punishes a breach of those standards as a crime. This chapter introduces the means by which government protects people and businesses from prohibited conduct.

A. General Principles

Detailed criminal codes and statutes define crimes and specify their punishment. Crimes vary from state to state but still show the imprint of a common law background through similar elements and structure.

1. Nature and Classification of Crimes

A **crime** is conduct that is prohibited and punished by a government. Crimes are classified as *common law* or *statutory* according to their origin. Offenses punishable by less than one year in prison are called **misdemeanors**. More serious crimes are called **felonies**, including serious business crimes such as bribery and embezzlement, which are punishable by confinement in prison for more than one year. Misdemeanors include weighing goods with uninspected scales or operating without a sales tax license. An act may be a felony in one state and a misdemeanor in another.[1]

2. Basis of Criminal Liability

A crime generally consists of two elements: (1) a mental state (scienter or intent) and (2) an act or omission. Harm may occur as a result of a crime, but harm is not an essential element of a crime.

(A) Mental State. Mental state, or intent, does not require an awareness or knowledge of guilt. In most crimes, the voluntary commission of the act is sufficient for proving mental state. Ignorance that a law is being broken does not mean there is not mental state. **For Example,** dumping waste without a permit is still a criminal act even when the party releasing the waste did not know about the permit requirement.

(B) Act or Omission. Specific statutes define the conduct that, when coupled with sufficient mental

state, constitutes a crime. **For Example,** writing a check knowing you do not have the funds available is conduct that is a crime.

3. Responsibility for Criminal Acts

In some cases, persons who did not necessarily commit the criminal act itself are still held criminally responsible for acts committed by others.

(A) Corporate Liability. Corporations are held responsible for the acts of their employees. A corporation may also be held liable for crimes based on the failure of its employees to act. In the past decade, some of the nation's largest corporations have paid fines for crimes based on employees' failure to take action or for the actions they did take. **For Example,** AIG, the world's largest insurer, paid the largest fine in corporate history in the United States, $1.6 billion, for its questionable accounting practices and alleged sham insurance contracts undertaken for the purpose of boosting its earnings.[2]

(B) Officers and Agents of Corporations. One of the main differences between nonbusiness and business crimes is that more people in a company can be convicted for the same business crime. For nonbusiness crimes, only those who are actually involved in the act itself can be convicted of the crime. For business crimes, however, managers of firms whose employees commit criminal acts can be held liable if the managers authorized the conduct of the employees or knew about their conduct and did nothing or failed to act reasonably in their supervisory positions to prevent the employees from engaging in criminal conduct.

(C) Penalty for Crime: Forfeiture. When a defendant is convicted of a crime, the court may also declare that the defendant's rights in any property used or gained from a crime (an instrument of that crime) be confiscated. Some types of instruments of the crime are automatically forfeited, such as the tools of a crime. **For Example,** the U.S. government confiscated from confessed $50-billion-Ponzi schemer, Bernie Madoff, everything from his yacht to his bank

---

[1] Some states further define crimes by seriousness with different degrees of a crime, such as first-degree murder, second-degree murder, and so on. Misdemeanors may be differentiated by giving special names to minor misdemeanors.
[2] **www.sec.gov**.

U.S. v Erickson, 2009 WL 903387 (CA 10 2009)

Making Stuff Up for the Grand Jury

Kathryn Erickson was the general manager of the Uintah Special Services District (USSD), an entity created to use federal-mineral-lease revenues for road projects. She, along with her secretary, Cheryl McCurdy, administered the (USSD) from a small office in Vernal, Utah. Ms. Erickson's authority was limited and she was not permitted to enter into or modify contracts for or to expend more than $1,000 of USSD funds, without board approval.

Mitchell Construction was a major contractor for USSD. In 1998, USSD awarded Mitchell Construction a contract to haul gravel from a site called Hamaker Bottoms and another contract to carry out small asphalt-paving projects. Both contracts were to be completed within the 1998 construction year.

During 1999 and 2000 Mitchell Construction continued to perform work on the projects covered by its 1998 contracts with USSD, despite their expiration. It submitted invoices to USSD and was paid for this work.

In June 1999 a federal grand jury began to investigate contracting irregularities at USSD and the Uintah County Road Department and issued a subpoena duces tecum to USSD requesting copies of "project contracts, invoices" between USSD and contractors.

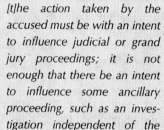

While the office was preparing the response for the grand jury subpoena, Ms. McCurdy saw Ms. Erickson prepare a handwritten change order for the Hamaker Bottoms contract and saw Ms. Erickson and Gilman N. Mitchell both sign it. The change order, which was backdated to January 13, 1999, extended the contract through December 31, 2000.

Ms. McCurdy later discovered that two other change orders had been created and backdated. She spent a day copying documents for the grand jury and recording, on a handwritten list, all of the documents that she had copied. However, she left Ms. Erickson in the office while she was working on the list in order to go home for dinner. Ms. Erickson called her and told her not to come back because all the copying was done. Later, Ms. McCurdy found on Ms. Erickson's desk a photocopy of the grand jury document list and saw that two entries not in her handwriting had been added. These entries were for change orders for contracts between Mitchell Construction and USSD. Ms. McCurdy reported the change to the government.

Ms. Erickson and Mr. Mitchell were each indicted by a grand jury in the U.S. District Court for the District of Utah on three counts of obstruction of justice by knowingly falsifying a document with the knowledge and intent that the grand jury would rely on it.

The jury returned a verdict of guilty against both Ms. Erickson and Mr. Mitchell on all three counts. The two appealed.

JUDICIAL OPINION

HARTZ, Circuit Judge … The Defendants were convicted of violating 18 U.S.C. § 1503, which prohibits "corruptly … influenc[ing], obstruct[ing], or imped[ing], or endeavor[ing] to influence, obstruct, or impede, the due administration of justice." We have identified three "core" elements of this offense: "(1) There must be a pending judicial proceeding; (2) the defendant must have knowledge or notice of the pending proceeding; and (3) the defendant must have acted corruptly with the specific intent to obstruct or impede the proceeding in its due administration of justice." In construing the elements of the offense, the Supreme Court has endorsed a nexus test, requiring that

> [t]he action taken by the accused must be with an intent to influence judicial or grand jury proceedings; it is not enough that there be an intent to influence some ancillary proceeding, such as an investigation independent of the court's or grand jury's authority…. [T]he act must have a relationship in time, causation, or logic with the judicial proceedings. In other words, the endeavor must have the natural and probable effect of interfering with the due administration of justice…. [I]f the defendant lacks knowledge that his actions are likely to affect the judicial proceeding, he lacks the requisite intent to obstruct.

"The nexus limitation is best understood as an articulation of the proof of wrongful intent that will satisfy the *mens rea* requirement of 'corruptly' obstructing or endeavoring to obstruct." *United States v. Quattrone*, 441 F.3d 153, 170 (2d Cir.2006).

Ms. Erickson and Mr. Mitchell concede that the first two elements of the offense are not at issue: A grand-jury proceeding was pending at the time of the charged conduct and both Defendants knew of it. Moreover, although Defendants' briefs occasionally speak in general terms of the absence of evidence of intent, their specific arguments focus

Continued

on the issue of nexus. The essence of their various arguments is that the government failed to show how their conduct affected the grand-jury investigation.

We are not persuaded. Indeed, the Supreme Court opinion adopting the nexus requirement described a circumstance very much like the one before us to exemplify how the nexus requirement could be satisfied.

As the Second Circuit has said:

> A defendant's awareness that a subpoena seeks documents, coupled with his actions taken to place those documents beyond the grand jury's reach clearly would meet the ... nexus requirement.... [I]t is enough if he knows that a subpoena calls for a category of documents, or even one particular document, and then takes steps to place those documents beyond the reach of the grand jury.

Here, the Defendants created false documents to deliver to the grand jury in response to its subpoena. The evidence was sufficient to satisfy the nexus requirement.

Both Defendants insist that the government failed to present evidence that the grand jury was misled or otherwise affected by their submission of falsified change orders. But the required nexus is only that the charged conduct "have the natural and probable effect of interfering with the due administration of justice." Success is not necessary; "an 'endeavor' suffices." *Id.*

Ms. Erickson also asserts that the backdated change orders did no more than memorialize the reality of what had happened during 1999 and 2000; that reality, she says, was

that Mitchell Construction continued to do work for USSD and to submit invoices that its board duly paid. But a reasonable jury could reject this innocent explanation for the change orders. USSD board member Merlin Sinfield testified that the board trusted Ms. Erickson and did not scrutinize the paperwork she presented to it, which typically included multiple invoices for each check. Sinfield also testified that the board had not known of the change orders and that he now recognized that it was improper for USSD to pay Mitchell Construction after the Hamaker Bottoms and small-paving contracts had run. In any event, the fraudulent documents compromised the grand jury's ability to make its own determination whether the work in 1999 and 2000 was authorized. A grand jury is obstructed whenever it is presented with manufactured evidence, even if the manufacturer thinks that the evidence supports "reality." Ms. Erickson's challenge to the sufficiency of the evidence on this ground fails.

In brief, we hold that knowingly submitting fraudulent documents in response to a grand-jury subpoena constitutes obstruction of justice, when, as here, a grand-jury proceeding is underway and the defendant knows of it. The evidence was therefore sufficient to convict Defendants of violating § 1503.

QUESTIONS

1. List the three requirements for proving an obstruction of justice case.

2. How does the court respond to the defendants' arguments that no one was hurt by what was done?

3. What would be an effective business policy for responding to subpoenas?

---

accounts to his seat on NASDAQ. Confiscation is, in effect, an increased penalty for the defendant's crime.

(D) PENALTIES FOR BUSINESS AND WHITE-COLLAR CRIMES. Most common law criminal penalties were created with "natural" persons in mind, as opposed to "artificial" or corporate persons. A $100,000 fine may be significant to an individual but to a corporation with $3 billion in assets and hundreds of millions in income, such a fine could be viewed as a minimal cost of doing business.

Criminal penalties for corporations have been reformed to address this need for deterrence. Rather than using fixed-amount fines, statutes and courts apply percentage of revenue penalties. **For Example,** a bad decision on a product line would cost a company 10 percent to 20 percent of its earnings. A criminal penalty could be imposed in the same percentage fashion with the idea that the company simply made a bad legal decision that should be reflected in earnings.

Another change in penalties for business and white-collar crimes has been the requirement for mandatory prison sentences for officers and directors

United States v Park, 421 US 658 (1975)

Rats In the Warehouse and a CEO with a Fine

Acme Markets, Inc., was a national food retail chain headquartered in Philadelphia, Pennsylvania. At the time of the government action, John R. Park [respondent] was president of Acme, which employed 36,000 people and operated 16 warehouses.

In 1970, the Food and Drug Administration (FDA) forwarded a letter to Mr. Park describing, in detail, problems with rodent infestation in Acme's Philadelphia warehouse facility. In December 1971, the FDA found the same types of conditions in Acme's Baltimore warehouse facility. In January 1972, the FDA's chief of compliance for its Baltimore office wrote to Mr. Park about the inspection. The letter included the following language:

We note with much concern that the old and new warehouse areas used for food storage were actively and extensively inhabited by live rodents. Of even more concern was the observation that such reprehensible conditions obviously existed for a prolonged period of time without any detection, or were completely ignored.

We trust this letter will serve to direct your attention to the seriousness of the problem and formally advise you of the urgent need to initiate whatever measures are necessary to prevent recurrence and ensure compliance with the law.

After Mr. Park received the letter, he met with the vice president for legal affairs for Acme and was assured that he was "investigating the situation immediately and would be taking corrective action."

When the FDA inspected the Baltimore warehouse in March 1972, there was some improvement in the facility, but there was still rodent infestation. Acme and Park were both charged with violations of the Federal Food, Drug, and Cosmetic Act. Acme pleaded guilty. Mr. Park was convicted and fined $500; he appealed based on error in the judge's instruction, given as follows:

The individual is or could be liable under the statute, even if he did not consciously do wrong. However, the fact that the Defendant is president and is a chief executive officer of the Acme Markets does not require a finding of guilt. Though, he need not have personally participated in the situation, he must have had a responsible relationship to the issue. The issue is, in this case, whether the Defendant, John R. Park, by virtue of his position in the company, had a position of authority and responsibility in the situation out of which these charges arose.

The court of appeals reversed Mr. Park's conviction, and the government appealed.

JUDICIAL OPINION

BURGER, C. J..... Central to the Court's conclusion [in *United States v Dotterweich*], 320 U.S. 277 (1943), that individuals other than proprietors are subject to the criminal provisions of the Act was the reality that "the only way in which a corporation can act is through the individuals who act on its behalf."

At the same time, however, the Court was aware of the concern... that literal enforcement "might operate too harshly by sweeping within its condemnation any person however remotely entangled in the proscribed shipment." A limiting principle, in the form of "settled doctrines of criminal law" defining those who "are responsible for the commission of a misdemeanor," was available. In this context, the Court concluded, those doctrines dictated that the offense was committed "by all who have... a responsible share in the furtherance of the transaction which the statute outlaws."

The Act does not, as we observed in *Dotterweich*, make criminal liability turn on "awareness of some wrongdoing" or "conscious fraud." The duty imposed by Congress on responsible corporate agents is, we emphasize, one that requires the highest standard of foresight and vigilance, but the Act, in its criminal aspect, does not require that which is objectively impossible. The theory upon which responsible corporate agents are held criminally accountable for "causing" violations of the Act permits a claim that a defendant was "powerless" to prevent or correct the violation to "be raised defensively at a trial on the merits." *U.S. v Wiesenfield Warehouse Co.*, 376 U.S. 86 (1964). If such a claim is made, the defendant has the burden of coming forward with evidence, but this does not alter the Government's ultimate burden of proving beyond a

Continued

reasonable doubt the defendant's guilt, including his power, in light of the duty imposed by the Act, to prevent or correct the prohibited condition.

Turning to the jury charge in this case, it is of course arguable that isolated parts can be read as intimating that a finding of guilt could be predicated solely on respondent's corporate position.... Viewed as a whole, the charge did not permit the jury to find guilt solely on the basis of respondent's position in the corporation; rather, it fairly advised the jury that to find guilt it must find respondent "had a responsible relation to the situation," and "by virtue of his position …had authority and responsibility" to deal with the situation. The situation referred to could only be "foods… held in unsanitary conditions in a warehouse with the result that it consisted, in part, of filth or… may have been contaminated with filth."

Park testified in his defense that he had employed a system in which he relied upon his subordinates, and that he was ultimately responsible for this system. He testified further that he had found these subordinates to be "dependable" and had "great confidence" in them.

[The rebuttal] evidence was not offered to show that respondent had a propensity to commit criminal acts, that the crime charged had been committed; its purpose was to demonstrate that respondent was on notice that he could not rely on his system of delegation to subordinates to prevent or correct unsanitary conditions at Acme's warehouses, and that he must have been aware of the deficiencies of this system before the Baltimore violations were discovered. The evidence was therefore relevant since it served to rebut Park's defense that he had justifiably relied upon subordinates to handle sanitation matters.

"[Reversed]"

QUESTIONS

1. How long had Mr. Park known about the rats in the warehouse?

2. Does it matter that a subordinate did not respond?

3. Do officers need to be certain their subordinates are reliable in order to avoid criminal liability?

who are convicted of crimes committed as they led their corporations. In 2009, a federal judge required an executive who entered a guilty plea to spend his two years of probation writing a book about what he did and offer guidance to business executives so that they can avoid his missteps. He is then required to publish and distribute the book.[3] The human element of the corporation is then punished for the crimes that the business committed. The U.S. Sentencing Commission, established by Congress in 1984, has developed both federal sentencing guidelines and a carrot-and-stick approach to fighting business crime. If the managers of a company are involved and working to prevent criminal misconduct in the company and a crime occurs, the guidelines permit sentence reductions for the managers' efforts. If the managers do not adequately supervise conduct and do not encourage compliance with the law, the guidelines require judges to impose harsher sentences and fines. The guidelines, referred to as the **Federal Sentencing Guidelines** (or the *U.S. Sentencing Guidelines*), apply

to federal crimes such as securities fraud, antitrust violations, racketeering, theft (embezzlement), Medicare fraud, and other business crimes. The sentencing guidelines permit a judge to place a guilty company on probation, with the length of the probation controlled by whether the company had prevention programs in place.

Following the collapse of companies such as Enron, WorldCom, and Adelphia, the U.S. Sentencing Commission (USSC) piloted the passage of the 2001 Economic Crime Package: Consolidation, Clarification, and Certainty. Amended guidelines, post-Enron, address the increased corporate and white-collar criminal penalties enacted under Sarbanes-Oxley (SOX), and consider the seriousness of the offense, the company's history of violations, its cooperation in the investigation, the effectiveness of its compliance program (often called an *ethics program*), and the role of senior management in the wrongdoing. Corporate managers found to have masterminded any criminal activity must be

---

[3] Natasha Singer, "Judge Orders Former Bristol-Myers Executive to Write Book," *New York Times*, June 9, 2009, p. B3.

sentenced to prison time.[4] Figure 8.1 is a summary of the current penalties for federal crimes. Under a U.S. Supreme Court decision in 2005, *U.S. v Booker*, judges may only use the guidelines as just that, guidelines; the sentencing ranges are no longer mandatory for judges.[5] Going outside those ranges, however, is carefully reviewed by appellate courts.[6] Federal judges can consider only the evidence

FIGURE 8-1	*Roster of White-Collar Criminal Charges*	

COMPANY/PERSON	ISSUE	STATUS
Andrew Fastow, former CFO of Enron (2004)	Multimillion-dollar earnings from serving as principal in SPEs of Enron created to keep debts off the company books; significant sales of shares during the time frame preceding company collapse	Resigned as CFO; appeared before Congress and took the Fifth Amendment; entered guilty plea to securities and wire fraud; sentence of 6 years
Bear Stearns	Sale of mortgage-based securities without full disclosure of risk	Two of its long-term fund managers under indictment; company's demise
Bernie Ebbers (2005) Former CEO, WorldCom	Fraud	Convicted; sentenced to 25 years
Computer Associates (2004)	Criminal investigation pending on securities fraud and obstruction following $2.2 billion restatement in sales	Pending investigations; former CEO entered guilty plea to felony charges
Countrywide Mortgage (2009)	Insider trading; securities fraud	Former CEO Angelo Mozilo charged with insider trading, CFO and COO charged with failure to disclose firm's relaxed lending standards
Enron (2001)	Earnings overstated through mark-to-market accounting; off-the-book/special-purpose entities (SPEs) carried significant amounts of Enron debt not reflected in the financial statements; significant offshore SPEs (881 of 3,000 SPEs were offshore, primarily in Cayman Islands)	Company in bankruptcy; impetus for SOX; CFO Andrew Fastow and others entered guilty pleas; see Lea Fastow, Kenneth Lay, and Jeffrey Skilling
HealthSouth (2003)	$2.7 billion accounting fraud; overstatement of revenues	16 former executives indicted; 5 plead guilty; see Richard Scrushy
KPMG (2006)	Tax shelter fraud	Settled by paying a penalty of $456 million fine in lieu of indictment; 16 former partners and employees indicted; most charges dismissed

[4] *U.S. v Booker*, 543 US 220 (2005).
[5] *U.S. v Skilling*, 554 F3d 529 (CA 5 2009).
[6] *Gall v U.S.*, 552 US 38.

FIGURE 8-1 | **Continued**

COMPANY/PERSON	ISSUE	STATUS
L. Dennis Kozlowski, former CEO of Tyco (2003)	Accused of improper use of company funds	Indicted in New York for failure to pay sales tax on transactions in fine art; hung jury on charges of looting Tyco; convicted on retrial with 15-25-year sentence
Bernard Madoff (2009)	Ran a $50-billion Ponzi scheme through Madoff Securities	Entered guilty plea to all charges and refused to cooperate with investigators; 150-year sentence (at age of 71 in 2009, it is the equivalent of a life sentence)
Marsh & McLennan (2005)	Price-fixing	Paid $850 million in restitution to end investigation of its brokerage practices
Martha Stewart, CEO of Martha Stewart Living, Omnimedia, Inc., and close friend of Dr. Waksal (2003)	Sold 5,000 shares of ImClone one day before public announcement of negative FDA action on Erbitux	Indicted and convicted, along with her broker at Merrill Lynch, of making false statements and conspiracy; served sentence and probation
Richard Scrushy (2003)	Indicted for fraud and bribery for HealthSouth accounting fraud	Acquitted of all charges related to HealthSouth; convicted of bribing former governor of Alabama
Stanford Securities (2009)	$9 billion Ponzi scheme	Indictments of 4 top officers, including Stanford, the controller, the chief accounting officer, the chief investment officer, and an official from Antigua for mail, wire, and securities fraud

presented at trial and may not consider evidence of previous convictions, but not evidence that has not been proven at trial.[7]

(E) SARBANES-OXLEY REFORMS TO CRIMINAL PENALTIES. Part of SOX, passed by Congress following the collapses of Enron and WorldCom corporations, was the **White-Collar Crime Penalty Enhancement Act of 2002**.[8] This act increases penalties substantially. **For Example,** the penalties for mail and wire fraud are increased from a maximum of 5 years to a maximum of 20

years. Penalties for violation of pension laws increased from 1 year to 10 years and the fines increased from $5,000 to $100,000.[9]

4. Indemnification of Crime Victims

Penalties are paid to the government. Typically, the victim of a crime does not benefit from the criminal prosecution and conviction of the wrongdoer, although courts can order that restitution be paid to victims.

[7] Mary Kreiner Ramirez, "Just in Crime: Guiding Economic Crime Reform after the Sarbanes-Oxley Act of 2002," 34 *Loyola University of Chicago Law Journal* 359, 387 (2003).
[8] 18 USC § 1314 *et seq.*
[9] 18 USC §§ 1341 and 1343; 29 USC § 1131.

thinking things through

Employees Obeying Orders—Employer Liable?

Lauro Ortega was digging a foundation at a Lattarulo construction site. The Lattarulo site involved digging a foundation next to another building, but the Lattarulo building required a deeper dig. The result was that the foundation of the building next to the site was weakened and required support until the Lattarulo concrete was poured to provide the substitute for the former ground support. A consultant working nearby did warn Mr. Williams Lattarulo, the owner, about the foundation's risk of collapse once the digging went deeper. Mr. Ortega also raised his concerns to Mr. Lattarulo. Mr. Lattarulo told him to keep digging. Mr. Ortega's co-workers also warned Mr. Lattarulo that the trench was unsafe and needed to have some supports placed in it to prevent a collapse. When he was warned a second time by his workers he said, "Don't worry about it."

Shortly thereafter, the adjoining building's foundation collapsed onto Mr. Ortega. Mr. Ortega's head was all that was uncovered when the foundation collapsed, but the pressure of the dirt and debris that rendered him immobile constricted his chest and made him unable to breathe. He

suffocated to death as his co-workers tried to dig him out from the debris.

While Mr. Lattarulo listed a company as a safety consultant for the site (something required by code), he did not actually have or pay a consultant, something that saved him $90,000 on the job. On the day of the collapse, a building inspector for the city visited the site where the fatality had occurred and said there were "shoddy work conditions." She also found eight violations of city code at the site.

The city brought manslaughter charges against Mr. Lattarulo. Mr. Lattarulo maintained that there was just an accident on a job site and he cannot be held criminally liable. However, the Building Department commissioner said that when there are clear rules and warnings—as there were in the case for the required support for digging trenches—and those rules and warnings are not followed, there will be criminal sanctions. When is an owner criminally liable for actions and work conducted by employees?

Source: Michael Wilson, "Manslaughter Charge for Builder in Brooklyn Collapse," *New York Times*, October 12, 2008, A24.

Several states have adopted statutes providing a limited degree of indemnification to victims of crime to compensate them for the harm or loss sustained.[10] Under some criminal victim indemnification statutes, dependents of a deceased victim are entitled to recover the amount of support they were deprived of by the victim's death. The Victims of Crime Act of 1984 creates a federal Crime Victims Fund. Using the fines paid into the federal courts as well as other monies, the federal government makes grants to the states to assist them in financing programs to provide assistance for victims of crime.[11] The Victim and

Witness Protection Act of 1982 authorizes the sentencing judge in a federal district court to order, in certain cases, that the defendant make restitution (restoration) to the victim or pay the victim the amount of medical expenses or loss of income caused by the crime.[12]

(A) ACTION FOR DAMAGES. The criminal prosecution of a wrongdoer is not undertaken primarily for the financial benefit of the victim of the crime, but the victim is typically entitled to bring a civil action for damages against the wrongdoer for the harm

---

[10] A 1973 Uniform Crime Victims Reparations Act was adopted in Kansas, Louisiana, Montana, North Dakota, Ohio, and Utah. This act has been superseded by the Uniform Victims of Crime Act of 1992 adopted only in Montana, with variations.

[11] 18 USC § 1401 *et seq.*

[12] 18 USC § 3579, as amended by 18 USC § 18.18; see *Hughey v United States*, 495 US 411 (1990). Some states likewise provide for payment into a special fund. *Ex parte* Lewis, 556 So 2d 370 (Ala 1989). In 2002, Congress passed another victims' compensation statute, with this one providing relief and assistance to the victims of terrorist attacks in the United States. 42 USCA § 10603b.

sustained. Statutes creating business crimes often give the victim the right to sue for damages. **For Example,** a company or individual violating federal antitrust laws is liable to the victim for three times the damages actually sustained.

(B) INDEMNIFICATION OF UNJUSTLY CONVICTED. If an innocent person is convicted of a crime, the state legislature typically pays the person damages to compensate for the wrong that has been done. In some states, this right to indemnity is expressly established by statute, as in the case of the New York Unjust Conviction and Imprisonment Act. The fact that a person has been imprisoned while awaiting trial and is then acquitted does not entitle that person to compensation under such a statute because an acquittal does not mean that the person was found innocent. It means only that the government was not able to prove guilt beyond a reasonable doubt.[13]

B. WHITE-COLLAR CRIMES

White-collar crime is generally considered business crime, the type committed without physical threats or acts.

5. Conspiracies

Prior to the commission of an intended crime, a person may engage in conduct that is itself a crime, such as a conspiracy. A **conspiracy** is an agreement between two or more persons to commit an unlawful act or to use unlawful means to achieve an otherwise lawful result. The crime is the agreement itself; generally, it is immaterial that nothing is done to carry out the agreement, although some conspiracy statutes do require that some act is done to carry out the agreement before the crime of conspiracy is committed.

6. Crimes Related to Production, Competition, and Marketing

(A) IMPROPER USE OF INTERSTATE COMMERCE. The shipment of improper goods or the transmission of improper information in interstate commerce is a federal crime. **For Example,** knowingly shipping food with salmonella would be a violation of the federal law that prohibits shipping adulterated foods, drugs, or cosmetics in interstate commerce.

The Communications Act of 1934, as amended, makes it a crime to manufacture or sell devices knowing their primary use is to unscramble satellite telecasts without having paid for the right to do so.[14]

(B) SECURITIES CRIMES. To protect the investing public, both state and federal laws have regulated the issuance and public sale of stocks and bonds. Between 1933 and 1940, Congress adopted seven such regulatory statutes. These statutes and the crimes associated with sales of securities are covered in Chapter 46.

7. Money Laundering

The federal government has adopted a Money Laundering Control Act (MLCA).[15] The act prohibits the knowing and willful participation in a financial transaction involving unlawful proceeds when the transaction is designed to conceal or disguise the source of the funds. The so-called *USA Patriot Act* that was passed on October 26, 2001, less than two months after the destruction of the World Trade Center and the damage to the Pentagon on September 11, 2001, includes a substantial number of changes and amendments to the Money Laundering Control Act and the Bank Secrecy Act (BSA).[16] Both statutes have been used as means to control bribery, tax evasion, and money laundering. Their changes and amendments were designed to curb the funding of terrorist activities in the United States.

The Patriot Act expands the coverage of the law from banks and financial institutions to anyone involved in financial transactions, which includes securities brokers; travel agents; those who close real

---

[13] *People v Neff*, 731 NY S 2d 269 (2001).
[14] 47 USC § 705(d)(1), (e)(4), 47 USC § 605 (d)(1), (e)(4); *United States v Harrell*, 983 F 2d 36 (5th Cir 1993); but see *DIRECTV, Inc. v Robson*, 420 F 3d 532 (5th Cir 2005).
[15] 18 USC §§ 1956–1957 (2000). *U.S. v Prince*, 214 F 3d 740 (6th Cir 2000).
[16] 31 USC § 531(h).

estate transactions; insurance companies; loan or finance companies; casinos; currency exchanges; check-cashing firms; auto, plane, and boat dealers; and branches and agencies of foreign banks located in the United States. The amendments make even small businesses subject to the requirements of disclosure under MLCA and BSA, such as reporting cash transactions in excess of $10,000.

In addition, the types of accounts covered have been expanded. The accounts covered are not only securities accounts but also money market accounts. Furthermore, banks are now more actively involved in supervising accounts and following through on government information furnished to the bank on suspicious transactions and activities as well as individuals. Banks are required to implement new policies to prevent the types of transactions tagged by the government noted and conduct internal investigations for suspicious transactions. Because of the required close-watch provisions of these laws, banks and others covered under the federal statutes have developed anti-money-laundering programs. These programs must include a "Know Your Customer" training segment that teaches employees how to spot suspicious customers and transactions.

8. Racketeering

Congress passed the **Racketeer Influenced and Corrupt Organizations (RICO) Act**[17] in 1970 as part of the Organized Crime Control Act. The law was designed primarily to prevent individuals involved in organized crime from investing money obtained through racketeering in legitimate businesses. However, the broad language of the act, coupled with a provision that allows individuals and businesses to sue for treble damages, has resulted in an increasing number of lawsuits against ordinary businesspersons not associated with organized crime.

(A) CRIMINAL AND CIVIL APPLICATIONS. RICO authorizes criminal and civil actions against persons who use any income derived from racketeering activity to invest in, control, or conduct an enterprise through a pattern of *racketeering activity*.[18] In criminal and civil actions under RICO, a pattern of racketeering activity must be established by proving that at least two acts of racketeering activity—so-called *predicate acts*—have been committed within 10 years.[19] Conviction under RICO's criminal provisions may result in a $25,000 fine and up to 20 years' imprisonment as well as forfeiture of the property involved. A successful civil plaintiff may recover three times the actual damages suffered and attorney fees.[20]

(B) EXPANDING USAGE. Civil RICO actions have been successful against business entities, such as accounting firms, labor unions, insurance companies, commercial banks, and stock brokerage firms. However, under the Private Securities Litigation Reform Act of 1995, securities fraud is eliminated as a **predicate act**, or a qualifying underlying offense, for private RICO actions, absent a prior criminal conviction.[21]

9. Bribery

Bribery is the act of giving money, property, or any benefit to a particular person to influence that person's judgment in favor of the giver. At common

---

[17] 18 USC §§ 1961–1968.
[18] § 1961. Definitions:
  (1) "Racketeering activity" means any act or threat involving murder, kidnapping, gambling, arson, robbery, bribery, extortion, dealing in obscene matter, dealing in a controlled substance or listed chemical, or sports bribery; counterfeiting; theft from interstate shipment; embezzlement from pension and welfare funds; extortionate credit transactions; fraud; wire fraud; mail fraud; procurement of citizenship or nationalization unlawfully; reproduction of naturalization or citizenship papers; obstruction of justice; tampering with a witness, victim, or an informant; retaliating against a witness, victim, or an informant; false statement in application and use of passport; forgery or false use of passport; fraud and misuse of visas, permits and other documents; racketeering; unlawful welfare fund payments; laundering of monetary instruments; use of interstate commerce facilities in the commission of murder-for-hire; sexual exploitation of children; interstate transportation of stolen motor vehicles; interstate transportation of stolen property; trafficking in counterfeit labels of phonorecords, computer programs or computer program documentation, or packaging and copies of motion pictures or other audiovisual works; criminal infringement of a copyright; trafficking in contraband cigarettes; and white slave traffic.
[19] Brian Slocum, "RICO and the Legislative Supremacy Approach to Federal Criminal Lawmaking," 31 *Loyola Univ. Chicago Law Journal* 639 (2000).
[20] 18 U.S.C. § 1963.
[21] Connecticut's commercial bribery statute is a good example. It provides: *A person is guilty of commercial bribery when he confers, or agrees to confer, any benefit upon any employee, agent or fiduciary without the consent of the latter's employer or principal, with intent to influence his conduct in relation to his employer's or principal's affairs.* CGSA § 53a-160 (2002). Other examples of commercial bribery statues can be found at Minn. Stat Ann § 6-9.86 (Minnesota 2001); NH Rev Stat § 638:8 (New Hampshire 2001); Alaska Stat 11.45.670 (Alaska 2001); and Ala. Code § 13A-11-120 (Alabama 2001). Mississippi prohibits commercial bribery as well as sports bribery, which is paying the agent of a sports team in order to influence the outcome of a sporting event. Miss. Code Ann § 97-9-10 (2001).

law, the crime was limited to doing such acts to influence a public official.

The giving and the receiving of a bribe constitute separate crimes. In addition, the act of trying to obtain a bribe may be a crime of solicitation of bribery in some states, while in other states bribery is broadly defined to include solicitation of bribes.

10. Commercial Bribery

Commercial bribery is a form of bribery in which an agent for another is paid or given something of value in order to make a decision on behalf of his or her principal that benefits the party paying the agent. **For Example,** a napkin supplier who pays a restaurant agent $500 in exchange for that agent's decision to award the restaurant's napkin contract to that supplier has engaged in commercial bribery.[22]

11. Extortion and Blackmail

Extortion and *blackmail* are crimes in which money is exchanged for either specific actions or restraint in taking action.

(A) Extortion. When a public officer makes an illegal demand, the officer has committed the crime of **extortion. For Example,** if a health inspector threatens to close down a restaurant on a false sanitation law charge unless the restaurant pays the inspector a sum of money, the inspector has committed extortion. (If the restaurant voluntarily offers the inspector the money to prevent the restaurant from being shut down because of actual violations of the sanitation laws, the crime committed would be bribery.) Extortion has been expanded beyond the public law officer requirement of the common law. Most states have expanded extortion to include obtaining anything of value by threat, which might be, for example, loan sharking. In a number of states, statutes extend the extortion concept to include making terrorist threats.[23]

(B) Blackmail. In jurisdictions where extortion is limited to the conduct of public officials, a nonofficial commits **blackmail** by making demands that would

be extortion if made by a public official. Ordinarily, blackmail is the act of threatening someone with publicity about a matter that would damage the victim's personal or business reputation.

12. Corrupt Influence

Legislative bodies have increasingly outlawed certain practices that exert a corrupting influence on business transactions.

(A) Improper Political Influence. At the federal and state levels, it is a crime for one who holds public office to hold a financial interest in or to receive money from an enterprise that seeks to do business with the government. Such conduct is a conflict of interest between the official's duty to citizens and his or her personal financial interests. **For Example,** the former governor of Illinois, Rod Blagojevich, was charged with seeking funds, fundraisers, and positions in exchange for political favors. To keep officials' conduct transparent, lobbyists must register in Washington, D.C.,[24] and adhere to statutory limits on gifts and contributions to political campaigns. Public officials must file annual disclosure forms about their financial positions as well as provide a disclosure of all gifts and their value.

(B) Foreign Corrupt Practices Act. The **Foreign Corrupt Practices Act (FCPA)** is a federal criminal statute that applies to businesses whose principal offices are in the United States; it is an antibribery and anticorruption statute covering these companies' international operations.[25] The FCPA prohibits making, authorizing, or promising payments or gifts of money or anything of value with the intent to corrupt. This prohibition applies to payments or gifts designed to influence official acts of foreign officials, parties, party officials, candidates for office, nongovernmental organizations (NGOs), or any person who transmits the gift or money to these types of persons.

The FCPA does not prohibit **grease** or **facilitation payments**. These are payments made only to get officials to perform their normal duties or to perform them in a timely manner. Facilitation payments are

---

[22] 15 USC § 78(a), (n)–(t).
[23] *Pennsylvania v Bunting*, 426 A2d 130 (Pa 1981).

[24] Foreign Agents Registration Act, 22 USC § 611 *et seq.*, as amended.
[25] 15 USC § 78dd-1 *et seq.*

ethics&the law

Why Regulate Bribes?

In 1999, a scandal involving the International Olympic Committee (IOC) erupted when it was discovered that members of the Salt Lake City Olympic Committee had given extensive gifts to members of the IOC to win the 2002 Winter Olympics for Salt Lake City. The gifts included everything from college tuition to medical care to entertainment. The attitude at the time toward the Salt Lake City revelations was, "It's always been done this way," or

"Everybody does this," or "It doesn't really hurt anyone."

Why should criminal indictments be brought against the U.S. citizens who bribed IOC members?* Why do we care?

* The criminal charges against two members of the Salt Lake City Olympic Committee were dismissed by the court but were reinstated by the Tenth Circuit. U.S. v Welch, 327 F3d 1081 (10th Cir 2003). The federal charges were again dismissed for lack of evidence.

those made to (1) secure a permit or a license, (2) obtain paper processing, (3) secure police protection, (4) provide phone, water, or power services, or (5) obtain any other similar action.

13. Counterfeiting

Counterfeiting is making, with fraudulent intent, a document or coin that appears to be genuine but is not because the person making it did not have the authority to make it. It is a federal crime to make, to possess with intent to transfer, or to transfer counterfeit coins, bank notes, or obligations or other securities of the United States. Various states also have statutes prohibiting the making and passing of counterfeit coins and bank notes. These statutes often provide, as does the federal statute, a punishment for the mutilation of bank notes or the lightening (of the weight) or mutilation of coins.

14. Forgery

Forgery consists of the fraudulent making or material altering of an instrument, such as a check, that attempts to create or changes a legal liability of another person.[26] Ordinarily, **forgery** consists of signing another's name with intent to defraud, but it

may also consist of making an entire instrument or altering an existing one. It may result from signing a fictitious name or the offender's own name with the intent to defraud.

The issuing or delivery of a forged instrument to another person constitutes the crime of **uttering** a forged instrument. Any sending of a forged check through the channels of commerce or of bank collection constitutes an uttering of a forged instrument. The act of depositing a forged check into the forger's bank account by depositing it in an automatic teller machine constitutes uttering within the meaning of a forgery statute.[27]

15. Perjury

Perjury consists of knowingly giving false testimony in a judicial proceeding after having been sworn to tell the truth. Knowingly making false answers on any form filed with a government typically constitutes perjury or is subjected to the same punishment as perjury. In some jurisdictions, the false answers given in a situation other than in court or the litigation process is called the crime of *false swearing*. The penalties for perjury were increased substantially following the collapse of Enron with the passage of SOX.

---

[26] Misrepresenting the nature of a document in order to obtain their signature on it is forgery. *State v Martinez*, 74 Cal Rptr 3d 409 (2008).
[27] *Wisconsin v Tolliver*, 440 NW2d 571 (Wis App 1989).

16. False Claims and Pretenses

Many statutes make it a crime to submit false claims or to obtain goods by false pretenses.

(A) FALSE CLAIMS. Some statutes provide that making a false claim to an insurance company or government office is a crime. The federal false statement statute makes it a crime to knowingly and willfully make a false material statement about any matter within the jurisdiction of any department or agency of the United States. For example, it is a crime for a contractor to make a false claim against the United States for payment for work that was never performed. It is also a crime to make false statements about income and assets on a student's application for federal financial aid.

(B) OBTAINING GOODS BY FALSE PRETENSES. Almost all states have statutes that forbid obtaining money or goods under false pretenses.[28] Sometimes they are directed against a particular form of deception, such as using a bad check. An intent to defraud is an essential element of obtaining property by false pretenses.[29]

Examples of false pretense include delivering a check knowing that there is insufficient money in the bank account to cover the check.[30] False representations as to future profits in a business are also forms of false pretenses.

Failing to perform on a contract is not a false pretense crime unless the contract had been entered into with the intent of not performing it.[31]

(C) UNAUTHORIZED USE OF AUTOMATED TELLER MACHINE. Obtaining money from an automated teller machine (ATM) by the unauthorized use of the depositor's ATM card is a federal crime.

(D) FALSE INFORMATION SUBMITTED TO BANKS. Knowingly making false statements in a loan application to a federally insured bank is a federal crime.[32] It is also a crime for a landowner to put a false value on land transferred to a bank as security for a loan.[33]

For Example, many of the initial criminal charges in the subprime mortgage market collapse have involved mortgage brokers and appraisers who misrepresented property value or applicants' income in their mortgage applications for federally insured loans.

17. Bad Checks

The use of a bad check is commonly made a crime by statute. In the absence of a bad check statute, the use of a bad check could generally be prosecuted under a false pretenses statute.

Under a bad check statute, it is a crime to use or pass a check with the intent to defraud with the knowledge that there are insufficient funds in the bank to pay the check when it is presented for payment. Knowledge that the bad check will not be paid when presented to the bank is an essential element of the crime. The bad check statutes typically provide that if the check is not made good within a specified number of days after payment by the bank is refused, it is presumed that the defendant acted with the intent to defraud.[34] For more information on checks, see Chapter 28.

18. Credit Card Crimes

It is a crime to steal a credit card and, in some states, to possess the credit card of another person without that person's consent. Using a credit card without the permission of the card owner is the crime of obtaining goods or services by false pretenses or with the intent to defraud. Likewise, a person who continues to use a credit card with the knowledge that it has been canceled is guilty of the crime of obtaining goods by false pretenses.

When, without permission, someone signs the name of the card owner for the credit card transaction, she has committed the crime of forgery.

The Credit Card Fraud Act of 1984[35] makes it a federal crime to obtain anything of value in excess of $1,000 in a year by means of a counterfeit credit card,

---

[28] *Mass. v Cheromcka*, 850 NE2d 1088 (Mass App 2006).
[29] *State v Moore*, 903 A2d 669 (Conn App 2006).
[30] *U.S. v Tudeme*, 457 F 3d 577 (Fed App 2006).
[31] *Jacobs v State*, 230 SW 3d 225 (Tex App 2006).
[32] 18 USC § 1014. See *United States v Autorino*, 381 F 3d 48 (2d Cir 2004).
[33] *United States v Faulkner*, 17 F 3d 745 (5th Cir 1994).

[34] *McMillan v First Nat. Bank of Berwick*, A2d, 2009 WL 1966952 (Pa Super).
[35] 18 USC § 1029.

to make or sell such cards, or to possess more than 15 counterfeit cards at one time.

19. Embezzlement

Embezzlement is the fraudulent conversion of another's property or money by a person to whom it has been entrusted.[36] Employees who take their employer's property or funds for personal use have committed the crime of embezzlement. An agent employee commits embezzlement when he receives and keeps payments from third persons—payments the agent should have turned over to the principal. **For Example,** when an insured gives money to an insurance agent to pay the insurance company but the insurance agent uses the money to pay premiums on the policies of other persons, the agent is guilty of embezzlement. Generally, the fact that the defendant intends to return the property or money embezzled or does in fact do so is no defense.

Today, every jurisdiction has not only a general embezzlement statute but also various statutes applicable to particular situations. **For Example,** statutes cover embezzlement by government officials and employees.

20. Obstruction of Justice: Sarbanes-Oxley

Another Sarbanes-Oxley Act of 2002 provision clarifies what constitutes obstruction of justice and increases the penalties for such an act. The new section makes it a felony for anyone, including company employees, auditors, attorneys, and consultants,

> to alter, destroy, mutilate, conceal, cover up, falsify or make a false entry with the "intent to impede, obstruct, or influence the investigation or proper administration of any matter within the jurisdiction of any department or agency of the United States."[37]

The statute goes on to address audit records specifically and requires auditors to retain their work papers related to a client's audit for at least five years.

Any destruction of documents prior to that time constitutes a felony and carries a penalty of up to 10 years. The statute was passed in response to the conduct of Arthur Andersen, the audit firm for the collapsed Enron Corporation. Many of the firm's audit papers on Enron were destroyed, but the firm and partner-in-charge escaped criminal liability because the government could not establish that the senior managers in Andersen were aware of the shredding.[38]

21. Corporate Fraud: Sarbanes-Oxley

SOX also created a new form of mail and wire fraud. Ordinarily, mail or wire fraud consists of the use of the mail or telephones for purposes of defrauding someone of money and/or property. However, the SOX form of mail or wire fraud is based on new requirements imposed on corporate officers to certify their financial statements when they are issued. If a corporate officer fails to comply with all requirements for financial statement certification or certifies financial statements that contain false material information, the officer and company have committed corporate fraud with penalties that range from fines of $1,000,000 and/or 10 years to $5,000,000 and/or 20 years for willful violation of the certification requirements.

22. The Common Law Crimes

In contrast to white-collar crimes, *common law crimes* are crimes that involve the use of force or the threat of force or cause injury to persons or damage to property. The following sections discuss crimes of force and crimes against property that affect businesses.

(A) LARCENY. *Larceny* is the wrongful or fraudulent taking of the personal property of another by any person with fraudulent intent. Shoplifting is a common form of larceny. In many states, shoplifting is made a separate crime. In some states, all forms of larceny and robbery are consolidated into a statutory

---

[36] *State v Weaver*, 607 SE2d 599 (NC 2005).
[37] 18 USC § 1519. The newly defined and expanded crime of obstruction carries an unspecified fine and a sentence of up to 20 years.
[38] *Arthur Andersen LLP v U.S.*, 544 US 696 (2005).

sports & entertainment law

The NBA Referee, Gambling, and Some Tossed Games

Tim Donaghy, a referee for the NBA, entered a guilty plea to two federal felony charges in connection with his bets and tips on NBA games. The charges are conspiracy to engage in wire fraud and transmitting betting information via interstate commerce. Mr. Donaghy picked teams to win in games he was scheduled to referee. Experts have said that Donaghy committed the equivalent of insider trading on Wall Street by providing outsiders with information about games, players, and referees. He got $5,000 from his tippees for correct picks.

According to the indictments, Donaghy began betting on games in 2003, but in December 2006 began passing along inside information to others who were also charged in the conspiracy. The communication was in code via cell phone. Through his lawyer, Donaghy indicated that he had a gambling addiction problem and was currently on medication and under the treatment of a psychiatrist.

The NBA Commissioner, David Stern, referred to Donaghy as a "rogue referee," but said that the gambling charges were a wake-up call for the NBA and that it must not be "complacent."*

Mr. Donaghy's missteps were discovered as the federal government was conducting an investigation into the Gambino crime family, based in Brooklyn.

Commissioner Stern said that the NBA would be looking at the checks and balances that the NFL has built into its system including Las Vegas travel prohibitions on referees. The NFL also has significant background checks and ongoing monitoring of its referees.

Mr. Donaghy ran a basketball clinic for developmentally disabled boys in Springfield, P.A. (Mr. Donaghy's hometown) for almost a decade. He was a graduate of Villanova and had worked his way up to being one of the NBA's top referees, coming through the ranks of refereeing in both high school and the Continental Basketball Association. Mr. Donaghy had a wife and four children. His salary with the NBA during 2006 was $260,000. Mr. Donaghy was sentenced to 15 months in prison.

Why do you think Mr. Donaghy was engaged in gambling? Doesn't his civic activity paint a different picture of his character?

* Roscoe Nance, "Scandal Is a 'Wakeup Call,' Stern Says," *USA Today*, August 16, 2007, 2C.

---

crime of theft. At common law, there was no crime known as theft.

(B) ROBBERY. *Robbery* is the taking of personal property from the presence of the victim by use of force or fear. Most states have aggravated forms of robbery, such as robbery with a deadly weapon. Snatching a necklace from the neck of the victim involves sufficient force to constitute robbery. When the unlawful taking is not by force or fear, as when the victim does not know that the property is being taken, the offense is larceny, but it cannot be robbery.

Some statutes may be aimed at a particular kind of robbery, **For Example,** carjacking is a federal crime under the Anti-Car Theft Act of 1992.[39]

(C) BURGLARY. At common law, *burglary* was the breaking and entering during the night into the dwelling house of another with the intent to commit a felony. Inserting the automatic teller card of another, without their knowledge or permission, into an automatic teller machine set in the wall of the bank may constitute an entry into the bank for the purpose of committing burglary.[40] Some states word

[39] 18 USC § 2119. *U.S. v Bell*, 608, F Supp 2d 1257 (Kan 2009)
[40] *California v Ravenscroft*, 243 Cal Rptr 827 (Ct App 1988).

their burglary statutes, however, so that there is no burglary in this automatic teller case. This act would be covered by other criminal statutes.

Modern statutes have eliminated many of the elements of the common law definition so that under some statutes it is now immaterial when or whether there was an entry to commit a felony. The elements of breaking and entering are frequently omitted. Under some statutes, the offense is aggravated and the penalty is increased, depending on the place where the offense was committed, such as a bank building, freight car, or warehouse. Related statutory offenses, such as the crime of possessing burglars' tools, have been created.

(D) ARSON. At common law, *arson* was the willful and malicious burning of another's dwelling. The law was originally designed to protect human life, although arson has been committed just with the burning of the building even if no one is actually hurt. In most states, arson is a felony, so if someone is killed in the resulting fire, the offense is considered a felony-murder. Under the felony-murder rule, homicide, however unintended, occurring in the commission of a felony is automatically classified as murder. Virtually every state has created a special offense of burning to defraud an insurer.

(E) RIOTS AND CIVIL DISORDERS. Damage to property in the course of a riot or civil disorder is ordinarily covered by other types of crimes such as the crime of larceny or arson. In addition, the act of assembling as a riotous mob and engaging in civil disorders is generally some form of crime in itself under either common law concepts of disturbing the peace or modern antiriot statutes, even without destruction or theft of property. However, statutes on civil disorders must be carefully drawn to avoid infringing on constitutionally protected free speech.

C. CRIMINAL LAW AND THE COMPUTER

In some situations, ordinary crimes cover computer crimes situations. In other situations, new criminal law statutes are required.

23. What is a Computer Crime?

Generally, the term **computer crime** is used to refer to a crime that can be committed only by a person having some knowledge of the operation of a computer. Just as stealing an automobile requires knowledge of how to operate and drive a car, so the typical computer crime requires the knowledge of how the computer works.

Because the more serious and costly wrongs relating to computers do not fit into the ordinary definitions of crime, there are now computer-specific criminal statutes: Computer crimes can be committed against the computer, using the computer, or through the computer.

24. The Computer as Victim

A traditional crime may be committed by stealing or intentionally damaging a computer.

(A) THEFT OF HARDWARE. When a computer itself is stolen, the ordinary law relating to theft crimes should apply. Theft of a computer is subject to the same law as the theft of a truck or a desk.

(B) THEFT OF SOFTWARE. When a thief takes software, whether in the form of a program written on paper or a program on a disk or memory stick, something has been taken, but it is not tangible property as larceny requires. At common law, the value of stolen software would be determined by the value of the tangible substance on which the program was recorded. Under a traditional concept of property, which would ignore the value of the intangible program, theft of software would be only petty larceny. Now, however, virtually every state makes stealing software a crime. Chapter 11 provides more information on crimes, software, and the internet.

(C) INTENTIONAL DAMAGE. The computer may be the "victim" of a crime when it is intentionally destroyed or harmed. In the most elementary form of damage, the computer could be harmed if it was smashed with an ax or destroyed in an explosion or a fire. In such cases, the purpose of the intentional damage is to cause the computer's owner the financial loss of the computer and the destruction of the information that is stored in it.

Intentional damage can result from more subtle means. Gaining access to the computer and then erasing or altering the data is also the crime of intentional damage. Likewise, interfering with the air conditioning so computers are damaged or malfunction would also be covered under intentional damage statutes. Planting a bug or virus in the software, causing the program to malfunction or to give incorrect output, is a form of intentional damage. Angry employees, former employees, and competitors have all been convicted of intentional damage.

25. Unauthorized Use of Computers

The unlawful use of a computer belonging to someone else is also a crime in some states. There are specific statutes at the state and federal levels that make it unlawful to use government computers without permission.

26. Computer Raiding

Taking information from a computer without the consent of the owner is a crime. Whether theft is accomplished by instructing the computer to make a printout of stored information or by tapping into its data bank by electronic means is not important. In some states, taking information is known as the crime of "computer trespass."[41]

Both Congress and state legislatures have adopted statutes that make it a crime to gain unauthorized access to a computer or use information so gained to cause harm to the computer or its rightful user.[42]

27. Diverted Delivery by Computer

In many industries, a computer controls the delivery of goods. The person in charge of that computer or someone unlawfully gaining access to it may cause the computer to direct delivery to an improper place. That is, instead of shipping goods to the customers to whom they should go, the wrongdoer diverts the goods to a different place, where the wrongdoer or a confederate receives them.

In precomputer days, written orders were sent from the sales department to the shipping department. The shipping department then sent the ordered goods to the proper places. If the person in the sales department or the person in the shipping department was dishonest, either one could divert the goods from the proper destination. Today, instructing the computer to give false directions can cause this fraudulent diversion of goods. Basically, the crime has not changed. The computer is merely the new instrument by which the old crime is committed. This old crime has taken on a new social significance because of the amazingly large dollar value of the thefts. In one case, several hundred loaded freight cars disappeared. In another case, a loaded oil tanker was diverted to unload into a fleet of tank trucks operated by an accomplice of the computer operator.

28. Economic Espionage by Computer

The **Economic Espionage Act (EEA)** is a federal law[43] passed in response to several cases in which high-level executives took downloaded proprietary information from their computers to their new employers. The EEA makes it a felony to steal, appropriate, or take a trade secret as well as to copy, duplicate, sketch, draw, photograph, download, upload, alter, destroy, replicate, transmit, deliver, send, mail, or communicate a trade secret. The penalties for EEA violations are up to $500,000 and 15 years in prison for individuals and $10 million for organizations. When employees take new positions with another company, their former employers are permitted to check the departing employees' computer e-mails and hard drives to determine whether the employees have engaged in computer espionage.

29. Electronic Fund Transfer Crimes

The Electronic Fund Transfers Act (EFTA)[44] makes it a crime to use any counterfeit, stolen, or

---

[41] *Washington v Riley*, 846 P2d 1365 (Wash 1993).
[42] The Counterfeit Access Device and Computer Fraud Act of 1984, 18 USC § 1030 *et seq.*; Computer Fraud and Abuse Act of 1986, as amended in 1999, 18 USC § 1001; Electronic Communications Privacy Act of 1986, Act of 1986, 18 USC § 2510; Computer Fraud Act of 1987, 15 USC §§ 272, 278, 40 USC § 759; National Information Infrastructure Protection Act, 18 USC § 1030 (protecting confidentiality and integrity on the Internet).
[43] 18 USC § 1831.
[44] 15 USC § 1693(n).

e-commerce&cyberlaw

They Were Bullies: Mean Girls in Cyberspace

It has been called the MySpace suicide case. On May 14, 2008, a federal grand jury indicted Lori Drew, 49, of Missouri, the so-called cyber bully. Ms. Drew had created a MySpace site for Josh Evans, a fictitious teen boy she used as a means of getting information from Megan Meier, a 13-year-old girl with whom Ms. Drew's daughter had had a falling-out. Josh pretended to be interested in Megan, but then said that she was "fat" and that the world would be a better place without her. Megan hanged herself within an hour of receiving the final comments from "Josh."

Ms. Drew was charged with one count of conspiracy and two counts of accessing computers without authorization and was convicted of three lesser charges.

When the indictment was made public, Salvador Hernandez, assistant director of the FBI in Los Angeles, said, "Whether we characterize this tragic case as 'cyberbullying,' cyberabuse, or illegal computer access, it should serve as a reminder that our children use the Internet for social interaction and that technology has altered the way they conduct their daily activities. As adults, we must be sensitive to the potential dangers posed by the use of the Internet by our children."*

Some states have now passed specific statutes to make cyber-bullying a crime.

Is there a computer crime statute that covers Ms. Drew's conduct?

Not yet.

* K. C. Jones, "Missouri Mom Indicted in MySpace Cyber-Bullying Suicide Case," **www.informationweek.com**. May 15, 2008.

---

fraudulently obtained card, code, or other device to obtain money or goods in excess of a specified amount through an electronic fund transfer system. The EFTA also makes it a crime to ship in interstate commerce devices or goods so obtained or to knowingly receive goods that have been obtained by means of the fraudulent use of the transfer system.

30. Circumventing Copyright Protection Devices Via Computer

The Digital Millennium Copyright Act (DMCA)[45] makes it a federal offense to circumvent or create programs to circumvent encryption devices that copyright holders place on copyrighted material to prevent unauthorized copying. **For Example,** circumventing the encryption devices on software or CDs or DVDs is a violation of the DMCA.

For example, Dmitry Sklyarov, a Russian computer programmer, was the first person to be charged with a violation of the DMCA. Mr. Sklyarov was arrested in early 2002 at a computer show after giving a speech in Las Vegas at the Defcon convention on his product that he had developed to permit the circumvention of security devices on copyrighted materials. His program unlocks password-protected e-books and PDF files. He gave his speech and was returned to Russia in exchange for his agreement to testify in a case that will determine the constitutionality of DMCA.

31. Spamming

More states are addressing the use of computers to send unsolicited e-mails. Nevada was the first state to regulate spam and California, Washington, and Virginia followed shortly after. Criminal regulation began with very narrowly tailored statutes such as one in Washington that made it a crime to send an e-mail with a misleading title line.[46] The specific

[45] 17 USC § (1998).
[46] Saul Hansell, "Total Up the Bill for Spam," *New York Times*, July 28, 2003, C1, C4.

ethics & the law

Ethics and the Tobacco Class-Action Lawyer

Class-action lawyer Dickie Scruggs was portrayed in the 1999 movie "The Insider," which starred Russell Crowe as Jeffrey Wigand, the tobacco industry whistle-blower who obtained a $206 billion settlement from the tobacco companies (Mr. Scruggs's fee for the case was $1 billion). Almost a decade after the movie that made him a hero came out, Scruggs entered a guilty plea to bribery and was sentenced to five years in prison for his role in an attempt to bribe a federal judge.

Mr. Scruggs was representing insurance claimants against insurers for their damages from Hurricane Katrina. The judge presiding over the case contacted the FBI about a bribery attempt. One of the four lawyers working with Scruggs was approached by the FBI and agreed to wear a wire to catch Scruggs. The content of the tapes revealed both *actus reus* and *scienter*. Zachary Scruggs, Dickie's son, also entered a guilty plea. All of the remaining lawyers involved in the bribery scheme entered guilty pleas as well.

Those in the legal profession said they did not understand Scruggs's actions because he had the skill to win any case. "He didn't need to cheat," was the comment of a representative from the American Trial Lawyers Association. Scruggs's words at his sentencing were poignant: "I could not be more ashamed to be where I am today, mixed up in a judicial bribery scheme.... I realized I was getting mixed up in it. And I will go to my grave wondering why. I have disappointed everyone in my life–my wife, my family, my son, particularly.... I deeply regret my conduct. It is a scar and a stain on my soul that will be there forever."

Source: Abha Bhattarai, "Class-Action Lawyer Given 5 Years in a Bribery Case," New York Times, June 28, 2008, B3.

criminal statutes on spamming are evolving, and Virginia became the first state to pass a criminal antispamming law. The statute prohibits sending "unsolicited bulk electronic mail" or spam and makes the offense a felony based on the level of activity.[47] Thirty-six states now have some form of spamming regulation. The penalties range from fines to imprisonment.

D. CRIMINAL PROCEDURE RIGHTS FOR BUSINESSES

Business criminals are treated the same procedurally as other criminals. They have the same rights under the criminal justice system. The U.S. Constitution guarantees the protection of individual rights within the criminal justice system.

32. Fourth Amendment Rights for Businesses

(A) SEARCH AND SEIZURE: WARRANTS. The **Fourth Amendment** of the U.S. Constitution provides that "the right of the people to be secure in their persons, houses, papers, and effects, against unreasonable searches and seizures, shall not be violated." This amendment protects individual privacy by preventing unreasonable searches and seizures. Before a government agency can seize the property of individuals or businesses, it must obtain a valid **search warrant** issued by a judge or magistrate, based on probable cause, or an exception to this warrant requirement must apply. In other words, there must be good reason to search the location named. The Fourth Amendment applies equally to individuals and corporations. If an improper search is conducted, evidence obtained during the course of that search

---

[47] *Id.*

may be inadmissible in the criminal proceedings for the resulting criminal charges.[48]

(B) EXCEPTIONS TO THE WARRANT REQUIREMENT. Exceptions to the warrant requirement are emergencies, such as a burning building, and the "plain-view" exception, which allows law enforcement officials to take any property that anyone can see, for no privacy rights are violated when items and property are left in the open for members of the public to see. **For Example,** you have an expectation of privacy in the garbage in your garbage can when it is in your house. However, once you move that garbage can onto the public sidewalk for pickup, you no longer have the expectation of privacy because you have left your garbage out in plain view of the public.

Another exception allows officers to enter when they are needed to give aid because of an ongoing criminal act. **For Example,** officers who are able to see a fight through the windows of a house and resulting injuries can enter to render help. Another exception would be that the person who lives in the property to be searched has given permission for the search.

(C) BUSINESS RECORDS AND SEARCHES. In many business crimes, the records that prove a crime was committed are not in the hands of the person who committed that crime. Accountants, attorneys, and other third parties may have the business records in their possession. In addition to the Fourth Amendment issues involved in seizing these records (a warrant is still required), there may be protections for the business defendants. The next section covers those protections.

(D) PROTECTIONS FOR PRIVILEGED RECORDS AND DOCUMENTS. All states recognize an attorney-client privilege, which means that an individual's conversations with her lawyer and the notes of those conversations are not subject to seizure unless the privilege is waived. In many of the prosecutions of companies, the Justice Department has asked companies to waive the attorney/client privilege so that it can have access to information that is then used to find other companies that may have participated in criminal activity. Some states recognize an accountant-client privilege and

other privileges, such as those between priest and parishioner or doctor and patient. A privileged relationship is one in which the records and notes resulting from the contact between individuals cannot be seized even with a warrant (with some exceptions).

33. Fifth Amendment Self-Incrimination Rights for Businesses

(A) SELF-INCRIMINATION. The words "I take the Fifth" are used to invoke the constitutional protections against self-incrimination provided under the **Fifth Amendment** that prevents compelling a person to be a witness against himself. **For Example,** Mark McGwire, the former St. Louis baseball player, invoked the Fifth Amendment in his testimony during Congressional hearings on steroid use. Ken Lay, former CEO and chairman of Enron, took the Fifth Amendment before Congress when asked to testify–as did Bernie Ebbers, former CEO of WorldCom. However, both Lay and Ebbers took the witness stand in their own trials. They were not required to, but hoped to help their cases. The Fifth Amendment protection applies only to individuals; corporations are not given Fifth Amendment protection. A corporation cannot prevent the disclosure of its books and records on the grounds of self-incrimination. The officers and employees of a corporation can assert the Fifth Amendment, but the records of the corporation belong to the corporation, not to them.

(B) MIRANDA RIGHTS. The famous **Miranda warnings** come from a case interpreting the extent of Fifth Amendment rights. In *Miranda v Arizona*,[49] the U.S. Supreme Court ruled that certain warnings must be given to persons who face custodial interrogation for the purposes of possible criminal proceedings. The warnings consist of an explanation to individuals that they have the right to remain silent; that if they do speak, anything they say can be used against them; that they have the right to have an attorney present; and that if they cannot afford an attorney, one will be provided for them. Failure to give the *Miranda* warnings means that any statements, including a confession, obtained while the individual was being

---

[48] See, Arizona v Gant, 129 SCt 1710 (2009) in which the U.S. Supreme Court held that evidence obtained searching the vehicle of a suspect who is handcuffed and locked in a police car cannot be used. A search warrant is needed when the suspect has no access to the evidence to destroy it.
[49] 384 US 436 (1966).

Dow Chemical Co. v United States, 476 US 1819 (1986)

Low-Flying Aircraft Bearing Federal Agents with Cameras

Dow Chemical (petitioner) operates a 2,000-acre chemical plant at Midland, Michigan. The facility, with numerous buildings, conduits, and pipes, is visible from the air. Dow has maintained ground security at the facility and has investigated flyovers by other, unauthorized aircraft. However, none of the buildings or manufacturing equipment is concealed.

In 1978, the Environmental Protection Agency (EPA) conducted an inspection of Dow. The EPA requested a second inspection, but Dow denied the request. The EPA then employed a commercial aerial photographer to take photos of the plant from 12,000, 3,000, and 1,200 feet. The EPA had no warrant, but the plane was always within navigable air space when the photos were taken.

When Dow became aware of the EPA photographer, it brought suit in federal district court and challenged the action as a violation of its Fourth Amendment rights. The district court found that the EPA had violated Dow's rights and issued an injunction prohibiting further use of the aircraft. The Court of Appeals reversed and Dow appealed.

JUDICIAL OPINION

BURGER, Chief Justice.... The photographs at issue in this case are essentially like those used in map-making. Any person with an airplane and an aerial camera could readily duplicate them. In common with much else, the technology of photography has changed in this century. These developments have enhanced industrial processes, and indeed all areas of life; they have also enhanced enforcement techniques. Whether they may be employed by competitors to penetrate trade secrets is not a question presented in this case. Governments do not generally seek to appropriate trade secrets of the private sector, and the right to be free of appropriation of trade secrets is protected by law.

That such photography might be barred by state law with regard to competitors, however, is irrelevant to the questions presented here. State tort law governing unfair competition does not define the limits of the Fourth Amendment. The Government is seeking these photographs in order to regulate, not compete with, Dow.

Dow claims first the EPA has no authority to use aerial photography to implement its statutory authority of "site inspection" under the Clean Air Act.

Congress has vested in EPA certain investigatory and enforcement authority, without spelling out precisely how this authority was to be exercised in all the myriad circumstances that might arise in monitoring matters relating to clean air and water standards.

Regulatory or enforcement authority generally carries with it all the modes of inquiry and investigation traditionally employed or useful to execute the authority granted. Environmental standards cannot be enforced only in libraries and laboratories, helpful as those institutions may be.

The EPA, as a regulatory and enforcement agency, needs no explicit statutory provisions to employ methods of observation commonly available to the public at large; we hold that the use of aerial photography is within the EPA's statutory authority.

DISSENTING OPINION

POWELL, MARSHALL, BRENNAN, and BLACKMUN, Justices... The Fourth Amendment protects private citizens from arbitrary surveillance by their Government. Today, in

the context of administrative aerial photography of commercial premises, the Court retreats from that standard. It holds that the photography was not a Fourth Amendment "search" because it was not accompanied by a physical trespass and because the equipment used was not the most highly sophisticated form of technology available to the Government. Under this holding the existence of an asserted privacy interest apparently will be decided solely by reference to the manner of surveillance used to intrude on that interest. Such an inquiry will not protect Fourth Amendment rights, but rather will permit their gradual decay as technology advances.

EPA's aerial photography penetrated into a private commercial enclave, an area in which society has recognized that privacy interests may legitimately be claimed. The photographs captured highly confidential information that Dow had taken reasonable and objective steps to preserve as private.

QUESTIONS

1. Of what significance is the fact that Dow's plant could be seen from the air?

2. Did the EPA need a warrant for taking its aerial photographs?

3. What objections does the dissent raise to the decision?

Georgia v Randolph, 2006 WL 707380 (2006)

A Man's Home Is His Castle, but His Wife Can Still Turn on Him

Scott Randolph and his wife, Janet, separated in late May 2001, when she left their Americus, Georgia, home and went to stay with her parents in Canada, taking their son and some belongings. In July, she returned to the Americus house with the child. No one is sure whether she had returned to reconcile or whether she had come to gather her remaining possessions.

On July 6, 2001, Janet called police and told them that there were "items of drug evidence" in the house. Sergeant Murray asked Scott Randolph for permission to search the house, which he refused.

The sergeant turned to Janet for consent to search, which she readily gave. She led the officer upstairs to a bedroom that she identified as Scott's, where the sergeant noticed a section of a drinking straw with a powdery residue he suspected was cocaine. He then left the house to get an evidence bag from his car and to call the district attorney's office, which instructed him to stop the search and apply for a warrant.

When Sergeant Murray returned to the house, Janet Randolph withdrew her consent. The police took the straw and the Randolphs to the police station. After getting a search warrant, the police returned to the house and seized further evidence of drug use, which served as the basis of Scott's indictment for possession of cocaine.

Scott Randolph moved to suppress the evidence, as products of a warrantless search. The trial court denied the motion, ruling that Janet had common authority to consent to the search.

The Court of Appeals of Georgia reversed, and the Georgia Supreme Court sustained the reversal. The state of Georgia appealed, and the U.S. Supreme Court granted *certiorari*.

JUDICIAL OPINION

SOUTER, Justice… To the Fourth Amendment rule ordinarily prohibiting the warrantless entry of a person's house as unreasonable per se, one "jealously and carefully drawn" exception recognizes the validity of searches with the voluntary consent of an individual possessing authority. None of our co-occupant consent-to-search cases, however, has presented the further fact of a second occupant physically present and refusing permission to search, and later moving to suppress evidence so obtained.

[S]hared tenancy is understood to include an "assumption of risk," on which police officers are entitled to rely, and although some group living together might make an exceptional arrangement that no one could admit a guest without

the agreement of all, the chance of such an eccentric scheme is too remote to expect visitors to investigate a particular household's rules before accepting an invitation to come in. So, *Matlock* relied on what was usual and placed no burden on the police to eliminate the possibility of atypical arrangements, in the absence of reason to doubt that the regular scheme was in place.

The want of any recognized superior authority among disagreeing tenants is also reflected in the law's response when the disagreements cannot be resolved. The law does not ask who has the better side of the conflict; it simply provides a right to any co-tenant, even the most unreasonable, to obtain a decree partitioning the property and terminating the relationship. And while a decree of partition is not the answer to disagreement among rental tenants, this situation resembles co-ownership in lacking the benefit of any understanding that one or the other rental co-tenant has a superior claim to control the use of the quarters they occupy together. In sum, there is no common understanding that one co-tenant generally has a right or authority to prevail over the express wishes of another, whether the issue is the color of the curtains or invitations to outsiders.

Since we hold to the "centuries-old principle of respect for the privacy of the home," "it is beyond dispute that the home is entitled to special protection as the center of the private lives of our people." We have, after all, lived our whole national history with an understanding of "the ancient adage that a man's home is his castle [to the point that t]he poorest man may in his cottage bid defiance to all the forces of the Crown."

Disputed permission is thus no match for this central value of the Fourth Amendment, and the State's other countervailing claims do not add up to outweigh it. Yes, we recognize the consenting tenant's interest as a citizen in bringing criminal activity to light. And we understand a co-tenant's legitimate self-interest in siding with the police to deflect suspicion raised by sharing quarters with a criminal.

Nor should this established policy of Fourth Amendment law be undermined by the principal dissent's claim that it shields spousal abusers and other violent co-tenants who will refuse to allow the police to enter a dwelling when their victims ask the police for help. It is not that the dissent exaggerates violence in the home; we recognize that domestic abuse is a serious problem in the United States. But this case has no bearing on the capacity of the police to protect domestic victims. The dissent's argument rests on the failure

Continued

to distinguish two different issues: when the police may enter without committing a trespass, and when the police may enter to search for evidence. No question has been raised, or reasonably could be, about the authority of the police to enter a dwelling to protect a resident from domestic violence; so long as they have good reason to believe such a threat exists, it would be silly to suggest that the police would commit a tort by entering, say, to give a complaining tenant the opportunity to collect belongings and get out safely, or to determine whether violence (or threat of violence) has just occurred or is about to (or soon will) occur, however much a spouse or other co-tenant objected. Thus, the question whether the police might lawfully enter over objection in order to provide any protection that might be reasonable is easily answered yes.

This case invites a straightforward application of the rule that a physically present inhabitant's express refusal of consent to a police search is dispositive as to him, regardless of the consent of a fellow occupant. Scott Randolph's refusal is clear, and nothing in the record justifies the search on grounds independent of Janet Randolph's consent. The State does not argue that she gave any indication to the police of a need for protection inside the house that might have justified entry into the portion of the premises where the police found the powdery straw (which, if lawfully seized, could have been used when attempting to establish probable cause for the warrant issued later).

The judgment of the Supreme Court of Georgia is therefore affirmed.

DISSENTING OPINION

Chief Justice ROBERTS, with whom Justice SCALIA joins, dissenting.

The Court creates constitutional law by surmising what is typical when a social guest encounters an entirely atypical situation. The rule the majority fashions does not implement the high office of the Fourth Amendment to protect privacy, but instead provides protection on a random and happenstance basis, protecting, for example, a co-occupant who happens to be at the front door when the other occupant consents to a search, but not one napping or watching television in the next room. And the cost of affording such random protection is great, as demonstrated by the recurring cases in which abused spouses seek to authorize police entry into a home they share with a nonconsenting abuser.

The correct approach to the question presented is clearly mapped out in our precedents: The Fourth Amendment protects privacy. If an individual shares information, papers, or places with another, he assumes the risk that the other person will in turn share access to that information or those

papers or places with the government. And just as an individual who has shared illegal plans or incriminating documents with another cannot interpose an objection when that other person turns the information over to the government, just because the individual happens to be present at the time, so too someone who shares a place with another cannot interpose an objection when that person decides to grant access to the police, simply because the objecting individual happens to be present.

A warrantless search is reasonable if police obtain the voluntary consent of a person authorized to give it. Co-occupants have "assumed the risk that one of their number might permit [a] common area to be searched." Just as Mrs. Randolph could walk upstairs, come down, and turn her husband's cocaine straw over to the police, she can consent to police entry and search of what is, after all, her home, too.

The majority's assumption about voluntary accommodation simply leads to the common stalemate of two gentlemen insisting that the other enter a room first.

The fact is that a wide variety of differing social situations can readily be imagined, giving rise to quite different social expectations. A relative or good friend of one of two feuding roommates might well enter the apartment over the objection of the other roommate. The reason the invitee appeared at the door also affects expectations: A guest who came to celebrate an occupant's birthday, or one who had traveled some distance for a particular reason, might not readily turn away simply because of a roommate's objection. The nature of the place itself is also pertinent: Invitees may react one way if the feuding roommates share one room, differently if there are common areas from which the objecting roommate could readily be expected to absent himself. Altering the numbers might well change the social expectations: Invitees might enter if two of three co-occupants encourage them to do so, over one dissenter.

The possible scenarios are limitless, and slight variations in the fact pattern yield vastly different expectations about whether the invitee might be expected to enter or to go away. Such shifting expectations are not a promising foundation on which to ground a constitutional rule, particularly because the majority has no support for its basic assumption—that an invited guest encountering two disagreeing co-occupants would flee—beyond a hunch about how people would typically act in an atypical situation.

If two friends share a locker and one keeps contraband inside, he might trust that his friend will not let others look inside. But by sharing private space, privacy has "already been frustrated" with respect to the lockermate. If two roommates share a computer and one keeps pirated software on a shared drive, he might assume that his roommate will not inform the

Continued

government. But that person has given up his privacy with respect to his roommate by saving the software on their shared computer.

The same analysis applies to the question whether our privacy can be compromised by those with whom we share common living space. If a person keeps contraband in common areas of his home, he runs the risk that his co-occupants will deliver the contraband to the police.

In this sense, the risk assumed by a joint occupant is comparable to the risk assumed by one who reveals private information to another. If a person has incriminating information, he can keep it private in the face of a request from police to share it, because he has that right under the Fifth Amendment. If a person occupies a house with incriminating information in it, he can keep that information private in the face of a request from police to search the house, because he has that right under the Fourth Amendment. But if he shares the information—or the house—with another, that other can grant access to the police in each instance.

QUESTIONS

1. What factors in the case caused such strong opinions by the majority and dissenting judges?

2. What role did the issue of property law play in the decision and opinions?

3. Why did the issue of domestic violence come up in the opinion?

---

interrogated cannot be used as evidence against that individual. The prosecution will have to rely on evidence other than the statements made in violation of *Miranda*, if such evidence exists.

34. Due Process Rights for Businesses

Also included in the Fifth Amendment is the language of due process. **Due process** is the right to be heard, question witnesses, and present evidence before any criminal conviction can occur. Due process in criminal cases consists of an initial appearance at which the charges and the defendant's rights are outlined; a preliminary hearing or grand jury proceeding in which the evidence is determined to be sufficient to warrant a trial; an arraignment for entering a plea and setting a trial date when the defendant pleads innocent; a period of discovery for obtaining evidence; and a trial at which witnesses for the prosecution can be cross-examined and evidence presented to refute the charges. In addition to these procedural steps, the **Sixth Amendment** guarantees

that the entire process will be completed in a timely fashion because this amendment guarantees a speedy trial.

lawflix

Double Jeopardy (2000) R

Ashley Judd plays a woman on the run for false charges of killing her husband. But her husband faked his death and then she finds and kills him – can she be tried again?

Columbo (Seasons 1–6)

Detective Columbo is the bumbling, brilliant sleuth who crosses a few Fourth and Fifth Amendment lines here and there.

Check out LawFlix at **www.cengage.com/ blaw/dvl** to access movie clips that illustrate business law concepts.

MAKE THE CONNECTION

SUMMARY

When a person does not live up to the standards set by law, this punishable conduct, called *crime*, may be common law or statutory in origin. Crimes are classified as *felonies*, which generally carry greater sentences and more long-term consequences, and *misdemeanors.*

Employers and corporations may be criminally responsible for their acts and the acts of their employees. The federal sentencing guidelines provide parameters for sentences for federal crimes and allow judges to consider whether the fact that a business promotes compliance with the law is a reason to reduce a sentence.

White-collar crimes include those relating to financial fraud. Sarbanes-Oxley reforms increased the penalties for financial fraud and added fraudulent financial statement certification as a crime. Other white-collar crimes include bribery, extortion, blackmail, and corrupt influence in politics and in business. Also included as white-collar crimes are counterfeiting, forgery, perjury, making false claims against the government, obtaining goods or money by false pretenses, using bad checks, false financial reporting, and embezzlement. The common law crimes include those that involve injury to person and/or property, such as arson and murder.

Statutes have expanded the area of criminal law to meet situations in which computers are involved. Both federal and state statutes make the unauthorized taking of information from a computer a crime. The diversion of deliveries of goods and the transfer of funds, the theft of software, and the raiding of computers are made crimes to some extent by federal laws. Newer federal statutes that apply to computers are the Economic Espionage Act, which prohibits downloading or copying information via computer to give to a competitor, and the Digital Millennium Copyright Act that prohibits circumventing or designing programs to circumvent encryption devices.

Criminal procedure is dictated by the Fourth, Fifth, and Sixth Amendments. The Fourth Amendment protects against unreasonable searches, the Fifth Amendment protects against self-incrimination and provides due process, and the Sixth Amendment guarantees a speedy trial.

LEARNING OUTCOMES

After studying this chapter, you should be able to

A. GENERAL PRINCIPLES

LO.1 Discuss the nature and classification of crimes
See the discussion of crimes and misdemeanors on p. 142.

LO.2 Describe the basis of criminal liability
See the **For Example** discussion of dumping waste and intent on p. 142.
See *U.S. v Erickson* on p. 143.

LO.3 Identify who is responsible for criminal acts
See *U.S. v Park* on p. 145.
See Thinking Things Through on p. 149.

LO.4 Explain the penalties for crimes and the sentencing for corporate crimes

See the discussion of the sentencing guidelines and the various cases related to them on p. 146.

B. WHITE-COLLAR CRIMES

LO.5 List examples of white-collar crimes and their elements
See the discussion that begins on p. 150.
See the Sports & Entertainment Law discussion of the NBA referee on p. 156.

LO.6 Describe the common law crimes
See the discussion that begins on p. 155.
See the E-Commerce & Cyberlaw discussion of cyber-bullying on p. 159.

C. CRIMINAL LAW AND THE COMPUTER

LO.7 Discuss crimes related to computers
See the discussion that begins on p. 157.

D. CRIMINAL PROCEDURE RIGHTS FOR BUSINESSES

LO.8 Describe the rights of businesses charged with crimes and the constitutional protections afforded them
See the *Dow* case on p. 162.

KEY TERMS

blackmail
computer crime
conspiracy
crime
due process
Economic Espionage Act (EEA)
embezzlement
extortion
facilitation payments
Federal Sentencing Guidelines

felonies
Fifth Amendment
Foreign Corrupt Practices Act (FCPA)
forgery
Fourth Amendment
grease
Miranda warnings
misdemeanors
predicate act

Racketeer Influenced and Corrupt Organizations (RICO) Act
search warrant
Sixth Amendment
uttering
White-Collar Crime Penalty Enhancement Act of 2002
white-collar crime

QUESTIONS AND CASE PROBLEMS

1. Bernard Flinn operated a business known as Harvey Investment Co., Inc./High Risk Loans. Flinn worked as a loan broker, matching those who came to him with lenders willing to loan them money given their credit history and the amount involved. From 1982 through 1985, Flinn found loans for five people. Indiana requires that persons engaged in the business of brokering loans obtain a license from the state. Flinn was prosecuted for brokering loans without having a license. He raised the defense that he did not know that a license was required and that, accordingly, he lacked the criminal intent to broker loans without having a license. Does Flinn have a good defense? [*Flinn v Indiana,* 563 NE2d 536 (Ind)]

2. H. J., Inc., and other customers of Northwestern Bell Corp. alleged that Northwestern Bell had furnished cash and tickets for air travel, plays, and sporting events and had offered employment to members of the Minnesota Public Utilities Commission in exchange for favorable treatment in rate cases before the commission. A Minnesota statute makes it a felony to bribe public officials. H. J. and other customers brought suit against Northwestern for violating the criminal bribery statute. Can the customers bring a criminal action? [*H. J., Inc. v Northwestern Bell Corp.,* 420 NW2d 673 (Minn App)]

3. Baker and others entered a Wal-Mart store shortly after 3:00 A.M. by cutting through the metal door with an acetylene torch. They had moved some of the merchandise in the store to the rear door, but the police arrived before the merchandise could be taken from the store. Baker was prosecuted for larceny. He raised the defense that he was not guilty of larceny because no merchandise had ever left the store. Is there enough intent and action for a crime? [*Tennessee v Baker,* 751 SW2d 154 (Tenn App)]

4. Gail drove her automobile after having had dinner and several drinks. She fell asleep at the wheel and ran over and killed a pedestrian. Prosecuted for manslaughter, she raised the defense that she did not intend to hurt anyone and because of the drinks did not know what she was doing. Was this a valid defense?

5. Dr. Doyle E. Campbell, an ophthalmologist, established his practice in southern Ohio in 1971. Many of Dr. Campbell's patients are elderly people who qualify for federal Medicare benefits and state Medicaid benefits. Under the existing financing system, a doctor who treats a Medicare patient is required to submit a "Medicare Health Insurance Claim Form" (HCFA Form 1500). The doctor is required to certify that "the services shown on this form were medically indicated and necessary for the health of the patient and were personally rendered by me or were rendered incident to my professional service by my employees." Claims Dr. Campbell submitted for his elderly patients ranged from $900 to $950, of which $530 to $680 were covered by the Medicare program. The government alleged that Dr. Campbell billed Medicare for several treatments that were either not performed or not necessary. Dr. Campbell was charged with fraud for the paperwork he submitted. Has he committed a crime? [*United States v Campbell*, 845 F 2d 1374 (6th Cir)]

6. In the late 1980s, Life Energy Resources, Ltd. (LER), a New York corporation, was a multilevel marketing network. LER's marketing plan provided that members of the general public could purchase its products only through an official LER distributor or by becoming LER distributors themselves. Each potential distributor had to be sponsored by an existing distributor and was required to sign a distributorship agreement with LER stating that he or she would not make medical claims or use unofficial literature or marketing aids to promote LER products.

Ballistrea and his partner Michael Ricotta were at the top of the LER distribution network. Two products sold by LER were the REM SuperPro Frequency Generator (REM) and the Lifemax Miracle Cream (Miracle Cream). The REM, which sold for $1,350 to distributors, was a small box powered by electricity that ran currents through the feet and body of the user.

Ballistrea and Ricotta distributed literature and audiotapes to many potential downstream distributors and customers—some of whom were undercover government agents—touting the REM and the Miracle Cream. Other literature claimed that the Miracle Cream could alleviate the discomforts of premenstrual syndrome and reverse the effects of osteoporosis. The Food and Drug Administration charged Ballistrea and Ricotta with violating federal law for making medical claims concerning LER products. Their defense is that they never sold any of the products. They simply earned commissions as part of the marketing scheme and could not be held criminally liable on the charges. Are they correct? [*United States v Ballistrea*, 101 F 3d 827 (2d Cir)]

7. Carriage Homes, Inc. was a general contractor that built multifamily residential and land-development projects in Minnesota. John Arkell was Carriage Homes' chief executive officer, president, and sole shareholder. Carriage Homes built Southwinds, a condominium development of 38 residential units in Austin, Minnesota. The foundation elevations of some of the Southwinds units were lower than permitted under the State Building Code, causing storm water to pool in the units' driveways and garages. The city of Austin's development director sent Arkell a series of seven letters in 1999 and 2001 concerning the elevation problems, and Arkell gave the letters to the project managers, who failed to resolve the problems.

Minnesota makes a violation of the State Building Code a misdemeanor. On May 30, 2001, the state charged Carriage Homes and Arkell with three misdemeanor counts each, alleging a violation of the Uniform Building Code (UBC).

Carriage Homes pleaded guilty and was sentenced to a $1,000 fine. But Arkell pleaded not guilty, asserting that he could not be held criminally responsible for the violation. After a bench trial, the district court found Arkell guilty. He was sentenced to pay a fine, pay restitution to the condominium owners, and serve 90 days in jail, with 80 days stayed pending his compliance with sentencing conditions. Mr. Arkell appealed on the grounds that the employees and subcontractors had simply not followed his orders and he was not responsible for their failures. Is he correct? [*State v Arkell*, 657 NW2d 883 (Minn. App. 2003)]

8. James Durham runs an art gallery. He has several paintings from unknown artists that he has listed for sale. The paintings always sell at his weekly auction for $20,000 to $50,000 above what James believes them to be worth. James learns that the bidders at the auctions are employed by an olive distributor located near the shipping yards of the city. What concerns should Durham have about the art, the bidders and the large purchase prices?

9. Jennings operated a courier service to collect and deliver money. The contract with his customers allowed him a day or so to deliver the money that had been collected. Instead of holding collections until delivered, Jennings made short-term investments with the money. He always made deliveries to the customers on time, but because he kept the profit from the investments for himself, Jennings was prosecuted for embezzlement. Was he guilty? [*New York v Jennings*, 504 NE2d 1079 (NY)]

10. In 2000, former investment banker Frank Quattrone was head of the technology division of Credit Suisse First Boston Corporation (CSFB), earning about $120 million per year. Quattrone and his Tech Group did the initial public offerings (IPOs) for a great many of the dotcoms. Because of questions about those IPOs, there were several state and federal grand jury investigations of CSFB pending in the fall of 2000. On December 5, 2000, Quattrone sent the following e-mail "endorsement":

    [H]aving been a key witness in a securities litigation case in south texas (miniscribe) i strongly advise you to follow these procedures.

Quattrone then added an e-mail from Richard Char, another investment banker, that read:

Subject: Time to clean up those files …

With the recent tumble in stock prices, and many deals now trading below issue price, the securities litigation bar is expected to [sic] an all out assault on broken tech IPOs.

In the spirit of the end of the year (and the slow down in corporate finance work), we want to remind you of the CSFB document retention policy [the policy was reproduced here].

Note that if a lawsuit is instituted, our normal document retention policy is suspended and any cleaning of files is prohibited under the CSFB guidelines (since it constitutes the destruction of evidence). We strongly suggest that before you leave for the holidays, you should catch up on file cleanup.

As a result of the Quattrone e-mail, at least some Tech Group bankers began or continued "cleaning" their files. Quattrone was indicted for obstruction of justice in connection with the investigations. Did he obstruct justice? [*U.S. v Quattrone*, 441 F 3d 153 (2d Cir 2006)]

11. Grabert ran Beck's, an amusement center in Louisiana. He held a license for video gambling machines. Louisiana makes it illegal to allow a minor to play a video gambling machine. A mother came into Grabert's center carrying her 23-month-old baby in her arms. She sat at the video poker machine with her child on her lap and proceeded to play. State troopers witnessed the baby pushing the buttons on the machine at least three times. The Department of Public Safety and Corrections revoked Grabert's video gaming license because a minor had been allowed to play the machines, and Grabert sought judicial review. The trial court reversed, and the department appealed. Has Grabert committed the crime of allowing a minor to engage in gaming? Is this the crime of allowing a minor to gamble? [*Grabert v Department of Public Safety & Corrections*, 680 So2d 764 (La App) *cert. denied; Grabert v State through Dept. of Public Safety and Corrections*, 685 So2d 126 (La.)]

12. The Banco Central administered a humanitarian plan for the government of Ecuador. Fernando

Banderas and his wife presented false claims that the bank paid. After the fraud was discovered, the bank sued Banderas and his wife for damages for fraud and treble damages under the Florida version of RICO. Banderas and his wife asserted that they were not liable for RICO damages because there was no proof that they were related to organized crime and because the wrong they had committed was merely ordinary fraud. They had not used any racketeering methods. Is involvement with organized crime a requirement for liability under RICO? [*Banderas v Banco Central del Ecuador*, 461 So2d 265 (Fla App)]

13. Kravitz owned 100 percent of the stock of American Health Programs, Inc. (AHP). To obtain the Philadelphia Fraternal Order of Police as a customer for AHP, Kravitz paid money bribes to persons who he thought were officers of that organization but who in fact were federal undercover agents. He was prosecuted for violating RICO. He was convicted, and the court ordered the forfeiture of all of Kravitz's shares of AHP stock. Can a forfeiture be ordered? [*United States v Kravitz*, 738 F 2d 102 (3d Cir)]   *yes*

14. Howell made long-distance telephone calls through the telephone company's computer-controlled switching system to solicit funding for a nonexistent business enterprise. What crimes did Howell commit? [*New Mexico v Howell*, 895 P 2d 232 (NM App)]

Chapter 9

Torts

The law of torts permits individuals and companies to recover from other individuals and companies for wrongs committed against them. Tort law provides rights and remedies for conduct that meets the elements required to establish that a wrong has occurred.

A. General Principles

Civil, or noncriminal, wrongs that are not breaches of contract are governed by tort law. This chapter covers the types of civil wrongs that constitute torts and the remedies available for those wrongs.

1. What Is a Tort?

Tort comes from the Latin term *tortus,* which means "crooked, dubious, twisted." Torts are actions that are not straight but are crooked, or civil, wrongs. A tort is an interference with someone's person or property. **For Example,** entering someone's house without his or her permission is an interference and constitutes the tort of trespass. Causing someone's character to be questioned is a wrong against the person and is the tort of defamation. The law provides protection against these harms in the form of remedies awarded after the wrongs are committed. These remedies are civil remedies for the acts of interference by others.

2. Tort and Crime Distinguished

A *crime* is a wrong that arises from a violation of a public duty, whereas a *tort* is a wrong that arises from a violation of a private duty. A crime is a wrong of such a serious nature that the appropriate level of government steps in to prosecute and punish the wrongdoer to deter others from engaging in the same type of conduct. However, whenever the act that is committed as a crime causes harm to an identifiable person, that person may recover from the wrongdoer for monetary damages to compensate for the harm. For the person who experiences the direct harm, the act is called a *tort*; for the government, the same act is called a *crime*.

When the same act is both a crime and a tort, the government may prosecute the wrongdoer for a violation of criminal law, and the individual who experiences the direct harm may recover damages. **For Example,** O. J. Simpson was charged by the state of California with the murder of his ex-wife, Nicole Brown Simpson, and her friend Ron Goldman. A criminal trial was held in which O. J. Simpson was acquitted. Simpson was subsequently sued civilly by the families of Nicole Simpson and Ron Goldman for the tort of wrongful death. The jury in the civil case found Simpson civilly liable and the court ordered him to pay nearly $20 million in damages plus interest. Only $382,000 of this judgment has actually been paid to the families.

3. Types of Torts

There are three types of torts: intentional torts, negligence, and strict liability. **Intentional torts** are those that occur when wrongdoers engage in intentional conduct. **For Example,** striking another person in a fight is an intentional act and would be the tort of battery and possibly also the crime of battery. Your arm striking another person's nose in a fast-moving crowd of people at a rock concert is not a tort or crime because your arm was pushed unintentionally by the force of the crowd. If you stretched out your arms in that crowd or began to swing your arms about and struck another person, you would be behaving carelessly in a crowd of people; and, although you may not have committed an intentional tort, it is possible that your careless conduct constitutes the tort of **negligence**. Careless actions, or actions taken without thinking through their consequences, constitute negligence. The harm to the other person's nose may not have been intended, but there is liability for these accidental harms under negligence. **For Example,** if you run a red light, hit another car, and injure its driver, you did not intend the result. However, your careless behavior of disregarding a traffic signal resulted in the injury, and you would have liability for your negligence to that driver.

Strict liability is another type of tort that imposes liability without regard to whether there was any intent to harm or any negligence occurred. Strict liability is imposed without regard to fault. Strict or absolute liability is imposed because the activity involved is so dangerous that there must be full accountability.

Nonetheless, the activity is necessary and cannot be prohibited. The compromise is to allow the activity but ensure that its dangers and resulting damages are fully covered through the imposition of full liability for all injuries that result. **For Example,** contractors often need to use dynamite to take a roadway through a mountainside or demolish a building that has become a hazard. When the dynamite is used, noise, debris, and possibly dangerous pieces of earth and building will descend on others' land and possibly on people. In most states, contractors are held strictly liable for the resulting damage from the use of dynamite. The activity is necessary and not illegal, but those who use dynamite must be prepared to compensate those who are injured as a result.

Other areas in which there is strict liability for activity include the storage of flammable materials and crop dusting. The federal government and the states have pure food laws that impose absolute liability on manufacturers who fail to meet the statutory standards for their products. Another area of strict liability is *product liability,* which is covered in Chapter 25.

B. Intentional Torts

4. Assault

An *assault* is intentional conduct that threatens a person with a well-founded fear of imminent harm coupled with the present ability to carry out the threat of harm. **For Example,** the angry assertion "I'm going to kick your butt" along with aggressive movement in the direction of the victim with the intent to carry out the threat is an assault, even though a third person intervenes to stop the intended action. Mere words, however, although insulting, are ordinarily insufficient to constitute an assault.

5. Battery

A *battery* is the intentional, wrongful touching of another person without that person's consent. Thus, a threat to use force is an assault, and the actual use of force is the battery. The single action of striking an individual can be both a crime and a tort. A lawsuit

for the tort of battery provides a plaintiff with the opportunity to recover damages resulting from the battery. The plaintiff must prove damages, however.

6. False Imprisonment

False imprisonment is the intentional detention of a person without that person's consent.[1] The detention need not be for any specified period of time, for any detention against one's will is false imprisonment. False imprisonment is often called the *shopkeeper's tort* because so much liability has been imposed on store owners for their unreasonable detention of customers suspected of shoplifting. Requiring a customer to sit in the manager's office or not allowing a customer to leave the store can constitute the tort of false imprisonment. Shop owners do, however, need the opportunity to investigate possible thefts in their stores. As a result, all states have some form of privilege or protection for store owners called a *shopkeeper's privilege.*

The **shopkeeper's privilege** permits the store owner to detain a suspected shoplifter based on reasonable suspicion for a reasonable time without resulting liability for false imprisonment to the accused customer.[2] The privilege applies even if the store owner was wrong about the customer being a shoplifter, so long as the store owner acted based on reasonable suspicions and treated the accused shoplifter in a reasonable manner. These privilege statutes do not protect the store owner from liability for unnecessary physical force or for invasion of privacy.

7. Intentional Infliction of Emotional Distress

The **intentional infliction of emotional distress** (IIED) is a tort involving conduct that goes beyond all bounds of decency and produces mental anguish in the harmed individual. This tort requires proof of outrageous conduct and resulting emotional distress in the victim. **For Example,** Erica Schoen, a 16-year employee of Freightliner, returned to work on light duty after surgery for a work-related shoulder injury. She was assigned to work out of the nurse's station under two

---

[1] *Forgie-Buccioni v Hannaford Bros. Inc.,* 413 F3d 175 (1st Cir 2005).
[2] *Limited Stores, Inc. v Wilson-Robinson,* 876 SW2d 248 (Ark 1994); see also *Wal-Mart Stores, Inc. v Binns,* 15 SW3d 320 (Ark 2000).

employees who intentionally worked her beyond her restrictions, assigned her to humiliating work, repeatedly called her worthless, and used her as a personal servant—ordering her to get snacks, sodas, and lunches for them and not reimbursing her. After five months of this treatment, Erica brought the matter to the human resources manager, who told her, in part, "Nobody wants you. You're worthless. We build trucks down here. . . ." Erica became hysterical and thereafter required psychiatric care. The jury awarded $250,000 for IIED, and it was upheld on appeal because the repetitive misconduct and its duration, ratified by the human resource manager, was intolerable.[3]

8. Invasion of Privacy

The right of privacy is the right to be free of unreasonable intrusion into one's private affairs. The tort of **invasion of privacy** actually consists of three different torts: (1) intrusion into the plaintiff's private affairs (for example, planting a microphone in an office or home); (2) public disclosure of private facts (for example, disclosing private financial information, such as a business posting returned checks from customers near its cash register in a public display); and (3) appropriation of another's name, likeness, or image for commercial advantage. This form of invasion of privacy is generally referred to as the *right of publicity*. The elements of this tort are (1) appropriation of the plaintiff's name or likeness for the value associated with it, and not in an incidental manner or for a newsworthy purpose, (2) identification of the plaintiff in the publication, and (3) an advantage or benefit to the defendant. The right of publicity is designed to protect the commercial interest of celebrities in their identities. **For Example,** popular and critically acclaimed rock and roll musician Don Henley, the founder and member of the band The Eagles, successfully sued a department store chain that ran an international newspaper advertisement for its Henley shirt, which stated in large letters as the focus of the ad "This is Don's henley." The ad (1) used the value associated with the famous name Don Henley to get consumers to read

it, (2) the plaintiff was identifiable in the ad, and (3) the ad was created with the belief that use of the words "Don's henley" would help sell the product.[4]

9. Defamation

Defamation is an untrue statement by one party about another to a third party. **Slander** is oral or spoken defamation, and **libel** is written (and in some cases broadcast) defamation. The elements for defamation are (1) a statement about a person's reputation, honesty, or integrity that is untrue; (2) publication (which is accomplished when a third party hears or reads the defamatory statement); (3) a statement that is directed at a particular person; and (4) damages that result from the statement.

For Example, a false statement by the owner of a business that the former manager was fired for stealing when he was not would be defamation, and the former manager's damages could be his inability to find another position because of the statement's impact on his reputation.

In cases in which the victim is a public figure, such as a Hollywood celebrity or a professional sports player, another element is required, the element of malice, which means that what was said or written was done with the knowledge that the information was false or with reckless disregard for whether it was true or false.

The defenses to defamation include the truth. If the statement is true, even if it is harmful to the victim, it is not the tort of defamation.[5]

Some statements are privileged, and this privilege provides a full or partial defense to the tort of defamation. **For Example,** members of Congress enjoy an **absolute privilege** when they are speaking on the floor of the Senate or the House because public policy requires a free dialogue on the issues pending in a legislative body. The same absolute privilege applies to witnesses in court proceedings to encourage witnesses with information to come forward and testify. Where a witness granted immunity from prosecution testifies before a governmental agency, the witness is entitled to immunity from defamation lawsuits, as set forth in the *Clemens* case.

[3] *Schoen v Freightliner LLC*, 199 P3d 332 (Or App 2008).
[4] *Henley v Dillard Department Stores*, 46 F Supp 2d 587 (ND Tex 1999).
[5] See *Stark v Zeta Phi Beta Sorority Inc.*, 587 F Supp 2d 170 (D DC 2008).

Clemens v McNamee, 638 F Supp 2d 742 (SD Tex 2009)

Roger Clemens Strikes Out in Texas Court

Roger Clemens sued his former trainer Brian McNamee for defamation. He alleged that McNamee falsely stated to the "Mitchell Commission," a congressional investigatory body looking into the use of performance-enhancing drugs in major league baseball, that Clemens had used steroids and human growth hormones during his professional baseball career. Clemens's complaint alleged that McNamee's statements to the Commission "injured Clemens's reputation and exposed him to public hatred, contempt, ridicule, and financial injuries." McNamee filed a motion to dismiss for lack of personal jurisdiction and privilege.

JUDICIAL OPINION

Ellison, District Judge . . . McNamee argues that his statements to the Mitchell Commission are privileged, and therefore cannot form the basis for a defamation action. The Court has already determined that it does not have personal jurisdiction over McNamee with respect to his statements to Mitchell. In the alternative, the Court now finds that McNamee's statements to Mitchell should be treated with immunity.

Based on statements made by McNamee's counsel at oral argument, the Court requested that McNamee submit additional evidence of a judicial proceeding, including statements from the prosecutors and investigators involved, any judicial records, and evidence that McNamee's statements were not voluntary. In response, McNamee submitted three declarations, including two declarations from his own counsel and one from Assistant United States Attorney Matthew A. Parrella. . . .

Under Texas law, statements made to government agencies as part of legislative, judicial, or quasi-judicial proceedings are entitled to absolute immunity so long as they are made as part of an ongoing proceeding, they are not unsolicited, and they are made to an agency whose findings need not be approved or ratified by another agency. . . .

In *Shanks v. Allied Signal Inc.,* the Fifth Circuit considered whether such immunity should be given to statements made during the context of a National Transportation Safety Board investigation. After reviewing Texas law, the Fifth Circuit determined that, even though the Texas Supreme Court had never spoken to the specific issue of whether statements made to NTSB investigators were

protected by absolute immunity, the Court would most likely find these statements to be covered. In coming to this conclusion, the Fifth Circuit recognized that, when communications relate to an ongoing proceeding, absolute immunity applies. It thus held that, under Texas law, statements made to NTSB investigators were subject to absolute immunity.

According to Assistant United States Attorney Parrella, he interviewed McNamee as part of an investigation into the distribution of anabolic steroids, human growth hormones, and money laundering. McNamee and his counsel met with Parrella, FBI agents, and IRS agents numerous times. McNamee was told, prior to the interviews, that he was not a target of the investigation, but that his "witness status would be subject to review if he chose not to co-operate." McNamee's statements during the interview were given use immunity, and he was told that he was subject to prosecution for making false statements.

It was Parrella who requested that McNamee speak to the Mitchell Commission. Parrella told McNamee that speaking to the Mitchell Commission was part of his cooperation with the investigation in order to maintain his witness status. Prior to the interviews with the Mitchell Commission, Parrella told McNamee that the proffer agreement would cover the interviews and that he could face prosecution for any false material statements. McNamee agreed to these terms, and he participated in three interviews with the Mitchell Commission. The interviews were all arranged by either agents or Assistant United States Attorneys. Agents and Assistant United States Attorneys participated, either in person or via phone, in all interviews between McNamee and the Mitchell Commission.

Parrella's investigation, much like the NTSB investigation at issue in *Shanks,* was an ongoing proceeding. All of McNamee's interviews with Mitchell were scheduled by prosecutors or federal agents. Parrella compelled McNamee to speak to Mitchell, in effect, by warning him that, if he did not cooperate, his witness status could change. Parrella also warned McNamee that, if he lied to Mitchell, he could be subject to a federal prosecution. As a matter of public policy, McNamee's statements to Mitchell should be protected. As the court observed in *Darrah v. Hinds,* "the proper administration of justice requires full disclosure from witnesses without fear of

Continued

retaliatory lawsuits for defamation of any sort." 720 S.W.2d 689, 691 (Tex. App.-Fort Worth 1986, ref. n.r.e.).

. . .Since Clemens does not dispute Parrella's Declaration, the Court finds, pursuant to Rule 56, that McNamee was compelled to make his statements to Mitchell as part of a judicial proceeding. . . .

[Authors' Note: The court dismissed for lack of personal jurisdiction Clemens's allegations regarding statements made by McNamee to *Sports Illustrated* because they were not made in Texas. A charge of defamation regarding alleged statements made by McNamee to pitcher Andy Pettitte in Texas is still pending before the court.]

[*It is so ordered.*]

QUESTIONS

1. What condition applies to witnesses who are granted immunity from prosecution by federal prosecutors?

2. What is the rationale for prosecutors granting immunity to witnesses testifying in governmental proceedings?

The media enjoy a **qualified privilege** for stories that turn out to be false. Their qualified privilege is a defense to defamation so long as the information was released without malice and a retraction or correction is made when the matter is brought to their attention.

A *qualified privilege* to make a defamatory statement in the workplace exists when the statement is made to protect the interests of the private employer on a work-related matter, especially when reporting actual or suspected wrongdoing. **For Example,** Neda Lewis was fired from her job at Carson Oil Company for allegedly stealing toilet paper. The employee in charge of supplies noticed toilet paper was regularly missing from the ladies room, and one evening from a third-floor window overlooking the parking lot, she observed that the plaintiff's bag contained two rolls of toilet paper. She reported the matter to the executive secretary, who reported it to both the president and the CEO of the firm, who decided to fire her. Two other employees were also informed. The employer was able to successfully raise the defense of a qualified privilege to Ms. Lewis' defamation action for "false accusations of theft" since all of the employees involved were participants in the investigation and termination of the employee.[6]

A new statutory privilege has been evolving with respect to letters of recommendation and references given by employers for employees who are applying for jobs at other companies. Most companies, because of concerns about liability for defamation, will only confirm that a former employee did work at their firm and will provide the time period during which the person was employed. However, many employees who had histories that should have been revealed for safety reasons have been hired because no negative information was released. Numerous states now have statutes that provide employers a qualified privilege with respect to references and recommendations. So long as the employer acts in good faith in providing information, there is no liability for defamation to the former employee as a result of the information provided.

10. Product Disparagement

Although the comparison of products and services is healthy for competition, false statements about another's products constitute a form of slander called **slander of title** or libel called **trade libel**; collectively, these are known as **product disparagement**, which occurs when someone makes false statements about another business, its products, or its abilities.[7] The elements of product disparagement are (1) a false statement about a particular business product or

---

[6] *Lewis v Carson Oil Co.*, 127 P3d 1207 (Or App 2006).
[7] *Sannerud v Brantz*, 879 P2d 341 (Wyo 1994). See *Suzuki Motor Corp. v Consumers Union*, 230 F3d 1110 (9th Cir 2003), *cert denied* 540 US 983 (2003), for an example of the complexity of a product disparagement action.

about its service in terms of honesty, reputation, ability, or integrity; (2) communication of the statement to a third party; and (3) damages.

11. Wrongful Interference with Contracts

The tort of **contract interference** or (tortious interference with contracts) occurs when parties are not allowed the freedom to contract without interference from third parties. While the elements required to establish the tort of contract interference are complex, a basic definition is that the law affords a remedy when a third party intentionally causes another to break a contract already in existence. **For Example,** Nikke Finke, a newspaper reporter who had a contract with the *New York Post* to write stories about the entertainment industry for the *Post's* business section, wrote two articles about a lawsuit involving a literary agent and the Walt Disney Company over merchandising rights to the Winnie-the-Pooh characters. Finke reported that the trial court sanctioned Disney for engaging in "misuse of the discovery process" and acting in "bad faith" and ordered Disney to pay fees and costs of $90,000. Disney's president, Robert Iger, sent a letter to the *Post's* editor-in-chief, Col Allan, calling Finke's reporting an "absolute distortion" of the record and "absolutely false." Approximately two weeks after the Pooh articles were published, the *Post* fired Finke; her editor told her she was being fired for the Pooh articles. She sued Disney on numerous tort theories, including interference with her contract with the *Post.* Disney sought to have the complaint dismissed, which motion was denied by the court. The Court of Appeals concluded that Finke demonstrated a reasonable probability of proving that Iger's allegations that she made false statements in her article were themselves false; and it concluded that a jury could find Disney liable for intentional interference with contractual relations based on circumstantial evidence and negligent interference with contractual relations because it was reasonably foreseeable to Disney that

the nature of its accusations against Finke would result in her termination from employment.[8]

12. Trespass

A **trespass** is an unauthorized action with respect to land or personal property. A *trespass to land* is any unpermitted entry below, on, across, or above the land of another. **For Example,** Joyce Ameral's home abuts the mid-way point of the 240-yard, par-4 ninth hole of the public Middlebrook Country Club. Balls sliced and hooked by golfers have damaged her windows and screens, dented her car, and made her deck too dangerous for daytime use. Her landscapers are forced to wear hard hats when cutting her lawn. In her lawsuit against the country club owner, the court ruled that the projection of golf balls onto Ameral's property constituted a continuing trespass and it enjoined the trespass.[9]

A *trespass to personal property* is the invasion of personal property without the permission of the owner. **For Example,** the use of someone's car without that person's permission is a trespass to personal property.

C. NEGLIGENCE

The widest range of tort liability today arises in the field of negligence. Accidents happen! Property is damaged, and/or injuries result. The fact that an individual suffers an injury does not necessarily mean that the individual will be able to recover damages for the injury. **For Example,** Rhonda Nichols was shopping in the outdoor garden center at a Lowe's Home Center when a "wild bird" flew into the back of her head, causing injuries. Her negligence lawsuit against Lowe's was dismissed because the owner did not have a duty to protect her from a wild bird attack because it was not reasonably foreseeable.[10] Jane Costa was passively watching a Boston Red Sox baseball game at Fenway Park when a foul ball struck her in the face, causing severe and permanent injuries.

[8] *Finke v The Walt Disney Co.,* 2 Cal Rptr 3d 436 (Cal App 2003).
[9] *Ameral v Pray,* 831 NE2d 915 (Mass App 2005).
[10] *Nichols v Lowe's Home Center, Inc.,* 407 F Supp 2d 979 (SD Ill 2006).

Her negligence lawsuit against the Boston Red Sox was unsuccessful because it was held that the owners had no duty to warn Ms. Costa of the obvious danger of foul balls being hit into the stands.[11] Although cases involving injury to spectators at baseball games in other jurisdictions have turned on other tort doctrines, injured fans, like Ms. Costa, are left to bear the costs of their injuries. Only when an injured person can demonstrate the following four elements of negligence is a right to recover established: (1) a duty, (2) breach of duty, (3) causation, and (4) damages.[12] Several defenses may be raised in a negligence lawsuit.

13. Elements of Negligence

(A) DUTY TO EXERCISE REASONABLE CARE. The first element of negligence is a *duty*. There is a general duty of care imposed to act as a reasonably prudent person would in similar circumstances. **For Example,** Gustavo Guzman worked for a subcontractor as a chicken catcher at various poultry farms where a Tyson Foods employee, Brian Jones, operated a forklift and worked with the catchers setting up cages to collect birds for processing at a Tyson plant. Contrary to Tyson's instructions "never to allow catchers to move behind the forklift or otherwise out of sight," Brian moved his forklift and struck Guzman, who suffered a serious spinal injury. A general contractor, Tyson Foods, owes a duty to exercise reasonable care to a subcontractor's employee, Gustavo Guzman.[13]

Professionals have a duty to perform their jobs at the level of a reasonable professional. For a professional such as an accountant, doctor, lawyer, dentist, or architect to avoid liability for **malpractice,** the professional must perform his or her skill in the same manner as, and at the level of, other professionals in the same field.

Those who own real property have a duty of care to keep their property in a condition that does not create hazards for guests. Businesses have a duty to inspect and repair their property so that their customers are not injured by hazards, such as spills on the floor or uneven walking areas. When customer safety is a concern, businesses have a duty to provide adequate security, such as security patrols in mall parking lots.

(B) BREACH OF DUTY. The second element of negligence is the breach of duty imposed by statute or by the application of the reasonable person standard. The defendant's conduct is evaluated against what a reasonable person would have done under the circumstances. That is, when there is sufficient proof to raise a jury question, the jury decides whether the defendant breached the duty to the injured person from a reasonable person's perspective.[14] **For Example,** the jury in Guzman's lawsuit against Tyson Foods (the *Tyson* case), after weighing all of the facts and circumstances, determined that Tyson's employee's operation of the forklift constituted a breach of Tyson's duty of care to Guzman.

(C) CAUSATION. A third element of negligence is *causation,* the element that connects the duty and the breach of duty to the injuries to the plaintiff. **For Example,** in Guzman's lawsuit, the forklift operator's careless conduct was the cause in fact of this worker's injuries. A "but for" test for causation is used. *But for* Tyson employee Brian Jones' negligent conduct in moving the forklift under the circumstances surrounding the accident, Guzman would not have been injured.

Once the cause in fact is established, the plaintiff must establish *proximate cause*. That is, it must establish that the harm suffered by the injured person was a foreseeable consequence of the defendant's negligent actions. Foreseeability requires only the general danger to be foreseeable. In the *Tyson* case, the court determined that while there was some evidence that a jury could possibly infer that Tyson could not foresee an accident similar to the one involving

---

[11] *Costa v Boston Red Sox Baseball Club,* 809 NE2d 1090 (Mass App 2004).
[12] *Alfred v Capital Area Soccer League, Inc.,* 669 SE2d 277 (NC App 2008).
[13] *Tyson Foods Inc. v Guzman,* 116 SW3d 233 (Tex App 2003).
[14] A breach of duty may be established by the very nature of the harm to the plaintiff. The doctrine of *res ipsa loquitur* ("the event speaks for itself") provides a rebuttable presumption that the defendant was negligent when a defendant owes a duty to the plaintiff, the nature of the harm caused the plaintiff is such that it ordinarily does not happen in the absence of negligence, and the instrument causing the injury was in the defendant's exclusive control. An example of the doctrine is a lawsuit against a surgeon after a surgical device is discovered in a former patient months after the surgery by another physician seeking the cause of the patient's continuing pain subsequent to the operation.

Guzman, the evidence was legally sufficient to support the jury's finding that Tyson's negligence was foreseeable and the cause in fact of Guzman's injuries.

The landmark *Palsgraf v Long Island Rail Road Co.* case established a limitation on liability for unforeseeable or unusual consequences following a negligent act.

Palsgraf v Long Island Ry. Co., 162 NE 99 (NY 1928)

The Scales Tipped on Causation

Helen Palsgraf (plaintiff) had purchased a ticket to travel to Rockaway Beach on the Long Island Railway (defendant). While she was standing on a platform at the defendant's station waiting for the train, another train stopped at the station. Two men ran to catch the train, which began moving as they were running. One of the men made it onto the train without difficulty but the other man who was carrying a package, was unsteady as he tried to jump aboard. Employees of the defendant helped pull the man in and push him onto the train car, but in the process the package was dropped. The package contained fireworks, and when it was dropped, it exploded. The vibrations from the explosion caused some scales (located at the end of the platform on which Palsgraf was standing) to fall. As they fell, they hit Palsgraf, who was injured. Palsgraf filed suit against the railroad for negligence.

JUDICIAL OPINION

CARDOZO, C. J. . . . The conduct of the defendant's guard, if a wrong in its relation to the holder of the package, was not a wrong in its relation to the plaintiff, standing far away. Nothing in the situation gave notice that the falling package had in it the potency of peril to persons thus removed. Negligence is not actionable unless it involves the invasion of a legally protected interest, the violation of a right. "Proof of negligence in the air, so to speak, will not do." The plaintiff, as she stood upon the platform of the station, might claim to be protected against intentional invasion of her bodily security. Such invasion is not charged. She might claim to be protected against unintentional invasion by conduct involving in the thought of reasonable men an unreasonable hazard that such invasion would ensue. These, from the point of view of the law, were the bounds of her immunity, with perhaps some rare exceptions, survivals for the most part of ancient forms of liability, where conduct is held to be at the peril of the actor. If no hazard was apparent to the eye of ordinary vigilance, an act innocent and harmless, at least to outward seeming, with reference to her, did not take to itself the quality of a tort because it happened to be a wrong, though apparently not one involving the risk of bodily insecurity, with reference to some one else.

A different conclusion will involve us, and swiftly too, in a maze of contradictions. A guard stumbles over a package which has been left upon a platform. It seems to be a bundle of newspapers. It turns out to be a can of dynamite. To the eye of ordinary vigilance, the bundle is abandoned waste, which may be kicked or trod on with impunity. Is a passenger at the other end of the platform protected by the law against the unsuspected hazard concealed beneath the waste? If not, is the result to be any different, so far as the distant passenger is concerned, when the guard stumbles over a valise which a truckman or a porter has left upon the walk? The passenger far away, if the victim of a wrong at all, has a cause of action, not derivative, but original and primary. His claim to be protected against invasion of his bodily security is neither greater nor less because the act resulting in the invasion is a wrong to another far removed. In this case, the rights that are said to have been violated, the interests said to have been invaded, are not even of the same order. The man was not injured in his person or even put in danger. The purpose of the act, as well as its effect, was to make his person safe. If there was a wrong to him at all, which may very well be doubted, it was a wrong to a property interest only, the safety of his package. Out of this wrong to property, which threatened injury to nothing else, there has passed, we are told, to the plaintiff by derivation or succession a right of action for the invasion of an interest of another order, the right to bodily security. The diversity of interests emphasizes the futility of the effort to build the plaintiff's right upon the basis of a wrong to some one else. The gain is one of emphasis, for a like result would follow if the interests were the same. Even then, the orbit of the danger as disclosed to the eye of reasonable vigilance would be the orbit of the duty. One who jostles one's neighbor in a crowd does not invade the rights of others standing at the outer fringe when the unintended contact casts a bomb upon the ground. The wrongdoer as to them is the man who carries the bomb, not the one who explodes it without suspicion of the danger. Life will have to be made over, and human nature transformed, before prevision so extravagant can be accepted as the norm of conduct, the customary standard to which behavior must conform.

Continued

The risk reasonably to be perceived defines the duty to be obeyed, and risk imports relation; it is risk to another or to others within the range of apprehension. Here, by concession, there was nothing in the situation to suggest to the most cautious mind that the parcel wrapped in newspaper would spread wreckage through the station. If the guard had thrown it down knowingly and willfully, he would not have threatened the plaintiff's safety, so far as appearances could warn him. His conduct would not have involved, even then, an unreasonable probability of invasion of her bodily security. Liability can be no greater where the act is inadvertent.

DISSENTING OPINION

ANDREWS, J. . . . The proposition is this: Every one owes to the world at large the duty of refraining from those acts that may unreasonably threaten the safety of others. Such an act occurs. Not only is he wronged to whom harm might reasonably be expected to result, but he also who is in fact injured, even if he be outside what would generally be thought the danger zone.

As we have said, we cannot trace the effect of an act to the end, if end there is. Again, however, we may trace it part of the way. An overturned lantern may burn all Chicago. We may follow the fire from the shed to the last building. We rightly say the fire started by the lantern caused its destruction. A cause, but not the proximate cause. What we do mean by the word "proximate" is that, because of convenience, of public policy of a rough sense of justice, the law arbitrarily declines to trace a series of events beyond a certain point. This is not logic. It is practical politics.

The act upon which defendant's liability rests is knocking an apparently harmless package onto the platform. The act was negligent. For its proximate consequences the defendant is liable. If its contents were broken, to the owner; if it fell upon and crushed a passenger's foot, then to him; if it exploded and injured one in the immediate vicinity, to him. Mrs. Palsgraf was standing some distance away. How far cannot be told from the record—apparently 25 to 30 feet, perhaps less. Except for the explosion, she would not have been injured. . . . The only intervening cause was that, instead of blowing her to the ground, the concussion smashed the weighing machine which in turn fell upon her. There was no remoteness in time, little in space. And surely, given such an explosion as here, it needed no great foresight to predict that the natural result would be to injure one on the platform at no greater distance from its scene than was the plaintiff. Just how no one might be able to predict. Whether by flying fragments, by broken glass, by wreckage of machines or structures no one could say. But injury in some form was most probable.

Under these circumstances I cannot say as a matter of law that the plaintiff's injuries were not the proximate result of the negligence.

QUESTIONS

1. Do you think helping someone onto a moving train is a breach of duty? Do reasonable people do this?

2. Was Mrs. Palsgraf's injury foreseeable?

3. What is the court choosing to limit?

(D) DAMAGES. The plaintiff in a personal injury negligence lawsuit must establish the actual losses caused by the defendant's breach of duty of care and is entitled to be made whole for all losses. The successful plaintiff is entitled to compensation for (1) past and future pain and suffering (mental anguish), (2) past and future physical impairment, (3) past and future medical care, and (4) past and future loss of earning capacity. Life and work life expectancy are critical factors to consider in assessing damage involving permanent disabilities with loss of earning capacity. Expert witnesses are utilized at trial to present evidence based on worklife tables and present value tables to deal with these economic issues. The jury considers all of the evidence in the context of the elements necessary to prove negligence and all defenses raised, and it renders a verdict.

For Example, in the *Tyson* case, the defendant presented evidence and argued that Gustavo Guzman was himself negligent regarding the accident. The jury found that both parties were negligent and attributed 80 percent of the fault to Tyson and 20 percent to Guzman (this is called *comparative negligence* and is discussed in the following section). The jury awarded Guzman $931,870.51 in damages ($425,000.00 for past physical pain and mental anguish, $150,000.00 for future physical pain and mental anguish, $10,000.00 for past physical impairment, $10,000.00 for future physical impairment, $51,870.51 for past medical care, $5,000.00

for future medical care, $70,000.00 for past lost earning capacity, and $210,000.00 for future lost earning capacity). After deducting 20 percent of the total jury award for Guzman's own negligence, the trial court's final judgment awarded Guzman $745,496.41.

In some situations, the independent actions of two defendants occur to cause harm. **For Example,** Penny Shipler was rendered a quadriplegic as a result of a Chevrolet S-10 Blazer rollover accident. She sued the driver Kenneth Long for negligence and General Motors for negligent design of the Blazer's roof. She was awarded $18.5 million in damages. Because two causes provided a single indivisible injury, the two defendants were held jointly and severally liable.[15] Under *joint and several liability,* each defendant may be held liable to pay the entire judgment. However, should one defendant pay the entire judgment, that party may sue the other for "contribution" for its proportionate share.

In some cases in which the breach of duty was shocking, plaintiffs may be awarded *punitive damages.* However, punitive (also called *exemplary*) damages are ordinarily applied when the defendant's tortious conduct is attended by circumstances of fraud, malice, or willful or wanton conduct.[16]

14. Defenses to Negligence

(A) CONTRIBUTORY NEGLIGENCE. A plaintiff who is also negligent gives the defendant the opportunity to raise the defense of **contributory negligence,** which the defendant establishes by utilizing the elements of negligence previously discussed, including the plaintiff's duty to exercise reasonable care for his or her own safety, the breach of that duty, causation, and harm. Under common law, the defense of contributory negligence, if established, is a complete bar to recovery of damages from the defendant. The *Hardesty* case involves the application of the contributory negligence defense.

Hardesty v American Seating Co., 194 F Supp 2d 447 (D Md 2002)

Keep Your Eye on the Ball in Sports: Keep Your Eye on the 300-Pound Boxes in Trucking

Lawrence Hardesty is an over-the-road tractor-trailer truck driver who picked up a load of stadium seating equipment for the NFL stadium under construction in Baltimore. The equipment was packaged in large corrugated cardboard boxes weighing several hundred pounds. The shipper, American Seating Co., loaded the trailer while Hardesty remained in the cab of his truck doing "paperwork" and napping. Considerable open space existed between the boxes and the rear door of the trailer. The evidence showed that Hardesty failed to properly examine the load bars used to secure the boxes from movement during transit. When Hardesty arrived at the Baltimore destination, he opened the rear trailer door and boxes at the end of the trailer fell out and injured him. Hardesty brought a personal injury negligence action against the shipper. American Seating Co. responded that Hardesty was contributorily negligent, thus barring his negligence claim.

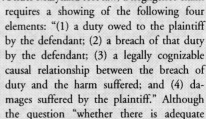

JUDICIAL OPINION

DAVIS, D. J. . . . Under Maryland tort law, a negligence claim requires a showing of the following four elements: "(1) a duty owed to the plaintiff by the defendant; (2) a breach of that duty by the defendant; (3) a legally cognizable causal relationship between the breach of duty and the harm suffered; and (4) damages suffered by the plaintiff." Although the question "whether there is adequate proof of the required elements needed to succeed in a negligence action is [generally] a question of fact to be determined by the fact finder, . . . *the existence of a legal duty is a question of law to be decided by the court.*" Contributory negligence, "that degree of reasonable and ordinary care that a plaintiff fails to undertake in the face of an appreciable risk which cooperates with the defendant's negligence in bringing about the plaintiff's harm," is a complete bar to recovery. . . .

---

[15] *Shipler v General Motors Corp.,* 710 NW2d 807 (Neb 2006).
[16] See *Eden Electrical, Ltd. v Amana Co.,* 370 F3d 824 (8th Cir 2004); and *University of Colorado v American Cyanamid Co.,* 342 F3d 1298 (Fed Cir 2003).

Continued

As a matter of law, Plaintiff's claim is barred by his own contributory negligence. . . .

QUESTIONS

1. How does the court define contributory negligence?

2. Is contributory negligence a complete bar to Hardesty's recovery of damages for his injuries in this case?

3. If Maryland applied a "comparative negligence" defense, as set forth in the following section of the text, rather than contributory negligence, would a more fair or just result have been reached in this case?

The contributory negligence defense has given way to the defense of comparative negligence in most states.

(B) COMPARATIVE NEGLIGENCE. Because contributory negligence produced harsh results with no recovery of damages for an injured plaintiff, most states have adopted a fairer approach to handling situations in which both the plaintiff and the defendant are negligent; it is called *comparative negligence.* Comparative negligence is a defense that permits a negligent plaintiff to recover some damages but only in proportion to the defendant's degree of fault.[17] **For Example,** in the *Tyson* case, both the defendant and the plaintiff were found to be negligent. The jury attributed 80 percent of the fault for the plaintiff's injury to Tyson and 20 percent of the fault to the plaintiff, Guzman. While Guzman's total damages were $931,870, they were reduced by 20 percent, and the final judgment awarded Guzman was $745,496.

Some comparative negligence states refuse to allow the plaintiff to recover damages if the plaintiff's fault was more than 50 percent of the cause of the harm.[18]

(C) ASSUMPTION OF THE RISK. The assumption of the risk defense has two categories. *Express assumption of the risk* involves a written exculpatory agreement under which a plaintiff acknowledges the risks involved in certain activities and releases the defendant from prospective liability for personal injuries sustained as a result of the defendant's negligent conduct. Examples include ski lift tickets, white water rafting contracts, permission for high school

cheerleading activities, and parking lot claim checks. In most jurisdictions these agreements are enforceable as written. However, in some jurisdictions they may be considered unenforceable because they violate public policy. **For Example,** Gregory Hanks sued the Powder Ridge Ski Resort for negligence regarding serious injuries he sustained while snowtubing at the defendant's facility. He had signed a release which explicitly provided that the snowtuber: *["fully] assume[s] all risks associated with [s]nowtubing,* even if due to the NEGLIGENCE" of the defendants [emphasis in original]. The Supreme Court of Connecticut found that the release was unenforceable because it violated the public policy by shifting the risk of negligence to the weaker bargainer.[19]

Implied primary assumption of the risk arises when a plaintiff has impliedly consented, often in advance of any negligence by the defendant, to relieve a defendant of a duty to the plaintiff regarding specific known and appreciated risks. It is a subjective standard, one specific to the plaintiff and his or her situation. **For Example,** baseball mom Delinda Taylor took her two boys to a Seattle Mariners baseball game and was injured during the pregame warm-up when a ball thrown by José Mesa got past Freddie Garcia, striking Taylor in the face and causing serious injuries. The defendant baseball team successfully raised the affirmative defense of implied primary assumption of the risk by showing that Mrs. Taylor had full subjective understanding of the specific risk of getting hit by a thrown baseball, and she voluntarily chose to encounter that risk.[20]

---

[17] *City of Chicago v M/V Morgan,* 375 F3d 563 (7th Cir 2004).
[18] *Davenport v Cotton Hope Plantation,* 482 SE2d 569 (SC App 1997).
[19] *Hanks v Powder Ridge,* 885 A2d 734 (Conn 2005).
[20] *Taylor v Baseball Club of Seattle,* 130 P3d 835 (Wash App 2006).

A number of states have either abolished the defense of assumption of the risk, reclassifying the defense as comparative negligence so as not to completely bar a plaintiff's recovery of damages, or have eliminated the use of the assumption of the risk terminology and handle cases under the duty, breach of duty, causation, and harm elements of negligence previously discussed.[21]

(D) IMMUNITY. Governments are generally immune from tort liability.[22] This rule has been eroded by decisions and in some instances by statutes, such as the Federal Tort Claims Act. Subject to certain exceptions, this act permits the recovery of damages from the United States for property damage, personal injury, or death action claims arising from the negligent act or omission of any employee of the United States under such circumstances that the United States, if a private person, would be liable to the claimant in accordance with the law of the place where the act or omission occurred. A rapidly growing number of states have abolished governmental immunity, although many still recognize it.

Until the early 1900s, charities were immune from tort liability, and children and parents and spouses

sports&entertainment law

Liability for Injuries Under the Sports Exception Doctrine

Charles "Booby" Clark played football for the Cincinnati Bengals as a running back on offense. Dale Hackbart played defensive free safety for the Denver Broncos. As a consequence of an interception by the Broncos, Hackbart became an offensive player, threw a block, and was watching the play with one knee on the ground when Clark "acting out of anger and frustration, but without a specific intent to injure," stepped forward and struck a blow to the back of Hackbart's head and neck, causing a serious neck fracture. Is relief precluded for injuries occurring during a professional football game? The answer is no. While proof of mere negligence is insufficient to establish liability during such an athletic contest, liability must instead be premised on heightened proof of reckless or intentional conduct on the part of the defendant. In the *Hackbart* case, the court determined that if the evidence established that the injury was the result of acts of Clark that were in reckless disregard of Hackbart's safety, Hackbart is

entitled to damages.* Why didn't Hackbart pursue recovery under negligence law, contending that Clark had a general duty of care to act as a reasonably prudent person would in similar circumstances? Because football and other contact sports contain within the rules of the games inherent *unreasonable* risks of harm, a negligence theory is not applicable. What contact sports do you believe qualify under this "sports exception" doctrine for which proof of negligence is insufficient to establish liability for injuries sustained during the athletic contest?

PGA golfer Walter Mallin sued PGA golfer John Paesani for injuries that Mallin sustained while competing in a PGA golf tournament when Paesani drove a golf ball that struck Mallin in the head on his right temple. Paesani contends that the "sports exception" doctrine applies and the negligence case must be dismissed. How would you decide this case?**

* *Hackbart v Cincinnati Bengals, Inc.*, 601 F2d 516 (10th Cir 1979).
** *Mallin v Paesani*, 892 A2d 1043 (Conn Super, 2005).

---

[21] See, for example, *Costa v The Boston Red Sox Baseball Club*, 809 NE2d 1090 (Mass App 2004), where the court cites state precedent that" . . . the abolishment of assumption of the risk as an affirmative defense did not alter the plaintiff's burden . . . to prove the defendant owed [the plaintiff] a duty of care . . . and thus left intact the open and obvious damages rule, which operates to negate the existence of a duty to care."
[22] *Kirby v Macon County*, 892 SW2d 403 (Tenn 1994).

could not sue each other. These immunities are fast disappearing. **For Example,** if a father's negligent driving of his car causes injuries to his minor child passenger, the child may recover from the father for his injuries.[23]

D. STRICT LIABILITY

The final form of tort liability is known as *strict liability*. When the standards of strict liability apply, very few defenses are available. Strict liability was developed to provide guaranteed protection for those who are injured by conduct the law deems both serious and inexcusable.

15. What is Strict Liability?

Strict liability is an absolute standard of liability imposed by the law in circumstances the courts or legislatures have determined require a high degree of protection. When strict liability is imposed, the result is that the company or person who has caused injury or damages by the conduct will be required to compensate for those damages in an absolute sense. Few, if any, defenses apply in a situation in which the law imposes a strict liability standard. **For Example,** as noted earlier in the chapter, engaging in ultrahazardous activities, such as using dynamite to excavate a site for new construction, results in strict liability for the contractor performing the demolition. Any

---

thinking things through

Torts and Public Policy

Over a decade ago, a jury awarded 81-year-old Stella Liebeck nearly $3 million because she was burned after she spilled a cup of McDonald's coffee on her lap. Based on these limited facts, a national discussion ensued about a need for tort reform, and to this day "Stella Awards" are given on Web sites for apparently frivolous or excessive lawsuits. Consider the following additional facts and the actual damages awarded Stella Liebeck. Decide whether her recovery was just.

- McDonald's coffee was brewed at 195 to 205 degrees.

- McDonald's quality assurance manager "was aware of the risk [of burns] . . . and had no plans to turn down the heat."

- Mrs. Liebeck spent seven days in the hospital with third degree burns and had skin grafts. Gruesome photos of burns of the inner thighs, groin, and buttocks were entered as evidence.

- The compensatory damages were $200,000, which were reduced to $160,000 because Mrs. Liebeck was determined to be 20 percent at fault.

- The jury awarded $2.7 million in punitive damages. The trial court judge reduced this amount to $480,000.

- The total recovery at the trial court for Mrs. Liebeck was $640,000. Both parties appealed, and a settlement was reached at what is believed to be close to the $640,000 figure.

Tort remedies have evolved because of public policy incentives for the protection of individuals from physical, mental, and economic damage. Tort remedies provide economic motivation for individuals and businesses to avoid conduct that could harm others.

The amount of the compensation and the circumstances in which compensation for torts should be paid are issues that courts, juries, and legislatures review. Many legislatures have examined and

---

[23] *Cates v Cates,* 588 NE2d 330 (Ill App 1992); see also *Doe v McKay,* 700 NE2d 1018 (Ill 1998).

thinking things through

Continued

continue to review the standards for tort liability and damages.

The U.S. Supreme Court devoted several decisions in recent years to dealing with excessive punitive damages in civil litigation, and it has set "guideposts" to be used by courts in assessing punitive damages.* In *State Farm Mutual Automobile Insurance Co. v Campbell*, compensatory damages for the plaintiffs at the trial court level

---

* *BMW of North America v Gore*, 517 US 559 (1996); *Cooper Industries v Leatherman Tool Group, Inc.*, 532 US 424 (2001); *State Farm Insurance v Campbell*, 538 US 408 (2003); and *Exxon Shipping Co. v Baker*, 128 S Ct 2605, 2621 (2008).

were $1 million, and punitive damages, based in part on evidence that State Farm's nationwide policy was to underpay claims regardless of merit to enhance profits, were assessed at $145 million. The Supreme Court concluded that the facts of *Campbell* would likely justify a punitive damages award only at or near the amount of compensatory damages. Thus, even those who act very badly as State Farm Insurance did have a constitutionally protected right under the Due Process Clause of the Fourteenth Amendment to have civil law damages assessed in accordance with the Supreme Court's guideposts.

---

damages resulting from the explosion are the responsibility of that contractor, so the contractor is strictly liable.

16. Imposing Strict Liability

Strict liability arises in a number of different circumstances, but the most common are in those situations in which a statutory duty is imposed and in product liability. For example at both the state and federal levels, there are requirements for the use, transportation, and sale of radioactive materials, as well as the disposal of biomedical materials and tools. Any violation of these rules and regulations would result in strict liability for the company or person in violation.

Product liability, while more fully covered in Chapter 25, is another example of strict liability. A product that is defective through its design, manufacture, or instructions and that injures someone results in strict liability for the manufacturer.

lawflix

Class Action (1991) (R)

This movie depicts the magnitude of damages and recovery when multiple injuries occur. The film provides insights on tort reform and the ethics of lawyers. You can learn about the magnitude of discovery and evidence.

Check out LawFlix at **www.cengage.com/blaw/dvl** to access movie clips that illustrate business law concepts.

Notting Hill (1999) (PG-13)

A story of famous star gets guy, dumps guy, gets guy back, dumps guy again, and then guy dumps famous star, and on and on. But, the guy owns a bookstore that sells travel books and he has a shoplifter. Hugh Grant, as the guy, illustrates perfection in exercising the shopkeeper's privilege.

You can view a clip of this movie and others that illustrate business law concepts at the LawFlix site, located at **www.cengage.com/blaw/dvl**.

MAKE THE CONNECTION

SUMMARY

A *tort* is a civil wrong that affords recovery for damages that result. The three forms of torts are intentional torts, negligence, and strict liability. A tort differs from a crime in the nature of its remedy. Fines and imprisonment result from criminal violations, whereas money damages are paid to those who are damaged by conduct that constitutes a tort. An action may be both a crime and a tort, but the tort remedy is civil in nature.

Selected intentional torts are false imprisonment, defamation, product disparagement, contract interference or tortious interference, and trespass. False imprisonment is the detention of another without his or her permission. False imprisonment is often called the *shopkeeper's tort* because store owners detain suspected shoplifters. Many states provide a privilege to store owners if they detain shoplifting suspects based on reasonable cause and in a reasonable manner. Defamation is slander (oral) or libel (written) and consists of false statements about another that damage the person's reputation or integrity.

Truth is an absolute defense to defamation, and there are some privileges that protect against defamation lawsuits, such as those for witnesses at trial and for members of Congress during debates on the floor. There is a developing privilege for employers when they give references for former employees. Invasion of privacy is intrusion into private affairs; public disclosure of private facts; or appropriation of someone's name, image, or likeness for commercial purposes.

To establish the tort of negligence, one must show that there has been a breach of duty in the form of a violation of a statute or professional competency standards or of behavior that does not rise to the level of that of a reasonable person. That breach of duty must have caused the foreseeable injuries to the plaintiff, and the plaintiff must be able to quantify the damages that resulted. Possible defenses to negligence include contributory negligence, comparative negligence, and assumption of risk.

Strict liability is absolute liability with few defenses.

LEARNING OUTCOMES

After studying this chapter, you should be able to

A. GENERAL PRINCIPLES

LO.1 Explain the difference between torts and crimes
See the discussion on wrongs that are a violation of a private duty as torts, and wrongs that are a violation of a public duty as crimes, p 172.
See the O.J. Simpson example of his acquittal of the crimes of murder and his civil liability for the torts of wrongful death, on p. 172.

B. INTENTIONAL TORTS

LO.2 Distinguish between an assault and a battery
See the "kick your butt" threat example of an assault on p. 173

LO.3 Explain the three different torts of invasion of privacy
See the discussion of the intrusion into a person' private affairs, public disclosure of private facts, and right of publicity torts beginning on p. 174.

LO.4 Explain the torts of defamation and defenses
See the discussion of slander, libel, and trade libel beginning on p. 174.
See the discussion of the requirement of the enhanced element of malice for cases in which the victim is a public figure, p. 174.
See the defense of privilege raised in the *Clemens* case on p. 175.

C. NEGLIGENCE

LO.5 Explain the elements of negligence and defenses

See the discussion of the elements of negligence: duty, breach of duty, and causation and damages beginning on p. 178.

See the discussion of the defenses of contributory negligence, comparative negligence, assumption of risk, and immunity beginning on p. 181.

D. STRICT LIABILITY

LO.6 Explain the tort of strict liability and why very few defenses are avaliable

See the dynamite excavation example, holding the contractor liable for any damages with no defenses because of the hazardous activity, p. 184.

KEY TERMS

absolute privilege
contract interference
contributory negligence,
defamation
false imprisonment
intentional infliction of
  emotional distress
intentional torts

invasion of privacy
libel
malpractice,
negligence
product disparagement
qualified privilege
shopkeeper's privilege
slander of title

slander
strict liability
tort
trade libel
trespass

QUESTIONS AND CASE PROBLEMS

1. Christensen Shipyards built a 155-foot yacht for Tiger Woods at its Vancouver, Washington, facilities. It used Tiger's name and photographs relating to the building of the yacht in promotional materials for the shipyard without seeking his permission. Was this a right of publicity tort because Tiger could assert that his name and photos were used to attract attention to the shipyard to obtain commercial advantage? Did the shipyard have a First Amendment right to present the truthful facts regarding their building of the yacht and the owner's identity as promotional materials? Does the fact that the yacht was named *Privacy* have an impact on this case? Would it make a difference as to the outcome of this case if the contract for building the yacht had a clause prohibiting the use of Tiger's name or photo without his permission?

2. ESPN held its Action Sports and Music Awards ceremony in April, at which celebrities in the fields of extreme sports and popular music such as rap and heavy metal converged. Well-known musicians Ben Harper and James Hetfield were there, as were popular rappers Busta Rhymes and LL Cool J. Famed motorcycle stuntman Evel Knievel, who is commonly thought of as the "father of extreme sports," and his wife Krystal were photographed. The photograph depicted Evel, who was wearing a motorcycle jacket and rose-tinted sunglasses, with his right arm around Krystal and his left arm around another young woman. ESPN published the photograph on its "extreme sports" Web site with a caption that read "Evel Knievel proves that you're never too old to be a pimp." The Knievels brought suit against ESPN, contending that the photograph and caption were defamatory because they accused Evel of soliciting prostitution and implied that Krystal was a prostitute. ESPN contends that the caption was a figurative and slang usage and was not defamatory as a matter of law. Decide. [*Knievel v ESPN,* 393 F3d 1068 (9th Cir)]

3. While snowboarding down a slope at Mammoth Mountain Ski Area (Mammoth), 17-year-old

David Graham was engaged in a snowball fight with his 14-year-old brother. As he was "preparing to throw a snowball" at his brother, David slammed into Liam Madigan, who was working as a ski school instructor for Mammoth, and injured him. Madigan sued Graham for damages for reckless and dangerous behavior. The defense contended that the claim was barred under the doctrine of assumption of the risk, applicable in the state, arising from the risk inherent in the sport that allows for vigorous participation and frees a participant from a legal duty to act with due care. Decide. [*Mammoth Mountain Ski Area v Graham*, 38 Cal Rptr 3d 422 (Cal App)]

4. Following a visit to her hometown of Coalinga, Cynthia wrote "An Ode to Coalinga"(Ode) and posted it in her online journal on MySpace.com. Her last name did not appear online. Her page included her picture. The Ode opens with "The older I get, the more I realize how much I despise Coalinga" and then proceeds to make a number of extremely negative comments about Coalinga and its inhabitants. Six days later, Cynthia removed the Ode from her journal. At the time, Cynthia was a student at UC Berkeley, and her parents and sister were living in Coalinga. The Coalinga High School principal, Roger Campbell, submitted the Ode to the local newspaper, the *Coalinga Record*, and it was published in the Letters to the Editor section, using Cynthia's full name. The community reacted violently to the Ode, forcing the family to close its business and move. Cynthia and her family sued Campbell and the newpaper on the right-of-privacy theory of public disclosure of private facts. What are the essential elements of this theory? Were Cynthia and her family's rights of privacy violated? No [*Moreno v Hanford Sentinel, Inc.*, 91 Cal Rptr 3d 858 (Cal App 2009)]

5. JoKatherine Page and her 14-year-old son Jason were robbed at their bank's ATM at 9:30 P.M. one evening by a group of four thugs. The thieves took $300, struck Mrs. Page in the face with a gun, and ran. Mrs. Page and her son filed suit against the bank for its failure to provide adequate security. Should the bank be held liable? [*Page v American National Bank & Trust Co.*, 850 SW2d 133 (Tenn)]

6. A Barberton Glass Co. truck was transporting large sheets of glass down the highway. Elliot Schultz was driving his automobile some distance behind the truck. Because of the negligent way that the sheets of glass were fastened in the truck, a large sheet fell off the truck, shattered on hitting the highway, and then bounced up and broke the windshield of Shultz's car. He was not injured but suffered great emotional shock. He sued Barberton to recover damages for this shock. Barberton denied liability on the ground that Schultz had not sustained any physical injury at the time or as the result of the shock. Should he be able to recover? [*Schultz v Barberton Glass Co.*, 447 NE2d 109 (Ohio)]

7. Mallinckrodt produces nuclear and radioactive medical pharmaceuticals and supplies. Maryland Heights Leasing, an adjoining business owner, claimed that low-level radiation emissions from Mallinckrodt damaged its property and caused a loss in earnings. What remedy should Maryland Heights have? What torts are involved here? [*Maryland Heights Leasing, Inc. v Mallinckrodt, Inc.*, 706 SW2d 218 (Mo App)]

8. An owner abandoned his van in an alley in Chicago. In spite of repeated complaints to the police, the van was allowed to remain in the alley. After several months, it was stripped of most of the parts that could be removed. Jamin Ortiz, age 11, was walking down the alley when the van's gas tank exploded. The flames from the explosion set fire to Jamin's clothing, and he was severely burned. Jamin and his family brought suit brought against the city of Chicago to recover damages for his injuries. Could the city be held responsible for injuries caused by property owned by someone else? Why or why not? [*Ortiz v Chicago*, 398 NE2d 1007 (Ill App)]

9. Carrigan, a district manager of Simples Time Recorder Co., was investigating complaints of

mismanagement of the company's Jackson office. He called at the home of Hooks, the secretary of that office, who expressed the opinion that part of the trouble was caused by the theft of parts and equipment by McCall, another employee. McCall was later discharged and sued Hooks for slander. Was she liable? [*Hooks v McCall*, 272 So 2d 925 (Miss)]

10. Defendant no. 1 parked his truck in the street near the bottom of a ditch on a dark, foggy night. Iron pipes carried in the truck projected nine feet beyond the truck in back. Neither the truck nor the pipes carried any warning light or flag, in violation of both a city ordinance and a state statute. Defendant no. 2 was a taxicab owner whose taxicab was negligently driven at an excessive speed. Defendant no. 2 ran into the pipes, thereby killing the passenger in the taxicab. The plaintiff brought an action for the passenger's death against both defendants. Defendant no. 1 claimed he was not liable because it was Defendant no. 2's negligence that had caused the harm. Was this defense valid? [*Bumbardner v Allison*, 78 SE2d 752 (NC)]

11. Carl Kindrich's father, a member of the Long Beach Yacht Club before he died, expressed a wish to be "buried at sea." The Yacht Club permitted the Kindrich family the use of one of its boats, without charge, for the ceremony, and Mr. Fuller —a good friend of Carl's father—piloted the boat. Portable stairs on the dock assisted the attendees in boarding. Upon returning, Fuller asked for help to tie up the boat. The steps were not there, and Carl broke his leg while disembarking to help tie up the boat. Carl sued the Yacht Club for negligence in failing to have someone on the dock to ensure that the portable steps were available. The Yacht Club contended that it was not liable because Carl made the conscious decision to jump from the moving vessel to the dock, a primary assumption of risk in the sport of boating. The plaintiff contended that he was not involved in the sport of boating, and at most his actions constituted minimal comparative negligence, the type which a jury could weigh in conjunction with the defendant's negligence in

assessing damages. Decide. [*Kindrich v Long Beach Yacht Club*, 84 Cal Rptr 3d 824 (Cal App 2008).]

12. Hegyes was driving her car when it was negligently struck by a Unjian Enterprises truck. She was injured, and an implant was placed in her body to counteract the injuries. She sued Unjian, and the case was settled. Two years later Hegyes became pregnant. The growing fetus pressed against the implant, making it necessary for her doctor to deliver the child 51 days prematurely by Cesarean section. Because of its premature birth, the child had a breathing handicap. Suit was brought against Unjian Enterprises for the harm sustained by the child. Was the defendant liable? [*Hegyes v Unjian Enterprises, Inc.*, 286 Cal Rptr 85 (Cal App)]

13. Kendra Knight took part in a friendly game of touch football. She had played before and was familiar with football. Michael Jewett was on her team. In the course of play, Michael bumped into Kendra and knocked her to the ground. He stepped on her hand, causing injury to a little finger that later required its amputation. She sued Michael for damages. He defended on the ground that she had assumed the risk. Kendra claimed that assumption of risk could not be raised as a defense because the state legislature had adopted the standard of comparative negligence. What happens if contributory negligence applies? What happens if the defense of comparative negligence applies?

14. A passenger on a cruise ship was injured by a rope thrown while the ship was docking. The passenger was sitting on a lounge chair on the third deck when she was struck by the weighted end of a rope thrown by an employee of Port Everglades, where the boat was docking. These ropes, or heaving lines, were being thrown from the dock to the second deck, and the passenger was injured by a line that was thrown too high.

The trial court granted the cruise line's motion for directed verdict on the ground there was no evidence that the cruise line knew or should have known of the danger. The cruise line contended that it had no notice that this "freak accident" could occur. What is the duty of a cruise ship line to its passengers? Is there liability here? Does it matter that an employee of the port city, not the cruise lines, caused the injury? Should the passenger be able to recover? Why or why not? [*Kalendareva v Discovery Cruise Line Partnership*, 798 So 2d 804 (Fla App)]

15. Blaylock was a voluntary psychiatric outpatient treated by Dr. Burglass, who became aware that Blaylock was violence prone. Blaylock told Dr. Burglass that he intended to do serious harm to Wayne Boynton, Jr., and shortly thereafter he killed Wayne. Wayne's parents then sued Dr. Burglass on grounds that he was liable for the death of their son because he failed to give warning or to notify the police of Blaylock's threat and nature. Was a duty breached here? Should Dr. Burglass be held liable? [*Boynton v Burglass*, 590 So 2d 446 (Fla App)]

Chapter 10

INTELLECTUAL PROPERTY RIGHTS AND THE INTERNET

Intellectual property comes in many forms: the writing by an author or the software developed by an employee, the new product or process developed by an inventor, the company name Hewlett-Packard, and the secret formula used to make Coca-Cola. Federal law provides rights to owners of these works, products, company names, and secret formulas that are called *copyrights, patents, trademarks,* and *trade secrets.* State laws provide protection for trade secrets. These basic legal principles are also applicable in an Internet and e-commerce context. This chapter discusses the federal and state laws governing intellectual property rights and their Internet context.

A. TRADEMARKS AND SERVICE MARKS

The Lanham Act, a federal law, grants a producer the exclusive right to register a trademark and prevent competitors from using that mark. This law helps assure a producer that it, not an imitating competitor, will reap the financial, reputation-related rewards of a desirable product. And trademarks reduce consumers' search costs, allowing them to make decisions that more closely coincide with their preferences.

1. Introduction

A mark is any word, name, symbol, device, or combination of these used to identify a product or service.[1] If the mark identifies a product, such as an automobile or soap, it is called a **trademark**. If it identifies a service, such as an airline or dry cleaner, it is called a **service mark**.

The owner of a mark may obtain protection from others using it by registering the mark in accordance with federal law at the Patent and Trademark Office (PTO) in Washington, D.C.[2] To be registered, a mark must distinguish the goods or services of the applicant from those of others. Under the federal Lanham Act, a register, called the Principal Register, is maintained for recording such marks. Inclusion on the Principal Register grants the registrant the exclusive right to use the mark. Challenges may be made to the registrant's right within five years of registration, but after five years, the right of the registrant is incontestable.

A mark may be "reserved" before starting a business by filing an application for registration on the basis of the applicant's good-faith intent to use the mark. Once the mark is used in trade, then the PTO will actually issue the registration with a priority date retroactive to the date the application was filed. The applicant has a maximum period of 36 months to get the business started and demonstrate that the mark is in "use in commerce."

2. International Registration

Under the Madrid System of International Registration of Marks (the Madrid Protocol), the United States became a party to a treaty providing for the international registration of marks in November 2003. Now U.S. companies that sell products and provide services in foreign countries may register their marks and obtain protection for them in more than 60 signatory countries by filing a single application in English for each mark with the U.S. Patent and Trademark Office.[3] Before the mark can be the subject of an international application, it must have already been registered or applied for with the U.S. Patent and Trademark Office (PTO). A change in ownership of a mark can be accomplished by a single filing. Renewal is required every 10 years by paying a single renewal fee.

3. Registrable Marks

Trademark law categorizes marks along a spectrum of **distinctiveness**, based on their capacity to serve a source-identifying function. A mark is classified as (1) coined or fanciful (most distinctive), (2) arbitrary, (3) suggestive, (4) descriptive, and (5) generic (least distinctive). **For Example,** the mark EXXON is fanciful because it was designed by its owner to designate petroleum and related products. The name

---

[1] 15 USC § 1127.
[2] *Lanham Act,* 15 USC §§ 1050–1127.
[3] Signatory countries include most U.S. trading partners with the exception of Canada and Mexico.

KODAK is a coined creation of the owner of this trademark and has no other meaning in English, but it serves to distinguish the goods of its owner from all others. The mark APPLE for computers, an arbitrary mark, consists of a word in common usage that is arbitrarily applied in such a way that it is not descriptive or suggestive. The mark COPPERTONE for suntan lotion is a suggestive mark—requiring some imagination to reach a conclusion about the nature of the product. Coined or fanciful, arbitrary, and suggestive marks may be registered on the Principal Register under the Lanham Act without producing any actual evidence of the source-identifying attribution or the public perception of these marks.

Descriptive marks are those that convey an immediate idea of the ingredients, qualities, or characteristics of the goods or service, such as SPORTS ILLUSTRATED for a sports magazine. Because descriptive marks are not inherently capable of serving as source identifiers, such marks may only be registered on the Principal Register after the owner has provided sufficient evidence to establish that the public associates the term or phrase not only with a specific feature or quality, but also with a single commercial source. When a descriptive phrase becomes associated with a single commercial source, the phrase is said to possess "**acquired distinctiveness**" or "**secondary meaning**," and therefore functions as a trademark. **For Example,** when the public perceives the phrase SPORTS ILLUSTRATED as a particular sports magazine in addition to its primary meaning as a description of a specific feature or element, the phrase has "acquired distinctiveness" or "secondary meaning" and may receive trademark protection.

Generic terms that describe a "genus" or class of goods such as soap, car, cola, or rosé wine are never registrable because they do not have a capacity to serve as a source identifier.

In the *Harley-Davidson* case, the motorcycle manufacturer sought to appropriate the word *hog* as its trademark, and a local motorcyle shop sought to parody Harley's logo to promote its own products and services.

Harley-Davidson, Inc. v Grottanelli, 164 F3d 987 (2d Cir 1999)

No Hogging Generic Terms

Harley-Davidson obtained a judgment against Ronald Grottanelli in the U.S. District for the Western District of New York for infringement of its bar-and-shield trademark, and the court enjoined his future use of that mark. The judgment also enjoined Grottanelli from using the word "hog" in reference to some of his products and services. Both parties appealed.

JUDICIAL OPINION

NEWMAN, J. . . .

1. The word "Hog" Applied to Motorcycles

Public use of the word "hog." In the late 1960s and early 1970s, the word "hog" was used by motorcycle enthusiasts to refer to motorcycles generally and to large motorcycles in particular. The word was used that way in the press at least as early as 1965, and frequently thereafter, prior to the 1980s when Harley first attempted to make trademark use of the term. Several dictionaries include a definition of "hog" as a motorcycle, especially a large one. The October 1975 issue of *Street Chopper* contained an article entitled "Honda Hog," indicating that the word "hog" was generic as to motorcycles and needed a tradename adjective.

Beginning around the early 1970s and into the early 1980s, motorcyclists increasingly came to use the word "hog" when referring to Harley-Davidson motorcycles. However, for several years, as Harley-Davidson's Manager of Trademark Enforcement acknowledged, the company attempted to disassociate itself from the word "hog." The Magistrate judge drew the reasonable inference that the company wished to distance itself from the connection between "hog" as applied to motorcycles and unsavory elements of the population, such as Hell's Angels, who were among those applying the term to Harley-Davidson motorcycles.

Harley-Davidson's use of the word "hog." In 1981, Harley-Davidson's new owners recognized that the term "hog" had financial value and began using the term in connection with its merchandise, accessories, advertising, and promotions. In 1983, it formed the Harley Owners' Group, pointedly using the acronym "H.O.G." In 1987, it registered the acronym in conjunction with various logos. It subsequently registered the mark "HOG" for motorcycles. That registration lists Harley-Davidson's first use as occurring in 1990.

Continued

Grottanelli's use of the word "hog." Grottanelli opened a motorcycle repair shop under the name "The Hog Farm" in 1969. Since that time his shop has been located at various sites in western New York. At some point after 1981, Grottanelli also began using the word "hog" in connection with events and merchandise. He has sponsored an event alternatively known as "Hog Holidays" and "Hog Farm Holidays," and sold products such as "Hog Wash" engine degreaser and a "Hog Trivia" board game.

2. The Bar-and-Shield Logo

Harley-Davidson's use of the logo. Since approximately 1909, Harley-Davidson has used variations of its bar-and-shield logo—a shield traversed across the middle by a horizontal bar. The words "Motor" and "Cycles" (or sometimes "Company") appear at the chief and base of the shield, respectively, and the name "Harley-Davidson" appears on the horizontal bar. Variations of the bar-and-shield logo were registered with the United States Patent and Trademark Office in 1982 and thereafter.

Grottanelli's use of the logo. By 1979, Grottanelli had begun using variants of Harley-Davidson's bar-and-shield logo. His 1979 advertisements include a hand-drawn copy of the bar-and-shield logo, with the name "Harley-Davidson" displayed on the horizontal bar. Since 1982, in response to letters of protest from Harley-Davidson, Grottanelli has replaced the words "Harley-Davidson" on the horizontal bar of his logo with the words "American-Made." He has also placed a banner at the bottom of his logo with the words "UNAUTHORIZED DEALER." In 1986, Grottanelli began using his current logo, which adds an eagle's wings behind the shield. This addition was apparently patterned after Harley-Davidson's bicentennial logo design mark, which included an eagle above the shield. Grottanelli's 1986 version of his logo also features a drawing of a pig wearing sunglasses. Grottanelli acknowledged at trial that his bar-and-shield logo is his version of Harley-Davidson's logo and that his version is "supposed to be similar, but confusing . . . [t]o a Harley-Davidson bar and shield." . . .

DISCUSSION

1. USE OF THE WORD "HOG"

. . . No manufacturer can take out of the language a word, even a slang term, that has generic meaning as to a category of products and appropriate it for its own trademark use. . . .

. . . In this case, one dictionary cites a generic use of "hog" to mean a large motorcycle as early as 1967, long before Harley's first trademark use of the word, and the recent dictionary editions continuing to define the word to mean a large motorcycle indicate that the word has not lost its generic meaning. We have observed that newspaper and magazine use of a word in a generic sense is "a strong indication of the general public's perception" that the word is generic. In this case, media use of "hog" to mean a large motorcycle began as early as 1935 and continued thereafter.

However, rather than recognize that the word "hog," originally generic as applied to motorcycles, cannot subsequently be appropriated for trademark use, the Magistrate Judge upheld Harley-Davidson's anti-dilution claim on the ground that its "HOG" mark has become a strong trademark. This was error. Even the presumption of validity arising from federal registration, *see Reese Publishing Co. v Hampton International Communications, Inc.,*620 F.2d 7, 11 [205 USPQ 585] (2d Cir. 1980), cannot protect a mark that is shown on strong evidence to be generic as to the relevant category of products prior to the proprietor's trademark use and registration. . . .

. . . Harley-Davidson suggests . . . that it is entitled to trademark use of "HOG" as applied to motorcycles because a substantial segment of the relevant consumers began to use the term specifically to refer to Harley-Davidson motorcycles before the company made trademark use of the term. Some decisions have invoked this principle to accord a company priority as to its subsequent trademark use of a term. *See National Cable Television Ass'n, Inc. v American Cinema Editors, Inc.,*937 F.2d 1572 [19 USPQ2d 1424] (Fed. Cir. 1991) (mark "ACE"); *Volkswagenwerk AG v Hoffman,* 489 F. Supp. 678 [209 USPQ 398] (D.S.C. 1980) (mark "BUG"). Whether or not we would agree with these decisions, they present a significantly different situation. Neither "ACE" nor "BUG" was a generic term in the language as applied, respectively, to a category of film editors or a category of automobiles prior to the public's use of the terms to refer to the American Cinema Editors and Volkswagen cars. By contrast, "hog" was a generic term in the language as applied to large motorcycles before the public (or at least some segments of it) began using the word to refer to Harley-Davidson motorcycles. The public has no more right than a manufacturer to withdraw from the language a generic term, already applicable to the relevant category of products, and accord it trademark significance, at least as long as the term retains some generic meaning.

For all of these reasons, Harley-Davidson may not prohibit Grottanelli from using "hog" to identify his motorcycle products and services. Like any other manufacturer with a product identified by a word that is generic, Harley-Davidson will have to rely on all or a portion of its tradename (or other protectable marks) to identify its brand of motorcycles, *e.g.,* "Harley Hogs."

II. BAR-AND-SHIELD LOGO

Parody defense. Grottanelli admits that his use of his bar-and-shield logo "purposefully suggests an association with Harley," but argues that his use is a protectable parody. We have accorded considerable leeway to parodists whose expressive works aim their parodic commentary at a trademark or a trademarked product, *see, e.g., Cliffs Notes, Inc. v Bantam*

Continued

Doubleday Dell Publishing Group, Inc., 886 F.2d 490, 493–95 (2d Cir. 1989), *cf. Rogers, v Grimaldi,* 875 F.2d 994, 998 (2d Cir. 1989), but have not hesitated to prevent a manufacturer from using an alleged parody of a competitor's mark to sell a competing product, *see Deere & Co. v MTD Products, Inc.,* 41 F.3d 39 (2d Cir. 1994) (applying New York's anti-dilution statute). Grottanelli uses his bar-and-shield logo on the signage of his business, in his newsletter, and on T-shirts. The signage on his business is, in effect, trademark use for a competing service, since, Harley-Davidson offers motorcycle repair services through its authorized dealers, and Grottanelli's placement of his bar-and-shield logo on his newsletter and T-shirts promotes his repair and parts business. In this context, parodic use is sharply limited. *See Deere,* 41 F.3d at 45 (citing *Wendy's International, Inc. v Big Bite, Inc.,* 576 F. Supp. 816 (S.D. Ohio 1983)).

In light of our ruling, we need not consider, with respect to Grottanelli's use of the term "hog," his defense of laches or both parties' challenge to the geographic scope of the injunction.

. . . Grottanelli's mark makes no comment on Harley's mark; it simply uses it somewhat humorously to promote his own products and services, which is not a permitted trademark parody use. . . .

Disclaimer defense. Grottanelli gains no protection by coyly adding to his version of the bar-and-shield logo the wording "UNAUTHORIZED DEALER." We have alluded to commentary questioning the capacity of brief negating words like "not" or "no" in disclaimers adequately to avoid confusion.

. . . Whatever the worth of such disclaimers in other contexts, the use of the prefix "UN" before "AUTHORIZED DEALER" provides Grottanelli with no defense when used on signage designed to attract speeding motorcyclists. *See* Restatement (Third) of Unfair Competition § 21 cmt. c (noting that "[a]lthough in theory *prominent* disclaimer of association with the prior user can reduce or eliminate confusion, the courts have ordinarily found the use of disclaimers insufficient to avoid liability for infringement") [emphasis added]. . . .

For all of these reasons, Grottanelli was properly enjoined from using his current bar-and-shield logo and any mark that so resembles Harley-Davidson's trademarked logo as to be likely to cause confusion.

CONCLUSION: The judgment of the District Court is affirmed to the extent it enjoined Grottanelli's use of his bar-and-shield logo and reversed to the extent that it enjoined his use of the word "hog.". . .

[Judgment affirmed]

QUESTIONS

1. If a term is classified as generic, may a manufacturer enforce trademark usage of that term if it shows that a substantial segment of the relevant consumer population believes the term refers to the products of that manufacturer?

2. Did the court accept Grottanelli's parody defense?

3. Did Grottanelli's disclaimer that he was an unauthorized dealer enable him to avoid liability for infringement of Harley's bar-and-shield logo?

Ordinarily geographic terms are not registrable on the Principal Register. **For Example,** BOSTON BEER was denied trademark protection because it was a geographic term.[4] However if a geographic term has acquired a secondary meaning, it would be registrable. **For Example,** the geographic term *Philadelphia* has acquired secondary meaning when applied to cream cheese products.

A personal name can acquire trademark protection if the name has acquired secondary meaning. **For Example,** the name "Paul Frank" is a personal name and as a trademark had acquired significant recognition and fame in the sale of t-shirts, clothing, and accessories designed by Paul Frank Sunich. Mr. Sunich had a falling out with Paul Frank Industries Inc. (PFI), and started his own t-shirt business using his own personal name, Paul Frank Sunich. The court rejected Mr. Sunich's contention that he had a right to use his full name as a trademark, because it was likely to cause consumer confusion with the established famous mark, and the court preliminarily enjoined him from using his "Paul Frank Sunich" mark with the sale of clothing or accessories. It did, however, permit him to use his full name, Paul Frank Sunich, in signatures, business meetings, and other such contexts where the name did not resemble a trademark or trade name, and did not appear on goods similar to those sold by PFI. Where Mr. Sunich's full name was used, there also had to be some clear explanation that Mr. Sunich was no longer affiliated with PFI. For example, his use of the Web site

---

[4] *Boston Beer Co. v Slesar Bros. Brewing Co.,* 9 F3d 812 (1st Cir 1994).

domain name **www.paulfranksunich.com** was not enjoined so long as it maintained a message explaining that Mr. Sunich no longer worked for or with PFI.[5]

With a limited number of colors available for use by competitors, along with possible shade confusion, courts had held for some 90 years that color alone could not function as a trademark. The U.S. Supreme Court has overturned this rule, and now if a color serves as a symbol that distinguishes a firm's goods and identifies their source without serving any other significant function, it may, sometimes at least, meet the basic legal requirements for use as a trademark.[6] **For Example,** Owens-Corning Fiberglass Corp. has been allowed to register the color pink as a trademark for its fiberglass insulation products.

4. Remedies for Improper Use of Marks

A person who has the right to use a mark may obtain an injunction prohibiting a competitor from imitating or duplicating the mark. The basic question in such litigation is whether the general public is likely to be confused by the mark of the defendant and to believe wrongly that it identifies the plaintiff's mark.[7] If there is this danger of confusion, the court will enjoin the defendant from using the particular mark.

In some cases, the fact that the products of the plaintiff and the defendant did not compete in the same market was held to entitle the defendant to use a mark that would have been prohibited as confusingly similar if the defendant manufactured the same product as the plaintiff. **For Example,** it has been held that Cadillac, as applied to boats, is not confusingly similar to Cadillac as applied to automobiles; therefore, its use cannot be enjoined.[8]

In addition to broad injunctive relief, the prevailing party may recover lost profits and other actual damages. In cases of willful violations, the court has full discretion to award the plaintiff up to treble damages. In "exceptional cases" the court has discretion to award attorney's fees.

The *Venture Tape Corp.* case deals with an improper use of a mark and the judicial remedies applied.

Venture Tape Corp. v McGills Glass Warehouse, 540 F3d 56 (1st Cir 2008)

But . . . What's Wrong with Diverting Traffic?

In 1996, Venture Tape Corporation, a manufacturer of specialty adhesive tapes and foils used in the stained-glass industry, procured two federal trademark registrations for products called "Venture Tape" and "Venture Foil," respectively. Over the next 15 years, Venture expended hundreds of thousands of dollars to promote the two marks in both print and Internet advertising. Consequently, its products gained considerable popularity, prestige, and goodwill in the worldwide stained-glass market.

Through its Internet Web site, McGills Glass Warehouse also sells adhesive tapes and foils that directly compete with "Venture Tape" and "Venture Foil." Beginning in 2000, and without obtaining Venture's permission or paying it any compensation, McGills owner Donald Gallagher intentionally "embedded" the Venture marks in the McGills Web site, both by including the marks on the Web site's metatags—a component of a Web page's programming containing descriptive information about the Web page that is typically not observed when the Web page is displayed in a Web browser—and in white lettering on a white background screen, similarly invisible to persons viewing the Web page.

Gallagher admittedly took these actions because he had heard that Venture's marks would attract people using Internet search engines to the McGills Web site, people who might buy McGills products. Upon discovery, Venture sued McGills for trademark infringement. McGills contends that it had no way of knowing whether the Venture marks had lured any Internet consumers to the Web site, and so there was no proven confusion of source, and thus no

---

[5] *Paul Frank Industries Inc. v Paul Sunich,* 502 F Supp 2d 1094 (CD Cal 2007).
[6] *Qualitex Co. v Jacobson Products Co., Inc.,* 514 US 159 (1995).
[7] *Resource Lenders, Inc. v Source Solutions, Inc.,* 404 F Supp 2d 1232 (ED Cal 2005).
[8] *General Motors Corp. v Cadillac Marine and Boat Co.,* 140 USPQ (BNA) 447 (1964). See also *Amstar Corp. v Domino's Pizza Inc.,* 615 F2d 252 (5th Cir 1980), where the mark Domino as applied to pizza was not held to be confusingly similar to Domino as applied to sugar.

Continued

liability. And it asserts that Gallagher was unaware that the use of the marks was illegal. From a judgment for Venture, McGills appealed.

JUDICIAL OPINION

LIPEZ, C. J. . . . "The purpose of a trademark is to identify and distinguish the goods of one party from those of another. To the purchasing public, a trademark 'signi[fies] that all goods bearing the trademark' originated from the same source and that 'all goods bearing the trademark are of an equal level of quality.'" *Id.* (quoting 1 J. Thomas McCarthy, *McCarthy on Trademarks and Unfair Competition*, 3:2 (4th ed. 2007)). To establish trademark infringement under the Lanham Act, Venture was required to prove that: (1) it owns and uses the "Venture Tape" and "Venture Foil" marks; (2) McGills used the same or similar marks without Venture's permission; and (3) McGills' use of the Venture marks likely confused internet consumers, thereby causing Venture harm (e.g., lost sales). The parties agree that no genuine factual dispute exists concerning the first two elements of proof.

Our focus then becomes the "likelihood of confusion" among internet consumers. This inquiry requires us to assess eight criteria: (1) the similarity of Venture's and McGills' marks; (2) the similarity of their goods; (3) the relationship between their channels of trade (e.g., internet-based commerce); (4) the relationship between their advertising; (5) the classes of their prospective purchasers; (6) any evidence of actual confusion of internet consumers; (7) McGills' subjective intent in using Venture's marks; and (8) the overall strength of Venture's marks. (*Pignons S.A de Mecanique de Precision v. Polaroid Corp.*, 657 F.2d 482, 487 (1st Cir. 1981)) [hereinafter "*Pignons* factors"]. No single criterion is necessarily dispositive in this circumstantial inquiry.

. . . McGills effectively admitted seven of the eight elements of the *Pignons* analysis. The record contains numerous admissions that metatags and invisible background text on McGills' website incorporated Venture's exact marks. In his deposition, Gallagher admitted that the parties are direct competitors in the stained glass industry and that both companies use websites to promote and market their products. Gallagher even admitted that he intentionally used Venture Tape's marks on McGills' website for the express purpose of attracting customers to McGills' website and that he chose "Venture Tape" because of its strong reputation in the stained glass industry. These admissions illustrate the similarity (indeed identity) of the marks used, the similarity of the goods, the close relationship

between the channels of trade and advertising, and the similarity in the classes of prospective purchasers. They also support the conclusions that McGills acted with a subjective intent to trade on Venture's reputation and that Venture's mark is strong. Accordingly, only the sixth factor—evidence of actual consumer confusion—is potentially in disupute.

On appeal, McGills argues that Gallagher had no way of knowing whether or not his use of the Venture marks on the McGills website had been successful, i.e., whether the marks actually lured any Internet consumer to the website. Thus, the company contends that summary judgment in Venture's favor was improper because there was no evidence of actual confusion. . . .

"[A] trademark holder's burden is to show likelihood of confusion, not actual confusion. While evidence of actual confusion is 'often deemed the best evidence of possible future confusion, proof of actual confusion is not essential to finding likelihood of confusion,'" *Borinquen Biscuit*, 443 F .3d at 120; *see also Brookfield Communs., Inc. v. West Coast Entertainment Corp.*, 174 F .3d 1036, 1050 (9th Cir. 1999) ("[D]ifficulties in gathering evidence of actual confusion make its absence generally unnoteworty."). . . .

McGills' admissions regarding the other seven *Pignons* factors, particularly Gallagher's admission that his *purpose* in using the Venture marks was to lure customers to his site, permit us to conclude that no genuine dispute exists regarding the likelihood of confusion. As a result, Venture was entitled to summary judgment on the liability issue.

[AUTHORS' NOTE: The court awarded Venture an equitable share of the defendant's profits, some $230,339.17, as a rough measure of the likely harm incurred, along with attorney's fees of $188,583.06 and $7,564.75 in costs.]

[Judgment affirmed]

QUESTIONS

1. What factors are considered by the court in determining whether McGills' use of Venture's marks created a "likelihood of confusion" among Internet consumers?

2. Since no evidence whatsoever was entered of actual confusion, and with the defendant genuinely being uncertain as to whether the marks actually lured Internet consumers to the Web site, is it inherently unfair for the court to speculate on the plaintiff's lost profits?

3. Comment on the defendant's assertion that he did not know it was illegal to use Venture's mark.

5. Abandonment of Exclusive Right to Mark

An owner who has an exclusive right to use a mark may lose that right. If other persons are permitted to use that mark, it loses its exclusive character and is said to pass into the English language and become generic. Examples of formerly enforceable marks that have made this transition into the general language are *aspirin, thermos, cellophane,* and *shredded wheat.* Nonuse for three consecutive years is prima facie evidence of abandonment.[9]

6. Trade Dress Protection

Firms invest significant resources to develop and promote the appearance of their products and the packages in which these products are sold so that they are clearly recognizable by consumers.

Trade dress involves a product's total image and, in the case of consumer goods, includes the overall packaging look in which each product is sold.

When a competitor adopts a confusingly similar trade dress, it dilutes the first user's investment and goodwill and deceives consumers, hindering their ability to distinguish between competing brands. The law of trade dress protection was initially settled by the U.S. Supreme Court in 1992,[10] and courts have subsequently become more receptive to claims of trade dress infringement under Section 43(a) of the Lanham Act. To prevail, a plaintiff must prove that its trade dress is distinctive and nonfunctional and the defendant's trade dress is confusingly similar to the plaintiff's.[11] Thus a competitor who copied the Marlboro cigarettes package for its Gunsmoke brand of cigarettes was found to have infringed on the trade dress of the Marlboro brand.[12] Trade dress protection under the Lanham Act is the same as that provided a qualified unregistered trademark and does not provide all the protection available to the holder of a registered trademark.

7. Limited Lanham Act Protection of Product Design

Trade dress originally included only the packaging and "dressing" of a product, but in recent years, federal courts of appeals' decisions have expanded trade dress to encompass the design of a product itself. Some manufacturers have been successful in asserting Section 43(a) Lanham Act protection against "knockoffs"— that is, copies of their furniture designs, sweater designs, and handbag designs. In this context Samara Brothers, Inc., discovered that Wal-Mart Stores, Inc., had contacted a supplier to manufacture children's outfits based on photographs of Samara garments, and Wal-Mart was selling these so-called knockoffs. Samara sued Wal-Mart, claiming infringement of unregistered trade dress under Section 43(a) of the Lanham Act. The matter progressed to the U.S. Supreme Court, which considered whether a product's design can be distinctive and, therefore, protectable under Section 43 (a) of the Lanham Act. The Court set aside the trial court's decision in favor of Samara Brothers and concluded that a product's design is not inherently distinctive and can only meet the "distinctiveness" element required in a Section 43(a) case by a showing of secondary meaning. That is, the manufacturer must show that the design has come to be known by the public as identifying the product in question and its origin. The matter was remanded for further proceeding consistent with the Court's decision.[13]

It is clear from the Supreme Court's *Wal-Mart Stores, Inc. v Samara Bros, Inc.* decision that ordinarily only famous designers whose works are widely recognized by the public by their design alone, such as certain Tommy Hilfiger and Ralph Lauren garments, Dooney & Bourke handbags, and Movado watches, will be able to successfully pursue Section 43(a) trade dress protection for their designs against knockoff versions of their work sold under Wal-Mart or other private labels. Of course if a manufacturer's design is copied along with the manufacturer's labels or logo, the makers and sellers of these counterfeit goods are

---

[9] *Doeblers' Pennsylvania Hybrids, Inc. v Doebler,* 442 F3d 812 (3rd Cir 2006).
[10] *Two Pesos, Inc. v Taco Cabana, Inc.,* 505 US 763 (1992).
[11] *Clicks Billiards v Sixshooters, Inc.,* 251 F3d 1252 (9th Cir 2001); and *Woodsland Furniture, LLC v Larsen,* 124 P3d, 1016 (Idaho 2005).
[12] *Philip Morris, Inc. v Star Tobacco Corp.,* 879 F Supp 379 (SDNY 1995).
[13] *Wal-Mart Stores, Inc. v Samara Bros, Inc.,* 529 US 205 (2000).

always in clear violation of the Lanham Act. As discussed later, design patents also have limited applicability and protect new and nonobvious ornamental features of a product.

8. Prevention of Dilution of Famous Marks

The Federal Trademark Dilution Act of 1995 (FTDA)[14] provides a cause of action against the "commercial use" of another's famous mark or trade name when it results in a "dilution of the distinctive quality of the mark." The act protects against discordant uses, such as Du Pont shoes, Buick aspirin, and Kodak pianos. Unlike an ordinary trademark infringement action, a dilution action applies in the absence of competition and likelihood of confusion. The act was amended in 2005 to provide that a plaintiff need not prove actual injury to the economic value of the famous mark to prevail in the lawsuit. In addition, the revised act permits truthful comparative advertising and a "fair use" defense for parodying a famous mark.[15]

9. Internet Domain Names and Trademark Rights

An *Internet domain name* is a unique address by which an Internet resource can be identified and found by a Web browser accessing the Internet. Examples of commercial Internet domain names are "Amazon.com," "Priceline.com," and the publisher of this book, "Cengage.com." These domain names match the names of their respective businesses, and these domain names are also trademarks.

Any unused domain name can be registered on a first-come, first-served basis for a rather modest fee, so long as the name differs from a previously registered name by at least one character. With such quick and inexpensive registration and with the addition of new registrars and new global suffixes such as ".biz" (small businesses), ".info" (resources), ".name" (individuals),

and ".pro" (professionals) to relieve ".com" (commerce) overcrowding, there exists an ever-increasing chance of intentional and unintentional trademark infringement.

(A) CYBERSQUATTERS. **Cybersquatters** are individuals who register and set up domain names on the Internet that are identical, or confusingly similar, to existing trademarks that belong to others or are the personal names of famous persons. The cybersquatter hopes to sell or "ransom" the domain name to the trademark owner or the famous individual.

Because the extent of the legal remedies available to famous companies or famous individuals who have been victims of cybersquatters has not always been certain, Congress passed the Federal Anticybersquatting Consumer Protection Act (ACPA)[16] in 1999 to prohibit the practice of cybersquatting and cyberpiracy and to provide clear and certain remedies. However, to be successful in an ACPA lawsuit, the plaintiff must prove that the name is famous and that the domain name was registered in bad faith.[17] Remedies include (1) injunctive relief preventing the use of the name, (2) forfeiture of the domain name, and (3) attorney fees and costs. In addition, trademark owners may obtain damages and the profits that cybersquatters made from the use of the name.

A safe harbor exists under the ACPA for defendants who both "believed and had reasonable grounds to believe that the use of the domain name was fair use or otherwise lawful."[18] A defendant who acts even partially in bad faith in registering a domain name is not entitled to the shelter of the safe harbor provision. **For Example,** Howard Goldberg, the president of Artco, is an operator of Web sites that sell women's lingerie and other merchandise. He registered a domain name **http://www.victoriassecrets.net** to divert consumers to his Web sites to try to sell them his goods. The court rejected his ACPA safe harbor defense that he intended in good faith to have customers compare his company's products with

---

[14] 15 USC § 125(c)(1).
[15] Trademark Dilution Revision Act (2005).
[16] Pub L 106, 113 Stat 1536, 15 USC § 1051.
[17] A plaintiff must meet the burden of proof, however that its mark is "famous," in order to come within the protection of the ACPA, with the courts requiring the marks be highly distinctive and thus well known throughout the country. Among the marks courts have ruled not to be distinctive are "Blue Man Group," the performing group; "Clue," the board game; and "Trek," for bicycles. In contrast, marks that have been ruled famous include "Nike," "Pepsi," and "Victoria's Secret." See *Philbrick v eNom Inc.*, 593 F Supp 2d 352, 367 (D NH 2009).
[18] 15 USC § 1125(d)(1)(B)(ii).

those of Victoria's Secret. The fact that Victoria's Secret is a distinctive or famous mark deserving of the highest degree of trademark protection, coupled with the fact that the defendant added a mere *s* to that mark and gave false contact information when he requested the domain name, indicates that he and his company acted in bad faith and intended to profit from the famous mark.[19]

(B) DISPUTE AVOIDANCE. To avoid the expense of trademark litigation, it is prudent to determine whether the Internet domain name selected for your new business is an existing registered trademark or an existing domain name owned by another. Commercial firms provide comprehensive trademark searches for less than $500. Determining whether a domain name is owned by another may be done online at **www.internic.net/whois.html**.

The Internet Corporation for Assigned Names and Numbers (ICANN) provides fast-track arbitration procedures to protect trademark owners from conflicting online domain names under the auspices of the World Intellectual Property Organization (WIPO). **For Example,** Victoria's Secret stores arbitrated the "victoriassecrets.net" domain name held by Howard Goldberg's company, and the arbitration panel transferred the ownership of the name to Victoria's Secret stores. Victoria's Secret stores subsequently brought an action against Goldberg and Artco for damages and injunctive relief under trademark law and the ACPA.

B. COPYRIGHTS

A **copyright** is the exclusive right given by federal statute to the creator of a literary or an artistic work to use, reproduce, and display the work. Under the

---

e-commerce&cyberlaw

Metatags describe the contents of a Web site using keywords. Some search engines search metatags to identify Web sites related to a search. In *Playboy Enterprises, Inc. (PEI) v WELLES,** PEI sued "Playmate of the year 1981" Terri Welles for using that and other phrases involving PEI's trademarks on her Internet Web site metatags. Some search engines that use their own summaries of Web sites, or that search the entire text of sites, would be likely to identify Welles's site as relevant to a search for "Playboy" or "Playmate," thus allowing Welles to trade on PEI's marks, PEI asserted. Remembering that the purpose of a trademark is not to provide a windfall monopoly to the mark owner but to prevent confusion over the source of products or services, the court applied a three-factor test for normative use to this

case: (1) the product or service must be one not readily identifiable without the use of the mark, (2) only so much of the mark may be used as reasonably necessary to identify the product or service, and (3) the user must not suggest sponsorship or endorsement by the trademark holder.

Welles had no practical way of describing herself without using the trademark terms. The court stated, "We can hardly expect someone searching for Welles's site . . . to describe Welles without referring to Playboy—as the nude model selected by Mr. Hefner's organization."

The court stated that there is no descriptive substitute for the trademarks used in Welles's metatags, and to preclude their use would inhibit the free flow of information on the Internet, which is not a goal of trademark law. Moreover, the metatag use was reasonable use to identify her products and services and did not suggest sponsorship, thus satisfying the second and third elements of the court's test.

* *Playboy Enterprises, Inc. v Welles*, 279 F3d 796 (9th Cir 2002). See *ESS Entertainment 2000, Inc. v Rockstar Videos Inc.*, 2008 US App, LEXIS 23294 (9th Cir).

---

[19] *Victoria's Secret Stores v Artco*, 194 F Supp 2d 204 (SD Ohio 2002).

international treaty called the *Berne Convention*, copyright of the works of all U.S. authors is protected automatically in all Berne Convention nations that have agreed under the treaty to treat nationals of other member countries like their own nationals.

A copyright prevents not the copying of an idea but only the copying of the way the idea is expressed.[20] That is, the copyright is violated when there is a duplication of the words, pictures, or other form of expression of the creator but not when there is just use of the idea those words, pictures, or other formats express.

The Copyright Act does not apply extraterritorially. However, if the infringement is completed in the United States and the copied work is then disseminated overseas, there is liability under the act for the resulting extraterritorial damages. **For Example,** the Los Angeles News Service (LANS), an independent news organization, produced two copyrighted videotapes of the beating of Reginald Denny during the Los Angeles riots of April 1992, and LANS licensed them to NBC for use on the *Today Show* in New York. Visnews taped the works and transmitted them by satellite to Reuters in London, which provided copies to its overseas subscribers. The infringement by Visnews occurred in New York, and Visnews was liable for the extraterritorial damages that resulted from the overseas dissemination of the work.[21]

It is a violation of U.S. copyright law for satellite carriers to capture signals of network stations in the United States and transmit them abroad. **For Example,** PrimeTime's satellite retransmission of copyrighted NFL football games to satellite dish owners in Canada was held to be a violation of U.S. copyright law, notwithstanding testimony of PrimeTime's CEO that a law firm in Washington, D.C., told him that U.S. law did not pertain to the distribution of products in Canada. The NFL was awarded $2,557,500 in statutory damages.[22]

10. Duration of Copyright

Article 1, Section 8, of the U.S. Constitution empowered Congress to

> *promote the Progress of Science and useful Arts, by securing for limited times to Authors and Inventors the exclusive Right to their respective Writings and Discoveries.*

The first U.S. copyright statute was enacted soon after in 1790 and provided protection for any "book, map or chart" for 14 years, with a privilege to renew for an additional 14 years. In 1831, the initial 14-year term was extended to 28 years, with a privilege for an additional 14 years. Under the 1909 Copyright Act, the protection period was for 28 years, with a right of renewal for an additional 28 years.

The Copyright Act of 1976 set the duration of a copyright at the life of the creator of the work plus 50 years. Under the Sonny Bono Copyright Term Extension Act of 1998, the duration has been extended to the life of the creator plus 70 years.[23] If a work is a "work made for hire"—that is, a business pays an individual to create the work—the business employing the creator registers the copyright. Under the 1998 Extension Act, such a copyright has been extended by 20 years and now runs for 120 years from creation or 95 years from publication of the work, whichever period is shorter. After a copyright has expired, the work is in the public domain and may be used by anyone without cost.[24]

11. Copyright Notice

Prior to March 1, 1989, the author of an original work secured a copyright by placing a copyright notice on the work, consisting of the word *copyright* or the symbol, the year of first publication, and the name or pseudonym of the author. The author was also required to register the copyright with the Copyright Office. Under the Berne

---

[20] *Attia v New York Hospital*, 201 F3d 50 (2d Cir 2000).
[21] *Los Angeles News Service v Reuters*, 149 F3d 987 (9th Cir 1998).
[22] *National Football League v PrimeTime 24 Joint Venture*, 131 F Supp 2d 458 (SDNY 2001).
[23] PL 105-298, 112 Stat 2827, 17 USC § 302(b).
[24] Without the Sonny Bono Extension Act of 1998, the copyright on Mickey Mouse, created by Walt Disney Co. in 1928, was set to expire in 2003 and enter the public domain. Pluto, Goofy, and Donald Duck would have followed soon after.

Convention Implementation Act of 1988,[25] a law that adjusts U.S. copyright law to conform to the Berne Convention, it is no longer mandatory that works published after March 1, 1989, contain a notice of copyright. However, placing a notice of copyright on published works is strongly recommended. This notice prevents an infringer from claiming innocent infringement of the work, which would reduce the amount of damages owed. To bring a copyright infringement suit for a work of U.S. origin, the owner must have submitted two copies of the work to the Copyright Office in Washington, D.C., for registration.

12. What is Copyrightable?

Copyrights protect literary, musical, dramatic, and artistic work. Protected are books and periodicals; musical and dramatic compositions; choreographic works; maps; works of art, such as paintings, sculptures, and photographs; motion pictures and other audiovisual works; sound recordings; architectural works; and computer programs.

The work must be original, independently created by the author, and possess at least some minimal degree of creativity.[26] **For Example,** William Darden, a Web page designer, challenged the Copyright Office's denial of a copyright registration for a series of existing maps with some changes in the nature of shading, coloring, or font. A court found that the Copyright Office acted within its discretion when it denied Darden's registration with the finding by the examiner from the Visual Arts Section that the maps were "representations of the preexisting census maps in which the creative spark is utterly lacking or so trivial as to be virtually nonexistent."[27]

13. Copyright Ownership and the Internet

Businesses today commonly use offsite programming services to create copyrightable software, with the delivery of code over the Internet. As set forth

previously, when a business pays an employee to create a copyrightable work, it is a "work for hire" and the business employing the creator owns and may register the copyright. On the other hand, if a freelancer is employed offsite to create software for a fixed fee without a contract setting forth the ownership of the work, the freelancer owns the work product and the company utilizing the freelancer has a license to use the work product but does not have ownership of it. To avoid disputes about ownership of custom software, a written contract that addresses these ownership and license questions is necessary.

14. Rights of Copyright Holders

A copyright holder has the exclusive right to (1) reproduce the work; (2) prepare derivative works, such as a script from the original work; (3) distribute copies of recordings of the work; (4) publicly perform the work, in the case of plays and motion pictures; and (5) publicly display the work, in the case of paintings, sculptures, and photographs.

The copyright owner may assign or license some of the rights listed and will receive royalty payments as part of the agreement. The copyright law also ensures royalty payments. **For Example,** Jessie Riviera is a songwriter whose songs are sung at public performances and are recorded by performers on records, tapes, and CDs. Jessie is entitled to royalties from the public performance of her works. Such royalties are collected by two performing rights societies, the American Society of Composers, Authors, and Publishers (ASCAP) and Broadcast Music, Inc. (BMI), who act on behalf of the copyright holders. Jessie is also entitled to so-called mechanical royalties that refer to the royalty stream derived from "mechanically" reproduced records, tapes, and CDs.[28] The principal payers of mechanical royalties are record companies, and the rates are set by the Copyright Royalty Tribunal.

In addition to rights under the copyright law and international treaties, federal and state laws prohibit record and tape piracy.

---

[25] PL 100-568, 102 Stat 2854, 17 USC § 101 et seq.
[26] *Feist Publications Inc. v Rural Telephone Services Co.*, 499 US 340 (1991).
[27] *Darden v Peters*, 402 F Supp 2d 638 (ED NC 2005).
[28] The ASCAP was formed in 1914 by eminent American composers including Victor Herbert and John Philip Sousa. BMI was formed in 1939. Public performance royalties collected by these societies exceed $1.5 billion per year and are distributed according to elaborate formulas.

15. Limitation on Exclusive Character of Copyright

A limitation on the exclusive rights of copyright owners exists under the principle of *fair use*, which allows limited use of copyrighted material in connection with criticism, news reporting, teaching, and research. Four important factors to consider when judging whether the use made in a particular case is fair use include the following:

1. The purpose and character of the use, including whether such use is of a commercial nature or is for nonprofit educational purposes[29]

2. The nature of the copyrighted work

3. The amount and substantiality of the portion used in relation to the copyrighted work as a whole

4. The effect of the use on the potential market for or value of the copyrighted work[30]

In *American Geophysical Union v Texas, Inc.*, the court applied the four statutory standards to determine whether the defendant's photocopying of scientific journal articles was fair use.

American Geophysical Union v Texaco, Inc., 60 F3d 913 (2d Cir 1995)

Fair Use or Not Fair Use—That Is the Question

The American Geophysical Union and 82 other publishers of scientific and technical journals brought a class-action lawsuit against Texaco claiming that Texaco's unauthorized photocopying of articles from their journals constituted a copyright infringement. Texaco's defense was that the copying was fair use under Section 107 of the Copyright Act of 1976. To avoid extensive discovery, the parties agreed to focus on one randomly selected Texaco scientist, Dr. Donald Chickering, who had photocopies of eight articles from the *Journal of Catalysis* in his files. The trial court judge held that the copying of the eight articles did not constitute fair use, and Texaco appealed.

JUDICIAL OPINION

NEWMAN, C. J. . . . Burdens of Proof and Standard of Review

Fair use serves as an affirmative defense to a claim of copyright infringement, and thus the party claiming that its secondary use of the original copyrighted work constitutes a fair use typically carries the burden of proof as to all issues in the dispute. Moreover, since fair use is a "mixed question of law and fact," *Harper & Row*, 471 U.S. at 560, 105 S.Ct. at 2230, we review the District Court's conclusions on this issue *de novo*, though we accept its subsidiary findings of fact unless clearly erroneous, see *Twin Peaks*, 996 F.2d at 1374. . . .

FIRST FACTOR: PURPOSE AND CHARACTER OF USE

The first factor listed in section 107 is "the purpose and character of the use, including whether such use is of a commercial nature or is for nonprofit educational purposes." Especially pertinent to an assessment of the first fair use factor are the precise circumstances under which copies of the eight *Catalysis* articles were made. After noticing six of these articles when the original copy of the journal issue containing each of them was circulated to him, Chickering had them photocopied, at least initially, for the same basic purpose that one would normally seek to obtain the original—to have it available on his shelf for ready reference if and when he needed to look at it. The library circulated one copy and invited all the researchers to make their own photocopies. It is a reasonable inference that the library staff wanted each journal issue moved around the building quickly and returned to the library so that it would be available for others to look at. Making copies enabled all researchers who might one day be interested in examining the contents of an article in the issue to have the article readily available in their own offices. In Chickering's own words, the copies of the articles were made for "my personal convenience," since it is "far more convenient to have access in my office to a photocopy

---

[29] In *Princeton University Press v Michigan Document Services, Inc.*, 99 F3d 1381 (6th Cir 1996), a commercial copyshop reproduced "coursepacks" and sold them to students attending the University of Michigan. The court refused to consider the "use" as one for nonprofit educational purposes because the use challenged was that of the copyshop, a for-profit corporation that had decided to duplicate copyrighted material for sale to maximize its profits and give itself a competitive edge over other copyshops by declining to pay the royalties requested by the holders of the copyrights.

[30] See fair use analysis in *Perfect 10 v Amazon.com, Inc.*, 487 F3d 701, 719 – 725 (9th Cir 2007).

Continued

of an article than to have to go to the library each time I wanted to refer to it." Affidavit of Donald Chickering at 11 (submitted as direct trial testimony) [hereinafter *Chickering testimony*]. Significantly, Chickering did not even have occasion to use five of the photocopied articles at all, further revealing that the photocopies of the eight *Catalysis* articles were primarily made just for "future retrieval and reference." *Id.* . . .

The photocopying of these eight *Catalysis* articles may be characterized as "archival"—*i.e.,* done for the primary purpose of providing numerous Texaco scientists (for whom Chickering served as an example) each with his or her own personal copy of each article without Texaco's having to purchase another original journal. . . .

On balance, we agree with the District Court that the first factor favors the publishers; primarily because the dominant purpose of the use is a systematic institutional policy of multiplying the available number of copies of pertinent copyrighted articles by circulating the journals among employed scientists for them to make copies, thereby serving the same purpose for which additional subscriptions are normally sold, or, as will be discussed, for which photocopying licenses may be obtained.

SECOND FACTOR: NATURE OF COPYRIGHTED WORK

The second statutory fair use factor is "the nature of the copyrighted work." In assessing this factor, the District Court noted that the articles in *Catalysis* "are created for publication with the purpose and intention of benefiting from the protection of the copyright law," and that copyright protection "is vitally necessary to the dissemination of scientific articles of the sort that are at issue." 802 F.Supp. at 16. Nevertheless, the Court ultimately concluded that this factor favored Texaco because the photocopied articles were essentially factual in nature and the "scope of fair use is greater with respect to factual than nonfactual works." . . .

Ultimately . . . the manifestly factual character of the eight articles precludes us from considering the articles as "within the core of the copyright's protective purposes," *Campbell,* 114 S.Ct. at 1175; see also *Harper & Row,* 471 U. S. at 563, 105 S.Ct. at 2232 ("The law generally recognizes a greater need to disseminate factual works than works of fiction or fantasy."). Thus, in agreement with the District Court, we conclude that the second factor favors Texaco.

THIRD FACTOR: AMOUNT AND SUBSTANTIABILITY OF PORTION USED

The third statutory fair use factor is "the amount and substantiality of the portion used in relation to the copyrighted work as a whole." The District Court concluded that

this factor clearly favors the publishers because Texaco copied the eight articles from *Catalysis* in their entirety. . . .

Despite Texaco's claims that we consider its amount of copying "minuscule" in relation to the entirety of *Catalysis,* we conclude, as did the District Court, that Texaco has copied entire works. Though this conclusion does not preclude a finding of fair use, it militates against such a finding, see *Sony,* 464 U.S. at 449–50, 104 S.Ct. at 792–93, and weights the third factor in favor of the publishers. . . .

FOURTH FACTOR: EFFECT UPON POTENTIAL MARKET OR VALUE

The fourth statutory fair use factor is "the effect of the use upon the potential market for or value of the copyrighted work." Assessing this factor, the District Court detailed the range of procedures Texaco could use to obtain authorized copies of the articles that it photocopied and found that "whatever combination of procedure Texaco used, the publishers' revenues would grow significantly." The Court concluded that the publishers "powerfully demonstrated entitlement to prevail as to the fourth factor," since they had shown "a substantial harm to the value of their copyrights" as the consequence of Texaco's copying. See *id.* at 18–21.

Prior to *Campbell,* the Supreme Court had characterized the fourth factor as "the single most important element of fair use," *Harper & Row,* 471 U.S. at 566, 105 S.Ct. at 2233. However, *Campbell's* discussion of the fourth factor conspicuously omits this phrasing. Apparently abandoning the idea that any factor enjoys primacy, *Campbell* instructs that '[a]ll [four factors] are to be explored, and the results weighed together, in light of the purposes of copyright.' 114 S.Ct. at 1171. . . .

Primarily because of lost licensing revenue, and to a minor extent because of lost subscription revenue, we agree with the District Court that "the publishers have demonstrated a substantial harm to the value of their copyrights through [Texco's] copying," 802 F.Supp. at 21, and thus conclude that the fourth statutory factor favors the publishers.

AGGREGATE ASSESSMENT

We conclude that three of the four statutory factors, including the important first and the fourth factors, favor the publishers. . . . We therefore agree with the District Court's conclusion that Texaco's photocopying of eight particular articles from the *Journal of Catalysis* was not fair use.

Though we recognize the force of many observations made in Judge Jacob's dissenting opinion, we are not dissuaded by his dire predictions that our ruling in this case "has ended fair-use photocopying with respect to a large population of journals," 60 F.3d at 938–39, or, to the extent that the transactional licensing scheme is used, "would seem to require that an

Continued

intellectual property lawyer be posted at each copy machine," *id.* at 937–38. Our ruling does not consider photocopying for personal use by an individual. Our ruling is confined to the institutional, systematic, archival multiplication of copies revealed by the record—the precise copying that the parties stipulated should be the basis for the District Court's decision now on appeal and for which licenses are in fact available. And the claim that lawyers need to be stationed at copy machines is belied by the ease with which music royalties have been collected and distributed for performances at thousands of cabarets, without the attendance of intellectual property lawyers in any capacity other than as customers. . . .

[*Affirmed*]

QUESTIONS

1. Assess Texaco's position that the purpose and character of its use of the eight articles were for the legitimate reason of use in Dr. Chickering's research and they were not photocopied for resale.

2. Is the "market-effect" factor the single most important element of fair use?

3. Do you believe that the result of this decision will lead to the dire consequences of the posting of intellectual property lawyers at every copy machine, trying to enforce licensing schemes?

First Amendment privileges of freedom of speech and the press are preserved through the doctrine of *fair use*, which allows for use of portions of another's copyrighted work for matters such as comment and criticism. Parodies and caricatures are the most penetrating forms of criticism and are protected under the fair use doctrine. Moreover, while injunctive relief is appropriate in the vast majority of copyright infringement cases because the infringements are simply piracy, in the case of parodies and caricatures where there are reasonable contentions of fair use, preliminary injunctions to prevent publication are inappropriate. The copyright owner can be adequately protected by an award of damages should infringement be found. **For Example,** Suntrust Bank, the trustee of a trust that holds the copyright to Margaret Mitchell's *Gone with the Wind*, one of the all-time best-selling books in the world, obtained a preliminary injunction preventing Houghton Mifflin Co. from publishing Alice Randall's *The Wind Done Gone*. The Randall book is an irreverent parody that turns old ideas upside down. The Court of Appeals set aside the injunction of the federal district court because Houghton Mifflin had a viable fair use defense.[31]

16. Secondary Liability for Infringement

An entity that distributes a device with the object of promoting its use to infringe copyrights as shown by

clear expression or other active steps taken to foster the resulting acts of infringement is liable for these acts of infringement by third parties, regardless of the device's lawful uses. **For Example,** Grokster, Ltd., and Stream-Cast Networks, Inc., distributed free software products that allow all computer users to share electronic files through peer-to-peer networks, so called because users' computers communicate directly with each other, not through central servers. When these firms distributed their free software, each clearly voiced the objective that the recipients use the software to download copyrighted works. These firms derived profits from selling advertising space and streaming ads to the software users. Liability for infringement was established under the secondary liability doctrines of contributory or vicarious infringement.[32]

17. Digital Millennium Copyright Act

The Digital Millennium Copyright Act of 1998 (DMCA)[33] was enacted to curb the pirating of software and other copyrighted works, such as books, films, videos, and recordings, by creating civil and criminal penalties for anyone who circumvents encryption software. The law also prohibits the manufacture, import, sale, or distribution of circumvention devices.

Title II of the DMCA provides a "safe harbor" for Internet Service Providers (ISP) from liability for direct, vicarious, and contributory infringement of

---

[31] *Suntrust Bank v Houghton Mifflin Co.*, 268 F3d 1257 (11th Cir 2001).
[32] *Metro-Goldwyn-Mayer Studios, Inc. v Grokster, Ltd.*, 545 US 913 (2005).
[33] 17 USC § 1201.

ethics & the law

The Death of Journalism?

Washington Post columnist Ian Shapira wrote a column entitled "How Gawker Ripped off My Newspaper Story."* He had written a profile on Washington based "business coach" Anne Loehr, an expert on how people in their 20s and late teens behave in the workplace. He conducted an extensive phone interview with Loehr, attended one of her "Get Wise with Gen Ys" sessions and spent an additional day writing the story. Shapira is provided a living wage, health care, and retirement benefits by The Post. Gawker's eight paragraph posting condensed Loehr's biography with a link to Shapira's story, and

utilized Loehr's own words on various points of interest, followed by a "cut and paste" of Shapira's "stuff." It ended with the hyperlinked words "Washington Post."

The newspaper industry is in financial peril. Is there a line that can be drawn between the "fair use" doctrine allowing appropriate quoting and linking, and "parasitic" free-rider Web sites? Shapira asserts that current law allows "the Gawker's of the world to appropriate others' work, repurpose it and sell ads against it with no payment to or legal recourse for the company that [paid the originator of the story]." Should the copyright law be amended to require those who sell ads against heavily excerpted articles to pay a fee to the originator? Is this payment the ethical thing to do?

* http://www.washingtonpost.com/wp-dyn/content/article/2009/07/31/. . .

---

copyrights provided the ISP (1) does not have actual knowledge of the infringing activity or expeditiously removed access to the problematic material upon obtaining knowledge of infringing activity, (2) does not receive financial benefit directly attributable to the infringing activity, and (3) responded expeditiously upon notification of the claimed infringement.

C. PATENTS

Under Article 1, Section 8, of the U.S. Constitution, the founding fathers of our country empowered Congress to promote the progress of science by securing for limited times to inventors the exclusive rights to their discoveries. Federal patent laws established under Article 1, Section 8, protect inventors just as authors are protected under copyright law authorized by the same section of the U.S. Constitution.

18. Types, Duration, and Notice

There are three types of patents, the rights to which may be obtained by proper filing with the Patent and

Trademark Office (PTO) in Washington, D.C. The types and duration of patents are as follows.

(A) UTILITY PATENTS. Inventions classified as *utility* or *functional patents* grant inventors of any new and useful process, machine, manufacture, or composition of matter or any new and useful improvement of such devices the right to obtain a patent.[34] Prior to 1995, utility patents had a life of 17 years from the date of grant. Under the Uruguay Round Trade Agreement Act, effective June 8, 1995, the duration of U.S. utility patents was changed from 17 years from the date of grant to 20 years from the date of filing to be consistent with the patent law of World Trade Organization (WTO) member states.

(B) DESIGN PATENTS. A second kind of patent exists under U.S. patent law that protects new and nonobvious ornamental features that appear in connection with an article of manufacture.[35] These patents are called *design patents* and have a duration of 14 years. In order to establish design patent infringement, the patent holder has the difficult task of

---

[34] 35 USC § 101.
[35] 35 USC § 173.

proving, by a preponderance of the evidence, that an ordinary observer (and not the eye of an expert) taking into account the prior art would believe the accused design to be the same as the patented design.[36] **For Example,** the Court of Appeals for the Federal Circuit (CAFC) held that defendant Swisa's Nail Buffer, which features buffer surfaces on all four of its sides, was not "the same as" and thus did not infringe on Egyptian Goddess, Inc.'s patented nail buffer design, which features buffer surfaces on three of its four sides.[37]

(C) PLANT PATENTS. A third type of patent, called a *plant patent*, protects the inventors of asexually reproduced new varieties of plants. The duration is 20 years from the date of filing, the same duration applied to utility patents.

(D) NOTICE. The owner of a patent is required to mark the patented item or device using the word *patent* and must list the patent number on the device to recover damages from an infringer of the patent.

19. Patentability

Section 101 of the 1952 Patent Act recognizes four categories of subject matter for patent eligibility: (1) processes, (2) machines, (3) manufactures, and (4) compositions of matter. However, even if a claim may be deemed to fit one of these categories, it may not be patent eligible. Phenomena of nature, though just discovered; mental processes; and abstract intellectual concepts are not patentable because they are the basic tools of scientific and technological work.[38]

Once it is established that an invention is patent eligible, a patent may be obtained if the invention is something that is *new and not obvious* to a person of ordinary skill and knowledge in the art or technology to which the invention is related. Whether an invention is new and not obvious in its field may lead to highly technical proceedings before a patent examiner, the PTO's Board of Patent Appeals, and

the U.S. Court of Appeals for the Federal Circuit (CAFC). **For Example,** Thomas Devel's application for a patent on complementary DNA (cDNA) molecules encoding proteins that stimulated cell division was rejected by a patent examiner as "obvious" and the rejection was affirmed by the PTO's Board of Patent Appeals. However, after a full hearing before the CAFC, which focused on the state of research in the field as applied to the patent application, Devel's patent claims were determined to be "not invalid because of obviousness."[39]

Once approved by the Patent and Trademark Office, a patent is presumed valid. However, a defendant in a patent infringement lawsuit may assert a patent's invalidity as a defense to an infringement claim by showing the invention as a whole would have been obvious to a person of ordinary skill in the art when the invention was patented. This showing is called **prior art**. **For Example,** Ron Rogers invented and patented a tree-trimming device that is essentially a chain saw releasably mounted on the end of a telescoping pole. Rogers sued Desa International, Inc. (DIA) for patent infringement after DIA introduced the Remington Pole Saw, a chain saw releasably mounted on the end of a telescoping pole. DIA provided evidence of prior art, citing four preexisting patents dealing with "trimming tools on extension poles" that correlated with Rogers's patent. The court nullified Rogers's patent because it concluded the DIA had met its heavy burden of proof that releasably mounting a lightweight chain saw on the end of a telescoping pole assembly to trim trees would be obvious to a person of ordinary skill in the art.[40]

Patent law has expanded to include human-made microorganisms as patent-eligible subject matter, since such compositions are not nature's handiwork, but the inventor's own work.

20. Patentable Business Methods

A 1998 Court of Appeals for the Federal Circuit (CAFC) decision recognized "business methods" as a

---

[36] *Gorham v White*, 81 US 511 (1871).

[37] *Egyptian Goddess, Inc. v SWISA, Inc.*, 545 F3d 665 (Fed Cir 2008).

[38] *Gottschalk v. Benson*, 409 US 63, 67 (1972).

[39] *In re Devel*, 51 F3d 1552 (Fed Cir 1995).

[40] *Rogers v Desa International, Inc.*, 166 F Supp 2d 1202 (ED Mich 2001). See *KRS International Co. v Teleflex, Inc.*, 550 US 398, 401 (2007) for the Supreme Court's recent "obviousness" patent decision, where the Court held that mounting an available sensor on a fixed pivot point of the prior art pedal was a design step well within the grasp of a person of ordinary skill in the relevant art and that the benefit of doing so would be obvious.

patent-eligible "process" under Section 101 of the Patent Act.[41] A burgeoning number of business-method patents followed, with the U.S. Supreme Court referencing in its *eBay v MercExchange* decision the "potential vagueness and suspect validity of some of these patents." A pure business-method patent consists basically of a series of steps related to performing a business process. **For Example,** Patent No. 6,846,131 sets forth a method of doing business with steps for Producing Revenue from Gypsum-Based Refuse Sites. So-called junk patents have also been issued as business-method patents. **For Example,** Patent No. 4,022,227, Method of Concealing Baldness, contains a series of steps for combing one's hair that amount to what is best known as a *comb-over*. Business methods are often in the form of software programs and encompass e-commerce applications.

Recent decisions of the Federal Circuit Court of Appeals contain a much more restrictive approach to evaluating the patentability of business methods under Section 101 of the Patent Act. **For Example,** Bernard Bilski's "business method" of hedging risk in the field of commodities trading was found not to be patent eligible because it was neither "tied to a machine or apparatus," nor did it transform anything.[42]

Believing that many business-method patents are obvious to persons of ordinary skill in their respective fields and have a chilling effect on consumer and public interests, a number of organizations have filed multiple reexamination requests with the PTO to invalidate these patents.[43]

21. Infringement

The patent owner has the exclusive right to make, use, or sell the invention. The owner may bring suit for patent infringement for unauthorized use of a patent and obtain appropriate monetary damages and injunctive relief. The Patent Act provides for the enhancement of damages upon proof of willful infringement and the award of reasonable attorney's fees in "exceptional cases."[44]

Under the act, the owner has "the right to exclude others from making, using, offering for sale or selling the invention."[45] In *eBay, Inc. v MercExchange, LLC,* the U.S. Supreme Court dealt with the question of whether the patent holder had the right to obtain the permanent injunctive relief of stopping a business entity from "using" the patented technology in addition to obtaining damages for the patent violation. The threat of a court order may be used to seek high and often unreasonable licensing fees. Major technology companies contended that trial courts should consider multiple factors in deciding whether to issue a permanent injunction.

EBay, Inc. v MercExchange, LLC, 547 US 388 (2006)

"Squeeze Play" Averted

eBay and its subsidiary half.com operate popular Internet Web sites that allow private sellers to list goods they wish to sell at either an auction or a fixed price (its "Buy it Now" feature). MercExchange, LLC, sought to license its business-method patent to eBay, but no agreement was reached. In MercExchange's subsequent patent infringement suit, a jury found that its patent was valid, that

eBay had infringed the patent, and $29.5 million in damages were appropriate. However, the District Court denied MercExchange's motion for permanent injunctions against patent infringement absent exceptional circumstances. MercExchange appealed. The Federal Circuit Court of Appeals reversed, and the U.S. Supreme Court granted *certiorari*.

---

[41] *State Street Bank v Signature Financial Group* 149 F3d 1368 (Fed Cir 1998).
[42] *In re Bilski,* 545 F3d 943 (Fed Cir 2008) (en banc).
[43] See Electronic Frontier Foundation, Patent Busting Project at **www.eff.org/patent/wanted** (April 2009).
[44] *See In re Seagate Technology, LLC,* 497 F3d 1360 (Fed. Cir. 2007), where the CAFC set a higher "willfulness" standard, requiring at least a showing of objective recklessness on the part of the infringer.
[45] 35 USC § 154(a)(1).

Continued

JUDICIAL OPINION

THOMAS, A.J. . . . According to well-established principles of equity, a plaintiff seeking a permanent injunction must satisfy a four-factor test before a court may grant such relief. A plaintiff must demonstrate: (1) that it has suffered an irreparable injury; (2) that remedies available at law, such as monetary damages, are inadequate to compensate for that injury; (3) that, considering the balance of hardships between the plaintiff and defendant, a remedy in equity is warranted; and (4) that the public interest would not be disserved by a permanent injunction. . . . The decision to grant or deny permanent injunctive relief is an act of equitable discretion by the district court, reviewable on appeal for abuse of discretion.

These familiar principles apply with equal force to disputes arising under the Patent Act. . . . To be sure, the Patent Act also declares that "patents shall have the attributes of personal property," § 261, including "the right to exclude others from making, using, offering for sale, or selling the invention," § 154(a)(1). According to the Court of Appeals, this statutory right to exclude alone justifies its general rule in favor of permanent injunctive relief. But the creation of a right is distinct from the provision of remedies for violations of that right. Indeed, the Patent Act itself indicates that patents shall have the attributes of personal property "[s]ubject to the provisions of this title," 35 U.S.C. § 261, including, presumably, the provision that injunctive relief "may" issue only "in accordance with the principles of equity," § 283. . . .

Because we conclude that neither court below correctly applied the traditional four-factor framework that governs the award of injunctive relief, we vacate the judgment of the Court of Appeals, so that the District Court may apply that framework in the first instance. In doing so, we take no position on whether permanent injunctive relief should or should not issue in this particular case, or indeed in any number of other disputes arising under the Patent Act. . . .

[Reversed and Remanded]

Chief Justice Roberts, with whom Justice Scalia and Justice Ginsburg join, concurring. I agree with the Court's holding that "the decision whether to grant or deny injunctive relief rests within the equitable discretion of the district courts, and that such discretion must be exercised consistent with traditional principles of equity, in patent disputes no less than in other cases governed by such standards," *ante,* at 1841, and I

join the opinion of the Court. That opinion rightly rests on the proposition that "a major departure from the long tradition of equity practice should not be lightly implied.". . .

Justice Kennedy, with whom Justice Stevens, Justice Souter, and Justice Breyer join, concurring. . . . To the extent earlier cases establish a pattern of granting an injunction against patent infringers almost as a matter of course, this pattern simply illustrates the result of the four-factor test in the contexts then prevalent. The lesson of the historical practice, therefore, is most helpful and instructive when the circumstances of a case bear substantial parallels to litigation the courts have confronted before.

In cases now arising trial courts should bear in mind that in many instances the nature of the patent being enforced and the economic function of the patent holder present considerations quite unlike earlier cases. An industry has developed in which firms use patents not as a basis for producing and selling goods but, instead, primarily for obtaining licensing fees. See FTC, To Promote Innovation: The Proper Balance of Competition and Patent Law and Policy, ch. 3, pp. 38–39 (Oct. 2003). For these firms, an injunction, and the potentially serious sanctions arising from its violation, can be employed as a bargaining tool to charge exorbitant fees to companies that seek to buy licenses to practice the patent. When the patented invention is but a small component of the product the companies seek to produce and the threat of an injunction is employed simply for undue leverage in negotiations, legal damages may well be sufficient to compensate for the infringement and an injunction may not serve the public interest. In addition injunctive relief may have different consequences for the burgeoning number of patents over business methods, which were not of much economic and legal significance in earlier times. The potential vagueness and suspect validity of some of these patents may affect the calculus under the four-factor test. . . .

QUESTIONS

1. What classification of patent is involved in this decision?

2. Did eBay win on the issue before the Supreme Court? Explain.

3. Summarize the position set forth in Justice Kennedy's concurring opinion.

Under the Supreme Court's "doctrine of equivalents," infringers may not avoid liability for patent infringement by substituting insubstantial differences for some of the elements of the patented product or process. The test for infringement requires an essential inquiry: Does the accused product or process contain elements identical or equivalent to each claimed element of the patented invention?[46]

D. SECRET BUSINESS INFORMATION

A business may have developed information that is not generally known but that cannot be protected under federal law, or a business may want to avoid the disclosure required to obtain a patent or copyright protection of computer software. As long as such information is kept secret, it will be protected under state law relating to trade secrets.[47]

22. Trade Secrets

A **trade secret** may consist of any formula, device, or compilation of information that is used in one's business and is of such a nature that it provides an advantage over competitors who do not have the information. It may be a formula for a chemical compound; a process of manufacturing, treating, or preserving materials; or, to a limited extent, certain confidential customer lists.[48]

Courts will not protect customer lists if customer identities are readily ascertainable from industry or public sources or if products or services are sold to a wide group of purchasers based on their individual needs.[49]

23. Loss of Protection

When secret business information is made public, it loses the protection it had while secret. This loss of protection occurs when the information is made known without any restrictions. In contrast, there is no loss of protection when secret information is shared or communicated for a special purpose and the person receiving the information knows that it is not to be made known to others.

When a product or process is unprotected by a patent or a copyright and is sold in significant numbers to the public, whose members are free to resell to whomever they choose, competitors are free to reverse engineer (start with the known product and work backward to discover the process) or copy the article. For Example, Crosby Yacht Co., a boatbuilder on Cape Cod, developed a hull design that is not patented. Maine Boatbuilders, Inc. (MBI), purchased one of Crosby's boats and copied the hull by creating a mold from the boat it purchased. MBI is free to build and sell boats utilizing the copied hull.

24. Defensive Measures

Employers seek to avoid the expense of trade secret litigation by limiting disclosure of trade secrets to employees with a "need to know." Employers also have employees sign nondisclosure agreements, and they conduct exit interviews when employees with confidential information leave, reminding the employees of the employer's intent to enforce the nondisclosure agreement. In addition, employers have adopted industrial security plans to protect their unique knowledge from "outsiders," who may engage in theft, trespass, wiretapping, or other forms of commercial espionage.

25. Criminal Sanctions

Under the federal Industrial Espionage Act of 1996,[50] knowingly stealing, soliciting, or obtaining trade secrets by copying, downloading, or uploading via electronic means or otherwise with the intention that

---

[46] *Warner-Jenkinson v Hilton Davis Chemical Co.*, 520 US 17 (1997). But see *Festo Corp. v Shoketsu*, 493 F3d 1368 (Fed Cir 2007).

[47] The Uniform Trade Secrets Act was officially amended in 1985. It is now in force in Alabama, Alaska, Arizona, Arkansas, California, Colorado, Connecticut, Delaware, Florida, Georgia, Hawaii, Idaho, Illinois, Indiana, Iowa, Kansas, Kentucky, Louisiana, Maine, Minnesota, Mississippi, Montana, Nebraska, Nevada, New Hampshire, New Mexico, North Dakota, Ohio, Oklahoma, Oregon, Rhode Island, South Carolina, South Dakota, Utah, Vermont, Virginia, Washington, West Virginia, and Wisconsin. Trade secrets are protected in all states either under the uniform act or common law and under both criminal and civil statutes.

[48] Restatement (Second) of Torts § 757 cmt b. See *Home Pride Foods, Inc. v Johnson*, 634 NW2d 774 (Neb 2001).

[49] *Xpert Automation Systems Corp. v Vibromatic Co.*, 569 NE2d 351 (Ind App 1990).

[50] PL 104–294, 18 USC § 1831 et seq. (1996).

it will benefit a foreign government or agent is a crime. This act also applies to the stealing or purchasing of trade secrets by U.S. companies or individuals who intend to convert trade secrets to the economic benefit of anyone other than the owner. The definition of trade secret is closely modeled on the Uniform Trade Secrets Act and includes all forms and types of financial, business, scientific, technical, economic, and engineering information. The law requires the owner to have taken "reasonable and proper" measures to keep the information secret. Offenders are subject to fines of up to $500,000 or twice the value of the proprietary information involved, whichever is greater, and imprisonment for up to 15 years.

Corporations may be fined up to $10,000,000 or twice the value of the secret involved, whichever is greater. In addition, the offender's property is subject to forfeiture to the U.S. government, and import-export sanctions may be imposed.

E. Protection of Computer Software and Mask Works

Computer programs, chip designs, and mask works are protected from infringement with varying degrees of success by federal statutes, restrictive licensing, and trade secrecy.

CPA   26. Copyright Protection of Computer Programs

Under the Computer Software Copyright Act of 1980,[51] a written program is given the same protection as any other copyrighted material regardless of whether the program is written in source code (ordinary language) or object code (machine language). **For Example,** Franklin Computer Corp. copied certain operating-system computer programs that had been copyrighted by Apple Computer, Inc.

When Apple sued Franklin for copyright infringement, Franklin argued that the object code on which its programs had relied was an uncopyrightable "method of operation." The Third Circuit held that computer programs, whether in source code or in object code embedded on ROM chips, are protected under the act.[52]

In determining whether there is a copyright violation under the Computer Software Copyright Act, courts will examine the two programs in question to compare their structure, flow, sequence, and organization. Moreover, the courts in their infringement analysis look to see whether the most *significant* steps of the program are similar rather than whether most of the program's steps are similar. To illustrate a copyright violation, substantial similarity in the structure of two computer programs for dental laboratory record-keeping was found—even though the programs were dissimilar in a number of respects—because five particularly important subroutines within both programs performed almost identically."[53]

The protection afforded software by the copyright law is not entirely satisfactory to software developers because of the distinction made by the copyright law of protecting expressions but not ideas. Also, Section 102(b) of the 1980 Computer Software Copyright Act does not provide protection for "methods of operation." A court has allowed a competitor to copy the identical menu tree of a copyrighted spreadsheet program because it was a noncopyrightable method of operation.[54]

As set forth previously, the Digital Millennium Copyright Act of 1998 was enacted to curb the pirating of a wide range of works, including software.

CPA   27. Patent Protection of Programs

Patents have been granted for computer programs; for example, a method of using a computer to carry out

---

[51] Act of December 12, 1980, PL 96–517, 94 Stat 3015, 17 USC §§ 101, 117. (Note: CPA Exam content changes in January 2011.)
[52] *Apple Computer Inc. v Franklin Computer Corp.*, 714 F2d 1240 (3d Cir 1983).
[53] *Whelen Associates v Jaslow Dental Laboratory*, 797 F2d 1222 (3d Cir 1986).
[54] *Lotus Development Corp. v Borland International Inc.*, 49 F3d 807 (1st Cir 1995), aff'd, 516 US 233 (1996).

translations from one language to another has been held patentable.

The disadvantage of patenting a program is that the program is placed in the public records and may thus be examined by anyone. This practice poses a potential danger that the program will be copied. To detect patent violators and bring legal action is difficult and costly.[55]

28. Trade Secrets

While primary protection for computer software is found in the Computer Software Copyright Act, industry also uses trade secret law to protect computer programs. When software containing trade secrets is unlawfully appropriated by a former employee, the employee is guilty of trade secret theft.[56]

FIGURE 10-1 | *Summary Comparison of Intellectual Property Rights*

TYPE OF INTELLECTUAL PROPERTY	TRADEMARKS	COPYRIGHTS	PATENTS	TRADE SECRETS
PROTECTION	WORDS, NAMES, SYMBOLS, OR DEVICES USED TO IDENTIFY A PRODUCT OR SERVICE	ORIGINAL CREATIVE WORKS OF AUTHORSHIP, SUCH AS WRITINGS, MOVIES, RECORDS, AND COMPUTER SOFTWARE	UTILITY, DESIGN, AND PLANT PATENTS	ADVANTAGEOUS FORMULAS, DEVICES, OR COMPILATION OF INFORMATION
APPLICABLE STANDARD	IDENTIFIES AND DISTINGUISHES A PRODUCT OR SERVICE	ORIGINAL CREATIVE WORKS IN WRITING OR IN ANOTHER FORMAT	NEW AND NONOBVIOUS, ADVANCED IN THE ART	NOT READILY ASCERTAINABLE, NOT DISCLOSED TO THE PUBLIC
WHERE TO APPLY	PATENT AND TRADEMARK OFFICE	REGISTER OF COPYRIGHTS	PATENT AND TRADEMARK OFFICE	NO PUBLIC REGISTRATION NECESSARY
DURATION	INDEFINITE SO LONG AS IT CONTINUES TO BE USED	LIFE OF AUTHOR PLUS 70 YEARS, OR 95 YEARS FROM PUBLICATION FOR "WORKS FOR HIRE"	UTILITY AND PLANT PATENTS, 20 YEARS FROM DATE OF APPLICATION; DESIGN PATENTS, 14 YEARS	INDEFINITE SO LONG AS SECRET IS NOT DISCLOSED TO PUBLIC

[55] The PTO has adopted guidelines for the examination of computer-related inventions, 61 CFR §§ 7478–7502.

[56] The National Conference of Commissioners on Uniform State Laws (NCCUSL) has promulgated a new uniform law, the Uniform Computer Information Transactions Act (UCITA), to govern contracts involving the sale, licensing, maintenance, and support of computer software and books in digital form. This uniform act had been identified as Article 2B and was part of the comprehensive revisions to Article 2 of the Uniform Commercial Code. The act is supported by software publishers and opposed by software developers and buyers. The act can be obtained from the NCCUSL at **www.nccusl.org.** Information for and against the UCITA can be found at **www.ucitaonline.com.** The act has been adopted by Maryland and Virginia.

29. Restrictive Licensing

To retain greater control over proprietary software, it is common for the creator of the software to license its use to others rather than selling it to them. Such licensing agreements typically include restrictions on the use of the software by the licensee and give the licensor greater protection than that provided by copyright law. These restrictions commonly prohibit the licensee from providing, in any manner whatsoever, the software to third persons or subjecting the software to reverse engineering.[57]

30. Semiconductor Chip Protection

The Semiconductor Chip Protection Act (SCPA) of 1984[58] created a new form of industrial intellectual property by protecting mask works and the semiconductor chip products in which they are embodied against chip piracy. A **mask work** refers to the specific form of expression embodied in chip design, including the stencils used in manufacturing semiconductor chip products. A **semiconductor chip product** is a product placed on a piece of semiconductor material in accordance with a predetermined pattern that is intended to perform electronic circuitry functions. These chips operate microwave ovens, televisions, computers, robots, x-ray machines, and countless other devices. This definition of semiconductor chip products includes such products as analog chips, logic function chips like microprocessors, and memory chips like RAMS and ROMs.

(A) DURATION AND QUALIFICATIONS FOR PROTECTION. The SCPA provides the owner of a mask work fixed in semiconductor chip products the exclusive right for 10 years to reproduce and distribute the products in the United States and to import them into the United States. The protection of the act applies only to those works that, when considered as a whole, are not commonplace, staple, or familiar in the semiconductor industry.

(B) LIMITATION ON EXCLUSIVE RIGHTS. Under the SCPA's reverse engineering exemption, competitors may not only study mask works but may also use the results of that study to design their own semiconductor chip products embodying their own original masks even if the masks are substantially similar (but not substantially identical) so long as their products are the result of substantial study and analysis, not merely the result of plagiarism.

Innocent infringers are not liable for infringements occurring before notice of protection is given them and are liable for reasonable royalties on each unit distributed after notice has been given them. However, the continued purchasing of infringing semiconductors after notice has been given can result in penalties of up to $250,000.

(C) REMEDIES. The SCPA provides that an infringer will be liable for actual damages and will forfeit its profits to the owner. As an alternative, the owner may elect to receive statutory damages of up to $250,000 as determined by a court. The court may also order destruction or other disposition of the products and equipment used to make the products. **For Example,** Altera Corporation manufactures programmable logic devices. It was successful in the lawsuit against its competitor Clear Logic, Inc., which works from a different business model. Altera was successful in its lawsuit against Clear Logic under the SCPA, asserting that Clear Logic had copied the layout design of its registered mask works. It also was successful in its claim that Clear Logic induced breach of software licenses with Altera customers. Damages were assessed at $36 million.[59]

The Jerk (1979) (R)

Steve Martin invents a special handle for eyeglasses that is mass marketed by a businessman who gives him a percentage of the royalties from sales. Should Martin be paid?

Check out LawFlix at **www.cengage.com/blaw/dvl** to acces movie clips that illustrate business law concepts.

[57] See *Fonar Corp. v Domenick*, 105 F3d 99 (2d Cir 1997).
[58] PL 98-620, 98 Stat 3347, 17 USC § 901.
[59] *Altera Corp. v Clear Logic Inc.*, 424 F3d 1079 (9th Cir 2005).

MAKE THE CONNECTION

SUMMARY

Property rights in trademarks, copyrights, and patents are acquired as provided primarily in federal statutes. A trademark or service mark is any word, symbol, design, or combination of these used to identify a product (in the case of a trademark) or a service (in the case of a service mark). Terms will fall into one of four categories: (1) generic, (2) descriptive, (3) suggestive, or (4) arbitrary or fanciful. Generic terms are never registrable. However, if a descriptive term has acquired a secondary meaning, it is registrable. Suggestive and arbitrary or fanciful marks are registrable as well. If there is likelihood of confusion, a court will enjoin the second user from using a particular mark.

A copyright is the exclusive right given by federal statute to the creator of a literary or an artistic work to use, reproduce, or display the work for the life of the creator and 70 years after the creator's death.

A patent gives the inventor an exclusive right for 20 years from the date of application to make, use, and sell an invention that is new and useful but not obvious to those in the business to which the invention is related. Trade secrets that give an owner an advantage over competitors are protected under state law for an unlimited period so long as they are not made public.

Protection of computer programs and the design of computer chips and mask works is commonly obtained, subject to certain limitations, by complying with federal statutes, by using the law of trade secrets, and by requiring restrictive licensing agreements. Many software developers pursue all of these means to protect their proprietary interests in their programs.

LEARNING OUTCOMES

After studying this chapter, you should be able to clearly explain:

A. TRADEMARKS AND SERVICE MARKS

LO.1 Explain the spectrum of distinctiveness used to classify trademarks and explain why distinctiveness is important

> See the Kodak example, a coined most distinctive mark, p. 193.
> See the Sports Illustrated example, a descriptive mark with acquired distinctiveness, p. 193.
> See the *Harley Davidson* case where "hog" was found to be generic and not distinctive at all, p. 194.

LO.2 Explain how personal names can acquire trademark protection

> See the Paul Frank example on p. 195.

LO.3 List the remedies available for improper use of trademarks

> See the remedies applied in the *Venture Tape* case on p. 196, injunctive relief, lost profits and attorney's fees.

B. COPYRIGHTS

LO.4 Explain what is and is not copyrightable; explain the fair use defense

> See the discussion on what is copyrightable on p. 202.
> See the *Darden* example of a denial of a copyright because of lack of creativity, p. 202.
> See the *Wind Done Gone* example of fair use parody on p. 205.

C. PATENTS

LO.5 Explain the "new and not obvious" requirement necessary to obtain a patent

> See the cDNA "not obvious" example on p. 207.
> See the mounted chain saw "obvious" example on p. 207.

D. SECRET BUSINESS INFORMATION

LO.6 List and explain the defensive measures employers take to preserve confidential business information

See the discussion on signing and enforcing nondisclosure agreements on p. 210.

E. PROTECTION OF COMPUTER SOFTWARE AND MASK WORKS

LO.7 Explain the extent of protection provided owners of software

See the *Apple Computer* example on p. 211.

KEY TERMS

acquired distinctiveness
copyright
cybersquatters
distinctiveness

mask work
prior art
secondary meaning
semiconductor chip

service mark
trade dress
trade secret
trademark

QUESTIONS AND CASE PROBLEMS

1. China is a signatory country to the Madrid Protocol on the international registration of trademarks. Starbucks opened its first café in China in 1999 and has added outlets in numerous locations including Shanghai and at the Great Wall and the imperial palace in Beijing. Xingbake Café Corp. Ltd. has imitated the designs of Starbuck's cafés in its business coffee café locations in Shanghai. *Xing* (pronounced "Shing") means star, and *bake*, or "bak kuh" is pronounced like "bucks." Does the Seattle, Washington, Starbucks Corporation have standing to bring suit in China against Xingbake Café Corp. Ltd? If so, on what theory? Decide. (*Boston Globe*, January 3, 2006, 1)

2. Cable News Network with its principal place of business in Atlanta, Georgia, is the owner of the trademark CNN in connection with providing news and information services to people worldwide through cable and satellite television networks, Web sites, and news services. Its services are also available worldwide on the Internet at the domain name CNN.com. Maya Online Broadband Network (Maya HK) is a Chinese company. It registered the domain name CNNEWS.com with Network Solutions, Inc. The CNNews.com Web site was designed to provide news and information to Chinese-speaking individuals worldwide,

making significant use of the terms *CNNews* and *CNNews.com* as brand names and logos that the Atlanta company contends resembles its logos. Maya HK has admitted that CNNews in fact stands for China Network News abbreviated as CNN. The Atlanta company had notified Maya HK of its legal right to the CNN mark before the Chinese company registered the CNNews.com domain name. Does the federal Anticybersquatting Consumer Protection Act apply to this case? If so, does a "safe harbor" exist under the ACPA for Maya HK in that most people who access its Web site in China have never heard of CNN? Decide. [*Cable News Network v CNN News.com*, 177 F Supp 2d 506 (ED Va)]

3. Banion manufacturers semiconductor chips. He wants to obtain protection for his mask works under federal law, particularly so that competitors will be prohibited from reverse engineering these works. Advise Banion of his legal options, if any, to accomplish his objective.

4. Jim and Eric work for Audio Visual Services (AVS) at Cramer University in Casper, Wyoming. For "expenses" of $5, Jim and Eric used AVS facilities after hours to burn discs of Pearl Jam's CD *Vitology* for 25 friends or friends of friends from school. When Mrs. Mullen, who is in charge of AVS, discovered this and confronted

them, Jim, a classics major, defended their actions, telling her, "It's *de minimus*. . . I mean, who cares?" Explain to Jim and Eric the legal and ethical ramifications of their actions.

5. Sullivan sold t-shirts with the name *Boston Marathon* and the year of the race imprinted on them. The Boston Athletic Association (BAA) sponsors and administers the Boston Marathon and has used the name *Boston Marathon* since 1917. The BAA registered the name *Boston Marathon* on the Principal Register. In 1986, the BAA entered into an exclusive license with Image, Inc., to use its service mark on shirts and other apparel. Thereafter, when Sullivan continued to sell shirts imprinted with the name *Boston Marathon*, the BAA sought an injunction. Sullivan's defense was that the general public was not being misled into thinking that his shirts were officially sponsored by the BAA. Without this confusion of source, he contended, no injunction should be issued. Decide. [*Boston Athletic Ass'n v Sullivan*, 867 F2d 22 (1st Cir)]

6. The University of Georgia Athletic Association (UGAA) brought suit against beer wholesaler Bill Laite for marketing Battlin' Bulldog Beer. The UGAA claimed that the cans infringed its symbol for its athletic teams. The symbol, which depicted an English Bulldog wearing a sweater with a G and the word BULLDOGS on it, had been registered as a service mark. Soon after the beer appeared on the market, the university received telephone calls from friends of the university who were concerned that Battlin' Bulldog Beer was not the sort of product that should in any way be related to the University of Georgia. The university's suit was based on the theory of false designation of origin in violation of the Lanham Act. Laite contended that there was no likelihood of confusion because his bulldog was different from the university's and his cans bore the disclaimer "Not associated with the University of Georgia." Decide. [*University of Georgia Athletic Ass'n v Laite*, 756 F2d 1535 (11th Cir)]

7. Twentieth Century Fox (Fox) owned and distributed the successful motion picture *The Commitments*. The film tells the story of a group of young

Irish men and women who form a soul music band. In the film, the leader of the band, Jimmy, tries to teach the band members what it takes to be successful soul music performers. Toward that end, Jimmy shows the band members a videotape of James Brown's energetic performance of the song "Please, Please, Please." This performance came from Brown's appearance in 1965 on a television program called the *TAMI Show*. Portions of the 1965 performance are shown in *The Commitments* in seven separate "cuts" for a total of 27 seconds. Sometimes the cuts are in the background of a scene, and sometimes they occupy the entire screen. Brown's name is not mentioned at all during these relatively brief cuts. His name is mentioned only once later in the film, when Jimmy urges the band members to abandon their current musical interests and tune in to the great soul performers, including James Brown: "Listen, from now on I don't want you listening to Guns & Roses and The Soup Dragons. I want you on a strict diet of soul. James Brown for the growls, Otis Redding for the moans, Smokey Robinson for the whines, and Aretha for the whole lot put together." Would it be fair use under U.S. copyright law for Fox to use just 27 seconds of James Brown cuts in the film without formally obtaining permission to use the cuts? Advise Fox as to what, if anything, would be necessary to protect it from a lawsuit. [See *Brown v Twentieth Century Fox Film Corp.*, 799 F Supp 166 (DDC)]

8. The Greenwich Bank & Trust Co. (GB&T) opened in 1998 and by 2008 had expanded to a total of four branches in the Greenwich, Connecticut, community of 62,000 residents. A competitor using the name Bank of Greenwich (BOG) opened in December 2006. GB&T's parent entity sued BOG for trademark violation under the Lanham Act. BOG argued that GB&T's service mark is generic and is simply not entitled to Lanham Act protection because it combines the generic term "bank" and the geographic term "Greenwich." GB&T asserted that it had been the only bank in Greenwich using the word *Greenwich* in its name and had done so exclusively for nine years. It asserted that a geographic term is entitled to protection if it acquires secondary meaning.

GB&T introduced evidence regarding its advertising expenditures, sales success, and length of exclusivity of use along with evidence of actual consumer confusion. Decide. [*Connecticut Community Bank v The Bank of Greenwich*, 578 F Supp 2d 405 (D Conn 2008)].

9. The menu commands on the Lotus 1-2-3 spreadsheet program enable users to perform accounting functions by using such commands as "Copy," "Print," and "Quit." Borland International, Inc., released its Quattro spreadsheet, a program superior to Lotus 1-2-3 that did, however, use an identical copy of the entire Lotus 1-2-3 menu tree but did not copy any of Lotus's computer code. Lotus believed that its copyright in Lotus 1-2-3 had been violated. Borland insisted that the Lotus menu command was not copyrightable because it is a method of operation foreclosed from protection under Section 102(b) of the Copyright Act of 1976. Decide. [*Lotus Development Corp. v Borland International, Inc.*, 49 F3d 807 (1st Cir), aff'd, 516 US 233]

10. Diehr devised a computerized process for curing rubber that was based on a well-known mathematical formula related to the cure time, and he devised numerous other steps in his synthetic rubber-curing process. The patent examiner determined that because abstract ideas, the laws of nature, and mathematical formulas are not patentable subject matter, the process in this case (based on a known mathematical formula) was also not patentable. Diehr contended that all of the steps in his rubber-curing process were new and not obvious to the art of rubber curing. He contended also that he did not seek an exclusive patent on the mathematical formula, except for its use in the rubber-curing process. Decide. [*Diamond v Diehr*, 450 US 175]

11. Aries Information Systems, Inc., develops and markets computer software specifically designed to meet the financial accounting and reporting requirements of such public bodies as school districts and county governments. One of Aries's principal products is the POBAS III accounting program. Pacific Management Systems Corporation was organized by Scott Dahmer, John Laugan, and Roman Rowan for marketing a financial accounting and budgeting system known as FAMIS. Dahmer, Laugan, and Rowan were Aries employees before, during, and shortly after they organized Pacific. As employees, they each gained access to Aries's software materials (including the POBAS III system) and had information about Aries's existing and prospective clients. Proprietary notices appeared on every client contract, source code list, and magnetic tape. Dahmer, Laugan, and Rowan signed an Employee Confidential Information Agreement after beginning employment with Aries. While still employees of Aries, they submitted a bid on behalf of Pacific to Rock County and were awarded the contract. Pacific's FAMIS software system is substantially identical to Aries's proprietary POBAS III system. Aries sued Pacific to recover damages for misappropriation of its trade secrets. Pacific's defense was that no "secrets" were misappropriated because many employees knew the information in question. Decide. [*Aries Information Systems, Inc. v Pacific Management Systems Corp.*, 366 NW2d 366 (Minn App)]

12. The plaintiff, Herbert Rosenthal Jewelry Corporation, and the defendant, Kalpakian, manufactured jewelry. The plaintiff obtained a copyright registration of a jeweled pin in the shape of a bee. Kalpakian made a similar pin. Rosenthal sued Kalpakian for infringement of copyright registration. Kalpakian raised the defense that he was only copying the idea, not the way the idea was expressed. Was he liable for infringement of the plaintiff's copyright? [*Herbert Rosenthal Jewelry Corp. v Kalpakian*, 446 F2d 738 (9th Cir)]

13. Mineral Deposits, Ltd. (MD, Ltd.), an Australian company, manufactures the Reichert Spiral, a device used for recovering gold particles from sand and gravel. The spiral was patented in Australia, and MD, Ltd., had applied for a patent in the United States. Theodore Zigan contacted MD, Ltd., stating he was interested in purchasing up to 200 devices for use in his gravel pit. MD, Ltd., agreed to lend Zigan a spiral for testing its efficiency. Zigan made molds of the spiral's components and proceeded to manufacture 170 copies of the device.

When MD, Ltd., found out that copies were being made, it demanded the return of the spiral. MD, Ltd., also sought lost profits for the 170 spirals manufactured by Zigan. Recovery was sought on a theory of misappropriation of trade secrets. Zigan offered to pay for the spiral lent him by MD, Ltd. He argued that trade secret protection was lost by the public sale of the spiral. What ethical values are involved? Was Zigan's conduct a violation of trade secret law? [*Mineral Deposits, Ltd. v Zigan*, 773 P2d 609 (Colo App)]

14. Village Voice Media, owners of the famous *Village Voice* newspaper in New York City, sent a letter to *The Cape Cod Voice*, a year-old publication located in Orleans, Massachusetts, objecting to the use of the word *Voice* in the title of its publication. It warned that the Cape Cod publication could cause "confusion as to the source affiliation with the famous Village Voice marks." The publisher of *The Cape Cod Voice* responded that "small places have a right to their own voices." The use of the word *Voice* was thus in dispute between these parties. Would you classify it as generic, descriptive, suggestive, arbitrary, or fanciful? How would you resolve this controversy? [*Cape Cod Times* Business Section, Amy Zipkin, *The New York Times*, October 16, 2004, G-1].

CPA QUESTIONS

1. Multicomp Company wishes to protect software it has developed. It is concerned about others copying this software and taking away some of its profits. Which of the following is true concerning the current state of the law?

   a. Computer software is generally copyrightable.

   b. To receive protection, the software must have a conspicuous copyright notice.

   c. Software in human readable source code is copyrightable but machine language object code is not.

   d. Software can be copyrighted for a period not to exceed 20 years.

2. Which of the following is not correct concerning computer software purchased by Gultch Company from Softtouch Company? Softtouch originally created this software.

   a. Gultch can make backup copies in case of machine failure.

   b. Softtouch can typically copyright its software for at least 75 years.

   c. If the software consists of compiled computer databases, it cannot be copyrighted.

   d. Computer programs are generally copyrightable.

3. Using his computer, Professor Bell makes 15 copies (to distribute to his accounting class) of a database in some software he has purchased for his personal research. The creator of this software is claiming copyright. Which of the following is correct?

   a. This is an infringement of copyright, since he bought the software for personal use.

   b. This is not an infringement of copyright, since databases cannot be copyrighted.

   c. This is not an infringement of copyright because the copies were made using a computer.

   d. This is not an infringement of copyright because of the fair use doctrine.

4. Intellectual property rights included in software may be protected under which of the following?

   a. Patent law

   b. Copyright law

   c. Both of the above

   d. None of the above

Chapter 11

CYBERLAW

A. INTRODUCTION TO CYBERLAW

1. What is Cyberlaw?

The World Wide Web has enabled businesses to move goods and services through commerce at lightning speed. In many ways, the changes in technology and resulting changes in business practices have occurred at speeds that have not permitted the law to keep pace with them. As a result, this new world of business has caused some distress among managers, law professors, and students as they wonder, "Are there laws that cover this new way of doing business?"

The answer to the question is both yes and no. Although certainly some new laws govern aspects of using and operating systems in the new economy and cyberspace, body of law and precedent—the same body of law and precedent that has seen businesses through many economic and technological revolutions—remains. This same body of law and its characteristics are again a resource for resolving the new economy's legal issues. Examining how the law applies to the new technology provides further evidence of the law's stability, innovation, and flexibility. (See Chapter 1 for more discussion of the characteristics of law.) The rise of the Internet and its pervasive use in business is not the first time the law has had to change to keep pace with technological revolutions. **For Example,** the new clarity of satellite pictures and observation techniques such as thermal scanning have raised new issues concerning searches and the requirements for warrants. The law adjusts and survives through a balancing of the interests at stake as issues arise from the use of new technologies.

Even though the law that is applied to resolve the problems of the new technologies and the new economy is often referred to as **cyberlaw**, you need not fear that you will be required to learn a whole new body of law. There have been and will continue to be changes in the law to accommodate new ways of doing business, but there has also been and will

continue to be reliance on the fundamental principles that underlie our laws and the rights they protect. This chapter simply examines the issues and concerns in cyberspace and covers their resolution through a brief overview of new and existing laws. Other chapters provide more details on these rights and protections. This chapter provides a framework for both the challenges of legal issues in **cyberspace** as well as how the law is adjusting to and absorbing the changes business brings through innovation.

2. What are the Issues in Cyberlaw?

The legal issues of cyberspace can be broken down into six areas: **tort** issues, contract issues, intellectual property issues, criminal law issues, constitutional restraints and protections, and securities law issues. Within each of these six areas of existing law are a number of new legal issues that have arisen because of the nature of cyberspace and the conduct of business there. That various cyberlaw issues can be grouped into traditional areas of law demonstrates the not-so-new nature of cyberlaw in the new economy. The following sections focus on these six main areas.

B. TORT ISSUES IN CYBERSPACE

The tort issues in cyberlaw are privacy, appropriation, and defamation.

3. Employer/Employee Privacy Issues in Cyberlaw

E-mail use and Internet surfing for personal reasons in the workplace is a nearly universal practice. A 2007 study found that employees spend about 20 percent of their work day on social use of the Internet, which includes personal e-mails and Web surfing.[1] An earlier survey concluded that 30 percent of employees have used company e-mail systems to send racist, pornographic, sexist, or otherwise discriminatory messages.[2] Blogging has introduced yet another way

---

[1] **www.salary.com**, July 2007.
[2] W. Michael Hoffman, Laura P. Hartman, and Mark Rowe, "You've Got Mail . . . And the Boss Knows: A Survey by the Center for Business Ethics of Companies' Email and Internet Monitoring," 108 Business and Society 285 (2003). See also **http://www.elronsoftware.com** for more information on employee use of e-mail.

the Internet is used by employees—often to disclose private and/or negative information about their companies. Tweeting is instant and ongoing communication that could reveal, prematurely, information that the company does not want public. E-mails, Internet surfing, and blogging require a delicate balancing of rights and interests.

(A) Employers Are Accountable for Employee E-Mail Content. Employers are held responsible for the content of employee e-mails and employers must have access and control rights as a result. For example, e-mails that contain off-color jokes or suggestive comments create an atmosphere of harassment. (See Chapter 40 for more information on sexual harassment).[3] Employers are also responsible when employees use e-mail or the Internet at work to violate intellectual property rights (see pp. 226 and 231 in this chapter for more discussion on this topic). Employers are also held accountable when employees use e-mails and blogs to defame fellow employees or competitors, vendors, or even customers.

Employee e-mail is spontaneous, candid, and discoverable. As a result, the content of employees' e-mail is often fertile territory for prosecutors who can find evidence of intent in employee e-mails and blogs. For example, in 2008, investigators uncovered e-mails of employees at Standard & Poor's, the investment rating agency, that indicated that while the employee/ analysts were rating debt instruments as AAA, they were also having their doubts about them. One employee wrote, "These deals could have been structured by cows and we would still rate them."[4] Another e-mail read, "Rating agencies continue to create [an] even bigger monster—the CDO market. Let's hope we are all wealthy and retired by the time this house of cards falters."[5] These candid e-mails were a foundation for settlements paid by the analysts' firms and resulted in general reforms of the analyst industry.

In 2005, Marsh & McLennan settled its price-fixing case with New York's attorney general after e-mails showing that employees were concerned about possible antitrust violations emerged. One employee had written, "I am not some Goody Two Shoes who believes that truth is absolute, but I do feel I have a pretty strict ethical code about being truthful and honest. This idea of 'throwing the quote' by quoting artificially high numbers in some predetermined arrangement for us to lose is repugnant to me, not so much because I hate to lose, but because it is basically dishonest. And I basically agree with the comments of others that it comes awfully close to collusion and price-fixing."[6] Marsh settled the case for $850 million.

(B) Types of Employer Monitoring: What's Legal. Because they are held accountable for what employees do in cyberspace, employers use various methods for monitoring employees including using key-stroking software that allows the employer to see those messages employees typed but did not send, using blocking software that limits sites employees can visit, monitoring and searching e-mails, checking blogs for content, and examining items posted on Facebook and YouTube.

There were some efforts in the early days of cyberspace to apply existing law to ensure e-mail privacy. The Electronic Communications Privacy Act of 1986 (ECPA) prohibits the unauthorized access of "live" communications, as when someone uses a listening device to intercept a telephone conversation. However, e-mail is stored information, and the question of this act's application for resolving the privacy issue is doubtful.[7] ECPA also has an exception for consensual interception. The Stored Communication Act (SCA) prohibits the unauthorized interception of electronic communications, generally meaning stored communication, not ongoing communication such as text messaging, tweeting, and instant messaging. However, the courts have held

---

[3] See *Garrity v John Hancock Mut. Life Ins. Co.,* (D Mass 2002) (memorandum opinion), in which an employer's termination of an employee for sending an e-mail entitled, "The Top Ten Reasons Cookie Dough Is Better Than Men" was upheld on grounds that such content created an atmosphere of harassment.

[4] Summary Report of Issues Identified in the Commission's Examination of Select Credit Rating Agencies, July 8, 2008.

[5] Ibid.

[6] Alex Berenson, "Once Again, Spitzer Follows E-Mail Trail," *New York Times,* Oct. 18, 2004, C1, C2.

[7] "Every circuit court to have considered the matter has held that an 'intercept' under the ECPA must occur contemporaneously with transmission." See *Fraser v Nationwide Mut. Ins. Co.,* 352 F3d 107, 113 (3d Cir 2003).

consistently that employees give consent to such monitoring, and there are no statutory violations when employers do live listening, interception, or recovery of sent communication that is stored and available electronically.[8] When employers have informal policies or policies that allow employees to reimburse their employers for private use of text services, the courts have held that monitoring and disclosure of those messages is a violation of the law.

(c) PRIVACY AND EMPLOYER SCREENING OF APPLICANTS. If the employer will be doing prehiring monitoring, such as looking at MySpace.com and Facebook—and/or "Googling" the applicant's name—the applicant must be told of this monitoring at the time of the application. The information that we post on publicly available sites is not considered private, so employers, as long as they are maintaining consistent standards for all applicants, can examine what you have posted on the Internet.

Employers are also using Google and other Internet sources to track employee work excuses. One company's human resources official was on the phone with the company employment lawyer seeking to determine what action could be taken against an employee who was absent frequently but who claimed he was absent to care for his ill grandmother. While they were talking, the lawyer "Googled" the employee's name and found that he was being arraigned in federal court.

Schools, employment counselors, and lawyers are offering the following warnings about the dangers of Internet personal postings:[9]

1. Nothing is private on the Internet. People can see everything.

2. Be careful what you blog.

3. Protect your identity when in chat rooms.

4. Assume that everything you write and post will be seen.

5. You can clean up your name on Google using several services, but having no hits at all can lead to suspicions.

6. Think before you write, blog, post, or do anything on the Internet.

(D) PRIVACY TORTS AND EMPLOYERS' RIGHT OF ACCESS TO EMPLOYEE E-MAILS AND INTERNET USE. Because employers are accountable for the content of employee e-mail, it is not a breach of privacy for employers to monitor employee e-mail and Internet usage. Monitoring the content of employee e-mails is important for keeping companies out of legal difficulties. However, employees may believe they have an expectation of privacy in their e-mails, even when those e-mails are sent from work. That belief may spring from the tort standards that protect private lives, communications, and information. The tort of **invasion of privacy**, or intrusion into private affairs, has application to cyberspace communication. Internet disclosure, without permission, of private information is a breach of privacy. Employers generally require employees to sign a document in which they acknowledge that by working at the company and using the company's e-mail and server that they have waived their right to privacy. Former Sun Microsoft Systems CEO, Scott McNealy, summed up employee rights to privacy when it comes to Internet use: "You have zero privacy. Get over it."[10]

Employers can monitor electronic communications from employees that are marked as private; e-mails that are sent from home and from private computers that use the company server; e-mails that do not involve company business; text messages sent using company phones; and tweets sent over company iPhones, BlackBerries, and other phone communication systems. Even an employee's communications to his or her lawyer are not private if the company has a "no personal use" policy that employees agree to follow.[11]

---

[8] Meir S. Hornung, "Think Before You Type: A Look at E-mail Privacy in the Workplace," 11 *Fordham Journal of Corporate & Financial Law*, 115, 154 (2005).
[9] From Michelle Conlin, "You Are What You Post," *Business Week*, March 27, 2006, 52–53. For a discussion of research on blogging, see Rainie, "The State of Blogging," Pew Internet and American Life Project, November 2005; available at **www.pewinternet.org/pdfs/PIP_blogging_data.pdf**, and **www.technorati .com**.
[10] A. Michael Froomkin, "The Death of Privacy," 52 *Stanford Law Review*, 1461, 1462 (2000). Presented at the *Cyberspace and Privacy: A New Legal Paradigm?* Symposium, Stanford, CA, 2000.
[11] *Scott v Beth Israel Med. Ctr.*, 847 NYS2d 436 (2007).

Quon v Arch Wireless Operating Co., Inc., 529 F3d 892 (CA 9 2008) cert. granted 2009 WL 1146443 (U.S.)

When You Pay for the Texting, It Belongs to You

Jeff Quon, a sergeant and member of the city of Ontario's SWAT team "texted" Sergeant Steve Trujillo, dispatcher April Florio, and his wife Jerilyn Quon using Arch Wireless text-messaging services that were provided for him through the city of Ontario's contract with Arch.

The city had no official policy directly addressing the use of text messaging. However, the city did have a general "Computer Usage, Internet, and E-mail Policy" applicable to all employees. The policy provided that all software, programs, networks, Internet, e-mail, and other systems were to be used only for city of Ontario–related business. The policy also states, "Users should have no expectation of privacy or confidentiality when using these resources," and indicated that usages were monitored and recorded. Quon attended a meeting during which SWAT team members and others were told that text messages would fall under the city's policy as public information, and be therefore eligible for auditing.

Under the city's contract with Arch Wireless, each pager was allotted 25,000 characters, after which the city was required to pay overage charges. Quon's supervisor told him that he was over by more than 15,000 characters and that he should reimburse the city for the overage charges so that he (the supervisor) would not have to audit the transmission and see how many messages were non–work related. Quon refused to pay and was told to cut down on his transmissions.

When Quon and another officer again exceeded the 25,000-character limit, his supervisor stated that he was "tired of being a bill collector with guys going over the allotted amount of characters on their text pagers." Ontario's chief of police, Chief Scharf, then requested an audit of the text messages.

Because city officials were not able to access the text messages themselves, they requested and obtained the messages from Arch Wireless. The audit of the messages revealed abuse of on-the-clock time through sheer numbers of personal texts and their sexually explicit content. The officers (appellants) were disciplined and subsequently challenged the discipline by claiming violation of their Fourth Amendment rights. The trial court found that there was a Fourth Amendment violation, but granted Arch Wireless a summary judgment on Quon's claims of invasion of privacy.

JUDICIAL OPINION

WARDLAW, Circuit Judge . . . The Stored Communications Act (SCA) was enacted because the advent of the Internet presented a host of potential privacy breaches that the Fourth Amendment does not address. Generally, the SCA prevents "providers" of communication services from divulging private communications to certain entities and/or individuals. Appellants challenge the district court's finding that Arch Wireless is a "remote computing service" ("RCS") as opposed to an "electronic communication service" ("ECS") under the SCA, §§ 2701-2711. The district court correctly concluded that if Arch Wireless is an ECS, it is liable as a matter of law, and that if it is an RCS, it is not liable.

When Arch Wireless released to the City the transcripts of Appellants' messages, Arch Wireless potentially ran afoul of the SCA. This is because both an ECS and RCS can release private information to, or with the lawful consent of, "an addressee or intended recipient of such communication," id. § 2702(b)(1), (b)(3), whereas only an RCS can release such information "with the lawful consent of . . . the subscriber." Id. § 2702(b)(3). It is undisputed that the City was not an "addressee or intended recipient," and that the City was a "subscriber."

We hold that Arch Wireless provided an "electronic communication service" to the City. The parties do not dispute that Arch Wireless acted "knowingly" when it released the transcripts to the City. When Arch Wireless knowingly turned over the text-messaging transcripts to the City, which was a "subscriber," not "an addressee or intended recipient of such communication," it violated the SCA, 18 U.S.C. § 2702(a)(1). Accordingly, judgment in Appellants' favor on their claims against Arch Wireless is appropriate as a matter of law, and we remand to the district court for proceedings consistent with this holding.

Appellants assert that they are entitled to summary judgment on their Fourth Amendment claim against the City, the Department, and Scharf, and on their California constitutional privacy claim against the City, the Department, Scharf, and Glenn. Specifically, Appellants agree with the district court's conclusion that they had a reasonable expectation of privacy in the text messages. However, they argue that the issue regarding Chief Scharf's intent in authorizing the search never should have gone to trial because the search was unreasonable as a matter of law. We agree.

The extent to which the Fourth Amendment provides protection for the contents of electronic communications in the Internet age is an open question. The recently minted

Continued

standard of electronic communication via e-mails, text messages, and other means opens a new frontier in Fourth Amendment jurisprudence that has been little explored. Here, we must first answer the threshold question: Do users of text messaging services such as those provided by Arch Wireless have a reasonable expectation of privacy in their text messages stored on the service provider's network? We hold that they do.

Our Internet jurisprudence is instructive. In *United States v Forrester*, we held that "e-mail . . . users have no expectation of privacy in the to/from addresses of their messages . . . because they should know that this information is provided to and used by Internet service providers for the specific purpose of directing the routing of information." *United States v Forrester*, 512 F.3d 500, 510 (9th Cir.2008). Thus, we have extended the pen register and outside-of-envelope rationales to the "to/from" line of e-mails. But we have not ruled on whether persons have a reasonable expectation of privacy in the content of e-mails.

We see no meaningful difference between the e-mails at issue in Forrester and the text messages at issue here. Both are sent from user to user via a service provider that stores the messages on its servers. Similarly, as i.n Forrester, we also see no meaningful distinction between text messages and letters. As with letters and e-mails, it is not reasonable to expect privacy in the information used to "address" a text message, such as the dialing of a phone number to send a message. However, users do have a reasonable expectation of privacy in the content of their text messages vis-a-vis the service provider. That Arch Wireless may have been able to access the contents of the messages for its own purposes is irrelevant. Appellants did not expect that Arch Wireless would monitor their text messages, much less turn over the messages to third parties without Appellants' consent.

We do not endorse a monolithic view of text message users' reasonable expectation of privacy, as this is necessarily a context-sensitive inquiry. Absent an agreement to the contrary, Trujillo, Florio, and Jerilyn Quon had no reasonable expectation that Jeff Quon would maintain the private nature of their text messages, or vice versa. Had Jeff Quon voluntarily permitted the Department to review his text messages, the remaining Appellants would have no claims. Nevertheless, the OPD surreptitiously reviewed messages that all parties reasonably believed were free from third-party review. As a matter of law, Trujillo, Florio, and Jerilyn Quon had a reasonable expectation that the Department would not review their messages absent consent from either a sender or recipient of the text messages.

The Department's general "Computer Usage, Internet and E-mail Policy" stated both that the use of computers "for personal benefit is a significant violation of City of Ontario

Policy" and that "[u]sers should have no expectation of privacy or confidentiality when using these resources." Quon signed this Policy and attended a meeting in which it was made clear that the Policy also applied to use of the pagers.

As the district court made clear, however, such was not the "operational reality" at the Department. The district court reasoned:

> Lieutenant Duke made it clear to the staff, and to Quon in particular, that he would not audit their pagers so long as they agreed to pay for any overages. Given that Lieutenant Duke was the one in charge of administering the use of the city-owned pagers, his statements carry a great deal of weight. Indeed, before the events that transpired in this case the department did not audit any employee's use of the pager for the eight months the pagers had been in use.

Even more telling, Quon had exceeded the 25,000 character limit "three or four times," and had paid for the overages every time without anyone reviewing the text of the messages. This demonstrated that the OPD followed its "informal policy" and that Quon reasonably relied on it. Nevertheless, without warning, his text messages were audited by the Department. Under these circumstances, Quon had a reasonable expectation of privacy in the text messages archived on Arch Wireless's server.

A search is reasonable "at its inception" if there are "reasonable grounds for suspecting . . . that the search is necessary for a noninvestigatory work-related purpose such as to retrieve a needed file." Here, the purpose was to ensure that officers were not being required to pay for work-related expenses. This is a legitimate work-related rationale, as the district court acknowledged.

However, the search was not reasonable in scope. As O'Connor makes clear, a search is reasonable in scope "when the measures adopted are reasonably related to the objectives of the search and not excessively intrusive in light of . . . the nature of the [misconduct]."

There were a host of simple ways to verify the efficacy of the 25,000-character limit (if that, indeed, was the intended purpose) without intruding on Appellants' Fourth Amendment rights. For example, the Department could have warned Quon that for the month of September he was forbidden from using his pager for personal communications, and that the contents of all of his messages would be reviewed to ensure the pager was used only for work-related purposes during that time frame. Alternatively, if the Department wanted to review past usage, it could have asked Quon to

Continued

count the characters himself, or asked him to redact personal messages and grant permission to the Department to review the redacted transcript. Under this process, Quon would have an incentive to be truthful because he may have previously paid for work-related overages and presumably would want the limit increased to avoid paying for such overages in the future. These are just a few of the ways in which the Department could have conducted a search that was reasonable in scope. Instead, the Department opted to review the contents of all the messages, work-related and personal, without the consent of Quon or the remaining Appellants.

This was excessively intrusive in light of the noninvestigatory object of the search, and because Appellants had a reasonable expectation of privacy in those messages, the search violated their Fourth Amendment rights.

QUESTIONS

1. What did the police department do wrong in handling its cyberspace policies?

2. What alternatives does the court propose that would have made the search of the Quon text messages reasonable?

4. Web User Information and Privacy

A second privacy issue in cyberlaw is the use of information that Web sites have gleaned from their users. **For Example,** if you use an airline's Web site to book your travel arrangements, that Web site has a profile of your travel habits. The airline knows how frequently you travel and where you travel. That type of targeted customer information is something other Web sites and retailers are willing to pay dearly for because they know their product is being considered by those most likely to purchase it. If you use Amazon.com to buy books, that Web site has relevant information about the types of books you read, your interests, and even some indications about your income level based on your spending habits.

---

e-commerce&cyberlaw

Ten Commandments for Avoiding Workplace Exposure

1. Publish policies regarding employee use of e-mail, the Internet, and any employer-issued hardware or software.

2. Have employees sign off on the policy each year.

3. Tell employees that the company will monitor e-mail, Internet use, and any other use of employer-issued computers. Be sure to cover all new technology, such as Palm Pilots, BlackBerries, and two-way text-messaging systems.

4. Create a style guide for writing business e-mails.

5. Train all employees on how to write appropriate business e-mails.

6. Develop a document/e-mail retention policy.

7. Tell employees you will cooperate with law enforcement officials and turn over any evidence of illegal activities.

8. Enforce all policies in an even-handed manner.

9. Keep current on new technology in the marketplace and how it can be used and monitored.

10. Re-evaluate all technology-related policies annually.*

* Frank C. Morris, Jr., "The Electronic Platform: Email and Other Privacy Issues in the Workplace," 20 *Computer & Internet Law* (no. 8), 1–20.

Even though this issue of privacy may seem new and peculiar to cyberspace, it is, in fact, a rather old issue that has long been a concern of credit card companies. These companies' use and sale of information about their customers are restricted. Customers must be given the right to refuse such use of their names and other information for sale as part of lists for target marketing. Some state attorneys general are utilizing these credit card privacy rights to enforce privacy rights against Web site owners who sell information about their users. The Federal Trade Commission (FTC) has begun to take positions that are identical to its stances on other types of commerce issues. **For Example,** if catalog companies are required to provide notice to customers about delays in shipment of goods to customers, Internet companies must comply with the same notification rules.

(A) FREEDOM OF SPEECH, SCREEN NAMES, AND PRIVACY. Another privacy issue that has arisen is whether plaintiffs in suits for defamation can successfully subpoena Internet Service Providers (ISPs) to obtain the identity of individuals who post statements in chat rooms and across the Internet, make defamatory remarks over the Internet, facilitate the downloading of music through their sites, and even allow the sharing of exam information that is proprietary. Music companies' actions against individuals who download music but do not pay for their songs requires the discovery of the identity of those who are doing the downloading. Can the music companies require the ISPs to disclose the names of their customers for purposes of preventing copyright infringement? There are now clear standards for determining disclosure of identity that tend to favor disclosure.[12] Access to ISP identity information is now relatively routine.[13]

Sony Music Entertainment Inc. v Does 1–40, 326 F SUPP 2D 556 (SDNY 2004)

The Ratfink ISP: Telling Who's Doing The Downloading

Sony and others (Plaintiffs) own the copyrights and exclusive licenses to the various sound recordings. Forty Does (defendants), without permission, used "Fast Track," an online media distribution system-or "peer to peer" ("P2P") file copying network—to download hundreds or thousands of copyrighted sound recordings. Sony was able to identify Cablevision as the Internet service provider ("ISP") to which the Does subscribed. Sony did so by using a publicly available database to trace the Internet Protocol ("IP") address for each Doe. An ISP can identify the computer from which the alleged infringement occurred and the name and address of the subscriber controlling the computer when it is provided with a user's IP address and the date and time of the allegedly infringing activity.

As a condition of providing its Internet service, Cablevision requires its subscribers to agree to its "Terms of Service" under which "[t]ransmission or distribution of any material in violation of any applicable law or regulation is prohibited. This includes, without limitation, material protected by copyright, trademark, trade secret or other intellectual property right used without proper authorization."

On January 26, 2004, the court issued an order granting Sony the right to serve a subpoena upon Cablevision to obtain the identity of each Doe by requesting the name, address, telephone number, email address, and Media Access Control address for each defendant.

On February 2, 2004, *amici curiae* Electronic Frontier Foundation, Public Citizen, and the American Civil Liberties Union ("*amici*") submitted a letter to the court objecting to the grant of the subpoena. The court affirmed its order for a subpoena.

Cablevision sent notice to all affected subscribers. Cablevision's letter stated,

Unless we hear from you, or your attorney, in writing by February 20, 2004 that you have filed the appropriate papers with the U.S. District Court for the Southern District of New York to have the subpoena set aside, we will disclose your subscriber information to the plaintiffs, as required by the enclosed subpoena.

---

[12] *Columbia Pictures, Inc. v Bunnell*, 245 FRD 443 (CD Cal 2007).
[13] See, e.g., *Laface Records, LLC v Atlantic Recording Corp.*, 2007 WL 4286189, (WD Mich Sept. 27, 2007) (not reported in F Supp 2d).

Continued

On February 20, 2004, Cablevision received a letter from one of the subscriber's attorney stating that he represented one of Cablevision's subscribers and that he "would expect that Cablevision will make every effort to quash the subpoena or otherwise limit the scope of the requested discovery so . . . as not to infringe on [his] client's privacy rights."

On February 23, 2004, Cablevision complied with the subpoena and provided relevant identifying information for about thirty-six Does. The Does filed a motion to quash the subpoena.

JUDICIAL OPINION

CHIN, District Judge . . . Jane Doe moves to quash the subpoena.

A. The First Amendment

Defendants' motions raise two First Amendment issues: (1) whether a person who uses the Internet to download or distribute copyrighted music without permission is engaging in the exercise of speech; and (2) if so, whether such a person's identity is protected from disclosure by the First Amendment.

The Supreme Court has recognized that the First Amendment protects anonymous speech. It is well-settled that the First Amendment's protection extends to the Internet. Courts have recognized the Internet as a valuable forum for robust exchange and debate. The Internet is a particularly effective forum for the dissemination of anonymous speech. Anonymous speech, like speech from identifiable sources, does not have absolute protection. The First Amendment for example, does not protect copyright infringement, and the Supreme Court, accordingly, has rejected First Amendment challenges to copyright infringement actions. Parties may not use the First Amendment to encroach upon the intellectual property rights of others.

Against the backdrop of First Amendment protection for anonymous speech, courts have held that civil subpoenas seeking information regarding anonymous individuals raise First Amendment concerns. For example, in *NAACP v Alabama ex rel. Patterson*, 357 U.S. 449, 462, 78 S.Ct. 1163, 2 L.Ed.2d 1488 (1958), the Supreme Court held that a discovery order requiring the NAACP to disclose its membership list interfered with the First Amendment's freedom of assembly. Similarly, in *NLRB v Midland Daily News*, 151 F.3d 472, 475 (6th Cir.1998), the Sixth Circuit declined on First Amendment grounds to enforce a subpoena duces tecum issued by the National Labor Relations Board seeking to require a newspaper publisher to disclose the identity of an anonymous advertiser.

As a threshold matter, I address whether the use of P2P file copying networks to download, distribute, or make available for distribution copyrighted sound recordings, without permission, is an exercise of speech. I conclude that this conduct qualifies as speech, but only to a degree.

In contrast to many cases involving First Amendment rights on the Internet, a person who engages in P2P file sharing is not engaging in true expression. Such an individual is not seeking to communicate a thought or convey an idea. Instead, the individual's real purpose is to obtain music for free.

Arguably, however, a file sharer is making a statement by downloading and making available to others copyrighted music without charge and without license to do so. Alternatively, the file sharer may be expressing himself or herself through the music selected and made available to others. Although this is not "political expression" entitled to the "broadest protection" of the First Amendment, the file sharer's speech is still entitled to "some level of First Amendment protection."

I conclude, accordingly, that the use of P2P file copying networks to download, distribute, or make sound recordings available qualifies as speech entitled to First Amendment protection. That protection, however, is limited, and is subject to other considerations.

Plaintiffs have alleged ownership of the copyrights or exclusive rights of copyrighted sound recordings at issue in this case sufficiently to satisfy the first element of copyright infringement. Plaintiffs have attached to the complaint a partial list of the sound recordings the rights to which defendants have allegedly infringed. Each of the copyrighted recordings on the list is the subject of a valid Certificate of Copyright Registration issued by the Register of Copyrights to one of the record company plaintiffs. Plaintiffs also allege that among the exclusive rights granted to each plaintiff under the Copyright Act are the exclusive rights to reproduce and distribute to the public the copyrighted recordings. Defendants have failed to refute in any way plaintiffs' allegations of ownership.

Plaintiffs have submitted supporting evidence listing the copyrighted songs downloaded or distributed by defendants using P2P systems. The lists also specify the date and time at which defendants' allegedly infringing activity occurred and the IP address assigned to each defendant at the time. Moreover, the use of P2P systems to download and distribute copyrighted music has been held to constitute copyright infringement. Accordingly, plaintiffs have sufficiently pled copyright infringement to establish a prima facie claim.

Plaintiffs' discovery request is also sufficiently specific to establish a reasonable likelihood that the discovery request would lead to identifying information that would make possible service upon particular defendants who could be sued in federal court. Plaintiffs seek identifying information about particular Cablevision subscribers, based on the specific

Continued

times and dates when they downloaded specific copyrighted and licensed songs. Such information will enable plaintiffs to serve process on defendants.

Plaintiffs have also established that they lack other means to obtain the subpoenaed information by specifying in their ex parte application for expedited discovery and papers in opposition to Jane Doe's motion to quash the steps they have taken to locate the Doe defendants. These include using a publicly available database to trace the IP address for each defendant, based on the times of infringement.

Plaintiff have also demonstrated that the subpoenaed information is centrally needed for plaintiffs to advance their copyright infringement claims. Ascertaining the identities and residences of the Doe defendants is critical to plaintiffs' ability to pursue litigation, for without this information, plaintiffs will be unable to serve process.

Plaintiffs are also entitled to discovery in light of defendants' minimal expectation of privacy . . . [t]he Terms of Service state that "Cablevision has the right . . . to disclose

any information as necessary to satisfy any law, regulation or other governmental request." Accordingly, defendants have little expectation of privacy in downloading and distributing copyrighted songs without permission.

In sum, defendants' First Amendment right to remain anonymous must give way to plaintiffs' right to use the judicial process to pursue what appear to be meritorious copyright infringement claims.

For the reasons set forth above, defendants' motions to quash the subpoena are denied and the arguments raised by *amici* are rejected.

QUESTIONS

1. List the factors a court considers in determining whether to require identification of users by an ISP.

2. What is the level of privacy ISP subscribers have for their use of that service?

(B) COOKIES AND PRIVACY. Technology has permitted companies to plant "cookies" on the computers of those who are using certain Internet sites. With those "cookies" in place, the Web site owner has a way to track the computer owner's activity. At least one court has held that a Web site operator's placing cookies on a user's computer is a violation of an unauthorized access statute that would provide the computer owner a right of action for that breach of the statute and privacy.[14]

(C) STATUTORY PROTECTIONS FOR PRIVACY IN CYBERSPACE. Several federal laws and some state laws provide privacy protections, although somewhat limited, for Internet users. The Privacy Act of 1974 controls the use of information gathered about consumers, but it applies only to government-collected data such as information gathered by the Social Security Administration or the Internal Revenue Service. Furthermore, there are exceptions for the agencies for

"routine use."[15] Some segments of the Computer Fraud and Abuse Act (CFAA) and the ECPA provide privacy protection for certain types of communications, such as financial information and its use and transfer.[16] These privacy laws are not general protections but address specific issues. For example, the Children's Online Privacy Protection Act (COPPA) targets online informational privacy but applies only to Web sites that collect information from children.[17]

Numerous state laws on privacy exist; the problem comes in enforcing those laws against Web site sponsors who have no presence in the state. (See the discussion of long-arm jurisdiction over these Internet players in Section 13, "Due Process Issues in Cyberspace.")

5. Appropriation in Cyberspace

The tort of **appropriation** involves taking an image, likeness, or name for purposes of commercial

---

[14] *In re Intuit Privacy Litigation*, 138 F Supp 2d 1272 (CD Cal 2001); see also *In re Toys R Us, Inc., Privacy Litig.*, 2001 WL 34517252 (ND Cal) (not reported in F Supp 2d), in which the court reached a different conclusion. However, tapping into sites to gain competitive or proprietary information is a breach of privacy. *Creative Computing v Getloaded.com LLC*, 386 F3d 930 (CA 9 2004).
[15] 5 USC § 552a (2000).
[16] 18 USC § 1030 and 18 USC §§ 2510–2520, 2701 (1997).
[17] 15 USC §§ 6501–6506.

advantage. A business cannot use someone's name or likeness for advertising or endorsement without permission. The use of that name or image in cyberspace does not change the nature of the protection that this form of the privacy tort provides. **For Example,** the use of Tiger Woods's name or picture on the Web site of a yacht company, without his permission, is appropriation, even if Mr. Woods actually owns one of the companys' yachts. A screen saver program that uses a likeness of Richard, the million-dollar winner on the CBS television program *Survivor,* without his permission has violated his privacy rights. The use of his likeness for the Conniver screen saver program with the *Survivor* logo was appropriation. The method of appropriation may be different, but the elements are the same. Appropriation in cyberspace is still the tort of appropriation.

6. Defamation in Cyberspace

(A) DEFAMATION AND DAMAGES. The elements of **defamation** remain the same in cyberspace. (See Chapter 9 for more details.) You must show that someone said or wrote something false that portrayed you in a bad light and that the statement, written or oral, was published, heard, or read by others. That the defamation occurs in a chat room does not change the application of tort law. However, the pervasive nature of the Internet could increase the damages for defamation because of the large number of people who obtain the information quickly, and damage can be done rapidly. **For Example,** Mark S. Jakob, a securities trader who had lost $100,000 in August 2000 with poor trades in Emulex, Inc., decided to correct his declining earnings trend by posting a false press release on the Internet that Emulex's earnings were overstated and that its CEO would resign. The fake news release resulted in an overall loss in the value of Emulex stock of $2.5 billion before trading was stopped. As a result of this action, Jakob made $240,000 through a short position.[18] The tort of defamation would permit the investors to recover their losses.

(B) DEFAMATION AND BLOGGING. By 2009, there were approximately 112.5 million blogs, not including the 72 million in China. While blogs may be personal, there are tort issues that arise when employees begin posting information about their companies or their companies' competitors on their personal blogs. Even when employees discuss what has happened at work, the company can be portrayed in a negative or untruthful way that could be defamatory. For example, an employee discussing disciplinary action at work might present a view of what happened that leaves out information and results in damage to the company.

Because the blogging phenomenon is so new, there is scant case law on the rights of companies against blogging employees. However, there are some situations in which employees have been fired or disciplined because of their postings on their blogs. **For Example,** a Delta flight attendant was suspended and later fired because she had posted a photo on her "Queen of the Sky" blog that showed her in her Delta flight attendant uniform.[19] Delta's reasons for her termination, also known as "doocing," or being fired for blogging, were related to its logo and name being associated with the content of the blog, something over which it had no control. A Starbucks employee who was not permitted to leave work when he was sick was also terminated by the company for his posting of a negative story about his rugged boss.

Concealed identity bloggers can wreak havoc on competitors. John Mackey, the CEO of Whole Foods, using the name Rahodeb (his wife's name, Deborah, jumbled), posted over 1,000 messages in chat rooms that were dedicated to stock trading. During the period that Mr. Mackey was posting messages, Whole Foods stock quadrupled in value. The messages were flattering to Whole Foods and negative about Wild Oats, a competitor. On February 24, 2005, Mackey posted the following comment about Wild Oats CEO Perry Odak: "Perhaps the OATS Board will wake up and dump Odak and bring in a visionary and highly competent CEO [like Mackey]." Referred to as "sock-puppeting," this common practice also raises ethical issues.

[18] Alex Berenson, "Man Charged in Stock Fraud Based on Fake News," *New York Times,* September 1, 2000, C1, C2.
[19] *Simonetti v Delta Air Lines Inc.,* No. 1: 05-CV-2321, 2005 WL 2407621 (ND Ga 2005).

---

ethics & the law

The Blogger Who Kissed and Told on Capitol Hill

Jessica Cutler, a staff member for Senator Mike DeWine, began a blog that detailed her sexual encounters with various government officials in Washington, D.C. Ms. Cutler did not identify anyone by name in her blog, but the level of detail in her posts had most of Washington figuring out who was who in the Cutler blog. Ms. Cutler was fired for "misusing an office computer." What ethical issues

exist in Ms. Cutler's public revelations? Was it legal for the senator to terminate her employment? What advice could you offer employers that would come from this experience? What about defamation if her partners are not identified by name?

Source: April Witt, "Blog Interrupted," *Washington Post*, Apr. 15, 2004, W12.

C. CONTRACT ISSUES IN CYBERSPACE

7. Formation of Contracts in Cyberspace

Formation of a **contract** in cyberspace is simply the result of the desire for speed and better communication in business. If you wanted to form a contract with a New York seller 20 years ago and you were in Los Angeles, you drafted a proposal and mailed it to the seller. The back-and-forth negotiations took time through the mail. Then overnight delivery service arrived to speed up your cross-country negotiations. Next came faxes and their instantaneous exchanges of terms and negotiations. The amount of paperwork involved in transactions was still unchanged. Paperless contracts were born with the availability of electronic digital interchange (EDI). EDI is simply the electronic exchange of business forms. Contracts are formed using purchase orders and invoices submitted via computer.[20]

With the Internet, e-mail, and the ability to attach documents, cyberspace has provided business yet another method for forming contracts. And while the method is different, the rules for formation have not changed. The same laws that apply when contracts are formed in a business office govern the formation of contracts in cyberspace: there must be offer and acceptance.

Some issues that arise in contract formation in the new economy are, for example, whether a contract is formed when someone downloads a program from the Internet. The person may have paid for the program by credit card and simply downloaded it on the computer. Acceptance occurs when the click occurs—a contract is formed.[21] (See Chapters 12–17 for more information on contracts in cyberspace.)

The Electronic Signatures in Global and National Commerce Act (called **E-sign**) is a federal law that recognizes digital signatures as authentic for purposes of contract formation. Even though E-sign recognizes the validity of electronic signatures, states laws regulate the authenticity and security of signatures. The Uniform Electronic Transactions Act (UETA) and the Uniform Computer Information Transaction Act (UCITA) are two model laws drafted to allow states to adopt a uniform position. UETA is a uniform law that 46 states plus the District of Columbia have adopted;[22] two states have adopted UCITA.[23]

---

[20] L. J. Kutten, Bernard D. Reams, and Allen E. Strehler, *Electronic Contracting Law* (Clark Boardman, 1991).

[21] A.V. *v iParadigms, Ltd. Liability Co.*, 544 F Supp 2d 473 (ED Va 2008).

[22] Forty-six jurisdictions have adopted UETA. The states that have not adopted it are Georgia, Illinois, New York, and Washington.

[23] Maryland Commercial Law §§ 22-101 to 22-816, and Virginia Code §§ 59.1-501.1 to 59.1-509.2. Both laws can be found online: **www.uetaonline.com** and **www.ucitaonline.com**.

8. Misrepresentation and Fraud in Cyberspace

The types of **misrepresentation** and fraud on the Internet range from promises of delivery not fulfilled to promises of performance not met. The majority of the fraud complaints received by the FBI relate to Internet auctions. These issues are not new legal issues; only the form of misrepresentation or fraud has changed. For Example, seven retailers signed a consent decree with the FTC, which requires them to pay fines totaling $1.5 million to settle a complaint against them for late delivery of Christmas merchandise ordered over the Web. Macys.com, Toysrus.com, and CDNOW all signed the consent decree that was based on the FTC mail-and-telephone rule requiring retailers to let customers know when they do not have a product or that there will be a delay in the shipment. The existing notification rule was simply applied to Internet transactions.

In marketing **search engines**, some companies have misrepresented the capabilities of their products or have failed to disclose the methods they use to give preference to certain links and their order of listing when the search engine is used. The remedy for such misrepresentations and fraud on the Internet is the same as the remedy in situations with paper contracts. Misrepresentation and fraud are defenses to formation and entitle the party who was misled or defrauded to rescind the agreement and/or collect money damages.

In addition to contract remedies available for misrepresenting the nature of the search engine product and capabilities, a small group of search engine companies has proposed a code of ethics for search engine firms. Headed by Mike Adams, founder and owner of WebSeed.com, the rules are called "Search Engine Promotion Code of Ethics." Adams says that his industry needs reform and gave the following example of Dotsubmit.com, a former company that claimed it would submit its clients' Web sites to 10,000 search engines. Other problems include the lack of limitations on the number of pages from any domain, which means there is so much space used that consumers have difficulty finding what they are looking for.

Key provisions of the search engine code of ethics cover claims about search engine performance as well as the honoring of submission guidelines that impose requirements on Web sites seeking to be listed.

D. INTELLECTUAL PROPERTY ISSUES IN CYBERSPACE

Intellectual property rights have not changed—simply because the Internet has facilitated the ability to copy everything from trademarks to songs with great ease. As noted in Chapter 10, intellectual property rights are protected for the sake of innovation. As in the other areas of law discussed to this point, the Internet simply presents new challenges for interpretation of copyright law. The ease of posting items to the Internet and the ability to copy them quickly does not change the rights of copyright ownership. As with all other reproductions of work, permission to reproduce copyrighted work, either using a copy machine or the Internet, is required.[24]

Perhaps no case has brought to a head the discussion of intellectual property rights and their application to cyberspace than that of Napster. Shawn Fanning and Sean Parker, two college students who were then 19 and 20 years old, respectively, founded this company. Napster developed a software program that enabled users to download music files over the Internet at no cost. The music industry filed suit against Napster, Grokster, and other companies and all have either been settled or fully litigated with arrangements for music companies to charge fees for access to music and then pay those fees to the copyright holders.

The Recording Industry Association of America (RIAA) has undertaken an aggressive litigation strategy against music downloaders. The RIAA estimates that 11 million home computers actively share music files in one month. The RIAA and others have moved into international markets as well. Gottfrid Svartholm Warg, Peter Sunde, Fredrik Neij, and Carl

---

[24] See *Lowry's Reports, Inc. v Legg Mason, Inc.*, 271 F Supp 2d 737 (D Md 2003) in which the employer was found liable for copyright infringement by its employees who posted subscription e-mail of financial newsletter on employer's intranet using employer's equipment and on company time, even though employees violated employer's policy not to do so.

Lundstrom, the four Swedish lads who were the operators and financiers of the Pirate Bay Web site, were convicted in Sweden of copyright infringement in April 2009. Pirate Bay, a site that allows free access to copyrighted movies, music, and more, has been shut down.

The legal question in the music cases, as with all other Internet infringement cases, is: Is it **fair use** or **infringement** to provide a link on a Web site to another Web site for copyrighted materials there? The Digital Millennium Copyright Act (DMCA)[25] was enacted as an amendment to federal copyright laws and makes it a federal offense to circumvent or create programs to circumvent encryption devices placed in copyrighted material to prevent unauthorized copying. **For Example,** circumventing the encryption devices on software or DVDs violates the DMCA. (See Chapter 10 for more information.)

Another issue that has resulted because of the universal access and availability of the Internet is that of disputes over names for Internet sites. In October 1999, the Internet Corporation for Assigned Names and Numbers (ICANN) approved the Uniform Domain Name Dispute Resolution Policy (UDRP). Prior to this policy, Network Solutions Inc. (NSI) had followed a policy of allowing trademark holders to halt the use of trademarked names for Web sites until the issue of ownership was resolved.

Under UDRP, the parties go through arbitration, and the current user continues to use the name until the matter is resolved. The UDRP also does not require a registration for a complainant to bring proceedings—the party can bring the action without registration and can base a complaint on a Web site's name being deceptively similar.

In addition to the use of this international registration system, existing U.S. laws can help protect the identity and property of businesses. **For Example,** the Federal Trademark Dilution Act permits a company whose name is harmed or diluted through its use by another to bring suit for injunctions and damages. Also,

the FTC's rules on trademark protection are equally applicable to the Internet.

E. Criminal Law Issues in Cyberspace

9. Nature and Types of Cyberspace Crimes

The FBI has labeled **cybercrime** "epidemic."[26] More than 25 percent of the Fortune 500 companies have fallen victim to computer crime.[27] As one expert put it, computer viruses cost the United States more than the total cost of the war in Afghanistan. One virus, known as the "Love Letter" virus, cost U.S. businesses $10 billion.[28] In 1999, one man was able to perpetrate a fraud of $45 million by simply making credit card charges to various credit cards from around the world with information he had gleaned by searching Web sites with consumer information.[29]

Computer crime is simply a more conventional crime carried out through the use of a computer. In other words, using someone else's credit card is fraud, whether you steal the credit card and hand it to the clerk or you use the card number through a transaction on the Web. Some crimes, however, owe their existence to the Internet. **For Example,** rerouting users from the domain they were trying to access to a pornographic Web site does not fit the elements of any particular common law crime, but it is a wrongful use of a computer and its systems. Likewise, using a computer to ensure that your call to a radio station will be answered before other callers' calls is wrongful use and an unlawful trespass into the radio station's system, but no common law crime covers it. Special computer crime statutes must be developed to deal with the use of computers to carry out new forms of fraud and unfair advantage.[30] Computers can be tools of the crime (**identity theft**), targets of crime (hacking into a system of another), or incidental to a crime (as when they are used for money laundering).

[25] 17 USC § 1201 *et seq.*
[26] **http://www.emergency.com**
[27] **http://www.jaring.my**
[28] **http://www.computereconomics.com**
[29] **http://www.computerworld.com/news/1999/**
[30] *United States v Peterson,* 98 F3d 502 (9th Cir 1996).

Several new crimes have arisen as technology has evolved that are variations of the theft statutes. *Phishing* refers to sending e-mails that appear to be from banks and other account sources to get consumers to respond with their private financial information. *Pharming* is the term for a new tool that redirects consumers to another Web site (even when they have correctly entered the right address) so the redirected site can obtain financial information from the consumers.

Finally, the *evil twins phenomenon* consists of wireless networks that lure consumers to the networks by appearing to be legitimate Wi-Fi networks available in locations such as Starbucks, airports, and hotels. The Wi-Fi networks seem to be original and legitimate. However, they are simply created by hackers as the evil twin of the good Wi-Fi sites. The evil twin manipulators/hackers are just seeking

financial information and passwords. Evil twins have also been known to infect computers with viruses.

There are criminal laws that are specifically applicable to computer crime that were covered in Chapter 8 and include the Computer Fraud and Abuse Act[31] and the Economic Espionage Act (EEA).[32]

10. Criminal Procedure and Rights in Cyberspace

Another issue that arises because of cyberspace relates to **warrants**. The Fourth Amendment applies not only to searches of offices and homes but also to searches of computers. Indeed, when a warrant specifies that the officers search computers and files, at least one court has ordered that the warrant be specific as to whether it includes home and/or office

---

thinking things through
Free-Riders and Piggybacking

A new issue that has evolved because of technology could require legal steps. Neighbors are *piggybacking* or tapping into their neighbors' wireless Internet connection. The original subscriber pays a monthly fee for the service but, without security, people in the area are able to tap into the wireless network and bog down the speed of the service. Once limited to geeks and hackers, the practice is now common among ordinary folk who just want free Internet service.

One college student said, "I don't think it's stealing. I always find people out there who aren't protecting their connection, so I just feel free to go ahead and use it."* According to a recent survey, only about 30 percent of the 4,500 wireless networks onto which the surveyors logged were encrypted.

An apartment dweller said she leaves her connection wide open because, "I'm sticking it to the man. I open up my network, leave it wide open for anyone to jump on." One of the users of another's wireless network said, "I feel sort of bad about it, but I do it anyway. It just seems harmless." She said that if she gets caught, "I'm a grandmother. They're not going to yell at an old lady. I'll just play the dumb card."

Some neighbors offer to pay those with wireless service in exchange for their occasional use rather than paying a wireless company for full-blown service. However, the original subscribers do not really want to run their own Internet service.

What possible crimes could be committed here? Do you think we need new legislation to cover this activity? What do you think of the users' statements?

* Michael Marriott, "Hey Neighbor, Stop Piggybacking on My Wireless," *New York Times*, March 5, 2006, A1, A23.

---

[31] 18 USC § 1030 (2002).
[32] 18 USC § 1831 et seq. (2002).

computers and files.[33] The protection against unlawful searches and seizures has not changed; only the objects being searched have become more sophisticated, and a warrant can include them as well, so long as it specifies the extent of the computer and file search. Just as in the case of the employer access and the music downloaders, the question for the courts is whether Internet users who are identified only by their screen names have an expectation of privacy.

U.S. v King, 509 F3d 1338 (CA 11 2007)

Shared Drive + Shared Access = No Privacy

In February 2003, while serving as a civilian contractor, Michael D. King resided in a dormitory at the Prince Sultan Air Base in Saudi Arabia. During his stay in the dormitory, King kept his personal laptop computer in his room and connected it to the base network. All users of the base network signed agreements indicating that they understood their communications over and use of the base network were subject to monitoring. King believed that he had secured his computer so that others could not access the contents of its hard drive.

On February 23, 2003, an enlisted airman was searching the base network for music files when he came across King's computer on the network. The airman was able to access King's hard drive because it was a "shared" drive. In addition to finding music files on King's computer, the airman also discovered a pornographic movie and text files "of a pornographic nature." The airman reported his discovery to a military investigator who in turn referred the matter to a computer specialist. This specialist located King's computer and hard drive on the base network and verified the presence of pornographic videos and explicit text files on the computer. She also discovered a folder on the hard drive labeled "pedophilia." The computer specialist did not employ any "special means" to access King's computer because "everybody on the entire network" could obtain the same access.

The computer specialist then filed a report with the investigator detailing what she had found, and the investigator obtained a search warrant for King's room. During a search of his room, military officials seized King's computer and also found CDs containing child pornography. They then referred the matter to the FBI for investigation and King left Saudi Arabia and returned to Montgomery, Alabama.

Two years later, the government obtained an indictment charging King with possession of child pornography. After his arrest, the government searched his residence pursuant to a search warrant and found additional CDs and hard drives containing over 30,000 images of child pornography.

King entered a guilty plea and was sentenced to 108 months in prison. King then appealed his conviction on the grounds that there had been an illegal search and seizure of his computer and files.

PER CURIMA

King contends that the district court denied his motions to suppress based on the erroneous finding that he did not have a reasonable expectation of privacy in his computer files that were remotely accessed over a military computer network, because the search of those files by the computer specialist exceeded the scope of her authority to monitor usage of the base network. King asserts that he sought to protect his computer files through security settings, he never knowingly exposed them to the public, and he was unaware that the files were shared on the network. King further challenges the district court's alternative finding that the military officials conducted a proper workplace search, arguing that this was a criminal investigation into King's personal computer located in his private dorm room. Finally, King asserts that the subsequent search warrant was invalid, as it was based on information that was obtained improperly through the remote search of his computer files.

The Fourth Amendment's prohibition against unreasonable searches and seizures "protects an individual in those places where [he] can demonstrate a reasonable expectation of privacy against government intrusion," and "only individuals who actually enjoy the reasonable expectation of privacy have standing to challenge the validity of a government search." Accordingly, the threshold issue in this case is whether King had a legitimate expectation of privacy in the contents of his personal laptop computer when it was connected to the base network from his dorm room.

We have held that tenants of a multiunit apartment building do not have a reasonable expectation of privacy in the common areas of the building, where the lock on the front door is "undependable" and "inoperable." We have also held

---

[33] *United States v Hunter*, 13 F Supp 2d 574 (D Vt 1998).

Continued

that even though a company has a subjective expectation of privacy in documents that are shredded and disposed of in a garbage bag that is placed within a private dumpster, the company's "subjective expectation of privacy is not one that society is prepared to accept as objectively reasonable" when the company fails to "take sufficient steps to restrict the public's access to its discarded garbage."

King has not shown a legitimate expectation of privacy in his computer files. His experience with computer security and the affirmative steps he took to install security settings demonstrate a subjective expectation of privacy in the files, so the question becomes "whether society is prepared to accept [King's] subjective expectation of privacy as objectively reasonable."

It is undisputed that King's files were "shared" over the entire base network, and that everyone on the network had access to all of his files and could observe them in exactly the same manner as the computer specialist did. As the district court observed, rather than analyzing the military official's actions as a search of King's personal computer in his private dorm room, it is more accurate to say that the authorities conducted a search of the military network, and King's computer files were a part of that network. King's files were exposed to thousands of individuals with network access, and the military authorities encountered the files without employing any special means or intruding into any area which King could reasonably expect would remain private. The contents of his computer's hard drive were akin to items stored in the unsecured common areas of a multiunit apartment building or put in a dumpster accessible to the public.

Because his expectation of privacy was unreasonable King suffered no violation of his Fourth Amendment rights when his computer files were searched through the computer's connection to the base network. It follows that his additional claim that the later search warrant was invalid because it incorporated information obtained from the search of his computer files also lacks merit.

Affirmed

QUESTIONS

1. Why does the court draw the comparisons with non-cyber searches?

2. What lessons should contractors learn from this case?

F. CONSTITUTIONAL RESTRAINTS AND PROTECTIONS IN CYBERSPACE

The constitutional issues that have arisen as a result of Internet technology cover everything from the First Amendment to the commerce clause and involve issues ranging from pornography to taxation.

11. First Amendment Rights in Cyberspace

Some speech on the Internet is commercial, but other forms of speech involve communications relating to voting and ballot initiatives. Speech on the Internet enjoys constitutional protection, but the Internet has also facilitated the transport of pornography with great ease because photos can be sent from computer to computer. The presence of pornography on the Internet and the ease of access that children have to that material have presented challenges for regulation. The Child Pornography Prevention Act[34] made it a crime to knowingly sell, possess, or distribute child pornography on the Web. However, the U.S. Supreme Court ruled that the statute was void for both vagueness and violating First Amendment rights.[35]

Other First Amendment issues in cyberspace include whether a blogger is a journalist for purposes of asserting the defense of protecting a source. At least one court has held that bloggers are entitled to that journalistic defense.[36]

---

[34] 18 USC § 2252 *et seq.* (2002).
[35] *United States v Hilton*, 167 F3d 61 (1st Cir 1999), *cert denied*, 528 US 844 (1999); *United States v Acheson*, 195 F3d 645 (11th Cir 1999); and *Free Speech Coalition v Reno*, 220 F3d 1113 (9th Cir 1999), *cert granted as Ashcroft v Free Speech Coalition*, 535 US 234 (2002).
[36] *Doe v Cahill*, 884 A2d 451 (Del 2005).

12. Commerce Clause Issues in Cyberspace

The commerce clause has also come into play with the Internet because of the desire of both the states and the federal government to tax the transactions taking place via the Internet. The U.S. Constitution requires that there be some "nexus" between the taxing authority and the business paying the tax (see Chapter 4 for more information on constitutional issues in taxation), and many questions arise about the constitutionality of taxing Internet sales because of the lack of "bricks and mortar" in these businesses. Some Internet retailers are located in one state and have no contact, physically, with any other states. Their only contact is through the computers of their customers, who may be located in all 50 states. Is it constitutional for Colorado to tax a New Jersey company operating out of a small office in Trenton? Courts will simply apply the standards of fairness and allocation that they have relied on in other eras as businesses grew in reach even though their physical locations did not change.

The Internet Tax Freedom Act (ITFA)[37] has been renewed. The ITFA provides that states and local governments cannot tax Internet access. Contrary to popular belief, ITFA does not suspend sales taxes on transactions over the Internet. To tax Internet sales, the seller must have some physical presence in the state or a pattern of distribution and doing business there. **For Example,** Nordstrom might not have stores located in a particular state, but it would be required to collect sales taxes from sales to residents of that state if it had warehouse facilities in that state. Refer to Chapter 3 for a full discussion of the Internet and sales tax.

13. Due Process Issues in Cyberspace

Related to the nexus doctrine and taxation of Internet sales is the issue of whether an Internet business site with few physical facilities and no real presence in other states can be required to travel to the states where its customers are to litigate cases brought by those customers. The notion of long-arm jurisdiction (see Chapter 4) becomes even more critical because of the Internet. When does a company have a sufficient presence in a state that requires it to defend a lawsuit in that state? The answer is the same as the answer for the presence of a "bricks and mortar" business. Is requiring the Internet retailer to come to a state to defend a lawsuit fair, or does it offend notions of justice and fair play? Is reaching out to customers in a state through the Internet sufficient to require the Internet company to come to that state and defend lawsuits brought by those customers, or should the customers be required to travel to the state where the Internet company is located?

G. Securities Law Issues in Cyberspace

The Internet has facilitated access to the capital markets. The existence of computers has led to *day traders,* investors who have online second-by-second financial information about companies as well as the ability to track trades in order to buy and sell stock. However, this universal access means an increase in the players in the market, and those players have often used tactics not entirely within the boundaries of the existing legal framework or the level playing field so important in the stock markets.

One practice that has begun is **pump-and-dump** through which a trader buys a certain stock and then posts information on the Web to increase interest in it, which drives up its price. When the price has climbed to a sufficiently high level, the trader sells it and walks away with the profits earned by the hype created on the Web. The tactic is new and the response time faster, but the practice of pump-and-dump is nothing more than securities fraud. Pump-and-dump allowed 15-year-old Jonathan Lebed to turn his $8,000 in savings into $800,000 in stock gains. He became the first minor ever charged by the Securities and Exchange Commission (SEC) with securities fraud. His penalty was to repay the gains that he made.[38]

Many CEOs and CFOs have developed their own blogs or have begun "tweeting" as a means of

---

[37] Pub. L. No. 105-277, originally enacted on October 21, 1998, and renewed on November 16, 2001.
[38] Gretchen Morgenson, "S.E.C. Says Teenager Had After-School Hobby: Online Stock Fraud," *New York Times*, September 21, 2000, A1, C10.

staying in touch with concerned shareholders and employees. However, securities lawyers have been monitoring the blogs and tweets closely because of the concern that these executives would unwittingly disclose information that was not yet ready for public disclosure. For example, a tweet that discloses a luncheon meeting might prematurely reveal merger discussions.

Existing securities laws also cover other issues that have emerged with cyberspace companies. **For Example,** America Online entered into a consent decree with the SEC for its accounting practices in which the company predicted sales and booked income on the basis of advertising expenses. The SEC found the model for predicting sales untested and misleading. Even though doing business on the Internet was new with no historical financial data,

the SEC held that financial projections must be based on adequate information.[39]

The Net (1995) (PG-13)

In a movie that was ahead of its time, a computer programmer becomes a victim of identity theft when she holds too much information about the software companies for which she has done consulting work.

Check out LawFlix at **www.cengage.com/blaw/dvl** to access movie clips that illustrate business law concepts.

MAKE THE CONNECTION

SUMMARY

The term *cyberlaw* seems to indicate a new body of law that exists or is being created to manage all of the legal issues of the cybereconomy, cyberspace, and cybertechnology. Even though some new criminal statutes have been enacted to address specific types of computer crimes, the law, with its great flexibility, has been able to easily adapt to address many of the legal issues that affect the new economy in cyberspace.

Six existing areas of law apply to cyberspace: tort issues, contract issues, intellectual property issues, criminal violations, constitutional restraints and protections, and securities law issues.

In tort law, the issues that arise on the Internet relate to privacy and defamation. In contracts, the issues center on formation and signatures, as well as the need for diligence in handling fraud and misrepresentation in the course of formation of contracts. Infringement and fair use are the key topics

of intellectual property law that arise through the Internet. Although some peculiar issues such as linking Web sites and copyrighted materials or the types of domain names that may be used exist, the laws to address these new ways of possible infringement of others' intellectual property rights are in place. Criminal violations remain centered on the crimes of trespass and theft. Computers are either used to commit crimes or become the object of crimes, and both old criminal statutes and new ones protect property from harm, even on the Internet. The Constitution still applies to questions of jurisdiction and taxation. The standards of fairness still apply, and courts simply face the issue of whether a company is present because the Internet is available in every state and country. Finally, securities fraud is securities fraud whether committed face-to-face, by paper, by phone, or by chat room.

[39] Floyd Norris, "AOL Pays a Fine to Settle a Charge That It Inflated Profits," *New York Times*, May 16, 2000, C6.

LEARNING OUTCOMES

After studying this chapter, you should be able to clearly explain:

A. INTRODUCTION TO CYBERLAW

LO.1 Identify the privacy rights of employees and obligations of employees with regard to the Internet, their e-mails, and servers

See the Standard & Poor's example on p. 221.

See E-Commerce & Cyberlaw, "Ten Commandments for Avoiding Workplace Exposure," on p. 225.

See *Quon v Arch Wireless Operating Co., Inc.,* on p. 223.

B. TORT ISSUES IN CYBERSPACE

LO.2 Discuss the issue of defamation on the Web

See the Ethics & the Law discussion of the blogger who kissed and told, p. 230.

C. CONTRACT ISSUES IN CYBERSPACE

LO.3 Explain the obligations of service providers to reveal identity and content

See *Sony Music Entertainment Inc. v Does 1– 40* on p. 226.

LO.4 Discuss the constitutional law issues that have resulted from cyberspace

See *U.S. v King* on p. 234.

D. INTELLECTUAL PROPERTY ISSUES IN CYBERSPACE

LO.5 Describe the intellectual property issues in cyberspace

See *Sony Music Entertainment Inc. v Does* on p. 226.

E. CRIMINAL LAW ISSUES IN CYBERSPACE

F. CONSTITUTIONAL RESTRAINTS AND PROTECTIONS IN CYBERSPACE

LO.6 Explain the concerns and legal issues blogging raises

See the John Mackey example on p. 229.

See the Delta and Starbucks examples on p. 229.

G. SECURITIES LAW ISSUES IN CYBERSPACE

LO.7 Give an example of securities law issues in cyberspace.

See the AOL example on booking ad revenues on p. 237.

KEY TERMS

appropriation	e-sign	misrepresentation
contract	fair use	pump-and-dump
cybercrime	identity theft	search engines
cyberlaw	infringement	tort
cyberspace	intellectual property rights	warrants
defamation	invasion of privacy	

QUESTIONS AND CASE PROBLEMS

1. Discuss whether employees would have the right of privacy in the following e-mail situations:

   a. E-mail sent in a company in which there is no warning given about the lack of privacy in e-mails. [*Smyth v Pillsbury*, 914 F Supp 97 (ED Pa 1996)]

   b. An e-mail sent to co-workers from home using the employee's AOL account.

c. An e-mail sent from a laptop while the employee is traveling for the company.

d. An e-mail sent to a coworker over a company Internet system in a company in which the employer has promised privacy in e-mail. [*Commonwealth v Proetto*, 771 A2d 823 (Pa Super Ct 2001)]

e. Employer monitoring of the e-mails of any employee when those e-mails were stored in a file folder marked "Personal." [*Mclaren v Microsoft Corp.*, 1999 WL 339015 (Tex App–Dallas 1999)]

f. Employees using company e-mail for union organization purposes. [*Pratt & Whitney*, National Labor Relations Board General Counsel Advisory Memorandum Cases 12-CA-18446, 12-CA-18722, 12-CS-18863 (February 23, 1998)]

2. In the midst of the litigation surrounding its program for downloading music, Napster, Inc., discovered that a company was selling t-shirts with its logo on them. Can Napster do anything to prevent the use of its logo? Is the use of the logo for t-shirts any different from the use of songs for purposes of downloading for individual listening?

3. The *New York Times* discovered that 24 of the employees in its payroll processing center were sending "inappropriate and offensive e-mail in violation of corporate policy." Do the employees have any right to privacy with regard to the jokes they send over their e-mail accounts at work? No Applying what you have learned about the nature of cyberlaw, determine whether, under existing sexual harassment laws, a company could be held liable for harassment via e-mails. yes.

4. Daniel Dagesse suffered serious injuries when he slipped and fell in his hotel room at the Aruba Marriott Resort (the Plant Hotel). He sued Plant Hotel N.V., the limited liability company that owns the resort; Oranjestad Property Management N.V., Plant Hotel's parent company; Marriott Aruba N.V., the company that manages the resort; and Marriott International, Inc., a corporation that was the agent and management company for Plant Hotel and Oranjestad. Elaine Dagesse, Daniel's wife, also filed suit against the same companies alleging loss of consortium. The Dagesses filed suit in federal district court in New Hampshire, seeking to have the companies come and defend the lawsuit there. The companies filed a motion to dismiss on the grounds that they had no physical presence in the state of New Hampshire. The Dagesses contended that all of the companies operated an interactive Web site to which they went and through which they made their reservations as they sat in their home in New Hampshire, and that this Web site resulted in New Hampshire's jurisdiction over the companies. Were they correct? [*Dagesse v Plant Hotel N.V.*, 113 F Supp 2d 211 (D NH)]

5. Colleges and universities continue to work to help students understand that what they post on the Web is not private information and can often have unintended consequences. The following examples resulted in student disciplinary proceedings:

- Several students at The Ohio State University boasted on Facebook (a networking/socializing site) that they had stormed the field after Ohio State beat Penn State and had taken part in what erupted into a riot. Law enforcement officials were able to trace the students through the university system, and 50 Ohio State students were referred to the office of judicial affairs.

- Students at the University of Mississippi stated on an open site that they wanted to have sex with a professor.

- A student at Fisher College threatened to take steps to silence a campus police officer.

Another problem with the open sites is that the students are posting personal information with which stalkers and others can access them. These nefarious individuals can then easily obtain students' cell phone numbers, addresses, whereabouts, and other information.

The most popular college site, Facebook, indicates that students spend an average of 17 minutes per day on the site. A great deal of information can be conveyed during that time period. Students do so without thinking through the possibility that outsiders with bad intentions could be seeking and using information about them that is posted there.

What legal and ethical issues do you see in the types of comments that students make on these sites and in the sites themselves? Why and how can the colleges and universities obtain information from these sites without a warrant?

6. On July 24, 2002, the Recording Industry Association of America (RIAA) served its first subpoena to obtain the identity of a Verizon subscriber alleged to have made more than 600 copyrighted songs available for downloading over the Internet through peer-to-peer file transfer software provided by KaZaA. Verizon claimed that because RIAA's subpoena related to material transmitted over Verizon's network—rather than stored on it—it fell outside the scope of the subpoena power. Should the subpoena be quashed as Verizon requests, or should it be honored? [*In re Verizon Internet Services, Inc.*, 257 F Supp 2d 244 (DDC)]

7. Glenayre Electronics announced to its employees that it could inspect the laptops it furnished for its employees to use. An employee challenged the inspection of his laptop as a violation of his privacy. Could the company search the laptops? [*Muick v Glenayre Electronics*, 280 F3d 741 (7th Cir)]

8. A state university provided a written notice to employees that their computers could be monitored and added a splash screen with the same notice that appears on the computers each time employees start their computers. Has the university done enough to allow monitoring without invading employee privacy? Would it make any difference if the employees had a password for their e-mail access and computer access? What about state public records law? Would employee e-mails be subject to public disclosure because the e-mails would be considered public record? [*U.S. v Angevine*, 281 F3d 1130 (10th Cir)]

9. APTC, a publicly traded corporation, filed a complaint, captioned "*Anonymous Publicly Traded Company v John Does 1 through 5,*" asserting that the John Doe defendants, whose identities and residences were unknown, "made defamatory and disparaging material misrepresentations" about APTC in Internet chat rooms. APTC asserted its belief that the John Doe defendants were current and/or former employees who breached their fiduciary duties and contractual obligations by publishing "confidential material insider information" about APTC on the Internet. Although it did not specify what harm would be incurred by identifying itself, APTC contended that it had to proceed anonymously "because disclosure of its true company name will cause it irreparable harm." APTC wanted the court to issue subpoenas to the ISP to determine the identity of the John Does. How do you think the court will decide on the issue of the John Does' identity? [*America Online, Inc. v Anonymous Publicly Traded Co.*, 542 SE2d 377 (Va)]

10. In response to legal cases in which companies have had their internal e-mails used to their disadvantage, several companies have developed programs that automatically destroy e-mails once they have been opened and read on the other end. Is it legal and ethical to destroy e-mails on a regular basis such as this? To visit an e-mail destruction site, go to **www.authentica.com** or **www.qvtech.com**.

11. Immunomedics, Inc., has discovered sensitive information about its technology posted on various Web sites and chat rooms. The information is so proprietary that it could have come only from company employees, all of whom have signed agreements not to disclose such information. Those who posted the information used screen names, and Immunomedics has asked the court to issue a subpoena to the ISP so that it can determine the identity of those posting the information and recover for breach of contract and trade secret infringement. Should the court

issue the subpoena? *yes.* [*Immunomedics, Inc. v Does 1–10*, 2001 WL 770389 (NJ Super 2001)]

12. Jane Doe filed a complaint against Richard Lee Russell and America Online (AOL) to recover for alleged emotional injuries suffered by her son, John Doe. Doe claimed that in 1994, Russell lured John Doe, who was then 11 years old, and two other minor males to engage in sexual activity with each other and with Russell. She asserted that Russell photographed and video-taped these acts and used AOL's chat rooms to market the photographs and videotapes and to sell a videotape. In her six-count complaint, Doe claimed that AOL violated criminal statutes and that AOL was negligent *per se* in distributing an advertisement offering "a visual depiction of sexual conduct involving [John Doe]" and by allowing Russell to sell or arrange to sell child pornography, thus aiding in the sale and distribution of child pornography, including obscene images of John Doe. Does Mrs. Doe have a cause of action? What laws discussed in this chapter apply? [*Doe v America Online, Inc.*, 783 So2d 1010 (Fla)]

13. Customers of a chat room are using the chat room, Maphia, for access to each other and to transfer Sega games to each other. They are able to avoid paying the $19 to $60 the games cost for purchase in the stores. The users say they are simply transferring files and that there is no crime. The chat room says it cannot stop customers from interacting. Do you think there are any civil or criminal law violations in their conduct? [*Sega Enterprises, Ltd. v Maphia*, 857 F Supp 679 (ND Cal)]

Part 2
CONTRACTS

Chapter 12

NATURE AND CLASSES OF CONTRACTS: CONTRACTING ON THE INTERNET

Practically every business transaction affecting people involves a contract.

A. Nature of Contracts

This introductory chapter will familiarize you with the terminology needed to work with contract law. In addition, the chapter introduces quasi contracts, which are not true contracts but obligations imposed by law.

1. Definition of a Contract

A **contract** is a legally binding agreement.[1] By one definition, "a contract is a promise or a set of promises for the breach of which the law gives a remedy, or the performance of which the law in some way recognizes as a duty."[2] Contracts arise out of agreements, so a contract may be defined as an agreement creating an obligation.

The substance of the definition of a contract is that by mutual agreement or assent, the parties create enforceable duties or obligations. That is, each party is legally bound to do or to refrain from doing certain acts.

2. Elements of a Contract

The elements of a contract are (1) an agreement (2) between competent parties (3) based on the genuine assent of the parties that is (4) supported by consideration, (5) made for a lawful objective, and (6) in the form required by law, if any. These elements will be considered in the chapters that follow.

3. Subject Matter of Contracts

The subject matter of a contract may relate to the performance of personal services, such as contracts of employment to work developing computer software or to play professional football. A contract may provide for the transfer of ownership of property, such as a house (real property) or an automobile (personal property), from one person to another.

4. Parties to a Contract

The person who makes a promise is the **promisor**, and the person to whom the promise is made is the **promisee**. If the promise is binding, it imposes on the promisor a duty or obligation, and the promisor may be called the **obligor**. The promisee who can claim the benefit of the obligation is called the **obligee**. The parties to a contract are said to stand in **privity** with each other, and the relationship between them is termed **privity of contract**. For Example, when the state of North Carolina and the architectural firm of O'Brien/Atkins Associates executed a contract for the construction of a new building at the University of North Carolina, Chapel Hill, these parties were in privity of contract. However, a building contractor, RPR & Associates, who worked on the project did not have standing to sue on the contract between the architect and the state because the contractor was not in privity of contract.[3]

In written contracts, parties may be referred to by name. More often, however, they are given special names that better identify each party. For example, consider a contract by which one person agrees that another may occupy a house upon the payment of money. The parties to this contract are called *landlord* and *tenant*, or *lessor* and *lessee*, and the contract between them is known as a *lease*. Parties to other types of contracts also have distinctive names, such as *vendor* and *vendee* for the parties to a sales contract, *shipper* and *carrier* for the parties to a transportation contract, and *insurer* and *insured* for the parties to an insurance policy.

---

[1] The Uniform Commercial Code defines *contract* as "the total legal obligation which results from the parties' agreement as affected by [the UCC] and any other applicable rules of law." UCC § 1–201(11).

[2] Restatement (Second) of Contracts § 1.

[3] *RPR & Associates v O'Brien/Atkins Associates, P.A.*, 24 F Supp 2d 515 (MDNC 1998). See also *Roof Techs Int. Inc. v State*, 57P3d 538 (Kan App 2002), where a layer of litigation was avoided regarding lawsuits involving the renovation of the Farrell Library at Kansas State University. The state was the only party in privity of contract with the architectural firm and would thus have to bring claims against the architectural firm on behalf of all of the contractors. Two subcontractors, the general contractor, and the owner of the library, the state of Kansas, used a settlement and liquidation agreement assigning all of the state's claims against the architect to the general contractor.

A party to a contract may be an individual, a partnership, a limited liability company, a corporation, or a government.[4] One or more persons may be on each side of a contract. Some contracts are three-sided, as in a credit card transaction, which involves the company issuing the card, the holder of the card, and the business furnishing goods and services on the basis of the credit card.

If a contract is written, the persons who are the parties and who are bound by it can ordinarily be determined by reading what the document says and seeing how it is signed. A contract binds only the parties to the contract. It cannot impose a duty on a person who is not a party to it. Ordinarily, only a party to a contract has any rights against another party to the contract.[5] In some cases, third persons have rights on a contract as third-party beneficiaries or assignees. A person cannot be bound, however, by the terms of a contract to which that person is not a party.[6]

CPA   5. How a Contract Arises

A contract is based on an agreement. An agreement arises when one person, the **offeror**, makes an offer and the person to whom the offer is made, the **offeree**, accepts. There must be both an offer and an acceptance. If either is lacking, there is no contract.

6. Intent to Make a Binding Agreement

Because a contract is based on the consent of the parties and is a legally binding agreement, it follows that the parties must have an intent to enter into an agreement that is binding. Sometimes the parties are in agreement, but their agreement does not produce a contract. Sometimes there is merely a preliminary agreement, but the parties never actually make a contract, or there is merely an agreement as to future plans or intentions without any contractual obligation to carry out those plans or intentions.

7. Freedom of Contract

In the absence of some ground for declaring a contract void or voidable, parties may make such contracts as they choose. The law does not require parties to be fair, or kind, or reasonable, or to share gains or losses equitably.

B. CLASSES OF CONTRACTS

Contracts may be classified according to their form, the way in which they were created, their binding character, and the extent to which they have been performed.

CPA   8. Formal and Informal Contracts

Contracts can be classified as formal or informal.

(A) FORMAL CONTRACTS. **Formal contracts** are enforced because the formality with which they are executed is considered sufficient to signify that the parties intend to be bound by their terms. Formal contracts include (1) **contracts under seal** where a person's signature or a corporation's name is followed by a scroll, the word *seal*, or the letters *L.S.*;[7] (2) contracts of record, which are obligations that have been entered before a court of record, sometimes called a **recognizance**; and (3) negotiable instruments.

CPA   (B) INFORMAL CONTRACTS. All contracts other than formal contracts are called **informal** (or simple) **contracts** without regard to whether they are oral or written. These contracts are enforceable, not because of the form of the transaction but because they represent agreement of the parties.

9. Express and Implied Contracts

Simple contracts may be classified as express *contracts* or *implied contracts* according to the way they are created.

---

[4] See *Purina Mills, LLC v Less*, 295 F Supp 2d 1017 (ND Iowa 2003) in which the pig-seller plaintiff, which converted from a corporation to a limited liability company (LLC) while the contract was in effect, was a proper party in interest and could maintain a contract action against defendant buyers.
[5] *Hooper v Yakima County*, 904 P2d 1193 (Wash App 1995).
[6] *Walsh v Telesector Resources Group, Inc.*, 662 NE2d 1043 (Mass App 1996).
[7] Some authorities explain *L.S.* as an abbreviation for *locus sigilium* (place for the seal).

FIGURE 12-1 | *Contractual Liability*

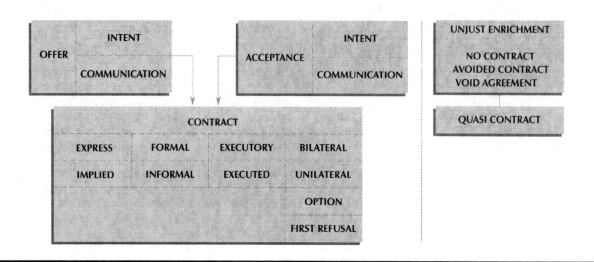

(A) EXPRESS CONTRACTS. An **express contract** is one in which the terms of the agreement of the parties are manifested by their words, whether spoken or written.

(B) IMPLIED CONTRACTS. An **implied contract** (or, as sometimes stated, a *contract implied in fact*) is one in which the agreement is shown not by words, written or spoken, but by the acts and conduct of the parties.[8] Such a contract arises when (1) a person renders services under circumstances indicating that payment for them is expected and (2) the other person, knowing such circumstances, accepts the benefit of those services. **For Example,** when a building owner requests a professional roofer to make emergency repairs to the roof of a building, an obligation arises to pay the reasonable value of such services, although no agreement has been made about compensation.

An implied contract cannot arise when there is an existing express contract on the same subject.[9] However, the existence of a written contract does not bar recovery on an implied contract for extra work that was not covered by the contract.

CPA 10. Valid and Voidable Contracts and Void Agreements

Contracts may be classified in terms of enforceability or validity.

(A) VALID CONTRACTS. A **valid contract** is an agreement that is binding and enforceable.

(B) VOIDABLE CONTRACTS. A **voidable contract** is an agreement that is otherwise binding and enforceable, but because of the circumstances surrounding its execution or the lack of capacity of one of the parties, it may be rejected at the option of one of the parties. **For Example,** a person who has been forced to sign an agreement that that person would not have voluntarily signed may, in some instances, avoid the contract.

(C) VOID AGREEMENTS. A **void agreement** is without legal effect. An agreement that contemplates the performance of an act prohibited by law is usually incapable of enforcement; hence it is void. Likewise, it cannot be made binding by later approval or ratification.

---

[8] *Lindquist Ford, Inc. v Middleton Motors, Inc.*, 557 F3d 469, 481 (7th Cir 2009).
[9] *Pepsi-Cola Bottling Co. of Pittsburgh, Inc., v PepsiCo, Inc.*, 431 F3d 1241 (10th Cir 2000).

11. Executed and Executory Contracts

Contracts may be classified as *executed contracts* and *executory contracts* according to the extent to which they have been performed.

(A) EXECUTED CONTRACTS. An **executed contract** is one that has been completely performed. In other words, an executed contract is one under which nothing remains to be done by either party.[10] A contract may be executed immediately, as in the case of a cash sale, or it may be executed or performed in the future.

(B) EXECUTORY CONTRACTS. In an **executory contract**, something remains to be done by one or both parties.[11] **For Example,** on July 10, Mark agreed to sell to Chris his Pearl drum set for $600, the terms being $200 upon delivery on July 14, with $200 to be paid on July 21, and the final $200 being due July 28. Prior to the July 14 delivery of the drums to Chris, the contract was entirely executory. After the delivery by Mark, the contract was executed as to Mark and executory as to Chris until the final payment was received on July 28.

12. Bilateral and Unilateral Contracts

In making an offer, the offeror is in effect extending a promise to do something, such as pay a sum of money, if the offeree will do what the offeror requests. Contracts are classified as *bilateral* or *unilateral*. Some bilateral contracts look ahead to the making of a later contract. Depending on their terms, these are called *option contracts* or *first-refusal contracts*.

CPA   (A) BILATERAL CONTRACT. If the offeror extends a promise and asks for a promise in return and if the offeree accepts the offer by making the promise, the contract is called a **bilateral contract**. One promise is given in exchange for another, and each party is bound by the obligation. **For Example,** when the house painter offers to paint the owner's house for $3,700 and the owner promises to pay $3,700 for the job, there is an exchange of promises, and the agreement gives rise to a bilateral contract.

(B) UNILATERAL CONTRACT. In contrast with a bilateral contract, the offeror may promise to do something or to pay a certain amount of money only when the offeree does an act.[12] Examples of where **unilateral contracts** commonly appear are when a reward is offered, a contest is announced, or changes are made and disseminated in an employee manual. The offeree does not accept the offer by express agreement, but rather by performance. The *Aon Risk Services* case involved an assertion of the existence of a unilateral contract.

Aon Risk Services Inc. v Meadors, 267 SW3d 603 9 (Ark App 2007)

Unilateral Contract: Pretty Good Bonus!

Aon Risk Services, Inc. (ARS Arkansas), and Combined Insurance Companies are subsidiaries of Aon Corporation. The parent corporation issued an "Interdependency Memo" dated February 2000, which encouraged ARS brokerage offices to place insurance business with Aon-affiliated companies. It also set up a bonus pool for revenues generated under the plan, with Combined agreeing to pay "30% of annualized premium on all life products over 15-year term plus 15% 1st year for all other products." John Meadors saw the memo in February 2000, and believed it would entitle him to this compensation over and above his employment contract. Meadors put Combined in touch with Dillard's Department Stores and on March 24, 2000, Dillard's and Combined executed a five-year agreement whereby Dillard's employees could purchase life, disability, and other insurance policies through workplace enrollment. When Meadors did not receive bonus-pool money generated by the transaction, he sued his employer for breach of a unilateral contract. The

---

[10] *Marsh v Rheinecker*, 641 NE2d 1256 (Ill App 1994).
[11] *DiGeneraro v Rubbermaid, Inc.*, 214 F Supp 2d 1354 (SO Fla 2002).
[12] See *Young v Virginia Birth-Related Neurological Injury Compensation Program*, 620 SE2d 131 (Va App 2005).

Continued

employer's defense was that the memo was not sufficiently definite to constitute an offer.

JUDICIAL OPINION

VAUGHT, J. . . . Meadors's theory at trial was that the Interdependency Memo formed a unilateral contract. There are several instances where unilateral contracts commonly appear, such as where a reward is offered, *e.g., Ark. Bankers' Ass'n v. Ligon* 174 Ark. 234, 295 S.W. 4 (1927), where a contest is announced, *e.g., Mears v. Nationwide Mut. Ins. Co.* 91 F.3d 1118 (8th Cir. 1996), or where changes are made and disseminated in an employee manual. *See Crain Indus., Inc. v. Case* 305 Ark. 566, 810 S.W.2d 910 (1991). In those situations, the offeree does not accept the offer by express agreement but by his performance. For example, in the case of a reward, the offeree accepts by performing the particular task, such as the capture of a fugitive, for which the reward is offered. Even though he has not directly communicated his acceptance, a contract is formed as the result of his performance. *See Ligon, supra* (recognizing that a unilateral contract is composed of an offer that invites acceptance in the form of actual performance), 17A AM. JUR. 2D *Contracts* § 5 (2d ed. 1991) (stating that, if performance occurs, then the offer has been accepted, and a contract is formed). The performance also constitutes consideration for the contract. 17A AM. JUR 2D *Contracts* § 5.

Definiteness of offer

ARS Arkansas argues first that the interdependency Memo was not sufficiently definite to constitute an offer for a unilateral contract. An offer is the manifestation of willingness to enter into a bargain, so made as to justify another person in understanding that his assent to the bargain is invited and will conclude it. An offer cannot be accepted so as to form a contract unless the terms are reasonably certain. *Restatement (Second) of Contracts* § 33 (1981). To bind the employer, an offer must be definite in form and must be communicated to the offeree. *See Hardie v. Cotter & Co.* 849 F.2d 1097 (18th Cir. 1988); *Dumas v. Kessler & Maguire Funeral Home, Inc.* 380 N. W.2d 544 (Minn. Ct. App. 1986). Whether a proposal is meant to be an offer for a unilateral contract is determined by the outward manifestations of the parties, and

not by their subjective intentions. The principle issue is whether the employer's statements are intended as an offer and accepted as such or are merely statements of policy and practice. *id.* . . .

ARS . . . relies heavily on *Martens v. Minnesota Minning & Manufacturing Co.* 616 N.W. 2d 732 (Minn. 2000), but it is distinguishable. There, the Minnesota court held that a brochure touting equal compensation for technical and administrative employees was too indefinite to constitute an offer. The court noted that there was no suggestion that an individual would be entitled to specific pay, benefit level, or condition of employment, nor were there any criteria to determine when the rights to any benefits had been breached. Further, the prerogative to make decisions as to individual employee promotions, salaries, and so forth was clearly reserved to management based on an evaluation of the individual. By contrast, the interdependency Memo in this case does not merely set out general goals and philosophies of compensation. It sets out specific percentages of premiums that will go into the bonus pool as part of an "enhanced compensation structure." And, while no employee is entitled to a "formulaic" bonus and Managing Directors may decide how to allocate the bonus pool among their employees, their discretion is not unfettered. For example, managers cannot withhold payment of the pool amount; the Memo provides that the entire pool must be distributed annually. Thus, the mere inclusion of possible judgment calls by management as to the manner of distribution among its employees does not, under these circumstances, render the Memo too indefinite to operate as an offer for a unilateral contract. . . .

CONCLUSION

We affirm the jury's verdict for breach of a unilateral contract against ARS Arkansas and reinstate Meador's damages of $2,406,522.60 pertaining to the Dillard's transaction. . . .

QUESTIONS

1. Must an offeree accept an offer by express agreement in order for a legally enforceable contract to be formed?

2. Was the "Interdependency Memo" too indefinite to constitute an offer?

(C) OPTION AND FIRST-REFUSAL CONTRACTS. The parties may make a contract that gives a right to one of them to enter into a second contract at a later date. If one party has an absolute right to enter into the later

contract, the initial contract is called an **option contract**. Thus, a bilateral contract may be made today giving one of the parties the right to buy the other party's house for a specified amount. This is an option contract because the party with the privilege has the freedom of choice, or option, to buy or not buy. If the option is exercised, the other party to the contract must follow the terms of the option and enter into the second contract. If the option is never exercised, no second contract ever arises, and the offer protected by the option contract merely expires.

In contrast with an option contract, a contract may merely give a **right of first refusal**. This imposes only the duty to make the first offer to the party having the right of first refusal.

13. Quasi Contracts

In some cases, a court will impose an obligation even though there is no contract.[13] Such an obligation is

FIGURE 12-2 | *Contract*

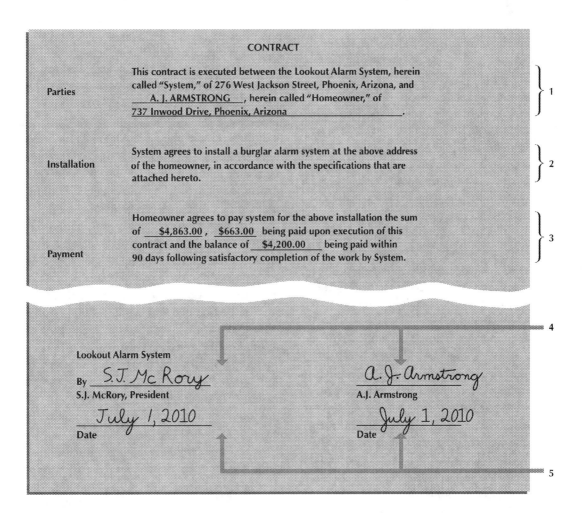

Note that this contract includes the following important information: (1) the name and address of each party, (2) the promise or consideration of the seller, (3) the promise or consideration of the buyer, (4) the signature of the two parties, and (5) the date.

[13] *Thayer v Dial Industrial Sales, Inc.*, 85 F Supp 2d 263 (SDNY 2000).

called a **quasi contract**, which is an obligation imposed by law.

(A) PREVENTION OF UNJUST ENRICHMENT. A quasi contract is not a true contract reflecting all of the elements of a contract set forth previously in this chapter. The court is not seeking to enforce the intentions of the parties contained in an agreement. Rather, when a person or enterprise receives a benefit from another, even in the absence of a promise to pay for the benefit, a court may impose an obligation to pay for the reasonable value of that benefit, to avoid *unjust enrichment*.

A successful claim for unjust enrichment usually requires (1) a benefit conferred on the defendant, (2) the defendant's knowledge of the benefit, and (3) a finding that it would be unjust for the defendant to retain the benefit without payment. The burden of proof is on the plaintiff to prove all of the elements of the claim. **For Example,** Hiram College sued Nicholas Courtad for $6,000 plus interest for tuition and other expenses. Because no evidence of a written contract was produced, the court considered it an unjust enrichment claim by the college. Courtad had attended classes for a few weeks and had not paid his tuition due to a problem with his financial aid package. Because he did not receive any credit hours toward a degree, which is the ultimate benefit of attending college, the court found that he did not receive a benefit and that a finding of unjust enrichment was not appropriate.[14]

Sometimes a contract may be unenforceable because of a failure to set forth the contract in writing in compliance with the statute of frauds. In other circumstances, no enforceable contract exists because of a lack of definite and certain terms. Yet in both situations, one party may have performed services for the benefit of the other party and the court will require payment of the reasonable value of services to avoid the unjust enrichment of the party receiving the services without paying for them. These damages are sometimes referred to as *restitution damages*. Some courts refer to this situation as an action or recovery in *quantum meruit* (as much as he or she deserved).

For Example, Arya Group, Inc. (Arya), sued the entertainer Cher for unjust enrichment. In June 1996, Cher negotiated an oral agreement with Arya to design and construct a house on her Malibu property for $4,217,529. The parties' oral agreement was set forth in a written contract with an August 1997 date and was delivered to Cher in October 1997. She never signed it. However, between June 1996 and November 1997, Arya performed and received payment for a number of services discharged under the unsigned contract. In August 1997, Cher requested Arya to meet with a home designer named Bussell who had previously worked with Cher on a Florida project, and Arya showed Bussell the plans and designs for the Malibu property and introduced her to his subcontractors. In November 1997, Cher terminated her agreement with Arya without paying the balance then due, as asserted by Arya, of $415,169.41. Arya claims that Cher and Bussell misappropriated the plans and designs Arya had prepared. Cher and the other defendants demurred to Arya's unjust enrichment complaint, pointing out that construction contracts must be evidenced in a writing signed by both parties under state law in order to be enforceable in a court of law. The appeals court determined that Arya's non-compliance with the state law requiring a signed written contract did not absolutely foreclose Arya from seeking damages for unjust enrichment if he could prove the assertions in the complaint that Cher was a sophisticated homeowner with previous involvement in residential construction who had legal representation in negotiating the agreement with Arya, and that Cher would be unjustly enriched if she were not required to compensate Arya for the reasonable value of the work already performed.[15]

A situation may arise over the mistaken conference of a benefit. **For Example,** Nantucket Island has a few approved colors for houses in its historic district. Using the approved gray color, Martin Kane and his crew began painting Sheldon Adams's house in the historic district as the result of a mistaken address. Adams observed the initiation of the work from his office across the street but did nothing to stop the painters. At the end of the day when the work was

[14] *Hiram College v Courtad*, 834 NE2d 432 (Ohio App 2005).
[15] *Arya Group, Inc. v Cher*, 91 Cal Rptr 2d 815 (Cal App 2d 2000). See also *Fischer v Flax*, 816 A2d 1 (2003).

thinking things through

Twelve Years of Litigation

Brown University accepted the bid of Marshall Contractors, Inc. (Marshall), to build the Pizzitola Sports Facility on its Providence, Rhode Island, campus. The parties intended to execute a formal written contract. Brown decided to pay $7,157,051 for the project, but Marshall sought additional payment for items it deemed extras and not contemplated in its bid. Because the parties were unable to agree on the scope of the project as compared to the price Brown was willing to pay, they never executed the formal written contract. Nevertheless, in the context of this disagreement over terms and price, construction began in May 1987. When the parties could not resolve their disagreements as the project neared completion in January 1989, Marshall sued Brown University, seeking to recover the costs for what it deemed "changes." Brown asserted that an implied-in-fact contract existed for all work at the $7,157,051 figure because the contractor went ahead with the project knowing the money Brown would pay. The litigation ended up in the Supreme Court of Rhode Island, and in 1997, the court concluded that no express or implied-in-fact contract had ever been reached by the parties concerning the scope of the project and what costs were to be included in the price stipulated by Brown. The case was remanded to the trial court for a new trial. After a trial on the theories of *quantum meruit* and unjust enrichment, a jury awarded Marshall $1.2 million dollars, which was some $3.1 million less than Marshall sought. Brown University appealed, and on November 21, 2001, the Supreme Court of Rhode Island affirmed the jury verdict for the contractor, determining that the proper measure of damages on unjust enrichment and *quantum meruit* theories was "the reasonable value of the work done."*

In May 1987 when the parties could not reach agreement enabling the execution of a formal written contract, thinking things through at that point in time should have exposed the potential for significant economic uncertainties to both parties in actually starting the building process under such circumstances. In the spring of 1987 when all parties were unable to reach agreement, mediation or expedited arbitration by construction experts may well have resolved the controversy and yielded an amicable written contract with little or no delay to the project. Instead, the unsettled cost issues during the building process could have had an adverse impact on the "job chemistry" between the contractor and the owner, which may have adversely affected the progress and quality of the job. The 12 years of litigation that, with its economic and human resource costs, yielded just $1.2 million for the contractor was a no-win result for both sides. A primary rule for all managers in projects of this scope is to make sure the written contracts are executed before performance begins! Relying on "implied-in-fact" or quasi-contract legal theories is simply a poor management practice.

* *ADP Marshall, Inc. v Brown University*, 784 A2d 309 (RI 2001).

---

done, Adams refused to pay for the work, saying, "I signed no contract and never approved this work." The law deems it inequitable that Adams should have received the benefit of this work, having observed the benefit being conferred and knowing that the painters expected payment. Adams would be unjustly enriched if he were allowed to retain the benefit without payment for the reasonable value of the work. If Adams did not have knowledge that the work was being done and thus that payment was expected, quasi-contractual liability would not be imposed.

The mistake that benefits the defendant may be the mistake of a third party.

(B) EXTENT OF RECOVERY. When recovery is allowed in quasi contract, the plaintiff recovers the reasonable value of the benefit conferred on the defendant,[16] or the fair and reasonable[17] value of the work performed, depending on the jurisdiction and the circumstances of the case itself. The customary method of calculating damages in construction contract cases is actual job costs plus an allowance for overhead and profits minus amount paid.[18]

C. Contracting on the Internet

Doing business online for consumers is very similar to doing business through a catalog purchase or by phone. Before placing an order, a buyer is commonly concerned about the reputation of the seller. The basic purchasing principle of *caveat emptor* still applies: buyer beware! The Internet provides valuable tools to allow a buyer to research the reputation of the seller and its products. Online evaluations of companies and their products can be found at Web sites, such as Consumer Reports (**www .consumerreports.org**), Consumers Digest (**www .consumersdigest.com**), or the Better Business Bureau (**www.bbb.org**). E-consumers may have access to categorized histories of comments by other e-consumers, such as Planet Feedback ratings at **www.planetfeedback.com.**

The intellectual property principles set forth in Chapter 10—as well as the contractual principles, the law of sales, and privacy laws you are about to study—all apply to e-commerce transactions. When you are purchasing an item online, you must carefully read all of the terms and conditions set forth on the seller's Web site when assessing whether to make a contemplated purchase. The proposed terms may require that any disputes be litigated in a distant state or be resolved through arbitration with restricted remedies, or there may be an unsatisfactory return policy, warranty limitations, or limitation of liability. Generally, the Web site terms become the contract of the parties and are legally enforceable.

The laws you have studied that prevent deceptive advertising by brick-and-mortar businesses also apply to Internet sites.[19] If an in-state site is engaging in false advertising, you may be able to exercise consumer protection rights through your state's attorney general's office, or you may find some therapeutic relief by reporting the misconduct to the Internet Scambusters site (**www.scambusters.com**).

From a seller's perspective, it is exceedingly helpful to have as much information as possible on your potential customers' buying habits. Federal law prohibits the collection of personal information from children without parental consent, and some states restrict the unauthorized collection of personal information. European Union countries have strict laws protecting the privacy of consumers. Sellers intending to collect personal information should obtain the consent of their customers, make certain that children are excluded, and make sure that the information is stored in a secure environment.

Advanced encryption technology has made the use of credit card payments through the Internet very safe. No computer system connected to the Internet is totally secure however. In the worst-case scenario, credit card issuers will not charge a user for more than the first $50 of unauthorized activity.

Internet contracts involve the same types of issues that are addressed in contracts offline but with certain technology-related nuances. The parties to the e-contracts must still negotiate their obligations in clear and unambiguous language, including such terms as quantity, quality, and price as well as warranties, indemnification responsibilities, limitations on liability, and termination procedures. The federal Electronic Signatures in Global and National Commerce Act (E-Sign) and the Uniform Electronic Transactions Act (UETA) mandate parity between paper and electronic contracts. The basic legal rules that govern contracts offline are the very same rules that govern online contracts, and basic civil procedure

---

[16] *Ramsey v Ellis*, 484 NW2d 331 (Wis 1992).
[17] *ADP Marshall, Inc. v Brown University*, 784 A2d 309 (RI 2001).
[18] *Mirano Contracting, Inc. v Perel*, 871 NYS2d 310 (AD 2008).
[19] See *MADCAP I, LLC v McNamee*, 702 NW2d 16 (Wis App 2005) in which the court found genuine issues of material fact as to whether a business Web site falsely represented the size and nature of its business to induce the public to purchase products and services described on its Web site in violation of the state's fraudulent representations statute.

rules apply. **For Example,** California buyer Paul Boschetto bought a 1964 Ford Galaxy that had been advertised on eBay to be "in awesome condition" from a Milton, Wisconsin resident, J. Hansing, for $34,106. On delivery Boschetto discovered that the car had rust, extensive dents, and would not start. His lawsuit against Hansing in U.S. District Court in California was dismissed for lack of personal jurisdiction.[20] (The formation of a contract with a nonresident defendant was not, standing alone, sufficient to create personal jurisdiction in California.)

Boxes identifying special Internet e-commerce topics are strategically placed throughout these chapters.

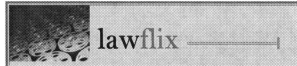

Paper Moon (1973) (PG)

In this movie for which Tatum O'Neal was given an Oscar, the ongoing issue between Annie and her alleged father is her recoupment of the money she says he promised. Discuss the contract issues (voidable [minor], formation, unilateral vs. bilateral, express, informal, etc.).

Check out LawFlix at **www.cengage.com/blaw/dvl** to access movie clips that illustrate business law concepts.

MAKE THE CONNECTION

SUMMARY

A contract is a binding agreement between two or more parties. A contract arises when an offer is accepted with contractual intent (the intent to make a binding agreement).

Contracts may be classified in a number of ways according to form, the way in which they were created, validity, and obligations. With respect to form, a contract may be either informal or formal, such as those under seal or those appearing on the records of courts. Contracts may be classified by the way they were created as those that are expressed by words—written or oral—and those that are implied or deduced from conduct. The question of validity requires distinguishing between contracts that are valid, those that are voidable, and those that are not contracts at all but are merely void agreements. Contracts can be distinguished on the basis of the obligations created as executed contracts, in which everything has been performed, and executory

contracts, in which something remains to be done. The bilateral contract is formed by exchanging a promise for a promise, so each party has the obligation of thereafter rendering the promised performance. In the unilateral contract, which is the doing of an act in exchange for a promise, no further performance is required of the offeree who performed the act.

In certain situations, the law regards it as unjust for a person to receive a benefit and not pay for it. In such a case, the law of quasi contracts allows the performing person to recover the reasonable value of the benefit conferred on the benefited person even though no contract between them requires any payment. Unjust enrichment, which a quasi contract is designed to prevent, sometimes arises when there was never any contract between the persons involved or when there was a contract, but for some reason it was avoided or held to be merely a void agreement.

---

[20] *Boschetto v. Hansing*, 539 F3d 1011 (9th Cir 2008).

LEARNING OUTCOMES

After studying this chapter, you should be able to clearly explain:

A. NATURE OF CONTRACTS

LO.1 Explain the meaning and importance of privity of a contract

See the example of the subcontractor, RPR & Associates, who worked on a project but could not sue the owner for payment, p. 246.

LO.2 Describe the way in which a contract arises

See the discussion on offer and acceptance on p. 247.

B. CLASSES OF CONTRACTS

LO.3 Distinguish between bilateral and unilateral contracts

See the example of the Nantucket painters on p. 252.

See the *AON Risk Services* case where an insurance agent won his case based on a unilateral contract theory, p. 249.

LO.4 Explain the reasoning behind quasi-contract recovery

See the example whereby Cher had to pay a home designer for certain work even though there was no contract, p. 252.

C. CONTRACTING ON THE INTERNET

LO.5 Explain how Internet contracts involve the same types of issues as offline contracts.

See the eBay example on p. 255.

KEY TERMS

bilateral contract	obligee	quantum meruit
contract	obligor	quasi contract
contracts under seal	offeree	recognizance
executed contract	offeror	right of first refusal
executory contract	option contract	unilateral contracts
express contract	privity	valid contract
formal contracts	privity of contract	void agreement
implied contract	promisee	voidable contract
informal contract	promisor	

QUESTIONS AND CASE PROBLEMS

1. What is a contract?

2. Fourteen applicants for a city of Providence, Rhode Island, police academy training class each received from the city a letter stating that it was a "conditional offer of employment" subject to successful completion of medical and psychological exams. The 14 applicants passed the medical and psychological exams. However, these applicants were replaced by others after the city changed the selection criteria. Can you identify an offer and acceptance in this case? Can you make

out a bilateral or unilateral contract? [*Ardito et al. v City of Providence,* 213 F Supp 2d 358 (D RI)]

3. Compare an implied contract with a quasi contract.

4. The Jordan Keys law firm represented the Greater Southeast Community Hospital of Washington, D.C., in a medical malpractice suit against the hospital. The hospital was self-insured for the first $1,000,000 of liability and the St. Paul Insurance Co. provided excess coverage up to $4,000,000. The law firm was owed $67,000

for its work on the malpractice suit when the hospital went into bankruptcy. The bankruptcy court ordered the law firm to release its files on the case to St. Paul to defend under the excess coverage insurance, and the Jordan Keys firm sued St. Paul for its legal fees of $67,000 expended prior to the bankruptcy under an "implied-in-fact contract" because the insurance company would have the benefit of all of its work. Decide. [*Jordan Keys v St. Paul Fire*, 870 A2d 58 (DC)]

5. Beck was the general manager of Chilkoot Lumber Co. Haines sold fuel to the company. To persuade Haines to sell on credit, Beck signed a paper by which he promised to pay any debt the lumber company owed Haines. He signed this paper with his name followed by "general manager." Haines later sued Beck on this promise, and Beck raised the defense that the addition of "general manager" showed that Beck, who was signing on behalf of Chilkoot, was not personally liable and did not intend to be bound by the paper. Was Beck liable on the paper? [*Beck v Haines Terminal and Highway Co.*, 843 P2d 1229 (Alaska)]

6. *A* made a contract to construct a house for *B*. Subsequently, *B* sued *A* for breach of contract. *A* raised the defense that the contract was not binding because it was not sealed. Is this a valid defense? [*Cooper v G. E. Construction Co.*, 158 SE2d 305 (Ga App)]

7. Edward Johnson III, the CEO and principal owner of the world's largest mutual fund company, Fidelity Investments, Inc., was a longtime tennis buddy of Richard Larson. In 1995, Johnson asked Larson, who had construction experience, to supervise the construction of a house on Long Pond, Mount Desert Island, Maine. Although they had no written contract, Larson agreed to take on the project for $6,700 per month plus lodging. At the end of the project in 1997, Johnson made a $175,000 cash payment to Larson, and he made arrangements for Larson to live rent-free on another Johnson property in the area called Pray's Meadow in

exchange for looking after Johnson's extensive property interests in Maine. In the late summer of 1999, Johnson initiated a new project on the Long Pond property. Johnson had discussions with Larson about doing this project, but Larson asked to be paid his former rate, and Johnson balked because he had already hired a project manager. According to Johnson, at a later date he again asked Larson to take on the "shop project" as a favor and in consideration of continued rent-free use of the Pray's Meadow home. Johnson stated that Larson agreed to do the job "pro bono" in exchange for the use of the house, and Johnson acknowledged that he told Larson he would "take care" of Larson at the end of the project, which could mean as much or as little as Johnson determined. Larson stated that Johnson told him that he would "take care of" Larson if he would do the project and told him to "trust the Great Oracle" (meaning Johnson, the highly successful businessperson). Larson sought payment in March 2000 and asked Johnson for "something on account" in April. Johnson offered Larson a loan. In August during a tennis match, Larson again asked Johnson to pay him. Johnson became incensed, and through an employee, he ended Larson's participation in the project and asked him to vacate Pray's Meadow. Larson complied and filed suit for payment for work performed at the rate of $6,700 per month. Did Larson have an express contract with Johnson? What legal theory or theories could Larson utilize in his lawsuit? How would you decide this case if you believed Larson's version of the facts? How would you decide the case if you believed Johnson's version of the facts? [*Larson v Johnson*, 196 F Supp 2d 38 (D.Me 2002)]

8. While Clara Novak was sick, her daughter Janie helped her in many ways. Clara died, and Janie then claimed that she was entitled to be paid for the services she had rendered her mother. This claim was opposed by three brothers and sisters who also rendered services to the mother. They claimed that Janie was barred because of the presumption that services rendered between family members are gratuitous. Janie claimed that

this presumption was not applicable because she had not lived with her mother but had her own house. Was Janie correct? [*In re Estate of Novak*, 398 NW2d 653 (Minn App)]

9. Dozier and his wife, daughter, and grandson lived in the house Dozier owned. At the request of the daughter and grandson, Paschall made some improvements to the house. Dozier did not authorize these, but he knew that the improvements were being made and did not object to them. Paschall sued Dozier for the reasonable value of the improvements, but Dozier argued that he had not made any contract for such improvements. Was he obligated to pay for such improvements? *Quasi Contract, unjust enrichment*

10. When Harriet went away for the summer, Landry, a house painter, painted her house. He had a contract to paint a neighbor's house but painted Harriet's house by mistake. When Harriet returned from vacation, Landry billed her for $3,100, which was a fair price for the work. She refused to pay. Landry claimed that she had a quasi-contractual liability for that amount. Was he correct?

11. *Not on test →* Margrethe and Charles Pyeatte, a married couple, agreed that she would work so that he could go to law school and that when he finished, she would go back to school for her master's degree. After Charles was admitted to the bar and before Margrethe went back to school, the two were divorced. She sued Charles, claiming that she was entitled to quasi-contractual recovery of the money that she had paid for Charles's support and law school tuition. He denied liability. Was she entitled to recover for the money she spent for Charles's maintenance and law school tuition? [*Pyeatte v Pyeatte*, 661 P2d 196 (Ariz App)]

12. Carriage Way was a real estate development of approximately 80 houses and 132 apartments. The property owners were members of the Carriage Way Property Owners Association.

Each year, the association would take care of certain open neighboring areas, including a nearby lake, that were used by the property owners. The board of directors of the association would make an assessment or charge against the property owners to cover the cost of this work. The property owners paid these assessments for a number of years and then refused to pay any more. In spite of this refusal, the association continued to take care of the areas in question. The association then sued the property owners and claimed that they were liable for the benefit that had been conferred on them. Were the owners liable? [*Board of Directors of Carriage Way Property Owners Ass'n v Western National Bank*, 487 NE2d 974 (Ill App)]

13. Lombard insured his car, and when it was damaged, the insurer sent the car to General Auto Service for repairs. The insurance company went bankrupt and did not pay the repair bill. General Auto Service then sued Lombard for the bill because he had benefited from the repair work. Was he liable?

14. When a college student complained about a particular course, the vice president of the college asked the teacher to prepare a detailed report about the course. The teacher did and then demanded additional compensation for the time spent in preparing the report. He claimed that the college was liable to provide compensation on an implied contract. Was he correct? [*Zadrozny v City Colleges of Chicago*, 581 NE2d 44 (Ill App)]

15. Smith made a contract to sell automatic rifles to a foreign country. Because the sale of such weapons to that country was illegal under an act of Congress, the U.S. government prosecuted Smith for making the contract. He raised the defense that because the contract was illegal, it was void and there is no binding obligation when a contract is void; therefore, no contract for which he could be prosecuted existed. Was he correct?

CPA QUESTIONS

1. Kay, an art collector, promised Hammer, an art student, that if Hammer could obtain certain rare artifacts within two weeks, Kay would pay for Hammer's postgraduate education. At considerable effort and expense, Hammer obtained the specified artifacts within the two-week period. When Hammer requested payment, Kay refused. Kay claimed that there was no consideration for the promise. Hammer would prevail against Kay based on:

   a. Unilateral contract

   b. Unjust enrichment

   c. Public policy

   d. Quasi contract

Chapter 13

FORMATION OF CONTRACTS: OFFER AND ACCEPTANCE

A *contract* consists of enforceable obligations that have been voluntarily assumed. Thus, one of the essential elements of a contract is an agreement. This chapter explains how the basic agreement arises, when there is a contract, and how there can be merely unsuccessful negotiations without a resulting contract.

A. REQUIREMENTS OF AN OFFER

An **offer** expresses the willingness of the offeror to enter into a contractual agreement regarding a particular subject. It is a promise that is conditional upon an act, a forbearance (a refraining from doing something one has a legal right to do), or a return promise.

CPA   1. Contractual Intention

To make an offer, the offeror must appear to intend to create a binding obligation. Whether this intent exists is determined by objective standards.[1] This intent may be shown by conduct.

For Example, when one party signs a written contract and sends it to the other party, such action is an offer to enter into a contract on the terms of the writing.

There is no contract when a social invitation is made or when an offer is made in obvious jest or excitement. A reasonable person would not regard such an offer as indicating a willingness to enter into a binding agreement.

(A) INVITATION TO NEGOTIATE. The first statement made by one of two persons is not necessarily an offer. In many instances, there may be a preliminary discussion or an invitation by one party to the other to negotiate or to make an offer. Thus, an inquiry by a school as to whether a teacher wished to continue the following year was merely a survey or invitation to negotiate and was not an offer that could be accepted. Therefore, the teacher's affirmative response did not create a contract.

Ordinarily, a seller sending out circulars or catalogs listing prices is not regarded as making an offer to sell at those prices. The seller is merely indicating a willingness to consider an offer made by a buyer on those terms. The reason for this rule is, in part, the practical consideration that because a seller does not have an unlimited supply of any commodity, the seller cannot possibly intend to make a contract with everyone who sees the circular. The same principle is applied to merchandise that is displayed with price tags in stores or store windows and to most advertisements. An advertisement in a newspaper is ordinarily considered an invitation to negotiate and is not an offer that can be accepted by a reader of the paper.[2] However, some court decisions have construed advertisements as offers that called for an act on the part of the customer thereby forming a unilateral contract, such as the advertisement of a reward for the return of lost property.

Quotations of prices, even when sent on request, are likewise not offers unless the parties have had previous dealings or unless a trade custom exists that would give the recipient of the quotation reason to believe that an offer was being made. Whether a price quotation is to be treated as an offer or merely an invitation to negotiate is a question of the intent of the party giving the quotation.[3]

(B) AGREEMENT TO MAKE A CONTRACT AT A FUTURE DATE. No contract arises when the parties merely agree that at a future date they will consider making a contract or will make a contract on terms to be agreed on at that time. In such a case, neither party is under any obligation until the future contract is made. Unless an agreement is reached on all material terms and conditions and nothing is left to future negotiations, a contract to enter a contract in the future is of no effect. **For Example,** Hewitt Associates provided employee benefits administrative services to Rollins, Inc. under a contract negotiated in 2001 to run through 2006. Prior to its expiration, the parties negotiated— seeking to agree to a multiyear extension of the 2001 agreement. They agreed to all of the material terms of the contract, except that Rollins balked at a

---

[1] *Glass Service Co. v State Farm Mutual Automobile Ins. Co.,* 530 NW2d 867 (Minn App 1995).
[2] *Pico v Cutter Dodge, Inc.,* 98 Hawaii 309 (2002).
[3] Statutes prohibiting false or misleading advertising may require adherence to advertised prices.

$1.8 million penalty clause. Rollins's employees told Hewitt that the extension "was going to be signed." However, Rollins did not sign and the 2001 agreement expired. Hewitt's contention that the agreement was enforceable at the moment Rollins told Hewitt it was going to sign the new agreement was rejected by the court, stating that an agreement to reach an agreement is a contradiction in terms and imposes no obligation on the parties.[4]

2. Definiteness

An offer, and the resulting contract, must be definite and certain.[5] If an offer is indefinite or vague or if an essential provision is lacking,[6] no contract arises from an attempt to accept it. The reason is that courts cannot tell what the parties are to do. Thus, an offer to conduct a business for as long as it is profitable is too vague to be a valid offer. The acceptance of such an offer does not result in a contract that can be enforced. Statements by a bank that it was "with" the debtors and would "support" them in their proposed business venture were too vague to be regarded as a promise by the bank to make necessary loans to the debtors.

The fact that minor, ministerial, and nonessential terms are left for future determination does not make an agreement too vague to be a contract.[7] In the *McCarthy* case, the court was faced with the question of whether a legally enforceable contract had been made where the parties expressed their intent to execute a subsequent purchase and sale agreement.

McCarthy v Tobin, 706 NE2d 629 (Mass 1999)

Offer to Purchase Is Controlling Legal Document

John McCarthy Jr. brought an action for specific performance against Ann Tobin claiming that the parties created a binding contract when they signed an offer to purchase (OTP) form on August 9, 1995. Robert DiMinico and his wife intervened because they thereafter agreed to purchase the property in question from Ms. Tobin. The trial court granted summary judgment for Tobin and the DiMinicos, which was vacated by the Appeals Court. The Supreme Judicial Court granted further appellate review.

JUDICIAL OPINION

ABRAMS, J. . . . The facts, which are undisputed, are as follows. On August 9, 1995, McCarthy executed an offer to purchase real estate on a pre-printed form generated by the Greater Boston Real Estate Board. The OTP contained, among other provisions, a description of the property, the price to be paid, deposit requirements, limited title requirements, and the time and place for closing. The OTP also included several provisions that are the basis of this dispute. The OTP required that the parties "shall, on or before 5 P.M. August 16, 1995, execute the applicable Standard Form Purchase and Sale Agreement recommended by the Greater Boston Real Estate Board . . . which, when executed, shall be the agreement between the parties hereto." . . . Finally, an unnumbered paragraph immediately above the signature line states: "NOTICE: This is a legal document that creates binding obligations. If not understood, consult an attorney." Tobin signed the OTP on August 11, 1995.

On August 16, 1995, sometime after 5 P.M., Tobin's lawyer sent a first draft of the purchase and sale agreement by facsimile transmission to McCarthy's lawyer. On August 21, McCarthy's lawyer sent a letter by facsimile transmission containing his comments and proposing several changes to Tobin's lawyer. The changes laid out the requirements for good title; imposed on Tobin the risk of casualty to the premises before sale; solicited indemnification, for title insurance purposes, regarding mechanics' liens, parties in possession, and hazardous materials; and sought an acknowledgment that the premises' systems were operational. The next day, the two lawyers discussed the proposed revisions. They did not discuss an extension of the deadline for signing the purchase and sale agreement, and

---

[4] *Hewitt Associates, LLC v Rollins, Inc.*, 669 SE2d 551 (Ga App 2008).

[5] *Graziano v Grant*, 744 A2d 156 (NJ Super AD 1999).

[6] *Peace v Doming Holdings Inc.*, 554 SE2d 314 (Ga App 2001).

[7] *Hsu v Vet-A-Mix, Inc.*, 479 NW2d 336 (Iowa App 1991). But see *Ocean Atlantic Development Corp v Aurora Christian Schools, Inc.*, 322 F3d 983 (7th Cir 2003), where letter offers to purchase (OTP) real estate were signed by both parties, but the offers conditioned the purchase and sale of each property upon the subsequent execution of a purchase and sale agreement. The court held that the parties thus left themselves room to walk away from the deal under Illinois law, and the OTPs were not enforced.

Continued

Tobin's lawyer did not object to the fact that the deadline had already passed. On August 23, Tobin's lawyer sent a second draft of the agreement to McCarthy's lawyer. On August 25, a Friday, McCarthy's lawyer informed Tobin's lawyer that the agreement was acceptable, McCarthy would sign it, and it would be delivered the following Monday. On Saturday, August 26, McCarthy signed the purchase and sale agreement. On the same day, Tobin accepted the DiMinicos' offer to purchase the property.

On August 28, McCarthy delivered the executed agreement and a deposit to Tobin's broker. The next day, Tobin's lawyer told McCarthy's lawyer that the agreement was late and that Tobin had already accepted the DiMinicos' offer. In September, 1995, Tobin and the DiMinicos executed a purchase and sale agreement. Before the deal closed, McCarthy filed this action for specific performance and damages.

1. *Firm offer.* The primary issue is whether the OTP executed by McCarthy and Tobin was a binding contract. Tobin and the DiMinicos argue that it was not because of the provision requiring the execution of a purchase and sale agreement. McCarthy urges that he and Tobin intended to be bound by the OTP and that execution of the purchase and sale agreement was merely a formality.

McCarthy argues that the OTP adequately described the property to be sold and the price to be paid. The remaining terms covered by the purchase and sale agreement were subsidiary matters which did not preclude the formation of a binding contract. We agree.

The controlling fact is the intention of the parties. . . . Tobin argues that language contemplating the execution of a final written agreement gives rise to a strong inference that she and McCarthy have not agreed to all material aspects of a transaction and thus that they do not intend to be bound. . . .

Although the provisions of the purchase and sale agreement can be the subject of negotiation, "norms exist for their customary resolution." . . .

The interveners argue that McCarthy departed from the customary resolution of any open issues, and therefore manifested his intent not to be bound, by requesting several additions to the purchase and sale agreement. We agree with the Appeals Court, however, that McCarthy's revisions were "ministerial and nonessential terms of the bargain." . . .

The inference that the OTP was binding is bolstered by the notice printed on the form. McCarthy and Tobin were alerted to the fact that the OTP "create[d] binding obligations." The question is what those obligations were. The DiMinicos argue that the OTP merely obligated the parties to negotiate the purchase and sale agreement in good faith. We disagree. The OTP employs familiar contractual language. It states that McCarthy "hereby offer[s] to buy" the property, and Tobin's signature indicates that "[t]his Offer is hereby accepted." The OTP also details the amount to be paid and when, describes the property bought, and specifies for how long the offer was open. This was a firm offer, the acceptance of which bound Tobin to sell and McCarthy to buy the subject property. We conclude that the OTP reflects the parties' intention to be bound.

[The court found that Tobin had waived the August 16 deadline by words and conduct attributable to her, including her lawyer's failure to object to the passage of the deadline and his continued dealing with McCarthy's lawyer to craft an agreement.]

2. *Specific performance.* . . . McCarthy's right to specific performance is unaltered by Tobin's execution of a purchase and sale agreement with the DiMinicos. McCarthy filed this action prior to the execution of that agreement. The DiMinicos had actual notice of McCarthy's claim to the property and assumed the risk of a result favorable to McCarthy. . . .

The judgment is vacated. The case is remanded to the Superior Court for the entry of a judgment in favor of McCarthy's claim for specific performance.

[Judgment for McCarthy]

QUESTIONS

1. State Tobin's position before the court.

2. Were there definite and certain terms agreed to by the parties regarding the purchase to Tobin's property?

3. Evaluate Ms. Tobin's strategy, after signing the OTP, of hiring an attorney to handle the purchase and sale agreement and closing.

The law does not favor the destruction of contracts because that would go against the social force of carrying out the intent of the parties.[8] Consequently, when it is claimed that a contract is too indefinite to be enforced, a court will do its best to find the intent of the parties and thereby reach the conclusion that the contract is not too indefinite. **For Example,** boxing promoter Don King had both a Promotional

[8] *Mears v Nationwide Mut, Inc. Co.,* 91 F3d 1118 (8th Cir 1996).

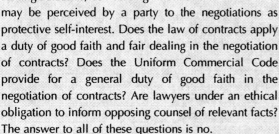

thinking things through
The Rules of Negotiations

Business agreements are often reached after much discussion, study, and posturing by both sides. Many statements may be made by both sides about the price or value placed on the subject of the transaction. Withholding information or presenting selective, self-serving information may be perceived by a party to the negotiations as protective self-interest. Does the law of contracts apply a duty of good faith and fair dealing in the negotiation of contracts? Does the Uniform Commercial Code provide for a general duty of good faith in the negotiation of contracts? Are lawyers under an ethical obligation to inform opposing counsel of relevant facts? The answer to all of these questions is no.

The Restatement (Second) of Contracts applies the duty of good faith and fair dealing to the performance and enforcement of contracts, not their negotiation;* so also does the UCC.** The American Bar Association's Model Rules of Professional Conduct, Rule 4.1 Comment 1 requires a lawyer to be "truthful" when dealing with others on a client's behalf, but it also states that generally a lawyer has "no affirmative duty to inform an opposing party of relevant facts."*** Comment 2 to Rule 4.1 contains an example of a "nonmaterial" statement of a lawyer as "estimates of price or value placed on the subject of a transaction."

The legal rules of negotiations state that—in the absence of fraud, special relationships, or statutory or contractual duties—negotiators are not obligated to divulge pertinent information to the other party to the negotiations. The parties to negotiations themselves must demand and analyze pertinent information and ultimately assess the fairness of the proposed transaction. Should a party conclude that the elements of a final proposal or offer are excessive or dishonest, that party's legal option is to walk away from the deal. Generally, the party has no basis to bring a lawsuit for lack of good faith and fair dealing in negotiations.

However, THINKING THINGS THROUGH, the ethical standards for negotiations set forth in Chapter 3 indicate that establishing a reputation for trustworthiness, candor, and reliability often leads to commercial success for a company's continuing negotiations with its customers, suppliers, distributors, lenders, unions, and employees.****

---

* Restatement (Second) of Contracts § 105, comment (c).
** Uniform Commercial Code § 1-203.
*** American Bar Association Model Rule of Professional Conduct 4.1 (a) Comment 1.

**** For a contrary example, consider the following story. The Atlanta Braves baseball team's general manager Frank Wren negotiated with free agent baseball player Rafael Furcal's agent Paul Kinzer. When all terms had been negotiated, Kinzer asked for a written terms-of-agreement sheet signed by the Braves, which to Wren meant an agreement had been reached. Kinzer took the sheet to the L.A. Dodgers, who then reached an agreement to sign the shortstop. Braves President John Schuerholz said, "The Atlanta Braves will no longer do business with that company—ever. I told Arn Tellem that we can't trust them to be honest and forthright." "Braves GM Blasts Furcal's Agents," Associated Press, *The Boston Globe*, December 20, 2008, C-7.

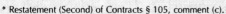

Agreement and a Bout Agreement with boxer Miguel Angel Goñzalez. The Bout Agreement for a boxing match held on March 7, 1998, with Julio Cesar Chavez gave King the option to promote the next four of Gonzalez's matches. The contract made clear that if Gonzalez won the Chavez match, he would receive at least $75,000 for the next fight unless the parties agreed otherwise, and if he lost, he would

receive at least $25,000 for the subsequent fight unless otherwise agreed. The agreement did not explicitly state the purse for the subsequent match in the event of a draw. The Chavez match ended in a draw, and Gonzalez contended that this omission rendered the contract so indefinite that it was unenforceable. The court disagreed, stating that striking down a contract as indefinite and in essence meaningless is at best a last resort. The court held that although the contract was poorly drafted, the Promotional Agreement contained explicit price terms for which a minimum purse for fights following a draw may be inferred.[9] A court may not rewrite the agreement of the parties in order to make it definite.

(A) DEFINITE BY INCORPORATION. An offer and the resulting contract that by themselves may appear "too indefinite" may be made definite by reference to another writing. **For Example,** a lease agreement that was too vague by itself was made definite because the parties agreed that the lease should follow the standard form with which both were familiar. An agreement may also be made definite by reference to the prior dealings of the parties and to trade practices.

(B) IMPLIED TERMS. Although an offer must be definite and certain, not all of its terms need to be expressed. Some omitted terms may be implied by law. **For Example,** an offer "to pay $400" for a certain Movado timepiece does not state the terms of payment. A court, however, would not condemn this provision as too vague but would hold that it required that cash be paid and that the payment be made on delivery of the watch. Likewise, terms may be implied from conduct. As an illustration, when borrowed money was given to the borrower by a check on which the word *loan* was written, the act of the borrower in endorsing the check constituted an agreement to repay the amount of the check.

(C) "BEST EFFORTS" CLAUSES. While decades ago it was generally accepted that a duty defined only in terms of "best efforts" was too indefinite to be enforced, such a view is no longer widely held. **For Example,** Thomas Hinc, an inventor, executed a contract with Lime-O-Sol Company (LOS) for LOS to produce and distribute Hinc's secret ingredient Stain Remover. Under the contract, Hinc was to receive $10 per gallon sold. The contract contained a clause obligating both parties to use their "best efforts" to market the product "in a manner that seems appropriate." Ultimately, LOS never produced, marketed, or sold Stain Remover for the duration of the contract. The court rejected the defense that the "best efforts" provision was vague and unenforceable stating "[b]est efforts, as commonly understood, means, at the very least *some* effort. It certainly does not mean

FIGURE 13-1 | *Offer and Acceptance*

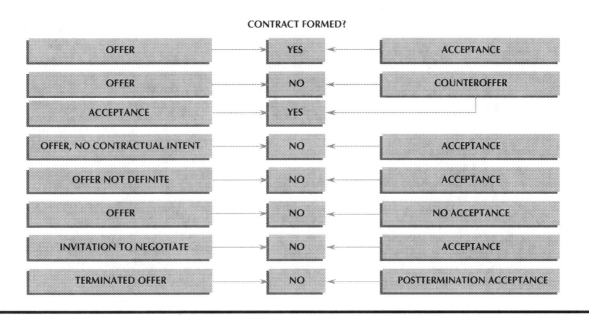

CONTRACT FORMED?

[9] *Gonzalez v Don King Productions, Inc.,* 17 F Supp 2d 313 (SDNY 1998); see also *Echols v Pelullo,* 377 F3d 272 (3rd Cir 2004).

zero effort—the construction LOS urges here to escape any obligation under its contract."[10]

(D) DIVISIBLE CONTRACTS. When the agreement consists of two or more parts and calls for corresponding performances of each part by the parties, the agreement is a **divisible contract**. Thus, in a promise to buy several separate articles at different prices at the same time, the agreement may be regarded as separate or divisible promises for the articles.

(E) EXCEPTIONS TO DEFINITENESS. The law has come to recognize certain situations in which the practical necessity of doing business makes it desirable to have a contract, yet the situation is such that it is either impossible or undesirable to adopt definite terms in advance. In these cases, the indefinite term is often tied to the concept of good-faith performance or to some independent factor that will be definitely ascertainable at some time in the future. The indefinite term might be tied to market price, cost to complete, production, or sales requirements. Thus, the law recognizes binding contracts in the case of a **requirements contract**—that is, a contract to buy all requirements of the buyer from the seller.[11] **For Example,** an agreement between Honeywell International Inc. and Air Products and Chemicals Inc. whereby Air Products would purchase its total requirements of wet process chemicals from Honeywell was held to be an enforceable requirements contract.[12] The law also recognizes as binding an **output contract**—that is, the contract of a producer to sell the entire production or output to a given buyer. These are binding contracts even though they do not state the exact quantity of goods that are to be bought or sold. The *Delphi Corporation* case contains an interpretation of a requirements contract allowing the buyer to control the timing and quantity of deliveries.

In re Delphi Corp., 2008 LEXIS 74207 (SDNY 2008)

GM—In The Driver's Seat On Quanity and Timing!

Automodular entered into a series of purchase orders that obligated Delphi to purchase and Automodular to provide all of Delphi's requirements deliverable to the original equipment manufacturer (OEM), General Motors. Automodular receives directions from the OEM's final assembly plants, regardless of whether Automodular is under contract to the OEM or Delphi. The purchase orders ("Contracts") incorporated Delphi's terms that the Buyer, GM, could require Automodular to implement changes to the specifications or design of the goods or to the scope of any services covered by the Contracts. GM informed Automodular that it needed fewer components and directed Automodular to, among other requirements, reduce shifts, change the assembly line speed, and change the length of workers' shifts (the "Delphi changes"). As a result, Automodular requested a price increase per unit assembled from Delphi because Automodular believed that such an increase was warranted pursuant to the Contract's change-in-scope provision. Delphi, however, refused to negotiate any price increase and the matter was litigated.

JUDICIAL OPINION

MARRERO, D.J. . . . In the instant matter, it was the clear intent of the parties to enter into requirement contracts. In a requirement contract, the parties do not fix a quantity term, but instead, the quantity will be the buyer's needs of the specific commodity over the contract's life. Specifically, this intent is demonstrated by language in the Contracts requiring Automodular to supply 100 percent of Delphi's particular subassembly needs, typically at a fixed price. Because the Contracts are requirement contracts, Delphi cannot generally be held liable under the Contracts for mere reductions in volume unless Delphi acted with bad faith. Automodular has not alleged that Delphi acted with bad faith in reducing its requirements, and the record clearly demonstrates that Delphi's reduced requirements were a result of GM's lowered demand, not bad faith on the part of Delphi.

Automodular counters that, although the Contracts may have been requirements contracts, it is entitled to an increase in price because the Delphi Changes altered the scope of

---

[10] *Hinc v Lime-O-Sol Company*, 382 F3d 716 (7th Cir 2004).
[11] *Simcala v American Coal Trade, Inc.*, 821 So2d 197 (Ala 2001).
[12] *Honeywell International Inc. v Air Products and Chemicals, Inc.*, 872 A2d 944 (Sup Ct Del 2005).

Continued

services and were not merely reductions in requirements. Section 3 of the Terms states that:

> *Buyer may at any time request [Automodular] to implement changes to the specifications or design of the goods or to the scope of any services or work covered by this Contract, including work related to inspection, testing or quality control . . . . Buyer will equitably determine any adjustment in price or delivery schedules resulting from such changes . . . .*

Automodular argues that by requiring the Delphi Changes, Delphi effectively altered the scope of the services or work covered by the Terms and that, pursuant to 3 of the Terms, Automodular is entitled to a price adjustment . . . .

Section 2.5 states in relevant part that "[d]eliveries will be made in the quantities, on the dates, and at the times specified by Buyer in this Contract or any subsequent releases or instructions Buyer issues under this Contract," and that "[i]f the requirements of Buyer's customers or market, economic or other conditions require changes in delivery schedules, Buyer may change the rate of scheduled shipments or direct temporary suspension of scheduled shipments without entitling [Automodular] to a price adjustment or other

compensation." (*Id.* § 2.5.) This provision demonstrates the intent of the parties to allow the buyer to effectively control the timing and quantity of deliveries without entitling Automodular to an adjustment in price.

. . . The express language in the Terms clearly demonstrates that the parties entered into requirement contracts, which did not allow for adjustments to price terms based on reductions in requirements . . . . Automodular is not entitled to a price adjustment pursuant to the Terms . . . .

[*Affirmed*]

QUESTIONS

1. Ordinarily, in requirement contracts, where the parties do not fix a quantity figure, is the Buyer held liable for breach of contract for reductions in volumes over previous years?

2. When GM directed Automodular to reduce shifts, change assembly line speed, and change the length of workers' shifts, in fairness, was not Automodular allowed, even entitled, to a price adjustment to reflect actual increases in its costs of production?

CPA   3. Communication of Offer to Offeree

An offer must be communicated to the offeree. Otherwise, the offeree cannot accept even though knowledge of the offer has been indirectly acquired. Internal management communications of an enterprise that are not intended for outsiders or employees do not constitute offers and cannot be accepted by them. Sometimes, particularly in the case of unilateral contracts, the offeree performs the act called for by the offeror without knowing of the offer's existence. Such performance does not constitute an acceptance. Thus, without knowing that a reward is offered for information leading to the arrest of a particular criminal, a person may provide information that leads to the arrest of the criminal. In most states, if that person subsequently learns of the reward, the reward cannot be recovered.[13]

Not only must the offer be communicated but also it must be communicated by the offeror or at the offeror's direction.

CPA   B. Termination of Offer

An offeree cannot accept a terminated offer. Offers may be terminated by revocation, counteroffer, rejection, lapse of time, death or disability of a party, or subsequent illegality.

CPA   4. Revocation of Offer by Offeror

Ordinarily, an offeror can revoke the offer before it is accepted. If this is done, the offeree cannot create a contract by accepting the revoked offer. Thus, the

---

[13] With respect to the offeror, it should not make any difference, as a practical matter, whether the services were rendered with or without knowledge of the existence of the offer. Only a small number of states have adopted this view, however.

bidder at an auction sale may withdraw (revoke) a bid (offer) before it is accepted, and the auctioneer cannot accept that bid later.

An ordinary offer may be revoked at any time before it is accepted even though the offeror has expressly promised that the offer will be good for a stated period and that period has not yet expired. It may also be revoked even though the offeror has expressly promised to the offeree that the offer would not be revoked before a specified later date.

The fact that the offeror expressly promised to keep the offer open has no effect when no consideration was given for that promise.

(A) WHAT CONSTITUTES A REVOCATION? No particular form or words are required to constitute a revocation. Any words indicating the offeror's termination of the offer are sufficient. A notice sent to the offeree that the property that is the subject of the offer has been sold to a third person is a revocation of the offer. A customer's order for goods, which is an offer to purchase at certain prices, is revoked by a notice to the seller of the cancellation of the order, provided that such notice is communicated before the order is accepted.

(B) COMMUNICATION OF REVOCATION. A revocation of an offer is ordinarily effective only when it is made known to the offeree.[14] Until it is communicated to the offeree, directly or indirectly, the offeree has reason to believe that there is still an offer that may be accepted, and the offeree may rely on this belief. A letter revoking an offer made to a particular offeree is not effective until the offeree receives it. It is not a revocation when the offeror writes it or even when it is mailed or dispatched. A written revocation is effective, however, when it is delivered to the offeree's agent or to the offeree's residence or place of business under such circumstances that the offeree may be reasonably expected to be aware of its receipt.

It is ordinarily held that there is a sufficient communication of the revocation when the offeree learns indirectly of the offeror's revocation. This is particularly true in a land sale when the seller-offeror, after making an offer to sell the land to the offeree, sells the land to a third person and the offeree indirectly learns of such sale. The offeree necessarily realizes that the seller cannot perform the original offer and therefore must be considered to have revoked it.

If the offeree accepts an offer before it is effectively revoked, a valid contract is created.

(C) OPTION CONTRACTS. An *option contract* is a binding promise to keep an offer open for a stated period of time or until a specified date. An option contract requires that the promisor receive consideration—that is, something, such as a sum of money—as the price for the promise to keep the offer open. In other words, the option is a contract to refrain from revoking an offer.

(D) FIRM OFFERS. As another exception to the rule that an offer can be revoked at any time before acceptance, statutes in some states provide that an offeror cannot revoke an offer prior to its expiration when the offeror makes a firm offer. A **firm offer** is an offer that states that it is to be irrevocable, or irrevocable for a stated period of time. Under the Uniform Commercial Code, this doctrine of firm offer applies to a merchant's signed, written offer to buy or sell goods but with a maximum of three months on its period of irrevocability.[15]

5. Counteroffer by Offeree

The offeree rejects the offer when she ignores the original offer and replies with a different offer.[16] If the offeree purports to accept an offer but in so doing makes any change to the terms of the offer, such action is a **counteroffer** that rejects the original offer. An "acceptance" that changes the terms of the offer or adds new terms is a rejection of the original offer and constitutes a counteroffer.[17]

Ordinarily, if *A* makes an offer, such as to sell a used automobile to *B* for $3,000, and *B* in reply makes an offer to buy at $2,500, the original offer is terminated. *B* is in effect indicating refusal of the original offer and in its place is making a different offer. Such an offer by the offeree is known as a *counteroffer*. No contract arises unless the original offeror accepts the counteroffer.

---

[14] *MD Drilling and Blasting, Inc. v MLS Construction, LLC,* 889 A2d 850 (Conn App 2006).
[15] UCC § 2-205.
[16] *Bourque v FDIC,* 42 F3d 704 (1st Cir 1994).
[17] *McLaughlin v Heikkila,* 697 NW2d 731 (Minn App 2005).

Counteroffers are not limited to offers that directly contradict the original offers. Any departure from or addition to the original offer is a counteroffer even though the original offer was silent on the point added by the counteroffer.

6. Rejection of Offer by Offeree

If the offeree rejects the offer and communicates this rejection to the offeror, the offer is terminated. Communication of a rejection terminates an offer even though the period for which the offeror agreed to keep the offer open has not yet expired. It may be that the offeror is willing to renew the offer, but unless this is done, there is no longer any offer for the offeree to accept.

7. Lapse of Time

When the offer states that it is open until a particular date, the offer terminates on that date if it has not yet been accepted. This is particularly so when the offeror declares that the offer shall be void after the expiration of the specified time. Such limitations are strictly construed.

If the offer contains a time limitation for acceptance, an attempted acceptance after the expiration of that time has no effect and does not give rise to a contract.[18] When a specified time limitation is imposed on an option, the option cannot be exercised after the expiration of that time, regardless of whether the option was exercised within what would have been held a reasonable time if no time period had been specified.

If the offer does not specify a time, it will terminate after the lapse of a reasonable time. What constitutes a reasonable time depends on the circumstances of each case—that is, on the nature of the subject matter, the nature of the market in which it is sold, the time of year, and other factors of supply and demand. If a commodity is perishable or fluctuates greatly in value, the reasonable time will be much shorter than if the subject matter is of a stable value. An offer to sell a harvested crop of tomatoes would expire within a very short time. When a seller purports to accept an offer after it has lapsed by the expiration of time, the seller's acceptance is merely a

counteroffer and does not create a contract unless the buyer accepts that counteroffer.

8. Death or Disability of Either Party

If either the offeror or offeree dies or becomes mentally incompetent before the offer is accepted, the offer is automatically terminated. **For Example,** Chet Wilson offers to sell his ranch to Interport, Inc., for $2.5 million. Five days later, Chet is killed in an aviation accident. Interport, Inc., subsequently writes to Chet Wilson Jr., an adult, that his father's offer is accepted. No contract is formed because the offer made by Chet died with him.

CPA 9. Subsequent Illegality

If the performance of the contract becomes illegal after the offer is made, the offer is terminated. **For Example,** if an offer is made to sell six semiautomatic handguns to a commercial firing range for $550 per weapon but a new law prohibiting such sales is enacted before the offer is accepted, the offer is terminated.

CPA C. ACCEPTANCE OF OFFER

An **acceptance** is the assent of the offeree to the terms of the offer. Objective standards determine whether there has been an agreement of the parties.

10. What Constitutes an Acceptance?

No particular form of words or mode of expression is required, but there must be a clear expression that the offeree agrees to be bound by the terms of the offer. If the offeree reserves the right to reject the offer, such action is not an acceptance.[19]

11. Privilege of Offeree

Ordinarily, the offeree may refuse to accept an offer. If there is no acceptance, by definition there is no contract. The fact that there had been a series of contracts between the parties and that one party's offer had always been accepted before by the other

[18] *Century 21 Pinetree Properties, Inc. v Cason,* 469 SE2d 458 (Ga App 1996).
[19] *Pantano v McGowan,* 530 NW2d 912 (Neb 1995).

does not create any legal obligation to continue to accept subsequent offers.

CPA 12. Effect of Acceptance

The acceptance of an offer creates a binding agreement or contract,[20] assuming that all of the other elements of a contract are present. Neither party can subsequently withdraw from or cancel the contract without the consent of the other party. **For Example,** James Gang refused to honor an oral stock purchase agreement he made with Moshen Sadeghi under terms he assented to and that were announced on the record to a court as a mutual settlement of a dispute. Gang was not allowed subsequently to withdraw from the agreement, because it was an enforceable contract.[21]

CPA 13. Nature of Acceptance

An *acceptance* is the offeree's manifestation of intent to enter into a binding agreement on the terms stated in the offer. Whether there is an acceptance depends on whether the offeree has manifested an intent to accept. It is the objective or outward appearance that is controlling rather than the subjective or unexpressed intent of the offeree.[22]

In the absence of a contrary requirement in the offer, an acceptance may be indicated by an informal "okay," by a mere affirmative nod of the head, or in the case of an offer of a unilateral contract, by performance of the act called for.

The acceptance must be absolute and unconditional. It must accept just what is offered.[23] If the offeree changes any terms of the offer or adds any new term, there is no acceptance because the offeree does not agree to what was offered.

When the offeree does not accept the offer exactly as made, the addition of any qualification converts the "acceptance" into a counteroffer, and no contract arises unless the original offeror accepts such a counteroffer.

CPA 14. Who May Accept?

Only the person to whom an offer is directed may accept it. If anyone else attempts to accept it, no agreement or contract with that person arises.

If the offer is directed to a particular class rather than a specified individual, anyone within that class may accept it. If the offer is made to the public at large, any member of the public at large having knowledge of the existence of the offer may accept it.

When a person to whom an offer was not made attempts to accept it, the attempted acceptance has the effect of an offer. If the original offeror is willing to accept this offer, a binding contract arises. If the original offeror does not accept the new offer, there is no contract.

CPA 15. Manner and Time of Acceptance

The offeror may specify the manner and time for accepting the offer. When the offeror specifies that there must be a written acceptance, no contract arises when the offeree makes an oral acceptance. If the offeror calls for acceptance by a specified time and date, a late acceptance has no legal effect, and a contract is not formed. Where no time is specified in the offer, the offeree has a reasonable period of time to accept the offer. After the time specified in the offer or a reasonable period of time expires (when no time is specified in the offer), the offeree's power to make a contract by accepting the offer "lapses."

When the offeror calls for the performance of an act or of certain conduct, the performance thereof is an acceptance of the offer and creates a unilateral contract.

When the offeror has specified a particular manner and time of acceptance, generally, the offeree cannot accept in any other way. The basic rule applied by the courts is that the offeror is the master of the offer![24]

CPA (A) SILENCE AS ACCEPTANCE. In most cases, the offeree's silence and failure to act cannot be regarded as an acceptance. Ordinarily, the offeror is not

---

[20] *Ochoa v Ford,* 641 NE2d 1042 (Ind App 1994).
[21] *Sadeghi v Gang,* 270 SW2d 773 (Tex App 2008).
[22] *Cowan v Mervin Mewes, Inc.,* 546 NW2d 104 (SD 1996).
[23] *Jones v Frickey,* 618 SE2d 29 (Ga App 2005).
[24] See *1-800 Contacts, Inc v Weigner,* 127 P3d 1241 (Utah App 2005).

permitted to frame an offer in such a way as to make the silence and inaction of the offeree operate as an acceptance. Nor can a party to an existing contract effect a modification of that agreement without the other party's actual acceptance or approval.

For Example, H. H. Taylor made a contract with Andy Stricker, a civil engineer, to design a small hotel. The parties agreed on an hourly rate with "total price not to exceed $7,200," and required that additional charges be presented to Taylor prior to proceeding with any changes. Andy was required to dedicate more hours to the project than anticipated but could not present

e-commerce&cyberlaw

Contract Formation on the Internet

It is not possible for an online service provider or seller to individually bargain with each person who visits its Web site. The Web site owner, therefore, as offeror, places its proposed terms on its Web site and requires visitors to assent to these terms in order to access the site, download software, or purchase a product or service.

In a written contract, the parties sign a paper document indicating their intention to be bound by the terms of the contract. Online, however, an agreement may be accomplished by the visitor-offeree simply typing the words "I Accept" in an onscreen box and then clicking a "send" or similar button that indicates acceptance. Or the individual clicks an "I Agree" or "I Accept" icon or check box. Access to the site is commonly denied those who do not agree to the terms. Such agreements have come to be known as *clickwrap* agreements and in the case of software license agreements, *SLAs*. The agreements contain fee schedules and other financial terms and may contain terms such as a notice of the proprietary nature of the material contained on the site and of any limitations on the use of the site and the downloading of software. Moreover, the clickwrap agreements may contain limitations on liability, including losses associated with the use of downloaded software or products or services purchased from the site.

To determine whether a clickwrap agreement is enforceable, courts apply traditional principles of contract law and focus on whether the plaintiffs had reasonable notice of and manifested assent to the clickwrap agreement. Failure to read an enforceable clickwrap agreement, as with any binding contract, will not excuse compliance with its terms.

In *Specht v Netscape Communications Corp.,** the Internet users were urged to click on a button to download free software, but the offer did not make clear to the user that clicking the download button would signify assent to restrictive contractual terms and conditions. The court, in its 2002 decision, declined to enforce this clickwrap agreement. Internet sellers and service providers generally learned from the *Specht* decision, and most clickwrap agreements now provide sufficient notice and means for clear assent. For example, in *Feldman v Google, Inc.,*** decided in 2007, the user was unsuccessful in challenging the terms of Google's "AdWords" Program clickwrap agreement. In order to activate an AdWords account, the user had to visit a Web page that displayed the agreement in a scrollable text box. The text of the agreement was immediately visible to the user, as was a prominent admonition in boldface to read the terms and conditions carefully, and with instructions to indicate assent if the user agreed to the terms.

Unlike the impermissible agreement in *Specht*, the user here had to take affirmative action and click the "Yes, I agree to the above terms and conditions" button in order to proceed to the next step. Clicking "Continue" without clicking the "Yes" button would have returned the user to the same Web page. If the user did not agree to all of the terms, he could not have activated his account, placed ads, or incurred charges.

* 306 F3d 17 (2d Cir 2002).
** *Feldman v Google. Inc.,* 513 F Supp 2d 229 (ED Pa 2007). See also *A. V. v Iparadigms, LLC,* 554 F Supp 2d 473 (ED Va 2008).

the additional charges to Taylor because Taylor would not return his phone calls. He billed Taylor $9,035 for his services. Taylor's failure to act in not returning phone calls is not a substitute for the assent needed to modify a contract. Stricker is thus only entitled to $7,200.[25]

(B) UNORDERED GOODS AND TICKETS. Sometimes a seller writes to a person with whom the seller has not had any prior dealings, stating that unless notified to the contrary, the seller will send specified merchandise and the recipient is obligated to pay for it at stated prices. There is no acceptance if the recipient of the letter ignores the offer and does nothing. The silence of the person receiving the letter is not an acceptance, and the sender, as a reasonable person, should recognize that none was intended.

This rule applies to all kinds of goods, books, magazines, and tickets sent through the mail when they have not been ordered. The fact that the items are not returned does not mean that they have been accepted; that is, the offeree is required neither to pay for nor to return the items. If desired, the recipient of the unordered goods may write "Return to Sender" on the unopened package and put the package back into the mail without any additional postage. The Postal Reorganization Act provides that the person who receives unordered mailed merchandise from a commercial sender has the right "to retain, use, discard, or dispose of it in any manner the recipient sees fit without any obligation whatsoever to the sender."[26] It provides further that any unordered merchandise that is mailed must have attached to it a clear and conspicuous statement of the recipient's right to treat the goods in this manner.

CPA   16. Communication of Acceptance

Acceptance by the offeree is the last step in the formation of a bilateral contract. Intuitively, the offeror's receipt of the acceptance should be the point in time when the contract is formed and its terms apply. When the parties are involved in face-to-face negotiations, a contract is formed upon the offeror's receipt of the acceptance. When the offeror hears the offeree's words of acceptance, the parties may shake hands, signifying their understanding that the contract has been formed.

CPA   (A) MAILBOX RULE. When the parties are negotiating at a distance from each other, special rules have developed as to when the acceptance takes effect based on the commercial expediency of creating a contract at the earliest period of time and the protection of the offeree. Under the so-called *mailbox rule,* a properly addressed, postage-paid mailed acceptance takes effect when the acceptance is placed into the control of the U.S. Postal Service[27] or, by judicial extension, is placed in the control of a private third-party carrier such as Federal Express or United Parcel Service.[28] That is, the acceptance is effective upon dispatch even before it is received by the offeror.

The offeror may avoid the application of this rule by stating in the offer that acceptance shall take effect upon receipt by the offeror.

CPA   (B) DETERMINING THE APPLICABLE MEANS OF COMMUNICATION. The modern rule on the selection of the appropriate medium of communication of acceptance is that unless otherwise unambiguously indicated in the offer, it shall be construed as inviting acceptance in any manner and by any medium reasonable under the circumstances.[29] A medium of communication is normally reasonable if it is one used by the offeror or if it is customary in similar transactions at the time and place the offer is received. Thus, if the offeror uses the mail to extend an offer, the offeree may accept by using the mail. Indeed, acceptance by mail is ordinarily reasonable when the parties are negotiating at a distance even if the offer is not made by mail.

---

[25] *Stricker v Taylor,* 975 P2d 930 (Or App 1999).
[26] Federal Postal Reorganization Act § 3009.
[27] See *Adams v Lindsell,* 106 Eng Rep 250 (KB 1818). Common law jurisdictions have unanimously adopted the mailbox rule, as has the Restatement (Second) of Contracts § 63, and the UCC [see UCC § 1-201(26),(38)].
[28] But see *Baca v. Trejo,* 902 NE2d 1108 (Ill App 2009) whereby an Illinois Court determined that a statute deeming a document to be filed with a state court on the date shown by the U.S. Postal Service cancellation mark—the mailbox rule—does not apply to documents consigned to a private carrier, UPS. The court reasoned that courts should not have the task of deciding which carriers are acceptable.
[29] Restatement (Second) of Contracts § 30; UCC § 2-206(1) (a).

CPA   (c) Telephone and Electronic Communication of Acceptance. Although telephonic communication is very similar to face-to-face communication, most U.S. courts, nevertheless, have applied the mailbox rule, holding that telephoned acceptances are effective where and when dispatched.

The courts have yet to address the applicability of the mailbox rule to e-mail. However, when the offeree's server is under the control of an independent entity, such as an online service provider, and the offeree cannot withdraw the message, it is anticipated that the courts will apply the mailbox rule, and acceptance will take effect on proper dispatch. In the case of companies that operate their own servers, the acceptance will take effect when the message is passed onto the Internet.

Facsimile transmissions are substantially instantaneous and could be treated as face-to-face communications. However, it is anticipated that U.S. courts, when called upon to deal with this issue, will apply the mailbox acceptance-upon-dispatch rule as they do with telephoned acceptances.

(d) Effects of the Mailbox Rule. If an offer requires that acceptance be communicated by a specific date and the acceptance is properly dispatched by the offeree on the final date, the acceptance is timely and the contract is formed, even though the offeror actually receives the acceptance well after the specified date has passed. **For Example,** by letter dated February 18, 1999, Morton's of Chicago mailed a certified letter to the Crab House accepting the Crab House's offer to terminate its restaurant lease. The Crab House, Inc., sought to revoke its offer to terminate the lease in a certified letter dated February 18, 1999 and by facsimile transmission to Morton's dated February 19, 1999. On February 22, 1999, the Crab House received Morton's acceptance letter; and on the same date Morton's received Crab House's letter revoking the offer to terminate the lease. Acceptance of an offer is effective upon dispatch to the Postal Service, and the contract springs into existence at the time of the mailing. Offers, revocations, and rejections are generally effective only upon

the offeree's receipt. Morton's dispatch of its acceptance letter on February 18 formed an agreement to terminate the lease, and the fax dispatched on February 19 was too late to revoke the offer to terminate the lease.[30]

17. Auction Sales

At an auction sale, the statements made by the auctioneer to draw forth bids are merely invitations to negotiate. Each bid is an offer, which is not accepted until the auctioneer indicates that a particular offer or bid is accepted. Usually, this is done by the fall of the auctioneer's hammer, indicating that the highest bid made has been accepted.[31] Because a bid is merely an offer, the bidder may withdraw the bid at any time before it is accepted by the auctioneer.

Ordinarily, the auctioneer who is not satisfied with the amounts of the bids that are being made may withdraw any article or all of the property from the sale. Once a bid is accepted, however, the auctioneer cannot cancel the sale. In addition, if it had been

lawflix

Funny Farm (1988) (PG)

Near the end of this Chevy Chase movie, two couples face a formation issue as one couple attempts to purchase a home. An offer, presented around a friendly kitchen table setting, is declined by the sellers. Do the buyers' threats to sue the sellers have any legal basis? While the buyers had made a special trip to see the land and felt that since they were offering more than the asking price that they had a contract, the sellers were free to reject the offer. Listing a house for a price is not an offer; it is an invitation for an offer.

Check out LawFlix at **www.cengage.com/ blaw/dvl** to access movie clips that illustrate business law concepts.

---

[30] *Morton's of Chicago v Crab House Inc.*, 746 NYS2d 317 (2002). *Kass v Grais*, 2007 NY Misc LEXIS 9017.
[31] *Dry Creek Cattle Co. v Harriet Bros. Limited Partnership*, 908 P2d 399 (Wyo 1995).

announced that the sale was to be made "without reserve," the property must be sold to the person making the highest bid regardless of how low that bid may be.

In an auction "with reserve," the auctioneer takes bids as agent for the seller with the understanding that no contract is formed until the seller accepts the transaction.[32]

MAKE THE CONNECTION

SUMMARY

Because a contract arises when an offer is accepted, it is necessary to find that there was an offer and that it was accepted. If either element is missing, there is no contract.

An offer does not exist unless the offeror has contractual intent. This intent is lacking if the statement of the person is merely an invitation to negotiate, a statement of intention, or an agreement to agree at a later date. Newspaper ads, price quotations, and catalog prices are ordinarily merely invitations to negotiate and cannot be accepted.

An offer must be definite. If an offer is indefinite, its acceptance will not create a contract because it will be held that the resulting agreement is too vague to enforce. In some cases, an offer that is by itself too indefinite is made definite because some writing or standard is incorporated by reference and made part of the offer. In some cases the offer is made definite by implying terms that were not stated. In other cases, the indefinite part of the offer is ignored when that part can be divided or separated from the balance of the offer.

Assuming that there is in fact an offer that is made with contractual intent and that it is sufficiently definite, it still does not have the legal effect of an offer unless it is communicated to the offeree by or at the direction of the offeror.

In some cases, there was an offer but it was terminated before it was accepted. By definition, an attempted acceptance made after the offer has been terminated has no effect. The offeror may revoke the

ordinary offer at any time. All that is required is the showing of the intent to revoke and the communication of that intent to the offeree. The offeror's power to revoke is barred by the existence of an option contract under common law or a firm offer under the Uniform Commercial Code. An offer is also terminated by the express rejection of the offer or by the making of a counteroffer, by the lapse of the time stated in the offer or of a reasonable time when none is stated, by the death or disability of either party, or by a change of law that makes illegal a contract based on the particular offer.

When the offer is accepted, a contract arises. Only the offeree can accept an offer, and the acceptance must be of the offer exactly as made without any qualification or change. Ordinarily, the offeree may accept or reject as the offeree chooses.

The acceptance is any manifestation of intent to agree to the terms of the offer. Ordinarily, silence or failure to act does not constitute acceptance. The recipient of unordered goods and tickets may dispose of the goods or use the goods without such action constituting an acceptance. An acceptance does not exist until the words or conduct demonstrating assent to the offer is communicated to the offeror. Acceptance by mail takes effect at the time and place when and where the letter is mailed or the fax is transmitted.

In an auction sale, the auctioneer asking for bids makes an invitation to negotiate. A person making a bid is making an offer, and the acceptance of the highest bid by the auctioneer is an acceptance of that offer and gives

[32] *Marten v Staab*, 543 NW2d 436 (Neb 1996). Statutes regulate auctions and auctioneers in all states. For example, state of Maine law prohibits an auctioneer from conducting an auction without first having a written contract with the consignor of any property to be sold, including (1) whether the auction is with reserve or without reserve, (2) the commission rate, and (3) a description of all items to be sold. See *Street v Board of Licensing of Auctioneers*, 889 A2d 319 ([Me] 2006).

rise to a contract. When the auction sale is without reserve, the auctioneer must accept the highest bid. If the auction is not expressly without reserve, the auctioneer may refuse to accept any of the bids.

LEARNING OUTCOMES

After studying this chapter, you should be able to clearly explain:

A. REQUIREMENTS OF AN OFFER

LO.1 Decide whether an offer contains definite and certain terms

> See the legal impact of a party's statement that the contract "was going to be signed" in the *Hewitt* example starting on p. 261.

B. TERMINATION OF AN OFFER

LO.2 Explain the exceptions the law makes to the requirement of definiteness

> See the *Delphi* case on requirements contracts, p. 266.

LO.3 Explain all the ways an offer can be terminated

> See the discussion of revocation, counteroffer, rejection, lapse of time, death or disability of a party, or subsequent illegality, starting on p. 267.

C. ACCEPTANCE OF AN OFFER

LO.4 Explain what constitutes the acceptance of an offer

> See the *Sadeghi* example where acceptance of an offer created a binding contract, p. 270.

LO.5 Explain the implications of failing to read a clickwrap agreement

> See the *Feldman* case as an example of an enforceable clickwrap agreement containing notice and manifested assent, p. 271.

KEY TERMS

acceptance	firm offer	requirements contract
counteroffer	offer	
divisible contract	output contract	

QUESTIONS AND CASE PROBLEMS

1. Bernie and Phil's Great American Surplus store placed an ad in the *Sunday Times* stating, "Next Saturday at 8:00 A.M. sharp, 3 brand new mink coats worth $5,000 each will be sold for $500 each! First come, First served." Marsha Lufklin was first in line when the store opened and went directly to the coat department, but the coats identified in the ad were not available for sale. She identified herself to the manager and pointed out that she was first in line in conformity with the store's advertised offer and that she was ready to pay the $500 price set forth in the store's offer. The manager responded that a newspaper ad is just an invitation to negotiate and that the store decided to withdraw "the mink coat promotion." Review the text on unilateral contracts in Section 12(b) of Chapter 12. Decide.

2. Brown made an offer to purchase Overman's house on a standard printed form. Underneath Brown's signature was the statement: "ACCEPTANCE ON REVERSE SIDE." Overman did not sign the offer on the back but sent Brown a letter accepting the offer. Later, Brown refused to perform the contract, and Overman sued him for breach of contract. Brown claimed there was no contract because the offer had not been accepted in the manner specified by the offer. Decide. [*Overman v Brown*, 372 NW2d 102 (Neb)]

3. Katherine mailed Paul an offer with definite and certain terms and that was legal in all respects stating that it was good for 10 days. Two days later she sent Paul a letter by certified mail (time stamped by the Postal Service at 1:14 P.M.) stating that the original offer was revoked. That evening Paul e-mailed acceptance of the offer to Katherine. She immediately phoned him to tell him that she had revoked the offer that afternoon, and he would surely receive it in tomorrow's mail. Was the offer revoked by Katherine?

4. Nelson wanted to sell his home. Baker sent him a written offer to purchase the home. Nelson made some changes to Baker's offer and wrote him that he, Nelson, was accepting the offer as amended. Baker notified Nelson that he was dropping out of the transaction. Nelson sued Baker for breach of contract. Decide. What social forces and ethical values are involved? [*Nelson v Baker*, 776 SW2d 52 (Mo App)]

5. Lessack Auctioneers advertised an auction sale that was open to the public and was to be conducted with reserve. Gordon attended the auction and bid $100 for a work of art that was worth much more. No higher bid, however, was made. Lessack refused to sell the item for $100 and withdrew the item from the sale. Gordon claimed that because he was the highest bidder, Lessack was required to sell the item to him. Was he correct? *No*

6. Willis Music Co. advertised a television set at $22.50 in the Sunday newspaper. Ehrlich ordered a set, but the company refused to deliver it on the grounds that the price in the newspaper ad was a mistake. Ehrlich sued the company. Was it liable? Why or why not? [*Ehrlich v Willis Music Co.*, 113 NE2d 252 (Ohio App)]

7. When a movement was organized to build Charles City College, Hauser and others signed pledges to contribute to the college. At the time of signing, Hauser inquired what would happen if he should die or be unable to pay. The representative of the college stated that the pledge would then not be binding and that it was merely a statement of intent. The college failed financially, and Pappas was appointed receiver to collect and liquidate the assets of the college corporation. He sued Hauser for the amount due on his pledge. Hauser raised the defense that the pledge was not a binding contract. Decide. What ethical values are involved? [*Pappas v Hauser*, 197 NW2d 607 (Iowa)]

8. *A* signed a contract agreeing to sell land he owned but reserved the right to take the hay from the land until the following October. He gave the contract form to *B*, a broker. *C*, a prospective buyer, agreed to buy the land and signed the contract but crossed out the provision regarding the hay crop. Was there a binding contract between *A* and *C*? *No, crossing out was a counteroffer*

9. A. H. Zehmer discussed selling a farm to Lucy. After a 40-minute discussion of the first draft of a contract, Zehmer and his wife, Ida, signed a second draft stating: "We hereby agree to sell to W. O. Lucy the Ferguson farm complete for $50,000 title satisfactory to buyer." Lucy agreed to purchase the farm on these terms. Thereafter, the Zehmers refused to transfer title to Lucy and claimed they had made the contract for sale as a joke. Lucy brought an action to compel performance of the contract. The Zehmers claimed there was no contract. Were they correct? [*Lucy v Zehmer*, 84 SE2d 516 (Va App)]

10. Wheeler operated an automobile service station, which he leased from W. C. Cornitius, Inc. The lease ran for three years. Although the lease did not contain any provision for renewal, it was in fact renewed six times for successive three-year terms. The landlord refused to renew the lease for a seventh time. Wheeler brought suit to compel the landlord to accept his offer to renew the lease. Decide. [*William C. Cornitius, Inc. v Wheeler*, 556 P2d 666 (Or)]

11. Buster Cogdill, a real estate developer, made an offer to the Bank of Benton to have the bank provide construction financing for the development of an outlet mall, with funds to be provided at prime rate plus two percentage points. The bank's president Julio Plunkett thanked Buster

for the proposal and said, "I will start the paperwork." Did Cogdill have a contract with the Bank of Benton? [*Bank of Benton v Cogdill,* 454 NE2d 1120 (Ill App)]

12. Ackerley Media Group, Inc., claimed to have a three-season advertising Team Sponsorship Agreement (TSA) with Sharp Electronics Corporation to promote Sharp products at all Seattle Supersonics NBA basketball home games. Sharp contended that a valid agreement did not exist for the third season (2000–2001) because a material price term was missing, thus resulting in an unenforceable "agreement to agree." The terms of the TSA for the 2000–2001 third season called for a base payment of $144,200 and an annual increase "not to exceed 6% [and] to be mutually agreed upon by the parties." No "mutually agreed" increase was negotiated by the parties. Ackerley seeks payment for the base price of $144,200 only. Sharp contends that since no price was agreed upon for the season, the entire TSA is unenforceable, and it is not obligated to pay for the 2000–2001 season. Is Sharp correct? [*Ackerley Media Group, Inc. v Sharp Electronics Corp.,* 170 F Supp 2d 445 (SDNY)]

13. L. B. Foster invited Tie and Track Systems Inc. to submit price quotes on items to be used in a railroad expansion project. Tie and Track responded by e-mail on August 11, 2006, with prices for nine items of steel ties. The e-mail concluded, "The above prices are delivered/Terms of Payment—to be agreed/Delivery—to be agreed/We hope you are successful with your bid. If you require any additional information please call." Just three of the nine items listed in Tie and Track's price quote were "accepted" by the project. L. B. Foster demanded that Tie and

Track provide the items at the price listed in the quote. Tie and Track refused. L. B. Foster sued for breach of contract. Did the August 11 e-mail constitute an offer, acceptance of which could bind the supplier to a contract? If so, was there a valid acceptance? [*L. B. Foster v Tie and Track Systems, Inc.,* 2009 WL 900993 (ND Ill)]

14. On August 15, 2003, Wilbert Heikkila signed an agreement with Kangas Realty to sell eight parcels of Heikkila's property. On September 8, 2003, David McLaughlin met with a Kangas agent who drafted McLaughlin's offer to purchase three of the parcels. McLaughlin signed the offer and gave the agent checks for each parcel. On September 9 and 10, 2003, the agent for Heikkila prepared three printed purchase agreements, one for each parcel. On September 14, 2003, David's wife, Joanne McLaughlin, met with the agent and signed the agreements. On September 16, 2003, Heikkila met with his real estate agent. Writing on the printed agreements, Heikkila changed the price of one parcel from $145,000 to $150,000, the price of another parcel from $32,000 to $45,000, and the price of the third parcel from $175,000 to $179,000. Neither of the McLaughlins signed an acceptance of Heikkila's changes to the printed agreements before Heikkila withdrew his offer to sell. The McLaughlins learned that Heikkila had withdrawn his offer on January 1, 2004, when the real estate agent returned the checks to them. Totally shocked at Heikkila's conduct, the McLaughlins brought action to compel specific performance of the purchase agreement signed by Joanne McLaughlin on their behalf. Decide. [*McLaughlin v Heikkila,* 697 NW2d 231 (Minn App)]

CPA QUESTIONS

1. Able Sofa, Inc., sent Noll a letter offering to sell Noll a custom-made sofa for $5,000. Noll immediately sent a telegram to Able purporting to accept the offer. However, the telegraph company erroneously delivered the telegram to Abel Soda, Inc. Three days later, Able mailed a

letter of revocation to Noll, which was received by Noll. Able refused to sell Noll the sofa. Noll sued Able for breach of contract. Able:

a. Would have been liable under the deposited acceptance rule only if Noll had accepted by mail

b. Will avoid liability since it revoked its offer prior to receiving Noll's acceptance

c. Will be liable for breach of contract

d. Will avoid liability due to the telegraph company's error (Law, #2, 9911)

2. On September 27, Summers sent Fox a letter offering to sell Fox a vacation home for $150,000. On October 2, Fox replied by mail agreeing to buy the home for $145,000. Summers did not reply to Fox. Do Fox and Summers have a binding contract?

a. No, because Fox failed to sign and return Summers's letter

b. No, because Fox's letter was a counteroffer

c. Yes, because Summers's offer was validly accepted

d. Yes, because Summers's silence is an implied acceptance of Fox's letter (Law, #2, 0462)

3. On June 15, Peters orally offered to sell a used lawn mower to Mason for $125. Peters specified that Mason had until June 20 to accept the offer. On June 16, Peters received an offer to purchase the lawn mower for $150 from Bronson, Mason's neighbor. Peters accepted Bronson's offer. On June 17, Mason saw Bronson using the lawn mower and was told the mower had been sold to Bronson. Mason immediately wrote to Peters to accept the June 15 offer. Which of the following statements is correct?

a. Mason's acceptance would be effective when received by Peters.

b. Mason's acceptance would be effective when mailed.

c. Peters's offer had been revoked and Mason's acceptance was ineffective.

d. Peters was obligated to keep the June 15 offer open until June 20. (Law, #13, 3095)

Chapter 14

CAPACITY AND GENUINE ASSENT

Acontract is a binding agreement. This agreement must be made between parties who have the capacity to do so. They must also truly agree so that all parties have really consented to the contract. This chapter explores the elements of contractual capacity of the parties and the genuineness of their assent.

A. CONTRACTUAL CAPACITY

Some persons lack contractual capacity, a lack that embraces both those who have a status incapacity, such as minors, and those who have a factual incapacity, such as persons who are insane.

1. Contractual Capacity Defined

Contractual capacity is the ability to understand that a contract is being made and to understand its general meaning. However, the fact that a person does not understand the full legal meaning of a contract does not mean that contractual capacity is lacking. Everyone is presumed to have capacity unless it is proven that capacity is lacking or there is status incapacity.[1] **For Example,** Jacqueline, aged 22, entered into a contract with Sunrise Storage Co. but later claimed it was not binding because she did not understand several clauses in the printed contract. The contract was binding. No evidence supported her claim that she lacked capacity to contract or to understand its subject. Contractual capacity can exist even though a party does not understand every provision of the contract.

(A) STATUS INCAPACITY. Over the centuries, the law has declared that some classes of persons lack contractual capacity. The purpose is to protect these classes by giving them the power to get out of unwise contracts. Of these classes, the most important today is the class identified as minors.

Until recent times, some other classes were held to lack contractual capacity in order to discriminate against them. Examples are married women and aliens. Still other classes, such as persons convicted of and sentenced for a felony, were held to lack contractual capacity in order to punish them. Today, these discriminatory and punitive incapacities have largely disappeared. Married women have the same contractual capacity as unmarried persons.[2]

By virtue of international treaties, the discrimination against aliens has been removed.

(B) FACTUAL INCAPACITY. A *factual incapacity* contrasts with incapacity imposed because of the class or group to which a person belongs. A factual incapacity may exist when, because of a mental condition caused by medication, drugs, alcohol, illness, or age, a person does not understand that a contract is being made or understand its general nature. However, mere mental weakness does not incapacitate a person from contracting. It is sufficient if the individual has enough mental capacity to understand, to a reasonable extent, the nature and effect of what he is doing.[3]

2. Minors

Minors may make contracts.[4] To protect them, however, the law has always treated minors as a class lacking contractual capacity.

(A) WHO IS A MINOR? At common law, any person, male or female, under 21 years of age was a minor. At common law, minority ended the day before the twenty-first birthday. The "day before the birthday" rule is still followed, but the age of majority has been reduced from 21 years to 18 years.

CPA (B) MINOR'S POWER TO AVOID CONTRACTS. With exceptions that will be noted later, a contract made by a minor is voidable at the election of the minor. The minor may affirm or ratify the contract on attaining majority by performing the contract, by expressly approving the contract, or by allowing a reasonable time to lapse without avoiding the contract.

---

[1] *In re Adoption of Smith*, 578 So2d 988 (La App 1991).
[2] A few states have a limitation that a married woman cannot make a binding contract to pay the debt of her husband if he fails to.
[3] *Fisher v Schefers*, 656 NW2d 591 (Minn App 2003).
[4] *Buffington v State Automobile Mut. Ins. Co.*, 384 SE2d 873 (Ga App 1989).

CPA   *(1) What Constitutes Avoidance?*

A minor may avoid or *disaffirm* a contract by any expression of an intention to repudiate the contract. Any act inconsistent with the continuing validity of the contract is also an avoidance.

CPA   *(2) Time for Avoidance.*

A minor can disaffirm a contract only during minority and for a reasonable time after attaining majority. After the lapse of a reasonable time, the contract is deemed ratified and cannot be avoided by the minor.

CPA   *(3) Minor's Misrepresentation of Age.*

Generally, the fact that the minor has misrepresented his or her age does not affect the minor's power to disaffirm the contract. Some states hold that such fraud of a minor bars contract avoidance. Some states permit the minor to disaffirm the contract in such a case but require the minor to pay for any damage to the property received under the contract.

In any case, the other party to the contract may disaffirm it because of the minor's fraud.

CPA   (c) Restitution by Minor after Avoidance.

When a minor disaffirms a contract, the question arises as to what the minor must return to the other contracting party.

(1) Original Consideration Intact.

When a minor still has what was received from the other party, the minor, on avoiding the contract, must return it to the other party or offer to do so. That is, the minor must put things back to the original position or, as it is called, restore the **status quo ante**.

(2) Original Consideration Damaged or Destroyed.

What happens if the minor cannot return what has been received because it has been spent, used, damaged, or destroyed? The minor's right to disaffirm the contract is not affected. The minor can still disaffirm the contract and is required to return only what remains. The fact that nothing remains or that what remains is damaged does not bar the right to disaffirm

the contract. In states that follow the common law rule, minors can thus refuse to pay for what has been received under a contract or can get back what had been paid or given even though they do not have anything to return or return property in a damaged condition. There is, however, a trend to limit this rule.

(d) Recovery of Property by Minor on Avoidance.

When a minor disaffirms a contract, the other contracting party must return the money received. Any property received from the minor must also be returned. If the property has been sold to a third person who did not know of the original seller's minority, the minor cannot get the property back. In such cases, however, the minor is entitled to recover the property's monetary value or the money received by the other contracting party.

CPA   (e) Contracts for Necessaries. A minor can disaffirm a contract for necessaries but must pay the reasonable value for furnished necessaries.

(1) What Constitutes Necessaries?

Originally, **necessaries** were limited to those things absolutely necessary for the sustenance and shelter of the minor. Thus limited, the term would extend only to food, clothing, and lodging. In the course of time, the rule was relaxed to extend generally to things relating to the health, education, and comfort of the minor. Thus, the rental of a house used by a married minor is a necessary.

(2) Liability of Parent or Guardian.

When a third person supplies the parents or guardian of a minor with goods or services that the minor needs, the minor is not liable for these necessaries because the third person's contract is with the parent or guardian, not with the minor.

When necessary medical care is provided a minor, a parent is liable at common law for the medical expenses provided the minor child. However, at common law, the child can be held contractually liable for her necessary medical expenses when the parent is unable or unwilling to pay. In the *Schmidt* case, the court dealt with the public policy considerations behind this rule.

Schmidt v Prince George's Hospital, 784 A 2d 1112 (Md 2001)

The Concussion and Legal Repercussion

On March 7, 1997, 16-year-old Michelle Schmidt was involved in a two-vehicle auto collision. She was transported to the Shock Trauma Unit at Prince George's Hospital, where she was initially admitted as "Jane Doe," without an emergency contact person or telephone number, because she was unconscious at the time of arrival. Although the hospital later was able to identify her name and address, it was only able to determine that her father was "Mr. Schmidt," and it obtained a telephone number for him. Due to the severity of her injuries sustained in the collision, the hospital provided necessary emergency medical care for a brain concussion and an open scalp wound. As of her discharge on March 8, 1997, she had incurred hospital expenses in the amount of $1,756.24. Ms. Schmidt was insured with personal injury protection (PIP) benefits through her father's insurance company, Erie Insurance Group. Erie issued a check in the amount of $1,756.24 to "Lewis A. Schmidt for Minor, Michelle Schmidt" in reference to "Prince George's Hospital Center, Service Date 03-07-1997 to 03-08-1997." The check was negotiated, but the funds were not used to pay the hospital; rather, the funds apparently were used to purchase a replacement automobile for Ms. Schmidt. After Ms. Schmidt attained her eighteenth birthday and failed to pay the hospital, it brought suit against her. From a judgement for the hospital, she appealed to the seven justice Court of Appeals.

JUDICIAL OPINION

HARRELL, J. . . .

A.

In the absence of a statute to the contrary, the prevailing modern rule is that a minor's contracts are voidable; nevertheless, it also is well established that a minor may be liable for the value of necessaries furnished to him or her. This doctrine, eponymously referred to as the doctrine of necessaries, is well recognized in Maryland law. In *Monumental Building Association v Herman*, 33 Md. 128, (1870), our venerable predecessor explained somewhat the breadth and application of this doctrine.

By the common law, persons, under the age of twenty-one years* are not bound by their contracts, *except for necessaries,* nor can they do any act, to the injury of their property, which they may not avoid, when arrived at full age.

---

* Effective 1 July 1973, the age of majority in Maryland was reduced from 21 to 18 years of age. Maryland Code (1957, 1998 Repl. Vol.), Art. 1 § 24.

. . . Infants have this indulgence from their supposed want of judgment in their transactions with others, and the law takes this care of them to prevent them from being imposed upon, or overreached by persons of more years and experience.

They are allowed to contract for their benefit with power in most cases, to recede from their contract when it may prove prejudicial to them, *but in their contract for necessaries, such as board, apparel, medical aid, teaching and instruction, and other necessaries, they are absolutely bound, and may be sued and charged in execution;* but it must appear that the things were absolutely necessary, and suitable to their circumstances, and whoever trusts them does so at his peril, or as it is said, deals with them at arms' length.

Their power, thus to contract for necessaries, is for their benefit, because the procurement of these things is essential to their existence, and if they were not permitted so to bind themselves they might suffer. *Monumental*, 33 Md. at 131–32 (emphasis added). . . .

The rationales underlying [named precedent cases] recognize that public policy and justice demand that an injured minor have the right to recover incurred medical expenses from a third-party tortfeasor, where the child's parents are unable or unwilling to pay for those expenses, *because the medical provider may sue to recover them,* either during the child's minority or within the statute of limitations after the child has reached the age of majority. By parity of reasoning, it would seem that such a child, upon attaining adulthood, may be liable in contract to pay for medical necessaries provided to him or her while a minor, if the parents were unable or unwilling to pay for such necessaries. Before we may reach such a holding, however, it seems prudent to examine how, if at all, our sister states regard the unwillingness prong of this aspect of the doctrine of necessaries.

B.

There appears to be no case elsewhere that supplies a user-friendly, all-purpose definition or scope of the term "unwilling to pay" in connection with the doctrine of necessaries. The vast majority of these cases share two common traits; they are bereft of detailed or substantive analysis of the "unwillingness" standard, and the varying outcomes are largely fact-driven. . . .

Some states appear to hold that, in order to find a parent "unwilling," thus making a child liable for his or her necessaries, a court should require hard and fast proof of default by the parents. Those states note that in order to meet the requirement of "unwilling," it must be shown that a parent was billed and/or sued and still refused to pay.

Continued

We shall not subscribe to that requirement as an essential prerequisite to a finding of unwillingness.

There are a significant number of states that interpret their version of the doctrine of necessaries as placing liability on a child *only* when his or her parents are financially unable to pay. . . .

. . . Overweighing the arguable unfairness to the minor in the balancing, at least in the present case, is the consideration of not placing hospitals and other emergency health care providers in a situation where apparently financially-able individuals may avoid paying for necessary medical treatment through a contrivance similar to that demonstrated on the record of this case.

. . . The doctrine of necessaries states that a minor may be held liable for the necessaries, including medical necessaries, which he or she is afforded when his or her parents are either unable or unwilling to pay. Consistent with this principle, Respondent, on the present facts, could have: (a) sued Petitioner, while she was still a minor, and her father; or, (b), as was done in the present case, sued Petitioner upon her reaching the age of majority.

. . . The father's refusal to apply the insurance proceeds to the debt owed Respondent—the existence of which he was well aware of as it was the facial premise for which he and Petitioner supplied to Erie in the first place—is a clear indication of his unwillingness to pay for Petitioner's medical expenses at a time fairly contemporaneous with the provision of the medical services, i.e., within 60 days. We agree with the Circuit Court, which found that, as an adult, Petitioner is liable for the medical treatment expenses which she incurred while a minor. We find no error in the Circuit Court's conclusions that Petitioner could be held liable for those medical expenditures provided for her benefit under the doctrine of necessaries, which trumps her defense that she was under the disability of minority when she entered into the implied promise to pay Respondent for the needed medical treatment. Lastly, we agree that the record supports that Petitioner's father was unwilling to pay for his then minor daughter's medical necessaries, which, in turn, left Petitioner primarily liable for the debt to Respondent.**

[Judgment affirmed]

DISSENTING OPINION

RAKER, J., dissenting, joined by BELL, C.J., and ELDRIDGE, J.:

The majority finds petitioner liable to respondent because her father was *unwilling* to pay for petitioner's medical expenses, not because her father was *unable* to pay. . . . The majority believes that the father's failure to use insurance proceeds to pay the hospital for his daughter's medical bills is a "clear indication" of his unwillingness to pay for petitioner's medical expenses. There is little case law in this State, or any other state, to help us decide when a parent is unwilling to pay for his or her child's necessary medical costs. What little law there is, however, suggests that where a child is supported by his or her parents, the parents' failure or default on single necessary expense does not usually render the child liable for that expense.

QUESTIONS

1. What is the historical policy basis for the modern rule that minors' contracts are voidable; and what is the basis for the exception that minors may be liable for necessaries?

2. In layperson's terms, explain the public policy utilized to support the court's decision to hold Ms. Schmidt liable for the unpaid emergency care provided to her while she was a minor?

3. What is the dissent's view of the case?

** On this record, Petitioner may have been able to implead her father in this litigation, whose parental duties during Petitioner's minority included paying for her necessaries, such as the medical expenses in issue. If Petitioner's father was able, but merely unwilling, to pay for her medical necessaries, it would not violate public policy for Petitioner, as an adult, to sue her parent for failure to provide for her necessaries . . .

CPA (F) Ratification of Former Minor's Voidable Contract. A former minor cannot disaffirm a contract that has been ratified after reaching majority.[5]

CPA *(1) What Constitutes Ratification?*
Ratification consists of any words or conduct of the former minor manifesting an intent to be bound by the terms of a contract made while a minor.

CPA *(2) Form of Ratification.*
Generally, no special form is required for ratification of a minor's voidable contract, although in some states a written ratification or declaration of intention is required.

CPA *(3) Time for Ratification.*
A person can disaffirm a contract any time during minority and for a reasonable time after that but, of

---

[5] *Fletcher v Marshall*, 632 NE2d 1105 (Ill App 1994).

necessity, can ratify a contract only after attaining majority. The minor must have attained majority, or the ratification would itself be regarded as voidable.

(G) Contracts That Minors Cannot Avoid. Statutes in many states deprive a minor of the right to avoid an educational loan;[6] a contract for medical care; a contract made while running a business; a contract approved by a court; a contract made in performance of a legal duty; and a contract relating to bank accounts, insurance policies, or corporate stock.

(H) Liability of Third Person for a Minor's Contract. The question arises as to whether parents are bound by the contract of their minor child. The question of whether a person cosigning a minor's contract is bound if the contract is avoided also arises.

(1) Liability of Parent.

Ordinarily, a parent is not liable on a contract made by a minor child. The parent may be liable, however, if the child is acting as the agent of the parent in making the contract. Also, the parent is liable to a seller for the reasonable value of necessaries supplied by the seller to the child if the parent had deserted the child.

(2) Liability of Cosigner.

When the minor makes a contract, another person, such as a parent or a friend, may sign along with the minor to make the contract more acceptable to the third person.

With respect to the other contracting party, the cosigner is bound independently of the minor. Consequently, if the minor disaffirms the contract, the cosigner remains bound by it. When the debt to the creditor is actually paid, the obligation of the cosigner is discharged.

If the minor disaffirms a sales contract but does not return the goods, the cosigner remains liable for the purchase price.

3. Mentally Incompetent Persons

A person with a mental disorder may be so disabled as to lack capacity to make a contract. If the person is so mentally incompetent as to be unable to understand that a contract is being made or the general nature of the contract, the person lacks contractual capacity.

(A) Effect of Incompetency. An incompetent person may ordinarily avoid a contract in the same manner as a minor. Upon the removal of the disability (that is, upon becoming competent), the formerly incompetent person can either ratify or disaffirm the contract.

A mentally incompetent person or his estate is liable for the reasonable value of all necessaries furnished that individual.

A current trend in the law is to treat an incompetent person's contract as binding when its terms and the surrounding circumstances are reasonable and the person is unable to restore the other contracting party to the status quo ante.

(B) Appointment of Guardian. If a court appoints a guardian for the incompetent person, a contract made by that person before the appointment may be ratified or, in some cases, disaffirmed by the guardian. If the incompetent person makes a contract after a guardian has been appointed, the contract is void and not merely voidable.

4. Intoxicated Persons

The capacity of a party to contract and the validity of the contract are not affected by the party's being impaired by alcohol at the time of making the contract so long as the party knew that a contract was being made.

If the degree of intoxication is such that a person does not know that a contract is being made, the contract is voidable by that person. The situation is the same as though the person were insane at the time and did not know what he or she was doing. On becoming sober, the individual may avoid or rescind the contract. However, an unreasonable delay in taking steps to set aside a known contract entered into while intoxicated may bar the intoxicated person from asserting this right.[7]

For Example, Edward made a contract while intoxicated. When he sobered up, he immediately disaffirmed the contract for lack of capacity as the result

---

[6] A Model Student Capacity to Borrow Act makes educational loans binding on minors in Arizona, Mississippi, New Mexico, North Dakota, Oklahoma, and Washington. This act was reclassified from a uniform act to a model act by the Commissioners on Uniform State Law, indicating that uniformity was viewed as unimportant and that the matter was primarily local in character.

[7] *Diedrich v Diedrich*, 424 NW2d 580 (Minn App 1988).

ethics & the law

Globe Life Insurance Company undertook a new sales program that targets neighborhoods in Los Angeles where drive-by shootings were a nightly occurrence. In two such shootings, children were killed as they sat in their living rooms.

Globe salespeople were instructed to "hit" the houses surrounding those where children were victims. They were also told to contact the parents of those children to sell policies for their other children.

Tom Raskin, an experienced Globe salesman, read of a drive-by shooting at Nancy Leonard's home, in which Leonard's five-year-old son was killed. The *Los Angeles Times* reported that Leonard was a single parent with four other children.

Raskin traveled to Leonard's home and described the benefits of a Globe policy for her other children. He offered her the $10,000 term life policy for each of the children for a total cost of $21 per month. Leonard was in the process of making funeral arrangements for her son, and Raskin noted, "See how much it costs for a funeral."

Leonard had been given several tranquilizers the night before by a physician at the hospital's emergency room. The physician had also given her 15 more tranquilizers to help her through the following week. She had taken one additional tranquilizer an hour before Raskin arrived, using a Coors Lite beer to take the pill.

Leonard signed the contract for the policy. After her son's funeral, she received the first month's bill for it and exclaimed, "I didn't buy any life insurance! Where did this come from?"

After you discuss Leonard's legal standing, discuss the ethical issues involved in Globe's sales program. Discuss the legal issues involved in Raskin's decision to target Leonard the day after her son's death.

---

of his intoxication. The other contracting party claimed that voluntary intoxication cannot void a contract, but Edward could disaffirm the contract because he lacked the legal capacity to enter a contract.

The courts treat impairment caused by the use of drugs the same as impairment caused by the excessive use of alcohol.

CPA B. Mistake

The validity of a contract may be affected by the fact that one or both of the parties made a mistake. In some cases, the mistake may be caused by the misconduct of one of the parties.

5. Unilateral Mistake

A *unilateral mistake*—that is, a mistake by only one of the parties—as to a fact does not affect the contract when the mistake is unknown to the other contracting party.[8] When a contract is made on the basis of a quoted price, the validity of the contract is not affected by the fact that the party furnishing the quotation made a mathematical mistake in computing the price if there was no reason for the other party to recognize that there had been a mistake.[9] The party making the mistake may avoid the contract if the other contracting party knew or should have known of the mistake.

6. Mutual Mistake

When both parties enter into a contract under a mutually mistaken understanding concerning a basic assumption of fact or law on which the contract is made, the contract is voidable by the adversely affected party if the mistake has a material effect on the agreed exchange.[10]

A contract based on *a mutual mistake in judgment* is not voidable by the adversely affected party.

[8] *Truck South Inc. v Patel,* 528 SE2d 424 (SC 2000).
[9] *Procan Construction Co. v Oceanside Development Corp.,* 539 NYS2d 437 (App Div 2d 1989).
[10] See *Browning v Howerton,* 966 P2d 367 (Wash App 1998).

FIGURE 14-1 | *Avoidance of Contract*

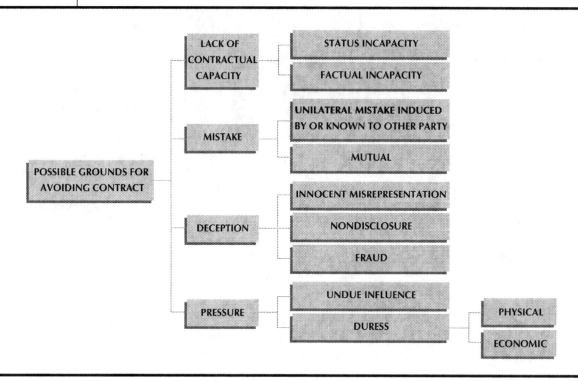

For Example, if both parties believe that a colt is not fast enough to develop into a competitive race horse and effect a sale accordingly, when the animal later develops into the winner of the Preakness as a three-year-old, the seller cannot rescind the contract based on mutual mistake because the mutual mistake was a mistake in judgment. In contrast, when two parties to a contract believe a cow to be barren at the time they contract for its sale, but before delivery of the animal to the buyer, it is discovered that the assumption was mistaken, such is a mutual mistake of fact making the contract void.[11]

7. Mistake in the Transcription or Printing of the Contract: Reformation

In some instances, the parties make an oral agreement, and in the process of committing it to writing or printing it from a manuscript, a phrase, term, or segment is inadvertently left out of the final, signed document. The aggrieved party may petition the court to **reform** the contract to reflect the actual agreement of the parties. However, the burden of proof is heightened to clear and convincing evidence that such a mistake was made. **For Example,** the Printers International Union reached agreement for a new three-year contract with a large regional printing company. As was their practice, the union negotiators then met with Sullivan Brothers Printers, Inc., a small specialty shop employing 10 union printers, and Sullivan Brothers and the union agreed to follow the contractual pattern set by the union and the large printer. That is, Sullivan Brothers agreed to give its workers all of the benefits negotiated for the employees of the large printing company. When the contract was typed, a new benefit of 75 percent employer-paid coverage for a dental plan was inadvertently omitted from the final contract that the parties signed. The

---

[11] See *Sherwood v Walker*, 66 Mich 568 (1887).

mistake was not discovered until later, and Sullivan Brothers, Inc., is now reluctant to assume the additional expense. Based on the clear and convincing evidence of a practice of following the contractual pattern set by the large printer and Sullivan's assent to again follow the pattern, a court or arbitrator will reform the contract.

C. Deception

One of the parties may have been misled by a fraudulent statement. In such situations, there is no true or genuine assent to the contract, and it is voidable at the innocent party's option.

8. Intentional Misrepresentation

Fraud is a generic term embracing all multifarious means that human ingenuity can devise and that are resorted to by one individual to get advantage over another. It is classified in the law as a *tort*. However, where a party is induced into making a contract by a material misrepresentation of fact, this form of fraudulent activity adversely affects the genuineness of the assent of the innocent party, and this type of fraud is the focus of our discussion in the chapters on contracts.

9. Fraud

Fraud is the making of a material misrepresentation (or false statement) of fact with (1) knowledge of its falsity or reckless indifference to its truth, (2) the intent that the listener rely on it, (3) the result that the listener does so rely, and (4) the consequence that the listener is harmed.[12]

The *Tschira* case deals with the tort of fraudulent misrepresentation and is a clear example of how fraud impacts on the genuineness of the contractual assent of the affected party. Note that the Tschiras did not seek to *rescind* (cancel) the two contracts they entered as a result of the fraudulent misrepresentations, which ordinarily is the first remedy sought in fraud cases, because they canceled the management agreement upon discovery of the fraud, and they later sold at a loss the property that was the subject of the second contract. The remedies they sought were the actual damages they suffered as a result of the fraud and punitive damages to punish and make an example of the perpetrators of the wrongdoings.

Tschira v Willingham, 135 F3d 1077 (6th Cir 1998)

Watch Out! Some People Have a Lot of Nerve

German citizens Klaus and Gerda Tschira brought suit against Corim, Inc., a U.S. real estate investment firm and its president Ben Willingham Jr. for fraudulent misrepresentation during a real estate transaction between the Tschiras and Corim. From a judgment for the Tschiras, Corim and Willingham appealed.

JUDICIAL OPINION

GIBSON, J. . . . In 1988, Klaus Tschira benefitted financially when the company he helped to create, SAP AG ("SAP"), went public in Germany. In search of investment opportunities, Klaus learned through a German real estate broker, Claus Schenk, that Appellants were soliciting investors for commercial property in the southeastern United States. Intrigued by this information. Klaus, who was joined by other SAP founders, attended a meeting in Walldorf, Germany at which Willingham, who speaks fluent German, made a presentation. According to trial testimony, Willingham explained that Corim proposed to obtain buildings for purchase by investors at a "fair market price"; Corim then intended to enter into management contracts with the new owners. By the terms of the management contracts, Corim and Willingham would lease the buildings from the investors and, in return, would then pay the investors a contractually established rent amounting to approximately eight percent annually of the purchase price of the building. Klaus testified that he

---

[12] *Maack v Resource Design & Construction, Inc.*, 875 P2d 570 (Utah 1994); *Bortz v Noon*, 729 A2d 555 (Pa 1999).

Continued

inquired as to how Willingham and Corim would earn a profit, and Willingham responded that Corim would receive revenue via the difference between the rents Corim would charge for its subleases and the rent Corim itself paid the investors.

The Tschiras found the investment attractive and initially agreed to buy four buildings in various southern cities and lease those properties back to Corim. The Tschiras did not procure independent American counsel for these transactions, as they claim to have regarded Willingham as their trusted agent. . . .

In late 1990, Schenk brought Klaus a Corim brochure about One Church Street, a Nashville, Tennessee property. The brochure advertised One Church Street as a five story commercial building erected in 1872, available for $1,985,000. The pamphlet described the property as having "a special architectural character" and said the building had been "recently renovated with substantial effort and expense." J.A. at 358. Corim guaranteed rent payments of $158,000 the first two years of the lease back, $165,000 the third and fourth years, and $171,000 the fifth year. The Tschiras expressed interest, and soon thereafter they received the Letter from Willingham. The document guaranteed that the building would be "insured sufficiently, so that it can be restored from the proceeds of the insurance in the event of destruction or damage." J.A. at 182. The final paragraph of the letter states that "[t]he powers of attorney given to us will only be used according to the forthcoming agreement." *Id.* Willingham had signed the copy of the Letter he mailed to the Tschiras. After reviewing the available materials, the Tschiras decided to invest in the property. They did not, however, secure independent counsel for the deal, visit One Church Street prior to the purchase, or obtain an appraisal from any source other than Corim.

The Tschiras and Corim subsequently entered into a Purchase Agreement for the Nashville property. They simultaneously executed a Management Agreement for the building. . . .

Several years later, the Tschiras discovered other details surrounding the sale of the Nashville building. Namely, they learned that two closings occurred on December 14, 1990. In the first, One Church Street, Inc., shell corporation owned by Corim and Willingham, purchased the property from its owner, First Atlanta Services Corporation. The selling price in this deal was $774,000. In the second transaction, One Church Street, Inc. sold the building to the Tschiras for $1,985,000. Schenk, the German national who referred the Tschiras to Corim, received a $79,400 commission from Corim for his part in the sale. Willingham admitted at trial that the Tschiras were never advised that the shell company purchased the property and then resold it for an instant profit of $1,211,000. When the Tschiras became aware of these facts

in the Spring of 1992, they canceled the Management Agreement with Corim and brought the instant lawsuit. In 1995, the Tschiras sold One Church Street for $665,000.

In their Complaint, the Tschiras claimed that Corim and Willingham. . . committed the tort of intentional misrepresentation. Two key pieces of evidence at trial were the title and liability insurance policies issued for One Church Street. The title insurance policy Willingham forwarded to the Tschiras indicated that the Ticor Title Insurance Company had provided protection up to $1,985,000. In actuality, Lisa Wilson, the local branch manager of Ticor, testified that the policy the company extended for the property was for only $774,000. Evidence also suggested that the liability insurance policy the Tschiras received, which purported to originate from Palmer Cay/Carswell and indicated coverage in the amount of $1,985,000, only provided protection up to $774,000. . . .

The jury awarded $1,420,000 in compensatory damages against Corim and Willingham, as well as $1,000,000 in punitive damages against Corim and $750,000 in punitive damages against Willingham. . . .

To establish a cause of action for fraudulent misrepresentation, a plaintiff must prove: (1) an intentional misrepresentation, (2) knowledge of the representation's falsity, (3) the plaintiff reasonably relied on the misrepresentation and suffered damages, and (4) the misrepresentation relates to an existing or past fact. See *Hill v John Banks Buick, Inc.*, 875 S.W.2d 667, 670 (Tenn.Ct.App.1993). The evidence presented at trial was sufficient to uphold the jury's finding of fraudulent misrepresentation. Willingham promised the Tschiras a fair market price for the property they were buying, as well as adequate title and property insurance to cover any losses. The evidence was sufficient to establish that, at the time Willingham promised this to the Tschiras, he knew the property's value was closer to $774,000, which is the price Corim paid for the property. The jury could have reasonably found that Willingham had knowledge of the false title and property insurance policies which only covered the property up to $774,000, while the Tschiras believed the property was covered up to $1,985,000—the price they paid for the property.

Appellants argue that the representations were not material because they provided a "guaranteed" return on the Tschiras' investment through the rental income. However, the jury could have reasonably found otherwise. The Tschiras believed they were paying "fair market price" for the purchase of the property, *in addition to* receiving a guaranteed return on their investment. The Tschiras believed, and the jury could have reasonably concluded, that the Tschiras actually paid $1,211,000 over the fair market price of the property and therefore lost that amount on their investment at the time of purchase. Finally, we conclude that the evidence was sufficient

Continued

to support the jury's determination that the Tschiras reasonably relied on the representations and suffered damages as a result of that reliance. The Tschiras believed, based on the letter of November 26, 1990, that Willingham was their trusted agent and would not sell them property for above the "fair market value." As a result of that belief, the Tschiras paid well over the "fair market price" for the property, thereby losing a great deal of money on the "investment." . . .

For the reasons set forth in this opinion, we affirm the district court's judgment in all respects.

[Judgment affirmed]

QUESTIONS

1. Identify the material misrepresentations of fact evident in this case.

2. What was the measure of damages received by the Tschiras?

3. Assess Corim, Inc., and Willingham's argument on appeal that the representations made were not material because they provided a "guaranteed" return on the Tschiras' investment through rental income.

To prove fraud, there must be a material misrepresentation of fact. Such a misrepresentation is one that is likely to induce a reasonable person to assent to a contract. **For Example,** Traci Hanson-Suminski purchased a used Honda Civic from Arlington Acura for $10,899. On a test drive with salesperson Mike Dobin, Traci noticed a vibration in the steering wheel and asked if the car had been in an accident. Dobin said, "No, it's fine." The dealer put new tires on the car and Traci bought it. Traci testified that she would not have purchased the car if she had known it had been in an accident. Eight months later when she sought to trade the car for another car, she was shown a Carfax Vehicle History Report which indicated the car had been in an accident. The dealer testified that all its sales associates are trained to respond to questions about vehicle history with "I don't know." It asserted that Dobin's statement was mere puffery. The court found that Dobin's statement was a material misrepresentation of the car's history, inducing the plaintiff to purchase the car. It rejected outright the dealer's assertion of puffery, which it defined as meaningless superlatives that no reasonable person would take seriously.[13]

(A) STATEMENT OF OPINION OR VALUE. Ordinarily, matters of opinion of value or opinions about future events are not regarded as fraudulent. Thus, statements that a building was "very good," it "required only normal maintenance," and the "deal was

excellent" were merely matters of opinion. Therefore, a court considered the sophistication and expertise of the parties and the commercial setting of the transaction and enforced the contract "as is." The theory is that the person hearing the statement recognizes or should recognize that it is merely the speaker's personal opinion, not a statement of fact. A statement that is mere sales talk cannot be the basis of fraud liability. **For Example,** CEO Bernard Ellis sent a memo to shareholders of his Internet-related services business some four days before the expiration of a lockup period during which these shareholders had agreed not to sell their stock. In the memo, he urged shareholders not to sell their stock on the release date because in the event of a massive sell-off "our stock could plummet." He also stated, "I think our share price will start to stabilize and then rise as our company's strong performance continues." Based on Ellis's "strong performance" statement, a major corporate shareholder did not sell. The price of the stock fell from $40 a share to 29 cents a share over the subsequent nine-month period. The shareholder sued Ellis for fraud, seeking $27 million in damages. The court held that the first half of the sentence in question was framed as a mere opinion as to future events and thus was nonactionable; and as to the characterization of the company's performance as "strong," such a self-congratulatory comment constituted mere puffery on which no reasonable investor would rely.[14]

---

[13] *Hanson-Suminski v. Rohrman Midwest Motors Inc.*, 858 NE2d 194 (Ill App 2008).
[14] *Next Century Communications v Ellis*, 318 F3d 1023 (11th Cir 2003).

A statement of opinion may be fraudulent when the speaker knows of past or present facts that make the opinion false. **For Example,** Biff Williams, the sales manager of Abrasives International (AI), sold an exclusive dealership selling AI products to Fred Farkas for $100,000 down and a 3 percent royalty on all gross proceeds. Williams told Farkas, "You have the potential to earn $300,000 to $400,000 a year in this territory." He later added, "We have four dealerships making that kind of money today." Farkas was thus persuaded by the business potential of the territory and executed the purchase contract. He later found out AI had a total of just four distributorships at that time, and the actual earnings of the highest producer was $43,000. Assertions of opinions about the future profit potential alone may not amount to fraud, but the assertion of present fact—that four dealerships were presently earning $300,000 to $400,000 a year—was a material misstatement of fact that made the forecast sales potential for Farkas's territory a material misstatement of fact as well. Because there were reliance and damages, Farkas can rescind the contract based on fraud and recover all damages resulting from it.[15]

(B) RELIANCE ON STATEMENT. A fraudulent statement made by one party has no importance unless the other party relies on the statement's truth. **For Example,** after making thorough tests of Nagel Company's pump, Allstate Services Company ordered 100 pumps. It later sued Nagel on the ground that advertising statements made about the pumps were false. Allstate Services cannot impose fraud liability on Nagel for the advertisements, even if they were false, because it had not relied on them in making the purchase but had acted on the basis of its own tests.

If the alleged victim of the fraud knew that the statements were false because the truth was commonly known, the victim cannot rely on the false statements. When the statements of a seller are so "indefinite and extravagant" that reasonable persons would not rely on them, the statements cannot be the basis of a claim of fraud.[16]

(C) PROOF OF HARM. For an individual to recover damages for fraud, proof of harm to that individual is required. The injured party may recover the actual losses suffered as a result of the fraud as well as punitive damages when the fraud is gross or oppressive. The injured party has the right to have the court order the rescission or cancellation of the contract that has been induced by fraud.[17]

10. Negligent Misrepresentation

While fraud requires the critical element of a known or recklessly made falsity, a claim of negligent misrepresentation contains similar elements except it is predicated on a negligently made false statement. That is, the speaker failed to exercise due care regarding material information communicated to the listener but did not intend to deceive. When the negligent misrepresentation of a material fact that the listener relies on results in harm to the listener, the contract is voidable at the option of the injured party. If fraud is proven, as opposed to misrepresentation, recovery of punitive damages in addition to actual damages can occur. Because it may be difficult to prove the intentional falsity required for fraud, it is common for a lawsuit to allege both a claim of fraud and a claim of negligent misrepresentation.

For Example, Marshall Armstrong worked for Fred Collins, owner of Collins Entertainment, Inc., a conglomerate that owns and operates video games. Collins Entertainment's core product video poker was hurt by a court ruling that prohibited cash payouts, which adversely affected its business and resulted in a debt of $13 to $20 million to SouthTrust bank. Chief operating officer Armstrong, on his own time, came up with the idea of modifying bingo machines as a new venture. To exploit this idea, Collins agreed to form a corporation called Skillpins Inc., that was unencumbered by the SouthTrust debt and to give Armstrong a 10 percent ownership interest. After a period, with some 300 Skillpins machines producing income, Armstrong discovered the revenues from the new venture on the debt-laden Collins Entertainment profit and loss statement, not that of Skillpins, Inc.

---

[15] The Federal Trade Commission and state agencies have franchise disclosure rules that will penalize the franchisor in this case. See Chapter 41.
[16] *Eckert v Flair Agency, Inc.*, 909 P2d 1201 (Okla App 1995) (seller's statement that house would never be flooded again).
[17] *Paden v Murray*, 523 SE2d 75 (Ga App 2000).

Armstrong's suit for both fraud and intentional misrepresentation was successful. In addition to actual damages, he received $1.8 million in punitive damages for fraud.[18]

11. Nondisclosure

Under certain circumstances, nondisclosure serves to make a contract voidable, especially when the nondisclosure consists of active concealment.

(A) GENERAL RULE OF NONLIABILITY. Ordinarily, a party to a contract has no duty to volunteer information to the other party. **For Example,** if Fox does not ask Tehan any questions, Tehan is not under any duty to make a full statement of material facts. Consequently, the nondisclosure of information that is not asked for does not impose fraud liability or impair the validity of a contract.

(B) EXCEPTIONS. The following exceptions to the general rule of nonliability for nondisclosure exist.

(1) Unknown Defect or Condition.

A duty may exist in some states for a seller who knows of a serious defect or condition to disclose that information to the other party where the defect or condition is unknown to the other person and is of such a nature that it is unlikely that the other person would discover it. However, a defendant who had no knowledge of the defect cannot be held liable for failure to disclose it.[19]

(2) Confidential Relationship.

If parties stand in a **confidential relationship**, failure to disclose information may be regarded as fraudulent. For example, in an attorney-client relationship,[20] the attorney has a duty to reveal anything that is material to the client's interest when dealing with the client. The attorney's silence has the same legal consequence as a knowingly made false statement that there was no material fact to be told the client.

(3) Active Concealment.

Nondisclosure may be more than the passive failure to volunteer information. It may consist of a positive act of hiding information from the other party by physical concealment, or it may consist of knowingly or recklessly furnishing the wrong information. Such conduct constitutes fraud. **For Example,** when Nigel wanted to sell his house, he covered the wooden cellar beams with plywood to hide extensive termite damage. He sold the house to Kuehne, who sued Nigel for damages on later discovering the termite damage. Nigel claimed he had no duty to volunteer information about the termites, but by covering the damage with plywood, he committed active fraud as if he had made a false statement that there were no termites.

D. PRESSURE

What appears to be an agreement may not in fact be voluntary because one of the parties entered into it as the result of undue influence or physical or economic duress.

CPA ## 12. Undue Influence

An aged parent may entrust all business affairs to a trusted child; a disabled person may rely on a nurse; a client may follow implicitly whatever an attorney recommends. The relationship may be such that for practical purposes, one person is helpless in the hands of the other. When such a confidential relationship exists, it is apparent that the parent, the disabled person, or the client is not exercising free will in making a contract suggested by the child, nurse, or attorney but is merely following the will of the other person. Because of the great possibility of unfair advantage, the law presumes that the dominating person exerts **undue influence** on the other person whenever the dominating person obtains any benefit from a contract made with the dominated person. The contract is then voidable. It may be set aside by the dominated person unless the dominating person can prove that, at the time the contract was made, no unfair advantage had been taken.

The class of confidential relationships is not well defined. It ordinarily includes the relationships of parent and child, guardian and ward, physician and patient, and attorney and client, and any other

[18] 621 SE2d 368 (SC App 2005).
[19] *Nesbitt v Dunn*, 672 So2d 226 (La App 1996).
[20] *In re Boss Trust*, 487 NW2d 256 (Minn App 1992).

relationship of trust and confidence in which one party exercises a control or influence over another.

Whether undue influence exists is a difficult question for courts (ordinarily juries) to determine. The law does not regard every influence as undue.

An essential element of undue influence is that the person making the contract does not exercise free will. In the absence of a recognized type of confidential relationship, such as that between parent and child, courts are likely to take the attitude that the person who claims to have been dominated was merely persuaded and there was therefore no undue influence.

CPA   13. Duress

A party may enter into a contract to avoid a threatened danger. The danger threatened may be a physical harm to person or property, called **physical duress**, or it may be a threat of financial loss, called **economic duress**.

(A) PHYSICAL DURESS. A person makes a contract under **duress** when there is such violence or threat of violence that the person is deprived of free will and makes the contract to avoid harm. The threatened harm may be directed either at a near relative of the contracting party or against the contracting party. If a contract is made under duress, the resulting agreement is voidable at the victim's election.

Agreements made to bring an end to mass disorder or violence are ordinarily not binding contracts because they were obtained by duress.

One may not void a contract on grounds of duress merely because it was entered into with great reluctance and proves to be very disadvantageous to that individual.[21]

(B) ECONOMIC DURESS. Economic duress is a condition in which one is induced by a wrongful act or threat of another to make a contract under circumstances that deprive one of the exercise of his own free will.[22] **For Example,** Richard Case, an importer of parts used to manufacture high-quality mountain bicycles, had a contractual duty to supply Katahdin Manufacturing Company's needs for specifically manufactured stainless steel brakes for the 2010 season. Katahdin's president, Bill Read, was in constant contact with Case about the

delay in delivery of the parts and the adverse consequences it was having on Katahdin's relationship with its retailers. Near the absolute deadline for meeting orders for the 2010 season, Case called Read and said, "I've got the parts in, but I'm not sure I'll be able to send them to you because I'm working on next year's contracts, and you haven't signed yours yet." Case's 2011 contract increased the cost of parts by 38 percent. Read signed the contract to obtain the delivery but later found a new supplier and gave notice to Case of this action. The defense of economic duress would apply in a breach of contract suit brought by Case on the 2011 contract because Case implicitly threatened to commit the wrongful act of not delivering parts due under the prior contract, and Katahdin Company had no means available to obtain parts elsewhere to prevent the economic loss that would occur if it did not receive those parts.

lawflix

Jerry Maguire (1996) (R)

Consider the marriage proposal, its validity, and Dorothy's later statement, "I did this. I made this happen. And the thing is, I can do something about it." What was Maguire's state of mind at the time of the proposal? Consider its possible hypothetical nature and the issues of whether it was a joke and the possible presence of undue influence (the young boy).

Matilda (1996) (PG)

A brilliant little girl with a strong moral compass who tries to instruct her family on many things erudite and her father specifically on what constitutes misrepresentation in selling used cars.

You can view a clip of this movie and others that illustrate business law concepts at the LawFlix site, located at **www.cengage.com/blaw/dvl**.

---

[21] *Miller v Calhoun Johnson Co.*, 497 SE2d 397 (Ga App 1998).
[22] *Hurd v Wildman, Harrold, Allen, and Dixon*, 707 NE2d 609 (Ill App 1999).

MAKE THE CONNECTION

SUMMARY

An agreement that otherwise appears to be a contract may not be binding because one of the parties lacks contractual capacity. In such a case, the contract is ordinarily voidable at the election of the party who lacks contractual capacity. In some cases, the contract is void. Ordinarily, contractual incapacity is the inability, for mental or physical reasons, to understand that a contract is being made and to understand its general terms and nature. This is typically the case when it is claimed that incapacity exists because of insanity, intoxication, or drug use. The incapacity of minors arises because society discriminates in favor of that class to protect them from unwise contracts.

The age of majority is 18. Minors can disaffirm most contracts. If a minor received anything from the other party, the minor, on avoiding the contract, must return what had been received from the other party if the minor still has it.

When a minor disaffirms a contract for a necessary, the minor must pay the reasonable value of any benefit received.

Minors only are liable for their contracts. Parents of a minor are not liable on the minor's contracts merely because they are the parents. Frequently, an adult enters into the contract as a coparty of the minor and is then liable without regard to whether the minor has avoided the contract.

The contract of an insane person is voidable to much the same extent as the contract of a minor. An important distinction is that if a guardian has been appointed for the insane person, a contract made by the insane person is void, not merely voidable.

An intoxicated person lacks contractual capacity if the intoxication is such that the person does not understand that a contract is being made.

The consent of a party to an agreement is not genuine or voluntary in certain cases of mistake, deception, or pressure. When this occurs, what appears to be a contract can be avoided by the victim of such circumstances or conduct.

As to mistake, it is necessary to distinguish between unilateral mistakes that are unknown to the other contracting party and those that are known. Mistakes that are unknown to the other party usually do not affect the binding character of the agreement. A unilateral mistake of which the other contracting party has knowledge or has reason to know makes the contract avoidable by the victim of the mistake.

The deception situation may be one of negligent misrepresentation or fraud. The law ordinarily does not attach any significance to nondisclosure. Contrary to this rule, there is a duty to volunteer information when a confidential relationship exists between the possessor of the knowledge and the other contracting party.

When concealment goes beyond mere silence and consists of actively taking steps to hide the truth, the conduct may be classified as fraud. A statement of opinion or value cannot ordinarily be the basis for fraud liability.

The voluntary character of a contract may be lacking because the agreement had been obtained by pressure. This may range from undue influence through the array of threats of extreme economic loss (called *economic duress*) to the threat of physical force that would cause serious personal injury or damage to property (called *physical duress*). When the voluntary character of an agreement has been destroyed by deception, or pressure, the victim may avoid or rescind the contract or may obtain money damages from the wrongdoer.

LEARNING OUTCOMES

After studying this chapter, you should be able to clearly explain:

A. CONTRACTUAL CAPACITY

LO.1 Define contractual capacity

See the example where Jacqueline, age 22, did not understand parts of a storage contract, p. 280.

LO.2 Explain the extent and effect of avoidance of a contract by a minor.

See the *Prince George's Hospital* case, where a minor had to pay for medical necessaries, on page 282.

B. MISTAKE

LO.3 Distinguish unilateral mistakes and mutual mistakes

See the example of the mutual mistake of fact regarding the fertility of a cow on p. 285.

C. DECEPTION

LO.4 Explain the difference between intentional misrepresentation, negligent misrepresentation and puffery.

See the example of the purchase of the used Honda where the misrepresentation was found to be fraud not puffery on p. 289.

D. PRESSURE

LO.5 Explain the difference between undue influence and duress

See the Katahdin bicycle example on economic duress, p. 292.

KEY TERMS

confidential relationship	fraud	status quo ante
contractual capacity	necessaries	undue influence
duress	physical duress	
economic duress	reform	

QUESTIONS AND CASE PROBLEMS

1. Lester purchased a used automobile from MacKintosh Motors. He asked the seller if the car had ever been in a wreck. The MacKintosh salesperson had never seen the car before that morning and knew nothing of its history but quickly answered Lester's question by stating: "No. It has never been in a wreck." In fact, the auto had been seriously damaged in a wreck and, although repaired, was worth much less than the value it would have had if there had been no wreck. When Lester learned the truth, he sued MacKintosh Motors and the salesperson for damages for fraud. They raised the defense that the salesperson did not know the statement was false and had not intended to deceive Lester. Did the conduct of the salesperson constitute fraud?

2. Helen, age 17, wanted to buy a Harley-Davidson "Sportster" motorcycle. She did not have the funds to pay cash but persuaded the dealer to sell the cycle to her on credit. The dealer did so partly because Helen said that she was 22 and showed the dealer an identification card that falsely stated her age as 22. Helen drove the motorcycle away. A few days later, she damaged it and then returned it to the dealer and stated that she disaffirmed the contract because she was a minor. The dealer said that she could not because (1) she had

misrepresented her age and (2) the motorcycle was damaged. Can she avoid the contract?

3. Paden signed an agreement dated May 28 to purchase the Murrays' home. The Murrays accepted Paden's offer the following day, and the sale closed on June 27. Paden and his family moved into the home on July 14, 1997. Paden had the home inspected prior to closing. The report listed four minor repairs needed by the home, the cost of which was less than $500. Although these repairs had not been completed at the time of closing, Paden decided to go through with the purchase. After moving into the home, Paden discovered a number of allegedly new defects, including a wooden foundation, electrical problems, and bat infestation. The sales agreement allowed extensive rights to inspect the property. The agreement provided:

Buyer . . . shall have the right to enter the property at Buyer's expense and at reasonable times . . . to thoroughly inspect, examine, test, and survey the Property. . . . Buyer shall have the right to request that Seller repair defects in the Property by providing Seller within 12 days from Binding Agreement Date with a copy of inspection report(s) and a written amendment to this agreement setting forth the defects in the report which Buyer requests to be repaired and/or replaced. . . . If Buyer does not timely present the written amendment and inspection report, Buyer shall be deemed to have accepted the Property "as is."

Paden sued the Murrays for fraudulent concealment and breach of the sales agreement. If Mr. Murray told Paden on May 26 that the house had a concrete foundation, would this be fraud? Decide. [*Paden v Murray*, 523 SE2d 75 (Ga App)]

4. High-Tech Collieries borrowed money from Holland. High-Tech later refused to be bound by the loan contract, claiming the contract was not binding because it had been obtained by duress. The evidence showed that the offer to make the loan was made on a take-it-or-leave-it basis. Was the defense of duress valid? [*Holland v High-Tech Collieries, Inc.*, 911 F Supp 1021 (DC WA)]

5. Thomas Bell, a minor, went to work in the Pittsburgh beauty parlor of Sam Pankas and agreed that when he left the employment, he would not work in or run a beauty parlor business within a 10-mile radius of downtown Pittsburgh for a period of two years. Contrary to this provision, Bell and another employee of Pankas's opened a beauty shop three blocks from Pankas's shop and advertised themselves as Pankas's former employees. Pankas sued Bell to stop the breach of the noncompetition, or restrictive, covenant. Bell claimed that he was not bound because he was a minor when he had agreed to the covenant. Was he bound by the covenant? [*Pankas v Bell*, 198 A2d 312 (Pa)]

6. Aldrich and Co. sold goods to Donovan on credit. The amount owed grew steadily, and finally Aldrich refused to sell any more to Donovan unless Donovan signed a promissory note for the amount due. Donovan did not want to but signed the note because he had no money and needed more goods. When Aldrich brought an action to enforce the note, Donovan claimed that the note was not binding because it had been obtained by economic duress. Was he correct? [*Aldrich & Co. v Donovan*, 778 P2d 397 (Mont)]

7. James Fitl purchased a 1952 Mickey Mantle Topps baseball card from baseball card dealer Mark Strek for $17,750 and placed it in a safe deposit box. Two years later, he had the card appraised, and he was told that the card had been refinished and trimmed, which rendered it valueless. Fitl sued Strek and testified that he had relied on Strek's position as a sports card dealer and on his representations that the baseball card was authentic. Strek contends that Fitl waited too long to give him notice of the defects that would have enabled Strek to contact the person who sold him the card and obtain relief. Strek asserts that he therefore is not liable. Advise Fitl concerning possible legal theories that apply to his case. How would you decide the case? [See *Fitl v Strek*, 690 NW2d 605 (Neb)]

8. An agent of Thor Food Service Corp. was seeking to sell Makofske a combination refrigerator-

freezer and food purchase plan. Makofske was married and had three children. After being informed of the eating habits of Makofske and his family, the agent stated that the cost of the freezer and food would be about $95 to $100 a month. Makofske carefully examined the agent's itemized estimate and made some changes to it. Makofske then signed the contract and purchased the refrigerator-freezer. The cost proved to be more than the estimated $95 to $100 a month, and Makofske claimed that the contract had been obtained by fraud. Decide. [*Thor Food Service Corp. v Makofske*, 218 NYS2d 93]

9. Blubaugh was a district manager of Schlumberger Well Services. Turner was an executive employee of Schlumberger. Blubaugh was told that he would be fired unless he chose to resign. He was also told that if he would resign and release the company and its employees from all claims for wrongful discharge, he would receive about $5,000 in addition to his regular severance pay of approximately $25,000 and would be given job-relocation counseling. He resigned, signed the release, and received about $40,000 and job counseling. Some time thereafter, he brought an action claiming that he had been wrongfully discharged. He claimed that the release did not protect the defendants because the release had been obtained by economic duress. Were the defendants protected by the release? [*Blubaugh v Turner*, 842 P2d 1072 (Wyo)]

10. Sippy was thinking of buying Christich's house. He noticed watermarks on the ceiling, but the agent showing the house stated that the roof had been repaired and was in good condition. Sippy was not told that the roof still leaked and that the repairs had not been able to stop the leaking. Sippy bought the house. Some time later, heavy rains caused water to leak into the house, and Sippy claimed that Christich was liable for damages. What theory would he rely on? Decide. [*Sippy v Christich*, 609 P2d 204 (Kan App)]

11. Pileggi owed Young money. Young threatened to bring suit against Pileggi for the amount due.

Pileggi feared the embarrassment of being sued and the possibility that he might be thrown into bankruptcy. To avoid being sued, Pileggi executed a promissory note to pay Young the amount due. He later asserted that the note was not binding because he had executed it under duress. Is this defense valid? [*Young v Pileggi*, 455 A2d 1228 (Pa Super)]

12. Office Supply Outlet, Inc., a single-store office equipment and supply retailer, ordered 100 model RVX-414 computers from Compuserve, Inc. A new staff member made a clerical error on the order form and ordered a quantity that was far in excess of what Office Supply could sell in a year. Office Supply realized the mistake when the delivery trucks arrived at its warehouse. Its manager called Compuserve and explained that it had intended to order just 10 computers. Compuserve declined to accept the return of the extra machines. Is the contract enforceable? What additional facts would allow the store to avoid the contract for the additional machines?

13. C&J Publishing Co. told a computer salesman that it wanted a computer system that would operate its printing presses. C&J specified that it wanted only new equipment and no used equipment would be acceptable. The seller delivered a system to C&J that was a combination of new and secondhand parts because it did not have sufficient new parts to fill the order. When C&J later learned what had happened, it sued the seller for fraud. The seller contended that no statement or warranty had been made that all parts of the system were new and that it would not therefore be liable for fraud. Decide.

14. The city of Salinas entered into a contract with Souza & McCue Construction Co. to construct a sewer. City officials knew unusual subsoil conditions (including extensive quicksand) existed that would make performance of the contract unusually difficult. This information was not disclosed when city officials advertised for bids. The advertisement for bids directed bidders to examine carefully the site of the work and declared that the submission of a bid would constitute

evidence that the bidder had made an examination. Souza & McCue was awarded the contract, but because of the subsoil conditions, it could not complete on time and was sued by Salinas for breach of contract. Souza & McCue counterclaimed on the basis that the city had not revealed its information on the subsoil conditions and was thus liable for the loss. Was the city liable? [*City of Salinas v Souza & McCue Construction Co.*, 424 P2d 921 (Cal App 3d)]

15. Vern Westby inherited a "ticket" from Anna Sjoblom, a survivor of the sinking of the *Titanic*, which had been pinned to the inside of her coat. He also inherited an album of postcards, some of which related to the *Titanic*. The ticket was a one-of-a-kind item in good condition. Westby needed cash and went to the biggest antique dealer in Tacoma, operated by Alan Gorsuch and his family, doing business as Sanford and Sons, and asked about the value of these items. Westby testified that after Alan Gorsuch examined the ticket, he said, "It's not worth nothing." Westby then inquired about the value of the postcard album, and Gorsuch advised him to come back later. On Westby's return, Gorsuch told Westby, "It ain't worth nothing." Gorsuch added that he "couldn't fetch $500 for the ticket." Since he needed money, Westby asked if Gorsuch would give him $1,000 for both the ticket and the album, and Gorsuch did so.

Six months later, Gorsuch sold the ticket at a nationally advertised auction for $110,000 and sold most of the postcards for $1,200. Westby sued Gorsuch for fraud. Testimony showed that Gorsuch was a major buyer in antiques and collectibles in the Puget Sound area and that he would have had an understanding of the value of the ticket. Gorsuch contends that all elements of fraud are not present since there was no evidence that Gorsuch intended that Westby rely on the alleged representations, nor did Westby rely on such. Rather, Gorsuch asserts, it was an arm's-length transaction and Westby had access to the same information as Gorsuch. Decide. [*Westby v Gorsuch*, 112 Wash App 558 (2002)]

CPA QUESTIONS

1. A building subcontractor submitted a bid for construction of a portion of a high-rise office building. The bid contained material computational errors. The general contractor accepted the bid with knowledge of the errors. Which of the following statements best represents the subcontractor's liability?

   a. Not liable, because the contractor knew of the errors

   b. Not liable, because the errors were a result of gross negligence

   c. Liable, because the errors were unilateral

   d. Liable, because the errors were material (5/95, Law, #17, 5351)

2. Egan, a minor, contracted with Baker to purchase Baker's used computer for $400. The computer was purchased for Egan's personal use. The agreement provided that Egan would pay $200 down on delivery and $200 thirty days later. Egan took delivery and paid the $200 down payment. Twenty days later, the computer was damaged seriously as a result of Egan's negligence. Five days after the damage occurred and one day after Egan reached the age of majority, Egan attempted to disaffirm the contract with Baker. Egan will:

   a. Be able to disaffirm despite the fact that Egan was *not* a minor at the time of disaffirmance

   b. Be able to disaffirm only if Egan does so in writing

   c. Not be able to disaffirm because Egan had failed to pay the balance of the purchase price

   d. Not be able to disaffirm because the computer was damaged as a result of Egan's negligence (11/93, Law, #21, 4318)

Chapter 15

CONSIDERATION

Will the law enforce every promise? Generally, a promise will not be enforced unless something is given or received for the promise.

A. General Principles

As a general rule, one of the elements needed to make an agreement binding is consideration.

1. Consideration Defined and Explained

Consideration is what each party to a contract gives up to the other in making their agreement.

(A) Bargained-for Exchange. *Consideration* is the bargained-for exchange between the parties to a contract. In order for consideration to exist, something of value must be given or promised in return for the performance or promise of performance of the other.[1] The value given or promised can be money, services, property, or the forbearance of a legal right.

For Example, Beth offers to pay Kerry $100 for her used skis, and Kerry accepts. Beth has promised something of value, $100, as consideration for Kerry's promise to sell the skis, and Kerry has promised Beth something of value, the skis, as consideration for the $100. If Kerry offered to *give* Beth the used skis and Beth accepted, these parties would have an agreement but not an enforceable contract because Beth did not provide any consideration in exchange for Kerry's promise of the skis. There was no *bargained-for exchange* because Kerry was not promised anything of value from Beth.

(B) Benefit-Detriment Approach. Some jurisdictions analyze consideration from the point of view of a *benefit-detriment approach,* defining *consideration* as a benefit received by the promisor or a detriment incurred by the promisee.

As an example of a unilateral contract analyzed from a benefit-detriment approach to consideration, Mr. Scully, a longtime summer resident of Falmouth, states to George Corfu, a college senior, "I will pay you $3,000 if you paint my summer home." George

in fact paints the house. The work of painting the house by George, the promisee, was a legal detriment to him. Also, the painting of the house was a legal benefit to Scully, the promisor. There was consideration in this case, and the agreement is enforceable.

2. Gifts

Promises to make a gift are unenforceable promises under the law of contracts because of lack of consideration, as illustrated previously in the scenario of Kerry promising to give her used skis to Beth without charge. There was no bargained-for exchange because Kerry was not promised anything of value from Beth. A completed gift, however, cannot be rescinded for lack of consideration.[2]

Charitable subscriptions by which individuals make pledges to finance the construction of a college building, a church, or another structure for charitable purposes are binding to the extent that the donor (promisor) should have reasonably realized that the charity was relying on the promise in undertaking the building program. Some states require proof that the charity has relied on the subscription.[3]

3. Adequacy of Consideration

Ordinarily, courts do not consider the adequacy of the consideration given for a promise. The fact that the consideration supplied by one party is slight when compared with the burden undertaken by the other party is immaterial. It is a matter for the parties to decide when they make their contract whether each is getting a fair return. In the absence of fraud or other misconduct, courts usually will not interfere to make sure that each side is getting a fair return.

Because the adequacy of consideration is ignored, it is immaterial that consideration is so slight that the transaction is in part a "gift." However, the Internal Revenue Service may view a given transaction as part consideration, part gift, and assess a gift tax as appropriate.

The fact that the consideration turns out to be disappointing does not affect the binding character of the contract. Thus, the fact that a business purchased

---

[1] *Brooksbank v Anderson,* 586 NW2d 789 (Minn App 1998).
[2] *Homes v O'Bryant,* 741 So 2d 366 (Miss App 1999).
[3] *King v Trustees of Boston University,* 647 NE2d 1176 (Ma 1995).

by a group of investors proves unprofitable does not constitute a failure of consideration that releases the buyers from their obligation to the seller.

4. Forbearance as Consideration

In most cases, consideration consists of the performance of an act such as providing a service, or the making of a promise to provide a service or goods, or paying money.[4] Consideration may also consist of **forbearance**, which is refraining from doing an act that an individual has a legal right to do, or it may consist of a promise of forbearance. In other words, the promisor may desire to buy the inaction or a promise of inaction of the other party.

The giving up of any legal right can be consideration for the promise of the other party to a contract. Thus, the relinquishment of a right to sue for damages will support a promise for the payment of money given in return for the promise to relinquish the right, if such is the agreement of the parties.

The promise of a creditor to forbear collecting a debt is consideration for the promise of the debtor to modify the terms of the transaction.

5. Illusory Promises

In a bilateral contract, each party makes a promise to the other. For a bilateral contract to be enforceable, there must be *mutuality of obligation*. That is, both parties must have created obligations to the other in their respective promises. If one party's promise contains either no obligation or only an apparent obligation to the other, this promise is an **illusory promise**. The party making such a promise is not bound because he or she has made no real promise. The effect is that the other party, who has made a real promise, is also not bound because he or she has received no consideration. It is said that the contract fails for lack of mutuality.

For Example, Mountain Coal Company promises to sell Midwest Power Company all the coal it may order for $48 per ton for the year 2010, and Midwest Power agrees to pay $48 for any coal it orders from Mountain Coal. Mountain Coal in its promise to Midwest Power has obligated itself to supply all coal

ordered at a stated price. However, Midwest Power's promise did not obligate it to buy any coal whatsoever from Mountain Coal (note that it was not a requirements contract). Because Midwest has no obligation to Mountain Coal under its promise, there is no mutuality of obligation, and Midwest cannot enforce Mountain Coal's promise when the market price of coal goes to $55 a ton in the winter of 2010 as the result of severe weather conditions.

Consider as well the example of the Jacksonville Fire soccer team's contract with Brazilian soccer star Edmundo. Edmundo signed a contract to play for the Jacksonville franchise of the new International Soccer League for five-years at $25 million. The extensive document signed by Edmundo set forth the details of the team's financial commitment and the details of Edmundo's obligations to the team and its fans. On page 4 of the document, the team inserted a clause reserving the right "to terminate the contract and team obligations at any time in its sole discretion." During the season, Edmundo received a $40 million five-year offer to play for Manchester United of the English Premier League, which he accepted. Because Jacksonville had a free way out of its obligation by the unrestricted cancellation provision in the contract, it thus made its promises to Edmundo illusory. Edmundo was not bound by the Jacksonville contract as a result of a lack of mutuality and was free to sign with Manchester United.

(A) CANCELLATION PROVISIONS. Although a promise must impose a binding obligation, it may authorize a party to cancel the agreement under certain circumstances on giving notice by a certain date. Such a provision does not make this party's promise illusory, for the party does not have a free way out and is limited to living up to the terms of the **cancellation provision**. For Example, actress Zsa Zsa Gabor made a contract with Hollywood Fantasy Corporation to appear at a fantasy vacation in San Antonio, Texas, on May 2–4, for a $10,000 appearance fee plus itemized (extravagant) expenses. The last paragraph of the agreement stated: "It is agreed that if a significant acting opportunity in a film comes up, Ms. Gabor will have the right to cancel her appearance in San Antonio by advising Hollywood Fantasy in writing by

---

[4] *Prenger v Baumhoer*, 914 SW2d 413 (Mo App 1996).

April 15, 1991." Ms. Gabor sent a telegram on April 15, 1991, canceling her appearance. During the May 2 through 4 period, Ms. Gabor's only acting activity was a 14-second cameo role during the opening credits of *Naked Gun 2½*. In a lawsuit for breach of contract that followed, the jury saw this portion of the movie and concluded that Ms. Gabor had not canceled her obligation on the basis of a "significant acting opportunity," and she was held liable for breach of contract.[5]

(B) CONDITIONAL PROMISES. A *conditional promise* is a promise that depends on the occurrence of a specified condition in order for the promise to be binding.

For Example, Mary Sparks, in contemplation of her signing a lease to take over a restaurant at Marina Bay, wanted to make certain that she had a highly qualified chef to run the restaurant's food service. She made a contract with John "Grumpy" White to serve as executive chef for a one-year period at a salary of $150,000. The contract set forth White's responsibilities and was conditioned on the successful negotiation of the restaurant lease with Marina Bay Management. Both parties signed it. Although the happening of the condition was within Mary's control because she could avoid the contract with Grumpy White by not acquiring the restaurant lease, she limited her future options by the contract with White. Her promise to White was not illusory because after signing the contract with him, if she acquired the restaurant lease, she was bound to hire White as her executive chef. Before signing the contract with White, she was free to sign any chef for the position. The contract was enforceable.

CPA   B. SPECIAL SITUATIONS

The following sections analyze certain common situations in which a lawsuit turns on whether the promisor received consideration for the promise sued on.

6. Preexisting Legal Obligation

Ordinarily, doing or promising to do what one is already under a legal obligation to do is not consideration.[6] Similarly, a promise to refrain from doing what one has no legal right to do is not consideration. This preexisting duty or legal obligation can be based on statute, on general principles of law, on responsibilities of an office held, or on a preexisting contract.

For Example, Officer Mary Rodgers is an undercover police officer in the city of Pasadena, California, assigned to weekend workdays. Officer Rodgers promised Elwood Farnsworth that she would diligently patrol the area of the Farnsworth estate on weekends to keep down the noise and drinking of rowdy young persons who gathered in this area, and Mr. Farnsworth promised to provide a $500 per month gratuity for this extra service. Farnsworth's promise is unenforceable because Officer Rodgers has a preexisting official duty as a police officer to protect citizens and enforce the antinoise and public drinking ordinances.

CPA (A) COMPLETION OF CONTRACT. Suppose that a contractor refuses to complete a building unless the owner promises a payment or bonus in addition to the sum specified in the original contract, and the owner promises to make that payment. The question then arises as to whether the owner's promise is binding. Most courts hold that the second promise of the owner is without consideration.

If the promise of the contractor is to do something that is not part of the first contract, then the promise of the other party is binding. **For Example,** if a bonus of $5,000 is promised in return for the promise of a contractor to complete the building at a date earlier than that specified in the original agreement, the promise to pay the bonus is binding.

CPA *(1) Good-Faith Adjustment*
A current trend is to enforce a second promise to pay a contractor a higher amount for the performance of the original contract when there are extraordinary circumstances caused by unforeseeable difficulties and when the additional amount promised the contractor is reasonable under the circumstances. The classic *Angel v Murray* decision involves a good-faith adjustment.

---

[5] *Hollywood Fantasy Corp. v Gabor*, 151 F2d 203 (5th Cir 1998).
[6] *Gardiner, Kamya & Associates v Jackson*, 369 F3d 1318 (Fed Cir 2004).

Angel v Murray, 113 RI 482, 322 A2d 630 (1974)

"You Had a Preexisting Legal Obligation," Said the Public Guardian, Mr. Angel.

John Murray was director of finance of the city of Newport. A contract was made with Alfred Maher to remove trash. Later, Maher requested that the city council increase his compensation. Maher's costs were greater than had been anticipated because 400 new dwelling units had been put into operation. The city council voted to pay Maher an additional $10,000 a year. After two such annual payments had been made, Angel and other citizens of the city sued Murray and Maher for a return of the $20,000. They said that Maher was already obligated by his contract to perform the work for the contract sum, and there was, accordingly, no consideration for the payment of the increased compensation. From a decision in favor of the plaintiffs, the city and Maher appealed.

JUDICIAL OPINION

ROBERTS, C. J. . . . It is generally held that a modification of a contract is itself a contract, which is unenforceable unless supported by consideration. . . .

The preexisting duty rule is followed by most jurisdictions. . . .

The primary purpose of the preexisting duty rule is to prevent what has been referred to as the "hold-up game." . . . A classic example of the "hold-up game" is found in *Alaska Packers' Ass'n v Domenico,* 117 F 99 (9th Cir 1902). There 21 seamen entered into a written contract with Domenico to sail from San Francisco to Pyramid Harbor, Alaska. They were to work as sailors and fishermen out of Pyramid Harbor during the fishing season of 1900. The contract specified that each man would be paid $50 plus two cents for each red salmon he caught. Subsequent to their arrival at Pyramid Harbor, the men stopped work and demanded an additional $50. They threatened to return to San Francisco if Domenico did not agree to their demand. Since it was impossible for Domenico to find other men, he agreed to pay the men an additional $50. After they returned to San Francisco, Domenico refused to pay the men an additional $50. The court found that the subsequent agreement to pay the men an additional $50 was not supported by consideration because the men had a preexisting duty to work on the ship under the original contract, and thus the subsequent agreement was unenforceable.

Another example of the "hold-up game" is found in the area of construction contracts. Frequently, a contractor will refuse to complete work under an unprofitable contract unless he is awarded additional compensation. The courts have generally held that a subsequent agreement to award additional compensation is unenforceable if the contractor is only performing work which would have been required of him under the original contract. . . .

These examples clearly illustrate that the courts will not enforce an agreement that has been procured by coercion or duress and will hold the parties to their original contract regardless of whether it is profitable or unprofitable. However, the courts have been reluctant to apply the preexisting duty rule when a party to a contract encounters unanticipated difficulties and the other party, not influenced by coercion or duress, voluntarily agrees to pay additional compensation for work already required to be performed under the contract. For example, the courts have found that the original contract was rescinded, . . . abandoned, . . . or waived.

Although the preexisting duty rule has served a useful purpose insofar as it deters parties from using coercion and duress to obtain additional compensation, it has been widely criticized as a general rule of law. . . . The modern trend appears to recognize the necessity that courts should enforce agreements modifying contracts when unexpected or unanticipated difficulties arise during the course of the performance of a contract, even though there is no consideration for the modification, as long as the parties agree voluntarily.

Under the Uniform Commercial Code, §2-209(1), . . . "an agreement modifying a contract [for the sale of goods] needs no consideration to be binding." . . . Although at first blush this section appears to validate modifications obtained by coercion and duress, the comments to this section indicate that a modification under this section must meet the test of good faith imposed by the Code, and a modification obtained by extortion without a legitimate commercial reason is unenforceable.

The modern trend away from a rigid application of the preexisting duty rule is reflected by § 89D(a) of the American Law Institute's Restatement Second of the Law of Contracts, which provides: "A promise modifying a duty under a contract not fully performed on either side is binding (a) if the modification is fair and equitable in view of circumstances not anticipated by the parties when the contract was made. . . ."

We believe that § 89D(a) is the proper rule of law and find it applicable to the facts of this case. It not only prohibits modifications obtained by coercion, duress, or extortion but also fulfills society's expectation that agreements entered into voluntarily will be enforced by the courts. . . .

Section 89D(a), of course, does not compel a modification of an unprofitable or unfair contract; it only enforces a modification if the parties voluntarily agree and if (1) the

Continued

promise modifying the original contract was made before the contract was fully performed on either side, (2) the underlying circumstances which prompted the modification were unanticipated by the parties, and (3) the modification is fair and equitable.

The evidence, which is uncontradicted, reveals that in June of 1968 Maher requested the city council to pay him an additional $10,000 for the year beginning on July 1, 1968, and ending on June 30, 1969. This request was made at a public meeting of the city council, where Maher explained in detail his reasons for making the request. Thereafter, the city council voted to authorize the Mayor to sign an amendment to the 1964 contract which provided that Maher would receive an additional $10,000 per year for the duration of the contract. Under such circumstances we have no doubt that the city voluntarily agreed to modify the 1964 contract.

Having determined the voluntariness of this agreement, we turn our attention to the three criteria delineated above. First, the modification was made in June of 1968 at a time when the five-year contract which was made in 1964 had not been fully performed by either party. Second, although the 1964 contract provided that Maher collect all refuse generated within the city, it appears this contract was premised on Maher's past

experience that the number of refuse-generating units would increase at a rate of 20 to 25 per year. Furthermore, the evidence is uncontradicted that the 1967–1968 increase of 400 units "went beyond any previous expectation." Clearly, the circumstances which prompted the city council to modify the 1964 contract were unanticipated. Third, although the evidence does not indicate what proportion of the total this increase comprised, the evidence does indicate that it was a "substantial" increase. In light of this, we cannot say that the council's agreement to pay Maher the $10,000 increase was not fair and equitable in the circumstances.

[Judgment reversed and action remanded]

QUESTIONS

1. What was the basis for the plaintiff's suit?

2. How would the *Angel* case have been decided under the common law rule as to consideration?

3. Can an adversely affected contractor compel a modification of an unprofitable contract under the *Angel v Murray* decision?

(2) Contract for Sale of Goods

When the contract is for the sale of goods, any modification made in good faith by the parties to the contract is binding without regard to the existence of consideration for the modification.

CPA   (B) Compromise and Release of Claims. The rule that doing or promising to do what one is already legally bound to do is not consideration applies to a part payment made in satisfaction of an admitted or *liquidated debt*. Thus, a promise to pay part of an amount that is admittedly owed is not consideration for a promise to discharge the balance. It will not prevent the creditor from demanding the remainder later. **For Example,** John owes Mark $100,000, which was due on March 1, 2010. On March 15, John offers to pay back $80,000 if Mark will agree to accept this amount as the discharge of the full amount owed. Mark agrees to this proposal, and it is set forth in writing signed by the parties. However, Mark later sues for the $20,000 balance. Mark will be successful

in the lawsuit because John's payment of the $80,000 is not consideration for Mark's promise to discharge the full amount owed because John was doing only what he had a preexisting legal duty to do.

If the debtor pays the part payment before the debt is due, there is consideration because, on the day when the payment was made, the creditor was not entitled to demand any payment. Likewise, if the creditor accepts some article (even of slight value) in addition to the part payment, consideration exists.

A debtor and creditor may have a bona fide dispute over the amount owed or whether any amount is owed. Such is called an *unliquidated debt*. In this case, payment by the debtor of less than the amount claimed by the creditor is consideration for the latter's agreement to release or settle the claim. It is generally regarded as sufficient if the claimant believes in the merit of the claim.[7]

(C) Part-Payment Checks. When there is a good-faith dispute about the amount of a debt and the debtor

---

[7] *F. H. Prince & Co. v Towers Financial Corp.,* 656 NE2d 142 (Ill App 1995).

tenders a check that states on its face "paid in full" and references the transaction in dispute, but the amount of the check is less than the full amount the creditor asserts is owed, the cashing of the check by the creditor discharges the entire debt.

(D) COMPOSITION OF CREDITORS. In a **composition of creditors**, the various creditors of one debtor mutually agree to accept a fractional part of their claims in full satisfaction of the claims. Such agreements are binding and are supported by consideration. When creditors agree to extend the due date of their debts, the promise of each creditor to forbear is likewise consideration for the promise of other creditors to forbear.

7. Past Consideration

A promise based on a party's past performance lacks consideration.[8] It is said that **past consideration** is no consideration. **For Example,** Fred O'Neal came up with the idea for the formation of the new community bank of Villa Rica and was active in its formation. Just prior to the execution of the documents creating the bank, the organizers discussed that once the bank was formed, it would hire O'Neal, giving him a three-year contract at $65,000 the first year, $67,000 the second year, and $70,000 the third. In a lawsuit against the bank for breach of contract, O'Neal testified that the consideration he gave in exchange for the three-year contract was his past effort to organize the bank. The court stated that past consideration generally will not support a subsequent promise and that the purported consideration was not rendered to the bank, which had not yet been established when his promotion and organization work took place.[9] The presence of a bargained-for exchange is not present when a promise is made in exchange for a past benefit.[10]

---

ethics & the law

Alan Fulkins, who owns a construction company that specializes in single-family residences, is constructing a small subdivision with 23 homes. Tretorn Plumbing, owned by Jason Tretorn, was awarded the contract for the plumbing work on the homes at a price of $4,300 per home.

Plumbing contractors complete their residential projects in three phases. Phase one consists of digging the lines for the plumbing and installing the pipes that are placed in the foundation of the house. Phase two consists of installing the pipes within the walls of the home, and phase three is installing of the surface plumbing, such as sinks and tubs. However, industry practice dictates that the plumbing contractor receive one-half of the contract amount after completion of phase one.

Tretorn completed the digs of phase one for Fulkins and received payment of $2,150. Tretorn then went to Fulkins and demanded an additional $600 per house to complete the work. Fulkins said, "But you already have a contract for $4,300!" Tretorn responded, "I know, but the costs are killing me. I need the additional $600."

Fulkins explained the hardship of the demand, "Look, I've already paid you half. If I hire someone else, I'll have to pay them two-thirds for the work not done. It'll cost me $5,000 per house."

Tretorn responded, "Exactly. I'm a bargain because the additional $600 I want only puts you at $4,900. If you don't pay it, I'll just lien the houses and then you'll be stuck without a way to close the sales. I've got the contract all drawn up. Just sign it and everything goes smoothly."

Should Fulkins sign the agreement? Does Tretorn have the right to the additional $600? Was it ethical for Tretorn to demand the $600? Is there any legal advice you can offer Fulkins?

---

[8] *Smith v Locklear*, 906 So2d 1273 (Fla App 2005).
[9] *O'Neal v Home Town Bank of Villa Rica*, 514 SE2d 669 (Ga App 1999).
[10] But see *United Resource Recovery Corp v Ranko Venture Management Inc.*, 854 F Supp 2d 645 (SDNY 2008) where a past work agreement was unenforceable because it was based on past consideration—however, the individual could recover under a signed consulting agreement for which no compensation had been paid. See also *Travis v Paepke*, 3 So3d 131 (Miss App 2009).

8. Moral Obligation

In most states, promises made to another based on "moral obligation" lack consideration and are not enforceable.[11] They are considered gratuitous promises and unenforceable. **For Example,** while on a fishing trip, Tom Snyder, a person of moderate means, met an elderly couple living in near-destitute conditions in a rural area of Texas. He returned to the area often, and he regularly purchased groceries for the couple and paid for their medical needs. Some two years later, the couple's son, David, discovered what Tom had been doing and promised to reimburse Snyder for what he had furnished his parents. This promise, based on a moral obligation, is unenforceable. A "past consideration" analysis also renders David's promise as unenforceable.

C. Exceptions to the Laws of Consideration

The ever-changing character of law clearly appears in the area of consideration as part of the developing law of contracts.

9. Exceptions to Consideration

By statute or decision, traditional consideration is not required in these situations:

(A) Charitable Subscriptions. Where individuals made pledges to finance the construction of buildings for charitable purposes, consideration is lacking according to technical standards applied in ordinary contract cases. For public policy reasons, the reliance of the charity on the pledge in undertaking the project is deemed a substitute for consideration.

(B) Uniform Commercial Code. In some situations, the Uniform Commercial Code abolishes the requirement of consideration. **For Example,** under the Code, consideration is not required for (1) a merchant's written, firm offer for goods stated to be irrevocable, (2) a written discharge of a claim for an alleged breach of a commercial contract, or (3) an agreement to modify a contract for the sale of goods.[12]

(C) Promissory Estoppel. Under the doctrine of **promissory estoppel**, a promisor may be prevented from asserting that his or her promise is unenforceable because the promisee gave no consideration for the

FIGURE 15-1 | ***Consideration and Promises***

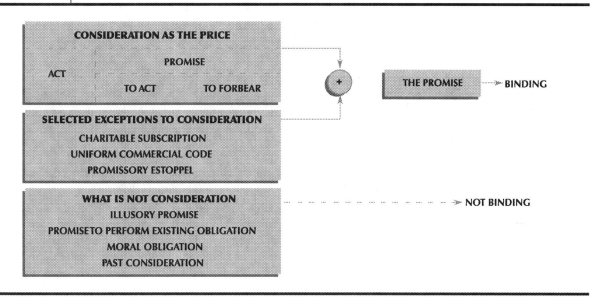

[11] *Production Credit Ass'n of Manaan v Rub,* 475 NW2d 532 (ND 1991). As to the Louisiana rule of moral consideration, see *Thomas v Bryant,* 596 So2d 1065 (La App 1992).
[12] UCC § 2-209(1).

promise. This doctrine, sometimes called the *doctrine of detrimental reliance,* is applicable when (1) the promisor makes a promise that lacks consideration, (2) the promisor intends or should reasonably expect that the promisee will rely on the promise, (3) the promisee in fact relies on the promise in some definite and substantial manner, and (4) enforcement of the promise is the only way to avoid injustice.[13]

Damages recoverable in a case of promissory estoppel are not the profits that the promisee expected, but only the amount necessary to restore the promisee to the position he or she would

have been in had the promisee not relied on the promise.[14]

Legal difficulties often arise because parties take certain things for granted. Frequently, they will be sure that they have agreed to everything and that they have a valid contract. Sometimes, however, they do not. The courts are then faced with the problem of leaving them with their broken dreams or coming to their rescue when promissory estoppel can be established. The *Chrysler* case is an example of the application of the doctrine of promissory estoppel.

Chrysler Corp. v Chaplake Holdings, Ltd., 822 A2d 1024 (Del 2003)

Brits Rescued by Promissory Estoppel

Portman Lamborghini, Ltd. (Portman), was owned by Chaplake Holdings, Ltd., a United Kingdom company, which was owned by David Jolliffe and David Lakeman as equal shareholders. Between 1984 and 1987, Portman sold approximately 30 new Lamborghinis each year through its exclusive concession contract with the car maker. It was then the largest Lamborghini dealer in the world, since Lamborghini's production was just 250 cars per year. These cars sold at a retail price between $200,000 and $300,000. In 1987, Chrysler Corporation bought Lamborghini, and its chairman, Lee Iacocca, presented a plan to escalate production to 5,000 units within five years. The plan included the introduction of a new model, the P140, with a retail price of $70,000. Between 1987 and 1991, all of the Chrysler/Lamborghini top executives with whom Jolliffe and Lakeman and their top advisors came in contact provided the same message to them —Chrysler was committed to the Expansion Plan, and in order for Portman to retain its exclusive U.K. market, it must expand its operational capacity from 35 cars in 1987 to 400 cars by 1992. Accordingly, Portman acquired additional financing, staff, and facilities and built a new distribution center. An economic downturn in the United States and major development and production problems at Lamborghini led Chrysler to reduce its expansion investment by two-thirds. Factory production delays eroded Portman's profitability and success, and it entered into receivership in April 1992. Suit was

brought on behalf of the Portman and Chaplake entities on a promissory estoppel theory against Chrysler, a Delaware corporation. The Jury awarded £569,321 to Portman for costs incurred in implementing the Expansion plan and awarded £462,686 to Chaplake for its investment in the plan. Chrysler appealed.

JUDICIAL OPINION

WALSH, J. . . . Under the doctrine of promissory estoppel a plaintiff must demonstrate by clear and convincing evidence that:

 (i) a promise was made;

 (ii) it was the reasonable expectation of the promisor to induce action or forbearance on the part of the promisee;

(iii) the promisee reasonably relied on the promise and took action to his detriment; and

(iv) such promise is binding because injustice can be avoided only by enforcement of the promise.

There were a series of promises made by Chrysler and its various representatives to Portman, Chaplake and their representatives. First, the comments of then-chairman Iacocca upon the acquisition of Lamborghini made clear Chrysler's

---

[13] *Neuhoff v Marvin Lumber and Cedar Co.,* 370 F3d 197 (1st Cir 2004).
[14] *Medistar Corp. v Schmidt,* 267 SW3d 150 (Tex App 2008).

Continued

plans to expand production over a period of five to six years. More importantly, between 1987 and 1991 [Chrysler/Lamborghini executives] Novaro, Richards, Molaschi and Levy made similar statements promising that the Lamborghini line would expand ten-fold, and that Portman would retain its exclusivity deal *only* if it expanded its operational capacity. By making these promises, Chrysler should have expected that Portman and Chaplake would be induced to expand its operations in accordance with the promised expansion of the Lamborghini line of automobiles.

Portman and Chaplake reasonably relied upon the promises made by Chrysler, and took action to their detriment. Over a period of several years, Portman and Chaplake were regularly updated regarding the progress of the Expansion Plan. Portman would not have implemented the Portman Plan in the absence of these promises. The reasonableness of Portman and Chaplake's reliance is bolstered by the fact that the promises emanated from many of the most senior officers involved with the Expansion Plan.

Lakeman and Jolliffe were sophisticated businessmen in their own right, and in crafting the Portman Plan they employed the services of highly sophisticated advisors. Nevertheless, the record establishes that *all* of the Chrysler/Lamborghini executives with whom Lakeman, Jolliffe, and their advisors came in contact provided the same message: Chrysler is committed to the Expansion Plan, and in order for Portman to retain its exclusivity in the U.K. market, it must expand its operational capacity accordingly. Therefore, it was not unreasonable for Lakeman and Jolliffe to rely upon the promises made by these executives.

Chrysler also argues that the existing written contracts between the parties governed the relationship, and therefore promissory estoppel is inapplicable. Here, Portman and Chaplake relied on promises from Chrysler executives. Those promises induced them to increase operational capacity and investment to a degree that would have been unnecessary *but for* the Expansion Plan and the role they were promised therein. The contracts governing other aspects of the business relationship are of no consequence to this analysis because the promises made regarding Portman's role in the Expansion Plan were in addition to the existing relationship. Finally, Chrysler correctly points out that the trial court failed to address the fourth element—or the so-called "avoidance of injustice" element—of the *Lord* test. . . .

The prevention of injustice is the "fundamental idea" underlying the doctrine of promissory estoppel. *See Chrysler v Quimby,* 144 A.2d 123, 133 (Del.1958). Accordingly, the trial judge implicitly found that this element was satisfied, and the court did not err by failing to submit this element of the *Lord* test to the jury.

[Judgment affirmed]. . .

CASE QUESTIONS

1. State the four elements of a promissory estoppel claim.

2. What is the significance of the fourth element of promissory estoppel, "avoidance of injustice"?

3. How did the court deal with Chrysler's assertion that existing written contracts between the parties preclude the application of promissory estoppel?

lawflix

Baby Boom (1987) (PG)

Review the scene near the end of the movie when Diane Keaton is presented with an offer for the purchase of her company, Country Baby. List the elements of consideration that Food Giant is paying for the company. Explain what Ms. Keaton's consideration is in exchange.

Check out LawFlix at **www.cengage.com/blaw/dvl** to access movie clips that illustrate business law concepts.

MAKE THE CONNECTION

SUMMARY

A promise is not binding if there is no consideration for the promise. Consideration is what the promisor requires as the price for his promise. That price may be doing an act, refraining from the doing of an act, or merely promising to do or to refrain. In a bilateral contract, it is necessary to find that the promise of each party is supported by consideration. If either promise is not so supported, it is not binding, and the agreement of the parties is not a contract. Consequently, the agreement cannot be enforced. When a promise is the consideration, it must be a binding promise. The binding character of a promise is not affected by the circumstance that there is a condition precedent to the performance promised. A promise to do what one is already obligated to do is not consideration, although some exceptions are made. Such exceptions include the rendering of a partial performance or a modified performance accepted as a good-faith adjustment to a changed situation, a compromise and release of claims,

a part-payment check, and a compromise of creditors. Because consideration is the price that is given to obtain the promise, past benefits conferred on the promisor cannot be consideration.

A promise to refrain from doing an act can be consideration. A promise to refrain from suing or asserting a particular claim can be consideration. When consideration is forbearance to assert a claim, it is immaterial whether the claim is valid as long as the claim has been asserted in the good-faith belief that it was valid.

When the promisor obtains the consideration specified for the promise, the law is not ordinarily concerned with the value or adequacy of that consideration.

Under the doctrine of promissory estoppel a court may enforce a promise lacking consideration where it is the only way to avoid injustice.

LEARNING OUTCOMES

After studying this chapter, you should be able to clearly explain:

A. GENERAL PRINCIPLES—CONSIDERATION

LO.1 Explain what constitutes consideration
See the "bargained for exchange" example involving Beth and Kerry, p. 299.
See the "benefit-detriment" approach to consideration example, p. 299.
See the discussion on forbearance as consideration on p. 300.

B. SPECIAL SITUATIONS

LO.2 Distinguish between a "preexisting legal obligation" and "past consideration"
See the preexisting duty example involving Officer Rogers on p. 301.
See the example involving Fred O'Neal where he found out the past consideration is no consideration rule, p. 304.

LO.3 Explain why promises based on moral obligations lack consideration.
See the example of the gratuitous deeds of Tom Synder on p. 305.

C. EXCEPTIONS TO THE LAWS OF CONSIDERATION

LO.4 List the exceptions to the requirement of consideration
See the discussion on charitable subscriptions, the UCC, and promissory estoppel starting on p. 305.

LO.5 Explain the "fundamental idea" underlying promissory estoppel
See the *Chaplake Holdings* case where the court enforced Chrysler's promise in order to correct an injustice, p. 306.

KEY TERMS

cancellation provision
composition of creditors
consideration

forbearance
illusory promise
past consideration

preexisting legal obligation
promissory estoppel

QUESTIONS AND CASE PROBLEMS

1. Sarah's house caught on fire. Through the prompt assistance of her neighbor Odessa, the fire was quickly extinguished. In gratitude, Sarah promised to pay Odessa $1,000. Can Odessa enforce this promise? No - moral obligation

2. William E. Story agreed to pay his nephew, William E. Story II, a large sum of money (roughly equivalent to $50,000 in 2007 dollars) "if he would refrain from drinking liquor, using tobacco, swearing, and playing cards or billiards for money until he should come to be 21 years of age." William II had been using tobacco and occasionally drank liquor but refrained from using these stimulants over several years until he was 21 and also lived up to the other requirements of his uncle's offer. Just after William II's 21st birthday, Story acknowledged that William II had fulfilled his part of the bargain and advised that the money would be invested for him with interest. Story died, and his executor, Sidway, refused to pay William II because he believed the contract between Story and William II was without consideration. Sidway asserted that Story received no benefit from William II's performance and William II suffered no detriment (in fact, by his refraining from the use of liquor and tobacco, William II was not harmed but benefited, Sidway asserted). Is there any theory of consideration that William II can rely on? How would you decide this case? [*Hamer v Sidway,* 124 NY 538]

Forbearance

3. Dale Dyer, who was employed by National By-Products, Inc., was seriously injured at work as the result of a job-related accident. He agreed to give up his right to sue the employer for damages in consideration of the employer's giving him a lifetime job. The employer later claimed that this agreement was not binding because Dyer's promise not to sue could not be consideration for the promise to employ on the ground that Dyer in fact had no right to sue. Dyer's only remedy was to make a claim under workers' compensation. Was the agreement binding? [*Dyer v National By-Products, Inc.,* 380 NW2d 732 (Iowa)]

4. Charles Sanarwari retained Stan Gissel to prepare his income tax return for the year 2006. The parties agreed on a fee of $400. Charles had done a rough estimate based on last year's return and believed he would owe the IRS approximately $2,000. When Stan's work was completed, it turned out that Charles would receive a $2,321 tax refund. Stan explained how certain legitimate advantages were used to reduce Charles's tax obligation. Charles paid for Stan's services and was so pleased with the work that he promised to pay Stan an additional $400 for the excellent job on the tax return when he received his tax refund. Thereafter, Stan and Charles had a falling out over a golf tournament where Charles was late for his tee time and Stan started without him, causing Charles to lose an opportunity to win the club championship. Stan was not paid the $400 promised for doing an excellent job on the tax return, and he sued Charles as a matter of principle. Decide.

5. Medistar is a real estate development company specializing in the development of medical facilities. Dr. Schmidt, the team physician for the San Antonio Spurs basketball team, sought to develop "The Texas Center for Athletes" medical center next to the Spurs facility and urged Medistar to obtain the real estate and develop the project on his group's behalf. Medistar spent more than $1 million and thousands of man-hours on the project from 2000 to July 12, 2004 when Dr. Schmidt's new group of investors purchased the property next to the Spur's facility for the project; subsequently, Medistar was

informed that it would have no role in the project. Medistar asserts that it relied on Dr. Schmidt's assurances that it would be the developer of the project—and after four years and the $1 million in time and expenses it spent, it is unconscionable to be excluded from the project. Dr. Schmidt and associates contend that Medistar has presented no contractual agreement tying it to any legal obligation to Medistar. Is there a viable legal theory available to Medistar? If so what is the remedy? [*Medistar v Schmidt*, 267 SW3d 150 (Tex App)]

6. Fedun rented a building to Gomer, who did business under the name of Mike's Cafe. Later, Gomer was about to sell the business to Brown and requested Fedun to release him from his liability under the lease. Fedun agreed to do so. Brown sold the business shortly thereafter. The balance of the rent due by Gomer under the original lease agreement was not paid, and Fedun sued Gomer on the rent claim. Could he collect after having released Gomer? [*Fedun v Mike's Cafe*, 204 A2d 776 (Pa Super)]

7. Alexander Proudfoot Co. was in the business of devising efficiency systems for industry. It told Sanitary Linen Service Co. that it could provide an improved system for Sanitary Linen that would save Sanitary Linen money. It made a contract with Sanitary Linen to provide a money-saving system. The system was put into operation, and Proudfoot was paid the amount due under the contract. The system failed to work and did not save money. Sanitary Linen sued to get the money back. Was it entitled to do so? [*Sanitary Linen Service Co. v Alexander Proudfoot Co.*, 435 F2d 292 (5th Cir)]

8. Sears, Roebuck and Co. promised to give Forrer permanent employment. Forrer sold his farm at a loss to take the job. Shortly after beginning work, he was discharged by Sears, which claimed that the contract could be terminated at will. Forrer claimed that promissory estoppel prevented Sears from terminating the contract. Was he correct? [*Forrer v Sears, Roebuck & Co.*, 153 NW2d 587 (Wis)]

9. Kemp leased a gas filling station from Baehr. Kemp, who was heavily indebted to Penn-O-Tex

Oil Corp., transferred to it his right to receive payments on all claims. When Baehr complained that the rent was not paid, he was assured by the corporation that the rent would be paid to him. Baehr did not sue Kemp for the overdue rent but later sued the corporation. The defense was raised that there was no consideration for the promise of the corporation. Decide. [*Baehr v Penn-O-Tex Corp.*, 104 NW2d 661 (Minn)]

10. Bogart owed several debts to Security Bank & Trust Co. and applied to the bank for a loan to pay the debts. The bank's employee stated that he would take the application for the loan to the loan committee and "within two or three days, we ought to have something here, ready for you to go with." The loan was not made. The bank sued Bogart for his debts. He filed a counterclaim on the theory that the bank had broken its contract to make a loan to him and that promissory estoppel prevented the bank from going back on what the employee had said. Was this counterclaim valid?

11. Kelsoe worked for International Wood Products, Inc., for a number of years. One day Hernandez, a director and major stockholder of the company, promised Kelsoe that the corporation would give her 5 percent of the company's stock. This promise was never kept, and Kelsoe sued International for breach of contract. Had the company broken its contract? [*Kelsoe v International Wood Products, Inc.*, 588 So2d 877 (Ala)]

12. Kathy left her classic 1978 Volkswagen convertible at Freddie's Service Station, requesting a "tune-up." When she returned that evening, Freddie's bill was $374. Kathy stated that Firestone and Sears advertise tune-ups for $70, and she asked Freddie, "How can you justify this bill?" Freddie responded, "Carburetor work." Kathy refused to pay the bill and left. That evening, when the station closed, she took her other set of keys and removed her car, after placing a check in the station's mail slot. The check was made out to Freddie's Service Station for $200 and stated on its face: "This check is in full payment of my account with you regarding the tune-up today on my 1978 Volkswagen

convertible." Freddie cashed the check in order to meet his business expenses and then sued Kathy for the difference owed. What result?

13. On the death of their mother, the children of Jane Smith gave their interests in their mother's estate to their father in consideration of his payment of $1 to each of them and his promise to leave them the property on his death. The father died without leaving them the property. The children sued their father's second wife to obtain the property in accordance with the agreement. The second wife claimed that the agreement was not a binding contract because the amount of $1 and future gifts given for the children's interests were so trivial and uncertain. Decide.

14. Radio Station KSCS broadcast a popular music program. It announced that it would pay $25,000 to any listener who detected that it did not play three consecutive songs. Steve Jennings listened to and heard a program in which two songs were followed by a commercial program. He claimed the $25,000. The station refused to pay on the ground that there was no consideration for its promise to pay that amount. Was the station liable? [*Jennings v Radio Station KSCS*, 708 SW2d 60 (Tex App)]

15. Hoffman wanted to acquire a franchise for a Red Owl grocery store. (Red Owl was a corporation that maintained a system of chain stores.) An agent of Red Owl informed Hoffman and his wife that if they would sell their bakery in Wautoma, acquire a certain tract of land in Chilton (another Wisconsin city), and put up $6,000, they would be given a franchise. In reliance on the agent's promise, Hoffman sold his business and acquired the land in Chilton, but he was never granted a franchise. He and his wife sued Red Owl. Red Owl raised the defense that there had been only an assurance that Hoffman would receive a franchise, but because there was no promise supported by consideration, there was no binding contract to give him a franchise. Decide. [*Hoffman v Red Owl Stores, Inc.*, 133 NW2d 267 (Wis)]

Chapter 16

LEGALITY AND PUBLIC POLICY

A court will not enforce a contract if it is illegal, contrary to public policy, or unconscionable.

A. GENERAL PRINCIPLES

An agreement is illegal either when its formation or performance is a crime or a tort or when it is contrary to public policy or unconscionable.

1. Effect of Illegality

Ordinarily, an illegal agreement is void. When an agreement is illegal, the parties are usually not entitled to the aid of the courts. Examples of illegal contracts where the courts have left the parties where they found them include a liquor store owner not being allowed to bring suit for money owed for goods (liquor) sold and delivered on credit in violation of statute and an unlicensed home improvement contractor not being allowed to enforce his contract for progress payments due him. If the illegal agreement has not been performed, neither party can sue the other to obtain performance or damages. If the agreement has been performed, neither party can sue the other to obtain damages or to set the agreement aside.[1]

Even if a contract appears to be legal on its face, it may be unenforceable if it was entered into for an illegal purpose. **For Example,** if zoning regulations in the special-purpose district of Washington, D.C., require that only a professional can lease space in a given building, and the rental agent suggests that two nonprofessionals take out the lease in their attorney's name, but all parties realize that the premises will be used only by the nonprofessionals, then the lease in question is illegal and unenforceable.[2]

2. Exceptions to Effect of Illegality

To avoid hardship, exceptions are made to the rules stated in Section 1.

(A) PROTECTION OF ONE PARTY. When the law that the agreement violates is intended to protect one of the parties, that party may seek relief. **For Example,** when, in order to protect the public, the law forbids the issuance of securities by certain classes of corporations, a person who has purchased them may recover the money paid.

(B) UNEQUAL GUILT. When the parties are not ***in pari delicto***—equally guilty—the least guilty party is granted relief when public interest is advanced by doing so. **For Example,** when a statute is adopted to protect one of the parties to a transaction, such as a usury law adopted to protect borrowers, the person to be protected will not be deemed to be *in pari delicto* with the wrongdoer when entering into a transaction that the statute prohibits.

3. Partial Illegality

An agreement may involve the performance of several promises, some of which are illegal and some legal. The legal parts of the agreement may be enforced provided that they can be separated from the parts that are illegal.

When the illegal provision of a contract may be ignored without defeating the contract's basic purpose, a court will merely ignore the illegal provision and enforce the balance of the contract. Consequently, when a provision for the payment of an attorney's fee in a car rental agreement was illegal because a local statute prohibited it, the court would merely ignore the fee provision and enforce the balance of the contract.[3]

If a contract is susceptible to two interpretations, one legal and the other illegal, the court will assume that the legal meaning was intended unless the contrary is clearly indicated.

4. Crimes and Civil Wrongs

An agreement is illegal, and therefore void, when it calls for the commission of any act that constitutes a crime. To illustrate, one cannot enforce an agreement by which the other party is to commit an assault, steal property, burn a house, or kill a person. A contract to obtain equipment for committing a crime is illegal

---

[1] *Sabia v Mattituck Inlet Marina, Inc.,* 805 NYS2d 346 (AD 2005).
[2] *McMahon v A, H, & B,* 728 A2d 656 (DC 1999).
[3] *Harbour v Arelco, Inc.,* 678 NE2d 381 (Ind 1997).

and cannot be enforced. Thus, a contract to manufacture and sell illegal slot machines is void.

An agreement that calls for the commission of a civil wrong is also illegal and void. Examples are agreements to slander a third person; defraud another; infringe another's patent, trademark, or copyright; or fix prices.

5. Good Faith and Fairness

Every contract has an implied obligation that neither party shall do anything that will have the effect of destroying or injuring the right of the other party to receive the fruits of the contract. This means that in every contract there exists an implied covenant of **good faith** and fair dealing. **For Example,** Katy Lesser entered into a 10-year lease of retail space to operate a natural food store in South Burlington, Vermont. Her business prospered and in April of 1999 she signed a lease for additional space. For five years, the landlord continually rebuffed her efforts to meet and discuss plans to renovate the 1999 space to expand the grocery store, motivated solely by a desire to pressure the tenant to pay a portion of his legal fees in an unrelated zoning case. The court found that the landlord breached the obligation of good faith and fair dealing, causing the 1999 space to be essentially unusable from 1999 to 2004. The court awarded the tenant the rent she paid for this period less a storage fee adjustment.[4]

6. Unconscionable Clauses

Ordinarily, a court will not consider whether a contract is fair or unfair, is wise or foolish, or operates unequally between the parties. **For Example,** the Kramper Family Farm sold 17.59 acres of land to Dakota Industrial Development, Inc. (DID), for $35,000 per acre if the buyer constructed a paved road along the property by December 31. The contract also provided that if the road was not completed by the date set forth in the contract, the price per acre would be $45,000. When the road was not completed by the December 31 date, Family Farm sued DID for the additional $10,000 per acre.

DID defended that to apply the contract according to its plain language would create an unconscionable result and was an unenforceable penalty provision contrary to public policy. The court refused to allow DID to escape its contractual obligations on the pretext of unconscionability and public policy arguments. The parties are at liberty to contract as they see fit, the court concluded, and generally, a court will not inquire into the adequacy of consideration inasmuch as the value of property is a matter of personal judgment by the parties to the contract. In this case, the price consisted of either $45,000 per acre, or $35,000 per acre with the road by a certain date.[5]

However, in certain unusual situations, the law may hold a contract provision unenforceable because it is too harsh or oppressive to one of the parties. This principle may be applied to invalidate a clause providing for the payment by one party of an excessive penalty on the breaking of a contract or a provision inserted by the dominant party that it shall not be liable for the consequences of intentional torts, fraud, or gross negligence. This principle is extended in connection with the sale of goods to provide that "if the court . . . finds the contract or any clause of the contract to have been unconscionable at the time it was made, the court may refuse to enforce the contract, or it may enforce the remainder of the contract without the unconscionable clause, or it may so limit the application of any unconscionable clause as to avoid any unconscionable result."[6]

(A) WHAT CONSTITUTES UNCONSCIONABILITY? A provision in a contract that gives what the court believes is too much of an advantage over a buyer may be held void as unconscionable.

(B) DETERMINATION OF UNCONSCIONABILITY. Some jurisdictions analyze unconscionability as having two separate elements: procedural and substantive. Both elements must be present for a court to refuse to enforce a contract provision. Other jurisdictions analyze unconscionability by considering the doctrine of adhesion and whether the clause in question is unduly oppressive.

---

[4] *Century Partners, LP v Lesser Goldsmith Enterprises,* 958 A2d 627 (Vt 2008).
[5] *Kramper Family Farm v Dakota Industrial Development, Inc.,* 603 NW2d 463 (Neb App 1999).
[6] UCC § 2-302(1).

Procedural unconscionability has to do with matters of freedom of assent resulting from inequality of bargaining power and the absence of real negotiations and meaningful choice or a surprise resulting from hiding a disputed term in an unduly long document or fine print. Companywide standardized form contracts imposed on a take-it-or-leave-it basis by a party with superior bargaining strength are called **contracts of adhesion**, and they may sometimes be deemed procedurally unconscionable.

Substantive unconscionability focuses on the actual terms of the contract itself. Such unconscionability is indicated when the contract terms are so one-sided as to shock the conscience or are so extreme as to appear unconscionable according to the mores and business practices of the time and place.

The U.S. Supreme Court has made clear that arbitration is an acceptable forum for the resolution of employment disputes between employees and their employers, including employment-related claims based on federal and state statutes.[7] The controlling arbitration agreement language is commonly devised and implemented by the employer. Under the Federal Arbitration Act (FAA), the employer can obtain a court order to stay court proceedings and compel arbitration according to the terms of the controlling arbitration agreement. The Supreme Court also made clear that in agreeing to arbitration of a statutory claim, a party does not forgo substantive rights afforded by the statute. In a growing number of court decisions, in effect employers are finding that courts will not enforce arbitration agreements in which the employer has devised an arbitration agreement that functions as a thumb on the employer's side of the scale.[8] The *Circuit City II* decision on remand from the U.S. Supreme Court contains an example of an unenforceable arbitration clause.

Circuit City Stores, Inc. v Adams (Circuit City II), 279 F3d 889 (9th Cir 2002)

Arbitration Agreement Short-Circuited

Saint Clair Adams completed an application to work as a sales person at Circuit City. As part of the application, Adams signed the "Circuit City Dispute Resolution Agreement" (DRA). The DRA requires employees to submit all claims and disputes to binding arbitration. Incorporated into the DRA are a set of "Dispute Resolution Rules and Procedures" that define the claims subject to arbitration, discovery rules, allocation of fees, and available remedies. Under these rules, the amount of damages is restricted: Back pay is limited to one year, front pay to two years, and punitive damages to the greater of the amount of front and back pay awarded or $5,000. In addition, the employee is required to split the cost of the arbitration, including the daily fees of the arbitrator, the cost of a reporter to transcribe the proceedings, and the expense of renting the room in which the arbitration is held, unless the employee prevails and the arbitrator decides to order Circuit City to pay the employee's share of the costs. Circuit City is not required under the agreement to arbitrate any claims against the employee. An employee cannot work at Circuit City without signing the DRA. Adams filed a state court lawsuit against Circuit City and three co-workers alleging sexual harassment, retaliation, constructive discharge, and intentional infliction of emotional distress under the California Fair Employment and Housing Act (FEHA). Adams sought compensatory, punitive, and emotional distress damages for alleged repeated harassment during his entire term of employment. Circuit City responded by filing a petition in federal district court to compel arbitration pursuant to the FAA. The petition was granted by the trial court, reversed by the Ninth Circuit Court of Appeals, which court was reversed by the U.S. Supreme Court (*Circuit City I*) and the case remanded to the Ninth Circuit Court of Appeals.

JUDICIAL OPINION

NELSON, C. J. . . . Circuit City has devised an arbitration agreement that functions as a thumb on Circuit City's side of

---

[7] *Gilmer v Interstate/Johnson Lane Corp.*, 500 US 20 (1991); *Circuit City Stores, Inc. v Adams*, 532 US 105 (2001).
[8] See *Vassilkouska v Woodfield Nissan Inc.*, 830 NE2d 619 (Ill App 2005).

Continued

the scale should an employment dispute ever arise between the company and one of its employees. We conclude that such an arrangement is unconscionable under California law.

A. Applicable Law

. . .Section 2 of the FAA provides that arbitration agreements "shall be valid, irrevocable, and enforceable, *save upon such grounds that exist at law or in equity for the revocation of any contract.*" 9 U.S.C. § 2 (emphasis added). In determining the validity of an agreement to arbitrate, federal courts "should apply ordinary state-law principles that govern the formation of contracts." *First Options of Chicago, Inc. v Kaplan* 514 U.S. 938, 944, (1995). . . . Thus general contact defenses such as fraud, duress, or unconscionability, grounded in state contract law, may operate to invalidate arbitration agreements. . . .

Under California law, a contract is unenforceable if it is both procedurally and substantively unconscionable. *Arinendariz v Found. Health Pshychcare Svcs., Inc.* 24 Cal.4th 83, 99 Cal.Rptr.2d 145, 6 P.3d 669, 690 (2000). . .

B. The DRA and Unconscionability

The DRA is procedurally unconscionable because it is a contract of adhesion: a standard form contract, drafted by the party with superior bargaining power, which relegates to the other party the option of either adhering to its terms without modification or rejecting the contract entirely. . . Circuit City, which possesses considerably more bargaining power than nearly all of its employees or applicants, drafted the contract and uses it as its standard arbitration agreement for all of its new employees. The agreement is a prerequisite to employment, and job applicants are not permitted to modify the agreement's terms—they must take the contract or leave it. . . .

The California Supreme Court's recent decision in *Armendariz* counsels in favor of finding that the Circuit City arbitration agreement is substantively unconscionable as well. . . .

We find the arbitration agreement at issue here virtually indistinguishable from the agreement the California Supreme Court found unconscionable in *Armendariz*. Like the agreemerit in *Armendariz*, the DRA unilaterally forces employees to arbitrate claims against the employer. The claims subject to arbitration under the DRA include "any and all employment-related legal disputes, controversies or claims *of an Associate* arising out of, or relating to, an Associate's application or candidacy for employment, employment or cessation of employment with Circuit City." (emphasis added). The provision does not require Circuit City to arbitrate its claims against employees. . . . This unjustified onesidedness deprives the DRA of the "modicum of bilaterality" that the California

Supreme Court requires for contracts to be enforceable under California law.

And again as in *Armendariz*, the asymmetry is compounded by the fact that the agreement limits the relief available to employees. Under the DRA, the remedies are limited to injunctive relief, up to one year of back pay and up to two years of front pay, compensatory damages, and punitive damages in an amount up to the greater of the amount of back pay and front pay awarded or $5,000. By contrast, a plaintiff in a civil suit for sexual harassment under the FEHA is eligible for all forms of relief that are generally available to civil litigants—including appropriate punitive damages and damages for emotional distress. The DRA also requires the employee to split the arbitrator's fees with Circuit City. This fee allocation scheme alone would render an arbitration agreement unenforceable. . . . In short, and just like the agreement invalidated by the California Supreme Court in *Armendariz*, the DRA forces Adams to arbitrate his statutory claims without affording him the benefit of the full range of statutory remedies.

In addition, our decision is entirely consistent with federal law concerning the enforceability of arbitration agreements. The Supreme Court, in *Gilmer v Interstate/ Johnson Lane Corp.* 500 U.S. 20, 26, 111 S.Ct. 1647, 114 L.Ed.2d 26(1991), held that "[b]y agreeing to arbitrate a statutory claim, [an employee] does not forgo the substantive rights afforded by the statute; [he] only submits to their resolution in an arbitral, rather than a judicial forum." While the Court in *Gilmer* affirmed that statutory rights can be resolved through arbitration, the decision also recognized that the arbitral forum must allow the employee to adequately pursue statutory rights. *Id.* at 28., 111 S. Ct. 1647

Courts have since interpreted *Gilmer* to require basic procedural and remedial protections so that claimants can effectively pursue their statutory rights. . . . We note that here, Circuit City's arbitration agreement . . . fails to provide for all of the types of relief that would otherwise be available in court, or to ensure that employees do not have to pay either unreasonable costs or. . . fees . . . as a condition of access to the arbitration forum. . . .

C. Severability

Under California law, courts have discretion to sever an unconscionable provision or refuse to enforce the contract in its entirety. . . .

In this case, as in *Armendariz*, the objectionable provisions pervade the entire contract. In addition to the damages limitation and the feesharing scheme, the unilateral aspect of the DRA runs throughout the agreement and defines the scope of the matters that are covered. Removing these provisions would go beyond mere excision to rewriting the

contract, which is not the proper role of this Court. Therefore, we find the entire arbitration agreement unenforceable.
[Reversed]

QUESTIONS

1. What body of law may courts use to examine the validity of arbitration agreements?

2. What reason does the Court of Appeals give for its determination that Circuit City's DRA was procedurally unconscionable?

3. What reason(s) did the Court of Appeals give for its determination that Circuit City's DRA was substantively unconscionable?

B. AGREEMENTS AFFECTING PUBLIC WELFARE

Agreements that may harm the public welfare are condemned as contrary to public policy and are not binding. Agreements that interfere with public service or the duties of public officials, obstruct legal process, or discriminate against classifications of individuals may be considered detrimental to public welfare and, as such, are not enforceable.

7. Agreements Contrary to Public Policy

A given agreement may not violate any statute but may still be so offensive to society that the courts feel that enforcing the contract would be contrary to public policy.

Public policy cannot be defined precisely but is loosely described as protection from that which tends to be injurious to the public or contrary to the public good or which violates any established interest of society. Contracts that may be unenforceable as contrary to public policy frequently relate to the protection of the public welfare, health, or safety; to the protection of the person; and to the protection of recognized social institutions. **For Example,** a woman entered into a services contract with a male in exchange for financial support. The record disclosed, however, that the association between the parties was one founded upon the exchange of money for sex. The court determined that the agreement for financial support in exchange for illicit sexual relations was violative of public policy and thus was unenforceable.[9] Courts are cautious in invalidating a contract on the ground that it is contrary to public policy because courts recognize that, on the one hand, they are applying a very vague standard and, on the other hand, they are restricting the freedom of the contracting parties to contract freely as they choose.[10]

8. Gambling, Wagers, and Lotteries

Gambling contracts are illegal. Largely as a result of the adoption of antigambling statutes, wagers or bets are generally illegal. Private **lotteries** involving the three elements of prize, chance, and consideration (or similar affairs of chance) are also generally held illegal. In many states, public lotteries (lotteries run by a state government) have been legalized by statute. Raffles are usually regarded as lotteries. In some states, bingo games, lotteries, and raffles are legalized by statute when the funds raised are used for a charitable purpose.

Sales promotion schemes calling for the distribution of property according to chance among the purchasers of goods are held illegal as lotteries without regard to whether the scheme is called a *guessing contest*, a *raffle*, or a *gift*.

Giveaway plans and games are lawful so long as it is not necessary to buy anything or give anything of value to participate. If participation is free, the

---

[9] *Anonymous v Anonymous,* 740 NYS2d 341 (App Div 2002).
[10] *Beacon Hill Civic Ass'n v Ristorante Toscano, Inc.,* 662 NE2d 1015 (Mass 1996).

element of consideration is lacking, and there is no lottery.

An activity is not gambling when the result is solely or predominantly a matter of skill. In contrast, it is gambling when the result is solely a matter of luck. Rarely is any activity 100 percent skill or 100 percent luck.

C. REGULATION OF BUSINESS

Local, state, and national laws regulate a wide variety of business activities and practices.

9. Effect of Violation

Whether an agreement made in connection with business conducted in violation of the law is binding or void depends on how strongly opposed the public policy is to the prohibited act. Some courts take the view that the agreement is not void unless the statute expressly specifies this. In some instances, a statute expressly preserves the validity of the contract. **For Example,** if someone fails to register a fictitious name under which a business is conducted, the violator, after registering the name as required by statute, is permitted to sue on a contract made while illegally conducting business.

10. Statutory Regulation of Contracts

To establish uniformity or to protect one of the parties to a contract, statutes frequently provide that contracts of a given class must follow a statutory model or must contain specified provisions. **For Example,** statutes commonly specify that particular clauses must be included in insurance policies to protect the persons insured and their beneficiaries. Other statutes require that contracts executed in connection with credit buying and loans contain particular provisions designed to protect the debtor.

Consumer protection legislation gives the consumer the right to rescind the contract in certain situations. Laws relating to truth in lending,

installment sales, and home improvement contracts commonly require that an installment-sale contract specify the cash price, the down payment, the trade-in value (if any), the cash balance, the insurance costs, and the interest and finance charges.

CPA 11. Licensed Callings or Dealings

Statutes frequently require that a person obtain a license, certificate, or diploma before practicing certain professions, such as law and medicine.[11] A license may also be required before carrying on a particular business or trade, such as that of a real estate broker, stockbroker, hotel keeper, or pawnbroker.

If a license is required to protect the public from unqualified persons, a contract made by an unlicensed person is unenforceable. **For Example,** a corporation that does not hold a required real estate broker's license cannot sue to recover fees for services as a broker. An unlicensed insurance broker who cannot recover a fee because of the absence of a license cannot evade the statutory requirement by having a friend who is a licensed broker bill for the services and collect the payment for him.

CPA 12. Contracts in Restraint of Trade

An agreement that unreasonably restrains trade is illegal and void on the ground that it is contrary to public policy. Such agreements take many forms, such as a combination to create a monopoly or to obtain a corner on the market or an association of merchants to increase prices. In addition to the illegality of the agreement based on general principles of law, statutes frequently declare monopolies illegal and subject the parties to various civil and criminal penalties.[12]

CPA 13. Agreements Not to Compete

In the absence of a valid restrictive covenant, the seller of a business may compete with the buyer, or an

---

[11] *Hakimi v Cantwell*, 855 NYS2d 273 (App Div 2008).
[12] Sherman Antitrust Act, 15 USC §§ 1–7; Clayton Act, 15 USC §§ 12–27; Federal Trade Commission Act, 15 USC §§ 41–58.

ex-employee may solicit customers of the former employer.

A noncompetition covenant may be held invalid because of vagueness concerning the duration and geographic area of the restriction.[13] Moreover, if the agreement not to compete is not properly executed in accordance with state law, it will not be enforced. **For Example,** Holly Martinez worked for Avis Rent-A-Car at the New Bern, North Carolina, airport. When hired, she printed her name on the top of the form containing an agreement not to compete but did not sign it. On December 17, she resigned her position to return to school, saying that she planned to get a part-time job. The next day, she began working for Hertz Rent-A-Car at the counter adjacent to the Avis counter. Avis was unsuccessful in obtaining a re-straining order to prevent Holly from working for its competitor because the agreement was not signed as required by state law.[14]

CPA   (A) SALE OF BUSINESS. When a going business is sold, it is commonly stated in the contract that the seller shall not go into the same or a similar business again within a certain geographic area or for a certain period of time, or both. In early times, such agreements were held void because they deprived the public of the service of the person who agreed not to compete, impaired the latter's means of earning a livelihood, reduced competition, and exposed the public to monopoly. To modern courts, the question is whether, under the circumstances, the restriction imposed on one party is reasonably necessary to protect the other party. If the restriction is reasonable, it is valid and enforceable. **For Example,** when Scott Gaddy, the majority stockholder of GWC Insurance Brokers, sold his business to Alliant for $4.1 million he agreed to refrain from competing in the insurance business in California for five years. Under California law, contracts not to compete are void, except for noncompetition covenants in connection with the sale of a business. The reason for the exception is to

prevent the seller from depriving the buyer of the full value of the acquisition, including the sold company's goodwill. The court enforced the covenant against Gaddy.[15]

(B) EMPLOYMENT CONTRACT. Restrictions to prevent competition by a former employee are held valid when reasonable and necessary to protect the interest of the former employer. **For Example,** a noncompete clause executed by Dr. Samuel Keeley that prohib-ited his "establishing a competing cardiovascular surgery practice within a 75-mile radius of Albany, Georgia, for a period of two years following the date of termination" was upheld in court and did not include more territory than necessary to protect the professional corporation's business interests.[16]

Public policy requires that noncompetition cove-nants be strictly construed in favor of freedom of action of the employee.[17] A restrictive covenant is not binding when it places a restriction on the employee that is broader than reasonably necessary to protect the employer. **For Example,** Illinois manufacturer Arcor's noncompete clause, which had a restricted area of "the United States and Canada" precluding competition by a former employee for a one-year period, was found to be unenforceable as an indus-trywide ban that constituted a "blanket prohibition on competition."[18] In determining the validity of a restrictive covenant binding an employee, the court balances the aim of protecting the legitimate interests of the employer with the right of the employee to follow gainful employment and provide services required by the public and other employers.

(C) EFFECT OF INVALIDITY. When a restriction of compe-tition agreed to by the parties is invalid because its scope as to time or geographic area is too great, how does this affect the contract? Some courts trim the restrictive covenant down to a scope they deem reasonable and require the parties to abide by that revision.[19] This rule is nicknamed the "blue-pencil rule."

[13] *Vukovich v Coleman,* 789 NE2d 520 (Ind App 2003).
[14] *New Hanover Rent-A-Car, Inc. v Martinez,* 525 SE2d 487 (NC App 2000).
[15] 72 Cal Rptr 3d 259 (Cal App 2008).
[16] *Keeley v CSA, P.C.,* 510 SE2d 880 (Ga App 1999).
[17] Noncompetition covenants are not valid in California. However, confidentiality agreements protecting trade secrets are enforceable in that state.
[18] *Arcor, Inc. v Haas,* 842 NE2d 265 (Ill App 2005).
[19] *Unisource Worldwide, Inc. v Valenti,* 196 F Supp 2d 269 (EDNY 2002).

thinking things through

Noncompete Clauses, Cause for Concern?

Some 10 states do not enforce noncompete clauses in employment contracts, according to the research of Matt Marx who has dedicated his doctoral studies at Harvard to this topic. The states are (from west to east): California, Washington, Nevada, Montana, North Dakota, Minnesota, Oklahoma, West Virginia, and Connecticut. (New York and Oregon have significantly limited their applicability). Marx had naively signed a two-year noncompete agreement out of MIT at SpeechWorks, a voice recognition start-up, and when he wanted to leave and continue in the voice recognition field, his options were to sit out the two-year noncompete period or go to work at a California firm, which he did. He is now researching whether enforcing noncompetes in a state can spur inventors, engineers, and entrepreneurs to move elsewhere to pursue development of their ideas.*

Does a state's innovation suffer when noncompete clauses handcuff employees to an employer, or force employees to take an unpaid leave for the noncompete period before continuing in their field with a new or start-up employer? THINKING THINGS THROUGH, prospective employees should carefully consider the impact noncompetes would have on their lives, and if they must sign one, carefully negotiate its duration and scope.

* *See* Scott Kirsner, "Why 'Noncompete' Means 'Don't Thrive,'" *Boston Globe*, December 30, 2007, E-1; Scott Kirsner, "Start-ups Stifled by Noncompetes," *Boston Globe*, June 21, 2009, G-1.

For Example, Julie Murray signed a noncompete agreement, which was validly assigned to the purchaser of the Accounting Center of Lucas County, Inc. When the new owner changed from an hourly wage to commission pay for her tax preparation work, she objected and was terminated. The court found the 24-month noncompete restriction exceeded what was reasonable to protect the employer's legitimate business interests, and modified the time period to one year.[20] In the *Arcor* case, the court refused to "blue pencil" the covenant because to render the clause reasonable, the court would in effect be writing a new agreement, which is inappropriate.[21]

Other courts refuse to apply the blue-pencil rule and hold that the restrictive covenant is void or that the entire contract is void.[22] There is also authority that a court should refuse to apply the blue-pencil rule when the restrictive covenant is manifestly unfair and would virtually keep the employee from earning a living.

14. Usurious Agreements

Usury is committed when money is loaned at a higher rate of interest than the law allows. Most states prohibit by statute charging more than a stated amount of interest. These statutes provide a maximum annual contract rate of interest that can be exacted under the law of a given state. In many states, the usury law does not apply to loans made to corporations.

When a lender incurs expenses in making a loan, such as the cost of appraising property or making a credit investigation of the borrower, the lender will require the borrower to pay the amount of such expenses. Any fee charged by a lender that goes

---

[20] *Murray v Accounting Center of Lucas County, Inc.*, 898 NE2d 89 (Ohio App 2008).
[21] *Arcor Inc.*, 847 NE2d at 374.
[22] *SWAT 24 v Bond*, 759 So2d 1047 (La App 2000). Under California law, any "contract by which anyone is restrained from engaging in a lawful profession, trade or business is to that extent void." Cal B&P Code § 16600. A noncompete provision is permitted, however, when "necessary to protect the employer's trade secrets." See *Lotona v Aetna U.S. Healthcare Inc.*, 82 F Supp 3d 1089 (CD Cal 1999), where Aetna was liable for wrongful termination when it fired a California employee for refusing to sign a noncompete agreement.

ethics&the law

William Stern and his wife were unable to have children because the wife suffered from multiple sclerosis and pregnancy posed a substantial health risk. Stern's family had been killed in the Holocaust, and he had a strong desire to continue his bloodline.

The Sterns entered into a surrogacy contract with Mary Beth Whitehead through the Infertility Center of New York (ICNY). William Stern and the Whiteheads (husband and wife) signed a contract for Mary Beth to be artificially inseminated and carry Stern's child to term, for which Stern was to pay Mary Beth $10,000 and ICNY $7,500.

Mary Beth was successfully artificially inseminated in 1985, and Baby M was born on March 27, 1986. To avoid publicity, the parents of Baby M were listed as "Mr. and Mrs. Whitehead," and the baby was called Sara Elizabeth Whitehead. On March 30, 1986, Mary Beth turned Baby M over to the Sterns at their home. They renamed the little girl Melissa.

Mary Beth became emotionally distraught and was unable to eat or sleep. The Sterns were so frightened by her behavior that they allowed her to take Baby M for one week to help her adjust. The Whiteheads took the baby and traveled throughout the East, staying in 20 different hotels and motels. Florida authorities found Baby M with Mary Beth's parents and returned her to the Sterns.

Mary Beth said the contract was one to buy a baby and was against public policy and therefore void. She also argued that the contract violated state laws on adoption and the severance of parental rights. The Sterns brought an action to have the contract declared valid and custody awarded to them.

Should the contract be valid or void? What types of behavior would be encouraged if the contract were declared valid? Is it ethical to "rent a womb"? Is it ethical to sell a child? See **In re Baby M, 537 A2d 15 (NJ 1988).**

thinking things through

Legality and Public Policy

Karl Llewellyn, the principal drafter of the law that governs nearly all sales of goods in the United States—the Uniform Commercial Code (UCC)—once wrote, "Covert tools are never reliable tools." He was referring to unfairness in a contract or between the contracting parties.

The original intent of declaring certain types of contracts void because of issues of imbalance was based in equity. Courts stepped in to help parties who found themselves bound under agreements that were not fair and open in both their written terms and the communications between the parties. One contracts scholar wrote that the original intent could be described as courts stepping in to help "presumptive sillies like sailors and heirs. . ." and others who, if not crazy, are "pretty peculiar."

However, as the sophistication of contracts and commercial transactions increased, the importance of accuracy, honesty, and fairness increased. Unconscionability is a contracts defense that permits courts to intervene where contracts, if enforced, would "affront the sense of decency." *unconscionability* is a term of ethics or moral philosophy used by courts to prevent exploitation and fraud.

beyond the reasonable expense of making the loan constitutes "interest" for the purposes of determining whether the transaction is usurious.[23]

Penalites for violating usury laws vary from state to state, with a number of states restricting the lender to the recovery of the loan but no interest whatsoever; other states allow recovery of the loan principal and interest up to the maximum contract rate. Some states also impose a penalty on the lender such as the payment of double the interest paid on a usurious loan.

As developed in the *Pinchuck* case, many states require forfeiture of the entire principal amount of the usurious loan.

Pinchuck V Canzoneri, 920 So2Nd 713 (Fla App 4, 2006)

A Needle of Usury in a Haystack of Subterfuge

Karen Canzoneri entered into two agreements with Howard Pinchuck. Under the first agreement Canzoneri advanced $50,000 to be repaid 12 percent per month for 12 consecutive months "as an investment profit." The second agreement required "$36,000 to be repaid on or before 6/1/01 with an investment profit of $36,000, total being $72,000." The annualized rate of return for the first transaction was 144 percent; and the annualized rate for the second transaction was 608 percent. The civil penalty for violating the state's maximum interest rate of 25 percent per annum is forfeiture of the entire principal amount. Canzoneri contends that the transactions were investments not subject to the usury law.

JUDICIAL OPINION

HAZOURI, J. . . . In *Jersey Palm–Gross, Inc. v Paper* 658 So.2d 531 (Fla. 1995), the supreme court stated:

The Florida Legislature enacted Chapter 687, Florida Statutes (1993), to protect borrowers from paying unfair and excessive interest to overreaching creditors. This chapter sets limits on interest rates and prescribes penalties for the violation of those limits. Section 687.071(2), Florida Statutes (1993), defines criminal usury as the willful and knowing charge or receipt of interest in excess of 25 percent per annum. Id. The civil penalty for violating this statute is forfeiture of the entire principal amount. § 687.071(7), Fla.Stat. (1993).

Jersey Palm–Gross, Inc. 658 So.2d at 534.

The four requirements of a usurious transaction are:

(1) that such transaction must be a loan, expressed or implied; (2) that an understanding must exist between the parties that the money lent shall be returned; (3) that for such loan, a greater rate of interest than is allowed by law shall be paid or agreed to be paid as the case may be; and (4) that there must exist a corrupt intention to take more than the legal rate for the use of the money loaned.

Diversified Enters., Inc. v West 141 So.2d 27, 29 (Fla. 2d DCA 1962).

The trial court found that the agreements included in counts I and V were valid and binding contracts. . . .

. . .Even though the agreements which were the subjects of counts I and V were put in terms of investment and the return is called profit, not interest, this does not change our conclusion that these were loans and the transactions were usurious.

It is well settled in Florida that the courts will look to the substance of the transaction rather than to the form to determine usury. See *Kay v Amendola* 129 So.2d 170 (Fla. 2d DCA 1961).

Our usury statutes show a clear legislative intent to prevent accomplishment of a usurious scheme by indirection, and the concealment of the needle of usury in a haystack of subterfuge will not avail to prevent its pricking the body of the law into action.

[Reversed and Remanded]

QUESTIONS

1. State the four elements of a usurious transaction.

2. How did the court decide this case?

3. Did the court order the borrower, Pinchuck, to repay the principal amount owed the lender, Canzoneri?

---

[23] *Lentimo v Cullen Center Bank and Trust Co.*, 919 SW2d 743 (Tex App 1996).

lawflix

Midnight Run (1988) (R)

Is the contract Robert DeNiro has for bringing in Charles Grodin, an embezzler, legal? Discuss the issues of consideration and ethics as the bail bondsman puts another bounty hunter on the case and DeNiro flees from law enforcement agents in order to collect his fee. And finally, discuss the legality of DeNiro's acceptance of money from Grodin and his release of Grodin at the end of the movie.

You can view a clip of this movie and others that illustrate business law concepts at the LawFlix site, located at **www.cengage.com/blaw/dvl**.

MAKE THE CONNECTION

SUMMARY

When an agreement is illegal, it is ordinarily void and no contract arises from it. Courts will not allow one party to an illegal agreement to bring suit against the other party. There are some exceptions to this, such as when the parties are not equally guilty or when the law's purpose in making the agreement illegal is to protect the person who is bringing suit. When possible, an agreement will be interpreted as being lawful. Even when a particular provision is held unlawful, the balance of the agreement may be saved so that the net result is a contract minus the clause that was held illegal.

The term *illegality* embraces situations in unconscionable contract clauses in which the courts hold that contract provisions are unenforceable because they are too harsh or oppressive to one of the parties to a transaction. If the clause is part of a standard form contract drafted by the party having superior bargaining power and is presented on a take-it-or-leave-it basis (a contract of adhesion) and the substantive terms of the clause itself are unduly oppressive, the clause will be found to be unconscionable and not enforced.

Whether a contract is contrary to public policy may be difficult to determine because public policy is not precisely defined. That which is harmful to the public welfare or general good is contrary to public policy. Contracts condemned as contrary to public policy include those designed to deprive the weaker party of a benefit that the lawmaker desired to provide, agreements injuring public service, and wagers and private lotteries. Statutes commonly make the wager illegal as a form of gambling. The private lottery is any plan under which, for a consideration, a person has a chance to win a prize.

Illegality may consist of the violation of a statute or administrative regulation adopted to regulate business. An agreement not to compete may be illegal as a restraint of trade except when reasonable in its terms and when it is incidental to the sale of a business or to a contract of employment.

The charging by a lender of a higher rate of interest than allowed by law is usury. Courts must examine transactions carefully to see whether a usurious loan is disguised as a legitimate transaction.

LEARNING OUTCOMES

After studying this chapter, you should be able to clearly explain:

A. GENERAL PRINCIPLES

LO.1 Explain the general contract principles on "illegality"

See the unenforceable illegal lease to nonprofessionals example on p. 313.
See the example where a contract to manufacture and sell illegal slot machines is void, p. 314.

LO.2 Explain the implied obligation on all parties of good faith and fair dealing

See the example of the Vermont landlord who deprived a tenant of her rights under a lease, p. 314.

B. AGREEMENTS AFFECTING PUBLIC WELFARE

LO.3 Understand that it is only in unusual situations that a contract provision will be unenforceable because it is unconscionable

See the *Kramper Family Farm* example where the court refused to consider whether the contract was fair or unfair, wise or foolish, p. 314.

C. REGULATION OF BUSINESS

LO.4 Explain the rationale for requiring licenses to carry on as a business, trade, or profession

See the discussion requiring licenses to protect the public from unqualified persons, p. 318.

LO.5 Distinguish between noncompete clauses after the sale of a business and noncompete clauses in employment contracts

See the example where the California court enforced a 5 year noncompete clause against the seller of a business, p. 319.
See the example involving Julie Murray's noncompete clause and why it was modified from 24 months to one year, p. 320.

KEY TERMS

contracts of adhesion
in pari delicto
good faith

lotteries
public policy

unconscionable clauses
usury

QUESTIONS AND CASE PROBLEMS

1. When are the parties to an illegal agreement *in pari delicto?*

2. John Iwen sued U.S. West Direct because of a negligently constructed yellow pages advertisement. U.S. West Direct moved to stay litigation and compel arbitration under the yellow pages order form, which required advertisers to resolve all controversies through arbitration, but allowed U.S. West (the publisher) to pursue judicial remedies to collect amounts due it. Under the arbitration provision, Iwen's sole remedy was a pro rata reduction or refund of the cost of the advertisement. The order form language was drafted by U.S. West Direct on a take-it-or-leave-it basis and stated in part:

   Any controversy or claim arising out of or relating to this Agreement, or breach thereof, other than an action by Publisher for the collection of amounts due under this Agreement, shall be settled by final, binding arbitration in accordance with the Commercial Arbitration rules of the American Arbitration Association.

   If forced to arbitration, Iwen would be unable to recover damages for the negligently constructed yellow pages ad, nor could he recover damages for infliction of emotional distress and punitive damages related to his many efforts to adjust the matter with the company, which were ignored or rejected. Must Iwen have his case resolved through arbitration rather than a court of law? [*Iwen v U.S. West Direct*, 977 P2d 989 (Mont)]

3. Sutcliffe Banton, dba Nemard Construction, furnished labor and materials (valued at $162,895) for improving Vicky Deafeamkpor's New York City residential property. She paid only $41,718, leaving $121,987 unpaid. Banton sued her and the jury awarded $90,000 in damages. Deafeamkpor moved for an order setting aside the jury's verdict because Banton was not properly licensed by New York City. Under NYC Code an unlicensed contractor may neither enforce a home improvement contract against an owner or recover in *quantum meruit*. The jury heard all the evidence regarding the materials and labor expended on Deafeamkpor's residence and concluded that the plaintiff performed satisfactory work valued at $90,000 for which he was not paid. Should the court allow the owner to take advantage of Banton and his employees and suppliers? What public policy would support such an outcome? Decide. [*Nemard Construction Corp. v Deafeamkpor*, 863 NYS2d 846]

4. Eugene McCarthy left his position as director of sales for Nike's Brand Jordan division in June 2003 to become vice president of U.S. footwear sales and merchandising at Reebok, one of Nike's competitors. Nike sought a preliminary injunction to prevent McCarthy from working for Reebok for a year, invoking a noncompete agreement McCarthy had signed in Oregon in 1997 when Nike had promoted him to his earlier position as a regional footwear sales manager. The agreement stated in pertinent part:

> *During EMPLOYEE'S employment by NIKE . . . and for one (1) year thereafter, ("the Restriction Period"), EMPLOYEE will not directly or indirectly . . . be employed by, consult for, or be connected in any manner with, any business engaged anywhere in the world in the athletic footwear, athletic*

> *apparel or sports equipment and accessories business, or any other business which directly competes with NIKE or any of its subsidiaries or affiliated corporations.*

McCarty contends that such a contract is a restraint of trade and should not be enforced. Nike contends that the agreement is fair and should be enforced. Decide. [*Nike, Inc. v McCarthy*, 379 F3d 576 (9th Cir)]

5. Ewing was employed by Presto-X-Co., a pest exterminator. His contract of employment specified that he would not solicit or attempt to solicit customers of Presto-X for two years after the termination of his employment. After working several years, his employment was terminated. Ewing then sent a letter to customers of Presto-X stating that he no longer worked for Presto-X and that he was still certified by the state. Ewing set forth his home address and phone number, which the customers did not previously have. The letter ended with the statement, "I thank you for your business throughout the past years." Presto-X brought an action to enjoin Ewing from sending such letters. He raised the defense that he was prohibited only from soliciting and there was nothing in the letters that constituted a seeking of customers. Decide. What ethical values are involved? [*Presto-X-Co. v Ewing*, 442 NW2d 85 (Iowa)]

6. The Minnesota adoption statute requires that any agency placing a child for adoption make a thorough investigation and not give a child to an applicant unless the placement is in the best interests of the child. Tibbetts applied to Cross-roads, Inc., a private adoption agency, for a child to adopt. He later sued the agency for breach of contract, claiming that the agency was obligated by contract to supply a child for adoption. The agency claimed that it was required only to use its best efforts to locate a child and was not required to supply a child to Tibbetts unless it found him to be a suitable parent. Decide. [*Tibbetts v Crossroads, Inc.*, 411 NW2d 535 (Minn App)]

7. Siddle purchased a quantity of fireworks from Red Devil Fireworks Co. The sale was illegal, however, because Siddle did not have a license to make the

purchase, which the seller knew because it had been so informed by the attorney general of the state. Siddle did not pay for the fireworks, and Red Devil sued him. He defended on the ground that the contract could not be enforced because it was illegal. Was the defense valid? [*Red Devil Fireworks Co. v Siddle*, 648 P2d 468 (Wash App)]

8. Onderdonk entered a retirement home operated by Presbyterian Homes. The contract between Onderdonk and the home required Onderdonk to make a specified monthly payment that could be increased by the home as the cost of operations increased. The contract and the payment plan were thoroughly explained to Onderdonk. As the cost of operations rose, the home continually raised the monthly payments to cover these costs. Onderdonk objected to the increases on the ground that the increases were far more than had been anticipated and that the contract was therefore unconscionable. Was his objection valid?

9. Smith was employed as a salesman for Borden, Inc., which sold food products in 63 counties in Arkansas, 2 counties in Missouri, 2 counties in Oklahoma, and 1 county in Texas. Smith's employment contract prohibited him from competing with Borden after leaving its employ. Smith left Borden and went to work for a competitor, Lady Baltimore Foods. Working for this second employer, Smith sold in 3 counties of Arkansas. He had sold in 2 of these counties while he worked for Borden. Borden brought an injunction action against Smith and Lady Baltimore to enforce the noncompete covenant in Smith's former contract. Was Borden entitled to the injunction? [*Borden, Inc. v Smith*, 478 SW2d 744 (Ark)]

10. Central Water Works Supply, a corporation, had a contract with its shareholders that they would not compete with it. There were only four shareholders, of whom William Fisher was one, but he was not an employee of the corporation. When he sold his shares in the corporation and began to compete with it, the corporation went to court to obtain an injunction to stop such competition. Fisher claimed that the corporation was not entitled to an injunction because he had

not obtained any confidential information or made customer contacts. The corporation claimed that such matters were relevant only when an employee had agreed not to compete but were not applicable when there was a noncompetitive covenant in the sale of a business and that the sale-of-a-business rule should be applied to a shareholder. Who was correct?

11. Vodra was employed as a salesperson and contracting agent for American Security Services. As part of his contract of employment, Vodra signed an agreement that for three years after leaving this employment, he would not solicit any customer of American. Vodra had no experience in the security field when he went to work for American. To the extent that he became known to American's customers, it was because of being American's representative rather than because of his own reputation in the security field. After some years, Vodra left American and organized a competing company that solicited American's customers. American sued him to enforce the restrictive covenant. Vodra claimed that the restrictive covenant was illegal and not binding. Was he correct? [*American Security Services, Inc. v Vodra*, 385 NW2d 73 (Neb)]

12. Potomac Leasing Co. leased an automatic telephone system to Vitality Centers. Claudene Cato signed the lease as guarantor of payments. When the rental was not paid, Potomac Leasing brought suit against Vitality and Cato. They raised the defense that the rented equipment was to be used for an illegal purpose—namely, the random sales solicitation by means of an automatic telephone in violation of state statute; that this purpose was known to Potomac Leasing; and that Potomac Leasing could therefore not enforce the lease. Was this defense valid? [*Potomac Leasing Co. v Vitality Centers, Inc.*, 718 SW2d 928 (Ark)]

13. The English publisher of a book called *Cambridge* gave a New York publisher permission to sell that book any place in the world except in England. The New York publisher made several bulk sales of the book to buyers who sold the book throughout the world, including England.

The English publisher sued the New York publisher and its customers for breach of the restriction prohibiting sales in England. Decide.

14. A state law required builders of homes to be licensed and declared that an unlicensed contractor could not recover compensation under a contract made for the construction of a residence. Although Annex Construction, Inc., did not have a license, it built a home for French. When he failed to pay what was owed, Annex sued him. He raised the defense that the unlicensed contractor could not recover for the contract price. Annex claimed that the lack of a license was not a bar because the president of the corporation was a licensed builder and the only shareholder of the corporation, and the construction had been properly performed. Was Annex entitled to recover?

15. Yarde Metals, Inc., owned six season tickets to New England Patriots football games. Gillette Stadium, where the games are played, had insufficient men's restrooms in use for football games at that time, which was the subject of numerous newspaper columns. On October 13, 2002, a guest of Yarde Metals, Mikel LaCroix, along with others, used available women's restrooms to answer the call of nature. As LaCroix left the restroom, however, he was arrested and charged with disorderly conduct. The Patriots organization terminated all six of Yarde's season ticket privileges, incorrectly giving as a reason that LaCroix was ejected "for throwing bottles in the seating section." Yarde sued, contending that "by terminating the plaintiff's season tickets for 2002 and for the future arbitrarily, without cause and based on false information," the Patriots had violated the implicit covenant of good faith and fair dealing of the season tickets contract. The back of each Patriots ticket states:

> *This ticket and all season tickets are revocable licenses. The Patriots reserve the right to revoke such licenses, in their sole discretion, at any time and for any reason.*

How would you decide this case? [*Yarde Metals, Inc. v New England Patriots Ltd.*, 834 NE2d 1233 (Mass App Ct)]

CPA QUESTIONS

1. West, an Indiana real estate broker, misrepresented to Zimmer that West was licensed in Kansas under the Kansas statute that regulates real estate brokers and requires all brokers to be licensed. Zimmer signed a contract agreeing to pay West a 5 percent commission for selling Zimmer's home in Kansas. West did not sign the contract. West sold Zimmer's home. If West sued Zimmer for nonpayment of commission, Zimmer would be:

   a. Liable to West only for the value of services rendered

   b. Liable to West for the full commission

   c. Not liable to West for any amount because West did not sign the contract

   d. Not liable to West for any amount because West violated the Kansas licensing requirements (5/92, Law, #25)

2. Blue purchased a travel agency business from Drye. The purchase price included payment for Drye's goodwill. The agreement contained a covenant prohibiting Drye from competing with Blue in the travel agency business. Which of the following statements regarding the covenant is *not* correct?

   a. The restraint must be *no* more extensive than is reasonably necessary to protect the goodwill purchased by Blue.

   b. The geographic area to which it applies must be reasonable.

   c. The time period for which it is to be effective must be reasonable.

   d. The value to be assigned to it is the excess of the price paid over the seller's cost of all tangible assets. (11/87, Law, #2)

Chapter 17

WRITING, ELECTRONIC FORMS, AND INTERPRETATION OF CONTRACTS

When must a contract be written? What is the effect of a written contract? These questions lead to the statute of frauds and the parol evidence rule.

A. STATUTE OF FRAUDS

A *contract* is a legally binding agreement. Must the agreement be evidenced by a writing?

1. Validity of Oral Contracts

In the absence of a statute requiring a writing, a contract may be oral or written. Managers and professionals should be more fully aware that their oral communications, including telephone conversations and dinner or breakfast discussions, may be deemed legally enforceable contracts. **For Example,** suppose that Mark Wahlberg, after reviewing a script tentatively entitled *The Bulger Boys*, meets with Steven Spielberg to discuss Mark's playing mobster James "Whitey" Bulger in the film. Steven states, "You *are* 'Whitey,' Marky! The nuns at Gate of Heaven Grammar School in South Boston—or maybe it was St. Augustine's—they don't send for the Boston Police when they are troubled about drug use in the schools; they send for you to talk to the kids. Nobody messes with you, and the kids know it. This is true stuff, I think, and this fugitive's brother Bill comes out of the Southie projects to be president of U Mass." Mark likes the script. Steven and Mark block out two months of time for shooting the film this fall. They agree on Mark's usual fee and a "piece of the action" based on a set percentage of the net income from the film. Thereafter, Mark's agent does not like the deal. He believes there are better scripts for Mark. Incredibly brutal things are coming out about "Whitey" that could severely tarnish the film. And with Hollywood accounting, a percentage of the "net" take is usually of little value. However, all of the essential terms of a contract have been agreed on, and such an oral agreement would be legally enforceable. As set forth in the following text, no writing is required for a services contract that can be performed within one year after the date of the agreement.

Certain contracts, on the other hand, must be evidenced by a writing to be legally enforceable. These contracts are covered by the **statute of frauds**.[1]

Because many oral contracts are legally enforceable, it is a good business practice in the preliminary stages of discussions to stipulate that no binding agreement is intended to be formed until a written contract is prepared and signed by the parties.

2. Contracts That Must Be Evidenced by a Writing

The statute of frauds requires that certain kinds of contracts be evidenced by a writing or they cannot be enforced. This means that either the contract itself must be in writing and signed by both parties or there must be a sufficient written memorandum of the oral contract signed by the person being sued for breach of contract. A *part performance* doctrine or exception to the statute of frauds may exist when the plaintiff's part performance is "unequivocally referable" to the oral agreement.[2]

(A) AGREEMENT THAT CANNOT BE PERFORMED WITHIN ONE YEAR AFTER THE CONTRACT IS MADE. A writing is required when the contract, by its terms or subject matter, cannot be performed within one year after the date of the agreement. An oral agreement to supply a line of credit for two years cannot be enforced because of the statute of frauds. Likewise, a joint venture agreement to construct a condominium complex was subject to the one-year provision of the statute of frauds when the contract could not reasonably have been performed within one year. The plans of the

---

[1] The name is derived from the original English Statute of Frauds and Perjuries, which was adopted in 1677 and became the pattern for similar legislation in America. The 17th section of that statute governed the sale of goods, and its modern counterpart is § 2-201 of the UCC. The 4th section of the English statute provided the pattern for U.S. legislation with respect to contracts other than for the sale of goods described in this section of the chapter. The English statute was repealed in 1954 except as to land sale and guarantee contracts. The U.S. statutes remain in force, but the liberalization by UCC § 2-201 of the pre-Code requirements with respect to contracts for the sale of goods lessens the applicability of the writing requirement. Additional movement away from the writing requirement is seen in the 1994 Revision of Article 8, Securities, which abolishes the statute of frauds provision of the original UCC § 8-319 and goes beyond by declaring that the one-year performance provision of the statute of frauds is not applicable to contracts for securities. UCC § 8-113 [1994 Revision].

[2] *Carey & Associates v Ernst*, 802 NYS2d 160 (AD 2005).

FIGURE 17-1 | *Hurdles in the Path of a Contract*

WRITING REQUIRED	
STATUTE OF FRAUDS	**EXCEPTIONS**
MORE THAN ONE YEAR TO PERFORM SALE OF LAND ANSWER FOR ANOTHER'S DEBT OR DEFAULT PERSONAL REPRESENTATIVE TO PAY DEBT OF DECEDENT FROM PERSONAL FUNDS PROMISE IN CONSIDERATION OF MARRIAGE SALE OF GOODS FOR $500 OR MORE MISCELLANEOUS	PART PERFORMANCE PROMISOR BENEFIT DETRIMENTAL RELIANCE
PAROL EVIDENCE RULE	**EXCEPTIONS**
EVERY COMPLETE, FINAL WRITTEN CONTRACT	INCOMPLETE CONTRACT AMBIGUOUS TERMS FRAUD, ACCIDENT, OR MISTAKE TO PROVE EXISTENCE OR NONBINDING CHARACTER OF CONTRACT MODIFICATION OF CONTRACT ILLEGALITY

parties projected a development over the course of three years.

The year runs from the time the oral contract is made rather than from the date when performance is to begin. In computing the year, the day on which the contract was made is excluded.

No *part performance* exception exists to validate an oral agreement not performable within one year. **For Example,** Babyback's Foods negotiated a multiyear oral agreement to comarket its barbecue meat products with the Coca-Cola Co. nationwide and arranged to have several coolers installed at area grocery stores in Louisville under the agreement.

Babyback's faxed to Coca-Cola a contract that summarized the oral agreement but Coca-Cola never signed it. Because Coca-Cola did not sign and no part performance exception exists for an oral agreement not performable within one year, Babyback's lawsuit was unsuccessful.[3]

When no time for performance is specified by the oral contract and complete performance could "conceivably occur" within one year, the statute of frauds is not applicable to the oral contract.[4]

When a contract may be terminated at will by either party, the statute of frauds is not applicable because the contract may be terminated within a year.

---

[3] *Coca-Cola Co. v Babyback's International Inc.,* 841 NE2d 557 (Ind 2006).
[4] *El Paso Healthcare System v Piping Rock Corp.,* 939 SW2d 695 (Tex App 1997).

For Example, David Ehrlich was hired as manager of Gravediggaz pursuant to an oral management agreement that was terminable at will by either Ehrlich or the group. He was entitled to receive 15 percent of the gross earnings of the group and each of its members, including rap artist Robert Diggs, professionally known as RZA, for all engagements entered into while he was manager under this oral agreement. Such an at-will contract is not barred by the statute of frauds.[5]

(1) Oral Extension of a Contract.

A contract in writing, but not required to be so by the statute of frauds because it is terminable at will, may be varied by a new oral contract, even if the original written contract provided that it should not be varied except by writing. However, the burden of proof on the party asserting the oral modification is a heavy one. The modification must be shown by "clear, unequivocal and convincing evidence, direct or implied." **For Example,** John Boyle is the sole shareholder of numerous entertainment-related companies called the Cellar Door Companies, valued at some $106,000,000. Through these companies, he controls much of the large concert business at outdoor amphitheaters in Virginia and North Carolina. Bill Reid worked for Boyle beginning in 1983 as president of one of Boyle's companies. Boyle conducted financial affairs with an "air of informality." Reid proposed to Boyle the need for an amphitheater in Virginia Beach, and Boyle promised him a "33 percent interest" "if he pulled it off." As a result of Reid's efforts, the 20,000-seat Virginia Beach Amphitheater opened in 1996. The Supreme Court of Virginia determined that clear and convincing evidence did support the oral modification of Reid's written contract, including the following excerpt from the Court's opinion:

> *Thomas J. Lyons, Jr., Boyle's friend for over 35 years, testified on behalf of Reid. Lyons and his wife attended a concert in July 1996 at the*

> *newly constructed Virginia Beach Amphitheater as guests of Boyle and his wife. Lyons complimented Boyle for the excellent work and effort that Reid had undertaken in making the amphitheater a reality. According to Lyons, Boyle stated: "Well that's why he's my partner . . . that's why he owns 35 percent in this—in the Amphitheater or this project." After Lyons finished his testimony, the chancellor remarked on the record that Boyle stood up from his seat and "hugged" Lyons, even though Lyons had just provided testimony detrimental to Boyle.*

Reid was thus entitled to a judgment equivalent to the value of his interest in the project, $3,566,343.[6]

(B) Agreement to Sell or a Sale of an Interest in Land. All contracts to sell land, buildings, or interests in land, such as mortgages, must be evidenced by a writing.[7] Leases are also interests in land and must be in writing, except in some states where leases for one year or less do not have to be in writing.[8] **For Example,** if Mrs. O'Toole orally agrees to sell her house to the Gillespies for $250,000 and, thereafter, her children convince her that she could obtain $280,000 for the property if she is patient, Mrs. O'Toole can raise the defense of the statute of frauds should she be sued for breach of the oral agreement. Under the *part performance doctrine,* an exception exists by which an oral contract for the sale of land will be enforced by a court of equity in a suit for specific performance if the buyer has taken possession of the land under an oral contract and has made substantial improvements, the value of which cannot easily be ascertained, or has taken possession and paid part of the purchase price.

(C) Promise to Answer for the Debt or Default of Another. If an individual *I* promises a creditor *C* to pay the debt of *D* if *D* does not do so, *I* is promising to answer for the debt of another. Such a promise is

---

[5] See *Ehrlich v Diggs,* 169 F Supp 2d 124 (EDNY 2001). See also *Sterling v Sterling,* 800 NYS2d 463 (AD 2005), in which the statute of frauds was no bar to an oral partnership agreement, deemed to be at will, that continued for an indefinite period of time.

[6] *Reid v Boyle,* 527 SE2d 137 (Va 2000).

[7] *Magnum Real Estate Services, Inc. v Associates, LLC,* 874 NYS2d 435 (App Div 2009).

[8] See, however, *BBQ Blues Texas, Ltd. v Affiliated Business,* 183 SW3d 543 (Tex App 2006), in which Eddie Calagero of Affiliated Business and the owners of BBQ Blues Texas, Ltd. entered an oral commission agreement to pay a 10 percent commission if he found a buyer for the restaurant, and he did so. The oral agreement was held to be outside the statute of frauds because this activity of finding a willing buyer did not involve the transfer of real estate. The second contract between the buyer and seller of the restaurant, which involved the transfer of a lease agreement, was a separate and distinct agreement over which Calagero had no control.

sometimes called a **suretyship** contract, and it must be in writing to be enforceable. *I*, the promisor, is obligated to pay only if *D* does not pay. *I*'s promise is a *collateral* or *secondary* promise, and such promises must be in writing under the statute of frauds.[9]

(1) Main Purpose of Exception.

When the main purpose of the promisor's promise to pay the debt of another is to benefit the promisor, the statute of frauds is not applicable, and the oral promise to pay the debt is binding.

For Example, an individual *I* hires a contractor *C* to repair *I*'s building, and the supplier *S* is unwilling to extend credit to *C*. In an oral promise by *I* to pay *S* what is owed for the supplies in question if *C* does not pay, *I* is promising to pay for the debt of another, *C*. However, the *main purpose* of *I*'s promise was not to aid *C* but to get his own house repaired. This promise is not within the statute of frauds.[10]

(D) Promise by the Executor or Administrator of a Decedent's Estate to Pay a Claim Against the Estate from Personal Funds. The **personal representative** (**executor** or **administrator**) has the duty of handling the affairs of a deceased person, paying the debts from the proceeds of the estate and distributing any balance remaining. The executor or administrator is not personally liable for the claims against the estate of the **decedent**. If the personal representative promises to pay the decedent's debts with his or her own money, the promise cannot be enforced unless it is evidenced by a writing.

If the personal representative makes a contract on behalf of the estate in the course of administering the estate, a writing is not required. The representative is then contracting on behalf of the estate. Thus, if the personal representative employs an attorney to settle the estate or makes a burial contract with an undertaker, no writing is required.

(E) Promises Made in Consideration of Marriage. Promises to pay a sum of money or give property to another in consideration of marriage must be in writing under the statute of frauds.

For Example, if Mr. John Bradley orally promises to provide Karl Radford $20,000 on Karl's marriage to Mr. Bradley's daughter Michelle—and Karl and Michelle marry—the agreement is not enforceable under the statute of frauds because it was not in writing.

Prenuptial or *antenuptial* agreements are entered into by the parties before their marriage. After full disclosure of each party's assets and liabilities, and in some states, income,[11] the parties set forth the rights of each partner regarding the property and, among other things, set forth rights and obligations should the marriage end in a separation or divorce. Such a contract must be in writing.

For Example, when Susan DeMatteo married her husband M. J. DeMatteo in 1990, she had a 1977 Nova and $5,000 in the bank. M. Joseph DeMatteo was worth as much as $112 million at that time, and he insisted that she sign a prenuptial agreement before their marriage. After full disclosure of each party's assets, the prenuptial agreement was signed and videotaped some five days before their marriage ceremony. The agreement gave Susan $35,000 a year plus cost-of-living increases, as well as a car and a house, should the marriage dissolve. After the couple divorced, Susan argued before the state's highest court that the agreement was not "fair or reasonable" because it gave her less than 1 percent of her former husband's wealth. The court upheld the agreement, however, pointing out that Susan was fully informed about her fiancé's net worth and was represented by counsel.[12] When there is full disclosure and representation, prenuptial agreements, like other contracts, cannot be set aside unless they are unconscionable, which in a domestic relations setting means leaving a former spouse unable to support herself or himself.

(F) Sale of Goods. As will be developed in Chapter 23, Nature and Form of Sales, contracts for

---

[9] See *Martin Printing, Inc. v Sone*, 873 A2d 232 (Conn App 2005), in which James Kuhe in writing personally guaranteed Martin Printing, Inc, to pay for printing expenses of *Pub Links Golfer Magazine*, if his corporation, Abbey Inc., failed to do so. When Abbey, Inc., failed to pay, the court enforced Kuhe's promise to pay.

[10] See *Christian v Smith*, 759 NW2d 447 (Neb 2008).

[11] See FLA. STAT § 732·702 (2).

[12] *DeMatteo v DeMatteo*, 762 NE2d 797 (Mass 2002). See also *Waton v Waton*, 887 So2d 419 (Fla App 2004).

the sale of goods priced at $500 or more must ordinarily be in writing under UCC § 2-201.[13]

(G) Promissory Estoppel. The statute of frauds may be circumvented when the party seeking to get around the statute of frauds is able to prove an enhanced promissory estoppel. While one element of a routine promissory estoppel case requires that the promisee rely on the promise in some definite and substantial manner, an enhanced level of reasonable reliance is necessary in order to have enhanced promissory estoppel, along with proof of an unconscionable injury or unjust enrichment. **For Example,** an Indiana bakery, Classic Cheesecake Inc., was able to interest several hotels and casinos in Las Vegas in buying its products. On July 27, 2004, its principals sought a loan from a local branch office of J. P. Morgan Chase Bank in order to establish a distribution center in Las Vegas. On September 17, local bank officer Dowling told Classic that the loan was a "go." When credit quality issues surfaced, Dowling continued to make assurances that the loan would be approved. On October 12, however, she told Classic that the loan had been turned down. Classic claimed that the bank's breach of its oral promise to make the loan and Classic's detrimental reliance on the promise caused it to lose more than $1 million. The Indiana statute of frauds requires agreements to lend money to be in writing. Classic contended that the oral agreement in this case must be enforced on the basis of promissory estoppel and the company's unconscionable injury. Judge Posner of the Seventh Circuit upheld the dismissal of the claim, writing (in part):

> . . .For the plaintiff to treat the bank loan as a certainty because they were told by the bank officer whom they were dealing with that it would be approved was unreasonable, especially if, as the plaintiffs' damages claim presupposes, the need for the loan was urgent. Rational businessmen know that there is many a slip 'twixt cup and lips,' that a loan is not approved until it is approved, that if a bank's employee tells you your loan application will be approved

> that is not the same as telling you it has been approved, and that if one does not have a loan commitment in writing yet the need for the loan is urgent one had better be negotiating with other potential lenders at the same time. . . .[14]

CPA   ### 3. Note or Memorandum

The statute of frauds requires a writing to evidence those contracts that come within its scope. This writing may be a note or memorandum as distinguished from a contract.[15] The statutory requirement is, of course, satisfied if there is a complete written contract signed by both parties.

(A) Signing. The note or memorandum must be signed by the party sought to be bound by the contract. **For Example,** in the previous scenario involving Mark Wahlberg and Steven Spielberg, suppose the parties agreed to do the film according to the same terms but agreed to begin shooting the film a year from next April, and Mark wrote the essential terms on a napkin, dated it, and had Steven sign it "to make sure I got it right." Mark then placed the napkin in his wallet for his records. Because the contract could not be performed within one year after the date of the agreement, a writing would be required. If Steven thereafter decided not to pursue the film because of new murder indictments against Whitey Bulger, Mark could enforce the contract against him because the napkin-note had been signed by the party to be bound or "sought to be charged," Steven. However, if Mark later decided not to appear in the film, the agreement to do the film could not be enforced against Mark because no writing existed signed by Mark, the party sought to be charged.

Some states require that the authorization of an agent to execute a contract coming within the statute of frauds must also be in writing. In the case of an auction, it is usual practice for the auctioneer to be the agent of both parties for the purpose of signing the memorandum.

The signature may be an ordinary one or any symbol that is adopted by the party as a signature.

---

[13] As will be presented in Chapter 23, under Revised Article 2, § 2-201, the $500 amount is increased to $5,000. This revision has not yet been adopted by any states.

[14] *Classic Cheesecake Co. Inc. v J. P. Morgan Chase Bank,* 546 F3d 839 (7th Cir 2008).

[15] *McLinden v Coco,* 765 NE2d 606 (Ind App 2002).

e–commerce&cyberlaw

Electronic Signatures in the Internet Age

A SIGNATURE authenticates a writing by identifying the signers through their distinctive marks. The act of signing a document calls to the attention of the signing parties the legal significance of their act and expresses authorization and assent to the body of the signed writing. An ELECTRONIC SIGNATURE, including technology

having digital or wireless capabilities, means any electronic sound, symbol, or process attached to, or logically associated with, a contract or other electronic record and executed with the intent to sign the record. An ELECTRONIC RECORD means any contract or other record created or stored in an electronic medium and retrievable in a perceivable form.

Conducting business electronically over the Internet has many advantages for consumers, businesses, and governments by allowing the instant purchase of goods, information, and services, and the reduction of sales, administrative, and overhead expenses. To facilitate the expansion of electronic commerce and place electronic signatures and electronic contracts on an equal footing with written signatures and paper contracts, Congress enacted a federal electronic signatures law.

Under the Electronic Signatures in Global and National Commerce Act (E-Sign),* electronically signed contracts cannot be denied legal effect because the signatures are in electronic form, nor can they be denied legal effect because they are delivered electronically. Contracts or documents requiring a notarized signature can be satisfied by the electronic signatures of the notaries coupled with the enclosure of all other required information as part of the record.

One of the goals of E-Sign was to spur states to enact the Uniform Electronic Transactions Act (UETA). Under E-Sign, a state may "modify, limit or supersede" the provisions of the federal act by enacting UETA "as approved and recommended for enactment in all the states" by the National Conference of Commissioners on Uniform State Laws or enacting a law that is consistent

with E-Sign.** Thus, for those states that enacted the official version of UETA or one consistent with E-Sign, the federal law is superceded by the state law. UETA is similar to E-Sign. It specifies that e-signatures and e-records can be used in contract formation, in audits, and as evidence. Selective differences between E-Sign and UETA are identified below. **For Example,** inventor Stewart Lamle sued toy maker Mattel, Inc., for breach of contract. The U.S. Court of Appeals for the Federal Circuit remanded the case for trial after resolving the motions before it. The facts reveal that after a June 11, 1997, meeting of the parties, Mattel employee Mike Bucher sent an e-mail dated June 26 to Lamle, which set forth the terms agreed to in principle at the meeting with the salutation "Best regards, Mike Bucher" appearing at the end of the e-mail. The court resolved the issue of whether an e-mail is a writing "subscribed by the party to be charged or the party's agent" in Lamle's favor. The court stated that under the UETA, the e-signature satisfies the state's (California's) Statute of Frauds. Because the e-mail was sent in 1997 prior to the effective date on the UETA, January 1, 2000, an evaluation of state common law was necessary. The court stated that it could see no meaningful difference between a typewritten signature on a telegram, which is sufficient to be a signature under state law, and the typed signature on the June 26 e-mail. It concluded that the e-mail satisfies the Statute of Frauds, assuming that there was a binding oral agreement on June 11.***

(a) General Rule of Parity. E-Sign provides for parity of electronic and paper signatures, contracts, and records. Electronic signatures and contracts satisfy the statute of frauds to the same extent they would if embodied as paper contracts with handwritten signatures. Internet contracts are neither more nor less valid, legal, and binding than are offline paper contracts. The rules are the same! The UETA is comparable to E-Sign in that it

---

*Pub L 106-229, 114 Stat 464, 15 USC § 7001.

**§ 102(a) and 102(a)(2). Forty-eight states and the District of Columbia have enacted the UETA in some form.
***Lamle v Mattel, Inc., 394 F3d 1355 (Fed Cir 2005); see also *Payout v Coral Mortgage Bankers*, 2009 WL 3526578 (D Colo 2009).

continued

treats e-signatures and e-records as if they were handwritten.[†]

(b) Identity Verification. Neither E-Sign nor UETA is a digital signature law in that neither requires security procedures or a certification authority for the verification of electronic signatures. The parties themselves determine how they will verify each other's identity. Some options are a credit card, a password or PIN, public-key cryptographic exchange of digital signatures, or biometric signatures.

(c) Exceptions. The E-Sign Act exempts documents and records on trust and estate law so that it does not cover wills, codicils, and testamentary trusts or commercial law matters such as checks, negotiable instruments, and letters of credit. The act also does not cover court documents and cancellation of health and life insurance. Generally, the UETA also does not apply to these documents and records set forth previously.

(d) Consumer Protection and Notice and Consent Requirements. Consumer protection laws remain intact under E-Sign. Protections exist for consumers to consent to receiving electronic contracts, records, and documents; and businesses must tell consumers of their right to receive hardcopy documents.

Consumers must consent to receiving documents electronically or confirm consent electronically. For example, a consumer and a business may have negotiated terms of a contract by telephone and agreed to execute their agreement by e-mail. The consumer is then sent an e-mail that contains a consent disclosure, which contains a hypertext markup language (HTML) link the consumer can use to test her ability to view the contract in HTML. The consumer then returns the e-mail message to the business, thereby confirming electronically her consent to use this electronic means.

[†]UETA § 7(a) and 7(b).

The UETA, like E-Sign, defers to existing substantive law regarding consumer protection.

(e) Time and Place of Sending and Receipt. E-Sign does not contain a provision addressing basic contract requirements such as sending and delivery, leaving such matters to existing contract law. However, the UETA provides that an electronic record is sent when it (1) is properly directed to an information processing system designated or used by the recipient to receive such records and from which the recipient may recover that record; (2) is in a form that the recipient's system is able to process; and (3) enters an information processing system that is in the control of the recipient but outside the control of the sender. An electronic record is received when (1) it enters an information processing system designated or used by the recipient to receive such records and from which the recipient is able to obtain the record and (2) it is in a form that the recipient's system can process.[††]

(f) Errors. Unlike E-Sign, which leaves matters relating to errors to be resolved by existing state contract law, UETA creates a system for dealing with errors. For example, when Marv Hale clicks on "buy" to make an online purchase of 12 bottles of Napa Valley Supreme Chardonnay at $12.90 per bottle, the computer will produce the equivalent of an invoice that includes the product's name, description, quantity, and price to enable Marv to avoid possible error when forming the electronic contract. This procedure gives the buyer an opportunity to identify and immediately correct an error. When such a procedure is not in effect and an error is later discovered, prompt notice to the other party can cure the error under Section 10 of the UETA.[†††]

[††]UETA § 15.
[†††]UETA § 10(2)(A)-(C).

It may consist of initials, figures, or a mark. In the absence of a local statute that provides otherwise, a signature may be made by pencil, pen, typewriter, print, or stamp. As will be discussed, electronic signatures have parity with on-paper signatures.

(B) CONTENT. The note or memorandum must contain all of the essential terms of the contract so the court can determine just what was agreed. If any essential term is missing, the writing is not sufficient. A writing evidencing a sale of land that does not describe the land or identify the buyer does not satisfy the statute of frauds. The subject matter must be identified either within the writing itself or in other writings to which it refers. A deposit check given by the buyer to the seller does not take an oral land sales contract out of the statute of frauds. This is so because the check does not set forth the terms of the sale.

The note or memorandum may consist of one writing or of separate papers, such as letters, or a combination of such papers. Separate writings cannot be considered together unless they are linked. Linkage may be express reference in each writing to the other or by the fact that each writing clearly deals with the same subject matter.

4. Effect of Noncompliance

The majority of states hold that a contract that does not comply with the statute of frauds is not enforceable.[16] If an action is brought to enforce the contract, the defendant can raise the defense that the alleged contract is not enforceable because it is not evidenced by a writing, as required by the statute of frauds.

(A) RECOVERY OF VALUE CONFERRED. In most instances, a person who is prevented from enforcing a contract because of the statute of frauds is nevertheless entitled to recover from the other party the value of any services or property furnished or money given under the oral contract. Recovery is not based on the terms of the contract but on a quasi-contractual obligation. The other party is to restore to the plaintiff what was received in order to prevent unjust enrichment at the plaintiff's expense. **For Example,** when an oral contract for services cannot be enforced because of the statute of frauds, the person performing the work may recover the reasonable value of the services rendered.

(B) WHO MAY RAISE THE DEFENSE OF NONCOMPLIANCE? Only a party to the oral contract may raise a defense that it is not binding because there is no writing that satisfies the statute of frauds. Third persons, such as an insurance company or the Internal Revenue Service, cannot claim that a contract is void because the statute of frauds was not satisfied.

B. PAROL EVIDENCE RULE

When the contract is evidenced by a writing, may the contract terms be changed by the testimony of witnesses?

5. Exclusion of Parol Evidence

The general rule is that parol or extrinsic evidence will not be allowed into evidence to add to, modify, or contradict the terms of a written contract that is fully integrated or complete on its face.[17] Evidence of an alleged earlier oral or written agreement within the scope of the fully integrated written contract or evidence of an alleged contemporaneous oral agreement within the scope of the fully integrated written contract is inadmissible as *parol evidence.*

Parol evidence is admissible, however, to show fraud, duress, or mistake and under certain other circumstances to be discussed in the following paragraphs.

The **parol evidence rule** is based on the theory that either there never was an oral agreement or, if there was, the parties abandoned it when they reached the stage in negotiations of executing their written contract. The social objective of the parol evidence rule is to give stability to contracts and to prevent the assertion of terms that did not exist or did not survive the bargaining of the parties so as to reach inclusion in the final written contract.

For Example, *L* (landlord), the owner of a new development containing a five-store mall, discusses leasing one of the stores to *T* (tenant), who is viewing the property with his sister *S,* a highly credible poverty worker on leave from her duties in Central America. *L,* in the presence of *S,* agrees to give *T* the exclusive right to sell coffee and soft drinks in the five-store mall. Soon *L* and *T* execute a detailed written lease for the store, which makes no provision for *T's* exclusive right to sell soft drinks and coffee in the mall. Subsequently, when two of the mall's new tenants begin to sell soft drinks and coffee, *T* brings suit against *L* for the breach of the oral promise granting him exclusive rights to sell soft drinks and coffee. *T* calls *S* as his first witness to prove the

---

[16] The UCC creates several statutes of frauds of limited applicability, in which it uses the phrase "not enforceable": §1-206 (sale of intangible personal property); § 2-201 (sale of goods); and § 8-319 (sale of securities).

[17] *Speed v Muhana,* 619 SE2d 324 (Ga App 2005).

existence of the oral promise. *L,* through his attorney, will object to the admission of any evidence of a prior oral agreement that would add to or amend the fully integrated written lease, which set forth all restrictions on the landlord and tenant as to uses of the premises. After study of the matter, the court, based on the parol evidence rule, will not hear testimony from either *S* or *T* about the oral promise *L* made to *T.* In order to preserve his exclusive right to sell the drinks in question, *T* should have made certain that this promise was made part of the lease. His lawsuit will not be successful.

6. When the Parol Evidence Rule Does Not Apply

The parol evidence rule will not apply in certain cases. The most common of these are discussed in the following paragraphs.

(A) AMBIGUITY. If a written contract is **ambiguous** or may have two or more different meanings, parol evidence may generally be admitted to clarify the meaning.[18]

Parol evidence may also be admitted to show that a word used in a contract has a special trade meaning or a meaning in the particular locality that differs from the common meaning of that word.

(B) FRAUD, DURESS, OR MISTAKE. A contract apparently complete on its face may have omitted a provision that should have been included. Parol evidence may be admitted to show that a provision was omitted as the result of fraud, duress, or mistake and to further show what that provision stated. Parol evidence is admissible to show that a provision of the written contract was a mutual mistake even though the written provision is unambiguous.[19] When one party claims to have been fraudulently induced by the other to enter into a contract, the parol evidence rule does not bar proof that there was a fraud.

For Example, the parol evidence rule does not bar proof that the seller of land intentionally misrepresented that the land was zoned to permit use as an industrial park. Such evidence does not contradict the terms of the contract but shows that the agreement is unenforceable.[20]

(C) MODIFICATION OF CONTRACT. The parol evidence rule prohibits only the contradiction of a complete written contract. It does not prohibit proof that the contract was thereafter modified or terminated. The *Bourg* case deals with an asserted oral modification of a written agreement.

Bourg v Bristol Boat Co., 705 A2d 969 (RI 1998)

All Sail and No Anchor

On April 2, 1990, Christian Bourg hired Bristol Boat Co., Inc., and Bristol Marine Co. (defendants) to construct and deliver a yacht on July 1, 1990. However, the defendants did not live up to their promises and the contract was breached. On October 22, 1990, the defendants executed a written settlement agreement whereby Bourg agreed to pay an additional sum of $135,000 for the delivery of the yacht and to provide the defendants a loan of $80,000 to complete the construction of the vessel. Referencing the settlement agreement, the defendants at the same time executed a promissory note obliging them to repay

the $80,000 loan plus interest in annual installments due on November 1 of each year, with the final payment due on November 1, 1994. The court stated in presenting the facts: "However, like the yacht itself, the settlement agreement soon proved to be just another hole in the water into which the plaintiff threw his money." Bourg sued the defendants after they failed to make certain payments on the note, and the court granted a motion for summary judgment in favor of Bourg for $59,081. The defendants appealed.

---

[18] *Berg v Hudesman,* 801 P2d 222 (Wash 1990). This is also the view followed by UCC § 2-202(a), which permits terms in a contract for the sale of goods to be "explained or supplemented by a course of dealing or usage of trade . . . or by course of performance." Such evidence is admissible not because there is an ambiguity but "in order that the true understanding of the parties as to the agreement may be reached." Official Code Comment to § 2-202.

[19] *Thompson v First Citizens Bank & Trust Co.*

[20] *Edwards v Centrex Real Estate Corp.,* 61 Cal Rptr 518 (Cal App 1997) 567 SE2d 184 (NC App 2002).

Continued

The defendants asserted that the trial court was in error because "at the time of the execution of the promissory note and settlement agreement upon which Plaintiff relies, it was understood and agreed that a substantial part of the note would be paid for by services rendered by the defendants. . . ."

JUDICIAL OPINION

FLANDERS, J. . . . [T]he statement in defendants' affidavit that the alleged oral modification was agreed to "[*at*] *the time of* the execution of the promissory note and settlement agreement" (emphasis added) eviscerates defendants' contention on appeal that it was in fact a subsequent oral modification. Rather, because the affidavit recites that the alleged oral side agreement was entered into *at the time of* the settlement agreement and promissory note, it would have constituted a contemporaneous modification that would merge into the integrated promissory note and settlement agreement and thus be barred from admission into evidence under the parol evidence rule. In short, this alleged contemporaneous oral modification was legally "immaterial in ascertaining the terms of the transaction" between plaintiff and defendants. *Fram Corp.*, 121 R.I. at 587–88, 401 A.2d at 1272.

Finally, although parties to an integrated written contract—that is, "one where the parties adopt a writing or writings as a final and complete expression of [their] agreement," *id.* at 587, 401 A.2d at 1272—can modify their understanding by a subsequent oral pact, to be legally effective there must be evidence of mutual assent to the essential terms of the modification and adequate consideration. Here the defendants adduced no competent evidence of either mutual assent to particular terms or of a specific consideration that would be sufficiently definite to constitute an enforceable subsequent oral modification to the parties' earlier written agreements. Thus legally this alleged oral alteration was all sail and no anchor.

[Judgment affirmed]

QUESTIONS

1. Did the parties have a fully integrated written contract concerning the loan of $80,000 and the promissory note?

2. Can a contemporaneous oral agreement that "it was understood and agreed that a substantial part of the note would be paid for by services rendered by the defendants" be given weight as evidence to contradict the 1990 written settlement agreement and note that called for annual cash payments to repay the $80,000 loan?

3. Must a subsequent oral modification to a written agreement meet the essential elements for contract formation, including an agreement, and consideration?

C. RULES OF CONSTRUCTION AND INTERPRETATION

In interpreting contracts, courts are aided by certain rules.

7. Intention of the Parties

When persons enter into an agreement, it is to be presumed that they intend for their agreement to have some effect. A court will strive to determine the intent of the parties and to give effect to it. A contract, therefore, is to be enforced according to its terms.[21] A court cannot remake or rewrite the contract of the parties under the pretense of interpreting.[22]

No particular form of words is required, and any words manifesting the intent of the parties are sufficient. In the absence of proof that a word has a peculiar meaning or that it was employed by the parties with a particular meaning, a common word is given its ordinary meaning.

(A) MEANING OF WORDS. Ordinary words are to be interpreted according to their ordinary meaning.[23] **For Example,** when a contract requires the gasoline dealer to pay the supplier for "gallons" supplied, the term *gallons* is unambiguous and does not require that an adjustment of the gallonage be made for the temperature.[24] When a contract calls for a business-person to pay a builder for the builder's "costs," the

[21] See *Greenwald v Kersh*, 621 SE2d 463 (Ga App 2005).
[22] *Abbot v Schnader, Harrison, Segal & Lewis, LLP*, 805 A2d 547 (Pa Super 2002).
[23] *Thorton v D.F.W. Christian Television, Inc.*, 925 SW2d 17 (Tex App 1995).
[24] *Hopkins v BP Oil, Inc.*, 81 F3d 1070 (11th Cir 1996).

term *costs* is unambiguous, meaning actual costs, not a lesser amount based on the builder's bid.[25]

If there is a common meaning to a term, that meaning will be followed even though the dictionary may contain additional meanings. If technical or trade terms are used in a contract, they are to be interpreted according to the area of technical knowledge or trade from which the terms are taken.

(B) INCORPORATION BY REFERENCE. The contract may not cover all of the agreed terms. The missing terms may be found in another document. Frequently, the parties executing the contract for storage will simply state that a storage contract is entered into and that the contract applies to the goods listed in the schedule attached to and made part of the contract. Likewise, a contract for the construction of a building may involve plans and specifications on file in a named city office. The contract will simply state that the building is to be constructed according to those plans and specifications that are "incorporated herein and made part of this contract." When there is such an **incorporation by reference**, the contract consists of both the original document and the detailed statement that is incorporated in it.

When a contract refers to another document, however, the contract must sufficiently describe the document or so much of it as is to be interpreted as part of the contract.

8. Whole Contract

The provisions of a contract must be construed as a whole in such a way that every part is given effect.

Every word of a contract is to be given effect if reasonably possible. The contract is to be construed as a whole, and if the plain language of the contract thus viewed solves the dispute, the court is to make no further analysis.[26]

9. Contradictory and Ambiguous Terms

One term in a contract may conflict with another term, or one term may have two different meanings. It is then necessary for the court to determine whether there is a contract and, if so, what the contract really means.

In the *Olander Contracting* case, the defendant City of Bismarck claimed that the contract was clear and unambiguous and that the trial judge, as a matter of law, should have decided in its favor. The contractor contended that the contract was ambiguous. It is the role of the judge—a question of law—to initially determine whether a contract is ambiguous. If the contract is ambiguous, it is the role of the jury—a question of fact—to determine which party's position is correct, with the aid of extrinsic evidence.

Olander Contracting v Wachter, 643 NW2d 29 (2002)

Who Pays the Piper?

Olander Contracting Co., developer Gail Wachter, and the City of Bismarck, North Dakota, entered into a water and sewer construction contract including, among other things, connecting a 10-inch sewer line from Wachter's housing development to the city's existing 36-inch concrete sewer main and installing a manhole at the connection, to be paid for by Wachter. Olander installed the manhole, but it collapsed within a few days. Olander installed a second manhole, with a large base supported by pilings, but it too failed a few days after it was installed. Olander then placed a rock bedding under the city's sewer main, replaced 78 feet of the existing  concrete pipe with PVC pipe, and installed a manhole a third time on a larger base. Olander sued Wachter and the City of Bismarck for damages of $456,536.25 for extra work it claims it was required to perform to complete its contract. Both defendants denied they were responsible for the amount sued under the contract. The jury returned a special verdict, finding that Olander performed "extra work/unforeseen work . . . for which it is entitled to be compensated in excess of the contract price" in the amount of $220,849.67, to be paid by the City of Bismarck. Appeals were taken.

---

[25] *Batzer Construction, Inc. v Boyer*, 125 P3d 773 (Or App 2006).
[26] *Covensky v Hannah Marine Corp.*, 903 NE2d 422 (Ill App 2009).

Continued

JUDICIAL OPINION

SANDSTROM, J. . . . Bismarck contends it should have been granted summary judgment of dismissal, arguing (a) the trial court erred in refusing to interpret the contract and in "pass[ing] the task of interpreting the contract to the jury"; (b) Bismarck had no duty to pay for Olander's work, because the contract placed responsibility for payment for all work on Wachter, . . . and "[n]o language in the contract allowed extra payments to Olander for mere completion of the contract work.". . .

We recently addressed the construction of written agreements:

> If the intent of the parties can be ascertained from the agreement alone, interpretation of the contract is a question of law. Thus, an unambiguous contract is particularly amenable to summary judgment. However, if the terms of the contract are ambiguous, extrinsic evidence regarding the parties' intent may be considered and the terms of the contract and parties' intent become questions of fact. When two good arguments can be made for either of two contrary positions as to the meaning of a term in a document, an ambiguity exists.

Garofalao v Saint Joseph's Hosp., 2000 ND 149, ¶ 7, 615 N.W.2d 160 (citations omitted). "Whether or not a contract is ambiguous is a question of law." *Des Lacs Valley Land Corp. v Herzig,* 2001 ND 17, ¶ 9, 621 N.W.2d 860. "A determination of ambiguity is but the starting point in the search for the parties' ambiguously expressed intentions, which are questions of fact to be determined with the aid of extrinsic evidence." *Bohn v Johnson,* 371 N.W.2d 781, 788 (N.D. 1985).

Section (6) of the contract provides, in part:

> The DEVELOPER [Wachter] will be responsible to pay the CONTRACTOR [Olander] for all of the contract work in accord with the plans, specifications, and proposal prepared by the DEVELOPER's Representative made a part of this contract.

Section (9) of the contract provides, in part:

> The CONTRACTOR shall guarantee all work against faulty materials and workmanship for a period of one year from the date of final payment. . . .

Section 126 of the General Provisions provides, in part:

> EXTRA WORK. The Contractor shall perform unfor[e]-seen work, for which there is no price included in the contract, whenever it is deemed necessary or desirable in order to complete fully the work as contemplated.

> Such work shall be performed in accordance with the specifications and as directed. When work not shown on the plans is to be performed by the Contractor the Engineer may order the work done on a force account basis when the measurement and pavement [sic] by unit prices becomes too cumbersome to be practicable, or when it is considered to be to the best interest of the City of Bismarck. Extra work will be paid for at the unit prices or lump sum stipulated in the order authorizing the work or the City of Bismarck may require the Contractor to do such work on a force account basis, to be compensated in the following manner. . . .

The contract requires Olander to "perform unfor[e]seen work, for which there is no price included in the contract, whenever it is deemed necessary or desirable in order to complete fully the work" and provides that "[e]xtra work will be paid for." The contract does not define unforeseen work or extra work, and does not specify which party is required to pay for such work. The parties have presented plausible arguments for contrary positions. The contract is, therefore, ambiguous, and there were genuine issues of material fact precluding summary judgment. We conclude the trial court properly received extrinsic evidence of the parties' ambiguously expressed intentions and properly submitted to the jury the factual questions of whether or not Olander performed extra work for which it was entitled to be paid and, if so, which party or parties were required to pay for it. . . .

Bismarck argues Olander failed to prove it had an enforceable agreement for payment for extra work, asserting "there is no language in the contract between the parties requiring Bismarck to pay anything for the work on this project." We have already determined the contract was ambiguous, and the trial court properly received extrinsic evidence about the parties' ambiguously expressed intentions and properly submitted to the jury the factual issue about extra work and which parties were to pay for it. . . .

Bismarck contends it should be granted a new trial because the trial court erred in conducting the trial by allowing the Jury to interpret the contract, and admitting evidence unfairly prejudicial to Bismarck. Bismarck's brief on these matters is very conclusory, with little or no supportive reasoning or citations to authorities. We have said that without supportive reasoning or citations to relevant authorities, an argument is without merit. . . .

We have already determined the trial court properly received extrinsic evidence of the parties' ambiguously expressed intentions, and properly submitted to the jury the factual questions of whether or not Olander performed extra work for which it was entitled to be paid and, if so, which party or

Continued

parties were required to pay for it. In doing so, the trial court did not improperly allow the jury to interpret the contract. . . .
[Judgment affirmed]

QUESTIONS

1. State the City of Bismarck's position on the intention of the parties' contract regarding payment to the contractor.

2. State the position of Olander Contracting.

3. What is the role of judge and jury in interpreting ambiguous and unambiguous contract language? What is the significance of a "question of law" and a "question of fact"? What is "extrinsic evidence" regarding the contract between Wachter, Olander, and the City of Bismarck?

In some instances, apparent conflict between the terms of a contract is eliminated by the introduction of parol evidence or by the application of an appropriate rule of construction.[27]

(A) NATURE OF WRITING. When a contract is partly a printed form or partly type-written and partly hand-written and the written part conflicts with the printed or typewritten part, the written part prevails. When there is a conflict between a printed part and a typewritten part, the latter prevails. Consequently, when a clause typewritten on a printed form conflicts with what is stated by the print, the conflicting print is ignored and the typewritten clause controls. This rule is based on the belief that the parties had given greater thought to what they typed or wrote for the particular contract as contrasted with printed words already in a form designed to cover many transactions. Thus, a typewritten provision to pay 90 cents per unit overrode a preprinted provision setting the price as 45 cents per unit.

When there is a conflict between an amount or quantity expressed both in words and figures, as on a check, the amount or quantity expressed in words prevails. Words control because there is less danger that a word will be wrong than a number.

(B) AMBIGUITY. A contract is *ambiguous* when the intent of the parties is uncertain and the contract is capable of more than one reasonable interpretation.[28] The background from which the contract and the dispute arose may help in determining the intention of the parties. **For Example,** when suit was brought in Minnesota on a Canadian insurance policy, the question arose whether the dollar limit of the policy referred to Canadian or U.S. dollars. The court concluded that Canadian dollars were intended. Both the insurer and the insured were Canadian corporations; the original policy, endorsements to the policy, and policy renewals were written in Canada; over the years, premiums had been paid in Canadian dollars; and a prior claim on the policy had been settled by the payment of an amount computed on the basis of Canadian dollars.

(C) STRICT CONSTRUCTION AGAINST DRAFTING PARTY. An ambiguous contract is interpreted strictly against the party who drafted it.[29] **For Example,** an insurance policy containing ambiguous language regarding coverage or exclusions is interpreted against the insurer and in favor of the insured when two interpretations are reasonably possible. This rule is a secondary rule that may be invoked only after all of the ordinary interpretive guides have been exhausted. The rule basically assigns the risk of an unresolvable ambiguity to the party creating it.[30]

---

[27] See *Wilkie v Eutice 36747, LLC,* 669 SE2d 155 (Ga App 2008) where the courts in this jurisdiction resolve contract interpretation issues by first determining whether the language is ambiguous. (1) If it is not, the trial court judge enforces the contract as written; (2) if the contract is ambiguous, the trial court judge will apply the rules of contract construction to resolve this ambiguity; and (3) if the ambiguity cannot be resolved in Step 2, a jury must decide what the parties intended and what the ambiguous language means.

[28] *Kaufman & Stewart v Weinbrenner Shoe Co.,* 589 NW2d 499 (Minn App 1999).

[29] *Idaho Migrant Council, Inc. v Warila,* 89 P2d 39 (Wyo 1995).

[30] *Premier Title Co. v Donahue,* 765 NE2d 513 (Ill App 2002).

10. Implied Terms

In some cases, a court will imply a term to cover a situation for which the parties failed to provide or, when needed, to give the contract a construction or meaning that is reasonable.

The court often implies details of the performance of a contract not expressly stated in the contract. In a contract to perform work, there is an implied promise to use such skill as is necessary to properly perform the work. When a contract does not specify the time for performance, a reasonable time is implied.

In every contract, there is an implied obligation that neither party shall do anything that will have the effect of destroying or injuring the right of the other party to receive the fruits of the contract. This means that in every contract there exists an implied covenant of **good faith** and fair dealing. When a contract may reasonably be interpreted in different ways, a court should make the interpretation that is in harmony with good faith and fair dealing. **For Example,** when a contract is made subject to the condition that one of the parties obtain financing, that party must make reasonable, good-faith efforts to obtain financing. The party is not permitted to do nothing and then claim that the contract is not binding because the condition has not been satisfied. Likewise, when a contract requires a party to obtain government approval, the party must use all reasonable means to obtain it.[31]

The Uniform Commercial Code imposes an obligation of good faith in the performance or enforcement of every contract.[32]

11. Conduct and Custom

The conduct of the parties and the customs and usages of a particular trade may give meaning to the words of the parties and thus aid in the interpretation of their contract.

(A) CONDUCT OF THE PARTIES. The conduct of the parties in carrying out the terms of a contract is the best guide to determine the parties' intent. When performance has been repeatedly tendered and accepted without protest, neither party will be permitted to claim that the contract was too indefinite to be binding. **For Example,** a travel agent made a contract with a hotel to arrange for trips to the hotel. After some 80 trips had already been arranged and paid for by the hotel at the contract price without any dispute about whether the contract obligation was satisfied, any claim by the travel agent that it could charge additional fees must be rejected

(B) CUSTOM AND USAGE OF TRADE. The customs and **usages of trade** or commercial activity to which the contract relates may be used to interpret the terms of a contract.[33] **For Example,** when a contract for the construction of a building calls for a "turn-key construction," industry usage is admissible to show what this means: a construction in which all the owner needs to do is to turn the key in the lock to open the building for use and in which all construction risks are assumed by the contractor.[34]

Custom and usage, however, cannot override express provisions of a contract that are inconsistent with custom and usage.

12. Avoidance of Hardship

As a general rule, a party is bound by a contract even though it proves to be a bad bargain. If possible, a court will interpret a contract to avoid hardship. Courts will, if possible, interpret a vague contact in a way to avoid any forfeiture of a party's interest.

When hardship arises because the contract makes no provision for the situation that has occurred, the court will sometimes imply a term to avoid the hardship.

In the *Perkins* case, the weaker party claimed that the court should imply or read into the contract a protective term that was not expressed in the written terms of the contract.

---

[31] *Kroboth v Brent,* 625 NYS2d 748 (App Div 1995).
[32] UCC §§ 1-201(19), 1-203.
[33] *Affiliated FM Ins. Co. v Constitution Reinsurance Corp.,* 626 NE2d 878 (Mass 1994).
[34] *Blue v R.L. Glossen Contracting, Inc.,* 327 SE2d 582 (Ga App 1985).

Perkins v Standard Oil Co., 383 P2d 107 (Or 1963)

Court Glides with Clyde

Standard Oil Co. made a jobbing, or wholesale, dealership contract with Clyde Perkins. The contract limited Perkins to selling Standard Oil's products and required him to maintain certain minimum prices. Standard Oil had the right to approve or disapprove Perkins' customers. In order to be able to perform under this contract, Perkins had to make a substantial monetary investment, and his only income was from commissions on sales of Standard Oil's products. Standard Oil made some sales directly to Perkins' customers. When Perkins protested, Standard Oil pointed out that the contract did not contain any provision making his rights exclusive. Perkins sued Standard Oil to compel it to stop dealing with his customers. From a decision in Standard Oil's favor, Perkins appealed.

JUDICIAL OPINION

ROSSMAN, J. . . . The contract authorized the plaintiff [Perkins] to sell without Standard's written consent "on a nonexclusive basis" the products which Standard consigned to him but only to service stations or consuming accounts. Standard's written consent was required before the plaintiff could sell to any other account. The plaintiff promised in the contract to use his "best efforts to promote the sale of products consigned hereunder" and to sell a specified minimum amount during each year. . . .

The plaintiff was required to deliver to Standard a complete list of the names and addresses of all his distributors and submit to it the names of any new potential distributors. . . .

The plaintiff claims that the contract by its very nature contains an implied condition that Standard would not solicit business directly from his (plaintiff's) customers. Standard protests that such an implied condition would be contrary to the express terms of the contract since the latter (1) provides that the plaintiff was authorized to sell Standard's products only "on a nonexclusive basis" and (2) reserved to Standard the "right to select its own customers." Plaintiff proposes a more restricted interpretation. . . . He concedes that the contract reserved to Standard the right to sell to any new accounts which it found, and to accept or reject any new accounts which he (the plaintiff) might obtain, but he insists that it does not permit Standard to solicit accounts which it had approved as his customers. . . .

In order to be successful in his business and to comply with the terms of his contract, the plaintiff was obliged to make substantial investments in storage facilities, delivery trucks, and other equipment. He was also obliged to hire employees. He was required to use his "best efforts" to promote the sale of Standard's products. Only if he sold Standard's products exclusively could it be said that he was using his best efforts to promote their sale. It is clear, then, that the contract limited his dealership to Standard products. Plaintiff was also required to sell a minimum quantity of other designated Standard petroleum products. If he at any time failed to sell the minimum quantity, Standard was at liberty to terminate its contract with him. Plaintiff's compensation was based exclusively on the sales he made to customers, which he secured through his own efforts. No compensation was available for the plaintiff if he obtained customers for Standard who bought directly from it. Nor does the contract obligate Standard to compensate him for sales made directly by Standard to plaintiff's customers. . . .

. . . A condition must be implied that Standard would not solicit customers which had been obtained through plaintiff's efforts. The interpretation of the contract for which Standard contends would leave plaintiff and others in a position similar to his completely at the mercy of Standard. . . .

"We cannot accept [Standard's] construction of its meaning. An intention to make so one-sided an agreement is not readily to be inferred. . . .

"In every contract there is an implied covenant that neither party shall do anything that will have the effect of destroying or injuring the right of the other party to receive the fruits of the contract, which means that in every contract there exists a covenant of good faith and fair dealing." . . . *3 Corbin* [*on Contracts* 278] 349–352 . . .

The implication of a condition finds support in many circumstances. . . . Plaintiff's only source of return on his substantial investments in the business was the sales he made to his customers. If Standard was at liberty to solicit his direct customers, as it contends. . . . plaintiff was in a state of economic servility; we do not believe that the parties intended such a result at the time the contract was signed. . . .

The contract before us is obviously a form contract prepared by Standard. It is a contract of "adhesion" in the sense that it is a take-it-or-leave-it whole. Such contracts are regarded by some authorities as anachronistic or inconsistent with real freedom of contract. At least they should be construed with an awareness of the inequality of the bargainers. . . .

[Judgment reversed]

QUESTIONS

1. What created the problem in the *Perkins* case?

2. Could the problem in the *Perkins* case have been avoided?

lawflix

The Santa Clause (1996) (PG)

When Scott Calvin (Tim Allen) tries on a Santa suit, he discovers that he has assumed all of Santa's responsibility. Calvin tries to challenge his acceptance of the terms of the agreement. Analyze the problems with offer, acceptance, and terms in very fine print (a magnifying glass is required). Do the terms of the suit contract apply when Calvin did not know them at the time he put on the suit?

For movie clips that illustrate business law concepts, see LawFlix at **www .cengage.com/blaw/dvl**.

MAKE THE CONNECTION

SUMMARY

An oral agreement may be a contract unless it is the intention of the parties that they should not be bound by the agreement without a writing executed by them. Certain contracts must be evidenced by a writing, however, or else they cannot be enforced. The statutes that declare this exception are called *statutes of frauds.* Statutes of frauds commonly require that a contract be evidenced by writing in the case of (1) an agreement that cannot be performed within one year after the contract is made, (2) an agreement to sell any interest in land, (3) a promise to answer for the debt or default of another, (4) a promise by the executor or administrator of a decedent's estate to pay a claim against the estate from personal funds, (5) a promise made in consideration of marriage, and (6) a contract for the sale of goods for a purchase price of $500 or more.

To evidence a contract to satisfy a statute of frauds, there must be a writing of all essential terms. The writing must be signed by the defendant against whom suit is brought for enforcement of the contract.

If the applicable statute of frauds is not satisfied, the oral contract cannot be enforced. To avoid unjust enrichment, a plaintiff barred from enforcing an oral contract may in most cases recover from the other contracting party the reasonable value of the benefits conferred by the plaintiff on the defendant.

When there is a written contract, the question arises whether that writing is the exclusive statement of the parties' agreement. If the writing is the complete and final statement of the contract, parol evidence as to matters agreed to before or at the time the writing was signed is not admissible to contradict the writing. This is called the *parol evidence rule.* In any case, the parol evidence rule does not bar parol evidence when (1) the writing is ambiguous, (2) the writing is not a true statement of the agreement of the parties because of fraud, duress, or mistake, or (3) the existence, modification, or illegality of a contract is in controversy.

Because a contract is based on the agreement of the parties, courts must determine the intent of the parties manifested in the contract. The intent that is to be enforced is the intent as it reasonably appears to a third person. This objective intent is followed.

In interpreting a contract, ordinary words are to be given their ordinary meanings. If trade or technical terms have been used, they are interpreted according to their technical meanings. The court must consider the whole contract and not read a particular part out of context. When different writings are executed as part of the same transaction, or one writing refers to or incorporates another, all of the writings are to be read together as the contract of the parties.

When provisions of a contract are contradictory, the court will try to reconcile or eliminate the conflict. If this cannot be done, the conclusion may be that there is no contract because the conflict makes the agreement indefinite as to a material matter. In some cases, conflict is solved by considering the form of conflicting terms. Handwriting prevails over typing and a printed form, and typing prevails over a printed form. Ambiguity will be eliminated in some cases by the admission of parol evidence or by interpreting the provision strictly against the party preparing the contract, particularly when that party has significantly greater bargaining power.

LEARNING OUTCOMES

After studying this chapter, you should be able to clearly explain:

A. STATUTE OF FRAUDS

LO.1 Explain when a contract must be evidenced by a writing

See the discussion and examples beginning on p. 329.

LO.2 Explain the effect of noncompliance with the statute of frauds

See the example in which an oral contract cannot be enforced because it is not in writing, but the plaintiff may recover the reasonable value of the services rendered, p. 336.

B. PAROL EVIDENCE RULE

LO.3 Explain the parol evidence rule and the exceptions to this rule

See the example in which the tenant is not allowed to call a witness to testify about a prior oral agreement that would add to and alter the written lease, p. 337.

See the exceptions based on ambiguity, fraud, duress, and mistake discussed on p. 337.

C. RULES OF CONSTRUCTION AND INTERPRETATION

LO.4 Understand the basic rule of contract construction that a contract is enforced according to its terms

See the example of the interpretation of the word "costs" on p. 338.

LO.5 State the rules for interpreting ambiguous terms in a contract

See the discussion on the nature of the writing beginning on p. 341.

KEY TERMS

administrator	good faith	statute of frauds
ambiguous	incorporation by reference	suretyship
decedent	parol evidence rule	usages of trade
executor	personal representative	

QUESTIONS AND CASE PROBLEMS

1. Kelly made a written contract to sell certain land to Brown and gave Brown a deed to the land. Thereafter, Kelly sued Brown to get back a 20-foot strip of the land. Kelly claimed that before making the written contract, it was agreed that Kelly would sell all of his land to Brown to

make it easier for Brown to get a building permit, but after that was done, the 20-foot strip would be reconveyed to Kelly. Was Kelly entitled to the 20-foot strip? What ethical values are involved? [*Brown v Kelly*, 545 So2d 518 (Fla App)]

2. Martin made an oral contract with Cresheim Garage to work as its manager for two years. Cresheim wrote Martin a letter stating that the oral contract had been made and setting forth all of its terms. Cresheim later refused to recognize the contract. Martin sued Cresheim for breach of the contract and offered Cresheim's letter in evidence as proof of the contract. Cresheim claimed that the oral contract was not binding because the contract was not in writing and the letter referring to the contract was not a contract but only a letter. Was the contract binding?

3. Lawrence loaned money to Moore, who died without repaying the loan. Lawrence claimed that when he mentioned the matter to Moore's widow, she promised to pay the debt. She did not pay it, and Lawrence sued her on her promise. Does she have any defense? [*Moore v Lawrence*, 480 SW2d 941 (Ark)]

4. Jackson signed an agreement to sell 79 acres of land to Devenyns. Jackson owned 80 acres and was apparently intending to keep for himself the acre on which his home was located. The written agreement also stated that "Devenyns shall have the option to buy on property _____," but nothing was stated in the blank space. Devenyns sued to enforce the agreement. Was it binding? [*In re Jackson's Estate*, 892 P2d 786 (Wyo)]

5. Boeing Airplane Co. contracted with Pittsburgh–Des Moines Steel Co. for the latter to construct a supersonic wind tunnel. R.H. Freitag Manufacturing Co. sold materials to York-Gillespie Co., which subcontracted to do part of the work. To persuade Freitag to keep supplying materials on credit, Boeing and the principal contractor both assured Freitag that he would be paid. When Freitag was not paid by the subcontractor, he sued Boeing and the contractor. They defended on the ground that the assurances given Freitag were not written. Decide. What ethical values are involved? [*R.H. Freitag Mfg. Co. v Boeing Airplane Co.*, 347 P2d 1074 (Wash)]

6. Louise Pulsifer owned a farm that she wanted to sell and ran an ad in the local newspaper. After Russell Gillespie agreed to purchase the farm, Pulsifer wrote him a letter stating that she would not sell it. He sued her to enforce the contract, and she raised the defense of the statute of frauds. The letter she had signed did not contain any of the terms of the sale. Gillespie, however, claimed that the newspaper ad could be combined with her letter to satisfy the statute of frauds. Was he correct? [*Gillespie v Pulsifer*, 655 SW2d 123 (Mo)]

7. In February or March, Corning Glass Works orally agreed to retain Hanan as management consultant from May 1 of that year to April 30 of the next year for a present value fee of $200,000. Was this agreement binding? Is this decision ethical? [*Hanan v Corning Glass Works*, 314 NYS2d 804 (App Div)] wasn't binding, b/c not in writing

8. Catherine (wife) and Peter (husband) Mallen had lived together unmarried for some four years when Catherine got pregnant and a marriage was arranged. Peter asked Catherine to sign a prenuptial agreement. Although his financial statement attached to the agreement did not state his income at $560,000 per year, it showed he was wealthy, and she had lived with him for four years and knew from their standard of living that he had significant income. Catherine contends that failure to disclose Peter's income was a nondisclosure of a material fact when the agreement was drawn up and that accordingly the agreement is not valid. Peter contends that he fully disclosed his net worth and that Catherine was well aware of his significant income. Further, he contends that disparities in the parties' financial status and business experience did not make the agreement unconscionable. Decide. [*Mallen v Mallen*, 622 SE2d 812 (Ga Sup Ct)] Catherine

9. Panasonic Industrial Co. (PIC) created a contract making Manchester Equipment Co., Inc. (MECI), a nonexclusive wholesale distributor of its products. The contract stated that PIC reserved the unrestricted right to solicit and make

direct sales of the products to anyone, anywhere. The contract also stated that it contained the entire agreement of the parties and that any prior agreement or statement was superseded by the contract. PIC subsequently began to make direct sales to two of MECI's established customers. MECI claimed that this was a breach of the distribution contract and sued PIC for damages. Decide. What ethical values are involved? [*Manchester Equipment Co. Inc. v Panasonic Industrial Co.,* 529 NYS2d 532 (App Div)]

10. A contract made for the sale of a farm stated that the buyer's deposit would be returned "if for any reason the farm cannot be sold." The seller later stated that she had changed her mind and would not sell, and she offered to return the deposit. The buyer refused to take the deposit back and brought suit to enforce the contract. The seller contended that the "any reason" provision extended to anything, including the seller's changing her mind. Was the buyer entitled to recover? [*Phillips v Rogers,* 200 SE2d 676 (W Va)]

11. Integrated, Inc., entered into a contract with the state of California to construct a building. It then subcontracted the electrical work to Alec Fergusson Electrical Contractors. The subcontract was a printed form with blanks filled in by typewriting. The printed payment clause required Integrated to pay Fergusson on the 15th day of the month following the submission of invoices by Fergusson. The typewritten part of the contract required Integrated to pay Fergusson "immediately following payment" (by the state) to the general contractor. When was payment required? [*Integrated, Inc. v Alec Fergusson Electrical Contractors,* 58 Cal Rptr 503 (Cal App)]

12. Norwest Bank had been lending money to Tresch to run a dairy farm. The balance due the bank after several years was $147,000. The loan agreement stated that Tresch would not buy any new equipment in excess of $500 without the express consent of the bank. Some time later, Tresch applied to the bank for a loan of $3,100 to purchase some equipment. The bank refused to make the loan because it did not believe the new equipment would correct the condition for which it would be bought and would not result in significant additional income. Tresch then sued the bank, claiming that its refusal to make the loan was a breach of the implied covenant of good faith and fair dealing. Decide. [*Tresch v Norwest Bank of Lewistown,* 778 P2d 874 (Mont)]

13. Physicians Mutual Insurance Co. issued a policy covering Brown's life. The policy declared that it did not cover any deaths resulting from "mental disorder, alcoholism, or drug addiction." Brown was killed when she fell while intoxicated. The insurance company refused to pay because of the quoted provision. Her executor, Savage, sued the insurance company. Did the insurance company have a defense? [*Physicians Mutual Ins. Co. v Savage,* 296 NE2d 165 (Ind App)]

14. The Dickinson Elks Club conducted an annual Labor Day golf tournament. Charbonneau Buick-Pontiac offered to give a new car as a prize to anyone making "a hole in one on hole no. 8." The golf course of the club was only nine holes. To play 18 holes, the players would go around the course twice, although they would play from different tees or locations for the second nine holes. On the second time around, what was originally the eighth hole became the seventeenth hole. Grove was a contestant in the tournament. He scored 3 on the no. 8 hole, but on approaching it for the second time as the seventeenth hole, he made a hole in one. He claimed the prize car from Charbonneau. The latter claimed that Grove had not won the prize because he did not make the hole in one on the eighth hole. Decide. [*Grove v Charbonneau Buick-Pontiac, Inc.,* 240 NW2d 8533 (ND)]

15. Tambe Electric Inc. entered into a written agreement with Home Depot to provide copper wire to Tambe at a price set forth in the writing, and allowing the contractor the option of paying for the wire over a period of time. Home Depot did not fulfill this written agreement and Tambe sued for $68,598, the additional cost it had to subsequently pay to obtain copper wire for its work. Home Depot defended that it had made

an oral condition precedent requiring payment in full by Tambe at the time it accepted the price quoted in the written agreement. Decide. [*Tambe Electric v Home Depot,* 856 NYS2d 373]

CPA QUESTIONS

1. Which of the following statements is true with regard to the statute of frauds?

   a. All contracts involving consideration of more than $500 must be in writing.

   b. The written contract must be signed by all parties.

   c. The statute of frauds applies to contracts that can be fully performed within one year from the date they are made.

   d. The contract terms may be stated in more than one document.

2. With regard to an agreement for the sale of real estate, the statute of frauds:

   a. Requires that the entire agreement be in a single writing

   b. Requires that the purchase price be fair and adequate in relation to the value of the real estate

   c. Does *not* require that the agreement be signed by all parties

   d. Does *not* apply if the value of the real estate is less than $500

3. In negotiations with Andrews for the lease of Kemp's warehouse, Kemp orally agreed to pay one-half of the cost of the utilities. The written lease, later prepared by Kemp's attorney, provided that Andrews pay all of the utilities. Andrews failed to carefully read the lease and signed it. When Kemp demanded that Andrews pay all of the utilities, Andrews refused, claiming that the lease did not accurately reflect the oral agreement. Andrews also learned that Kemp intentionally misrepresented the condition of the structure of the warehouse during the negotiations between the parties. Andrews sued to rescind the lease and intends to introduce evidence of the parties' oral agreement about sharing the utilities and the fraudulent statements made by Kemp. Will the parol evidence rule prevent the admission of evidence concerning each of the following?

	Oral agreement regarding who pays the utilities	Fraudulent statements by Kemp
a.	Yes	Yes
b.	No	Yes
c.	Yes	No
d.	No	No

Chapter
18

THIRD PERSONS AND CONTRACTS

A. Third-Party Beneficiary Contracts

Generally, only the parties to a contract may sue on it. However, in some cases a third person who is not a party to the contract may sue on the contract.

CPA 1. Definition

When a contract is intended to benefit a third person, such a person is an **intended beneficiary** and may bring suit on and enforce the contract. In some states, the right of the intended **third-party beneficiary** to sue on the contract is declared by statute.

For Example, Ibberson Co., the general contractor hired by AgGrow Oils, LLC to design and build an oilseed processing plant, contracted with subcontractor Anderson International Corp. to supply critical seed processing equipment for the project. Anderson's formal proposal to Ibberson identified the AgGrow Oils Project, and the proposal included drawings of the planned AgGrow plant. Under state law, this contract made between the contractor and subcontractor for the express benefit of the third-party AgGrow Oils could be enforced by the intended third-party beneficiary AgGrow Oils. The project was a failure. AgGrow was successful in the lawsuit against Anderson under the Anderson-Ibberson contract, having the standing to sue as an intended third-party beneficiary of that contract.[1]

(A) Creditor Beneficiary. The intended beneficiary is sometimes classified as a *creditor beneficiary* when the promisee's primary intent is to discharge a duty owed to the third party.[2] **For Example,** when Max Giordano sold his business, Sameway Laundry, to Harry Phinn, he had three years of payments totaling $14,500 owing to Davco, Inc., on a commercial Davco shirt drying and pressing machine purchased in 2006. Max

(the promisee) made a contract with Harry to sell the business for a stipulated sum. A provision in this contract selling the business called for Harry (the promisor) to make the Davco machine payments when due over the next three years. Should Harry fail to make payments, Davco, Inc., as an intended creditor beneficiary under the contract between Max and Harry, would have standing to sue Harry for breach of the payment provision in the contract.

CPA (B) Donee Beneficiary. The second type of intended beneficiary is a *donee beneficiary* to whom the promisee's primary intent in contracting is to give a benefit. A life insurance contract is such an intended third-party beneficiary contract. The promisee-insured pays premiums to the insurer under the contract of insurance so that, upon the death of the insured, the promisor-insurer would pay the sum designated in the contract to the beneficiary. The beneficiary's rights vest upon the insured's death, and the beneficiary can sue the insurance company upon the insured's death even though the insurance company never made any agreement directly with the beneficiary.

(C) Necessity of Intent. A third person does not have the status of an intended third-party beneficiary unless it is clear at the time the contract was formed that the parties intended to impose a direct obligation with respect to the third person.[3] In determining whether there is intent to benefit a third party, the surrounding circumstances as well as the contract may be examined.[4] There is a strong presumption that the parties to a contract intend to benefit only themselves.[5]

(D) Description. It is not necessary that the intended third-party beneficiary be identified by name. The beneficiary may be identified by class, with the result that any member of that class is a third-party

---

[1] *AgGrow Oils, LLC v National Union Fire Ins.*, 420 F3d 751 (8th Cir 2005).
[2] The Restatement (Second) of Contracts § 302 substitutes "intended beneficiary" for the terms "creditor" and "donee" beneficiary. However, some courts continue to use the classifications of creditor and donee third-party beneficiaries. Regardless of the terminology, the law continues to be the same. See *Continental Casualty v Zurich American Insurance*, 2009 WL 455285 (DC Or 2009).
[3] *American United Logistics, Inc. v Catellus*, 319 F3d 921 (7th Cir 2003).
[4] See *Becker v Crispell-Synder, Inc.*, 763 NW2d 192 (Wisc App 2009) for an example of complex circumstances surrounding a third-party beneficiary contract. The town of Somers, Wisconsin, entered into a contract with engineering firm Crispell-Synder (C-S) because it needed an engineering firm to oversee a new subdivision to be developed by the Beckers. Under this contract C-S would submit bills to the town for overseeing the development, and the town would pay C-S through a line of credit from the Beckers. The court held that the Beckers were third-party beneficiaries entitled to sue C-S for overcharging change orders.
[5] *Barney v Unity Paving, Inc.*, 639 NE2d 592 (Ill App 1994).

beneficiary. **For Example,** a contract between the promoter of an automobile stock car race and the owner of the racetrack contains a promise by the owner to pay specified sums of money to each driver racing a car in certain races. A person driving in one of the designated races is a third-party beneficiary and can sue the owner on the contract for the promised compensation.

2. Modification or Termination of Intended Third-Party Beneficiary Contract

Can the parties to the contract modify or terminate it so as to destroy the right of the intended third-party beneficiary? If the contract contains an express provision allowing a change of beneficiary or cancellation of the contract without the consent of the intended third-party beneficiary, the parties to the contract may destroy the rights of the intended beneficiary by acting in accordance with that contract provision.[6]

For Example, Roy obtained a life insurance policy from Phoenix Insurance Company that provided the beneficiary could be changed by the insured. Roy named his son, Harry, as the beneficiary. Later, Roy had a falling out with Harry and removed him as beneficiary. Roy could do this because the right to change the beneficiary was expressly reserved by the contract that created the status of the intended third-party beneficiary.

In addition, the rights of an intended third-party beneficiary are destroyed if the contract is discharged or ended by operation of law, for example, through bankruptcy proceedings.

3. Limitations on Intended Third-Party Beneficiary

Although the intended third-party beneficiary rule gives the third person the right to enforce the contract, it obviously gives no more rights than the

contract provides. That is, the intended third-party beneficiary must take the contract as it is. If there is a time limitation or any other restriction in the contract, the intended beneficiary cannot ignore it but is bound by it.

If the contract is not binding for any reason, that defense may be raised against the intended third-party beneficiary suing on the contract.[7]

CPA   4. Incidental Beneficiaries

Not everyone who benefits from the performance of a contract between other persons is entitled to sue as a third-party beneficiary. If the benefit was intended, the third person is an intended beneficiary with the rights described in the preceding sections. If the benefit was not intended, the third person is an *incidental beneficiary.* **For Example,** Ensil International (EI), a New York firm, entered a repair agreement in 1998 with a Canadian company, Ensil Canada (EC) to perform repair work relating to medical imaging devices. EI solicited repair business in the U.S. and shipped the items for repair to the Canadian firm. In 2001 BC Technical (BCT) shipped items for repair to EI who shipped them to EC for the actual repairs. The repair work was not successful and BCT sued both EI and EC under the 1998 repair agreement for damages. BC Technical was not an intended third-party beneficiary of the 1998 agreement that was undertaken several years before BCT and EI contracted for the repairs in 2001. BCT had no standing to sue the Canadian firm under the 1998 contract. BCT was an incidental beneficiary of the 1998 agreement.[8]

Whether or not a third party is an *intended* or *incidental* beneficiary, therefore, comes down to determining whether or not a reasonable person would believe that the promisee intended to confer on the beneficiary an enforceable benefit under the contract in question. The intent must be clear and definite or expressed in the contract itself or in the circumstances surrounding the contract's execution.

---

[6] A common form of reservation is the life insurance policy provision by which the insured reserves the right to change the beneficiary. Section 142 of the Restatement (Second) of Contracts provides that the promisor and the promisee may modify their contract and affect the right of the third-party beneficiary thereby unless the agreement expressly prohibits this or the third-party beneficiary has changed position in reliance on the promise or has manifested assent to it.

[7] *XL Disposal Corp. v John Sexton Contractors Co.,* 659 NE2d 1312 (Ill App 1995).

[8] *BC Technical Inc. v Ensil International,* 2007 WL 2908282 (D Utah 2007).

B. ASSIGNMENTS

The parties to a contract have both rights and duties. Can rights be transferred or sold to another person or entity? Can duties be transferred to another person?

5. Definitions

Contracts create **rights** and **duties** between the parties to the contract. An **assignment** is a transfer of contractual rights to a third party. The party owing a duty or debt under the contract is the **obligor** or **debtor**, and the party to whom the obligation is owed is the **obligee**. The party making the assignment is the **assignor**. The third party to whom the assignment is made is the **assignee**. **For Example,** Randy Marshall and Marilee Menendez own Huntington Beach Board (HBB) Company, LLC, a five-employee start-up company making top-of-the line surfboards. Marilee was able to sell 100 Duke Kahanamoku–inspired "longboards" to Watersports, Inc., a large retail sporting goods chain, for $140 per board. However, the best payment terms she could obtain were payment in full in 90 days. A contract containing these terms was executed, and the goods were delivered. To meet internal cash flow needs, HBB assigned its right to receive the $14,000 payment from the buyer to West Coast Financial Associates (Associates) and received $12,800 cash from Associates on execution of the assignment documents. Notice was given at that time to Watersports, Inc., of the assignment. The right to receive the payment due in 90 days under the sales contract has thus been transferred by the seller HBB (assignor) to the third party, Associates (the assignee), to whom the buyer, Watersports, Inc. (obligor), now owes the duty of payment. Under the law of assignments, Associates, the assignee, now has direct rights against the obligor, Watersports, Inc. (See Figure 18-1)

6. Form of Assignment

Generally, an assignment may be in any form. Statutes, however, may require that certain kinds of assignments be in writing or be executed in a particular form. Any words, whether written or spoken, that show an intention to transfer or assign will be given the effect of an assignment.[9]

7. Notice of Assignment

An assignment, if otherwise valid, takes effect the moment it is made. The assignee should give immediate notice of the assignment to the obligor, setting forth the obligor's duty to the assignee, in order to prevent improper payment.[10]

If the obligor is notified in any manner that there has been an assignment and that any money due must be paid to the assignee, the obligor's obligation can be discharged only by making payment to the assignee.

FIGURE 18-1 | **Surfboard Transaction Diagram**

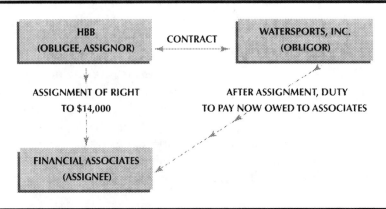

---

[9] *JOM Investments, LLC v Callahan Industries, Inc.*, 667 SE2d 429 (Ga App 2008).

[10] In some cases, an assignee will give notice of the assignment to the obligor in order to obtain priority over other persons who claim the same right or in order to limit the defenses that the obligor may raise against the assignee. UCC § 9-318.

If the obligor is not notified that there has been an assignment and that the money due must be paid to the assignee, any payment made by the obligor to the assignor reduces or cancels that portion of the debt. The only remedy for the assignee is to sue the assignor to recover the payments that were made by the obligor.

The Uniform Consumer Credit Code (UCCC) protects consumer-debtors making payments to an assignor without knowledge of the assignment[11] and imposes a penalty for using a contract term that would destroy this protection of consumers.[12]

8. Assignment of Right to Money

Assignments of contracts are generally made to raise money. **For Example,** an automobile dealer assigns a customer's credit contract to a finance company and receives cash for it. Sometimes assignments are made when an enterprise closes and transfers its business to a new owner.

A person entitled to receive money, such as payment for goods sold to a buyer or for work done under a contract, may generally assign that right to another person.[13] A **claim** or **cause of action** against another person may be assigned. Isaac Hayes, an Academy Award®–winning composer, producer, and the original voice of Chef in the television series South Park, assigned his copyright interests in several musical works in exchange for royalties from Stax Records.[14] A contractor entitled to receive payment from a building's owner can assign that right to a bank as security for a loan or can assign it to anyone else.

For Example, Celeste owed Roscoe Painters $5,000 for painting her house. Roscoe assigned this claim to the Main Street Bank. Celeste later refused to pay the bank because she had never consented to the assignment. The fact that Celeste had not consented is irrelevant. Roscoe was the owner of the claim and could transfer it to the bank. Celeste, therefore, is obligated to pay the assignee, Main Street Bank.

(A) FUTURE RIGHTS. By the modern rule, future and expected rights to money may be assigned. Thus, prior to the start of a building, a building contractor may assign its rights to money not yet due under an existing contract's payment on completion-phase schedule.

(B) PURPOSE OF ASSIGNMENT. The assignment of the right to money may be a complete transfer of the right that gives the assignee the right to collect and keep the money. In contrast, the assignment may be held for security. In this case, the assignee may hold the money only as a security for some specified obligation.

(C) PROHIBITION OF ASSIGNMENT OF RIGHTS. A clear and specific contractual prohibition against the assignment of rights is enforceable at common law. However, the UCC favors the assignment of contracts, and express contractual prohibitions on assignments are ineffective against (1) the assignment of rights to payment for goods or services, including accounts receivable,[15] and (2) the assignment of the rights to damages for breach of sales contracts.[16]

9. Nonassignable Rights

If the transfer of a right would materially affect or alter a duty or the rights of the obligor, an assignment is not permitted.[17]

(A) ASSIGNMENT INCREASING BURDEN OF PERFORMANCE. When the assignment of a right would increase the burden of the obligor in performing, an assignment is ordinarily not permitted. To illustrate, if the assignor has the right to buy a certain quantity of a stated article and to take such property from the seller's warehouse, this right can be assigned. However, if the sales contract stipulates that the seller should deliver to the buyer's premises and the assignee's premises are a substantial distance from the assignor's place of business, the assignment would not be given effect. In this case, the seller would be required to give a

[11] UCCC § 2.412.
[12] UCCC § 5.202.
[13] *Pravin Banker Associates v Banco Popular del Peru*, 109 F3d 850 (2d Cir 1997).
[14] *Hayes v Carlin America, Inc.*, 168 F Supp 2d 154 (SDNY 2001).
[15] UCC § 9-318(4). This section of the UCC is applicable to most commercial assignments.
[16] UCC § 2-210(2).
[17] *Aslakson v Home Savings Ass'n*, 416 NW2d 786 (Minn App 1987) (increase of credit risk).

FIGURE 18-2 | *Limitations on Transfer of Rights and Duties*

ASSIGNMENT OF RIGHT TO MONEY	ASSIGNMENT OF RIGHT TO PERFORMANCE	DELEGATION OF DUTIES
GENERALLY NO LIMITATION	INCREASE OF BURDEN PERSONAL SERVICES CREDIT TRANSACTION	PERSONAL OR NONSTANDARDIZED PERFORMANCE

different performance by providing greater transportation if the assignment were permitted.

(B) PERSONAL SERVICES. Contracts for personal services are generally not assignable. **For Example,** were golf instructor David Ledbetter to sign a one-year contract to provide instruction for professional golfer Davis Love III, David Ledbetter could not assign his first assistant to provide the instruction, nor could Davis Love assign a protégé to receive instruction from Ledbetter. Professional athletes and their agents commonly deal with assignment or trading rights of the athletes in their contracts with professional sports franchises.

There is a split among jurisdictions regarding whether employee noncompetition covenants are assignable to the new owner of a business absent employee consent. That is, some courts permit a successor employer to enforce an employee's noncompetition agreement as an assignee of the original employer. However, a majority of states that have considered this issue have concluded that restrictive covenants are personal in nature and not assignable. **For Example,** in September 2000, Philip Burkhardt signed a noncompetition agreement with his employer, NES Trench Shoring. On June 30, 2002, United Rentals Purchased NES with all contracts being assigned to United Rentals. Burkhardt stayed on with the new owner for five weeks and thereafter went to work for Traffic Control Services, a direct competitor of United. United was unsuccessful in its action to enforce the noncompetition covenant Burkhardt had signed with NES. Burkhardt's

covenant with NES did not contain a clause allowing the covenant to be assigned to a new owner, and the court refused to enforce it, absent an express clause permitting assignment.[18]

(C) CREDIT TRANSACTION. When a transaction is based on extending credit, the person to whom credit is extended cannot assign any rights under the contract to another. **For Example,** Jack Aldrich contracted to sell his summer camp on Lake Sunapee to Pat Norton for $200,000, with $100,000 in cash due at the closing and the balance due on an installment basis secured by a mortgage on the property to be executed by Norton. Several days later, Norton found a more desirable property, and her sister Meg was very pleased to take over the Sunapee contract. Pat assigned her rights to Meg. Jack Aldrich, having received a better offer after contracting with Pat, refused to consent to the assignment. In this situation, the assignment to Meg is prohibited because the assignee, Meg, is a different credit risk even though the property to serve as security remained unchanged.

CPA   10. Rights of Assignee

Unless restricted by the terms of the assignment or applicable law, the assignee acquires all the rights of the assignor.[19]

An assignee stands exactly in the position of the assignor. The assignee's rights are no more or less than those of the assignor. If the assigned right to payment is subject to a condition precedent, that same condition exists for the assignee. **For Example,** when a contractor is not entitled to receive the

---

[18] *Traffic Control Sources, Inc. v United Rentals Northwest, Inc.,* 87 P3d 1054 (Nov 2004).
[19] *Puget Sound National Bank v Washington Department of Revenue,* 868 P2d 127 (Wash 1994).

balance of money due under the contract until all bills of suppliers of materials have been paid, the assignee to whom the contractor assigns the balance due under the contract is subject to the same condition. As set forth previously, in some states the assignee of a business purchasing all of the assets and rights of the business has the right to enforce a confidentiality and noncompetition agreement against a former employee of the assignor, just as though it were the assignor.[20]

11. Continuing Liability of Assignor

The making of an assignment does not relieve the assignor of any obligation of the contract. In the absence of a contrary agreement, an assignor continues to be bound by the obligations of the original contract. **For Example,** boatbuilder Derecktor NY's assignment of obligations to a Connecticut boatbuilder did not release it from all liabilities under its boatbuilding contract with New York Water Taxi (NYWT); and NYWT was allowed to proceed against Derecktor NY for breach of contract–design and breach of contract–workmanship.[21]

When a lease is assigned, the assignee becomes the principal obligor for rent payments, and the leasee becomes a surety toward the lessor for the assignee's performance. **For Example,** Tri-State Chiropractic (TSC) held a five-year lease on premises at 6010 East Main Street in Columbus, Ohio. Without the leasor's consent, TSC assigned that lease to Dr. T. Wilson and Buckeye Chiropractic, LLC, prior to the expiration of the lease. TSC continues to be liable for rent as surety during the term of the lease, even if the leasor (owner)

had consented to the assignment or accepted payment from the assignee.[22] In order to avoid liability as a surety, TSC would have to obtain a discharge of the lease by **novation**, in which all three parties agree that the original contract (the lease) would be discharged and a new lease between Dr. Wilson and the owner would take effect. A novation allows for the discharge of a contractual obligation by the substitution of a new contract involving a new party.[23]

12. Liability of Assignee

It is necessary to distinguish between the question of whether the obligor can assert a particular defense against the assignee and the question of whether any person can sue the assignee. Ordinarily, the assignee is not subject to suit by virtue of the fact that the assignment has been made.

(A) CONSUMER PROTECTION LIABILITY OF ASSIGNEE. The assignee of the right to money may have no direct relationship to the original debtor except with respect to receiving payments. Consumer protection laws in most states, however, may subject the assignee to some liability for the assignor's misconduct.

In the *Jackson v Dewitt* case, the court was faced with deciding whether a finance company had an obligation to return money already paid to it by a homeowner under a retail installment security agreement between the homeowner and a contractor, which agreement had been assigned to the finance company by the contractor.

Jackson v Dewitt, 592 NW2d 262 (Wis App 1999)

The Pool and the Agreement Will Not Hold Any Water

Homeowner Michael Jackson entered into a contract for the construction of an in-ground lap pool with James DeWitt. The contract provided for a 12 ft. by 60 ft. pool at an estimated cost of $21,000. At the time the contract was signed, Jackson paid DeWitt

$11,400 in cash and financed $7,500 through a Retail Installment Security Agreement (RISA). Associates Financial Services Co. (Associates) provided DeWitt with all the forms necessary to document the financing of the home improvements. Consumer

[20] *Artromick International, Inc. v Koch,* 759 NE2d 385 (Ohio App 2001).
[21] *New York Trans Harbor, LLC v Derecktor Shipyards,* 841 NYS2d 821 (2007).
[22] *Schottenstein Trustees v Carano,* 2000 WL 1455425 (Ohio App 2000).
[23] See *Quicksilver Resources, Inc. v Eagle Drilling, LLC,* 2009 WL 1312598 (SD Tex 2009).

Continued

requests for financing were subject to Associates' approval, which was given for Jackson's lap pool. When the RISA was completed, DeWitt assigned it to Associates. Jackson made two monthly payments of $202.90 and a final payment of $7,094.20 while the lap pool was still under construction. When the pool was filled, it failed to hold water, and Jackson had the pool and deck removed. Jackson sued DeWitt for breach of contract. He asserted that all valid claims and defenses he had against DeWitt were also valid against the assignee, Associates. Jackson sought the return of the $7,500 he had financed from Associates. The trial court held that because Jackson had paid the entire balance of the loan before Associates knew of Jackson's claim he could not obtain relief from Associates under the consumer protection law § ATCP 110.06. Jackson appealed this decision.

JUDICIAL OPINION

ANDERSON, J . . . . WISCONSIN ADM.CODE § ATCP 110.06, governs home improvement contracts and provides:

1. *Every assignee of a home improvement contract takes subject to all claims and defenses of the buyer or successors in interest.*

2. *No seller shall enter into any home improvement contract wherein the buyer waives the right to assert against the seller or any assignee any claim or defense the buyer may have against the seller under the contract. . . .*

To subject all assignees or holders of "home improvement" contracts, including Associates, to the claims and defenses of the consumer, fulfills the intent of Wis. Adm. Code ch. ATCP 110. As one commentator has noted, ch. ATCP 110 "deals with a virtual laundry list of unfair or deceptive home improvement practices that have resulted in substantial financial losses to home owners over the years." Jeffries 57 Marq. L. Rev. at 578. The Wisconsin Supreme Court has also noted, "[T]he home improvement trade is subject to comprehensive and stringent rules designed to protect the consumer." To protect the homeowner when the contractor or seller has failed to fulfill the obligations imposed by ch. ATCP 110, the homeowner must be able to seek restitutionary relief wherever it is available. [It] provide[s] relief from the assignee or holder on a "home improvement contract" by making the assignee or holder subject to the claims and defenses of the buyer. . . .

We conclude, from the statute and regulation, that a homeowner may proceed under § 100.20(5), STATS., when he or she has suffered pecuniary loss as a result of violations of Wis. Adm. Code ch. ATCP 110. If the "home improvement contract" was financed with an "interlocking consumer loan," full payment before discovering the violations of the

regulation does not eliminate the consumer's cause of action against the assignee or holder of the "home improvement contract."

Excel Management, like this case, involved contracts for the sale of swimming pools to consumers. *See Excel Management*, 111 Wis.2d at 483, 331 N.W.2d at 314. In *Excel Management*, like this case, the complaint alleged that the contracts were obtained in violation of Wis. Adm. Code ch. ATCP 110. In *Excel Management*, like this case, the retailer used loan papers provided by the lender and assigned the completed contract to the lender. In *Excel Management*, like this case, the assigned contract contained a notice required by 16 C.F.R § 433.2, "Any holder of this consumer credit contract is subject to all claims and defenses which the debtor could assert against the seller of goods or services obtained pursuant hereto or with the proceeds hereof."

Considering these facts, the supreme court in *Excel Management*, readily concluded that although the contract was not a negotiable instrument, "[a]s an assignee of the contracts from Viking, First Savings takes each contract 'subject to all claims and defenses of the buyer of his successor in interest.'" . . . The supreme court commented that the warning language required by 16 C.F.R. § 433.2 clearly made the assignee of the contract aware that it took assignment of the contract subject to "any claims or defenses the buyer may assert." In *Excel Management*, the supreme court concluded that the consumers could bring actions against the assignees of their contracts for pecuniary losses stemming from the retailers' violations of the unfair trade statutes. *See id.* at 487, 331 N.W.2d at 316.

The factual similarity between this case and *Excel Management* requires us to reach a similar conclusion. Associates is an assignee of a "home improvement contract" that is governed by Wis. Adm. Code § ATCP 110.06. The regulation provides, "Every assignee of a home improvement contract takes subject to all claims and defenses of the buyer or successors in interest." Section ATCP 110.06(1). Therefore, as the assignee of the RISA, Associates is subject to any claims Jackson may assert, without regard to the negotiability of the contract. . . .

[Reversed]

QUESTIONS

1. Identify the parties to the retail installment sales agreement (RISA), identify their obligations, explain how Associates became involved, and identify Associates' legal status.

2. Assess the validity of this statement: "The contractor botched the pool installation job. The finance company merely facilitated the transaction for the benefit of both parties and is innocent of wrongdoing. The homeowner therefore should obtain relief solely from the contractor."

3. What did Jackson claim he was due from Associates?

FIGURE 18-3 | *Can a Third Person Sue on a Contract?*

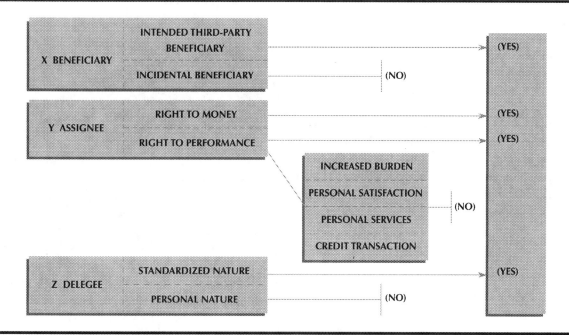

(B) DEFENSES AND SETOFFS. The assignee's rights are no greater than those of the assignor.[24] If the obligor could successfully defend against a suit brought by the assignor, the obligor will also prevail against the assignee.

The fact that the assignee has given value for the assignment does not give the assignee any immunity from defenses that the other party, the obligor, could have asserted against the assignor. The rights acquired by the assignee remain subject to any limitations imposed by the contract.

13. Warranties of Assignor

When the assignment is made for a consideration, the assignor is regarded as providing an **implied warranty** that the right assigned is valid. The assignor also warrants that the assignor is the owner of the claim or right assigned and that the assignor will not interfere with the assignee's enforcement of the obligation.

14. Delegation of Duties

A **delegation of duties** is a transfer of duties by a contracting party to another person who is to perform

them. Under certain circumstances, a contracting party may obtain someone else to do the work. When the performance is standardized and nonpersonal, so that it is not material who performs, the law will permit the **delegation** of the performance of the contract. In such cases, however, the contracting party remains liable in the case of default of the person doing the work just as though no delegation had been made.[25]

A contract may prohibit a party owing a duty of performance under a contract from delegating that duty to another.[26] **For Example,** Tom Joyce of Patriot Plumbing Co. contracts to install a new heating system for Mrs. Lawton. A notation on the sales contract that Tom Joyce will do the installation prohibits Patriot Plumbing from delegating the installation to another equally skilled plumber or to another company if a backlog of work occurs at Patriot Plumbing.

If the performance of a party to a contract involves personal skill, talents, judgment, or trust, the delegation of duties is barred unless consented to by the person entitled to the performance. Examples include performance by professionals such as physicians,

[24] *Shoreline Communications, Inc. v Norwich Taxi, LLC,* 797 A2d 1165 (Conn App 2002).
[25] *Orange Bowl Corp. v Warren,* 386 SE2d 293 (SC App 1989).
[26] See *Physical Distribution Services, Inc. v R. R. Donnelley,* 561 F3d 792 (8th Cir 2009).

dentists, lawyers, consultants, celebrities, artists, and craftpersons with unusual skills.

(A) INTENTION TO DELEGATE DUTIES. An assignment of rights does not in itself delegate the performance of duties to the assignee. In the absence of clear language in the assignment stating that duties are or are not delegated, all circumstances must be examined to determine whether there is a delegation. When the total picture is viewed, it may become clear what was intended. The fact that an assignment is made for security of the assignee is a strong indication there was no intent to delegate to the assignee the performance of any duty resting on the assignor.[27]

(B) DELEGATION OF DUTIES UNDER THE UCC. With respect to contracts for the sale of goods, "an assignment of 'the contract' or of 'all my rights under the contract' or an assignment in similar general terms is an assignment of rights and, unless the language or the circumstances (as in an assignment for security) indicate the contrary, it is a delegation of performance of the duties of the assignor, and its acceptance by the assignee

constitutes a promise . . . to perform those duties. This promise is enforceable by either the assignor or the other party to the original contract."[28]

lawflix

It Could Happen to You (1996) (PG)

Discuss the legal, ethical and contract issues involved in the first portion of the film in which a police officer (Nicholas Cage) promises to split a lottery ticket with a coffee shop waitress (Bridget Fonda) as her tip because he does not have enough money. The lottery ticket (purchased by Cage and his wife, Rosie Perez) is a winner, and Cage wrestles with his obligation to tell Fonda. You could discuss whether there was an assignment or whether Fonda was added as a third-party beneficiary after the fact.

Check out LawFlix at **www.cengage.com/ blaw/dvl** to access movie clips that illustrate business law concepts.

MAKE THE CONNECTION

SUMMARY

Ordinarily, only the parties to contracts have rights and duties with respect to such contracts. Exceptions are made in the case of third-party beneficiary contracts and assignments.

When a contract shows a clear intent to benefit a third person or class of persons, those persons are called *intended third-party beneficiaries*, and they may sue for breach of the contract. A third-party beneficiary is subject to any limitation or restriction found in the contract. A third-party beneficiary loses all rights when the original contract is terminated by

operation of law or if the contract reserves the right to change the beneficiary and such a change is made.

In contrast, an incidental beneficiary benefits from the performance of a contract, but the conferring of this benefit was not intended by the contracting parties. An incidental beneficiary cannot sue on the contract.

An assignment is a transfer of a right; the assignor transfers a right to the assignee. In the absence of a local statute, there are no formal requirements for an assignment. Any words manifesting the intent to

---

[27] *City National Bank of Fort Smith v First National Bank and Trust Co. of Rogers*, 732 SW2d 489 (Ark App 1987).
[28] UCC § 2-210(4).

transfer are sufficient to constitute an assignment. No consideration is required. Any right to money may be assigned, whether the assignor is entitled to the money at the time of the assignment or will be entitled or expects to be entitled at some time in the future.

A right to a performance may be assigned except when (1) it would increase the burden of performance, (2) the contract involves the performance of personal services, or (3) the transaction is based on extending credit.

When a valid assignment is made, the assignee has the same rights—and only the same rights—as the assignor. The assignee is also subject to the same defenses and setoffs as the assignor had been.

The performance of duties under a contract may be delegated to another person except when a personal element of skill or judgment of the original contracting party is involved. The intent to delegate duties may be expressly stated. The intent may also be found in an "assignment" of "the contract" unless the circumstances make it clear that only the right to money was intended to be transferred. The fact that there has been a delegation of duties does not release the assignor from responsibility for performance. The assignor is liable for breach of the contract if the assignee does not properly perform the delegated duties. In the absence of an effective delegation or the formation of a third-party beneficiary contract, an assignee of rights is not liable to the obligee of the contract for its performance by the assignor.

Notice is not required to effect an assignment. When notice of the assignment is given to the obligor together with a demand that future payments be made to the assignee, the obligor cannot discharge liability by payment to the assignor.

When an assignment is made for a consideration, the assignor makes implied warranties that the right assigned is valid and that the assignor owns that right and will not interfere with its enforcement by the assignee.

LEARNING OUTCOMES

After studying this chapter, you should be able to clearly explain:

A. THIRD-PARTY BENEFICIARY CONTRACTS

LO.1 Explain the two types of intended third-party beneficiaries

> See the Sameway Laundry example that illustrates how the "intended creditor beneficiary" can sue the buyer, p. 350.
> See the text discussion explaining that a life insurance contract is an "intended" donee third-party beneficiary contract, p. 350.

LO.2 Explain why an incidental beneficiary does not have the right to sue as a third-party beneficiary

> See the *Ensil* case in which the owner had no standing to sue as an incidental beneficiary, p. 351.

B. ASSIGNMENTS

LO.3 Define an assignment

> See the text discussion explaining that an assignment is the transfer of contractual rights to a third party, p. 352.
> See the *Huntington Beach Board* example that discusses the assignee's direct rights against the obligor, p. 352.

LO.4 Explain the general rule that a person entitled to receive money under a contract may generally assign that right to another person

> See the example of an automobile dealer assigning a customer's credit contract to a finance company in order to raise cash to buy more inventory, p. 353.

LO.5 List the nonassignable rights to performance

> See the text discussion regarding increase of burden, personal services, and credit transactions beginning on p. 354.

KEY TERMS

assignee	delegation of duties	obligee
assignment	delegation	obligor
assignor	duties	rights
cause of action	implied warranty	third-party beneficiary
claim	intended beneficiary	
debtor	novation	

QUESTIONS AND CASE PROBLEMS

1. Give an example of a third-party beneficiary contract.

2. A court order required John Baldassari to make specified payments for the support of his wife and child. His wife needed more money and applied for Pennsylvania welfare payments. In accordance with the law, she assigned to Pennsylvania her right to the support payments from her husband. Pennsylvania then increased her payments. Pennsylvania obtained a court order directing John, in accordance with the terms of the assignment from his wife, to make the support-order payments directly to the Pennsylvania Department of Public Welfare. John refused to pay on the ground that he had not been notified of the assignment or the hearing directing him to make payment to the assignee. Was he correct? [*Pennsylvania v Baldassari*, 421 A2d 306 (Pa Super)]

3. Lee contracts to paint Sally's two-story house for $2,500. Sally realizes that she will not have sufficient money, so she transfers her rights under this agreement to her neighbor Karen, who has a three-story house. Karen notifies Lee that Sally's contract has been assigned to her and demands that Lee paint Karen's house for $2,500. Is Lee required to do so?

4. Assume that Lee agrees to the assignment of the house-painting contract to Karen as stated in question 3. Thereafter, Lee fails to perform the contract to paint Karen's house. Karen sues Sally for damages. Is Sally liable?

5. Jessie borrows $1,000 from Thomas and agrees to repay the money in 30 days. Thomas assigns the right to the $1,000 to Douglas Finance Co. Douglas sues Jessie. Jessie argues that she had agreed to pay the money only to Thomas and that when she and Thomas had entered into the transaction, there was no intention to benefit Douglas Finance Co. Are these objections valid?

6. Washington purchased an automobile from Smithville Motors. The contract called for payment of the purchase price in installments and contained the defense preservation notice required by the Federal Trade Commission regulation. Smithville assigned the contract to Rustic Finance Co. The car was always in need of repairs, and by the time it was half paid for, it would no longer run. Washington canceled the contract. Meanwhile, Smithville had gone out of business. Washington sued Rustic for the amount she had paid Smithville. Rustic refused to pay on the grounds that it had not been at fault. Decide.

7. Helen obtained an insurance policy insuring her life and naming her niece Julie as beneficiary. Helen died, and about a year later the policy was found in her house. When Julie claimed the insurance money, the insurer refused to pay on the ground that the policy required that notice of death be given to it promptly following the death. Julie claimed that she was not bound by the time limitation because she had never agreed to it, as she was not a party to the insurance contract. Is Julie entitled to recover?

8. Lone Star Life Insurance Co. agreed to make a long-term loan to Five Forty Three Land, Inc., whenever that corporation requested one. Five Forty Three wanted this loan to pay off its short-term debts. The loan was never made, as it

was never requested by Five Forty Three, which owed the Exchange Bank & Trust Co. on a short-term debt. Exchange Bank then sued Lone Star for breach of its promise on the theory that the Exchange Bank was a third-party beneficiary of the contract to make the loan. Was the Exchange Bank correct? [*Exchange Bank & Trust Co. v Lone Star Life Ins. Co.,* 546 SW2d 948 (Tex App)]

9. The New Rochelle Humane Society made a contract with the city of New Rochelle to capture and impound all dogs running at large. Spiegler, a minor, was bitten by some dogs while in her schoolyard. She sued the school district of New Rochelle and the Humane Society. With respect to the Humane Society, she claimed that she was a third-party beneficiary of the contract that the Humane Society had made with the city. She claimed that she could therefore sue the Humane Society for its failure to capture the dogs that had bitten her. Was she entitled to recover? [*Spiegler v School District of the City of New Rochelle,* 242 NYS2d 430]

10. Zoya operated a store in premises rented from Peerless. The lease required Zoya to maintain liability insurance to protect Zoya and Peerless. Caswell entered the store, fell through a trap door, and was injured. She then sued Zoya and Peerless on the theory that she was a third-party beneficiary of the lease requirement to maintain liability insurance. Was she correct? [*Caswell v Zoya Int'l,* 654 NE2d 552 (Ill App)]

11. Henry was owed $10,000 by Jones Corp. In consideration of the many odd jobs performed for him over the years by his nephew, Henry assigned the $10,000 claim to his nephew Charles. Henry died, and his widow claimed that the assignment was ineffective so that the claim was part of Henry's estate. She based her assertion on the ground that the past performance rendered by the nephew was not consideration. Was the assignment effective?

12. Industrial Construction Co. wanted to raise money to construct a canning factory in Wisconsin. Various persons promised to subscribe the needed amount, which they agreed to pay when the construction was completed. The construction company assigned its rights and delegated its duties under the agreement to Johnson, who then built the cannery. Vickers, one of the subscribers, refused to pay the amount that he had subscribed on the ground that the contract could not be assigned. Was he correct?

13. The Ohio Department of Public Welfare made a contract with an accountant to audit the accounts of health care providers who were receiving funds under the Medicaid program. Windsor House, which operated six nursing homes, claimed that it was a third-party beneficiary of that contract and could sue for its breach. Was it correct? [*Thornton v Windsor House, Inc.,* 566 NE2d 1220 (Ohio)]

CPA QUESTIONS

1. On August 1, Neptune Fisheries contracted in writing with West Markets to deliver to West 3,000 pounds of lobster at $4.00 a pound. Delivery of the lobsters was due October 1, with payment due November 1. On August 4, Neptune entered into a contract with Deep Sea Lobster Farms that provided as follows: "Neptune Fisheries assigns all the rights under the contract with West Markets dated August 1 to Deep Sea Lobster Farms." The best interpretation of the August 4 contract would be that it was:

   a. Only an assignment of rights by Neptune

   b. Only a delegation of duties by Neptune

   c. An assignment of rights and a delegation of duties by Neptune

   d. An unenforceable third-party beneficiary contract

2. Graham contracted with the city of Harris to train and employ high school dropouts residing in Harris. Graham breached the contract. Long, a

resident of Harris and a high school dropout, sued Graham for damages. Under the circumstances, Long will:

a. Win, because Long is a third-party beneficiary entitled to enforce the contract

b. Win, because the intent of the contract was to confer a benefit on all high school dropouts residing in Harris

c. Lose, because Long is merely an incidental beneficiary of the contract

d. Lose, because Harris did not assign its contract rights to Long

3. Union Bank lent $200,000 to Wagner. Union required Wagner to obtain a life insurance policy naming Union as beneficiary. While the loan was outstanding, Wagner stopped paying the premiums on the policy. Union paid the premiums, adding the amounts paid to Wagner's loan. Wagner died, and the insurance company refused to pay the policy proceeds to Union. Union may:

a. Recover the policy proceeds because it is a creditor beneficiary

b. Not recover the policy proceeds because it is a donee beneficiary

c. Not recover the policy proceeds because it is not in privity of contract with the insurance company

d. Not recover the policy proceeds because it is only an incidental beneficiary

Chapter 19

DISCHARGE OF CONTRACTS

In the preceding chapters, you studied how a contract is formed, what a contract means, and who has rights under a contract. In this chapter, attention is turned to how a contract is ended or discharged. In other words, what puts an end to the rights and duties created by a contract?

A. CONDITIONS RELATING TO PERFORMANCE

As developed in the body of this chapter, the ordinary method of discharging obligations under a contract is by performance. Certain promises may be less than absolute and instead come into effect only upon the occurrence of a specified event, or an existing obligation may be extinguished when an event happens. These are conditional promises.

1. Classifications of Conditions

When the occurrence or nonoccurrence of an event, as expressed in a contract, affects the duty of a party to the contract to perform, the event is called a **condition**. Terms such as *if, provided that, when, after, as soon as, subject to,* and *on the condition that* indicate the creation of a condition.[1] Conditions are classified as *conditions precedent, conditions subsequent,* and *concurrent conditions.*

(A) CONDITION PRECEDENT. A **condition precedent** is a condition that must occur before a party to a contract has an obligation to perform under the contract. **For Example,** a condition precedent to a contractor's (MasTec's) obligation to pay a subcontractor (Mid-America) under a "pay-if-paid" by the owner (PathNet) clause in their subcontract agreement is the receipt of payment by MasTec from PathNet. The condition precedent—payment by the owner—did not occur due to bankruptcy, and therefore MasTec did not have an obligation to pay MidAmerica.[2]

(B) CONDITION SUBSEQUENT. The parties to a contract may agree that a party is obligated to perform a

certain act or pay a certain sum of money, but the contract contains a provision that relieves the obligation on the occurrence of a certain event. That is, on the happening of a **condition subsequent**, such an event extinguishes the duty to thereafter perform. **For Example,** Chad Newly served as the weekend anchor on *Channel 5 News* for several years. The station manager, Tom O'Brien, on reviewing tapes in connection with Newly's contract renewal, believed that Newly's speech on occasion was slightly slurred, and he suspected that it was from alcohol use. In the parties' contract discussions, O'Brien expressed his concerns about an alcohol problem and offered help. Newly denied there was a problem. O'Brien agreed to a new two-year contract with Newly at $167,000 for the first year and $175,000 for the second year with other benefits subject to "the condition" that the station reserved the right to make four unannounced drug-alcohol tests during the contract term; and should Newly test positive for drugs or alcohol under measurements set forth in the contract, then all of Channel 5's obligations to Newly under the contract would cease. When Newly subsequently failed a urinalysis test three months into the new contract, the happening of this event extinguished the station's obligation to employ and pay him under the contract.

(C) CONCURRENT CONDITION. In most bilateral contracts, the performances of the parties are *concurrent conditions.* That is, their mutual duties of performance under the contract are to take place simultaneously. **For Example,** concerning a contract for the sale and delivery of certain goods, the buyer must tender to the seller a certified check at the time of delivery as set forth in the contract, and the seller must tender the goods to the buyer at the same time.

B. DISCHARGE BY PERFORMANCE

When it is claimed that a contract is discharged by performance, questions arise as to the nature, time, and sufficiency of the performance.

---

[1] *Harmon Cable Communications v Scope Cable Television, Inc.,* 468 NW2d 350 (Neb 1990).
[2] *MidAmerica Construction Management, Inc. v MasTec North America, Inc.,* 436 F3d 1257 (10th Cir 2006).

sports&entertainment law

Endorsement Contracts

Sports marketing involves the use of famous athletes to promote the sale of products and services in our economy. Should an athlete's image be tarnished by allegations of immoral or illegal conduct, a company could be subject to financial losses and corporate embarrassment. Endorsement contracts may extend for multiyear periods, and should a "morals" issue arise, a company would be well served to have had a broad morals clause in its contract that would allow the company at its sole discretion to summarily terminate the endorsement contract. Representatives of athletes, on the other hand, seek narrow contractual language that allows for termination of endorsement contracts only upon the indictment for a crime, and they seek the right to have an arbitrator, as opposed to the employer, make the determination as to whether the morals clause was violated. Without any public discussion of the contractual obligations of the parties, consulting firm Accenture ended its association with Tiger Woods after widespread adverse publicity about his marital infidelities.* John Daly's endorsement contract with Callaway Golf was terminated by the company when he violated his behavior clause that restricted gambling and drinking activities; and when a photograph of Olympic gold medal swimmer Michael Phelps showed him with a marijuana pipe at a party at the University of South Carolina, Kellogg Co. dropped Phelps's endorsement deal.

Can the courts be utilized to resolve controversies over whether a "morals clause" has been violated? If so, is the occurrence of a morals clause violation a condition precedent or a condition subsequent?

---

* Tiger Woods had enormous bargaining power with sponsors prior to the infidelity disclosures in 2009. He earned over $100 million per year in sponsorships. To date no sponsor has disclosed its contractual relationship with him regarding behavior issues. It is speculated that any "morals clause" in a Woods sponsorship contract would probably require conviction of a felony before the contract would be terminated. Sponsors have stopped running Woods ads as they continue to assess his endorsements value for their brands.

2. Normal Discharge of Contracts

A contract is usually discharged by the performance of the terms of the agreement. In most cases, the parties perform their promises and the contract ceases to exist or is thereby discharged. A contract is also discharged by the expiration of the time period specified in the contract.[3]

3. Nature of Performance

Performance may be the doing of an act or the making of payment.

(A) TENDER. An offer to perform is known as a **tender**. If performance of the contract requires the doing of an act, the refusal of a tender discharges the party offering to perform and is a basis for that party to bring a lawsuit.

A valid tender of payment consists of an unconditional offer of the exact amount due on the date when due. A tender of payment is not just an expression of willingness to pay; it must be an actual offer to perform by making payment of the amount owed.

(B) PAYMENT. When the contract requires payment, performance consists of the payment of money.

(1) Application of Payments

If a debtor owes more than one debt to the creditor and pays money, a question may arise as to which debt has been paid. If the debtor specifies the debt to which the payment is to be applied and the creditor accepts the money, the creditor is bound to apply the

---

[3] *Washington National Ins. Co. v Sherwood Associates*, 795 P2d 665 (Utah App 1990).

money as specified.[4] Thus, if the debtor specifies that a payment is to be made for a current purchase, the creditor may not apply the payment to an older balance.

(2) Payment by Check

Payment by commercial paper, such as a check, is ordinarily a conditional payment. A check merely suspends the debt until the check is presented for payment. If payment is then made, the debt is discharged; if not paid, the suspension terminates, and suit may be brought on either the debt or the check. Frequently, payment must be made by a specified date. It is generally held that the payment is made on time if it is mailed on or before the final date for payment.

4. Time of Performance

When the date or period of time for performance is specified in the contract, performance should be made on that date or within that time period.

(A) No Time Specified. When the time for performance is not specified in the contract, an obligation to perform within a reasonable time is implied.[5] The fact that no time is specified neither impairs the contract on the ground that it is indefinite nor allows an endless time in which to perform. What constitutes a reasonable time is determined by the nature of the subject matter of the contract and the facts and circumstances surrounding the making of the contract.

(B) When Time Is Essential. If performance of the contract on or within the exact time specified is vital, it is said that "time is of the essence." Time is of the essence when the contract relates to property that is perishable or that is fluctuating rapidly in value. When a contract fixes by unambiguous language a time for performance and where there is no evidence showing that the parties did not intend that time should be of the essence, failure to perform within the specified time is a breach of contract entitling the innocent party to damages. **For Example,** Dixon and Gandhi agreed that Gandhi would close on the

purchase of a motel as follows: "Closing Date. The closing shall be held . . . on the date which is within twenty (20) days after the closing of Nomura Financing." Gandhi did not close within the time period specified, and Dixon was allowed to retain $100,000 in prepaid closing costs and fees as liquidated damages for Gandhi's breach of contract.[6]

(C) When Time Is Not Essential. Unless a contract so provides, time is ordinarily not of the essence, and performance within a reasonable time is sufficient. In the case of the sale of property, time is not regarded as of the essence when there has not been any appreciable change in the market value or condition of the property and when the person who delayed does not appear to have done so for the purpose of speculating on a change in market price.

(D) Waiver of Essence of Time Limitation. A provision that time is of the essence may be waived. It is waived when the specified time has expired but the party who could complain requests the delaying party to take steps necessary to perform the contract.

5. Adequacy of Performance

When a party renders exactly the performance called for by the contract, no question arises as to whether the contract has been performed. In other cases, there may not have been a perfect performance, or a question arises as to whether the performance satisfies the standard set by the contract.

CPA (A) Substantial Performance. Perfect performance of a contract is not always possible when dealing with construction projects. A party who in good faith has provided **substantial performance** of the contract may sue to recover the payment specified in the contract. However, because the performance was not perfect the performing party is subject to a counterclaim for the damages caused the other party. When a building contractor has substantially performed the contract to construct a building, the contractor is responsible for the cost of repairing or correcting the defects as an offset from the contract price.[7]

---

[4] *Oakes Logging, Inc. v Green Crow, Inc.,* 832 P2d 894 (Wash App 1992).
[5] *First National Bank v Clark,* 447 SE2d 558 (W Va 1994).
[6] *Woodhull Corp. v Saibaba Corp.,* 507 SE2d 493 (Ga App 1998).
[7] Substantial performance is not a defense to a breach of contract claim, however. See *Bentley Systems Inc. v Intergraph Corp.,* 922 So2d 61 (Ala 2005).

FIGURE 19-1 | *Causes of Contract Discharge*

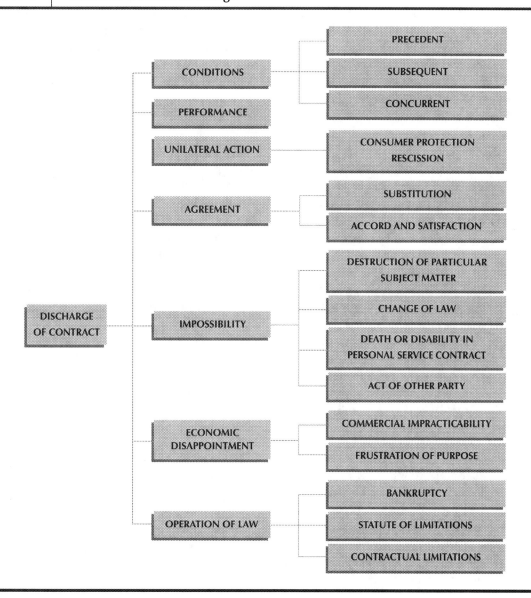

The measure of damages under these circumstances is known as "cost of completion" damages.[8] If, however, the cost of completion would be unreasonably disproportionate to the importance of the defect, the measure of damages is the diminution in value of the building due to the defective performance.

Whether there is substantial performance is a question of degree to be determined by all of the facts, including the particular type of structure involved, its intended purpose, and the nature and relative expense of repairs.

For Example, a certain building contractor (BC) and a certain owner (O) made a contract to construct a home overlooking Vineyard Sound on Martha's Vineyard according to plans and specifications that clearly called for the use of General Plumbing Blue Star piping. The contract price was $1,100,000. Upon inspecting the work before making the final

[8] *Hammer Construction Corp. v Phillips*, 994 So2d 1135 (Fla App 2008).

$400,000 payment and accepting the building, O discovered that BC had used Republic piping throughout the house. O explained to BC that his family had made its money by investing in General Plumbing, and he, therefore, would not make the final payment until the breach of contract was remedied. BC explained that Republic pipes were of the same industrial grade and quality as the Blue Star pipes. Moreover, BC estimated that it would cost nearly $300,000 to replace all of the pipes because of the destruction of walls and fixtures necessary to accomplish such a task. BC may sue O for $400,000 for breach of contract, claiming he had substantially performed the contract, and O may counterclaim for $300,000, seeking an offset for the cost of remedying the breach. The court will find in favor of the contractor and will not allow the $300,000 offset but will allow a "nominal" offset of perhaps $100 to $1,000 for the amount by which the Republic pipes diminished the value of the building. [9]

In most jurisdictions, the willfulness of the departure from the specifications of the contract does not by itself preclude some recovery for the contractor on the "cost of completion" basis but rather is a factor in consideration of whether there was substantial performance by the contractor. [10]

(B) FAULT OF COMPLAINING PARTY. A party cannot complain that a performance was defective when the performance follows the terms of the contract required by the complaining party. Thus, a homeowner who supplied the specifications for poured cement walls could not hold a contractor liable for damages when the walls that were poured in exact compliance with those specifications proved defective.

(C) PERFORMANCE TO THE SATISFACTION OF THE CONTRACTING PARTY OR A THIRD PARTY. Sometimes an agreement requires performance to the satisfaction, taste, or judgment of the other party to the contract. When the contract specifically stipulates that the performance must satisfy the contracting party, the courts will ordinarily enforce the plain meaning of the language of the parties and the work must satisfy the contracting

party—subject, of course, to the requirement that dissatisfaction be made in good faith. **For Example,** the Perrones' written contract to purchase the Hills' residence contained a clause making performance subject to inspection to the Perrones' satisfaction. During the house inspection, the inspector found a piece of wood in a crawl space that appeared to have been damaged by termites and had possibly been treated some 18 years before with chlordane. At the end of the inspection Mr. Perrone indicated that he would perform on the contract. Thereafter, he went on the Internet and found that chlordane is a highly toxic pesticide now banned from use as a termite treatment. As a result, the Perrones rescinded the contract under the buyer satisfaction clause. The Hills sued, believing that speculation about a pesticide treatment 18 years ago was absurd. They contended that the Perrones had breached the contract without a valid reason. The court decided for the Perrones, since they exercised the "satisfaction clause" in good faith. [11] Good-faith personal satisfaction is generally required when the subject matter of the contract is personal, such as interior design work, tailoring, or the painting of a portrait.

With respect to things mechanical or routine performances, courts require that the performance be such as would satisfy a reasonable person under the circumstances.

When work is to be done subject to the approval of an architect, engineer, or another expert, most courts apply the reasonable person test of satisfaction.

C. DISCHARGE BY ACTION OF PARTIES

Contracts may be discharged by the joint action of both contracting parties or, in some cases, by the action of one party alone.

6. Discharge by Unilateral Action

Ordinarily, a contract cannot be discharged by the action of either party alone. In some cases, however, the contract gives one of either party the right to cancel

[9] See *Jacob & Youngs, Inc. v Kent*, 230 NY 239 (1921).
[10] But see *USX Corp. v M. DeMatteo Construction Co.*, 315 F3d 43 (1st Cir 2002), for application of a common law rule that prohibits a construction contractor guilty of a willful breach of contract from maintaining any suit on the contract against the other party.
[11] *Hill v Perrones*, 42 P3d 210 (Kan App 2002).

the contract by unilateral action, such as by notice to the other party. Insurance policies covering loss commonly provide that the insurer may cancel the policy upon giving a specified number of days' notice.

(A) CONSUMER PROTECTION RESCISSION. A basic principle of contract law is that once made, a contract between competent persons is a binding obligation. Consumer protection legislation introduces into the law a contrary concept—that of giving the consumer a chance to think things over and to rescind the contract. Thus, the federal Consumer Credit Protection Act (CCPA) gives the debtor the right to rescind a credit transaction within three business days when the transaction would impose a lien on the debtor's home. **For Example,** a homeowner who mortgages his or her home to obtain a loan may cancel the transaction for any reason by notifying the lender before midnight of the third full business day after the loan is made.[12]

A Federal Trade Commission regulation gives the buyer three business days in which to cancel a home-solicited sale of goods or services costing more than $25.[13]

7. Discharge by Agreement

A contract may be discharged by the operation of one of its provisions or by a subsequent agreement. Thus, there may be a discharge by (1) the terms of the original contract, such as a provision that the contract should end on a specified date; (2) a mutual cancellation, in which the parties agree to end their contract; (3) a mutual **rescission**, in which the parties agree to annul the contract and return both parties to their original positions before the contract had been made; (4) the **substitution** of a new contract between the same parties; (5) a novation or substitution of a new contract involving a new party;[14] (6) an **accord and satisfaction**; (7) a release; or (8) a **waiver**.

(A) SUBSTITUTION. The parties may decide that their contract is not the one they want. They may then replace it with another contract. If they do, the original contract is discharged by substitution.[15]

(B) ACCORD AND SATISFACTION. When the parties have differing views as to the performance required by the terms of a contract, they may agree to a different performance. Such an agreement is called an *accord.* When the accord is performed or executed, there is an accord and satisfaction, which discharges the original obligation. To constitute an accord and satisfaction, there must be a bona fide dispute, a proposal to settle the dispute, and performance of the agreement. As seen in the *MKL Pre-Press* case, to constitute an accord and satisfaction, there must be a bona fide dispute, a proposal to settle the dispute, and performance of the agreement.

MKL Pre-Press Electronics v La Crosse Litho Supply, LLC, 840 NE2d 687 (Ill App 2005)

A Full Court Press to No Avail

In September 2002 La Crosse Litho Supply, LLC (La Crosse) entered a distribution agreement with MKL Pre-Press Electronics (MKL) for the distribution of MKL printing systems. La Crosse purchased a 7000 System unit from MKL for its end user Printing Plus with MKL technicians providing service and training for  the unit. The 7000 System at Printing Plus failed on three occasions and ultimately repairs were unsuccessful. On September 30, 2003 La Crosse cancelled the distribution agreement. On October 2, 2003 La Crosse sent a letter to MKL's Sales V.P. Bill Landwer setting forth an itemized

---

[12] If the owner is not informed of this right to cancel, the three-day period does not begin until that information is given. Consumer Credit Protection Act § 125, 15 USC § 1635(a), (e), (f).

[13] CFR § 429.1. This displaces state laws making similar provisions for rescission, such as UCCC § 2.502.

[14] *Eagle Industries, Inc. v Thompson,* 900 P2d 475 (Or 1995). In a few jurisdictions, the term *novation* is used to embrace the substitution of any new contract, whether between the original parties or not.

[15] *Shawnee Hospital Authority v Dow Construction, Inc.,* 812 P2d 1351 (Okla 1990).

Continued

accounting of what it owed MKL Pre-Press with deductions for the purchase price of the failed 7000 System and other offsets. MKL sent a subsequent bill for repairs and services, to which La Crosse objected and stated it would not pay them. MKL's attorney sent a demand letter for $26,453.31. La Crosse's president, Randall Peters, responded by letter dated December 30, 2003 explaining that with an offset for training and warranty work it performed, "we are sending you the final payment in the amount of $1,696.47." He added, "[w]ith this correspondence, we consider all open issues between La Crosse Litho Supply and MKL Pre Press closed." Enclosed with the letter was a check for $1,696.47 payable to MKL Pre-Press. In the remittance portion of the check, under the heading "Ref," was typed "FINAL PAYM." The check was endorsed and deposited on either January 26 or 27, 2004. MKL sued La Crosse for $24,756.84. La Crosse defended that the tender and subsequent deposit of the check for $1,696.47 constituted an accord and satisfaction. Jill Fleming, MKL's office manager, stated that it was her duty to process checks and that she did not read Peters' letter. From a judgment for La Crosse, MKL appealed.

JUDICIAL OPINION

GREIMAN, J. . . . An accord and satisfaction is a contractual method of discharging debts or claims between the parties to such an agreement. In order for such an arrangement to exist, there must be: (1) a *bonafide* dispute as to the claims pending between the parties; (2) an unliquidated sum owed; (3) consideration, (4) a shared mutual intent to compromise the claims; and (5) execution of the agreement. The accord is the actual agreement between the parties, while the satisfaction is its execution or performance. . . .

Where there is an honest dispute as to the amount owed and due between the parties and the debtor tenders an amount with the explicit understanding that it is full payment of all demands, the creditor's acceptance and negotiation of that amount constitutes an accord and satisfaction. *Koules v Euro–American Arbitrage, Inc.,* 689 N.E.2d 411 (1998). However, the partial payment of a fixed and certain demand due and not in dispute does not constitute satisfaction of the entire debt even where the creditor agrees to receive partial payment for the whole debt and gives a receipt for the whole demand. *Koules,* 689 N.E.2d 411.

As demonstrated by the October 2003 correspondence between Peters and Landwer concerning amounts still due and owing to plaintiff, plaintiff's subsequent invoices and Peters' objection there-to, and plaintiff's November 2003 demand letter, it is plainly apparent that a *bonafide* dispute existed as to the claims pending between the parties and an unliquidated sum

was owed by defendant to plaintiff. The tender of the check by defendant and its deposit by plaintiff constituted consideration and execution. The only element remaining is a shared mutual intent by the parties to compromise the claims between them. Intent can be inferred from conduct; the act of knowingly accepting and depositing a check upon which conditional language has been added indicates the existence of an accord and satisfaction. Where creditor takes and keeps a debtor's reduced payment with actual or constructive knowledge of the condition, the creditor has accepted the debtor's offer, and the original debt is settled for the reduced amount. . . .

Plaintiff additionally argues that the deposit of defendant's check by Fleming should not be imputed to it as an organization because Fleming had no responsibility to enter the organization into any sort of agreement like an accord and satisfaction and because the check contained no restrictive language indicating that it had been tendered in consideration of all claims pending between the parties. We disagree.

An organization's practice of authorizing its employee to endorse checks and deposit them into an account on its behalf cannot serve as a means of isolating the organization or its principals from the legal consequences that flow from the employee's actions in the scope of his or her duties. An employee whose authority includes depositing a check upon which restrictive language appeared will be presumed to have acted on behalf of the organization, and his or her acts will be imputed to the organization as a matter of law.

In this case, Fleming's affidavit clearly stated that it was within the scope of her duties to process and deposit checks on the plaintiff's behalf. She stated herself that she endorsed and deposited the check, the voucher portion of which clearly stated "FINAL PAYM." We cannot fathom what "FINAL PAYM" might mean, other than "final payment," meaning that defendant did not intend to send plaintiff any more money. Accordingly, we can only conclude that Fleming's conduct can and should be imputed to plaintiff and its principals, thereby constituting an accord and satisfaction. . . .

[Affirmed]

QUESTIONS

1. What are the elements of an "accord and satisfaction"?

2. Was there a shared mutual intent to compromise the claims between the parties?

3. Is it fair to expect an office manager to know that by processing a check for $1,696.47 marked "final payment" that her company could lose the right to pursue its position that it was owed an additional $24,756.84?

D. Discharge by External Causes

Circumstances beyond the control of the contracting parties may discharge the contract.

8. Discharge by Impossibility

To establish impossibility a party must show (1) the unexpected occurrence of an intervening act; (2) that the risk of the unexpected occurrence was not allocated by agreement or custom; and (3) that the occurrence made performance impossible. The doctrine of impossibility relieves nonperformance only in extreme circumstances.[16] The party asserting the defense of impossibility bears the burden of proving "a real impossibility and not a mere inconvenience or unexpected difficulty."[17] Moreover, courts will generally only excuse nonperformance where performance is objectively impossible—that is, incapable of performance by anyone. Financial inability to perform a contract that a party voluntarily entered into will rarely, if ever, excuse nonperformance. **For Example,** Ms. Robinson was employed by East Capital Community Development Group under a written employment contract for one year, but was terminated early for lack of funding. The contract did not reference that her continued employment was contingent on continued grant funding. The contract was objectively capable of performance. The defense of impossibility was rejected by the court.[18]

(A) Destruction of Particular Subject Matter. When parties contract expressly for, or with reference to, a particular subject matter, the contract is discharged if the subject matter is destroyed through no fault of either party. When a contract calls for the sale of a wheat crop growing on a specific parcel of land, the contract is discharged if that crop is destroyed by blight.

On the other hand, if there is merely a contract to sell a given quantity of a specified grade of wheat, the seller is not discharged when the seller's crop is destroyed by blight. The seller had made an unqualified undertaking to deliver wheat of a specified grade. No restrictions or qualifications were imposed as to the source. If the seller does not deliver the goods called for by the contract, the contract is broken, and the seller is liable for damages.

(B) Change of Law. A contract is discharged when its performance is made illegal by a subsequent change in the law. Thus, a contract to construct a nonfireproof building at a particular place is discharged by the adoption of a zoning law prohibiting such a building within that area. Mere inconvenience or temporary delay caused by the new law, however, does not excuse performance.

(C) Death or Disability. When the contract obligates a party to render or receive personal services requiring peculiar skill, the death, incapacity, or illness of the party that was either to render or receive the personal services excuses both sides from a duty to perform. It is sometimes said that "the death of either party is the death of the contract."

The rule does not apply, however, when the acts called for by the contract are of such a character that (1) the acts may be as well performed by others, such as the promisor's personal representatives, or (2) the contract's terms contemplate continuance of the obligations after the death of one of the parties. **For Example,** Lynn Jones was under contract to investor Ed Jenkins to operate certain Subway sandwich shops and to acquire new franchises with funding provided by Jenkins. After Jenkins's death, Jones claimed he was no longer bound under the contract and was free to pursue franchise opportunities on his own. The contract between Jones and Jenkins expressed that it was binding on the parties' "heirs and assigns" and that the contract embodied property rights that passed to Jenkins's widow. The agreement's provisions thus established that the agreement survived the death of Jenkins, and Jones was therefore obligated to remit profits from the franchise he acquired for himself after Jenkins's death.[19]

(D) Act of Other Party. Every contract contains "an implied covenant of good faith and fair dealing." As a

---

[16] *Island Development Corp. v District of Columbia,* 933 A2d 340, 350 (DC 2007).
[17] *Bergmann v Parker,* 216 A2d 581 (DC 1966).
[18] *East Capital View Community Development Corp. v Robinson,* 941 A2d 1036 (DC 2008).
[19] *Jenkins Subway, Inc. v Jones,* 990 SW2d 713 (Tenn App 1998).

result of this covenant, a promisee is under an obligation to do nothing that would interfere with the promisor's performance. When the promisee prevents performance or otherwise makes performance impossible, the promisor is discharged from the contract. Thus, a subcontractor is discharged from any obligation when it is unable to do the work because the principal contractor refuses to deliver the material, equipment, or money required by the subcontract. When the default of the other party consists of failing to supply goods or services, the duty may rest on the party claiming a discharge of the contract to show that substitute goods or services could not be obtained elsewhere.

9. Developing Doctrines

Commercial impracticability and frustration of purpose may excuse performance.

(A) COMMERCIAL IMPRACTICABILITY. The doctrine of *commercial impracticability* was developed to deal with the harsh rule that a party must perform its contracts unless it is absolutely impossible. However, not every type of impracticability is an excuse for

nonperformance. **For Example,** I. Patel was bound by his franchise agreement with Days Inn, Inc., to maintain his 60-room inn on old Route 66 in Lincoln, Illinois, to at least minimum quality assurance standards. His inn failed five consecutive quality inspections over two years, with the inspector noting damaged guest rooms, burns in the bedding, and severely stained carpets. Patel's defense when his franchise was cancelled after the fifth failed inspection was that bridge repairs on the road leading from I-55 to his inn had adversely affected his business and made it commercially impractical to live up to the franchise agreement. The court rejected his defense, determining that while the bridge work might have affected patronage, it had no effect on his duty to comply with the quality assurance standards of his franchise agreement.[20] Commercial impracticability is available only when the performance is made impractical by the subsequent occurrence of an event whose nonoccurrence was a basic assumption on which the contract was made.[21]

The *Specialty Tire* case deals with the application of the defense of impracticality.

Specialty Tires of America, Inc. v CIT, 82 F Supp 2d 434 (WD Pa 2000)

"Wait a Minute. . . . There's an Exception to the 'A Deal's a Deal' Doctrine!"

CIT, a major equipment leasing company, entered into a sale/leaseback contract with Condere Tire Corporation for 11 tire presses at Condere's tire plant in Natchez, Mississippi. Condere ceased making payments on these presses owned by CIT; and Condere filed for Chapter 11 bankruptcy. CIT thereafter contracted to sell the presses to Specialty Tires, Inc., for $250,000. When the contract was made, CIT, Condere, and Specialty Tires believed that CIT was the owner of the presses and was entitled to immediate possession. When CIT attempted to gain access to the presses to have them shipped, Condere changed its position and refused to allow the equipment to be removed from the plant. When the presses were not delivered, Specialty sued CIT for damages for nondelivery of the presses to date, and CIT asserted the defense of impracticability.

JUDICIAL OPINION

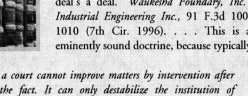

SMITH, D.J. . . . In the overwhelming majority of circumstances, contractual promises are to be performed, not avoided: *pacta sunt servanda,* or, as the Seventh Circuit loosely translated it, "a deal's a deal." *Waukesha Foundary, Inc. v Industrial Engineering Inc.,* 91 F.3d 1002, 1010 (7th Cir. 1996). . . . This is an eminently sound doctrine, because typically

a court cannot improve matters by intervention after the fact. It can only destabilize the institution of contract, increase risk, and make parties worse off. . . . Parties to contracts are entitled to seek, and retain, personal advantage; striving for that advantage is the source of much economic progress. Contract law does

---

[20] *Days Inn of America, Inc. v Patel,* 88 F Supp 2d 928 (CD Ill 2000).
[21] See Restatement (Second) of Contracts § 261; UCC § 2-615.

Continued

not require parties to be fair, or kind, or reasonable, or to share gains or losses equally.

Industrial Representation, Inc. v CP Clare Corp., 74 F.3d 128, 131–32 (7th Cir. 1996). Promisors are free to assume risks, even huge ones, and promisees are entitled to rely on those voluntary assumptions. . . .

Even so, courts have recognized, in an evolving line of cases from the common law down to the present, that there are limited instances in which unexpectedly and radically changed conditions render the judicial enforcement of certain promises of little or no utility. This has come to be known, for our purposes, as the doctrines of impossibility and impracticability.* Because of the unexpected nature of such occurrences, litigated cases usually involve, not interpretation of a contractual term, but the judicial filling of a lacuna in the parties agreement. *See* 2 E. Allan Farnsworth, *Farnsworth on Contracts* § 9.5, at 603 (2d ed. 1998); Such "gapfilling," however, must be understood for what it is: a court-ordered, as opposed to bargained-for, allocation of risk between the parties. . . .

Traditionally, there were three kinds of supervening events that would provide a legally cognizable excuse for failing to perform: death of the promisor (if the performance was personal), illegality of the performance, and destruction of the subject matter . . . beyond that the doctrine has grown to recognize that

> *relief is most justified if unexpected events inflict a loss on one party and provide a windfall gain for the other or where the excuse would save one party from an unexpected loss while leaving the other party in a position no worse than it would have without the contract.*

Calamari & Perillo, *supra* § 13.1, at 496; *see also* 2 Farnsworth, *supra* § 9.6, at 612. Thus, the Second Restatement of Contracts expresses the doctrine of impracticability this way:

> *Where, after a contract is made, a party's performance is made impracticable without his fault by the occurrence of an event the non-occurrence of which was a basic assumption on which the contract was made, his duty to render that performance is*

> *discharged, unless the language or the circumstances indicate the contrary.*

Restatement (Second) of Contracts § 261 (1981). Article 2 of the U.C.C., which applies to the sale of goods presented by the case *sub judice*, puts it similarly:

> *Delay in delivery or non-delivery in whole or in part by a seller . . . is not a breach of his duty under a contract for sale if performance as agreed has been made impracticable by the occurrence of a contingency the non-occurrence of which was a basic assumption on which the contract was made. . . .*

U.C.C. § 2–615(1)

The principal inquiry in an impracticability analysis, then, is whether there was a contingency the non-occurrence of which was a basic assumption underlying the contract. It is often said that this question turns on whether the contingency was "foreseeable." 2 Farnsworth, § 9.6, at 616, . . .

Generally speaking, while loss, destruction or a major price increase of fungible goods will not excuse the seller's duty to perform, the rule is different when the goods are unique, have been identified to the contract or are to be produced from a specific agreed-upon source. In such a case, the nonexistence or unavailability of a specific thing will establish a defense of impracticability. Murray, *supra*, § 113, at 649, 650; . . .

. . . CIT contracted to supply specific tire presses to Specialty. This was not a case of fungible goods; Specialty inspected, and bid for, certain identified, used presses located at the Natchez plant operated by Condere. All parties believed that CIT was the owner of the presses and was entitled to their immediate possession; Condere's representatives stated as much during the inspection visit. Neither Specialty nor CIT had any reason to believe that Condere would subsequently turn an about-face and assert a possessory interest in the presses. . . .

Thus, . . . it is clear that this is not the sort of risk that CIT should have expected to either bear or contract against. . . .

Plaintiff makes much of the argument that there was no "basic assumption" created by Condere upon which Specialty and CIT based their contract, stating that it relied upon CIT's representations alone. This is specious. As a matter of both law and logic, a basic assumption of any contract for the sale of specific, identified goods is that they are, in fact, available for sale. Accordingly, I reject this contention and conclude that the actions of Condere in detaining the presses presents sufficient grounds on which to base an impracticability defense. . . .

---

*The reported cases on this topic, unfortunately, are not characterized by either consistency or clarity of expression. As one respected treatise puts it, "Students who have concluded a first year contracts course in confusion about the doctrine of impossibility and have since . . . found that the cases somehow slip through their fingers when they try to apply them to new situations, may take some comfort in knowing that they are in good company." 1 White & Summers, *supra* § 3–10, at 164.

Continued

... While CIT did assume the risk of its own inability to perform, it did not assume the risk of Condere making it unable to perform by detaining the presses, any more than CIT assumed the risk that thieves would steal the presses from Condere before the latter could deliver them. In sum, this risk was not "sufficiently within the control of [CIT] that [it should be inferred that it was] assumed by that party." 2 Fransworth, *supra* § 9.6, at 619–20. It was completely within the control of Condere.

Accordingly, I conclude on this record that CIT has made out its defense of impracticability. ... CIT's performance is impracticable only in the temporary sense. Temporary impracticabilty only relieves the promisor of the obligation to perform as long as the impracticability lasts and for a reasonable time thereafter. ... Once it receives possession of the presses, CIT asserts that it stands ready and willing to perform its contract with Specialty. ... CIT is excused by the doctrine of impracticability and is entitled to full summary judgement.

[Judgment for CIT]

QUESTIONS

1. What is the rationale for the "a deal's a deal" doctrine, and what is its implication in the present case?

2. Summarize the Restatement (Second) Contracts expression of the defense of impracticality.

3. How did the court decide this case?

If a subsequent event occurs involving a severe shortage of raw materials or supplies that results in a marked increase in the cost of the materials or supplies and this event was foreseeable, the defense of commercial impracticability is not available.

(B) FRUSTRATION OF PURPOSE DOCTRINE. Because of a change in circumstances, the purpose of the contract may have no value to the party entitled to receive performance. In such a case, performance may be excused if both parties were aware of the purpose and the event that frustrated the purpose was unforeseeable.[22]

For Example, National Southern Bank rents a home near Willowbend Country Club on the southeastern shore of North Carolina for $75,000 a week to entertain business guests at the Ryder Cup matches scheduled for the week in question. Storm damage from Hurricane David the week before the event caused the closing of the course and the transfer of the tournament to another venue in a different state. The bank's duty to pay for the house may be excused by the doctrine of *frustration of purpose*, because the transfer of the tournament fully destroyed the value of the home rental, both parties were aware of the purpose of the rental, and the cancellation of the golf tournament was unforeseeable.

(C) COMPARISON TO COMMON LAW RULE. The traditional common law rule refuses to recognize commercial impracticability or frustration of purpose. By the common law rule, the losses and disappointments against which commercial impracticability and frustration of purpose give protection are merely the risks that one takes in entering into a contract. Moreover, the situations could have been guarded against by including an appropriate condition subsequent in the contract. A condition subsequent declares that the contract will be void if a specified event occurs.[23] The contract also could have provided for a readjustment of compensation if there was a basic change of circumstances. The common law approach also rejects these developing concepts because they weaken the stability of a contract.

An indication of a wider recognition of the concept that "extreme" changes of circumstances can discharge a contract is found in the Uniform Commercial Code. The UCC provides for the discharge of a

---

[22] The defense of frustration of purpose, or commercial frustration, is very difficult to invoke because the courts are extremely reluctant to allow parties to avoid obligations to which they have agreed. See *Wal-Mart Stores, Inc. v AIG Life Insurance Co.,* 872 A2d 611 (Del Ch 2005), denying application of the commercial frustration doctrine when the supervening event, the invalidation of hundreds of millions in tax deductions by the IRS, was reasonably foreseeable and could have been provided for in the contract.

[23] *Wermer v ABI,* 10 SW3d 575 (Mo App 2000).

contract for the sale of goods when a condition that the parties assumed existed, or would continue, ceases to exist.[24]

(D) FORCE MAJEURE. To avoid litigation over impossibility and impractability issues, modern contracting parties often contract around the doctrine of impossibility, specifying the failures that will excuse performance in their contracts. The clauses in which they do this are called *force majeure*—uncontrollable event—clauses. And as seen in the *Union Pacific Railroad* case, they are enforced by courts as written.

Wisconsin Electric Power Co. v Union Pacific Railroad Co., 557 F3d 504 (7th Cir 2009)

WEPCO Was Not Railroaded, It Was *Force Majeured*!

[handwritten: don't need case] *[handwritten: an act of god of]*

WEPCO, an electric utility, sued the Union Pacific Railroad Co. alleging that the railroad breached the *force majeure* provision of the parties' long-term coal-hauling contract, which ran from 1999 to 2005. The provision at issue provides that if the railroad is prevented by "an event of Force Majeure" from reloading its empty cars (after it has delivered coal to WEPCO) with iron ore destined for Geneva, Utah, it can charge the higher rate that the contract makes applicable to shipments that do not involve backhauling. The rate for coal shipped from one of the Colorado coal mines to WEPCO was specified as $13.20 per ton if there was a backhaul shipment but $15.63 if there was not. The iron ore that the railroad's freight trains would have picked up in Minnesota was intended for a steel mill in Utah. The steel company was bankrupt when the parties signed the contract. In November 2001 the steel mill shut down, and closed for good in February 2004. Two months later the railroad wrote WEPCO to declare "an event of Force Majeure" and that henceforth it would be charging WEPCO the higher rate applicable to shipments without a backhaul. WEPCO sued the railroad for breach of the force majeure provision in the contract.

JUDICIAL OPINION

POSNER, C.J. . . . The doctrine of impossibility in the common law of contracts excuses performance when it would be unreasonably costly (and sometimes downright impossible) for a party to carry out its contractual obligations. If the doctrine is successfully invoked, the contract is rescinded without liability. . . .

. . . Parties can, however, contract around the doctrine, because it is just a gap filler, 2 E. Allan Farnsworth, *Farnsworth on Contracts* § 9.6, p. 643 (3d ed.2004)—a guess at what the parties would have provided in their contract had they thought about the contingency that has arisen and has prevented performance or made it much more costly.

. . . "In the case of a binding promise that it shall rain tomorrow, the immediate legal effect of what the promisor does is, that he takes the risk of the event, within certain defined limits, as between himself and the promisee. He does no more when he promises to deliver a bale of cotton." O.W. Holmes, Jr., *The Common Law* 299-300 (1881). To defeat the application of the doctrine of impossibility the contract must state that the promisor must pay damages even if he commits a breach that could not have been prevented at a reasonable cost.

Modern contracting parties often do contract around the doctrine, though not by making the promisor liable for any and every failure to perform—rather by specifying the failures that will excuse performance. The clauses in which they do this are called force majeure ("superior force") clauses. The name suggests a purpose similar to that of the impossibility doctrine. But it is essential to an understanding of this case that a force majeure clause must always be interpreted in accordance with its language and context, like any other provision in a written contract, rather than with reference to its name. . . .

The provision at issue in this case does not specify circumstances that would make performance impossible or infeasible in any sense, and does not excuse the performing party (the railroad) from performing the contract. The prevision is part of Article XI of the contract, and some of the other provisions in the article do specify contingencies that would excuse performance, including certain "acts of God." But the provision at issue merely provides that if the railroad is prevented by "an event of Force Majeure" from reloading its empty cars (after it has delivered coal to WEPCO) with iron ore destined for Geneva, Utah, it can charge the higher rate that the contract makes applicable to shipments that do not involve backhauling.

. . . A couple of months after the final closing the railroad wrote WEPCO to declare "an event of Force Majeure" and

---

Continued

that henceforth it would be charging WEPCO the higher rate applicable to shipments without a backhaul. It did not attempt to make the rate change retroactive. Had it invoked the force majeure clause when the steel mill first shut down, WEPCO would have incurred an extra $7 million in shipping charges between then and the belated declaration of force majeure.

Despite this windfall, WEPCO argues that the railroad broke the contract by invoking the force majeure clause when it did. The fact that the railroad didn't invoke the clause earlier shows that the shutting down of the steel mill did not prevent the railroad from charging the low, backhaul

rate. Well of course not; it is never "impossible" to offer a discount. But what the contract says is that the railroad may charge the higher rate if it is prevented from reloading its cars, rather than if it is prevented from charging a lower rate. . . .

[*Summary judgement for the railroad affirmed*]

QUESTIONS

1. What is the purpose of a *force majeure* clause?

2. Did the court enforce the *force majeure* clause as written?

10. Temporary Impossibility

Ordinarily, a temporary impossibility suspends the duty to perform. If the obligation to perform is suspended, it is revived on the termination of the impossibility. If, however, performance at that later date would impose a substantially greater burden on the party obligated to perform, some courts discharge the obligor from the contract.

After the September 11, 2001, terrorist attack on the World Trade Center, New York City courts followed wartime precedents that had developed the law of temporary impossibility. Such impossibility, when of brief duration, excuses performance until it subsequently becomes possible to perform rather than excusing performance altogether. Thus, an individual who was unable to communicate her cancellation of travel 60 days prior to her scheduled travel as required by her contract, which needed to occur on or before September 14, 2001, could expect relief from a cancellation penalty provision in the contract based on credible testimony of attempted phone calls to the travel agent on and after September 12, 2001, even though the calls did not get through due to communication problems in New York City.[25]

(A) WEATHER. Acts of God, such as tornadoes, lightning, and floods, usually do not terminate a contract even though they make performance difficult. Thus, weather conditions constitute a risk that is assumed by a contracting party in the absence of a contrary agreement.

Consequently, extra expense sustained by a contractor because of weather conditions is a risk that the contractor assumes in the absence of an express provision for additional compensation in such a case. **For Example,** Danielo Contractors made a contract to construct a shopping mall for the Rubicon Center, with construction to begin November 1. Because of abnormal cold and blizzard conditions, Danielo was not able to begin work until April 1 and was five months late in completing the construction of the project. Rubicon sued Danielo for breach of contract by failing to perform on schedule. Danielo is liable. Because the contract included no provision covering delay caused by weather, Danielo bore the risk of the delay and resulting loss.

Modern contracts commonly contain a "weather clause" and reflect the parties' agreement on this matter. When the parties take the time to discuss weather issues, purchasing insurance coverage is a common resolution.

11. Discharge by Operation of Law

A contract is discharged by **operation of law** by (1) an alteration or a material change made by a party, (2) the destruction of the written contract with intent to discharge it, (3) bankruptcy, (4) the operation of a statute of limitations, or (5) a contractual limitation.

(A) BANKRUPTCY. As set forth in the chapter on bankruptcy, even though all creditors have not been paid in full, a discharge in **bankruptcy** eliminates ordinary contract claims against the debtor.

[25] See *Bugh v Protravel International, Inc.*, 746 NYS2d 290 (Civ Ct NYC 2002).

CPA (B) STATUTE OF LIMITATIONS. A **statute of limitations** provides that after a certain number of years have passed, a contract claim is barred. The time limitation provided by state statutes of limitations varies widely. The time period for bringing actions for breach of an oral contract is two to three years. The period may differ with the type of contract—ranging from a relatively short time for open accounts (ordinary customers' charge accounts) to four years for sales of goods.[26] A somewhat longer period exists for bringing actions for breach of written contracts (usually four to ten years). **For Example,** Prate Installations, Inc., sued homeowners Richard and Rebecca Thomas for failure to pay for a new roof installed by Prate. Prate had sent numerous invoices to the Thomases over a four-year period seeking payment to no avail. The Thomases moved to dismiss the case under a four-year limitation period. However, the court concluded that the state's ten-year limitations period on written contracts applied.[27] The maximum period for judgments of record is usually 10 to 20 years.

(C) CONTRACTUAL LIMITATIONS. Some contracts, particularly insurance contracts, contain a time limitation within which suit must be brought. This is in effect a private statute of limitations created by the agreement of the parties.

A contract may also require that notice of any claim be given within a specified time. A party who fails to give notice within the time specified by the contract is barred from suing on the contract.

A contract provision requiring that suit be brought within one year does not violate public policy, although the statute of limitations would allow two years in the absence of such a contract limitation.[28]

lawflix

Uncle Buck (1989) (PG-13)

John Candy plays ne'er-do-well Uncle Buck who promises to go to work at his girlfriend's tire store and marry her. When his brother calls in the middle of the night seeking help with his children, Buck tells his girlfriend (Chenise) that he can no longer honor his promise because he must go to the suburbs to care for his brother's children while his brother and sister-in-law travel to Indiana to be with his sister-in-law's very ill father.

Discuss Buck's excuse. Is it impossibility? Does the change in circumstances excuse Buck?

Check out LawFlix at **www.cengage.com/ blaw/dvl** to access movie clips that illustrate business law concepts.

MAKE THE CONNECTION

SUMMARY

A party's duty to perform under a contract can be affected by a condition precedent, which must occur before a party has an obligation to perform; a condition subsequent, that is, a condition or event that relieves the duty to thereafter perform; and concurrent conditions, which require mutual and often simultaneous performance.

Most contracts are discharged by performance. An offer to perform is called a *tender of performance.* If a tender of performance is wrongfully refused, the

[26] UCC § 2-725(1).
[27] *Prate Installations, Inc. v Thomas,* 842 NE2d 1205 (Ill App 2006).
[28] *Keiting v Skauge,* 543 NW2d 565 (Wis App 1995).

duty of the tenderer to perform is terminated. When the performance called for by the contract is the payment of money, it must be legal tender that is offered. In actual practice, it is common to pay and to accept payment by checks or other commercial paper.

When the debtor owes the creditor on several accounts and makes a payment, the debtor may specify which account is to be credited with the payment. If the debtor fails to specify, the creditor may choose which account to credit.

When a contract does not state when it is to be performed, it must be performed within a reasonable time. If time for performance is stated in the contract, the contract must be performed at the time specified if such time is essential (is of the essence). Ordinarily, a contract must be performed exactly in the manner specified by the contract. A less-than-perfect performance is allowed if it is a substantial performance and if damages are allowed the other party.

A contract cannot be discharged by unilateral action unless authorized by the contract itself or by statute, as in the case of consumer protection rescission.

Because a contract arises from an agreement, it may also be terminated by an agreement. A contract may also be discharged by the substitution of a new contract for the original contract; by a novation, or making a new contract with a new party; by accord and satisfaction; by release; or by waiver.

A contract is discharged when it is impossible to perform. Impossibility may result from the destruction of the subject matter of the contract, the adoption of a new law that prohibits performance, the death or disability of a party whose personal action was required for performance of the contract, or the act of the other party to the contract. Some courts will also hold that a contract is discharged when its performance is commercially impracticable or there is frustration of purpose. Temporary impossibility, such as a labor strike or bad weather, has no effect on a contract. It is common, though, to include protective clauses that excuse delay caused by temporary impossibility.

A contract may be discharged by operation of law. This occurs when (1) the liability arising from the contract is discharged by bankruptcy, (2) suit on the contract is barred by the applicable statute of limitations, or (3) a time limitation stated in the contract is exceeded.

LEARNING OUTCOMES

After studying this chapter, you should be able to clearly explain:

A. CONDITIONS RELATING TO PERFORMANCE

LO.1 List the three types of conditions that affect a party's duty to perform
    See the "pay-if-paid" condition-precedent example on p. 364.
    See the TV anchor's "failed urinalysis test" condition-subsequent example on p. 364.

B. DISCHARGE BY PERFORMANCE

LO.2 Explain the on-time performance rule
    See the "mailed payment" example on p. 366.
    See the "time is of the essence" example on p. 366.

C. DISCHARGE BY ACTION OF PARTIES

LO.3 Explain four ways a contract can be discharged by agreement of the parties
    See the text discussion on recession, cancellation, substitution, and novation on p. 369.

D. DISCHARGE BY EXTERNAL CAUSES

LO.4 State the effect on a contract of the death or disability of one of the contracting parties
    See the Subway Sandwich Shops example on p. 371.

LO.5 Explain when impossibility or impracticability may discharge a contract
    See the *Specialty Tire* impracticability case on p. 372.
    See the Ryder Cup frustration-of-purpose example on p. 374.

KEY TERMS

accord and satisfaction	condition	substantial performance
bankruptcy	operation of law	substitution
condition precedent	rescission	tender
condition subsequent	statute of limitations	waiver

QUESTIONS AND CASE PROBLEMS

1. McMullen Contractors made a contract with Richardson to build an apartment house for a specific price. A number of serious apartment house fires broke out in the city, and the city council adopted an ordinance increasing the fire precautions that had to be taken in the construction of a new building. Compliance with these new requirements would make the construction of the apartment house for Richardson more expensive than McMullen had originally contemplated. Is McMullen discharged from the contract to build the apartment house? *no*

2. Lymon Mitchell operated a Badcock Home Furnishings dealership, under which as dealer he was paid a commission on sales and Badcock retained title to merchandise on display. Mitchell sold his dealership to another and to facilitate the sale, Badcock prepared a summary of commissions owed with certain itemized offsets it claimed that Mitchell owed Badcock. Mitchell disagreed with the calculations, but he accepted them and signed the transfer documents closing the sale on the basis of the terms set forth in the summary and was paid accordingly. After pondering the offsets taken by Badcock and verifying the correctness of his position, he brought suit for the additional funds owed. What defense would you expect Badcock to raise? How would you decide the case? Explain fully. [*Mitchell v Badcock Corp.*, 496 SE2d 502 (Ga App)]

3. American Bank loaned Koplik $50,000 to buy equipment for a restaurant about to be opened by Casual Citchen Corp. The loan was not repaid, and Fast Foods, Inc., bought out the interest of Casual Citchen. As part of the transaction, Fast Foods agreed to pay the debt owed to American Bank, and the parties agreed to a new schedule of payments to be made by Fast Foods. Fast Foods did not make the payments, and American Bank sued Koplik. He contended that his obligation to repay $50,000 had been discharged by the execution of the agreement providing for the payment of the debt by Fast Foods. Was this defense valid? [*American Bank & Trust Co. v Koplik*, 451 NYS2d 426 (App Div)]

4. Metalcrafters made a contract to design a new earth-moving vehicle for Lamar Highway Construction Co. Metalcrafters was depending on the genius of Samet, the head of its research department, to design a new product. Shortly after the contract was made between Metalcrafters and Lamar, Samet was killed in an automobile accident. Metalcrafters was not able to design the product without Samet. Lamar sued Metalcrafters for damages for breach of the contract. Metalcrafters claimed that the contract was discharged by Samet's death. Is it correct? *no*

5. The Tinchers signed a contract to sell land to Creasy. The contract specified that the sales transaction was to be completed in 90 days. At the end of the 90 days, Creasy requested an extension of time. The Tinchers refused to grant an extension and stated that the contract was terminated. Creasy claimed that the 90-day clause was not binding because the contract did not state that time was of the essence. Was the contract terminated? [*Creasy v Tincher*, 173 SE2d 332 (W Va)] *yes*

6. Christopher Bloom received a medical school scholarship created by the U.S. Department of Health and Human Services to increase the number of doctors serving rural areas. In return for this assistance, Bloom agreed to practice four years in a region identified as being underserved by medical professionals. After some problem with his postgraduation assignment, Bloom requested a repayment schedule from the agency. Although no terms were offered, Bloom tendered to the agency two checks totaling $15,500 and marked "Final Payment." Neither check was cashed, and the government sued Bloom for $480,000, the value of the assistance provided. Bloom claimed that by tendering the checks to the agency, his liability had been discharged by an accord and satisfaction. Decide. [*United States v Bloom*, 112 F3d 200 (7th Cir)]

7. Dickson contracted to build a house for Moran. When it was approximately 25 percent to 40 percent completed, Moran would not let Dickson work any more because he was not following the building plans and specifications and there were many defects. Moran hired another contractor to correct the defects and finish the building. Dickson sued Moran for breach of contract, claiming that he had substantially performed the contract up to the point where he had been discharged. Was Dickson correct? [*Dickson v Moran*, 344 So2d 102 (La App)] *no*

8. A lessor leased a trailer park to a tenant. At the time, sewage was disposed of by a septic tank system that was not connected with the public sewage system. The tenant knew this, and the lease declared that the tenant had examined the premises and that the landlord made no representation or guarantee as to the condition of the premises. Some time thereafter, the septic tank system stopped working properly, and the county health department notified the tenant that he was required to connect the septic tank system with the public sewage system or else the department would close the trailer park. The tenant did not want to pay the additional cost involved in connecting with the public system. The tenant claimed that he was released from the lease and was entitled to a refund of the deposit that he had made. Was he correct? [*Glen R. Sewell Street Metal v Loverde*, 451 P2d 721 (Cal App)] *no*

9. Oneal was a teacher employed by the Colton Consolidated School District. Because of a diabetic condition, his eyesight deteriorated so much that he offered to resign if he would be given pay for a specified number of "sick leave" days. The school district refused to do this and discharged Oneal for nonperformance of his contract. He appealed to remove the discharge from his record. Decide. What ethical values are involved? [*Oneal v Colton Consolidated School District*, 557 P2d 11 (Wash App)]

10. Northwest Construction, Inc., made a contract with the state of Washington for highway construction. Part of the work was turned over under a subcontract to Yakima Asphalt Paving Co. The contract required that any claim be asserted within 180 days. Yakima brought an action for damages after the expiration of 180 days. The defense was that the claim was too late. Yakima replied that the action was brought within the time allowed by the statute of limitations and that the contractual limitation of 180 days was therefore not binding. Was Yakima correct? *no; the 180 days was binding*

11. The Metropolitan Park District of Tacoma gave Griffith a concession to run the district's parks. The agreement gave the right to occupy the parks and use any improvements found therein. The district later wished to set this agreement aside because it was not making sufficient money from the transaction. While it was seeking to set the agreement aside, a boathouse and a gift shop in one of the parks were destroyed by fire. The district then claimed that the concession contract with Griffith was discharged by impossibility of performance. Was it correct? [*Metropolitan Park District of Tacoma v Griffith*, 723 P2d 1093 (Wash)] *no*

12. Suburban Power Piping Corp., under contract to construct a building for LTV Steel Corp., made a subcontract with Power & Pollution Services, Inc., to do some of the work. The subcontract

provided that the subcontractor would be paid when the owner (LTV) paid the contractor. LTV went into bankruptcy before making the full payment to the contractor, who then refused to pay the subcontractor on the ground that the "pay-when-paid" provision of the subcontract made payment by the owner a condition precedent to the obligation of the contractor to pay the subcontractor. Was the contractor correct? [*Power & Pollution Services, Inc. v Suburban Power Piping Corp.,* 598 NE2d 69 (Ohio App)]

13. Ellen borrowed money from Farmers' Bank. As evidence of the loan, she signed a promissory note by which she promised to pay to the bank in installments the amount of the loan together with interest and administrative costs. She was unable to make the payments on the scheduled dates. She and the bank then executed a new agreement that gave her a longer period of time for making the payments. However, after two months, she was unable to pay on this new schedule. The bank then brought suit against her under the terms of the original agreement. She raised the defense that the original agreement had been discharged by the execution of the second agreement and could not be sued on. Decide.

14. Acme Hydraulic Press Co. manufactured large presses and sold them throughout the United States. The agreement-of-sale contract that Acme executed with its customers specified that they could make no claim for breach of contract unless notice of the breach was given within 10 days after the delivery of a press in question to the buyer and that no lawsuit could thereafter be brought if notice had not been given. Was this time limitation valid?

15. New Beginnings provides rehabilitation services for alcohol and drug abuse to both adults and adolescents. New Beginnings entered into negotiation with Adbar for the lease of a building in the city of St. Louis, and subsequently entered into a three-year lease. The total rent due for the three-year term was $273,000. After the lease was executed, the city denied an occupancy permit because Alderman Bosley and residents testified at a hearing in vigorous opposition to the presence of New Beginnings in the neighborhood. A court ordered the permit issued. Alderman Bosley thereafter contacted the chair of the state's appointment committee and asked her to pull the agency's funding. He received no commitment from her on this matter. After a meeting with the state director of Alcohol and Drug Abuse where it was asserted that the director said the funding would be pulled if New Beginnings moved into the Adbar location, New Beginnings's board decided not to occupy the building. Adbar brought suit for breach of the lease, and New Beginnings asserted it was excused from performance because of commercial impracticability and frustration of purpose. Do you believe the doctrine of commercial impracticability should be limited in its application so as to preserve the certainty of contracts? What rule of law applies to this case? Decide. [*Adbar v New Beginnings,* 103 SW2d 799 (Mo App)]

CPA QUESTIONS

1. Parc hired Glaze to remodel and furnish an office suite. Glaze submitted plans that Parc approved. After completing all the necessary construction and painting, Glaze purchased minor accessories that Parc rejected because they did not conform to the plans. Parc refused to allow Glaze to complete the project and refused to pay Glaze any part of the contract price. Glaze sued for the value of the work performed. Which of the following statements is correct?

   a. Glaze will lose because Glaze breached the contract by not completing performance.

   b. Glaze will win because Glaze substantially performed and Parc prevented complete performance.

382   Part 2   Contracts

c. Glaze will lose because Glaze materially breached the contract by buying the accessories.

d. Glaze will win because Parc committed anticipatory breach.

2. Ordinarily, in an action for breach of a construction contract, the statute of limitations time period would be computed from the date the contract is:

a. Negotiated

b. Breached

c. Begun

d. Signed

3. Which of the following will release all original parties to a contract but will maintain a contractual relationship?

	Novation	Substituted contract
a.	Yes	Yes
b.	Yes	No
c.	No	Yes
d.	No	No

Chapter 20

BREACH OF CONTRACT AND REMEDIES

What can be done when a contract is broken?

A. WHAT CONSTITUTES A BREACH OF CONTRACT?

The question of remedies does not become important until it is first determined that a contract has been violated or breached.

1. Definition of Breach

A **breach** is the failure to act or perform in the manner called for by the contract. When the contract calls for performance, such as painting an owner's home, the failure to paint or to paint properly is a *breach of contract*. If the contract calls for a creditor's forbearance, the creditor's action in bringing a lawsuit is a breach of the contract.

2. Anticipatory Breach

When the contract calls for performance, a party may make it clear before the time for performance arrives that the contract will not be performed. This is referred to as an **anticipatory breach**.

(A) ANTICIPATORY REPUDIATION. When a party expressly declares that performance will not be made when required, this declaration is called an **anticipatory repudiation** of the contract. To constitute such a repudiation, there must be a clear, absolute, unequivocal refusal to perform the contract according to its terms. **For Example,** Procter & Gamble (P&G) sought payment on four letters of credit issued by a Serbian bank, Investbanka. P&G presented two letters by June 8, prior to their expiration dates, with the necessary documentation for payment to Beogradska Bank New York, Investbanka's New York agent. A June 11 letter from Beogradska Bank broadly and unequivocally stated that the bank would not pay the letters of credit. Two additional letters of credit totaling $20,000 issued by Investbanka that expired by June 30 were not thereafter submitted to the New York agent bank by P&G. However, a court found that the bank had anticipatorily breached its obligations under those letters of credit by its broad renouncements in the June 11 letter, and judgments were rendered in favor of P&G.[1]

The *Tips* case deals with the issue of anticipatory repudiation and damages.

Tips v Hartland Developers, Inc., 961 SW2d 618 (Tex App 1998)

Splitting Tips—Contract Price Less Cost of Completion

In 1985, Hartland Developers, Inc., agreed to build an airplane hangar for Robert Tips of San Antonio for $300,000, payable in three installments of $100,000, with the final payment due upon the completion of the building and the issuance of a certificate of completion by the engineer representing Tips. The evidence shows that Tips's representative Mr. Lavelle instructed Hartland to cease work on the building because Tips could no longer afford to make payments. Hartland ceased work as instructed before the completion of the building, having been paid $200,000 at that time. He sued Tips for breach of contract. On May 6, 1996, the trial court allowed Hartland the amount owing on the contract, $100,000, less the cost of completing the building according to the contract, $65,000,

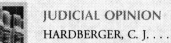

plus attorneys' fees and prejudgment and postjudgment interest. Tips appealed.

JUDICIAL OPINION

HARDBERGER, C. J. . . .

Substantial Performance

Tips claims that the evidence is legally or factually insufficient to support the trial court's finding that Hartland had substantially performed under the agreement. . . .

We agree with Tips that Hartland had not substantially performed under the contract. However, we find this point irrelevant to the resolution of this case. Substantial performance is a doctrine that allows *breaching* parties who have

---

[1] *Procter & Gamble v Investbanka*, 2000 WL 520630 (SDNY 2000).

Continued

substantially completed their obligations to recover on a contract. WHITE & SUMMERS, CONTRACTS § 11–18(b) (3rd ed 1987). Hartland was not a breaching party. A contractor can recover on a contract when the failure to substantially perform is the fault of the other party. A party injured by the anticipatory breach of another may elect to sue for damages under the contract, . . . (if owner repudiates construction contract, contractor may sue in damages or for restitution); *Taylor Pub. Co. v Systems Marketing Inc.* 686 S.W.2d 213, 217 (when party obligated to make fixed payment absolutely repudiates the agreement, the obligee is entitled to recover [in an] action for damages and receive the present value of the payments payable under the agreement).

The trial judge based his damage assessment on anticipatory repudiation of contract. The evidence that Tips's representative, Lavelle, instructed Hartland to cease work on the project because Tips no longer could afford to make payments was sufficient to support this finding. *See Tennessee Gas Pipeline Co. v Lenape Resources Corp.,* 870 S.W.2d 286, 302 (Tex App.—San Antonio 1993) (anticipatory repudiation occurs when a party repudiates a contract before time for performance), *aff'd in part, rev'd in part,* 925 S.W.2d 565 (Tex. 1996)

Offset Damages

Tips claims that the trial judge erred in not off-setting Hartland's award for its failure to provide electrical connections to the hangar. Tips also claims he should be compensated $11,000 for a temporary access ramp he was forced to construct in anticipation of a permanent ramp being installed. . . . [W]e find that the $65,000 offset for the construction of a permanent ramp is sufficient compensation for that deficiency. However, we agree with Tips that the damages award must be offset by the cost of providing electrical outlets to the hangar.

Tips is entitled to an offset for electrical connections under a breach of contract theory. Damages for breach of contract are the contract price, less, the cost of completion. *Sage Street Assoc. v Northdale Const. Co.* 937 S.W.2d 425, 426 (Tex. 1996). The trial judge did not address in his findings of fact and conclusions of law whether the electrical connections were contemplated by the contract, but there was testimony at trial that they were, and electrical wiring is listed among Hartland's duties in the contract. A witness for Hartland admitted under cross examination that the work was part of the agreement and that it had not been completed. Tips testified that he had spent $23,000 to install connections. Hartland's damages should be further offset by this amount.

[Judgment affirmed as modified]

QUESTIONS

1. What facts did Hartland rely on to assert the anticipatory repudiation of the contract?

2. What is the measure of damages for a breach of a construction contract? Calculate what is owed Hartland excluding attorneys' fees and interest.

3. Why is prejudgment and postjudgment interest appropriate in a breach of contract lawsuit?

A refusal to perform a contract that is made before performance is required unless the other party to the contract does an act or makes a concession that is not required by the contract, is an anticipatory repudiation of the contract.[2]

A party making an anticipatory repudiation may retract or take back the repudiation if the other party has not changed position in reliance on the repudiation. However, if the other party has changed position, the party making the anticipatory repudiation cannot retract it. **For Example,** if a buyer makes another purchase when the seller declares that the seller will not perform the contract, the buyer has acted in reliance on the seller's repudiation. The seller will therefore not be allowed to retract the repudiation.

(B) ANTICIPATORY REPUDIATION BY CONDUCT. The anticipatory repudiation may be expressed by conduct that makes it impossible for the repudiating party to perform subsequently. To illustrate, there is a repudiation by conduct if a farmer makes a contract to sell an identified quantity of potatoes nearly equivalent to his entire crop and then sells and delivers them to another buyer before the date specified for the delivery to the first buyer.

---

[2] *Chamberlain v Puckett Construction,* 921 P2d 1237 (Mont 1996).

sports & entertainment law

Get It While You Can?

In 2000, the cast of *Friends*, one of the hottest shows on television, demanded a pay increase. The demand was made with a valid contract in place and near the time NBC was to announce its fall lineup. The six stars demanded $1,000,000 each per episode. NBC settled for $750,000 per star, up from the stars' $150,000 per episode figure renegotiated in 1998.

When stars seek to renegotiate contracts before their expiration, the network can replace them if they fail to live up to their contracts, and it can enforce the standard contractual clause, which prohibits them from doing other television work until the expiration of their contracts. Recasting six stars for a highly successful show would not be feasible. To offset the stars' bargaining power, NBC prepared a television promotion that would relabel the last show for that season as the "series finale" and announce "See how it all ends on *Friends*." The cast were informed of NBC's threat to end the series in this manner. Renegotiations quickly ensued and led to the $750,000 agreement. Two years later the six stars obtained their goal of $1 million per episode paychecks. Was it ethical for the stars to threaten to strike just before the fall lineup announcements? When Jay Leno was asked about the tactics of the *Friends* stars, he responded, "You have to get what you can while you can in this business." Is Mr. Leno right? Is such an attitude ethical? When the new agreement was reached, was there a mutual rescission of the existing contract and the substitution of a new contract, or did the new contract fail for lack of consideration?

B. WAIVER OF BREACH

The breach of a contract may have no importance because the other party to the contract waives the breach.

3. Cure of Breach by Waiver

The fact that one party has broken a contract does not necessarily mean that there will be a lawsuit or a forfeiture of the contract. For practical business reasons, one party may be willing to ignore or waive the breach. When it is established that there has been a **waiver** of a breach, the party waiving the breach cannot take any action on the theory that the contract was broken. The waiver, in effect, erases the past breach. The contract continues as though the breach had not existed.

The waiver may be express or it may be implied from the continued recognition of the existence of the contract by the aggrieved party.[3] When the conduct of a party shows an intent to give up a right, it waives that right.[4]

4. Existence and Scope of Waiver

It is a question of fact whether there has been a waiver.

(A) EXISTENCE OF WAIVER. A party may express or declare that the breach of a contract is waived. A waiver of a breach is more often the result of an express forgiving of a breach. Thus, a party allowing the other party to continue performance without objecting that the performance is not satisfactory waives the right to raise that objection when sued for payment by the performing party.

For Example, a contract promising to sell back a parcel of commercial property to Jackson required Jackson to make a $500 payment to Massey's attorney on the first of the month for five months, December

---

[3] *Huger v Morrison*, 2000 La App LEXIS 241.
[4] *Stronghaven Inc. v Ingram*, 555 SE2d 49 (Ga App 2001).

through April. It was clearly understood that the payments would be "on time without fail." Jackson made the December payment on time. New Year's Day, a holiday, fell on a Friday, and Jackson made the second payment on January 4. He made $500 payments on February 1, March 1, and March 31, respectively, and the payments were accepted and a receipt issued on each occasion. However, Massey refused to convey title back to Jackson because "the January 4 payment was untimely and the parties' agreement had been breached." The court held that the doctrine of waiver applied due to Massey's acceptance of the late payment and the three subsequent payments without objection, and the court declared that Jackson was entitled to possession of the land.[5]

(B) Scope of Waiver. The waiver of a breach of contract extends only to the matter waived. It does not show any intent to ignore other provisions of the contract.

(C) Antimodification Clause. Modern contracts commonly specify that the terms of a contract shall not be deemed modified by waiver as to any breaches. This means that the original contract remains as agreed to. Either party may therefore return to, and insist on, compliance with the original contract.

In the example involving Jackson and Massey's contract, the trial court reviewed the contract to see whether the court was restricted by the contract from applying the waiver. It concluded: "In this case, the parties' contract did not contain any terms that could prevent the application of the doctrine of waiver to the acceptance of late payments."[6]

5. Reservation of Rights

It may be that a party is willing to accept a defective performance but does not wish to surrender any claim for damages for the breach. **For Example,** Midwest Utilities, Inc., accepted 20 carloads of Powder River Basin coal (sometimes called *Western coal*) from its supplier, Maney Enterprises, because its power plants were in short supply of coal. Midwest's requirements contract with Maney called for Appalachian coal, a low-sulfur, highly efficient fuel, which is sold at a premium price per ton. Midwest, in accepting the tendered performance with a **reservation of rights**, gave notice to Maney that it reserved all rights to pursue damages for the tender of a nonconforming shipment.

C. Remedies for Breach of Contract

One or more **remedies** may be available to the innocent party in the case of a breach of contract. There is also the possibility that arbitration or a streamlined out-of-court alternative dispute resolution procedure is available or required for determining the rights of the parties.

6. Remedies Upon Anticipatory Repudiation

When an anticipatory repudiation of a contract occurs, the aggrieved person has several options. He may (1) do nothing beyond stating that performance at the proper time will be required, (2) regard the contract as having been definitively broken and bring a lawsuit against the repudiating party without waiting to see whether there will be proper performance when the performance date arrives, or (3) regard the repudiation as an offer to cancel the contract. This offer can be accepted or rejected. If accepted, there is a discharge of the original contract by the subsequent cancellation agreement of the parties.

7. Remedies in General and the Measure of Damages

Courts provide a *quasi-contractual* or *restitution* remedy in which a contract is unenforceable because it lacked definite and certain terms or was not in compliance with the statute of frauds, yet one of the parties performed services for the other. The measure of damages in these and other quasi-contract cases is the reasonable value of the services performed, not an amount derived from the defective contract.

---

[5] *Massey v Jackson*, 726 So2d 656 (Ala Civ App 1998).
[6] Id., at 659.

FIGURE 20-1 | *What Follows the Breach*

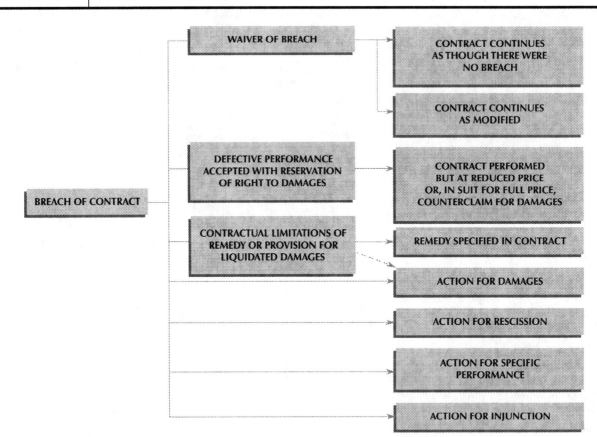

In cases when a person retains money or when a contemplated contract is not properly formed and no work is performed, the party retaining the benefit is obligated to make restitution to the person conferring the benefit. **For Example,** Kramer Associates, Inc. (KAI), a Washington D.C., consulting firm, accepted $75,000 from a Ghana-based corporation, Ikam, Ltd., to secure financing for a Ghana development project. No contract was ever executed, and KAI did virtually nothing to secure financing for the project. Restitution of the $75,000 was required.[7]

When there is a breach of contract, the regular remedy is an award of *monetary damages*. In unusual circumstances, when monetary damages are inadequate, the injured party may obtain **specific performance**, whereby the court will order that the contract terms be carried out.

The measure of monetary damages when there has been a breach of contract is the sum of money that will place the injured party in the same position that would have been attained if the contract had been performed.[8] That is, the injured party will be given the *benefit of the bargain* by the court. As seen in the *Tips v Hartland Developers* case, the non-breaching party, Hartland, was awarded the contract price less the cost of completion of the project, which had the effect of giving the builder the benefit of the bargain.

---

[7] *Kramer Associates, Inc. v IKAM, Ltd.,* 888 A2d 247 (DC 2005).
[8] *Leingang v City of Mandan Weed Board,* 468 NW2d 397 (ND 1991).

8. Monetary Damages

Monetary damages are commonly classified as compensatory damages, nominal damages, and punitive damages. **Compensatory damages** compensate the injured party for the damages incurred as a result of the breach of contract. Compensatory damages have two branches, *direct damages* and *consequential* (or *special*) *damages*.

Injured parties that do not sustain an actual loss because of a breach of contract are entitled to a judgment of a small sum of money such as $1; these damages are called **nominal damages**.

Damages in excess of actual loss, imposed for the purpose of punishing or making an example of the defendant, are known as **punitive damages** or *exemplary damages*. In contract actions, punitive damages are not ordinarily awarded.[9]

(A) Direct and Consequential Damages. **Direct damages** (sometimes called *general damages*) are those that naturally flow from the given type of breach of contract involved and include *incidental damages*, which are extra expenditures made by the injured party to rectify the breach or mitigate damages. **Consequential damages** (sometimes called *special damages*) are those that do not necessarily flow from the type of breach of contract involved but happen to do so in a particular case as a result of the injured party's particular circumstances.

Consequential damages may be recovered only if it was reasonably foreseeable to the defendant that the kind of loss in question could be sustained by the nonbreaching party if the contract were broken.

For Example, in early August, Spencer Adams ordered a four-wheel-drive GMC truck with a rear-end hydraulic lift for use on his Aroostook County, Maine, potato farm. The contract price was $58,500. He told Brad Jones, the owner of the dealership, that he had to have the truck by Labor Day so he could use it to bring in his crop from the fields before the first frost, and Brad nodded that he understood. The truck did not arrive by Labor Day as promised in the written contract. After a two-week period of gradually escalating recriminations with the dealership, Adams obtained the same model GMC truck at a dealership 40 minutes away in Houlton but at the cost of $60,500. He was also able to rent a similar truck from the Houlton dealer for $250 for the day while the new truck was being prepared. Farmhands had used other means of harvesting, but because of the lack of the truck, their work was set back by five days. As a result of the delays, 30 percent of the crop was still in the fields when the first frost came, causing damages expertly estimated at $320,000. The *direct damages* for the breach of contract in this case would be the difference between the contract price for the truck of $58,500 and the market price of $60,500, or $2,000. These direct damages naturally flow from the breach of contract for the purchase of a truck. Also, the *incidental damages* of $250 for the truck rental are recoverable direct damages. The $320,000 loss of the potato crop was a consequence of not having the truck, and this sum is arguably recoverable by Spencer Adams as *consequential or special damages*. Adams notified Brad Jones of the reason he needed to have the truck by Labor Day, and it should have been reasonably foreseeable to Jones that loss of a portion of the crop could occur if the truck contract was breached. However, because of Spencer Adams's obligation to mitigate damages (as discussed below), it is unlikely that Adams will recover the full consequential damages. Truck rental availability or the lack of availability within the rural area, alternative tractor usage, and the actual harvesting methods used by Adams all relate to the mitigation issue to be resolved by the jury.

(B) Mitigation of Damages. The injured party is under the duty to mitigate damages if reasonably possible.[10] In other words, damages must not be permitted to increase if an increase can be prevented by reasonable efforts. This means that the injured party must generally stop any performance under the contract to avoid running up a larger bill. The duty to mitigate damages may require an injured party to buy or rent elsewhere the goods that the wrongdoer was obligated to deliver under the contract. In the case of breach of an employment contract by the employer,

[9] A party who is not awarded actual damages but wins nominal damages can be considered a "prevailing party" for the purposes of a contractual attorney fee-shifting provision. *Brock v King*, 629 SE2d 829 (Ga App 2006).
[10] *West Pinal Family Health Center, Inc. v McBride*, 785 P2d 66 (Ariz 1989).

the employee is required to seek other similar employment. The wages earned from other employment must be deducted from the damages claimed. The discharged employee, however, is not required to take employment of less-than-comparable work.

(1) Effect of Failure to Mitigate Damages

The effect of the requirement of mitigating damages is to limit recovery by the nonbreaching party to the damages that would have been sustained had this party mitigated the damages where it was possible to do so. **For Example,** self-described "sports nut" Gary Baker signed up for a three-year club-seat "package" that entitled him and a companion to tickets for 41 Boston Bruins hockey games and 41 Boston Celtics basketball games at the New Boston Garden Corporation's Fleet Center for approximately $18,000 per year. After one year, Baker stopped paying for the tickets, thinking that he would simply lose his $5,000 security deposit. Baker, a CPA, tried to work out a compromise settlement to no avail. New Boston sued Baker for breach of contract, seeking the balance due on the tickets of $34,866. At trial, Baker argued to the jury that although he had breached his contract, New Boston had an obligation to mitigate damages, for example, by treating his empty seats and those of others in the same situation as "rush seats" shortly before game time and selling them at a discount. New Boston argued that just as a used luxury car cannot be returned for a refund, a season ticket cannot be canceled without consequences. The jury accepted Baker's position on mitigation and reduced the amount owed New Boston by $21,176 to $13,690.[11]

9. Rescission   ~rescind=cancel~

When one party commits a material breach of the contract, the other party may rescind the contract; if the party in default objects, the aggrieved party may bring an action for rescission. A breach is *material* when it is so substantial that it defeats the object of the parties in making the contract.[12]

An injured party who rescinds a contract after having performed services may recover the reasonable value of the performance rendered under restitutionary or quasi-contractual damages. Money paid by the injured party may also be recovered. The purpose is to restore the injured party to the position occupied before the contract was made. However, the party seeking restitutionary damages must also return what this party has received from the party in default.

For Example, Pedro Morena purchased real estate from Jason Alexander after Alexander had assured him that the property did not have a flooding problem. In fact, the property regularly flooded after ordinary rainstorms. Morena was entitled to the return of the purchase price and payment for the reasonable value of the improvements he made to the property. Alexander was entitled to a setoff for the reasonable rental value of the property during the time Morena was in possession of this property.

10. Action for Specific Performance

Under special circumstances, an injured party may obtain the equitable remedy of specific performance, which compels the other party to carry out the terms of a contract. Specific performance is ordinarily granted only if the subject matter of the contract is "unique," thereby making an award of money damages an inadequate remedy. Contracts for the purchase of land will be specifically enforced.[13]

Specific performance of a contract to sell personal property can be obtained only if the article is of unusual age, beauty, unique history, or other distinction. **For Example,** Maurice owned a rare Revolutionary War musket that he agreed to sell to Herb. Maurice then changed his mind because of the uniqueness of the musket. Herb can sue and win, requesting the remedy of specific performance of the contract because of the unique nature of the goods.

When the damages sustained by the plaintiff can be measured in monetary terms, specific performance will be refused. Consequently, a contract to sell a television station will not be specifically enforced when the buyer had made a contract to resell the station to a third person; the damages caused by the

[11] Sacha Pfeiffer, "Disenchanted Fan Scores Win in Ticket Fight," *Boston Globe*, August 28, 1999, B-4.
[12] *Greentree Properties, Inc. v Kissee*, 92 SW3d 289 (Mo App 2003).
[13] *English v Muller*, 514 SE2d 195 (Ga 1999).

breach of the first contract would be the loss sustained by being unable to make the resale, and such damages would be adequate compensation to the original buyer.[14]

Ordinarily, contracts for the performance of personal services are not specifically ordered. This is because of the difficulty of supervision by the court and the restriction of the U.S. Constitution's Thirteenth Amendment prohibiting involuntary servitude except as criminal punishment.

11. Action for an Injunction

When a breach of contract consists of doing an act prohibited by the contract, a possible remedy is an **injunction** against doing the act. **For Example,** when the obligation in an employee's contract is to refrain from competing after resigning from the company and the obligation is broken by competing, a court may order or enjoin the former employee to stop competing. Similarly, when a vocalist breaks a contract to record exclusively for a particular label, she may be enjoined from recording for any other company. This may have the indirect effect of compelling the vocalist to record for the plaintiff.

12. Reformation of Contract by a Court

At times, a written contract does not correctly state the agreement already made by the parties. When this occurs, either party may seek to have the court reform or correct the writing to state the agreement actually made.

A party seeking reformation of a contract must clearly prove both the grounds for reformation and what the agreement actually was. This burden is particularly great when the contract to be reformed is written. This is so because the general rule is that parties are presumed to have read their written contracts and to have intended to be bound by them when they signed the contracts.

When a unilateral mistake is made and it is of such consequence that enforcing the contract according to its terms would be unreasonable, a court may reform the contract to correct the mistake.

D. Contract Provisions Affecting Remedies and Damages

The contract of the parties may contain provisions that affect the remedies available or the recovery of damages.

13. Limitation of Remedies

The contract of the parties may limit the remedies of the aggrieved parties. **For Example,** the contract may give one party the right to repair or replace a defective item sold or to refund the contract price. The contract may require both parties to submit any dispute to arbitration or another streamlined out-of-court dispute resolution procedure.

14. Liquidated Damages

The parties may stipulate in their contract that a certain amount should be paid in case of a breach. This amount is known as liquidated damages and may be variously measured by the parties. When delay is possible, **liquidated damages** may be a fixed sum, such as $1,000 for each day of delay. When there is a total default, damages may be a percentage of the contract price or the amount of the down payment.

(A) VALIDITY. To be **valid**, a **liquidated damages clause** must satisfy two requirements: (1) The situation must be one in which it is difficult or impossible to determine the actual damages and (2) the amount specified must not be excessive when compared with the probable damages that would be sustained.[15] The validity of a liquidated damages clause is determined on the basis of the facts existing when the clause was agreed to.

(B) EFFECT. When a liquidated damages clause is held valid, the injured party cannot collect more than the amount specified by the clause. The defaulting party is bound to pay such damages once the fact is established that there has been a default. The injured party is not required to make any proof as to

---

[14] *Miller v LeSea Broadcasting, Inc.*, 87 F3d 224 (7th Cir 1996).
[15] *Southeast Alaska Construction Co. v Alaska*, 791 P2d 339 (Alaska 1990).

damages sustained, and the defendant is not permitted to show that the damages were not as great as the liquidated sum.

(c) Invalid Clauses. If the liquidated damages clause calls for the payment of a sum that is clearly unreasonably large and unrelated to the possible actual damages that might be sustained, the clause will be held to be void as a penalty. **For Example,** a settlement agreement between 27 plaintiffs seeking recovery for injuries resulting from faulty breast implants and the implants' manufacturer, Dow Corning Corp., called for seven $200,000 payments to each plaintiff. The agreement also called for a $100 per day payment to each plaintiff for any time when the payments were late as "liquidated damages." The court held that the $100 per day figure was not a reasonable estimate of anticipated damages. Rather, it was an unenforceable "penalty" provision.[16]

When a liquidated damages clause is held invalid, the effect is merely to erase the clause from the contract, and the injured party may proceed to recover damages for breach of the contract. Instead of recovering the liquidated damages amount, the injured party will recover whatever actual damages he can prove. **For Example,** JRC Trading Corp (JRC) bought computer software and hardware from Progressive Data Systems (PDS) for $167,935, which it paid in full, to track the movement of its trucks with inventory and to process transactions. The purchase agreement also called for a $7,500 per year licensing fee for an 18-year period, and it stated that in the event of default, PDS could "accelerate and declare all obligations of Customer as a liquidated sum." A dispute arose between the parties, and when the case was litigated, the only actual contract charges owed PDS were license fees of $7,500 for two years. The application of the liquidated damages clause would yield an additional $120,000 cash for PDS for the future fees for 16 years without any reduction for expenses or the present cash value for the not-yet-earned fees. Actual damages were clearly ascertainable and not difficult to determine, and the

amount sought was excessive. The court deemed the liquidated damages clause an unenforceable penalty and PDS was relegated to recovering its actual contractual damages.[17]

15. Attorneys' Fees

Attorneys' fees are a very significant factor in contract litigation. In Medistar Corporation's suit against Dr. David Schmidt, the jury awarded it $418,069 in damages under its promissory estoppel claim and in addition thereto the trial court judge allowed Medistar to recover $408,412 for its attorneys' fees. A state statute allows recovery of attorneys' fees for the prevailing party in a breach of partnership claim. On appeal the recovery of $408,412 in attorneys' fees was reversed since the jury awarded zero damages on Medistars' breach of partnership claim. The net result after payment of attorneys' fees—and not counting attorneys' fees for the appeal—was $9,657 for Medistar, after four years of "successful" litigation.[18]

The so-called "American rule" states that each party is responsible for its own attorneys' fees in the absence of an express contractual or statutory provision to the contrary.[19] Even in the event of a valid contractual provision for attorneys' fees, a trial court has the discretion to exercise its equitable control to allow only such sum as is reasonable, or the court may properly disallow attorneys' fees altogether on the basis that such recovery would be inequitable. **For Example,** although Evergreen Tree Care Services was awarded some monetary damages in its breach of contract suit against JHL, Inc., it was unsuccessful in its claim for attorneys' fees under a provision for attorneys' fees in the contract because the trial court exercised its equitable discretion, finding that both parties to the litigation came to court with "unclean hands," and that Evergreen failed to sufficiently itemize and exclude fees relating to its discovery abuses.[20]

[16] *Bear Stearns v Dow Corning Corp.*, 419 F3d 543 (6th Cir 2005). See *RKR Motors Inc. v Associated Uniform Rentals*, 995 So2d 588 (Fla App 2008).
[17] *Jefferson Randolf Corporation v PDS*, 553 SE2d 304 (Ga App 2001).
[18] *Medistar Corp. v Schmidt*, 267 SW3d 150 (Tex App 2008).
[19] *Centimark v Village Manor Associates, Ltd.*, 967 A2d 550 (Conn App 2009).
[20] *Stafford v JHL, Inc.*, 194 P3d 315 (Wyo 2008). See also *FNBC v Jennessey Group, LLC*, 759 NW2d 808 (Iowa App 2008).

16. Limitation of Liability Clauses

A contract may contain a provision stating that one of the parties shall not be liable for damages in case of breach. Such a provision is called an **exculpatory clause**, or when a monetary limit to damages for breach of contract is set forth in the contract, it may be referred to as a **limitation-of-liability clause**.

(A) CONTENT AND CONSTRUCTION. If an exculpatory clause or a limitation-of-liability clause limits liability for damages caused only by negligent conduct, liability is neither excluded nor limited if the conduct alleged is found to be grossly negligent, willful, or wanton. **For Example,** Security Guards Inc. (SGI) provided services to Dana Corporation, a truck frame manufacturer under a contract that contained a limitation-of-liability clause capping losses at $50,000 per occurrence for damages "caused solely by the negligence" of SGI or its employees. When a critical alarm was activated by a fire in the paint shop at 5:39 P.M., the SGI guard on duty did not follow appropriate procedures, which delayed notification to the fire department for 15 minutes. Royal Indemnity Co., Dana's insurer, paid Dana $16,535,882 for the fire loss and sued SGI for $7 million, contending that the SGI guard's actions were grossly negligent and caused the plant to suffer increased damages. The court held that if SGI were to be found grossly negligent, the liability would not be limited to $50,000, and a jury could find damages far exceeding that amount.[21]

(B) VALIDITY. As a general rule, experienced businesspersons are free to allocate liability in their contracts as they see fit. They have freedom to contract—even to make bad bargains or relinquish fundamental rights. However, courts in most states will not enforce a contract provision that *completely exonerates* a party from gross negligence or intentional acts.

(C) RELEASES. Release forms signed by participants in athletic and sporting events declaring that the sponsor, proprietor, or operator of the event shall not be liable for injuries sustained by participants because of its negligence are generally binding.[22] **For Example,** when Merav Sharon sued the city of Newton for negligence as a result of an injury received while participating in a high school cheerleading practice, the city successfully raised a signed exculpatory release as a defense.[23] So also the exculpatory contract Nathan Henderson signed releasing a white-water rafting expedition operator from liability for its negligence barred Henderson's negligence claim against the operator for an injury suffered disembarking from the operator's bus.[24]

lawflix

The Goodbye Girl (1977) (PG)

Richard Dreyfuss plays Elliott Garfield, a struggling Shakespearean actor who lands in New York with a sublease on an apartment still occupied by divorcee Marsha Mason and her daughter. The two work out living arrangements, split rent and food, and deal with the issue of whether Mason has any rights. Review all aspects of contracts as the characters discuss subleases, rent payment, living arrangements, and food costs.

Check out LawFlix at **www.cengage.com/blaw/dvl** to access movie clips that illustrate business law concepts.

---

[21] *Royal Indemnity Co. v Security Guards, Inc.*, 255 F Supp 2d 497 (ED Pa 2003).
[22] But see *Woodman v Kera, LLC*, 760 NW2d 641 (Mich App 2008) where the Court of Appeals of Michigan held that a preinjury waiver signed by a parent on behalf of a five-year-old child was invalid.
[23] *Sharon v City of Newton*, 437 Mass 99 (2002).
[24] *Henderson v Quest Expeditions, Inc.*, 174 SW3d 730 (Tenn App 2005).

MAKE THE CONNECTION

SUMMARY

When a party fails to perform a contract or performs improperly, the other contracting party may sue for damages caused by the breach. What may be recovered by the aggrieved person is stated in terms of being direct or consequential damages. Direct damages are those that ordinarily will result from the breach. Direct damages may be recovered on proof of causation and amount. Consequential damages can be recovered only if, in addition to proving causation and amount, it is shown that they were reasonably within the contemplation of the contracting parties as a probable result of a breach of the contract. The right to recover consequential damages is lost if the aggrieved party could reasonably have taken steps to avoid such damages. In other words, the aggrieved person has a duty to mitigate or reduce damages by reasonable means.

In any case, the damages recoverable for breach of contract may be limited to a specific amount by a liquidated damages clause.

In a limited number of situations, an aggrieved party may bring an action for specific performance to compel the other contracting party to perform the acts called for by the contract. Specific performance by the seller is always obtainable for the breach of a contract to sell land or real estate on the theory that such property has a unique value. With respect to other contracts, specific performance will not be ordered unless it is shown that there was some unique element present so that the aggrieved person would suffer a damage that could not be compensated for by the payment of money damages.

The aggrieved person also has the option of rescinding the contract if (1) the breach has been made concerning a material term and (2) the aggrieved party returns everything to the way it was before the contract was made.

Although there has been a breach of the contract, the effect of this breach is nullified if the aggrieved person by word or conduct waives the right to object to the breach. Conversely, an aggrieved party may accept a defective performance without thereby waiving a claim for breach if the party makes a reservation of rights. A reservation of rights can be made by stating that the defective performance is accepted "without prejudice," "under protest," or "with reservation of rights."

LEARNING OUTCOMES

After studying this chapter, you should be able to clearly explain:

A. WHAT CONSTITUTES A BREACH OF CONTRACT

LO.1 Explain what constitutes a breach of contract and an anticipatory breach of contract
See the illustration of a painting contractor's failure to properly paint a house, p. 384.
See the *Tips* case in which damages are assessed for anticipatory repudiation of a contract, p. 384.

B. WAIVER OF BREACH

LO.2 Describe the effect of a waiver of a breach

See the application of the waiver doctrine as applied in the Massey example on p. 386.

C. REMEDIES FOR BREACH OF CONTRACT

LO.3 Explain the range of remedies available for breach of contract
See Figure 20-1, "What Follows the Breach," on p. 388.
See the *Spenser Adams* example involving a range of monetary damages on p. 389.
See the *Pedro Morena* example involving rescission of a contract on p. 390.

See the rare Revolutionary War musket example of specific performance, p. 390.

D. CONTRACT PROVISIONS AFFECTING REMEDIES AND DAMAGES

LO.4 Explain when liquidated damages clauses are valid and invalid

See the Dow Corning faulty breast implants settlement agreement example in which liquidated damages of a $100 per day late payment were found to be an unenforceable penalty provision, p. 392.

LO.5 State when liability-limiting clauses and releases are valid

See the example in which the city of Newton successfully raised a signed exculpatory release as a defense in a high school cheerleading injury case, p. 393.

KEY TERMS

anticipatory breach
anticipatory repudiation
breach
compensatory damages
consequential damages
direct damages

exculpatory clause
injunction
limitation-of-liability clause
liquidated damages
nominal damages
punitive damages

remedies
reservation of rights
specific performance
valid
waiver

QUESTIONS AND CASE PROBLEMS

1. The Forsyth School District contracted with Textor Construction, Inc., to build certain additions and alter school facilities, including the grading of a future softball field. Under the contract, the work was to be completed by August 1. Various delays occurred at the outset of the project attributable to the school district, and the architect's representative on the job, Mr. Hamilton, told Textor's vice president, William Textor, not to be concerned about a clause in the contract of $250 per day liquidated damages for failure to complete the job by August 1. Textor sued the school district for breach of contract regarding payment for the grading of the softball field, and the District counterclaimed for liquidated damages for 84 days at $250 per day for failure to complete the project by the August 1 date. What legal basis exists for Textor to defend against the counter-claim for failure to complete the job on time? Was it ethical for the school district to bring this counterclaim based on the facts before you? [*Textor Construction, Inc. v Forsyth R-III School District*, 60 SW3d 692 (Mo App)]

2. Anthony makes a contract to sell a rare painting to Laura for $100,000. The written contract specifies that if Anthony should fail to perform the contract, he will pay Laura $5,000 as liquidated damages. Anthony fails to deliver the painting and is sued by Laura for $5,000. Can she recover this amount?

3. Rogers made a contract with Salisbury Brick Corp. that allowed it to remove earth and sand from land he owned. The contract ran for four years with provision to renew it for additional four-year terms up to a total of 96 years. The contract provided for compensation to Rogers based on the amount of earth and sand removed. By an unintentional mistake, Salisbury underpaid Rogers the amount of $863 for the months of November and December 1986. Salisbury offered this amount to Rogers, but he refused to accept it and claimed that he had been underpaid in other months. Rogers claimed that he was entitled to rescind the contract. Was he correct? [*Rogers v Salisbury Brick Corp.*, 882 SE2d 915 (SC)]

4. A contractor departed from the specifications at a number of points in a contract to build a house. The cost to put the house in the condition called for by the contract was approximately $14,000. The contractor was sued for $50,000 for breach of contract and emotional disturbance caused by the breach. Decide.

5. Protein Blenders, Inc., made a contract with Gingerich to buy from him the shares of stock of a small corporation. When the buyer refused to take and pay for the stock, Gingerich sued for specific performance of the contract on the ground that the value of the stock was unknown and could not be readily ascertained because it was not sold on the general market. Was he entitled to specific performance? [*Gingerich v Protein Blenders, Inc.*, 95 NW2d 522 (Iowa)]

6. The buyer of real estate made a down payment. The contract stated that the buyer would be liable for damages in an amount equal to the down payment if the buyer broke the contract. The buyer refused to go through with the contract and demanded his down payment back. The seller refused to return it and claimed that he was entitled to additional damages from the buyer because the damages that he had suffered were more than the amount of the down payment. Decide. [*Waters v Key Colony East, Inc.*, 345 So2d 367 (Fla App)]

7. Kuznicki made a contract for the installation of a fire detection system by Security Safety Corp. for $498. The contract was made one night and canceled at 9:00 the next morning. Security then claimed one-third of the purchase price from Kuznicki by virtue of a provision in the contract that "in the event of cancellation of this agreement . . . the owner agrees to pay $33^{1/3}$ percent of the contract price, as liquidated damages." Was Security Safety entitled to recover the amount claimed? [*Security Safety Corp. v Kuznicki*, 213 NE2d 866 (Mass)]

8. FNBC is a business brokerage firm that assists in the purchase and sale of businesses. Jennings and Hennessey were independent contractors working for FNBC. They left FNBC, and FNBC sued them for breach of their contracts with FNBC. The trial court issued a permanent injunction prohibiting the former contractors from using proprietary information and the court awarded attorneys' fees under a clause in the contract that would obligate Jennings and Hennessey to indemnify FNBC against claims "brought by persons not a party to the provision." Jennings and Hennessey appealed the decision on attorneys' fees. Decide. [*FNBC v Jennessey Group, LLC*, 759 NW2d 808 (Iowa Ap)]

9. Melodee Lane Lingerie Co. was a tenant in a building that was protected against fire by a sprinkler and alarm system maintained by the American District Telegraph Co. (ADT). Because of the latter's fault, the controls on the system were defective and allowed the discharge of water into the building, which damaged Melodee's property. When Melodee sued ADT, its defense was that its service contract limited its liability to 10 percent of the annual service charge made to the customer. Was this limitation valid? [*Melodee Lane Lingerie Co. v American District Telegraph Co.*, 218 NE2d 661 (NY)]

10. In May, a homeowner made a contract with a roofer to make repairs to her house by July 1. The roofer never came to repair the roof, and heavy rains in the fall damaged the interior of the house. The homeowner sued the roofer for breach of contract and claimed damages for the harm done to the interior of the house. Is the homeowner entitled to recover such damages?

11. Ken Sulejmanagic, aged 19, signed up for a course in scuba diving taught by Madison at the YMCA. Before the instruction began, Ken was required to sign a form releasing Madison and the YMCA from liability for any harm that might occur. At the end of the course, Madison, Ken, and another student went into deep water. After Ken made the final dive required by the course program, Madison left him alone in the water while he took the other student for a dive. When Madison returned, Ken could not be found, and it was later determined that he had drowned. Ken's parents sued Madison and the YMCA for

negligence in the performance of the teaching contract. The defendants raised the defense that the release Ken signed shielded them from liability. The plaintiffs claimed that the release was invalid. Who was correct? [*Madison v Superior Court*, 250 Cal Rptr 299 (Cal App)]

12. Wassenaar worked for Panos under a three-year contract stating that if the contract were terminated wrongfully by Panos before the end of the three years, he would pay as damages the salary for the remaining time that the contract had to run. After three months, Panos terminated the contract, and Wassenaar sued him for pay for the balance of the contract term. Panos claimed that this amount could not be recovered because the contract provision for the payment was a void penalty. Was this provision valid? [*Wassenaar v Panos*, 331 NW2d 357 (Wis)]

13. Soden, a contractor, made a contract to build a house for Clevert. The sales contract stated that "if either party defaults in the performance of this contract," that party would be liable to the other for attorneys' fees incurred in suing the defaulter. Soden was 61 days late in completing the contract, and some of the work was defective. In a suit by the buyer against the contractor, the contractor claimed that he was not liable for the buyer's attorneys' fees because he had made only a defective performance and because "default" in the phrase quoted meant "nonperformance of the contract." Was the contractor liable for the attorneys' fees? [*Clevert v Soden*, 400 SE2d 181 (Va)]

14. Protection Alarm Co. made a contract to provide burglar alarm security for Fretwell's home. The contract stated that the maximum liability of the alarm company was the actual loss sustained or $50, whichever was the lesser, and that this provision was agreed to "as liquidated damages and not as a penalty." When Fretwell's home was burglarized, he sued for the loss of approximately $12,000, claiming that the alarm company had been negligent. The alarm company asserted that its maximum liability was $50. Fretwell claimed that this was invalid because it bore no relationship to the loss that could have been foreseen when the contract was made or that in fact "had been sustained." Decide.

15. Shepherd-Will made a contract to sell Emma Cousar:

> *5 acres of land adjoining property owned by the purchaser and this being formerly land of Shepherd-Will, Inc., located on north side of Highway 223. This 5 acres to be surveyed at earliest time possible at which time plat will be attached and serve as further description on property.*

Shepherd-Will owned only one 100-acre tract of land that adjoined Emma's property. This tract had a common boundary with her property of 1,140 feet. Shepherd-Will failed to perform this contract. Emma sued for specific performance of the contract. Decide. [*Cousar v Shepherd-Will, Inc.*, 387 SE2d 723 (SC App)]

CPA QUESTIONS

1. Master Mfg., Inc., contracted with Accur Computer Repair Corp. to maintain Master's computer system. Master's manufacturing process depends on its computer system operating properly at all times. A liquidated damages clause in the contract provided that Accur pay $1,000 to Master for each day that Accur was late responding to a service request. On January 12, Accur was notified that Master's computer system had failed. Accur did not respond to Master's service request until January 15. If Master sues Accur under the liquidated damages provision of the contract, Master will:

   a. Win, unless the liquidated damage provision is determined to be a penalty

   b. Win, because under all circumstances liquidated damages provisions are enforceable

   c. Lose, because Accur's breach was *not* material

   d. Lose, because liquidated damage provisions violate public policy (5/93, Law, #25)

2. Jones, CPA, entered into a signed contract with Foster Corp. to perform accounting and review services. If Jones repudiates the contract prior to the date performance is due to begin, which of the following is *not* correct?

   a. Foster could successfully maintain an action for breach of contract after the date performance was due to begin.

   b. Foster can obtain a judgment ordering Jones to perform.

   c. Foster could successfully maintain an action for breach of contract prior to the date performance is due to begin.

   d. Foster can obtain a judgment for the monetary damages it incurred as a result of the repudiation. (5/89, Law, #35)

3. Which of the following concepts affect(s) the amount of monetary damages recoverable by the nonbreaching party when a contract is breached?

	Forseeability of damages	*Mitigation of damages*
a.	Yes	Yes
b.	Yes	No
c.	No	Yes
d.	No	No

glossary

A

abate—put a stop to a nuisance; reduce or cancel a legacy because the estate of the decedent is insufficient to make payment in full.

absolute guaranty—agreement that creates the same obligation for the guarantor as a suretyship does for the surety; a guaranty of payment creates an absolute guaranty.

absolute privilege—complete defense against the tort of defamation, as in the speeches of members of Congress on the floor and witnesses in a trial.

abstract of title—history of the transfers of title to a given piece of land, briefly stating the parties to and the effect of all deeds, wills, and judicial proceedings relating to the land.

acceptance—unqualified assent to the act or proposal of another; as the acceptance of a draft (bill of exchange), of an offer to make a contract, of goods delivered by the seller, or of a gift or deed.

acceptor—drawee who has accepted the liability of paying the amount of money specified in a draft.

accommodation party—person who signs an instrument to lend credit to another party to the paper.

accord and satisfaction—agreement to substitute for an existing debt some alternative form of discharging that debt, coupled with the actual discharge of the debt by the substituted performance.

acknowledgment—admission or confirmation, generally of an instrument and usually made before a person authorized to administer oaths, such as a notary public; used to establish that the instrument was executed by the person making the instrument, that it was a voluntary act, or that the instrument is recorded.

acquired distinctiveness—through advertising, use and association, over time, an ordinary descriptive word or phase has taken on a new source-identifying meaning and functions as a mark in the eyes of the public

act-of-state doctrine—doctrine whereby every sovereign state is bound to respect the independence of every other sovereign state, and the courts of one country will not sit in judgment of another government's acts done within its own territory.

adeemed—canceled; as in a specifically bequeathed property being sold or given away by the testator prior to death, thus canceling the bequest.

adjustable rate mortgage (ARM)—mortgage with variable financing charges over the life of the loan.

administrative agency—government body charged with administering and implementing legislation.

administrative law—law governing administrative agencies.

Administrative Procedure Act—federal law that establishes the operating rules for administrative agencies.

administrative regulations—rules made by state and federal administrative agencies.

administrator, administratrix—person (man, woman) appointed to wind up and settle the estate of a person who has died without a will.

admissibility—the quality of the evidence in a case that allows it to be presented to the jury.

adverse possession—hostile possession of real estate, which when actual, visible, notorious, exclusive, and continued for the required time, will vest the title to the land in the person in such adverse possession.

advising bank—bank that tells beneficiary that letter of credit has been issued.

affidavit—statement of facts set forth in written form and supported by the oath or affirmation of the person making the statement setting forth that such facts are true on the basis of actual knowledge or on information and belief. The affidavit is executed before a notary public or other person authorized to administer oaths.

affirm—action taken by an appellate court that approves the decision of the court below.

affirmative action plan (AAP)—plan to have a diverse and representative workforce.

after-acquired goods—goods acquired after a security interest has attached.

agency—the relationship that exists between a person identified as a principal and another by virtue of which the latter may make contracts with third persons on behalf of the principal. (Parties—principal, agent, third person)

agent—person or firm who is authorized by the principal or by operation of law to make contracts with third persons on behalf of the principal.

airbill—document of title issued to a shipper whose goods are being sent via air.

alteration—unauthorized change or completion of a negotiable instrument designed to modify the obligation of a party to the instrument.

alternative payees—those persons to whom a negotiable instrument is made payable, any one of whom may indorse and take delivery of it.

ambiguous—having more than one reasonable interpretation.

answer—what a defendant must file to admit or deny facts asserted by the plaintiff.

anticipatory breach—promisor's repudiation of the contract prior to the time that performance is required when such repudiation is accepted by the promisee as a breach of the contract.

anticipatory repudiation—repudiation made in advance of the time for performance of the contract obligations.

antilapse statutes—statutes providing that the children or heirs of a deceased beneficiary may take the legacy in the place of the deceased beneficiary.

apparent authority—appearance of authority created by the principal's words or conduct.

appeal—taking a case to a reviewing court to determine whether the judgment of the lower court or administrative agency was correct. (Parties—appellant, appellee)

appellate jurisdiction—the power of a court to hear and decide a given class of cases on appeal from another court or administrative agency.

appropriation—taking of an image, likeness, or name for commercial advantage.

arbitration—the settlement of disputed questions, whether of law or fact, by

one or more arbitrators by whose decision the parties agree to be bound.

Article 2—section of the Uniform Commercial Code that governs contracts for the sale of goods.

articles of copartnership—See *Partnership Agreement.*

articles of incorporation—document filed to create a corporation; the basic structure of a company and the rights of its owners.

articles of partnership—See *Partnership Agreement.*

assignee—third party to whom contract benefits are transferred.

assignment—transfer of a right. Generally used in connection with personal property rights, as rights under a contract, commercial paper, an insurance policy, a mortgage, or a lease. (Parties—assignor, assignee)

assignor—party who assigns contract rights to a third party.

association tribunal—a court created by a trade association or group for the resolution of disputes among its members.

assumption—mortgage transfers in which the transferee and mortgagor are liable and the property is subject to foreclosure by the mortgagee if payments are not made.

attestation clause—clause that indicates a witness has observed either the execution of the will or the testator's acknowledgment of the writing as the testator's will.

attorney in fact—agent authorized to act for another under a power of attorney.

attorney-client privilege—right of individual to have discussions with his/her attorney kept private and confidential

attractive nuisance doctrine—a rule imposing liability upon a landowner for injuries sustained by small children playing on the land when the

landowner permits a condition to exist or maintains equipment that a reasonable person should realize would attract small children who could not realize the danger. The rule does not apply if an unreasonable burden would be imposed upon the landowner in taking steps to protect the children.

authorities—corporations formed by government that perform public service.

automatic perfection—perfection given by statute without specific filing or possession requirements on the part of the creditor.

automatic stay—order to prevent creditors from taking action such as filing suits or seeking foreclosure against the debtor.

B

bad check laws—laws making it a criminal offense to issue a bad check with intent to defraud.

bailee—person who accepts possession of a property.

bailee's lien—specific, possessory lien of the bailee upon the goods for work done to them. Commonly extended by statute to any bailee's claim for compensation, eliminating the necessity of retention of possession.

bailment—relationship that exists when personal property is delivered into the possession of another under an agreement, express or implied, that the identical property will be returned or will be delivered in accordance with the agreement. (Parties—bailor, bailee)

bailment for mutual benefit—bailment in which the bailor and bailee derive a benefit from the bailment.

bailor—person who turns over the possession of a property.

balance sheet test—comparison of assets to liabilities made to determine solvency.

bankruptcy—procedure by which one unable to pay debts may surrender all assets in excess of any exemption claim to the court for administration and distribution to creditors, and the debtor is given a discharge that releases him from the unpaid balance due on most debts.

bankruptcy courts—court of special jurisdiction to determine bankruptcy issues.

battle of the forms—merchants' exchanges of invoices and purchase orders with differing boilerplate terms.

bearer—person in physical possession of commercial paper payable to bearer, a document of title directing delivery to bearer, or an investment security in bearer form.

bearer paper—instrument with no payee, payable to cash or payable to bearer.

bedrock view—a strict constructionist interpretation of a constitution.

beneficiary—person to whom the proceeds of a life insurance policy are payable, a person for whose benefit property is held in trust, or a person given property by a will; the ultimate recipient of the benefit of a funds transfer.

beneficiary's bank—the final bank, which carries out the payment order, in the chain of a transfer of funds.

bequest—gift of personal property by will.

bicameral—a two-house form of the legislative branch of government.

bilateral contract—agreement under which one promise is given in exchange for another.

bill of lading—document issued by a carrier acknowledging the receipt of goods and the terms of the contract of transportation.

bill of sale—writing signed by the seller reciting that the personal property therein described has been sold to the buyer.

blackmail—extortion demands made by a nonpublic official.

blank indorsement—an indorsement that does not name the person to whom the paper, document of title, or investment security is negotiated.

blocking laws—laws that prohibit the disclosure, copying, inspection, or removal of documents located in the enacting country in compliance with orders from foreign authorities.

blue sky laws—state statutes designed to protect the public from the sale of worthless stocks and bonds.

bona fide—in good faith; without any fraud or deceit.

bond—obligation or promise in writing and sealed, generally of corporations, personal representatives, and trustees; fidelity bonds.

bond indenture—agreement setting forth the contractual terms of a particular bond issue.

book value—value found by dividing the value of the corporate assets by the number of shares outstanding.

breach—failure to act or perform in the manner called for in a contract.

breach of the peace—violation of the law in the repossession of the collateral.

brownfields—land that is a designated Superfund cleanup site but which lies fallow because no one is willing to risk liability by buying the property, even when the hazardous waste has been removed or property no one is willing to spend the money to remove the hazardous waste.

bubble concept—method for determining total emissions in one area; all sources are considered in an area.

business ethics—balancing the goal of profits with values of individuals and society.

business judgment rule (BJR)—rule that allows management immunity from liability for corporate acts where there is a reasonable indication that the acts were made in good faith with due care.

bylaws—rules and regulations enacted by a corporation to govern the affairs of the corporation and its shareholders, directors, and officers.

C

cancellation provision—crossing out of a part of an instrument or a destruction of all legal effect of the instrument, whether by act of party, upon breach by the other party, or pursuant to agreement or decree of court.

capital stock—declared money value of the outstanding stock of the corporation.

cargo insurance—insurance that protects a cargo owner against financial loss if goods being shipped are lost or damaged at sea.

carrier—individual or organization undertaking the transportation of goods.

case law—law that includes principles that are expressed for the first time in court decisions.

cash surrender value—sum paid the insured upon the surrender of a policy to the insurer.

cash tender offer—general offer to all shareholders of a target corporation to purchase their shares for cash at a specified price.

cashier's check—draft drawn by a bank on itself.

cause of action—right to damages or other judicial relief when a legally protected right of the plaintiff is violated by an unlawful act of the defendant.

cease-and-desist order—order issued by a court or administrative agency to stop a practice that it decides is improper.

certificate of deposit (CD)—promise-to-pay instrument issued by a bank.

certificate of incorporation—written approval from the state or national government for a corporation to be formed.

certificate of stock—document evidencing a shareholder's ownership of stock issued by a corporation.

certified check—check for which the bank has set aside in a special account sufficient funds to pay it; payment is made when check is presented regardless of amount in drawer's account at that time; discharges all parties except certifying bank when holder requests certification.

cestui que trust—beneficiary or person for whose benefit the property is held in trust.

CF—cost and freight.

Chapter 11 bankruptcy—reorganization form of bankruptcy under federal law.

Chapter 7 bankruptcy—liquidation form of bankruptcy under federal law.

Chapter 13 bankruptcy—proceeding of consumer debt readjustment plan bankruptcy.

charging order—order by a court, after a business partner's personal assets are exhausted, requiring that the partner's share of the profits be paid to a creditor until the debt is discharged.

charter—grant of authority from a government to exist as a corporation. Generally replaced today by a certificate of incorporation approving the articles of incorporation.

check—order by a depositor on a bank to pay a sum of money to a payee; a bill of exchange drawn on a bank and payable on demand.

choice-of-law clause—clause in an agreement that specifies which law will govern should a dispute arise.

chose in action—intangible personal property in the nature of claims

against another, such as a claim for accounts receivable or wages.

CIF—cost, insurance, and freight.

civil disobedience—the term used when natural law proponents violate positive law.

claim—right to payment.

Clayton Act—a federal law that prohibits price discrimination.

Clean Air Act—federal legislation that establishes standards for air pollution levels and prevents further deterioration of air quality.

Clean Water Act—federal legislation that regulates water pollution through a control system.

close corporation—corporation whose shares are held by a single shareholder or a small group of shareholders.

close-connection doctrine—circumstantial evidence, such as an ongoing or a close relationship, that can serve as notice of a problem with an instrument.

COD—cash on delivery.

coinsurance clause—clause requiring the insured to maintain insurance on property up to a stated amount and providing that to the extent that this is not done, the insured is to be deemed a coinsurer with the insurer, so that the latter is liable only for its proportionate share of the amount of insurance required to be carried.

collateral—property pledged by a borrower as security for a debt.

comity—principle of international and national law that the laws of all nations and states deserve the respect legitimately demanded by equal participants.

commerce clause—that section of the U.S. Constitution allocating business regulation.

commercial impracticability—situation that occurs when costs of performance rise suddenly and performance of a contract will result in a substantial loss.

commercial lease—any nonconsumer lease.

commercial paper—written, transferable, signed promise or order to pay a specified sum of money; a negotiable instrument.

commercial unit—standard of the trade for shipment or packaging of a good.

commission merchant—bailee to whom goods are consigned for sale.

commission or factorage—consignee's compensation.

common carrier—carrier that holds out its facilities to serve the general public for compensation without discrimination.

common law—the body of unwritten principles originally based upon the usages and customs of the community that were recognized and enforced by the courts.

common stock—stock that has no right or priority over any other stock of the corporation as to dividends or distribution of assets upon dissolution.

community property—cotenancy held by husband and wife in property acquired during their marriage under the law of some of the states, principally in the southwestern United States.

comparative negligence—defense to negligence that allows plaintiff to recover reduced damages based on his level of fault.

compensatory damages—sum of money that will compensate an injured plaintiff for actual loss.

complaint—the initial pleading filed by the plaintiff in many actions, which in many states may be served as original process to acquire jurisdiction over the defendant.

composition of creditors—agreement among creditors that each shall accept a partial payment as full payment in consideration of the other creditors doing the same.

Comprehensive Environmental Response, Compensation, and Liability Act (CERCLA)—federal law that authorizes the president to issue funds for the cleanup of areas that were once disposal sites for hazardous wastes.

computer crimes—wrongs committed using a computer or with knowledge of computers.

concealment—failure to volunteer information not requested.

condition—stipulation or prerequisite in a contract, will, or other instrument.

condition precedent—event that if unsatisfied would mean that no rights would arise under a contract.

condition subsequent—event whose occurrence or lack thereof terminates a contract.

condominium—combination of co-ownership and individual ownership.

confidential relationship—relationship in which, because of the legal status of the parties or their respective physical or mental conditions or knowledge, one party places full confidence and trust in the other.

conflict of interest—conduct that compromises an employee's allegiance to that company.

conglomerate—relationship of a parent corporation to subsidiary corporations engaged in diversified fields of activity unrelated to the field of activity of the parent corporation.

consent decrees—informal settlements of enforcement actions brought by agencies.

consequential damages—damages the buyer experiences as a result of the seller's breach with respect to a third party; also called *special damages.*

consideration—promise or performance that the promisor demands as the price of the promise.

consignee—(1) person to whom goods are shipped, (2) dealer who sells goods for others.

consignment—bailment made for the purpose of sale by the bailee. (Parties—consignor, consignee)

consignor—(1) person who delivers goods to the carrier for shipment, (2) party with title who turns goods over to another for sale.

consolidation (of corporations)—combining of two or more corporations in which the corporate existence of each one ceases and a new corporation is created.

conspiracy—agreement between two or more persons to commit an unlawful act.

constitution—a body of principles that establishes the structure of a government and the relationship of the government to the people who are governed.

constructive bailment—bailment imposed by law as opposed to one created by contract, whereby the bailee must preserve the property and redeliver it to the owner.

constructive delivery—See *Symbolic Delivery.*

constructive eviction—act or omission of the landlord that substantially deprives the tenant of the use and enjoyment of the premises.

consumer—any buyer afforded special protections by statute or regulation.

consumer credit—credit for personal, family, and household use.

consumer goods—goods used or bought primarily for personal, family, or household use.

consumer lease—lease of goods by a natural person for personal, family, or household use.

Consumer Product Safety Improvement Act—federal law that sets standards for the types of paints used in toys; a response to the lead paint found in toys made in China; requires tracking for international production; increases penalties

contract—a binding agreement based on the genuine assent of the parties, made for a lawful object, between competent parties, in the form required by law, and generally supported by consideration.

contract carrier—carrier that transports on the basis of individual contracts that it makes with each shipper.

contract interference—tort in which a third party interferes with others' freedom to contract.

contract of adhesion—contract offered by a dominant party to a party with inferior bargaining power on a take-it-or-leave-it basis.

contract under seal—contract executed by affixing a seal or making an impression on the paper or on some adhering substance such as wax attached to the document.

contracting agent—agent with authority to make contracts; person with whom the buyer deals.

Contracts for the International Sale of Goods (CISG)—uniform international contract code contracts for international sale of goods.

contractual capacity—ability to understand that a contract is being made and to understand its general meaning.

contribution—right of a co-obligor who has paid more than a proportionate share to demand that the other obligor pay the amount of the excess payment made.

contributory negligence—negligence of the plaintiff that contributes to injury and at common law bars recovery from the defendant although the defendant may have been more negligent than the plaintiff.

conversion—act of taking personal property by a person not entitled to it and keeping it from its true owner or prior possessor without consent.

cooperative—group of two or more persons or enterprises that acts through a common agent with respect to a common objective, such as buying or selling.

copyright—exclusive right given by federal statute to the creator of a literary or an artistic work to use, reproduce, and display the work.

corporation—artificial being created by government grant, which for many purposes is treated as a natural person.

corporation by estoppel—corporation that comes about when parties estop themselves from denying that the corporation exists.

corporation de jure—corporation with a legal right to exist by virtue of law.

correspondent bank—will honor the letter of credit from the domestic bank of the buyer.

cost plus—method of determining the purchase price or contract price equal to the seller's or contractor's costs plus a stated percentage as the profit.

co-sureties—sureties for the same debtor and obligor.

cotenancy—when two or more persons hold concurrent rights and interests in the same property.

Council on Environmental Quality (CEQ)—federal agency that establishes national policies on environmental quality and then recommends legislation to implement these policies.

counterclaim—a claim that the defendant in an action may make against the plaintiff.

counteroffer—proposal by an offeree to the offeror that changes the terms of, and thus rejects, the original offer.

course of dealing—pattern of performance between two parties to a contract.

court—a tribunal established by government to hear and decide matters properly brought to it.

covenant against encumbrances—guarantee that conveyed land is not subject to any right or interest of a third person.

covenant of further assurances—promise that the grantor of an interest in land will execute any additional documents required to perfect the title of the grantee.

covenant of quiet enjoyment—covenant by the grantor of an interest in land to not disturb the grantee's possession of the land.

covenant of right to convey—guarantee that the grantor of an interest in land, if not the owner, has the right or authority to make the conveyance to a new owner.

covenant of seisin—guarantee that the grantor of an interest in land owns the estate conveyed to a new owner.

covenants of title—grantor's covenants of a deed that guarantee such matters as the right to make the conveyance, to ownership of the property, to freedom of the property from encumbrances, or that the grantee will not be disturbed in the quiet enjoyment of the land.

credit transfer—transaction in which a person making payment, such as a buyer, requests payment be made to the beneficiary's bank.

creditor—person (seller or lender) who is owed money; also may be a secured party.

crime—violation of the law that is punished as an offense against the state or government.

cross-examination—the examination made of a witness by the attorney for the adverse party.

cumulative voting—system of voting for directors in which each shareholder has as many votes as the number of voting shares owned multiplied by the number of directors to be elected, and such votes can be distributed for the various candidates as desired.

customary authority—authority of an agent to do any act that, according to the custom of the community, usually accompanies the transaction for which the agent is authorized to act.

cybercrime—crimes committed via the Internet.

cyberlaw—laws and precedent applicable to Internet transactions and communications.

cyberspace—World Wide Web and Internet communication.

cybersquatters—term for those who register and set up domain names on the Internet for resale to the famous users of the names in question.

D

de facto—existing in fact as distinguished from as of right, as in the case of an officer or a corporation purporting to act as such without being elected to the office or having been properly incorporated.

debenture—unsecured bond of a corporation, with no specific corporate assets pledged as security for payment.

debit transfer—transaction in which a beneficiary entitled to money requests payment from a bank according to a prior agreement.

debtor—buyer on credit (i.e., a borrower).

decedent—person whose estate is being administered.

deed—instrument by which the grantor (owner of land) conveys or transfers the title to a grantee.

defamation—untrue statement by one party about another to a third party.

defendant—party charged with a violation of civil or criminal law in a proceeding.

definite time—time of payment computable from the face of the instrument.

delegated powers—powers expressly granted the national government by the Constitution.

delegation—transfer to another of the right and power to do an act.

delegation of duties—transfer of duties by a contracting party to another person who is to perform them.

delivery—constructive or actual possession.

demand draft—draft that is payable upon presentment.

demurrer—a pleading to dismiss the adverse party's pleading for not stating a cause of action or a defense.

deposition—the testimony of a witness taken out of court before a person authorized to administer oaths.

depositor—person, or bailor, who gives property for storage.

derivative action—secondary action for damages or breach of contract brought by one or more corporate shareholders against directors, officers, or third persons.

development statement—statement that sets forth significant details of a real estate or property development as required by the federal Land Sales Act.

devise—gift of real estate made by will.

devisee—beneficiary of a devise.

direct damages—losses that are caused by breach of a contract.

direct examination—examination of a witness by his or her attorney.

directed verdict—a direction by the trial judge to the jury to return a verdict in favor of a specified party to the action.

disability—any incapacity resulting from bodily injury or disease to engage in any occupation for remuneration or profit.

discharge in bankruptcy—order of the bankruptcy court relieving the debtor from obligation to pay the unpaid balance of most claims.

disclosed principal—principal whose identity is made known by the agent as well as the fact that the agent is acting on the principal's behalf.

discovery—procedures for ascertaining facts prior to the time of trial in order to eliminate the element of surprise in litigation.

dishonor—status when the primary party refuses to pay the instrument according to its terms.

disinherited—excluded from sharing in the estate of a decedent.

Dispute Settlement Body—means, provided by the World Trade Organization, for member countries to resolve trade disputes rather than engage in unilateral trade sanctions or a trade war.

distinctiveness—capable of serving the source-identifying function of a mark.

distribution per stirpes—distribution of an estate made in as many equal parts as there are family lines represented in the nearest generation; also known as stirpital distribution.

distributor—entity that takes title to goods and bears the financial and commercial risks for the subsequent sale of the goods.

divestiture order—a court order to dispose of interests that could lead to a monopoly.

divisible contract—agreement consisting of two or more parts, each calling for corresponding performances of each part by the parties.

document of title—document treated as evidence that a person is entitled to receive, hold, and dispose of the document and the goods it covers.

domestic corporation—corporation that has been incorporated by the state in question as opposed to incorporation by another state.

dominant tenement—land that is benefited by an easement.

donee—recipient of a gift.

donor—person making a gift.

double indemnity—provision for payment of double the amount specified by the insurance contract if death is caused by an accident and occurs under specified circumstances.

draft or bill of exchange—an unconditional order in writing by one person upon another, signed by the person giving it, and ordering the person to whom it is directed to pay upon demand or at a definite time a sum certain in money to order or to bearer.

drawee—person to whom the draft is addressed and who is ordered to pay the amount of money specified in the draft.

drawer—person who writes out and creates a draft or bill of exchange, including a check.

due diligence—process of checking the environmental history and nature of land prior to purchase.

due process—the constitutional right to be heard, question witnesses, and present evidence.

due process clause—in the Fifth and Fourteenth Amendments, a guarantee of protection from unreasonable procedures and unreasonable laws.

dumping—selling goods in another country at less than their fair value.

duress—conduct that deprives the victim of free will and that generally gives the victim the right to set aside any transaction entered into under such circumstances.

duty—an obligation of law imposed on a person to perform or refrain from performing a certain act.

E

easement—permanent right that one has in the land of another, as the right to cross another's land or an easement of way.

easement by implication—easement not specifically created by deed that arises from the circumstances of the parties and the land location and access.

economic duress—threat of financial loss.

Economic Espionage Act (EEA)—federal law that makes it a felony to copy, download, transmit, or in any way transfer proprietary files, documents, and information from a computer to an unauthorized person.

economic strikers—union strikers trying to enforce bargaining demands when an impasse has been reached in the negotiation process for a collective bargaining agreement.

effects doctrine—doctrine that states that U.S. courts will assume jurisdiction and will apply antitrust laws to conduct outside of the United States when the activity of business firms has direct and substantial effect on U.S. commerce; the rule has been modified to require that the effect on U.S. commerce also be foreseeable.

effluent guidelines—EPA standards for maximum ranges of discharge into water.

electronic funds transfer (EFT)—any transfer of funds (other than a transaction originated by a check, draft, or similar paper instrument) that is initiated through an electronic terminal, telephone, computer, or magnetic tape so as to authorize a financial institution to debit or credit an account.

Electronic Funds Transfer Act (EFTA)—federal law that provides consumers with rights and protections in electronic funds transfers.

eleemosynary corporation—corporation organized for a charitable or benevolent purpose.

embezzlement—statutory offense consisting of the unlawful conversion of property entrusted to the wrongdoer.

eminent domain—power of government and certain kinds of corporations to take private property against the objection of the owner, provided the taking is for a public purpose and just compensation is made for it.

emissions offset policy—controls whether new factories can be built in a nonattainment area.

employment-at-will doctrine—doctrine in which the employer has historically been allowed to terminate the employment contract at any time for any reason or for no reason.

en banc—the term used when the full panel of judges on the appellate court hears a case.

encoding warranty—warranty made by any party who encodes electronic information on an instrument; a warranty of accuracy.

Endangered Species Act (ESA)—federal law that identifies and protects species that are endangered from development or other acts that threaten their existence.

endowment insurance—insurance that pays the face amount of the policy if the insured dies within the policy period.

environmental impact statement (EIS)—formal report prepared under NEPA to document findings on the impact of a federal project on the environment.

equitable title—beneficial interest in a trust.

equity—the body of principles that originally developed because of the inadequacy of the rules then applied by the common law courts of England.

escalation clause—provision for the automatic increase of the rent at periodic intervals.

escheat—transfer to the state of the title to a decedent's property when the owner of the property dies intestate and is not survived by anyone capable of taking the property as heir.

e-sign—signature over the Internet.

estate in fee—largest estate possible, in which the owner has absolute and entire interest in the land.

estoppel—principle by which a person is barred from pursuing a certain course of action or of disputing the truth of certain matters.

ethics—a branch of philosophy dealing with values that relate to the nature of human conduct and values associated with that conduct.

ex post facto *law*—a law making criminal an act that was lawful when done or that increases the penalty when done. Such laws are generally prohibited by constitutional provisions.

exculpatory clause—provision in a contract stating that one of the parties is not liable for damages in case of breach; also called *limitation-of-liability clause*.

executed contract—agreement that has been completely performed.

execution—the carrying out of a judgment of a court, generally directing that property owned by the defendant be sold and the proceeds first be used to pay the execution or judgment creditor.

executive branch—the branch of government (e.g., the president) formed to execute the laws.

executor, executrix—person (man, woman) named in a will to administer the estate of the decedent.

executory contract—agreement by which something remains to be done by one or both parties.

exhaustion of administrative remedies—requirement that an agency make its final decision before the parties can go to court.

existing goods—goods that physically exist and are owned by the seller at the time of a transaction.

exoneration—agreement or provision in an agreement that one party shall not be held liable for loss; the right of the surety to demand that those primarily liable pay the claim for which the surety is secondarily liable.

expert witness—one who has acquired special knowledge in a particular field as through practical experience or study, or both, whose opinion is admissible as an aid to the trier of fact.

export sale—direct sale to customers in a foreign country.

express authorization—authorization of an agent to perform a certain act.

express contract—agreement of the parties manifested by their words, whether spoken or written.

express warranty—statement by the defendant relating to the goods, which statement is part of the basis of the bargain.

extortion—illegal demand by a public officer acting with apparent authority.

F

facilitation payments—(or grease payments) legal payments to speed up or ensure performance of normal government duties.

factor—bailee to whom goods are consigned for sale.

fair use—principle that allows the limited use of copyrighted material for teaching, research, and news reporting.

false imprisonment—intentional detention of a person without that person's consent; called the shopkeeper's tort when shoplifters are unlawfully detained.

FAS—free alongside the named vessel.

federal district court—a general trial court of the federal system.

Federal Register—government publication issued five days a week that lists all administrative regulations, all presidential proclamations and executive orders, and other documents and classes of documents that the president or Congress direct to be published.

Federal Register Act—federal law requiring agencies to make public disclosure of proposed rules, passed rules, and activities.

Federal Sentencing Guidelines—federal standards used by judges in determining mandatory sentence terms for those convicted of federal crimes.

federal system—the system of government in which a central government is given power to administer to national concerns while individual states retain the power to administer to local concerns.

fee simple defeasibles—fee simple interest can be lost if restrictions on its use are violated.

fee simple estate—highest level of land ownership; full interest of unlimited duration.

felony—criminal offense that is punishable by confinement in prison for more than one year or by death, or that is expressly stated by statute to be a felony.

field warehousing—stored goods under the exclusive control of a warehouse but kept on the owner's premises rather than in a warehouse.

Fifth Amendment—constitutional protection against self-incrimination; also guarantees due process.

finance lease—three-party lease agreement in which there is a lessor, a lessee, and a financier.

financing statement—brief statement (record) that gives sufficient information to alert third persons that a particular creditor may have a security interest in the collateral described.

fire insurance policy—a contract that indemnifies the insured for property destruction or damage caused by fire.

firm offer—offer stated to be held open for a specified time, which must be so held in some states even in the absence of an option contract, or under the UCC, with respect to merchants.

first-in-time provision—creditor whose interest attached first has priority in the collateral when two creditors have a secured interest.

first-to-perfect basis—rule of priorities that holds that first in time in perfecting a security interest, mortgage, judgment, lien, or other property attachment right should have priority.

fixture—personal property that has become so attached to or adapted to real estate that it has lost its character as personal property and is part of the real estate.

floating lien—claim in a changing or shifting stock of goods of the buyer.

FOB place of destination—general commercial language for delivery to the buyer.

FOB place of shipment—"ship to" contract.

forbearance—refraining from doing an act.

forcible entry and detainer—action by the landlord to have the tenant removed for nonpayment of rent.

foreclosure—procedure for enforcing a mortgage resulting in the public sale of the mortgaged property and, less commonly, in merely barring the right of the mortgagor to redeem the property from the mortgage.

foreign corporation—corporation incorporated under the laws of another state.

Foreign Corrupt Practices Act (FCPA)—federal law that makes it a felony to influence decision makers in other countries for the purpose of obtaining business, such as contracts for sales and services; also imposes financial reporting requirements on certain U.S. corporations.

forged or unauthorized indorsement—instrument indorsed by an agent for a principal without authorization or authority.

forgery—fraudulently making or altering an instrument that apparently creates or alters a legal liability of another.

formal contracts—written contracts or agreements whose formality signifies the parties' intention to abide by the terms.

Fourth Amendment—privacy protection in the U.S. Constitution; prohibits unauthorized searches and seizures.

franchise—(1) privilege or authorization, generally exclusive, to engage in a particular activity within a particular geographic area, such as a government franchise to operate a taxi company within a specified city, or a private franchise as the grant by a manufacturer of a right to sell products within a particular territory or for a particular number of years; (2) right to vote.

franchise agreement—sets forth rights of franchisee to use trademarks, etc., of franchisor.

franchisee—person to whom franchise is granted.

franchising—granting of permission to use a trademark, trade name, or copyright under specified conditions; a form of licensing.

franchisor—party granting the franchise.

fraud—making of a false statement of a past or existing fact, with knowledge of its falsity or with reckless indifference as to its truth, with the intent to cause another to rely thereon, and such person does rely thereon and is harmed thereby.

fraud in factum—fraud committed through deception on documents or the nature of the transaction as opposed to the subject matter or parties in the transaction (fraud in the inducement).

fraud in the inducement—fraud that occurs when a person is persuaded or induced to execute an instrument because of fraudulent statements.

fraud-on-the-market—a theory that in an open and developed securities market, the price of a stock is determined by the information on the company available to the public, and misleading statements will defraud purchasers of stock even if they do not directly rely on these statements.

Freedom of Information Act—federal law permitting citizens to request documents and records from administrative agencies.

freight forwarder—one who contracts to have goods transported and, in turn, contracts with carriers for such transportation.

freight insurance—insures that shipowner will receive payment for transportation charges.

full warranty—obligation of a seller to fix or replace a defective product within a reasonable time without cost to the buyer.

funds transfer—communication of instructions or requests to pay a specific sum of money to the credit of a specified account or person without an actual physical passing of money.

fungible goods—homogeneous goods of which any unit is the equivalent of any other unit.

future goods—goods that exist physically but are not owned by the seller and goods that have not yet been produced.

G

garnishment—the name given in some states to attachment proceedings.

general agent—agent authorized by the principal to transact all affairs in connection with a particular type of business or trade or to transact all business at a certain place.

general corporation code—state's code listing certain requirements for creation of a corporation.

general jurisdiction—the power to hear and decide most controversies involving legal rights and duties.

general legacies—certain sums of money bequeathed to named persons by the testator; to be paid out of the decedent's assets generally without specifying any particular fund or source from which the payment is to be made.

general partnership—partnership in which the partners conduct as co-owners a business for profit, and each partner has a right to take part in the management of the business and has unlimited liability.

general partners—partners who publicly and actively engage in the transaction of firm business.

gift—title to an owner's personal property voluntarily transferred by a party not receiving anything in exchange.

gift causa mortis—gift, made by the donor in the belief that death was immediate and impending, that is revoked or is revocable under certain circumstances.

good faith—absence of knowledge of any defects in or problems; "pure heart and an empty head."

goods—anything movable at the time it is identified as the subject of a transaction.

grantee—new owner of a land conveyance.

grantor—owner who transfers or conveys an interest in land to a new owner.

gratuitous bailment—bailment in which the bailee does not receive any compensation or advantage.

gray market goods—foreign-made goods with U.S. trademarks brought into the United States by a third party without the consent of the trademark owners to compete with these owners.

grease payments—(or facilitation payments) legal payments to speed up or ensure performance of normal government duties.

guarantor—one who undertakes the obligation of guaranty.

guaranty—agreement or promise to answer for a debt; an undertaking to pay the debt of another if the creditor first sues the debtor.

guaranty of collection—form of guaranty in which creditor cannot proceed against guarantor until after proceeding against debtor.

guaranty of payment—absolute promise to pay when a debtor defaults.

guest—transient who contracts for a room or site at a hotel.

H

hearsay evidence—statements made out of court that are offered in court as proof of the information contained in the statements and that, subject to many exceptions, are not admissible in evidence.

holder—someone in possession of an instrument that runs to that person (i.e., is made payable to that person, is indorsed to that person, or is bearer paper).

holder in due course—a holder who has given value, taken in good faith without notice of dishonor, defenses, or that instrument is overdue, and who is afforded special rights or status.

holder through a holder in due course—holder of an instrument who attains holder-in-due-course status because a holder in due course has held it previous to him or her.

holographic will—unwitnessed will written by hand.

homeowners insurance policy—combination of standard fire insurance and comprehensive personal liability insurance.

hotelkeeper—one regularly engaged in the business of offering living accommodations to all transient persons.

hull insurance—insurance that covers physical damage on a freight-moving vessel.

I

identification—point in the transaction when the buyer acquires an interest in the goods subject to the contract.

identified—term applied to particular goods selected by either the buyer or the seller as the goods called for by the sales contract.

identity theft—use of another's credit tools, social security number, or other IDs to obtain cash, goods, or credit without permission.

illusory promise—promise that in fact does not impose any obligation on the promisor.

impeach—using prior inconsistent evidence to challenge the credibility of a witness.

implied contract—contract expressed by conduct or implied or deduced from the facts.

implied warranty—warranty that was not made but is implied by law.

implied warranty of merchantability—group of promises made by the seller, the most important of which is that the goods are fit for the ordinary purposes for which they are sold.

impostor rule—an exception to the rules on liability for forgery that covers situations such as the embezzling payroll clerk.

in pari delicto—equally guilty; used in reference to a transaction as to which relief will not be granted to either party because both are equally guilty of wrongdoing.

incidental authority—authority of an agent that is reasonably necessary to execute express authority.

incidental damages—incurred by the nonbreaching party as part of the process of trying to cover (buy substitute goods) or sell (selling subject matter of contract to another); includes storage fees, commissions, and the like.

income—money earned by the principal, or property in trust, and distributed by the trustee.

incontestability clause—provision that after the lapse of a specified time the insurer cannot dispute the policy on the ground of misrepresentation or fraud of the insured or similar wrongful conduct.

incorporation by reference—contract consisting of both the original or skeleton document and the detailed statement that is incorporated in it.

incorporator—one or more natural persons or corporations who sign and file appropriate incorporation forms with a designated government official.

indemnity—right of a person secondarily liable to require that a person primarily liable pay for loss sustained when the secondary party discharges the obligation that the primary party should have discharged; the right of an agent to be paid the amount of any loss or damage sustained without fault because of obedience to the principal's instructions; an undertaking by one person for a consideration to pay another person a sum of money to indemnify that person when a specified loss is incurred.

indemnity contract—agreement by one person, for consideration, to pay another person a sum of money in the event that the other person sustains a specified loss.

indenture trustee—usually a commercial banking institution, to represent the interests of the bondholders and ensure that the terms and covenants of the bond issue are met by the corporation.

independent contractor—contractor who undertakes to perform a specified task according to the terms of a contract but over whom the other contracting party has no control except as provided for by the contract.

indorsee—party to whom special indorsement is made.

indorsement—signature of the payee on an instrument.

indorser—secondary party (or obligor) on a note.

informal contract—simple oral or written contract.

informal settlements—negotiated disposition of a matter before an administrative agency, generally without public sanctions.

infringement—violation of trademarks, patents, or copyrights by copying or using material without permission.

injunction—order of a court of equity to refrain from doing (negative injunction) or to do

(affirmative or mandatory injunction) a specified act.

inland marine—insurance that covers domestic shipments of goods over land and inland waterways.

insider—full-time corporate employee or a director or their relatives.

insider information—privileged information on company business only known to employees.

insolvency—excess of debts and liabilities over assets, or inability to pay debts as they mature.

instruction—summary of the law given to jurors by the judge before deliberation begins.

insurable interest—the right to hold a valid insurance policy on a person or property.

insurance—a plan of security against risks by charging the loss against a fund created by the payments made by policyholders.

insurance agent—agent of an insurance company.

insurance broker—independent contractor who is not employed by any one insurance company.

insured—person to whom the promise in an insurance contract is made.

insurer—promisor in an insurance contract.

integrity—the adherence to one's values and principles despite the costs and consequences.

intellectual property rights—trademark, copyright, and patent rights protected by law.

intended beneficiary—third person of a contract whom the contract is intended to benefit.

intentional infliction of emotional distress—tort that produces mental anguish caused by conduct that exceeds all bounds of decency.

intentional tort—civil wrong that results from intentional conduct.

inter vivos gift—any transaction that takes place between living persons and creates rights prior to the death of any of them.

interest in the authority—form of agency in which an agent has been given or paid for the right to exercise authority.

interest in the subject matter—form of agency in which an agent is given an interest in the property with which that agent is dealing.

interlineation—writing between the lines or adding to the provisions of a document, the effect thereof depending upon the nature of the document.

intermediary bank—bank between the originator and the beneficiary bank in the transfer of funds.

interrogatories—written questions used as a discovery tool that must be answered under oath.

intestate—condition of dying without a will as to any property.

intestate succession—distribution, made as directed by statute, of a decedent's property not effectively disposed of by will.

invasion of privacy—tort of intentional intrusion into the private affairs of another.

investigative consumer report—report on a person based on personal investigation and interviews.

invitee—person who enters another's land by invitation.

involuntary bankruptcy—proceeding in which a creditor or creditors file the petition for relief with the bankruptcy court.

issuer—party who issues a document such as a letter of credit or a document of title such as a warehouse receipt or bill of lading.

J

joint tenancy—estate held jointly by two or more with the right of survivorship as between them, unless modified by statute.

joint venture—relationship in which two or more persons or firms combine their labor or property for a single undertaking and share profits and losses equally unless otherwise agreed.

judge—primary officer of the court.

judgment lien—lien by a creditor who has won a verdict against the landowner in court.

judgment n.o.v. (or *non obstante veredicto,* "notwithstanding the verdict") — a judgment entered after verdict upon the motion of the losing party on the ground that the verdict is so wrong that a judgment should be entered the opposite of the verdict.

judicial branch—the branch of government (courts) formed to interpret the laws.

judicial or execution sale—sale made under order of court by an officer appointed to make the sale or by an officer having such authority as incident to the office. The sale may have the effect of divesting liens on the property.

judicial triage—court management tool used by judges to expedite certain cases in which time is of the essence, such as asbestos cases in which the plaintiffs are gravely ill.

jurisdiction—the power of a court to hear and determine a given class of cases; the power to act over a particular defendant.

jurisdictional rule of reason—rule that balances the vital interests, including laws and policies, of the United States with those of a foreign country.

jury—a body of citizens sworn by a court to determine by verdict the issues of fact submitted to them.

L

land—earth, including all things embedded in or attached thereto, whether naturally or by the act of humans.

landlord—one who leases real property to another.

law—the order or pattern of rules that society establishes to govern the conduct of individuals and the relationships among them.

lease—agreement between the owner of property and a tenant by which the former agrees to give possession of the property to the latter in consideration of the payment of rent. (Parties—landlord or lessor, tenant or lessee)

leasehold estate—interest of a tenant in rented land.

legacy—gift of money made by will.

legal title—title held by the trustee in a trust situation.

legatee—beneficiary who receives a gift of personal property by will.

legislative branch—the branch of government (e.g., Congress) formed to make the laws.

lessee—one who has a possessory interest in real or personal property under a lease; a tenant.

lessor—one who conveys real or personal property by a lease; a landlord.

letter of credit—commercial device used to guarantee payment to a seller, primarily in an international business transaction.

letters of administration—written authorization given to an administrator of an estate as evidence of appointment and authority.

letters testamentary—written authorization given to an executor of an estate as evidence of appointment and authority.

liability insurance—covers the shipowner's liability if the ship causes damage to another ship or its cargo.

libel—written or visual defamation without legal justification.

license—personal privilege to do some act or series of acts upon the land of another, as the placing of a sign thereon, not amounting to an easement or a right of possession.

licensee—someone on another's premises with the permission of the occupier, whose duty is to warn the licensee of nonobvious dangers.

licensing—transfer of technology rights to a product so that it may be produced by a different business organization in a foreign country in exchange for royalties and other payments as agreed.

lien—claim or right, against property, existing by virtue of the entry of a judgment against its owner or by the entry of a judgment and a levy thereunder on the property, or because of the relationship of the claimant to the particular property, such as an unpaid seller.

life estate—an estate for the duration of a life.

limitation-of-liability clause—provision in a contract stating that one of the parties shall not be liable for damages in case of breach; also called an exculpatory clause.

limited covenant—any covenant that does not provide the complete protection of a full covenant.

limited defenses—defenses available to secondary parties if the presenting party is a holder in due course.

limited liability partnership (LLP)— partnership in which at least one partner has a liability limited to the loss of the capital contribution made to the partnership.

limited partner—partner who neither takes part in the management of the partnership nor appears to the public to be a general partner.

limited partnership—partnership that can be formed by "one or more general partners and one or more limited partners."

limited (special) jurisdiction—the authority to hear only particular kinds of cases.

limited warranty—any warranty that does not provide the complete protection of a full warranty.

lineals—relationship that exists when one person is a direct descendant of the other; also called lineal descendants.

liquidated damages—damages established in advance of breach as an alternative to establishing compensatory damages at the time of the breach.

liquidated damages clause—specification of exact compensation in case of a breach of contract.

liquidation—process of converting property into money whether of particular items of property or of all the assets of a business or an estate.

living trust—trust created to take effect within the lifetime of the settlor; also called inter vivos trust.

living will—document by which individuals may indicate that if they become unable to express their wishes and are in an irreversible, incurable condition, they do not want life-sustaining medical treatments.

living-document view—the term when a constitution is interpreted according to changes in conditions.

lottery—any plan by which a consideration is given for a chance to win a prize; it consists of three elements: (1) there must be a payment of money or something of value for an opportunity to win, (2) a prize must be available, and (3) the prize must be offered by lot or chance.

M

mailbox rule—timing for acceptance tied to proper acceptance.

maker—party who writes or creates a promissory note.

malpractice—when services are not properly rendered in accordance with commonly accepted standards; negligence by a professional in performing his or her skill.

marine insurance—policies that cover perils relating to the transportation of goods.

market power—the ability to control price and exclude competitors.

market value—price at which a share of stock can be voluntarily bought or sold in the open market.

mask work—specific form of expression embodied in a chip design, including the stencils used in manufacturing semiconductor chip products.

mass picketing—illegal tactic of employees massing together in great numbers to effectively shut down entrances of the employer's facility.

maturity date—date that a corporation is required to repay a loan to a bondholder.

means test—new standard under the Reform Act that requires the court to find that the debtor does not have the means to repay creditors; goes beyond the past requirement of petitions being granted on the simple assertion of the debtor saying, "I have debts."

mechanic's lien—protection afforded by statute to various kinds of laborers and persons supplying materials, by giving them a lien on the building and land that has been improved or added to by them.

mediation—the settlement of a dispute through the use of a messenger who carries to each side of the dispute the issues and offers in the case.

merchant—seller who deals in specific goods classified by the UCC.

merger (of corporations)—combining of corporations by which one absorbs the other and continues to exist, preserving its original charter and identity while the other corporation ceases to exist.

minitrial—a trial held on portions of the case or certain issues in the case.

Miranda *warnings*—warnings required to prevent self-incrimination in a criminal matter.

mirror image rule—common law contract rule on acceptance that requires language to be absolutely the same as the offer, unequivocal and unconditional.

misdemeanor—criminal offense with a sentence of less than one year that is neither treason nor a felony.

misrepresentation—false statement of fact made innocently without any intent to deceive.

mistrial—a court's declaration that terminates a trial and postpones it to a later date; commonly entered when evidence has been of a highly prejudicial character or when a juror has been guilty of misconduct.

money—medium of exchange.

money order—draft issued by a bank or a nonbank.

moral relativism—takes into account motivation and circumstance to determine whether an act was ethical.

mortgage—interest in land given by the owner to a creditor as security for the payment of the creditor for a debt, the nature of the interest depending upon the law of the state where the land is located. (Parties—mortgagor, mortgagee) *most-favored-nation clause*—clause in treaties between countries whereby any privilege subsequently granted to a third country in relation to a given treaty subject is extended to the other party to the treaty.

motion for summary judgment—request that the court decide a case on basis of law only because there are no material issues disputed by the parties.

motion to dismiss—a pleading that may be filed to attack the adverse party's pleading as not stating a cause of action or a defense.

N

National Environmental Policy Act (NEPA)—federal law that mandates study of a project's impact on the environment before it can be undertaken by any federal agency.

natural law—a system of principles to guide human conduct independent of, and sometimes contrary to, enacted law and discovered by man's rational intelligence.

necessaries—things indispensable or absolutely necessary for the sustenance of human life.

negligence—failure to exercise due care under the circumstances in consequence of which harm is proximately caused to one to whom the defendant owed a duty to exercise due care.

negotiability—quality of an instrument that affords special rights and standing.

negotiable bill of lading—document of title that by its terms calls for goods to be delivered "to the bearer" or "to the order of" a named person.

negotiable instruments—drafts, promissory notes, checks, and certificates of deposit that, in proper form, give special rights as "negotiable commercial paper."

negotiable warehouse receipt—receipt that states the covered goods will be delivered "to the bearer" or "to the order of."

negotiation—the transfer of commercial paper by indorsement and delivery by the person to whom it is then payable in the case of order paper and by physical transfer in the case of bearer paper.

Noise Control Act—federal law that controls noise emissions from low-flying aircraft.

nominal damages—nominal sum awarded the plaintiff in order to establish that legal rights have been violated although the plaintiff in fact has not sustained any actual loss or damages.

nonattainment areas—"dirty" areas that do not meet federal standards under the Clean Air Act.

nonconforming use—use of land that conflicts with a zoning ordinance at the time the ordinance goes into effect.

nonconsumer lease—lease that does not satisfy the definition of a consumer lease; also known as a commercial lease.

nonnegotiable bill of lading—See *Straight Bill of Lading.*

nonnegotiable instrument—contract, note, or draft that does not meet negotiability requirements of Article 3.

nonnegotiable warehouse receipt—receipt that states the covered goods received will be delivered to a specific person.

notice of dishonor—notice that an instrument has been dishonored; such notice can be oral, written, or electronic but is subject to time limitations.

notice statute—statute under which the last good faith or bona fide purchaser holds the title.

notice-race statute—statute under which the first bona fide purchaser to record the deed holds the title.

novation—substitution for an old contract with a new one that either replaces an existing obligation with a new obligation or replaces an original party with a new party.

nuisance—conduct that harms or prejudices another in the use of land or that harms or prejudices the public.

O

obligee—promisee who can claim the benefit of the obligation.

obligor—promisor.

ocean marine—policies that cover transportation of goods in vessels in international and coastal trade.

offer—expression of an offeror's willingness to enter into a contractual agreement.

offeree—person to whom an offer is made.

offeror—person who makes an offer.

Oil Pollution Act—federal law that assigns cleanup liability for oil spills in U.S. waters.

ombudsman—a government official or organization employee designated by statute or the organization/company to examine citizen and/or employee complaints.

open meeting law—law that requires advance notice of agency meeting and public access.

opening statements—statements by opposing attorneys that tell the jury what their cases will prove.

operation of law—attaching of certain consequences to certain facts because of legal principles that operate automatically as contrasted with consequences that arise because of the voluntary action of a party designed to create those consequences.

option contract—contract to hold an offer to make a contract open for a fixed period of time.

order of relief—the order from the bankruptcy judge that starts the protection for the debtor; when the order of relief is entered by the court, the debtor's creditors must stop all proceedings and work through the bankruptcy court to recover debts (if possible). Court finding that creditors have met the standards for bankruptcy petitions.

order paper—instrument payable to the order of a party.

original jurisdiction—the authority to hear a controversy when it is first brought to court.

originator—party who originates the funds transfer.

output contract—contract of a producer to sell its entire production or output to a buyer.

outstanding—name for shares of a company that have been issued to stockholders.

overdraft—negative balance in a drawer's account.

P

par value—specified monetary amount assigned by an issuing corporation for each share of its stock.

parol evidence rule—rule that prohibits the introduction into evidence of oral or written statements made prior to or contemporaneously with the execution of a complete written contract, deed, or instrument, in the absence of clear proof of fraud, accident, or mistake causing the omission of the statement in question.

partially disclosed principal—principal whose existence is made known but whose identity is not.

partner—one of two or more persons who jointly own and carry on a business for profit.

partnership—pooling of capital resources and the business or professional talents of two or more individuals (partners) with the goal of making a profit.

partnership agreement—document prepared to evidence the contract of the parties. (Parties—partners or general partners)

party—person involved in a legal transaction; may be a natural person, an artificial person (e.g., a corporation), or an unincorporated enterprise (e.g., a government agency).

past consideration—something that has been performed in the past and which, therefore, cannot be consideration for a promise made in the present.

payable to order—term stating that a negotiable instrument is payable to the order of any person described in it or to a person or order.

payee—party to whom payment is to be made.

payment order—direction given by an originator to his or her bank or by any bank to a subsequent bank to make a specified funds transfer.

per capita—method of distributing estate assets on an equal-per-person basis.

per stirpes—method for distribution of an estate that divides property equally down family lines.

perfected security interest—security interest with priority because of filing, possession, automatic or temporary priority status.

periodic tenancy—tenancy that continues indefinitely for a specified rental period until terminated; often called a month-to-month tenancy.

personal property—property that is movable or intangible, or rights in such things.

personal representative—administrator or executor who represents decedents under UPC.

physical duress—threat of physical harm to person or property.

plaintiff—the party who initiates a lawsuit.

pleadings—the papers filed by the parties in an action in order to set forth the facts and frame the issues to be tried, although, under some systems, the pleadings merely give notice or a general indication of the nature of the issues.

pledge—bailment given as security for the payment of a debt or the performance of an obligation owed to the pledgee. (Parties—pledgor, pledgee)

police power—the power to govern; the power to adopt laws for the protection of the public health, welfare, safety, and morals.

policy—paper evidencing the contract of insurance.

positive law—law enacted and codified by governmental authority.

possession—exclusive dominion and control of property.

possibility of reverter—nature of the interest held by the grantor after conveying land outright but subject to a condition or provision that may cause the grantee's interest to become forfeited and the interest to revert to the grantor or heirs.

postdate—to insert or place on an instrument a later date than the actual date on which it was executed.

power of attorney—written authorization to an agent by the principal.

precedent—a decision of a court that stands as the law for a particular problem in the future.

predatory lending—a practice on the part of the subprime lending market whereby lenders take advantage of less sophisticated consumers or those who are desperate for funds by using the lenders' superior bargaining positions to obtain credit terms that go well beyond compensating them for their risk.

predicate act—qualifying underlying offense for RICO liability.

preemption—the federal government's superior regulatory position over state laws on the same subject area.

preemptive right—shareholder's right upon the increase of a corporation's capital stock to be allowed to subscribe to such a percentage of the new shares as the shareholder's old shares bore to the former total capital stock.

preferences—transfers of property by a debtor to one or more specific creditors to enable these creditors to obtain payment for debts owed.

preferential transfers—certain transfers of money or security interests in the time frame just prior to bankruptcy that can be set aside if voidable.

preferred stock—stock that has a priority or preference as to payment of dividends or upon liquidation, or both.

prescription—acquisition of a right to use the land of another, as an easement, by making hostile, visible, and notorious use of the land, continuing for the period specified by the local law.

presentment—formal request for payment on an instrument.

price discrimination—the charging practice by a seller of different prices to different buyers for commodities of similar grade and quality, resulting in reduced competition or a tendency to create a monopoly.

prima facie—evidence that, if believed, is sufficient by itself to lead to a particular conclusion.

primary party—party to whom the holder or holder in due course must turn first to obtain payment.

primary picketing—legal presentations in front of a business notifying the public of a labor dispute.

primum non nocere—"above all do no harm."

principal—person or firm who employs an agent; person who, with

respect to a surety, is primarily liable to the third person or creditor; property held in trust.

principal debtor—original borrower or debtor.

prior art—a showing that an invention as a whole would have been obvious to a person of ordinary skill in the art when the invention was patented

private carrier—carrier owned by the shipper, such as a company's own fleet of trucks.

private corporation—corporation organized for charitable and benevolent purposes or for purposes of finance, industry, and commerce.

private law—the rules and regulations parties agree to as part of their contractual relationships.

private nuisance—nuisance that affects only one or a few individuals.

privileges and immunities clause—a clause that entitles a person going into another state to make contracts, own property, and engage in business to the same extent as citizens of that state.

privity—succession or chain of relationship to the same thing or right, such as privity of contract, privity of estate, privity of possession.

privity of contract—relationship between a promisor and the promisee.

privity rule—succession or chain of relationship to the same thing or right, such as privity of contract, privity of estate, privity of possession.

pro rata—proportionately, or divided according to a rate or standard.

probate—procedure for formally establishing or proving that a given writing is the last will and testament of the person who purportedly signed it.

procedural law—the law that must be followed in enforcing rights and liabilities.

process—paperwork served personally on a defendant in a civil case.

product disparagement—false statements made about a product or business.

profit—right to take a part of the soil or produce of another's land, such as timber or water.

promisee—person to whom a promise is made.

promisor—person who makes a promise.

promissory estoppel—doctrine that a promise will be enforced although it is not supported by consideration when the promisor should have reasonably expected that the promise would induce action or forbearance of a definite and substantial character on the part of the promised and injustice can be avoided only by enforcement of the promise.

promissory note—unconditional promise in writing made by one person to another, signed by the maker engaging to pay on demand, or at a definite time, a sum certain in money to order or to bearer. (Parties—maker, payee)

promoters—persons who plan the formation of the corporation and sell or promote the idea to others.

proof of claim—written statement, signed by the creditor or an authorized representative, setting forth any claim made against the debtor and the basis for it.

property report—condensed version of a property development statement filed with the secretary of HUD and given to a prospective customer at least 48 hours before signing a contract to buy or lease property.

prosecutor—party who originates a criminal proceeding.

prospectus—information provided to each potential purchaser of securities setting forth the key information contained in the registration statement.

proxy—written authorization by a shareholder to another person to vote the stock owned by the shareholder; the person who is the holder of such a written authorization.

public corporation—corporation that has been established for governmental purposes and for the administration of public affairs.

public nuisance—nuisance that affects the community or public at large.

public policy—certain objectives relating to health, morals, and integrity of government that the law seeks to advance by declaring invalid any contract that conflicts with those objectives even though there is no statute expressly declaring such a contract illegal.

public warehouses—entities that serve the public generally without discrimination.

pump-and-dump—self-touting a stock to drive its price up and then selling it.

punitive damages—damages, in excess of those required to compensate the plaintiff for the wrong done, that are imposed in order to punish the defendant because of the particularly wanton or willful character of wrongdoing; also called exemplary damages.

purchase money security interest (PMSI)—the security interest in the goods a seller sells on credit that become the collateral for the creditor/seller.

Q

qualified indorsement—an indorsement that includes words such as "without recourse" that disclaims certain liability of the indorser to a maker or a drawee.

qualified privilege—media privilege to print inaccurate information without liability for defamation, so long as a retraction is printed and there was no malice.

quantum meruit—"as much as deserved;" an action brought for the value of the services rendered the defendant when there was no express contract as to the purchase price.

quasi contract—court-imposed obligation to prevent unjust enrichment in the absence of a contract.

quasi-judicial proceedings—forms of hearings in which the rules of evidence and procedure are more relaxed but each side still has a chance to be heard.

quasi-public corporation—private corporation furnishing services on which the public is particularly dependent, for example, a gas and electric company.

quitclaim deed—deed by which the grantor purports to give up only whatever right or title the grantor may have in the property without specifying or warranting transfer of any particular interest.

quorum—minimum number of persons, shares represented, or directors who must be present at a meeting in order to lawfully transact business.

R

race statute—statute under which the first party to record the deed holds the title.

race-notice statute—See *Notice-Race Statute*.

Racketeer Influenced and Corrupt Organizations (RICO) Act—federal law, initially targeting organized crime, that has expanded in scope and provides penalties and civil recovery for multiple criminal offenses, or a pattern of racketeering.

real property—land and all rights in land.

recognizance—obligation entered into before a court to do some act, such as to appear at a later date for a hearing. Also called a *contract of record*.

recorder—public official in charge of deeds.

recross-examination—an examination by the other side's attorney that follows the redirect examination.

redemption—buying back of one's property, which has been sold because of a default, upon paying the amount that had been originally due together with interest and costs.

redirect examination—questioning after cross-examination, in which the attorney for the witness testifying may ask the same witness other questions to overcome effects of the cross-examination.

reference to a third person—settlement that allows a nonparty to resolve the dispute.

reformation—remedy by which a written instrument is corrected when it fails to express the actual intent of both parties because of fraud, accident, or mistake.

registered bonds—bonds held by owners whose names and addresses are registered on the books of the corporation.

registration requirements—provisions of the Securities Act of 1933 requiring advance disclosure to the public of a new securities issue through filing a statement with the SEC and sending a prospectus to each potential purchaser.

registration statement—document disclosing specific financial information regarding the security, the issuer, and the underwriter.

remainder interest—land interest that follows a life estate.

remand—term used when an appellate court sends a case back to trial court for additional hearings or a new trial.

remedy—action or procedure that is followed in order to enforce a right or to obtain damages for injury to a right.

rent-a-judge plan—dispute resolution through private courts with judges paid to be referees for the cases.

representative capacity—action taken by one on behalf of another, as the act of a personal representative on behalf of a decedent's estate, or action taken both on one's behalf and on behalf of others, as a shareholder bringing a representative action.

repudiation—result of a buyer or seller refusing to perform the contract as stated.

request for production of documents—discovery tool for uncovering paper evidence in a case.

requirements contract—contract in which the buyer buys its needs (requirements) from the seller.

rescission—action of one party to a contract to set the contract aside when the other party is guilty of a breach of the contract.

reservation of rights—assertion by a party to a contract that even though a tendered performance (e.g., a defective product) is accepted, the right to damages for nonconformity to the contract is reserved.

Resource Conservation and Recovery Act (RCRA)—federal law that regulates the disposal of potentially harmful substances and encourages resource conservation and recovery.

Resource Recovery Act—early federal solid waste disposal legislation that provided funding for states and local governments with recycling programs.

respondeat superior—doctrine that the principal or employer is vicariously liable for the unauthorized torts committed by an agent or employee while acting within the scope of the agency

or the course of the employment, respectively.

restrictive covenants—covenants in a deed by which the grantee agrees to refrain from doing specified acts.

restrictive indorsement—an indorsement that restricts further transfer, such as in trust for or to the use of some other person, is conditional, or for collection or deposit.

reverse—the term used when the appellate court sets aside the verdict or judgment of a lower court.

reverse mortgage—mortgage in which the owners get their equity out of their home over a period of time and return the house to the lender upon their deaths.

reversible error—an error or defect in court proceedings of so serious a nature that on appeal the appellate court will set aside the proceedings of the lower court.

reversionary interest—interest that a lessor has in property that is subject to an outstanding lease.

revoke—testator's act of taking back his or her will and its provisions.

right—legal capacity to require another person to perform or refrain from an action.

right of escheat—right of the state to take the property of a decedent that has not been distributed.

right of first refusal—right of a party to meet the terms of a proposed contract before it is executed, such as a real estate purchase agreement.

right of privacy—the right to be free from unreasonable intrusion by others.

right to cure—second chance for a seller to make a proper tender of conforming goods.

right-to-work laws—laws restricting unions and employees from negotiating clauses in their collective

bargaining agreements that make union membership compulsory.

risk—peril or contingency against which the insured is protected by the contract of insurance.

risk of loss—in contract performance, the cost of damage or injury to the goods contracted for.

Robinson-Patman Act—a federal statute designed to eliminate price discrimination in interstate commerce.

run with the land—concept that certain covenants in a deed to land are deemed to run or pass with the land so that whoever owns the land is bound by or entitled to the benefit of the covenants.

S

Safe Drinking Water Act—a federal law that establishes national standards for contaminants in drinking water.

sale on approval—term indicating that no sale takes place until the buyer approves or accepts the goods.

sale or return—sale in which the title to the property passes to the buyer at the time of the transaction but the buyer is given the option of returning the property and restoring the title to the seller.

search engine—Internet service used to locate Web sites.

search warrant—judicial authorization for a search of property where there is the expectation of privacy.

seasonable—timely.

secondary meaning—a legal term signifying the words in question have taken on a new meaning with the public, capable of serving a source-identifying function of a mark.

secondary parties—called secondary obligors under Revised Article 3; parties to an instrument to whom holders turn when the primary party, for whatever reason, fails to pay the instrument.

secondary picketing—picketing an employer with which a union has no dispute to persuade the employer to stop doing business with a party to the dispute; generally illegal under the NLRA.

secrecy laws—confidentiality laws applied to home-country banks.

secured party—person owed the money, whether as a seller or a lender, in a secured transaction in personal property.

secured transaction—credit sale of goods or a secured loan that provides special protection for the creditor.

securities—stocks and bonds issued by a corporation. Under some investor protection laws, the term includes any interest in an enterprise that provides unearned income to its owner.

security agreement—agreement of the creditor and the debtor that the creditor will have a security interest.

security interest—property right that enables the creditor to take possession of the property if the debtor does not pay the amount owed.

self-help repossession—creditor's right to repossess the collateral without judicial proceedings.

self-proved wills—wills that eliminate some formalities of proof by being executed according to statutory requirements.

selling on consignment—entrusting a person with possession of property for the purpose of sale.

semiconductor chip product—product placed on a piece of semiconductor material in accordance with a predetermined pattern that is intended to perform electronic circuitry functions.

service mark—mark that identifies a service.

servient tenement—land that is subject to an easement.

settlor—one who settles property in trust or creates a trust estate.

severalty—ownership of property by one person.

shared powers—powers that are held by both state and national governments.

Sherman Antitrust Act—a federal statute prohibiting combinations and contracts in restraint of interstate trade, now generally inapplicable to labor union activity.

shop right—right of an employer to use in business without charge an invention discovered by an employee during working hours and with the employer's material and equipment.

shopkeeper's privilege—right of a store owner to detain a suspected shoplifter based on reasonable cause and for a reasonable time without resulting liability for false imprisonment.

short-swing profit—profit realized by a corporate insider from selling securities less than six months after purchase.

sinking fund—fixed amount of money set aside each year by the borrowing corporation toward the ultimate payment of bonds.

situational ethics—a flexible standard of ethics that permits an examination of circumstances and motivation before attaching the label of right or wrong to conduct.

Sixth Amendment—the U.S. constitutional amendment that guarantees a speedy trial.

slander—defamation of character by spoken words or gestures.

slander of title—malicious making of false statements as to a seller's title.

small claims courts—courts that resolve disputes between parties when those disputes do not exceed a minimal

level; no lawyers are permitted; the parties represent themselves.

sole or individual proprietorship—form of business ownership in which one individual owns the business.

soliciting agent—salesperson.

sovereign compliance doctrine—doctrine that allows a defendant to raise as an affirmative defense to an antitrust action the fact that the defendant's actions were compelled by a foreign state.

sovereign immunity doctrine—doctrine that states that a foreign sovereign generally cannot be sued unless an exception to the Foreign Sovereign Immunities Act of 1976 applies.

special agent—agent authorized to transact a specific transaction or to do a specific act.

special drawing rights (SDRs)—rights that allow a country to borrow enough money from other International Money Fund (IMF) members to permit that country to maintain the stability of its currency's relationship to other world currencies.

special indorsement—an indorsement that specifies the person to whom the instrument is indorsed.

specific legacies—identified property bequeathed by a testator; also called specific devises.

specific lien—right of a creditor to hold particular property or assert a lien on particular property of the debtor because of the creditor's having done work on or having some other association with the property, as distinguished from having a lien generally against the assets of the debtor merely because the debtor is indebted to the lien holder.

specific performance—action brought to compel the adverse party to perform a contract on the theory that merely suing for damages for its breach will not be an adequate remedy.

spendthrift trust—a trust that, to varying degrees, provides that creditors of the beneficiary shall not be able to reach the principal or income held by the trustee and that the beneficiary shall not be able to assign any interest in the trust.

spot zoning—allowing individual variation in zoning.

stakeholder analysis—the term used when a decision maker views a problem from different perspectives and measures the impact of a decision on various groups.

stakeholders—those who have a stake, or interest, in the activities of a corporation; stakeholders include employees, members of the community in which the corporation operates, vendors, customers, and any others who are affected by the actions and decisions of the corporation.

stale check—a check whose date is longer than six months ago.

standby letter—letter of credit for a contractor ensuring he will complete the project as contracted.

stare decisis—"let the decision stand"; the principle that the decision of a court should serve as a guide or precedent and control the decision of a similar case in the future.

status quo ante—original positions of the parties.

statute of frauds—statute that, in order to prevent fraud through the use of perjured testimony, requires that certain kinds of transactions be evidenced in writing in order to be binding or enforceable.

statute of limitations—statute that restricts the period of time within which an action may be brought.

statutory law—legislative acts declaring, commanding, or prohibiting something.

stay of foreclosure—delay of foreclosure obtained by the mortgagor to prevent undue hardship.

stirpes—family lines; distribution per stirpes refers to the manner in which descendants take property by right of representation.

stock subscription—contract or agreement to buy a specific number and kind of shares when they are issued by the corporation.

stop payment order—order by a depositor to the bank to refuse to make payment of a check when presented for payment.

straight (or nonnegotiable) bill of lading—document of title that consigns transported goods to a named person.

strict liability—civil wrong for which there is absolute liability because of the inherent danger in the underlying activity, for example, the use of explosives.

strict tort liability—product liability theory that imposes liability upon the manufacturer, seller, or distributor of goods for harm caused by defective goods.

subject matter jurisdiction—judicial authority to hear a particular type of case.

sublease—a transfer of the premises by the lessee to a third person, the sublessee or subtenant, for a period of less than the term of the original lease.

sublessee—person with lease rights for a period of less than the term of the original lease; also known as subtenant.

subprime lending market—a credit market that makes loans to high-risk consumers (those who have bankruptcies, no credit history, or a poor credit history), often loaning money to pay off other debts the consumer has due.

subrogation—right of a party secondarily liable to stand in the place of the creditor after making payment to the creditor and to enforce the creditor's

right against the party primarily liable in order to obtain indemnity from such primary party.

substantial impairment—material defect in a good.

substantial performance—equitable rule that if a good-faith attempt to perform does not precisely meet the terms of the agreement, the agreement will still be considered complete if the essential purpose of the contract is accomplished.

substantive law—the law that defines rights and liabilities.

substitute check—electronic image of a paper check that a bank can create and that has the same legal effect as the original instrument.

substitution—substitution of a new contract between the same parties.

sum certain—amount due under an instrument that can be computed from its face with only reference to interest rates.

summary jury trial—a mock or dry-run trial for parties to get a feel for how their cases will play to a jury.

summation—the attorney address that follows all the evidence presented in court and sums up a case and recommends a particular verdict be returned by the jury.

Superfund Amendment and Reauthorization Act—federal law that authorizes the EPA to collect cleanup costs from those responsible for the ownership, leasing, dumping, or security of hazardous waste sites.

Superfund sites—areas designated by the EPA for cleanup of hazardous waste.

surety—obligor of a suretyship; primarily liable for the debt or obligation of the principal debtor.

suretyship—undertaking to pay the debt or be liable for the default of another.

symbolic delivery—delivery of goods by delivery of the means of control, such as a key or a relevant document of title, such as a negotiable bill of lading; also called constructive delivery.

T

takeover laws—laws that guard against unfairness in corporate takeover situations.

tariff—(1) domestically—government-approved schedule of charges that may be made by a regulated business, such as a common carrier or warehouser; (2) internationally—tax imposed by a country on goods crossing its borders, without regard to whether the purpose is to raise revenue or to discourage the traffic in the taxed goods.

tax lien—lien on property by a government agency for nonpayment of taxes.

teller's check—draft drawn by a bank on another bank in which it has an account.

temporary insider—someone retained by a corporation for professional services on an as-needed basis, such as an attorney, accountant, or investment banker.

temporary perfection—perfection given for a limited period of time to creditors.

tenancy at sufferance—lease arrangement in which the tenant occupies the property at the discretion of the landlord.

tenancy at will—holding of land for an indefinite period that may be terminated at any time by the landlord or by the landlord and tenant acting together.

tenancy by entirety or tenancy by entireties—transfer of property to both husband and wife.

tenancy for years—tenancy for a fixed period of time, even though the time is less than a year.

tenancy in common—relationship that exists when two or more persons own undivided interests in property.

tenancy in partnership—ownership relationship that exists between partners under the Uniform Partnership Act.

tenant—one who holds or possesses real property by any kind of right or title; one who pays rent for the temporary use and occupation of another's real property under a lease.

tender—goods have arrived, are available for pickup, and buyer is notified.

term insurance—policy written for a specified number of years that terminates at the end of that period.

termination statement—document (record), which may be requested by a paid-up debtor, stating that a security interest is no longer claimed under the specified financing statement.

testamentary capacity—sufficient mental capacity to understand that a writing being executed is a will and what that entails.

testamentary intent—designed to take effect at death, as by disposing of property or appointing a personal representative.

testamentary trust—trust that becomes effective only when the settlor's will takes effect after death.

testate—condition of leaving a will upon death.

testate distribution—distribution of an estate in accordance with the will of the decedent.

testator, testatrix—man, woman who makes a will.

third-party beneficiary—third person whom the parties to a contract intend to benefit by the making of the contract and to confer upon such person the right to sue for breach of contract.

time draft—bill of exchange payable at a stated time after sight or at a definite time.

tippee—individual who receives information about a corporation from an insider or temporary insider.

tort—civil wrong that interferes with one's property or person.

Toxic Substances Control Act (TOSCA)—first federal law to control the manufacture, use, and disposal of toxic substances.

trade dress—product's total image including its overall packaging look.

trade libel—written defamation about a product or service.

trade name—name under which a business is carried on and, if fictitious, must be registered.

trade secret—any formula, device, or compilation of information that is used in one's business and is of such a nature that it provides an advantage over competitors who do not have the information.

trademark—mark that identifies a product.

transferee—buyer or vendee.

traveler's check—check that is payable on demand provided it is countersigned by the person whose specimen signature appears on the check.

treasury stock—corporate stock that the corporation has reacquired.

treble damages—three times the damages actually sustained.

trespass—an unauthorized action with respect to person or property.

trial de novo—a trial required to preserve the constitutional right to a jury trial by allowing an appeal to proceed as though there never had been any prior hearing or decision.

tripartite—three-part division (of government).

trust—transfer of property by one person to another with the understanding or declaration that such property be held for the benefit of another; the holding of property by the owner in trust for another, upon a declaration of trust, without a transfer to another person. (Parties—settlor, trustee, beneficiary)

trust agreement—instrument creating a trust; also called deed of trust.

trust corpus—fund or property that is transferred to the trustee or held by the settlor as the body or subject matter of the trust; also called *trust fund, trust estate,* and *trust res.*

trustee—party who has legal title to estate and manages it.

trustee in bankruptcy—impartial person elected to administer the debtor's estate.

trustor—donor or settlor who is the owner of property and creates a trust in the property.

tying—the anticompetitive practice of requiring buyers to purchase one product in order to get another.

U

ultra vires—act or contract that the corporation does not have authority to do or make.

unconscionable—unreasonable, not guided or restrained by conscience and often referring to a contract grossly unfair to one party because of the superior bargaining powers of the other party.

underwriter—insurer.

undisclosed principal—principal on whose behalf an agent acts without disclosing to the third person the fact of agency or the identity of the principal.

undue influence—influence that is asserted upon another person by one who dominates that person.

Uniform Probate Code (UPC)—uniform statute on wills and administration of estates.

Uniform Simultaneous Death Act—law providing that when survivorship

cannot be established, the property of each person shall be disposed of as though he or she had survived the other.

unilateral contract—contract under which only one party makes a promise.

unincorporated association—combination of two or more persons for the furtherance of a common nonprofit purpose.

universal agent—agent authorized by the principal to do all acts that can lawfully be delegated to a representative.

universal defenses—defenses that are regarded as so basic that the social interest in preserving them outweighs the social interest of giving negotiable instruments the freely transferable qualities of money; accordingly, such defenses are given universal effect and may be raised against all holders.

USA Patriot Act—federal law that, among other things, imposes reporting requirements on banks.

usage of trade—language and customs of an industry.

usury—lending money at an interest rate that is higher than the maximum rate allowed by law.

uttering—crime of issuing or delivering a forged instrument to another person.

V

valid—legal.

valid contract—agreement that is binding and enforceable.

value—consideration or antecedent debt or security given in exchange for the transfer of a negotiable instrument or creation of a security interest.

variance—permission of a landowner to use the land in a specified manner that is inconsistent with the zoning ordinance.

vicarious liability—imposing liability for the fault of another.

void agreement—agreement that cannot be enforced.

voidable contract—agreement that is otherwise binding and enforceable but may be rejected at the option of one of the parties as the result of specific circumstances.

voidable title—title of goods that carries with it the contingency of an underlying problem.

voir dire examination—the preliminary examination of a juror or a witness to ascertain fitness to act as such.

voluntary bankruptcy—proceeding in which the debtor files the petition for relief.

voting by proxy—authorizing someone else to vote the shares owned by the shareholder.

voting trust—transfer by two or more persons of their shares of stock of a corporation to a trustee who is to vote the shares and act for such shareholders.

W

waiver—release or relinquishment of a known right or objection.

warehouse—entity engaged in the business of storing the goods of others for compensation.

warehouse receipt—receipt issued by the warehouse for stored goods. Regulated by the UCC, which clothes the receipt with some degree of negotiability.

warrant—authorization via court order to search private property for tools or evidence of a crime.

warranty—promise either express or implied about the nature, quality, or performance of the goods.

warranty against encumbrances—warranty that there are no liens or other encumbrances to goods except those noted by seller.

warranty deed—deed by which the grantor conveys a specific estate or interest to the grantee and makes one or more of the covenants of title.

warranty of habitability—implied warranty that the leased property is fit for dwelling by tenants.

warranty of title—implied warranty that title to the goods is good and transfer is proper.

wasting assets corporation—corporation designed to exhaust or use up the assets of the corporation, such as by extracting oil, coal, iron, and other ores.

way of necessity—grantee's right to use land retained by the grantor for going to and from the conveyed land.

White-Collar Crime Penalty Enhancement Act of 2002—federal reforms passed as a result of the collapses of companies such as Enron; provides for longer sentences and higher fines for both executives and companies.

white-collar crimes—crimes that do not use nor threaten to use force or violence or do not cause injury to persons or property.

whole life insurance—ordinary life insurance providing lifetime insurance protection.

will—instrument executed with the formality required by law by which a person makes a disposition of his or her property to take effect upon death.

writ of certiorari—order by the U.S. Supreme Court granting a right of review by the court of a lower court decision.

wrongfully dishonored—error by a bank in refusing to pay a check.

Z

zoning—restrictions imposed by government on the use of designated land to ensure an orderly physical development of the regulated area.

case index

Opinion cases are in italic type; cited cases are in roman type. Cases new to this edition are in color.